WHAT

ALSO BY

ERIC BENTLEY

THINKING ABOUT THE PLAYWRIGHT

THE KLEIST VARIATIONS

THE BRECHT COMMENTARIES

ARE YOU NOW OR HAVE YOU EVER BEEN? AND OTHER PLAYS

THEATRE OF WAR

THE THEATRE OF COMMITMENT

THE LIFE OF THE DRAMA

IN SEARCH OF THEATRE

BERNARD SHAW

THE PLAYWRIGHT AS THINKER

A CENTURY OF HERO WORSHIP

WHAT IS THEATRE?

INCORPORATING
THE DRAMATIC EVENT
AND OTHER REVIEWS
1944–1967

ERIC BENTLEY

HILL AND WANG
A DIVISION OF FARRAR, STRAUS AND GIROUX
NEW YORK

Hill and Wang
A division of Farrar, Straus and Giroux
19 Union Square West, New York 10003

Copyright © 2000 by Eric Bentley
Introduction copyright © 2000 by Donald Lyons
All rights reserved
Distributed in Canada by Douglas & McIntyre Ltd.
Printed in the United States of America
Designed by Harry Ford
First published in 1968 by Atheneum Publishers
Second edition published by Hill and Wang, 2000

Library of Congress Cataloging-in-Publication Data

Bentley, Eric. 1916–
    What is theatre? : incorporating the dramatic event and other reviews,
1944–1967 / Eric Bentley.—2nd ed.
        p. cm.
    Includes index.
    ISBN 0-8090-9695-1 (alk. paper)
    1. Theater—United States—History—20th century. 2. Theater—
United States—Reviews.
    I. Title.

PN2266.B48 2000
792.9'5'0973—dc21

                                                        99-087399

CONTENTS

INTRODUCTION BY DONALD LYONS   *ix*
PREFACE   *xxxiii*

The Dramatic Event

PROFESSIONAL PLAYGOING   *3*
PITY HIS SIMPLICITY   *8*
MERCHANT OF VENICE, LONG ISLAND   *12*
EUGENE O'NEILL'S PIETÀ   *16*
MAIMING THE BARD   *19*
PICKWICK IN LOVE   *22*
THE CASE OF O'CASEY   *25*
HITCH YOUR STAR TO A WAGON   *28*
WHAT IS ACTING?   *31*
CHARLIE CHAPLIN'S MEA CULPA   *34*
THE POET IN NEW YORK   *37*
IT'S ALL GREEK TO ME   *40*
THE PINK AND THE BLACK   *43*
I HAVE A BRIGHT IDEA   *46*
LILLIAN HELLMAN'S INDIGNATION   *49*
ACTING: NATURAL AND ARTIFICIAL   *52*
ACTING VS. RECITING   *55*
GUILDING THE LILLI   *58*
THE INNOCENCE OF ARTHUR MILLER   *62*
HANS ANDERSEN'S BOOMERANG   *65*
ON THE SUBLIME   *68*
PATHETIC PHALLUSES   *71*

CAMINO UNREAL   74
A MAJOR MUSICAL   78
FROM LEO X TO PIUS XII   81
PERSONALITY   84
ON BEING READ TO   87
WITHIN THIS WOODEN O   91
ON STAGING YEATS   94
GIVE MY REGARDS TO BROADWAY   97
SIR LAURENCE MACHEATH   100
JULIUS CAESAR, 1953   103
FOLKLORE ON FORTY-SEVENTH STREET   107
HOW DEEP ARE THE ROOTS?   110
THE PERFECT PLAY   114
NEW PLAYWRIGHT, NEW ACTRESS   117
GOD BLESS AMERICA   120
END AS A YES-MAN   123
THE ILL-MADE PLAY   127
PESSIMISM AS A PICK-ME-UP   131
SHAKESPEARE'S POLITICS   134
CAPTAIN BLIGH'S REVENGE   138
OLD POSSUM AT PLAY   141
THE IDEA OF A THEATRE   145
HOMOSEXUALITY   149
REIGEN COMES FULL CIRCLE   152
ACTING, SEX-APPEAL, DEMOCRACY   155
THE STANDARD STORY   159
TEA, SYMPATHY, AND THE NOBLE
  SAVAGE   162
WHO ARE YOU ROOTING FOR?   165
CRAFTY GODLINESS   169
THE PRESENCE OF MOZART   172
". . . AND CHRONICLE SMALL BEER"   175

What Is Theatre?

THE FAMILY, 1954   *183*

OFF BROADWAY   *186*

THE AMERICAN MUSICAL   *190*

A WHOLE THEORY OF THE DRAMA   *193*

JOSHUA LOGAN   *196*

A REAL WRITER   *200*

EILEEN HECKART AND OTHERS   *204*

POETRY OF THE THEATRE   *207*

THERE IS CHARM AND CHARM   *211*

BUT JUNK IS JUNK   *214*

WILD DUCK AND TAME PHOENIX   *218*

WHAT IS BEAUTY, SAITH MY SUFFER-
INGS, THEN?   *221*

TENNESSEE WILLIAMS AND NEW YORK
KAZAN   *224*

HOMAGE TO SCRIBE   *231*

ORSON WELLES AND TWO OTHELLOS   *235*

A GREAT BRONZE GONG   *238*

TWO HUNDRED YEARS OF MOWING   *242*

THE EXAMPLE OF THE COMÉDIE
FRANÇAISE   *245*

INACCURACY   *251*

THE ROAD FROM ROUEN TO NEW YORK   *254*

ON THE WATERFRONT   *258*

MARRIAGE, 1955   *261*

A FUNNY SORT OF RED   *265*

A DIRECTOR'S THEATRE   *269*

HOW NOT TO WRITE AN AUDIENCE   *272*

WHIMSY AND THE CULTURED CLASSES   *276*

THE LAST DRAWING-ROOM COMEDY   *279*

A DIRECTLY SENSUOUS PLEASURE   *283*

INACCURACY AGAIN   *286*

A LIQUID GRACE   *290*

UNDRAMATIC THEATRICALITY   *295*

THE OTHER ORSON WELLES   *304*

THE MISSING COMMUNIST   309
THIRTY-TWO NON-REVIEWS   315
OLIVIER ON DISK   330
DE FILIPPO ON THE SCREEN   335
MARTHA GRAHAM   338
MARCEL MARCEAU   342
JAMES AGATE   345

Other Reviews 1944–1967

DRAMA NOW   353
THE OLD VIC, THE OLD CRITICS,
    AND THE NEW GENERATION   362
BARRAULT: A DIALOGUE   368
PLAYWRIGHT OF THE FIFTIES   377
THE PEKING OPERA   382
OPERA IN NEW YORK   385
A TOUCH OF THE ADOLESCENT   394
COMEDY AND THE COMIC SPIRIT
    IN AMERICA   404
THE GERMAN THEATRE TODAY   414
EIGHT GERMAN PRODUCTIONS   423
CHARLIE CHAPLIN AND PEGGY HOPKINS
    JOYCE   434
THE CIVIL OBEDIENCE OF GALILEO GALILEI   443

AFTERTHOUGHTS (1952–1956)   453
INDEX   471

INTRODUCTION

by Donald Lyons

ERIC BENTLEY was the drama critic for *The New Republic* from 1952 to 1956. It was the only time in a long, prolific, and varied career that Bentley held a reviewing job, and the pieces in this book are, with some additions, the weekly essays he wrote for the magazine. While inspired by and descriptive of this or that play produced in New York, these essays far transcend what are normally thought of as play reviews. Bentley created meditations on theater, on America, on the fifties, on art and civilization. They are marvels of grace, clarity, and passion—grace of thought, clarity of phrase, and passion of soul. As deeply cultivated and ferociously concerned reports on the culture of America in mid-twentieth century, Bentley's theater reviews belong with those of two other weekly—and temporary—reviewers: James Agee on film and Edmund Wilson on books. As film critic, Agee had two voices: from 1941 to 1948 (anonymously) for *Time*, and from 1942 to 1948 for *The Nation*. W. H. Auden wrote that "his articles belong in that very select class—the music critiques of Berlioz and Shaw are the only other members I know—of newspaper work which has permanent literary value," and these words prefaced a 1944 volume of collected reviews.

Auden might have said the same about Edmund Wilson's *Classics and Commercials,* collected largely from his weekly notices for *The New Yorker*. It is with such books—essentially reflections on culture and society by writers who were somewhat fortuitously weekly critics—that *What Is Theatre?* (to give this book its omnibus title) should be classed.

Who is Eric Bentley, and how did he come to be asking "What is theater?" for *The New Republic*? He was born in 1916 in

Bolton, Lancashire, in the north of England, where his grandfather and father ran a successful moving-van business. His mother was a formidable and stern Victorian matriarch, a Baptist and a Puritan (they were not always the same thing).

Scholarships brought the bright boy to Oxford, where he studied with C. S. Lewis and, in the course of some amateur theatricals, got to wear Laurence Olivier's Toby Belch costume, beard, and mustache. Among the first plays he saw in London were *Richard of Bordeaux* and Chekhov's *Uncle Vanya*, both with John Gielgud. He has written of *Uncle Vanya* that "I'd never heard anyone talk like that, in or out of a theatre. I was enthralled. This was more real than all my realities. And I understood it, too: what adolescent wouldn't?"

A Commonwealth Fellowship in 1939 took Bentley to Yale (which he chose over Harvard because he could get a doctorate more quickly there). His doctoral thesis won the Porter Prize in 1941 for the best doctoral thesis of general human interest, and was later published as *A Century of Hero Worship* (1944).

Hero worship was then an appropriate subject for young Bentley, who was about to meet the great hero of his life. After Yale he took up a teaching job at UCLA, and while there became friendly with such leftist German exiles as the philosopher Theodor Adorno and the composer Hanns Eisler. Their words of admiration soon reached the ears of a German poet-playwright in need of a translator and hungry for success in America—Bertolt Brecht. Bentley was to become Brecht's translator, apostle, herald, director, friend, and son. He never shared the master's Stalinist politics, and he always saw Brecht's plays and poems as more supple and elusive, more humane and contradictory, than their creator's dogmas. In 1949 he sought out Brecht in Berlin, and in the Berliner Ensemble's productions of *Mother Courage* in East Berlin and later in Munich, he found the greatest theater he had ever seen, "a landmark in my life." It was a revelation matched only by the Berliner Ensemble's *Caucasian Chalk Circle* in 1956. When Brecht died in 1956, Bentley wrote that "there were times when I hated him, but there were no times when I did not love him."

Bentley's relationship to Brecht, to Brecht's work, to Brecht's entourage, and to what has over the years passed for Brechtianism is a (perhaps the) key thread in his life, and this is hardly the place to untangle it. What is of importance to insist on here is that Bentley was far more than Brecht's acolyte. His cultural geography was never narrow. For instance, he moved among and wrote for the New Critics, serving as a consulting editor for *The Kenyon Review*, in which (as well as in other quarterlies like *Partisan Review*) first appeared parts of Bentley's first great book, *The Playwright as Thinker* (1946). It may just be that the four words of that title—the playwright (of all people) as thinker (of all things)—are the most influential of the millions Bentley has written. The high discourse of literary modernism as it was constituted in the forties concerned itself with James and Joyce and Eliot and Conrad, with Pound and Rilke and Proust and Stein and Yeats the poet. With a stroke, Bentley introduced dramatists into the center of serious modernist discourse. The book posits Wagner and Ibsen as founders of modern tragic theater and goes on to characterize Wilde, Shaw, and Pirandello as "the three great wits of the modern stage." After a consideration of Strindberg, the book concludes with extended (and contrasting) treatments of Brecht and Sartre as avatars of, respectively, epic and existentialist theater. More than fifty years later, some of Bentley's emphases (Sartre) and relative omissions (Chekhov, Buechner, Wedekind, Kleist, O'Neill) seem odd, but the book's brio and brilliance endure. (And we now value some of these figures more highly precisely because of Bentley's tireless efforts to translate, appreciate, and quarrel with them.)

In 1947, Bentley wrote a short book on Shaw for New Directions' Makers of Modern Literature series. This clever and wise treatment set out to rescue Shaw from his reputation (in part self-created) as a slave to ideas both simple and simplistic. Instead, Bentley found in the chipper Irishman (then still living) a Jamesian savorer of life over ideas. "Shaw stands," argued Bentley, "for society against anti-social conspiracies . . . for style against fashion, for man against the machinery of living and for life—'life with a blessing'—against any particular idea whatsoever."

Influential writer though he was becoming, Bentley always thought of himself as a theater man. He wanted to, and did, direct; he wanted to, and eventually did, write plays. A theorist, however brilliant, needs to see and feel and get dirtied by actual stage experience. He also needs to write about what he sees. Hence Bentley the critic. He reported briefly on the Broadway seasons of 1945–48 for some literary reviews and for *Harper's*; from 1948 to 1951 he was in Europe, where he directed Lorca, Eliot, Brecht, and O'Neill and reported on theatre for *Theatre Arts* and *The Kenyon Review*. *In Search of Theatre* (1953) is Bentley's dazzlingly comprehensive chronicle of those years in which "I have roamed along the Boulevard Clichy looking for the Atelier. I have ridden a bicycle. . . . I have sat in the unlit Berlin S-Bahn during the blockade. . . . I have prowled around North London in the rain. . . . I have hunted down puppet theaters in the slums of Palermo."

Back in the United States, of which he was now a citizen, in late 1951, Bentley began to see that translating and occasional writing would not suffice for support. Happily, he received, and took, two offers of regular work—as a professor (later the Brander Matthews Professor of Dramatic Literature) at Columbia University, and as the drama critic for *The New Republic*. The magazine had had three previous drama critics: the very distinguished Stark Young, who had left the magazine after decades in 1947; briefly, the novelist Irwin Shaw; and the energetic, zestful, and elegant theater man Harold Clurman, founder of the Group Theatre. Robert Richman, the new literary editor of the magazine, eased out Clurman and replaced him with Bentley, who took the job warily and with a firm intention to quit after a short spell.

When Bentley took the reviewing job, he was regarded in some quarters as a Broadway-hating, Brecht-loving snob. In 1953, Walter Kerr, the programmatically philistine play critic at *The New York Herald Tribune* (and thus second in power only to Brooks Atkinson at the *Times*) sneered that "Brecht speaks only to Bentley, and Bentley speaks only to God." But one of the ironies of Bentley's tenure at *The New Republic* was that he was to have no opportunity to review Brecht. Of Brecht's four masterworks—*Galileo, Mother Courage, Good Woman of Setzuan*, and *Caucasian Chalk Circle*—the first had reached New York before 1952, and the other three late in or after 1956. (In fact, Bentley would direct the American premiere of *The Good Woman of Setzuan.*) So Bentley's Brechtianism was an undercurrent, a noise off.

What was the state of American theater during the years 1952–56? The most prestigious postwar playwrights, Tennessee Williams and Arthur Miller, had produced their masterworks (*All My Sons, Death of a Salesman, The Glass Menagerie,* and *A Streetcar Named Desire*) in the forties. On offer for Bentley to review were *Camino Real, Cat on a Hot Tin Roof,* and 27 *Wagons Full of Cotton* from Williams, and from Miller *The Crucible* and *A View from the Bridge.* Wonderful plays, but not now considered the authors' best. As for America's greatest playwright, Bentley reviewed the unproduced text of O'Neill's *A Moon for the Misbegotten.* The posthumous masterpiece *Long Day's Journey into Night* was produced in New York in the season after Bentley stopped reviewing. (He deals with it, and with the posthumous *More Stately Mansions,* in a 1964 review called "A Touch of the Adolescent," which is printed here among "Other Reviews.") Bentley's wrestlings with the achievement of O'Neill are chronicled in three essays: "Trying to Like O'Neill" (1951), printed in *In Search of Theater*; "A Touch of the Adolescent," published here; and "The Life and Hates of Eugene O'Neill" (1960), reprinted in *Thinking about the Playwright.* The only American play written after the forties that is regularly considered great— Edward Albee's *Who's Afraid of Virginia Woolf?* (1962)—is briefly mentioned in a 1964 talk for the Voice of America, also included here among "Other Reviews."

But if these were not years of new masterpieces, they were times of great cultural ferment. They were times, above all, of Communism and of anti-Communism. Not that—and Bentley had occasion to make this point again and again—there was overt Communism either on or off Broadway. (These were the first years of an artistically strong off-Broadway.) Bentley would have welcomed the open Stalinism (not the Stalinism, but the openness) of Brecht's *Caucasian Chalk Circle,* but instead the Broadway left preferred "mystification" and "evasion." "On Broadway, over the past quarter century, Communism has been the only political force with any real spread or any real staying power. Not that this is ever admitted, least of all by the Communists," he wrote. Rather, the characteristic trope of leftist plays was the false accusation—of Communism or of a surrogate for it. Lillian Hellman's revival of her 1934 play *The Children's Hour* provided a classic instance. In the play, "revived because of the current red scare," a teacher is falsely accused of lesbianism, discovers that she is a lesbian, and kills herself. Bentley made explicit the political analogy: "Mr. A, accused of Communism, indignantly denies it, only to admit it later." The same dishonest dramaturgy surfaced in Miller's *The Crucible*, which was ostensibly about witches; as Bentley pithily put it, "the analogy between 'red-baiting' and witch hunting can seem complete only to Communists, for only to them is the menace of Communism as fictitious as the menace of witches."

Bentley was not implying that Miller was a Communist. "For all I know," he drolly suggested Miller "may hate the Soviet state with all the ardor of Eisenhower." What Miller manifested was a fatuous liberal "innocence" that chose not to see. Miller's spurious evenhandedness is thus excoriated: "Arthur Miller, apparently desiring to break free from a Stalinism which he had never admitted to being in bondage to in the first place, can only condemn Soviet policy, if he quickly adds that America isn't very much better."

Like witchcraft and Communism, homosexuality was a frequent accusation on stage. *Cat on a Hot Tin Roof* contains one of those maybe-true accusations that were so thrilling to fifties audiences. "In the thirties," writes Bentley, "you felt the reassuring presence of the 'real' at the mention of a Worker. Today you feel it at the mention of a Homosexual." In *Tea and Sympathy*, a boy falsely accused of queerness is "cured" by sleeping with an older woman. The dramatization of Gide's *The Immoralist* seemed to face the issue honestly but then turned out to exemplify "a kind of liberalism which is safely reactionary"—the husband, if not innocent in the past, promises to abstain in the future. The review's final sentence offers a memorable snapshot of midtown New York in the fifties: "In the intermission you hear dowagers asking if such things can be; the male prostitutes on Times Square are easy to overlook for those who see New York through taxi windows." Bentley was not for more—or less—homosexuality or Communism on stage. He was for honesty and clarity. His point was that moral timidity and intellectual blur—how dare you call me a Commie/queer? . . . well, maybe I am one, but so what?—made for mediocre art.

Miller's *A View from the Bridge* contains another such accusation, "yet we don't feel the accusation is false." *A View from the Bridge* was Miller's play about informing on the New York waterfront, just as *On the Waterfront* was director Elia Kazan's movie about informing on the Hoboken waterfront. (Kazan had named names; Miller had not.) Bentley found both opposing works "obscured by a fog of false rhetoric."

In the early 1950s, Kazan was much more than a quondam Marxist; his cachet in New York and Hollywood made him "the incarnate spirit of the age." He was an artist whose "work means more to the American theater than that of any current writer whatsoever." Creator of a Freudianized Stanislavskianism, Kazan had directed *A Streetcar Named Desire* and *Death of a Salesman* and revolutionized acting with such performances as those of Marlon Brando in *Streetcar* and of James Dean in *East of Eden.* He specialized not in realism but in "phantasmagoria," the structuring of tense psychic tableaux alive with neurotic excitement. Bentley reviewed the Kazan touch in *Camino Real,* in *Tea and Sympathy,* and, supremely, in *Cat on a Hot Tin Roof,* about which he writes with devastating sympathy and precision. In his *Cat* staging, Kazan superimposed a drama of cleansing and redemptive sex upon a confused and ambivalent script—at least to Bentley's eye. (As always, Bentley exempts from his strictures what he finds best in Williams—his comedy, as realized in the character of "that old goat of a father.")

He was surprisingly (but maybe not, for a son of Bolton) shocked by the sexiness, the unhealthy obsession with sex as he saw it, evidenced in the work of Williams and Williams's epigone, William Inge. His review of Inge's *Picnic* was entitled "Pathetic Phalluses" and indicted the work's phallic worship. He even blamed poor Inge for the movie poster for *Come Back, Little Sheba,* which showed "a young man in his underwear gazing carnally at a girl." Reviewing Inge's *Bus Stop,* he cried, "Is it just that Mr. Inge's emphasis on sex, sex, sex shocks me? (It does.)" In another context, he laments that "the theatre which Shaw berated for its hedonism now lectures us on the sex prob-

lems of adolescents and the complexes of old maids." I suspect
Bentley would not express himself quite like this today—and
probably would not have then, if he had had the chance to review a great play about adolescent sexuality like Wedekind's
Spring's Awakening. In talking about *Cat,* he notes that " 'How
good is he (or she) in bed?' is what everyone asks of everyone
else. Now it seems to me that there are people, even in the
world of Tennessee Williams, who would not ask this question,
especially not of those who are near and dear. And what does
the query mean? A girl seems good in bed if you like *her*; otherwise, she seems bad in bed; and for most of us that is the heart
of the matter." There is a strange mixture, it seems to me, of
wisdom and priggishness in such comments. Bentley certainly
thought of himself as an opponent of puritanism, then in its
heyday in the person of Cardinal Spellman and in the institution of the Legion of Decency. But the fifties were a confused
and liminal decade; sexual discourse then had to be coded,
cryptic, and (in cases like those of Williams and Inge) closeted,
but it was for all that insistent and obsessive. Bentley objected
above all to the period's unhealthy disingenuousness. Looking
back now, after the triumph of overt sexual discourse, one is
less sure about what is healthy and what is unhealthy. Are the
confusions and contradictions of *Angels in America* any less than
those of *Cat on a Hot Tin Roof*?

If he was uncomfortable with sex as hinted at on Broadway,
Bentley was no friend to the fifties dream of the American family. "Family life," he cheerfully wrote in 1954, "is the most successful instrument of self-torture yet devised by an ingenious
and masochistic species, an exquisite compound of tedium, irritation, comic misunderstanding, and tragic suffering." But he
insisted that, in putting this on stage, "the petty reporting of
naturalism has got to be transformed and transcended either
by a larger realism or by poetic fantasy." This is exactly what
O'Neill did in *Long Day's Journey into Night,* of which Bentley's
words seem a proleptic description. In demanding "poetry" on
stage, Bentley did not have exquisiteness, or even verse, in
mind. Indeed, he excoriated Miller for his phony poeticizing in
A View from the Bridge, and he chided Paddy Chayefsky, "the
playwright of the age . . . this age of salesmanship and confor-

mity," for being mired in "averageness" of language and feeling. He found poetry in, of all people, Clifford Odets—"the poetry of the theatre, a poetry of the spoken word, the acted word, the word held up to the light to be stared at by a crowd, the word flung across footlights by actor-marksmen aiming straight at the heart of an audience."

If family was the constructing form of the American bourgeoisie, it did not enforce any sort of maturity. On the contrary. In 1964 Bentley saw "immaturity" as "a cult of modern civilization as a whole—Western, and, more particularly, American. . . . we live in a culture that does not believe in men and women but in Boys and Girls." JFK was our National Boy; Marilyn Monroe our National Girl, "a child with large breasts." The immediate occasion for these observations was the inveterate immaturity of O'Neill's characters (and of O'Neill) in the posthumously published *More Stately Mansions*. (The review is included here.)

It might be thought that Bentley, the disciple of the materialist Brecht, would not necessarily welcome genuine religion in drama. But there was in Bentley a disciple of Shaw and an admirer of F. R. Leavis, the editor of the magazine *Scrutiny*, famous for his insistence on "Life" as a religious dimension in literature. It should therefore not surprise us to hear Bentley finding in one play "no vision of evil, just a glimpse of neurosis, no profound moral life, but a violent palpitation by which alone one instant is joined to the next" or decrying "our friends of the East Sixties" as "being all too often without serious religion, art, or politics." "How good it is," he wrote, seeing a Graham Greene play, "to see religion shown on stage as, for better or worse, a substantial part of people's lives!" (He was, however, far from uncritical of the play as a whole or of its religiosity.) He found in Ansky's *The Dybbuk* something "religious in a broader, perhaps deeper sense [than orthodoxy]. Ansky makes real to us people whose religious tradition is perhaps the main thing in their lives and, like Chagall, he seems to tell us that we can be happy in the universe even if we are miserable in the world. There is a fine Dickensian mixture, in this Hasidism, of mysticism and jollity."

What about Bentley and actors? Perhaps knowing that his

reviews would appear after those of the daily critics—who did virtually nothing but describe the bodies, mannerisms, and attitudes of popular performers—Bentley is somewhat sparing in his evocations of actors. He prefers rather to map out the relationship of performer to role. How good a fit was it? Did the actor bring more or less than was wanted? When a beauty like Viveca Lindfors essays a classic role, Strindberg's Julie, Bentley clinically castigates her inadequacies: "No one listens to the play for Miss Lindfors is on stage, preparing to attack the prettiest wrist in America with a razor. . . . Miss Lindfors' hands and arms perform large gestures; one watches them perhaps with surprise, perhaps with incredulity, but hardly with pleasure." When, on the other hand, a great actress attacks a great role— Uta Hagen that of Turgenev's Natalia—Bentley can evoke her fineness: "She sweeps towards the footlights exclaiming: 'For the first time in my life I am in love!' and our hearts jump at the fine, free audacity of it. Like Turgenev himself, this actress is able to be both modern and traditional, subtle and broad, turned-in-toward-herself and turned-out-toward-the-public."

There were two regnant and antithetical styles of acting— English artifice and Method naturalism—that Bentley found many an occasion to describe and deplore. The former could turn easily into aestheticism and effeminacy, the latter into mere nervousness and fidgetiness. Laurence Olivier in the film of *Richard III* and Cyril Richard in *Peter Pan* do not escape censure. Tyrone Guthrie "stands too close to the rather chi-chi semiculture of more highbrow British theatre." Peter Brook and Oliver Messel produce shows "gorgeous and clever . . . seriously unserious, profoundly unprofound, and ungaily gay." Over here, Broadway had evolved what Bentley called "the new actress": she "brought onstage . . . a bizarre, neurasthenic quality . . . defined by grimaces and quiverings of the lip, by frequent sidelong glances, by jerky, syncopated movements of as many parts of the body as will move. The new actress cannot or will not keep still." He happens to be reviewing Jo Van Fleet, but assures us that "Jo Van Fleet is only one of her names. She has also called herself Maureen Stapleton, Geraldine Page, and Clarice Blackburn." Stapleton he later calls "the quintessence of Williamsism," reminding us that actors and playwrights were in harmony. Julie Harris he later finds "the very idea of a modern actress," although he calls her Joan of Arc more "Peter Pan than . . . grown-up patriot and capable strategist." Nor are the Method men spared. Paul Newman is advised to "watch some real roughnecks and stop watching (though, after all, this is impossible) Marlon Brando."

Evocation of a given performance is a skill (and Bentley has it), but I submit that evocation of the very spirit of a time, as manifested in a host of performances, is a more valuable accomplishment yet.

Wait a minute, I hear you ask. The fifties? Broadway? Wasn't that the last decade of the Golden Age of musicals? Where was Bentley on that subject? Not where he should have been, in my opinion. In theory, he "got" the American musical. "Plays!" he wrote in exasperation. "They start late, they end early, and two long intermissions offer poignant invitations to go home. Plays! . . . But the musicals start early, end late, and have a single intermission which is over before you can get to the men's room. . . . You can try anything; you *must* try many things. . . . here is the thick and slab gruel of American life." He was inspired to this rhapsody by a revival of *Guys and Dolls*. ("How pleasant to go from the fashionable psychopaths of Broadway's 'serious' drama to the nice old-fashioned delinquents of *Guys and Dolls*.") But *Guys and Dolls* had what Bentley demanded of musical comedy: comedy, frivolity. As soon as musicals got serious, Bentley got restless. In 1944, he found *Oklahoma!* "trite, cocksure, sentimental and vacuous," a deplorable representative of the "new Americanism." By 1953, he'd come to feel "much better" about *Oklahoma!*—but only if people stopped treating it seriously and calling it "the American *Magic Flute*."

With an imperious flourish, Bentley banished seriousness from the musical stage. "The last scene of *Carousel*," he declared, "is an impertinence; I refuse to be lectured by a musical comedy scriptwriter on the education of children, the nature of the good life, and the contribution of the American small town to the salvation of souls. I regard such a *gaffe* simply as an opportunity to get out of the theatre before the crowd. I deplore the death of the king in *The King and I*; it was definitely his duty to stay alive and amuse us. But *On Your Toes* is true musical comedy." This is Bentley in a rare Sheridan Whiteside/George Jean Nathan/James Agate vein, hurling grumpy dicta from the center aisle and brooking no contradiction from fools. It is sad to find such a gifted observer, and one who so regularly decried American immaturity, resisting maturity in a major American art form. The fifties were the last great decade for the musical, and much of what was happening in it goes unchronicled, let alone uncelebrated, here.

No one can be everywhere or see everything, of course. But Bentley writes warm and evocative appreciations of Martha Graham (both here and in *In Search of Theatre*), of Mozart and the Peking Opera. He is also interesting on film. He knows that the Shaw films, "as examples of cinematic art," are inferior to *The Maltese Falcon.* He has the reverence of an intellectual for Chaplin (he was enthusiastic about *Monsieur Verdoux* in *In Search of Theatre*) but takes the occasion of a review (included here) of Chaplin's *Limelight* (1952) to pinpoint the filmmaker's "return to the bosom of the bourgeoisie . . . expressed in the quintessentially bourgeois form of entertainment: sentimental domestic drama." He calls the film "a glorious failure." Today it is perhaps easier to see Chaplin's entire oeuvre as vitiated by sentimentality.

Most of the films that Bentley reviews here are Shakespeare films. The first occasion he seizes to write about Olivier is, however, not a Shakespeare movie but the cinematic version of *The Beggar's Opera*, directed by Peter Brook, adapted by Christopher Fry, and starring Olivier. Prone to resist Olivier in general, Bentley analyzes his "failure" in this "nullity of a film, which reduced a serious work with bite, point and anger to 'prunes and prisms' "—Bentley's shorthand for the exquisite "New Rococo" of British silliness. Looking back on Olivier's film of *Henry V*, which he dubs "mainly meritorious," Bentley notes the reduction of the play to the "picture-postcard effects" of "a jeu d'esprit." It's in a review of the sound track album to the movie of *Richard III* that Bentley attempts his fullest assessment of Olivier and his style. "His voice," Bentley writes," "is not grand, it is not rich, it is not warm. It fails, therefore, in most cases, to meet the demands of tragic drama." But his Richard is "superb," despite "the extreme lightness of the voice" and its "feeble falsetto." Bentley calls the movie "the finest achievement of Olivier in any field," for all his reservations about the style chosen for the film as a whole. ("British directors these days want their drama exquisite to the point of effeminacy.")

The Hollywood movie of *Julius Caesar* Bentley finds "arguably the best Shakespeare film to date." He is warmly sympathetic to Brando's "gallant" but "unready" stab at Antony. But he uses the film for a thrilling and profound investigation into the Shakespearean conception of "what is a man?" Shakespearean man was both a personal moral agent and a political being. In the thirties, Orson Welles had isolated the politics in *Julius Caesar* and played that alone; in 1953, Welles's ex-partner, John Houseman, the producer of the MGM *Julius Caesar*, cut out the politics—so to speak—and reduced the drama to one of personal jealousies. "By Marxist standards, Shakespeare's political studies are hopelessly unpolitical and subjective . . . by the anti-Marxist standards fashionable today [1953], they are much too political and objective." It only remains to add that the pendulum has today, in 1999–2000, swung the opposite way, and virtually all the Shakespeare we get is politicized and Marxised, often even set in the Hitlerian thirties, so we take the point.

Another John Houseman Shakespeare production—this time of *Coriolanus* on the stage—elicited another Bentley meditation on Shakespearean moral complexity. "You can't fully identify yourself with anyone in *Coriolanus*," notes the critic. "From the Broadway viewpoint, that is bad. From the human viewpoint, it is good. . . . The Evil is here in Rome, in Washington, in Coriolanus, in our classmate Alger Hiss, in me, and in you—*hypocrite lecteur*. The reference to Hiss will seem pretty callow to our Marxist friends, not only because he was quite right to be a spy for Moscow (or is it that he wasn't a spy? I forget), but also because they acknowledge no continuity between personal character and political action. The rest of us have been coming around from the Marxist position (if we ever held it) to the Shakespearean one." He thus establishes, electrifyingly, the relevance of *Coriolanus* to 1953 (and *mutatis mutandis* to 2000), and he praises, quite logically, the production's ability to "communicate a sense of [the play's] ancient and alien grandeur." Great theater must be at once remote and immediate.

Houseman's old crony Welles had a perhaps surprising place in Bentley's affections. Reviewing Welles's film of *Othello* in 1954, he lamented the waste of "a specifically theatrical imagination . . . that might have given the history of theater a different turn." It's a film of incidents, or rather of "arbitrary effects, visual and auditory, within incidents." "If there were a real mind in charge of the production as a whole, Orson Welles would be the greatest assistant director of all time."

On Welles's acting in the movie, Bentley is priceless: "Is Othello fat? Does he look as if he had a hangover? . . . An actor has to look sober when he is drunk; if Mr. Welles looks drunk when he is sober, he is all the less an actor. . . . He never acts, he is photographed—from near, from far, from above, from below, right side up, upside down." In general, "the film's artiness reveals that Welles has caught up with the Cocteau of 1920—or should one say with the Gordon Craig of 1910. . . . I don't know what *The Daily Worker* said, but it missed a trick if it didn't hold up Mr. Welles as a prize example of individualistic, bourgeois culture in decay."

When Welles directed *King Lear* onstage in 1956, he played the title role in a wheelchair, having broken not one but two ankles. Bentley, allowed to attend a few rehearsals, writes warmly about the "famous and magnificent Wellesian audacity" (for example, a huge map covering the whole stage). He sees, too, the self-destructiveness ("If Welles had three legs, he would have tripped three times") and the fatal fondness for bright ideas ("Theatre people should not have 'ideas' at all unless they are prepared to take the full responsibility, as Granville-Barker did, and become masters of ideas. . . . Mr. Welles has always been tempted to turn the theatre into a Notion and Novelty Store.") Orson Welles, lost leader though he was after being "born a theatrical genius," seems to figure in Bentley's mind as an anti-Kazan, a painter on vast canvases who disdained the psychological littlenesses beloved of the fifties.

If Bentley had gone abroad in search of theater in the late 1940s, world theater came to him in New York during his *New Republic* years. There were visits by groups like the Comédie Française, and there were local productions of foreign classics.

The Comédie Française he hoped would inspire an "organized theatre" here; the idea of establishing one, central, federally subsidized theater ("I cannot agree with those who are content to leave the American theatre to competitive enterprise") persisted for a long time, perhaps until diversified NEA and state grants—begun in the late sixties—emerged as a characteristically American, centrifugal experiment. That Bentley was no automatic admirer of visiting French companies is, however, evident from his caustic reaction (included here) to the 1957 visit of the Barrault-Renault Company. Structured as a Jamesian dialogue, the piece is severe both upon the company's distortions of Ben Jonson and Lope De Vega and upon the quality of the French plays chosen, like Jean Giraudoux's *Intermezzo* and Paul Claudel's *Christopher Columbus*, the latter pilloried by Bentley for daring to affirm the piety and goodness of Columbus's conquests.

Reviewing some tepid sample of Broadway whimsy, Bentley had cried, "Where is comedy—with its diabolical energy, its taut intellectuality, its moral severity?" He found those dangerous qualities not just in the Comédie Française's Molière but in a Sanford Meisner production (off Broadway, at the Neighborhood Playhouse) of Machiavelli's *Mandragola*, "a prime instance of uncorrupted comedy—a comedy in which character is defined, not by clever or graceful talk, but by plot." The Machiavelli review is a small masterpiece, an excited meditation on comedy, cynicism, and civilization.

Bentley was able, in the course of his duties, to see and think about some great European moderns—Ibsen, Strindberg, Pirandello, Turgenev, Chekhov. Seeing Ibsen's *The Master Builder* at the Phoenix on Second Avenue and Twelfth Street (probably the most prestigious off-Broadway house of the time), Bentley wonders how it is "you can spot the supremely great [dramatists] in the first scene of almost any of their plays." He decides it is "a quality of imagination by which they establish their own atmosphere, create their own world." From this particular production, "too much of Ibsen's poetry, his passion and his meaning is missing," but "if this is Ibsen and water, many theater evenings are water without Ibsen."

Strindberg's *Miss Julie* was done at the Phoenix but became

(as we saw) a vehicle for a star actress and elicited the rueful remark that "I like to hear the words of the masters spoken on
the Off Broadway stage, but not to the exclusion of their souls."
Drama critics, he insisted, must stop patting "the Off Broadway
people on the back" and start holding them to high standards.
But soon the Phoenix redeemed itself with a radiant staging of
Turgenev's only play, *A Month in the Country,* an "elusive masterpiece" in which "love seems to come curving at the characters
out of the air, like some dangerous, but deft, missile." Bentley
compares the Turgenev work to Racine's *Phèdre* as two of the
rare great plays about sexual passion. It's a thrilling review to
read—a sketch of a (nearly) utopian production of a great play.
Pirandello is here represented only in a review of *Six Characters*
as staged by the flamboyant impresario Tyrone Guthrie; this extraordinarily painful and tragic play (upon which Bentley has
written definitively elsewhere) became for Guthrie an occasion
for "revenge" on its author, "for his production inverts Pirandello's main thesis and proves . . . that directors and actors are
more real than a writer's characters."

Among the finest achievements of off-Broadway in the fifties,
still talked about by people who are not inveterate theatergoers,
were the productions of three Chekhov plays at the small, long,
narrow Fourth Street Theatre by a director named David Ross.
Inspired to think about the beauty of *The Three Sisters* ("There is
no more beautiful modern play"), Bentley ponders the nature
of Chekhovian beauty. "It is not," he decides, "an intended
beauty. It is a beauty that radiates from a beautiful spirit, and its
radiance is an irreducibly real love of his fellow man." The production space was small, but "a Beethoven sonata can be enjoyed even when it isn't played by Schnabel on a Steinway. This
is a great and lovely play, and its greatness and loveliness come
through instead of being obstructed and whittled away as I remember them to have been in the grandiose Broadway production of a dozen years ago. . . . It is made clear that the sisters are
small-town girls, not Park Avenue hostesses in disguise." The
next year, Bentley found Ross's *Cherry Orchard* in the same
space a failure, comparing the play—again in a musical simili-
tude—to "some exquisite and exact bit of tone-painting by Debussy" that must be performed with exactitude to register at all.

Chekhov's play itself struck him as weaker than *The Three Sisters*, a "masterpiece more in the mode of Chekhovism as popularly understood—a Chekhovism of nuance and innuendo, muted lyricism, gentle pathos and gentler humor." Such a description is not only valuably exact in itself but useful as a guide and warning for interpreters of Chekhov. Still less satisfying to Bentley was the Fourth Street Theatre's version of *Uncle Vanya*, which boasted a movie star (Franchot Tone, an actor in whom Bentley found much to praise) but sacrificed the play's soul for laughs. There resulted "a 'comic' Chekhov with the juice strained away, the juice of urgent emotion and serious significance." We can see in Bentley's comments here that, as early as the fifties, the revisionist bright idea that Chekhov must at all costs be funny was as facile, distorting, and one-sided as the old gloomy-Slavic-melancholy stereotype it was designed to overthrow.

If new Irish and English plays crowd New York stages today, it was contemporary French dramatists who were all the rage four decades ago. André Gide barely qualifies as a dramatist, but it was a dramatization (by Ruth and Augustus Goetz, who had earlier successfully dramatized Henry James's *Washington Square* as *The Heiress*) of his novel *The Immoralist* that sparked one of Bentley's most acute and urgent discussions of the timid and disingenuous presentation of homosexuality on the stage.

In a 1958 essay appended to this book, Bentley breezily calls Eugene Ionesco "the playwright of the fifties," but the remark looks quite hyperbolic today. To judge from this book, there were rather three French—or shall we say, two French and one Franco-Irish—playwrights who mattered in the New York of the fifties: Jean Anouilh, Jean Giraudoux, and Samuel Beckett. Of the three, Beckett is today a giant, one of the key dramatists (and writers) of the century; Giraudoux and Anouilh, when remembered at all, seem clever confectioners.

No less than four Anouilh plays were reviewed by Bentley for *The New Republic*, and he treated the playwright with seriousness, if with increasing suspicion. As early as 1949, in "God's Plenty in Paris" (reprinted in *In Search of Theatre*), Bentley had written that "every country's theater has its special weaknesses, its favorite way of being false"—instancing in America, Saroyan; in England, Priestley; in France, Anouilh. But when Anouilh's *The Rehearsal* was brought here by Jean Louis Barrault in 1952, Bentley called it a melodrama "salted with Gallic Sophistication and 'existentialist' psychology." *The Rehearsal*, about corrupt people rehearsing a Marivaux comedy called *Double Inconstancy*, is, to be sure, an ingeniously constructed artifact; but Bentley saw more: he saw it as issuing from a Pirandellesque theatrical imagination.

Bentley viewed Anouilh's *Mademoiselle Colombe*—in a translation by *Time* magazine critic Louis Kronenberger, under the direction of Harold Clurman, and with stars like Edna Best, Julie Harris, and Eli Wallach—as "the great tonic of the 1953–54 Broadway season," a pessimistic "tale of the futility of boy's meeting girl." Feeling perhaps that he had to stand against what he called "the anti-European newspaper fraternity," Bentley found the work "interesting" and likened it to Molière's *Misanthrope*, a play he said would be even more unpalatable to the rigid optimists of 1953.

Giving a mixed review to the off-Broadway production of Anouilh's *Thieves' Carnival* at the Cherry Lane, Bentley found the play, a jape about three burglars invading an aristocrat's house, "a short, slight masterpiece. . . . for charm, wit and sprightliness [it] constitutes one of the best plays of the past quarter century." He again situates Anouilh in a comic tradition embracing Musset, Marivaux, and Pirandello. Today, it is clearer that Anouilh owes at least as much to Irish dramatists like Wilde and Shaw and also that his debts to all influences are seldom repaid in the coin of living drama.

When *The Lark*, Anouilh's Joan of Arc play, came to Broadway (starring Julie Harris and translated by Lillian Hellman), Bentley dissented from the Frenchman's reduction of the character to a girl who "dies chiefly to avoid the coming of middle age." He now saw Anouilh's mind as narrowed by its "cold, comfortless, nauseated atheism." Rather amusingly, the tough-minded Hellman found herself trying to humanize and soften Anouilh's brittle cookie of a Joan. Anouilh's earlier version (so to speak) of Joan—that is, his neurotic, wartime *Antigone*—had been done on Broadway by the grand star Katharine Cornell before 1952. It too had been misleadingly presented in New York as a defense of "a partisan Antigone against a collaborationist Creon." As Bentley admits, the "politics of [*Antigone*] are by no means so unambiguous"; he might have gone further and confessed that the play is much closer to a defense of collaborationist Creon. Anouilh's shifty nihilism seems clearer—and less interesting—today.

The cleverness of Giraudoux, even as presented on Broadway in the fifties, looked wiser and riper than that of Anouilh. Giraudoux had not been mentioned in *The Playwright as Thinker*, and Bentley took the first occasion offered—a Broadway production of *Ondine*, a wan piece about sprites derived from German Romanticism—to redress this implied undervaluation. It was, however, not seeing *Ondine* in New York, but seeing Giraudoux as done all over Europe, that had changed Bentley's mind: "It is, alas, only since his death in 1944 that many of us have come to see that Giraudoux is a man to reckon with. . . . In Europe around 1950, Giraudoux confronted me wherever I went. . . . My eyes were opened to many things. I saw, for example, that . . . the mythological plays of Sartre and Anouilh are inconceivable without Giraudoux. More important, I had to grant that here was a first-rank man of letters consecrating his maturity to the theatre, finding in Louis Jouvet at once a great interpreter and a great instructor." In fact, seeing the Jouvet production of *Ondine* in Paris, with sets by Pavel Tchelichev, had prompted Bentley to write, in 1949, that "in France a Giraudoux style of performance has ripened and is now overripe; in America the fruit is still green." But in the event the Broadway production, directed by Mel Ferrer and starring Ferrer and his future wife Audrey Hepburn, prompted the observation that "I suppose the farthest you can get from Jouvet is a standard leading man from Hollywood, pleasant and uninteresting, handsome and helpless, the only trouble being that at this point you realize what a lot there was to be said for Jouvet. If he scarcely bothered with characterization, Jouvet at least knew what kind of a play he was in." Such stimulating and enlightening comparisons reflect not, as Bentley's detractors used to claim, a reflex anti-Broadwayism but a poised and civilized search for utopian theatrical experiences. Bentley liked Audrey

Hepburn, as he had liked Julie Harris, in Anouilh; those French dramatists knew how to write stellar roles for ingenues, as did, in their way, Williams and Inge. He had, however, some gentle admonitions: "The actress shouldn't stand like a *Harper's Bazaar* model—legs flung apart, chest out, arms akimbo, etc. In speaking poetic lines, the identical singsong shouldn't be so often repeated." (Rereading this, I retract any reservations I may have had about Bentley as a describer of performances. Can one not, from these few words, conjure up Hepburn's performance in the mind's eye? And yet this is not descriptive gush; it is sound advice.)

The great Giraudoux production in New York in the fifties was that of *Tiger at the Gates*, a play produced here in 1955 but written in 1935 and dealing with the efforts of the Trojan Hector and the Greek Ulysses to avert the coming conflict. While not uncritical ("If decadence means that individual cells have developed at the expense of the organism as a whole, the art of Giraudoux cannot escape the charge of decadence. In all his plays, language descends in such a torrent that the speeches, as it were, jump the banks of the drama"), Bentley praises both play and production. The play, one of "the two best anti-war plays" of the 1930s (the other being Brecht's *Mother Courage*), attempts to show that "in a universe so malign, defiance [like Hector's] is the supremely—perhaps the uniquely—admirable quality." The text, "written before Chamberlain went to Berchtesgaden in 1938," seemed to anticipate both that event and the Eisenhower-Khrushchev get-together in Geneva in 1955. The play "could," says Bentley, "have been written last week (though I don't know by whom)." The fifties, one can now easily forget, seemed then an apocalyptic time.

As for the performers, Bentley found Michael Redgrave, who played Hector, "rather more than a match for Jouvet," although he thought the production's Ulysses (Walter Fitzgerald) "no match for the great actor for whom the part was written (Pierre Renoir)." Tipping the balance to Broadway, Bentley confessed, "I cannot imagine even a French production's outdoing Diane Cilento's witty comment on Helen or Leueen MacGrath's pointed portrayal of Cassandra." He found Christopher Fry's translation flawed by "a certain upper-class British gush," noting that "the same weakening is to be observed in the rejection of Giraudoux's austere, ironic title 'The Trojan War Will Not Take Place' for Fry's florid, obvious one."

The experience of *Tiger at the Gates* prompted Bentley to one of his great flights: "What is great theatre? The component parts are brains, good taste, fine craftsmanship, high purpose, and so forth and so on, but the whole is greater than the sum of the parts and comes to us as a single impression which is at once intellectual satisfaction and emotional entrancement." There is, it seems to me, a reservation in this recipe. He is not saying, exactly, that *Tiger at the Gates* is a great play—like, say, *Coriolanus*—but that, when directed with vitality, as it was on Broadway by Harold Clurman, and acted with high intelligence, the play *makes for* great theater.

A far stranger and stronger play was to come from France the next year, Beckett's *Waiting for Godot.* Written in French in 1949 and translated by the author in 1952, the work, with its mix of vaudeville buffoonery and apocalyptic symbolism, was one of the key works of the postwar European avant-garde, along with Ingmar Bergman's films *Seventh Seal* (1956) and *Wild Strawberries* (1957) and the slightly later signature films of Antonioni and Fellini. Even before its arrival on Broadway, *Godot* sparked cultural warfare. As Bentley wrote, "the minute I saw, in the *New York Times*, the producer's statement that the play was not for casual theatergoers but for intellectuals, I could have written Walter Kerr's review for him. And I felt propelled into writing a defense of the play as if by its success or failure civilization would stand or fall."

And sure enough, Kerr declared in *The New York Herald Tribune* that *Waiting for Godot* is not a real carrot; it is a patiently painted, painstakingly formed plastic job for the intellectual fruitbowl." (Of course, carrots, real or otherwise, are not placed in fruitbowls, but Kerr didn't want to lose the insinuation in "fruitbowl.") The production was saved, for Kerr, by the clowning of Bert Lahr, whom he called "an artist with an eye to God's own truth."

Confronted with such demagogic philistinism, Bentley stood up for Beckett, countering that "Mr. Kerr gave Bert Lahr all the credit for a traditional yet rich clown characterization, which, however, had been skillfully put together by Mr. Beckett, as any reader may verify." Bentley liked the production but remarked, rather blithely, that "I have less reverence for the play than he [director Herbert Berghof], and would have lopped off the last bit of the first act."

What did Bentley think of the play itself? He was at first concerned to situate it in a French philosophic/dramatic tradition. He felt it derived from a "point of view . . . pretty close to that of Anouilh or Sartre. *Waiting for Godot* is a play that one of them ought to have written. It is the quintessence of 'existentialism' in the popular, and most relevant, sense of the term—a philosophy which underscores the incomprehensibility, and therefore the meaninglessness, of the universe, the nausea which man feels upon being confronted with the fact of existence, the praiseworthiness of the acts of defiance man may perform—acts which are taken, on faith, as self-justifying, while, rationally speaking, they have no justification because they have no possibility of success." The play was for him an illustration of "the problem of nausea as a playwright's conscious attitude to life."

Bentley can be felt resisting *Godot* throughout his very respectful review. "To me," he concludes, "the play did not come over with the force of revelation, nor with that of sheer greatness." He decides that Beckett is "over-influenced by Joyce" and that the play was "cut from those coats of many colors, *Ulysses* and *Finnegan's* [*sic*] *Wake*." In a 1958 piece on Ionesco (included here), Bentley calls Beckett "tiresome—when (let us say) he has cried out that the world is a terrible place for the seventeen hundredth time."

Why was Bentley so uncomfortable with *Godot*, surely the greatest new play he reviewed for *The New Republic*? I suspect, for one thing, that its novelty was blinding. With learning and subtlety, Bentley strove to place the play in a tradition of French nihilism, a tradition illustrated by the names of Sartre and Anouilh. And although he was no Marxist, Bentley was enough of a Brechtian (and a Leavisite, be it said) to reject nihilism (or "nausea," in the emotional register) as a possible ground of great art. Later in his review, though, Bentley contradicts himself by damning Beckett for an excessive discipleship to Joyce, whose *Ulysses* and *Finnegans Wake* are profoundly life-affirming—the very opposite of nihilistic.

Now, all these years and Beckett plays and Beckett productions and Beckett biographies later, it has become easy to see what Bentley missed in *Godot*. Above all, Beckett's is a play informed by Europe's (and the writer's) experiences in the Hitler war. It owes far more to the sufferings of the 1940s than to the now-negligible Sartre. And it achieves (*pace* Bentley) a perfectly dramatic articulation of its themes, which strike us as issuing not from nausea but from an idiosyncratic mix of despair and humor. And the humor is Irish in general and Beckett's in particular. In 1956, one of the few known facts about Beckett was that he had been for a time Joyce's secretary. That he was, but today the enormous differences between the two men are evident. Joyce was a tenderer soul, his humor running to the cerebral on the one hand and to the corporeal on the other. Beckett was a stony but suffering man who liked to strike a bleak gaiety out of the hard clash of character upon character.

Bentley's estimate of Beckett is doubtless different today. I note, for instance, that he wrote in 1998 that "it is not often that anything really happens in the history of drama, but at least twice in this our century, now about over, something did." The two occasions he means were the premiere of Pirandello's *Six Characters in Search of an Author* in Rome in 1921 and the premiere of *Waiting for Godot* in Paris in 1953.

To point to what was missing in Bentley's instant report on *Waiting for Godot* is to hold him to standards he has himself created. He is a wholly serious and profoundly learned man who has consecrated his life to thinking about and translating and making theater. He has taught me—and I'm sure, many others—how to think about drama. Regular drama criticism was for him a sort of halfway house between theory (exemplified by *The Playwright as Thinker*) and praxis (realized in his directing and, above all, in his very interesting plays, which often rethink the plays of earlier playwrights—his *The Fall of the Amazons*, for example, is a feminist revision of Kleist's *Penthesilea*, while his *Rondo* is a gay reworking of Schnitzler's *La Ronde*). But this particular halfway house turns out to be both sturdy and beautiful, luminously reflecting the taste of the architect and the weather of the times.

Eric Bentley, as is abundantly evident in this book, is not merely the twentieth century's best drama critic (how strong, except for Shaw, is the competition, after all?); he is one of its most bracing and witty writers.

PREFACE (1968)

I SERVED AS dramatic critic to *The New Republic* from 1952 to 1956. My reviews for the first two of these four seasons are collected under the title *The Dramatic Event*; those for the second two under the title *What Is Theatre?* At the end of the present volume, I have also ventured to look before and after. "Drama Now" and "The Old Vic, The Old Critics, and the New Generation," dating back more than twenty years, were my first contributions to dramatic criticism. Ten pieces follow, from the years 1957–1967. On the other hand, this volume is strictly limited to journalism. Three longer, more essayistic studies, originally smuggled into *The Dramatic Event* and *What Is Theatre?* respectively, have been taken out and included in another book, *The Theatre of Commitment*.

By way of preface to this collection, I propose to reprint a letter to the Off Broadway *Showbill* and a little article from the Broadway *Playbill*, both dating from 1957, the first year of my retirement from play reviewing:

1

A LETTER TO SHOWBILL

DEAR EDITORS: I haven't time to write you an article, but I know what worries me about Off Broadway, and I thought I'd simply tell you about it in a letter.

It is chiefly that Off Broadway is just the same as Broadway, only worse. Off Broadway has not the resources of Broadway, but it suffers under the same curse: dependence upon the so-called critics.

I have a proposal to make: that all these critics shoot themselves.

This measure, however, is dictated only by malice. It would have no salutary effect: the next team of "critics" would be just as silly.

So I have a substitute proposal: that all the "critics" resign. And, to show my good faith, I have myself resigned as a dramatic critic of *The New Republic* before sending this letter off to you. Will all those others who have made a similar decision for Christ please write in to the Off Broadway *Showbill*?

Meanwhile, I shall assume that *Showbill* will receive no correspondence from "critics" who have seen the error of their ways. So I have put together a substitute proposal—and one that I hope is more practical. This is that some Off Broadway house find a way of keeping a show going without "critical" endorsement. My idea is that the "critics" not be invited at all. The public would simply have to be informed by means of paid ads that the show was on. Or how else? I am not a managerial genius or else I would already have found the answer. I put the question to the managerial geniuses who will be reading your paper.

For only when Off Broadway makes itself independent can it again be what it was in its finest period (the late teens and early twenties of this century), namely, a place for experimental productions of plays that either are literally or virtually new. How distressing it is to think that nearly all (perhaps all?) the big Off Broadway successes are by well-established authors who have already reached a mass audience, often with the very play in question (*Threepenny Opera* and *Iceman Cometh* being prime examples). In the category of the virtually new, incidentally, I put old plays that have still not arrived in our city, like most of the plays of Strindberg. But even a Shakespeare play becomes new at a given moment in history. The big Shakespeare theatres are, quite properly, academic and, like the colleges, dole out Shakespeare plays indiscriminately all the time. It is for the Off Broadway people to seize the historic moment and bring off Shakespeare productions which would have quite another kind of resonance. Although I didn't see it, I am given to understand that Orson Welles' *Julius Caesar* (though technically *on* Broadway) was an effort of this sort. . . .

But I mustn't break my promise not to write you an article.

My best wishes for your magazine—provided it proves to be a thoroughly subversive affair.

Sincerely yours,
ERIC BENTLEY

2

THE POSSIBILITY OF
A DIFFERENT KIND OF THEATRE

WITHOUT SLIGHTING the achievements of the kind of theatre we do have—achievements like *Guys and Dolls* and *My Fair Lady* —I want to enquire if we could not have other kinds of theatre as well.

It will not be easy, for the whole weight of the entertainment industry goes into the effort to repeat former successes rather than create new ones. To duplicate, not to originate, is the aim and the method. Hence, if Broadway people take up a work that is different, they change it till it is the same. The Broadway critics have no higher praise for a classic than to say that it is as good as the latest commercial hit; and the Broadway producer's way with a classic is to make sure that it is identical with the latest commercial hit.

Take the style of presentation. The idea will be to do a Shakespeare comedy as if it were *Pajama Game*. Otherwise the critics will be bored and set the play down as minor Shakespeare, a rank, apparently, far below *Pajama Game*. A production has merit in the degree of its violence—the violence of its attack on the nervous system. The superlatives of newspaper critics, quite logically, are words like stunning, electric, overpowering, staggering, high voltage, "knocks you out of your seat." Even softer moods can be made violent—by sentimentality—and the merit of a softer piece can be measured in buckets-full of tears.

So the legitimate triumphs of commercial theatre are offset by its murderous onslaughts on everything that does not belong to the pattern—that is, by the Procrustean procedure of stretching or mutilating everything until it does conform. Comedy is treated as farce, and tragedy as melodrama. Cool drama of discussion is hotted up into phony-soulful romance. Shakespeare's most religious play turns into a varsity show. It is all as if someone decided that Mozart would only be interesting if played by Louis Armstrong.

Disorder reigns, and impurity. By impurity, I do not mean indecency, which has had a place in the theatre since Aristophanes and longer. I mean impurity in something closer to its chemical sense—a mixture of elements. In our theatre, you seldom see ANYTHING in its purity. Nearly always there is an effort, instead, to combine the best of both, and indeed all, worlds. Our lighter comedies are ruined by a moralism which has no proper place there. Musical comedies begin to put on the airs of operas, if not of oratorios. There is moral impurity in these mixtures, of course. And real dramatic critics have to spend a great deal of their space exposing the moral imposture —the equivocation—in commercial plays—from *Camille* and *The Second Mrs. Tanqueray* to *Tea and Sympathy* and *Cat on a Hot Tin Roof.*

The journalist-critics of our middle-class culture are, of course, *against* the indecency which the theatre needs and *for* the impurity from which it can only suffer. Healthy and delightful bawdry they will denounce as dirty and improper, while accepting real corruption provided it is sanctimoniously enough presented. Because they find impurity pure, they naturally find purity *im*pure. They have turned the moral and the aesthetic order topsy turvy.

One different theatre I should like to see is a THEATRE OF

PURITY. Yes, and even, in an aesthetic sense, a puritanic theatre, a theatre in which there is a place for simplicity, austerity, sincerity. Most of the masters of modern theatre have felt the need of something of the sort. Bernard Shaw, for example, called three of his plays "Plays for Puritans." In the usual sense, these plays seemed rather less puritanic than most, but they were puritanic in that they replaced the equivocations of popular prejudice with consistent and responsible attitudes. The theatre-goer was deprived of some of the titillations and indulgences he expected. Behind the good-natured Shavian dialogue there was a certain severity. Shaw said:

> The conception of theatrical art as the exploitation of popular superstition and ignorance, as the thrilling of poor bumpkins with ghosts and blood, exciting them with blows and stabs, duping them with tawdry affectations of rank and rhetoric, thriving parasitically on their moral diseases instead of purging their souls and refining their senses: this is the tradition that the theatre finds it so hard to get away from.

Purging their souls and refining their senses! Obviously, most theatre does just the opposite: it prevents the senses from developing any sensitivity by accepting them as they already are, and it either leaves their souls strictly alone or burdens them with moral duplicity.

Shaw fought for purity and for puritanism, and so did one of the great theatrical reformers of the next generation after Shaw—Jacques Copeau. He was less concerned with writing than with performance. His aim was to simplify the stage itself, and by implication his whole doctrine is in the single phrase *un tréteau nu*—a bare platform—which was his definition of the kind of stage he wanted. The actor comes out on a platform and acts. This is the essence of theatre. We should never get too far away from the essence. And, in a time of decadence, we should return to the essence.

The next example I will cite is that of a man who may at first seem to have nothing in common with Copeau, Bertolt Brecht. But wide apart as were their philosophies of life, they alike sought purity in theatre, and found it in plays and production for puritans. Brecht dismantled, as it were, the existing theatre, and started out from the ground up. One of the puritanic features of his stage is its refusal of all but white light. I would not defend this notion—at any rate not its exclusivity—but it has certainly been a very dramatic alternative to the decadent, over-colored and over-dark lighting of most modern theatre. I see it as a corrective, rather than a permanent replacement.

I have been preoccupied with the theatre of Brecht for a number of years just because it is the most carefully worked-out alternative to the kind of theatre I have been criticizing. In this latter theatre, nothing can be left as it is, it all has to be pumped up higher. *Inflation* is its chief characteristic. The children can't sit still, and the adults are all happy drunk. Each performance is full of an arbitrary energy known as Real Theatre. . . . But the theatre of Brecht is no less interesting when slow than when fast, when quiet than when loud, when calm than when excited. Though it is a theatre full of artistic delights, it is also a theatre in which statements are made and need not pretend to be more than statements. For a statement is a fine, clear, human thing, and shines by contrast in a world of pseudo-statement—a world of slogans, doubletalk, jargon, cant.

In politics, however, purity is impossible, and Brecht is a political playwright. If we seek an example of conspicuous purity, the man to cite would be not Brecht but Garcia Lorca. Unlike Brecht, Lorca had not been eaten away at by the nihilism of our time. There is a pristine, an unspoiled quality to his spirit: studying him one seems to understand the biblical expression "pure of heart." Here is something he wrote about the theatre:

Rather than do honor to poets and dramatists, I'd like to challenge and attack them passionately and roundly: "Are you afraid of this?" "Are you unable to express a man's fear of the sea?" "Do you shy off from a subject like the despair of soldiers who hate war?" The artist's soul whose foundation is critical love is tempered by necessity and struggle; by easy flattery it becomes effeminate and is destroyed. Our theatres are full of deceiving syrens, they are garlanded by hothouse roses, and the public is content, applauding dummy hearts and trivial dialogue. The dramatic poet who doesn't wish to be forgotten must not forget the open fields and wild roses, the fields where the farmers work, where dawn is wet on the grass, and where the pigeon, wounded by an unknown hunter, dies among the rushes with none to hear its grief.

Must not forget the open fields. The theatre is such a sophisticated place, and if the sophistication is that of a Wilde, we may not regret it. But mostly it is a sophistication rather shabby and third-rate, not a positive sophistication consisting in a certain conquest of life (if only by cynicism) but a negative sophistication consisting in hiding from life behind a barrage of hotels, cafes, nightclubs, agents' offices, that ersatz civilisation which Henry Miller calls the Air Conditioned Nightmare. Because of its apparently natural tendency towards the unnatural, the theatre has perpetually to be recalled to nature, to "real life" as it is called, which often in our time is taken to mean the sordid part of reality. Sordid reality easily turns to unreality when it is artificially separated from non-sordid reality, and nothing is more unreal than much of our realism. Lorca's phrase "the open fields" is much more helpfully suggestive. What a charming change it would be if a playwright, instead of knocking us out of our seats etcetera, would bring us the fragrance of a wild rose and the freedom of a field! What a joy, what a relief, if the freedom he proffered were not that of routine liberalism but that of an open field!

But what are the possibilities of our ever having such a theatre? In fact, Brecht and Lorca—though now generally acknowledged as two of the leading playwrights of this century—are almost unknown on our stage. This is not accidental. We have a theatre which has no place for such authors. We have a theatre which insists on one kind of thing, and these authors provided another kind of thing. A Lorca play would be as little at home on a Broadway stage as St. Francis at a table in the Stork Club.

Some people say that the Off Broadway theatre is the solution, but at present it is not. At present, it lives by the same

rules as Broadway. The Off Broadway theatres that have succeeded did so by the approval of the same half-dozen newspapermen from whom *My Fair Lady* got its start. Conversely,
when these gentlemen dislike an Off Broadway show, it has to
close down within a few days just like a Broadway show. So,
Off Broadway managers have felt compelled to limit themselves to authors who are favorites of Mr. Brooks Atkinson.
I am far from implying that these are not good authors. My
point is, rather, that it is grotesque to limit the repertoire of
a whole city to one man's personal favorites. The result is
that Off Broadway can get away with Chekhov and O'Neill
but not with quite a few authors equally distinguished. For,
Off Broadway, when one says "the critics," one means chiefly
a single critic, the critic of the *Times*. . . . What our city needs
is a couple of good permanent acting companies.

THE DRAMATIC
EVENT

Professional Playgoing

GEORGE JEAN NATHAN long ago established the right of the drama critic to leave after the first act. The time has now come for the critic to claim the right to stay away altogether. Deciding what we can do without is, after all, one of the great tasks of living, and, unlike some of the others, it can be performed rather efficiently. Having noted the way John Steinbeck is going—or Aldous Huxley—pick a name—I have decided not to read his next book. My decision may turn out to be mistaken. The next book may be a masterpiece. If it is, I shall hear about it, though; obviously I don't have time to read everything on the off-chance of stumbling on a masterpiece . . .

Few of the playwrights whose work is performed on Broadway have names one already knows. I decide whether to see their plays after reading the reviews of Brooks Atkinson, Walter Kerr, Richard Watts, William Hawkins, and whoever else is on sale at the nearest newsstand. When I've seen a play, I may realize I don't agree with any of these gentlemen. But I can figure out from what they say whether I *would* agree with them. I know, for example, what kind of play strikes me as sentimental and strikes Mr. X as charming, wholesome, heartwarming, beautiful, and morally inspiring. I know what kind of play strikes me as boringly trivial and strikes Mr. Y as quite splendid because it illustrates the view that the age of Ibsen is over, that drama should be free of preaching, that . . .

Still, if they all like it, I go; if they are divided in their opinions, I go; it is only when they all—or nearly all—*dis*like it that I deliberately stay away. The critics' rejections are far less misleading than their enthusiasms. And anyway it is better to be misled a few times than to go to the theatre too often. It

is important that a theatre critic see as few shows as possible:
the habit of regular attendance on complimentary tickets dis-
torts the whole experience of theatre-going and can even kill
the pleasure of it. For the man who is dragged almost nightly
to a show that begins forty minutes too early and which he
must "write up" by midnight, what is left of the pleasure he
had as a boy in Cleveland when he wrote to New York two
months ahead for a dollar-twenty ticket at a single show? Some
of my senior colleagues at the business tell me they try to atone
for the boredom they feel by writing up an ecstasy they do not
feel. That would explain pretty well the style in which theatre
reportage is couched. I prefer to leave when I am bored, to stay
at home when I think I *would* be bored, and in either event
not to go into print. That is why I am surprised when, having
taken issue with a play or a performance, I am told: "You
must have been bored." I take issue only when I am *not* bored.
Dissent, surely, is a proof of interest. If you were the playwright, wouldn't you rather have a critic take issue with your
play than be so ecstatic that you can tell he's making it up?

Of the many Broadway shows, 1952–1954, that are totally
ignored in this book, only a certain number belong to the
category, just defined, of plays I deliberately did not see.
Accident or illness kept me from others. There were some I
saw and found without sufficient interest to write on. There
were a few which would have drawn from me a mere repetition of what everyone else has said about them: why bother?
There were several cases in which some personal involvement
interfered too much; I could have written a notice that would,
in my opinion, have been honest; but I didn't always wish to
have my motives questioned by others; even though I might in
turn have questioned the motives of the questioners. After all,
a critic's motives are seldom questioned except by the criticized and their friends; and to impute bad motives to a critic is
the standard way of refusing to take criticism. "No, no, so-
and-so's criticism of my performance didn't hurt me in the
least, don't you know he wanted his wife to play the part?" In
general, the critic has to try to take this sort of thing, just as
the artist has to try to take criticism. I have sought to avoid
eliciting such comments only in cases where my personal in-

volvement was unusually delicate. In those circumstances, the critic can avoid the wildest calumny only by keeping silent; perhaps not even then.

I should not pretend that a critic's motives couldn't be bad; I merely observe that one imputation of motives leads to another. We are all sinners: it would be better to discuss the points at issue. Assume, if you like, that everyone's motives are perfectly vile.

I should not pretend, either, that the criticized artist can avoid being hurt and angry; I have been a criticized artist. But the critic cannot do his work without hurting; he resembles the dentist. Even to say that artist A is very good is to spread the rumor that artist B is not so good. Motive mongers will say the critic has a grudge against B's wife.

We are forever being disappointed because we insist on cherishing absurd expectations. We expect purity of motive in all mankind and from critics absolute justice into the bargain; and we howl like children when we don't get them; it is all a great waste of time. Nor are we much more sensible if we proceed from a tardy recognition of general fallibility to a demand for extreme reserve in public utterance. That we are tentative and skeptical in our philosophy is not to say that we have to be cagey and non-committal in discussion; that is the road, not to truth and joy, but to evasion and respectability. The critic is uncompromising, not because he regards himself as infallible, nor even because he feels very sure of himself, but because it is his job to be so. It is true, he enjoys this job; he enjoys a fight; his writing embodies his zest for living. Yet he doesn't enjoy all of the job. The constant infliction of pain is a burden to him, the price he has to pay for the right to practice his profession. For the journalist-critic, the only alternative to a sharp tongue is a mealy mouth.

I look nostalgically back to the nineteenth century, a more liberal time than ours, when dissent was decent, and an adverse criticism didn't have to be explained away by the imputation of jealous hostility or the sly whisper that the critic fell on his head at the age of two. Let us hope the day will again come when one man can say to another: "I think you are utterly wrong; I think your book—play—performance—is a hopeless failure; I am going to give you my reasons for think-ing so; you may retort that it is I who am completely mistaken; let us dine together on Tuesday."

What can the critic do? As I see it, his job is to use the verb *to be,* the adjectives *good* and *bad,* and the conjunctions *and* and *but.* He tells you what the show *is,* argues the *pros* and *cons* of it in a series of observations and counter observations, and announces if, in his opinion, the whole thing is any *good.* He will withstand the temptation to omit the *ands,* because he is interested in the additional fact that tips the scale. He will insist on the *buts,* because his mind is dialectical: he likes to see the other side of every coin. Since he cannot draw back from the act of appraisal, he will not substitute modish verbi-age, scientific or belle-lettristic, for plain *bads* and *goods.*

The theatre critic's concern is *theatre:* playwright and actor, director, scene designer, musician. But since all these work together to interpret *life,* the critic's approach will not be merely formal. Being a journalist, the drama critic will report the news. And we can judge him by the standards we apply to other journalists. Does he spot the essential things? Has he a nose for a new trend? At any rate we can't grumble at the recurrence of the word New. It is the critic's job to identify and describe the New Actress, the New Playwright, the New Rococo, the New Estheticism, the New Conformism, the New Conservatism—before they grow old.

As long as a critic has the qualities of his defects, no merely human being has the right to complain that he has the defects of his qualities. Even the limitations of the art he practices are not faults, provided he recognizes them and makes allowances. The limits of theatre criticism are soon reached. Here we have no lofty form of meditation conceived in solitude, recollected in tranquillity, and incorporated in large art-form or volumi-nous treatise. We have only a man's immediate response immediately recorded in the briefest bit of prose. Too often the *and* or *but* that would make the statement complete and comprehensive are missing; for *bad* we must read *good;* for *is, is not.* Practice the art of journalism, and even your remarks of a few months ago will surprise you. "Did I say that?" Reading reviews (including my own) of shows I have seen, I am given pause by many, all too many, distortions of the truth. The chief cause, I think, is *classification*. The New This and the New That are classes. The critic is all the time putting artists and works of art in categories. That is bad enough. The journalist critic goes one worse: rashly consigning his victims to this pigeonhole and that, he has to improvise even the pigeonholes. The critic of new art is all the time, says posterity, making mistaken judgments. The journalist-critic of new art goes one worse and maximizes his chances of error by rushing into print with his first hasty impression. He finds it interesting; that is his chief justification.[1] As the world goes, it is not a bad one: how little there is to be said for posterity's kind of wisdom! Nonetheless, I have been dismayed to see how often my snap categories have proved a bed of Procrustes for my poor authors and actors. I can only advise the reader in advance: our new actresses are often better than The New Actress or different, our new playwrights are better than The New Playwright or different . . . and so on.

After *classification* or *generality,* the chief source of error is something very like its opposite. Call it *immediacy*. What I have in mind is that the drama critic has blinkers on. He sees only what he sees; it is not very much; and he records it without asking questions such as: is this what I ought to have seen? Is it consistent with what I said I saw last week? When a dramatic critic looks back through a couple of dozen notices he has written, he is surprised not only by this remark or that but at totally unforeseen relationships between one remark and another. For example, the reader of the present volume might conclude that its author considers M. Anouilh flatly a better dramatist than Giraudoux. That is the impression given by separate reviews of *Colombe* and *Ondine*. Several factors

---

[1] In his important book *Buzz Buzz*, James Agate quotes C. E. Montague to the following effect: "And yet for old theatre notices there may be a kind of excuse. You wrote them in haste, it is true, with few books about you or moments to look a thing up; hot air and the dust of the playhouse were still in your lungs; you were sure to say things that would seem sorry gush or rant if you saw them again in the morning. How bad it all was for measure, containment, or balance! But that heat of the playhouse is not wholly harmful. Like sherris sack in the system of Falstaff, it hath a two-fold operation; 'it ascends me into the brain . . . makes it apprehensive, quick, forgetive, full of nimble, fiery and delectable shapes.' At least it sometimes gives you that illusion; below yourself in certain ways, you hope you are above yourself in others."

are involved. First, the author had no such comparison in mind. Second, he saw the plays not in Platonic purity but in particular productions. Third, there is the dual translation problem: does an author translate well? and: has he found the best possible translator? The reader is free to ask what questions he chooses; but in fairness he too should make allowances. Journalism is journalism. And there are times when consistency isn't worth a rap.

Something a critic says that is "wildly inconsistent with his whole theory" may be an inspiration. A drama critic must dare to say the things that don't fit if only because he is a reporter. He writes down what he in fact saw or what he in fact felt. For a dramatic critic the primary—I do not say the ultimate—experience is live contact with the actor.

I should be sorry, however, if the chronicle that follows is a mass of contradictions. I should like to think that if the phenomena reviewed are various, and my attitude to them subject both to chance variation and deliberate revision, the classifications have nevertheless some general validity and the judgments are the coherent product of a single, though limited, mind. Pirandello thought we were totally out of touch with other people and also with ourselves at all moments but the present one. We are each a hundred thousand moments and states of mind that are unrelated to each other.

I am hoping—and indeed assuming—that Pirandello was wrong.

Pity His Simplicity

> *"The few times I tried to read Truman Capote, I had to give up . . . His literature makes me nervous."*
>
> —WILLIAM FAULKNER

AT FIRST BLUSH Mr. Capote's play *The Grass Harp* is simply ridiculous: it is about living in trees. But it is saved from the ridiculous by the trite when, late in the evening, the conclusion is announced: "we can't live in trees, maybe some of us would like to, but none of us can."

It is true that the arboreal fable of *The Grass Harp* is meant to symbolize an escape from humdrum reality, that Mr. Capote's theme is the search for one's real self, and that such a theme is not to be stigmatized as trite merely because it is traditional. It has the effect of triteness in this play because it is in no way rendered active by Mr. Capote's art: when he has finished it still belongs to tradition; he has in no way made it his own; we hear only other voices echoing in other rooms. On occasion this may be partly blamed on the actors. In the large part of the bad but subsequently repentant sister, Ruth Nelson makes Mr. Capote's spreadeagle prose sound even more improbable than it need; as the Wise Southern Judge, Russell Collins seems to add an actor's unctuousness to an author's. Yet the one performer who contrives to remain real (by remaining herself) is forced to call attention to ham writing by making us feel she only speaks the lines because she has to. This is Mildred Natwick, without whom the play would have no adult existence.

The triteness is in the conclusions and at the core; in the premises and at the periphery all is ridiculous. Since the ridiculous is acceptable when it is funny and unpretentious, one can readily accept such minor characters as (in order of merit?) Buster the goldfish, the daft, if somewhat overacted, barber of Sterling Holloway, the headlong cosmetician of that superb zany Alice Pearce, and several other villagers who might be described as *by* Robert Lewis *out of* Charlie Chaplin. On the level of wise-cracking Broadway farce—on which the whole large part of the servant is played by Georgia Burke—Mr. Capote reveals a surprising talent. (The part itself is stolen from *Member of the Wedding;* Mr. Capote knows a good thing when he sees it.)

If only he would stay on the wise-cracking level! Instead, he follows what seems to be a new school of theatre and pursues the ridiculous high into the intense inane. Negatively described, this school is the latest revulsion against realism. It is usually presented in positive terms as a rebirth of poetic drama or at least as an assertion of fantasy and charm and theatricality over brute facts. Disparate authors come together to produce a somewhat coherent total result. The Eliot of *The Cocktail Party* joins hands with the Huxley of *The Gioconda Smile* to relieve the rich of their sexual guilt by appealing to a Higher Reality. Eliot and Huxley keep the framework of the drawing-room play; Anouilh and Fry, even when they present a drawing room, make sure that the place is filled with the fauna of a rococo fancy even if it is not actually decked with the flora of the new school in stage design. The new school in stage design is the counterpart of the new school in dramaturgy: elegant, dandified, and, it must be said, effeminate. The father of the school is the late Christian Bérard, a great designer though a highly specialized one. His specialty was costumes; his sets appeared to be costumes for the stage itself; the stage was a lovely woman.

This brings us back to *The Grass Harp* which has sets by Cecil Beaton, the English Bérard, who is, quite literally, a costumier turned stage designer. His work dominates the evening at the Martin Beck Theatre largely because it quite simply is what it is. It "is" the new style. It is what Mr. Capote and, I should judge, Robert Lewis aspire to and only partially, ambiguously, half-heartedly achieve. For example: there is nothing of the spirit of the South in Mr. Beaton's work, and why should there be? Art is a holiday, is itself, is silk shawls and luscious colors, is chintz and upholstery. He is happy in the realm that I have called the ridiculous; he does not need the trite. But Mr. Capote has to use words, can't get by with color and form, can't help being involved with life even if he is incapable of shaping it. It is almost as if he started with a realistic play and later—too much later—tried to transform it into a fantasy. In combination the realistic and fantastic elements became the trite and the ridiculous, respectively.

Had Mr. Lewis hewed to either line, realistic or fantastic, he might have made something of the play in actual production. As it is, the directing is non-committal and unsure without being discreet and unobtrusive. Mr. Lewis tries to cover up the ambiguity of the play, or his own ambiguous feelings about it, with apparatus: Cecil Beaton's costumes and decor, Virgil Thomson's music, and his own directorial gimmicks. Of the gimmicks the showiest is the shining of flashlights in Miss

Nelson's face when she wishes to make a pronouncement to the tree-dwellers: a shot is fired, everyone wonders who is hit, and the flashlights pick out the wounded man with magical unanimity. One could perhaps be rather amused by this sort of thing had not the simpler scenes been so neglected by comparison. I suppose the opening and closing scenes of the play could never be wholly convincing, yet they might have been at least interesting had Mr. Lewis helped the actors to bring a reality from themselves which the author had not managed to give them in his script. As things are, the domestic scenes are as wooden as the table they revolve around. Where something human might have been shaped and defined, Mr. Lewis fled into triviality and ostentation.

Admittedly no one would wish to banish triviality and ostentation from the theatre, their traditional home. What one protests against in the trivial, ostentatious work of today is its intellectual pretentiousness. Not long ago two very showy plays opened in New York, one from each of the principal schools of current practice, the Kazanian-realistic and the Beatonian-gorgeous: *Flight into Egypt* and *The Grass Harp*. In both cases the showiness would be in order were it not that we are meant to take both plays so very seriously. And in both cases the "bigness" of the production operates, not as delightful showmanship, but as a portentous frame for a very small picture. A mountain of production makes the squeal of the mouse that emerges the more plaintive and feeble.

Flight into Egypt might have had an identity had it been either a social drama by George Tabori or a psychological melodrama by Elia Kazan; it fell between the author's and the director's stools. The reason why *The Grass Harp* is so far out of tune is more fundamental. The play seems to me decadent —not, it is true, in the life depicted, but in the spirit of the depiction.

Although in *The Grass Harp* there is none of the scandalous subject-matter for which writers like Mr. Capote are known, and we are, on the contrary, in the company of virginal old ladies, innocent schoolgirls, and wistful widowers, this author's interest in innocence is in fact more extravagant than his interest in vice. His is a form of sentimentality—known and praised in the trade as Warmth and/or Humanity—which is the reverse side of unpleasant sophistication. Ostensibly, we are presented with purity, with simplicity. Yet when we try to describe these qualities in Mr. Capote's play, the word we feel the need of is *off;* for everything is slightly off color, off center, off key. What is Mr. Capote after? Is he fooling? It would be a relief to write him down the last bewilderer of the bourgeoisie. But Mr. Capote aims to please. He wants to be Warm and Human. I imagine him on his knees at that crossroads where *Harper's Bazaar* and Culture meet, addressing a prayer to Brooks Atkinson: "Gentle Critic Warm and Human / Look upon a Little Truman . . ."

Merchant of Venice, Long Island

IT BEGAN WITH a phone call some weeks ahead. I picked up the receiver, and a voice said it was Mike Todd's office and asked did I intend to see Mr. Todd's show at Jones Beach. Before I could hesitate, the voice added: "There'll be supper at the Stork Club before we drive you out there." The bait was irresistible. I would see Organization and Showmanship. I would see how the other half live.

There was something fishy about it from the start, only one is never warned. Two days before the show my tickets had not arrived, and when I phoned the Todd office I learned that on the second night (when weekly reviewers normally attend) there was no supper and no transportation. I was transferred to the first night when I said that otherwise I wouldn't go at all.

The streetdoor of the Stork Club opens just like any other door, we found, but as soon as we were inside it we found ourselves cornered by a close semicircle of severe gentlemen, one of whom snapped: "Yes?" and stared as if we had offered him an affront. We looked down to make sure we had clothes on. Or was it just that they weren't the right sort of clothes? I had been instructed to "look for Mr. G— in the Joquelin Room." But Mr. G—'s status was as unknown and therefore as non-existent to the snappy man at the door as our own. Had we not thought of the password MIKE TODD we might still be sweating on the sidewalk of 53rd Street.

The other half must have been in some other part of the club: the crowd in the Joquelin Room was not perceptibly of a different species from our own. Many of them looked up as we entered and quickly looked away again when they saw we weren't Aly Khan and Rita Hayworth. It was barely 5.30 but already the martinis were warm and watery. We could have had a nice time on lox canapés had not discretion prompted us to save our appetites for the kind of meal you see in the movies. By 6.25 we had plucked up courage to ask if perhaps supper was to be served in some other room—there being no signs of it within short range—and were dismayed to be told by a smiling waiter: "This party is leaving by bus at 6.30." No announcement was made, but at 6.30 an inner voice seemed to speak to many people at once. There was a general movement towards the elevator. As they passed one of the last tables each nudged his neighbor and pointed at a heavy-checked shirt beneath a moustache and whispered: "That's Brooks Atkinson —and he's eating!" People discussed whether he'd had to pay for his frankfurter or whether Mr. Todd had ordered supper for one.

I suppose the heat couldn't be blamed on our impresario; the weatherman is incorruptible. Still, many of us had visions of sleek, fast limousines and air-conditioned railway coaches. But no, we were assigned to buses, and they were fetid and slow.

Optimists in our party had heard that now at last food would be served: was there not a waiter aboard with a white tie and black sash? Unhappily, the man was a chronic deprecator. He disowned the whole enterprise and professed a preference for working on planes and trains. What had been done about food he really had no idea. To his surprise some ice-cream sticks—Good Humors, no less—were found and he consented to hand them round "as far as they'll go"—which was about two-thirds of the way down the bus. After dessert, the main course. Some sandwiches turned up, and husbands were asked if they'd mind sharing one with their wives. The Coca-Cola without which no banquet is complete was found in the aisle, none the worse for having been walked on. After most of it had been consumed warm, ice was unearthed. *Tout le confort américain.* Anyhow, man shall not live by bread alone. On every seat in the bus was a copy of the program. It contained several photographs of Mr. Todd, one of them occupying a full page (8⅓ by 11) on gold paper. "Mr. Todd is Mr. Showman," it said.

But is he? In the days of Johann Strauss (mentioned in the program, though in smaller type than Mr. Todd) it was fashionable to miss the first act. Is that why this opening of his *Night in Venice* was scheduled for eight while the press buses were driven in at nine? It can be interesting to figure out a story when you arrive in the middle—provided you can see and hear what happens after your arrival. At Jones Beach, the grand canal that flows between stage and auditorium remains, both physically and psychologically, an unbridged gap. You can't see faces and you don't feel part of the occasion. The public address system only makes matters worse. Being loud and tinny, it spoils the music. Being indistinct, it does not communicate the words. One is also very disturbed to see lips moving in one place and to hear the sound issue from quite another place. That is, one would be—if one could see lips. More often, one heard a great bellow from center stage and some seconds later discovered the singer on the outskirts.

I don't doubt that Strauss's *Night in Venice* could be pretty swish open-air entertainment if tricked out by theatre artists of the current Gorgeous School (Peter Brook, Oliver Messel *et al.*) ; it would be fancy but it would be fun. Yet we are letting Mr. Todd off much too lightly if we complain that he has no taste or sophistication: who ever said he had? *A Night in Venice* suffers more from helpless incomprehension, empty awe in the face of culture, than from philistine opposition to it. The dully obvious dancing, the anti-climactic glamor of the lighting, the cheap colors of the costumes, the tawdriness of the sets, the ham of the acting, all unmistakably belong to the tradition of "high" art. One has nothing against the idea of grandiose showmanship; one will even pay the price of a certain amount of vulgarity. *A Night in Venice* is not grandiose enough. The first act peters out in a disordered fizzing of quite ordinary rockets. At the première, the water ballet never took place at all; instead there were apologies on the microphone. Where is the showmanship of yesteryear? No one was entranced for a minute by all the awkward, mechanical approaches to romance in turrets and gondolas. There was a hopeful moment when the tumblers went to work—acrobatics, athletics, *something* physically thrilling was what the show needed—but they were hustled off stage before they got started. Mr. Todd was doing a highbrow show for lowbrows, and nobody seemed to like it. If he would do a lowbrow show well, even highbrows would like it.

Many of my journalist colleagues had had enough by intermission but there was no extracting the buses from the parking lots. My friend and I crept down from our high stadium seat to a point where the stage was a little less invisible, though we now had to stand. The chapter of mishaps continued on the return journey. The police proved as incorruptible as the weatherman and made our driver leave the parkway and find Manhattan by what looked to me like an Indian trail. It was two o'clock by the time we reached mid-town. During the ride, a newspaperman from New Jersey remarked: "And my wife said, '*I* have to stay home and put the baby to bed while *you* go gallivantin' off to the Stork Club!'" "Mike Todd had the right idea," was another comment, "supper at the Stork Club'll put 'em in the mood."

Are the critics more corruptible than the weatherman and the police? Mr. Todd might consider the case of the servant in *A Night in Venice*. Though he accepts a bribe of twenty scudi, he is scandalized at the idea of accepting five, ten, or fifteen. Now, suppose he had been offered twenty and not paid. Wouldn't he have been more scandalized still?

Eugene O'Neill's Pietà

BACK TO THE FARM. The New England farm of *Desire Under the Elms* and *Beyond the Horizon*. The issue is ownership. The villain of the piece tries to wrest it from the heroine and her father. He even gets the hero on his side. So heroine and father plot our hero's ruin: he is to be disgraced by being found in our heroine's bed. I am telling the story of Eugene O'Neill's *A Moon for the Misbegotten*,[1] and have come to the end of the second act. In Act Three comes a surprise. Our heroine has the opportunity of carrying out her revenge but she discovers that our hero is not on the villain's side after all, has not betrayed her. The occasion turns into a moonlit love scene, poetic and bedless. In Act Four, a second surprise follows. The heroine's father does not arrive with gun and witnesses as he had promised. We find he had known our hero's probity all along. He wanted to get the young couple into bed and couldn't think of a less unusual way to manage it. He knew heroes marry the girls they make love to, and he wanted to trap our hero into marriage. The play doesn't end with marriage, though. It ends with the heroine's wishing the hero an early, if painless, death. It doesn't have a happy ending, it has a happy middle. It is built round—written for the sake of —its third act, in which we see our hero as "a damned soul coming . . . in the moonlight to confess and be forgiven and find peace for a night."

A well-made melodrama in which the expectations of melodrama are deliberately disappointed: Bernard Shaw has familiarized us with the pattern and convinced us that the disappointment may be more apparent and formal than substantial and real. And O'Neill touches upon the central substances and realities of modern life and drama. In his preoccupation with death-in-life—modern man a living corpse—he reminds us of

[1] Destined to be the last play O'Neill published. Still unproduced in New York (Summer, 1954).

Ibsen. Like Strindberg, he shows people torturing each other with words; like Pirandello, he shows them torturing *themselves* with words. Stylistically, there is a kinship with O'Casey: especially in his climactic third act he attempts to transfigure his naturalistic prose into high poetry. And in stating his main theme—guilt—he seeks to place his play in the main stream of modern literature. (In the theatre its popularity, like that of *The Cocktail Party,* would depend on the degree to which it arouses and appeases the public's sense of guilt.)

Perhaps I've already made it apparent how close *A Moon for the Misbegotten* is to other work by O'Neill himself. It is closest to the last play he published, *The Iceman Cometh,* not only in style and lay-out but in having at its core a confession of guilt from a man who has wronged a woman. The "inner" climax which O'Neill substitutes for the expected melodramatic climax is his hero's confession that he was drunk when his dying mother last set eyes on him and that he slept with a whore in the train that carried his mother's corpse. Second to *The Iceman Cometh,* the most obvious and significant tie is with *Anna Christie.* In all three plays drinking and whoring are presented as the principal human pursuits, while above all three there hover the ideas of virginity and motherhood, associated in every case with Catholicism and Ireland.

Why not? The material is magnificent. If it appears ridiculous in O'Neill's plays it is because he has not succeeded in molding it. That his language, for example, is unequal to the tasks he assigns to it is generally admitted, though his admirers shrug the fact off with the observation that you can't blame him for not being Shakespeare. One might, however, expect so ambitious a writer to stand comparison with our more talented novelists. O'Neill has attempted the poetry of colloquial American speech, the poetry of the underworld, yet has never written a page to compare with *The Killers* or *A Clean, Well Lighted Place.* The tough talk of *A Moon for the Misbegotten* may be closer to the talk of 1923 (the date of the action) than I am equipped to say but anyone can see that the words have less vitality than even the worst of Hemingway. (Assignment for a linguist: how much of O'Neill's dialect and slang comes from life, how much from stage tradition and personal hunch?) Style is meaning. Hemingway's style has often succeeded in reaching in a few lines much the same sort of pessimism that O'Neill will circumnavigate for hundreds of pages.

What Europeans call the "American" style—i.e., the "tough" style—operates chiefly as an ironical mask for sensitivity. Undoubtedly O'Neill realized—with his brain,. that is—how much of American life there is in this contrast. The hero of *A Moon for the Misbegotten* "only acts [and, we may add, talks] like he's hard and shameless to get back at life when it's tormenting him—and who doesn't?" Unhappily, O'Neill himself shows that embarrassment in the face of life, that shame in the presence of the spirit, which is the source of the "American" way of talking. He is afraid to have anyone mention sin without having them add "Nuts with that sin bunk" or to quote a poem without at once denouncing "the old poetic bull."

The prime symptom—or perhaps prime cause—of this embarrassment is fear of sex—fear of woman as woman, longing for her as mother or as virgin. There was a moment (that of *Days Without End*) when O'Neill seemed to have settled for the Virgin Mother, like his Irish antecedents. In *A Moon for the Misbegotten*, he finds an equivalent in the terms of his own naturalistic mysticism, describing his heroine as "a virgin who bears a dead child in the night," and adding: "the dawn finds her still a virgin." The grandiosity here is that of adolescent poetry: corny words for corny conceptions. The heroine of *A Moon for the Misbegotten* is 5′ 11″ tall (to the hero's 5′ 9″) and weighs a hundred and eighty pounds. On the side of the comical-grotesque such a phenomenon has possibilities which are partly realized in one bravura scene in which she and her father bawl the villain out. Beyond that we inescapably have the impression of neurotic fantasy unorganized into art. In place of organization, clichés and formulae: Anna Christie was the whore with the heart of a virgin, this new heroine is the virgin-who-seems-to-be-a-whore-till-the-truth-comes-out. (Assignment for a director: cast this part. Having done so, cast the same actress in any other play.)

A Moon for the Misbegotten will change no one's opinion of

Eugene O'Neill. It is neither his worst work nor his best. If it is more serious, and in some ways more meritorious, than most recent plays, so much the worse for most recent plays. I rather think its central image—that of a giant virgin holding in her arms a dipsomaniac lecher with a heart of gold—may stand in all minds as O'Neill's monument; for admirers will find it characteristic in grandeur and poetry, while others will find in it, clinically speaking, neurotic fantasy indulged rather than exploited and, critically speaking, poetry strained after rather than achieved.

Maiming the Bard

SOME READERS felt that although, in my essay "Doing Shakespeare Wrong," [1] I provided clear enough examples of the under- and over-interpretation of Shakespeare's plays by modern stage directors, I gave no adequate definition of the happy medium.

The shoe pinches—but not only me. When not crying down all interpretation (and thus in practice under-interpreting) or crying up over-simple interpretation (and thus in practice over-interpreting), the theatrical profession acquiesces in Orson Welles' view: "Every single way of playing and staging Shakespeare—as long as the way is effective—is right." Now, unless it would always be "ineffective" to change an author's meaning, Mr. Welles is here accusing Shakespeare of having no meaning to change. If I thought that, I'd prefer Eugene O'Neill.

It must be the assumption of serious direction that Shakespeare meant something and did not mean something else. His meanings can be rejected only if one of the following three conditions obtains: (A) that they are unacceptable to a modern audience, (B) that they cannot be communicated to a

[1] In *In Search of Theater.*

modern audience, (C) that they are uninteresting to a modern audience. Total rejection means not producing a play at all; and there is a case for not producing *The Merchant of Venice* on grounds A and B or for not producing *Henry V* on grounds A, B, and C. Total rejection is simple. Difficulty arises when we reject a play in part, that is, when we produce it with cuts. If we may cut the whole, it would be reasonable to deduce that we could cut the parts—also on grounds of being unacceptable, incommunicable, or uninteresting—were not masterpieces organic and integrated structures. A passage may be "cuttable" on grounds A, B, or C, and yet necessary to the rhythm. Obviously there is a limit to the number of such enfeebled passages that any production can stand. It is when that limit is reached that the idea of production should be cancelled.

I think we must require that some ninety per cent of Shakespeare's meaning (the figure is arbitrary) come through. And here I intend the meaning the play had when first written, not any subsequent increment, and certainly not any separate "modern" meaning. The modernities I demand are not those which the director imposes on Shakespeare but those which he finds in Shakespeare. All he can impose is, at need, a modern frame to the picture, and even the modernity of the frame may often be only a more authentic historicity. *Finding* what is the positive significance in material which has passed the somewhat negative tests A, B, and C is the job. Here some have thought that I am "hedging." Again, it is granted that I have defined Scylla (the German and Russian left-wing Shakespeare) and Charybdis (the genteel British approach) without explaining how to steer in between.

What happens in *Hamlet*? What does a given play mean? Opinion on these matters has in our time been changed from top to bottom by reference to historical lore which our audiences know nothing about. It is implied that even the most popular and perennial of Shakespeare's plays can be rightly understood only in the light of Elizabethan history, psychology, physiology, demonology; the understanding of Shakespeare is limited to scholars, often in fact to the one scholar with the theory. Though at this extreme point our sense of humor rebels, we certainly wonder if ninety per cent is not much more of the original meaning than comes down to us.

We are disposed either to give up production altogether—or to jump to the other extreme, make larger cuts, believe that anything goes. Bertolt Brecht works through an Elizabethan play not only subtracting but adding as freely as did the Elizabethans themselves. He and Marlowe are, as it were, joint authors of the German *Edward II.* Judging by the fragment in the anthology *Theaterarbeit,* I'd say that he and Shakespeare are joint authors of the new *Coriolan.* This is legitimate but is a matter of playwriting, not directing, a matter of changing Shakespeare, not interpreting him. I maintain that the bulk of Shakespeare remains viable unchanged, if the responsibilities of interpretation are not shirked.

People tell me they were not shirked in the Stratford productions of the histories and appeal from my strictures to an official apologia, *Shakespeare's Histories at Stratford 1951,* by J. Dover Wilson and T. C. Worsley. In this lavishly illustrated, if expensive, 100-page pamphlet, Mr. Worsley and the many colleagues he quotes assume that the Stratford productions were guided by an adequate "conception" and that it only remains to discuss whether the conception confirms, or conflicts with, their established ideas of the characters. The argumentation is so urbane, the writing so sprightly, it may seem churlish to complain that the whole discussion stays comfortably within the boundaries of current British gentility—the same boundaries as those of the performances under review. The goldfish are agile and their fins flicker prettily, but the bowl, even if none of them know it exists, narrows their horizon. In an admirable introduction, Dover Wilson throws out suggestions that, had they been made in advance, might have driven the Stratford producers further along the road of interpretation. Looking back to the medieval tradition, he describes *Richard II* as a miracle, *Henry IV* as a morality. Looking forward to the present, he observes: "Never was non-moral statecraft more rampant . . . the Nazis and Stalinites have brought back to Europe the technique of Italian renaissance politics." Here to be sure is a basis for a modern production of the histories. In applying this idea we are not fitting Shakespeare with modern false limbs; on the contrary, we may accuse our genteel colleagues, for all their love of the bard, of maiming him.

Pickwick in Love

IN THE THEATRE, if we are amused, all else is forgiven and no questions are asked: amusement itself is a rare enough bird. We would not complain that a play is inferior to the novel it's based on if at least it provides us with a modicum of the special pleasure of theatre-going.

But why should we be lenient when we are not amused? Stanley Young's *Mr. Pickwick* at the Plymouth is a bad play badly performed. Since indeed it is so bad a play that it would probably not be performed at all but for certain circumstances outside its own boundaries, it is less pertinent to define the badness than the circumstances. The chief of these is that the play is "drawn from" a novel by Charles Dickens. It is Dickens' name, in fact, that brings the audience to the theatre. It is because his name is in the program that they laugh at many a line which would be greeted by stony silence if signed by me, you, or Stanley Young.

It should be superfluous to say that many lines in *The Pickwick Papers* are genuinely funny, that the book abounds in incidents and characters seen and provided with precise stage directions by one of the greatest dramatic geniuses in English history. Our complaint must not be that Mr. Young is so dependent on Dickens but that he is not dependent enough. Or, more precisely, that he draws on Dickens' prestige without drawing sufficiently on Dickens' work. The program tells us Mr. Young drew "freely" from Dickens, which turns out to mean not only that he adds things of his own but that even when he is merely "translating" he translates inaccurately and misses the force of the original. It is not Dickens he gives us but a dim and distorted image of Dickens which, having in mind that every great teacher is reduced by his disciples to an ism, we might call Dickensianism. The Dickensianism of the Dickens cult. The idea of a Dickens who is all warm sentiment and coy humor. A genteel Dickens in fact; the British director

John Burrell has attached an American playwright to that same genteel tradition which I have accused of handicapping British Shakespeare production. The tradition that maims the bard positively decapitates Dickens. The attempt to make a gentleman of Shakespeare can never quite succeed, but the attempt to make a lower-middle-class sentimentalist of Dickens has succeeded before it starts, for that, among other things, is what he is. It is of course for the "other things" that he has value; yet adaptors, directors, and actors can reduce him to nothing by reducing him to the only one of his dozen *personae* which is alternately uninteresting and objectionable. This is what has been done.

A man of sentiment, Mr. Pickwick is not a sentimental conception, though with a touch less of salt he would be so. (This of course is an unjustly negative way of putting it. Dickens' achievement is not that he avoided sentimentality but that he rendered sentiment with so special a delicacy; later he was to do bigger things; he never again did this thing.) Mr. Young has replaced Dickens' salt with the sugar of Dickensianism. If Dickens can transfigure a cliché, Mr. Young can reduce it to a cliché again; the coach of Cinderella turns back into a pumpkin.

Dickens' Pickwick has become a legendary figure, a piece of furniture in the mansion of the western mind. By dint of poetic imagination Dickens contrived to create one of those rare characters who have not only features and an identity but also a shimmering glamor; he hasn't only a face, one might say, he has an aureole too. Without his aureole, a character so poetically conceived, a character rendered by nuance and aroma, and wrought in gossamer, is little more than an old fool. On the stage, Mr. Pickwick (and with him Mr. Young) might possibly be saved by genius in the actor—which can have the same shimmer and insubstantiality. George Howe, who plays the part, is a fine performer. His Polonius was good when I first saw it eighteen years ago and it is still good, it is quite unchanged in fact, now that it is mis-named Pickwick. It has no aureole. It is not legendary.

Mr. Pickwick without his Pickwickian radiance is a poor forked animal indeed, yet Mr. Young adds insult to injury, imposition to deprivation, by also changing the animal's features. Transferring a piece of action, Hollywood-fashion, from one character to another he presents us with the only violent sensation of the evening: dismay at the discovery that his Pickwick is in love. He has been saddled with the egregious Mr. Tupman's passion for Rachel Wardle. Pickwick in Love! Queen Victoria might have asked for this as Queen Elizabeth is said to have asked for the similar degradation of Falstaff. She didn't, though; the Playwrights Company rushes in where an empress feared to tread.

That isn't all. The idea of Pickwick in love could only occur to someone who has rejected the idea of Pickwick. And someone who has rejected Pickwick need not stop at mere rejection. He can then take Pickwick and throw him into the Thames in a basket of soiled linen. The soiled linen in this case is the lady herself, and the Thames is the inanity of the whole relationship. True, Pickwick emerges from his bath of vapid sentimentality before he is done—but only because the lady has given up collecting moths (!) and instead has collected (!!) Stiggins.

One's quarrel with the Dickensians is not that they admire Dickens too much but that they don't admire him at all; they admire Dickensianism. They profess admiration for Dickens, yet, admiring him for little qualities, and being unable to think little of themselves, they cannot help taking a superior attitude to the supposed object of their veneration. So it is that what is meant for homage is really an affront. In the Young-Burrell production, for example, there is scarcely a walk, a gesture, an intonation, that is not an insult to the memory of a great artist. It's all meant to be charming, of course. But if you really believed Dickens to be charming you wouldn't strain like that to make him so. Anyway, Mr. Burrell should know that charm cannot be acted. It can only emanate from good acting as the aroma emanates from good brandy.

Would *Pickwick Papers* make a good play in any case? It seems doubtful. The dramatic nature of Dickens' genius is a lure to the theatrical adaptor—and a trap. Dramatic characters and incidents are not in themselves a play. In acknowledging that Dickens could have been a great dramatist one mustn't forget that what he did make of himself was—a great novelist. If I have implied that his dialogue often requires only a faithful copyist for adaptation to the stage, it is also true that none of his novels could become a great play without the collaboration of a great playwright.

The Case of O'Casey

THEY SAY THAT the critic of *The New York Times* is the dictator of serious drama on Broadway yet when he takes the unprecedented step of repeatedly writing articles to ask that Sean O'Casey be performed he doesn't get his way. Why is this?

The latest explanation to come to my ears is: "you can't raise the money, O'Casey is too close to communism." "Too close" is a very delicate expression, implying that some degree of closeness is permitted, or maybe some kind of closeness, or maybe closeness under certain conditions. Bernard Shaw is regularly performed though he never missed any opportunity of praising Stalin or calling himself a communist outright; he lived to support Wallace in '48 and to deplore American intervention in Korea. Charlie Chaplin, on the other hand, who does not call himself a communist, is called one by other people; and his film *Monsieur Verdoux* was ostracized in most parts of the country. Bertolt Brecht (to complete the list of the four leading comic talents of our time) has caused one potential Broadway backer to say: "his play is a masterpiece but I wouldn't produce it even if I knew it'd make a million." The long and short of it is that Shaw is given a hearing unreservedly, that Mr. Chaplin is given a hearing with reservations (*Monsieur Verdoux* was not kosher, but *City Lights* was), and that Mr. Brecht and Mr. O'Casey are not given a hearing at all.

The reason I've heard suggested for the approval of Shaw and Mr. Chaplin is that they've been in the business longer, they were established in public esteem long before Parnell

Thomas and Joseph McCarthy were heard of. Mr. Brecht and Mr. O'Casey, however, were also in the field before intolerance entered its present phase. Why didn't they find an audience in the twenties and thirties?

Mr. O'Casey tells his part of the story in *Inishfallen Fare Thee Well* and *Rose and Crown* (the fourth and fifth volumes of his autobiography). His three plays of the mid-twenties made enemies but they made powerful and numerous friends. They gave O'Casey an identity; and this proved precisely to be the problem when, a little later, he proceeded to write a little differently. To quote *Rose and Crown:*

> There was no importance in trying to do the same thing again . . . He wanted a change from what the Irish critics had called burlesque, photographic realism, or slices of life, though the manner and method of two of the plays were as realistic as the scents stealing from a gaudy bunch of blossoms.

Here, as so often in dramatic criticism, the word *realism* is ambiguous. Mr. O'Casey rightly implies that there is a sense in which even his early plays are not realistic. Conversely there is a sense in which it was the realism of the later plays that offended an influential section of the public. *The Silver Tassie* gave offence for not being *Journey's End*—that is, for exposing wounds instead of filming them over with gentility. *Within the Gates* gave offence for giving a close-up of a bishop instead of hiding him in a cloud of incense. *The Star Turns Red* gave offence for turning red—when the palette of a Cecil Beaton or an Oliver Messel had so many other colors to offer. It was opposed in England not for its brand of politics but for being political at all. The point of view is familiar to readers of Mr. O'Casey's arch-antagonist, James Agate, who, for example, complaining of J. B. Priestley, not that he wrote badly, but that he wrote politically, had clearly no means of distinguishing the Yorkshireman's defects from the Irishman's qualities.

One of the harshest terms of abuse in the metropolitan drama critic's vocabulary is expressionism, and James Agate was one of many who applied it to Mr. O'Casey. The word damaged him in the theatre world by hinting that he read books by foreign authors or spent his holidays beyond the Rhine. It damaged him by intimating that his later style was not his own. It furthered mystification by getting people to assume that there had been an obvious break in Mr. O'Casey's creative life—a gap, with his genius and his past on one side while his reading and his future were on the other. Mr. O'Casey observes plaintively that his residence in England was held accountable for the faults of a work which was conceived and begun before he left Ireland.

One cannot study this man's career without convicting the world around him of jealous meanness. First, they shelved his early works as "classics"; second, they took a stand which explained and dismissed his later works before they appeared. Between these two phases, there was one crucial and receptive moment, a moment when the O'Casey story, as Hollywood would call it, could have been given another turn, and by a single man. This was the moment when W. B. Yeats was reading *The Silver Tassie* for the Abbey Theatre. Not understanding the crucial nature of this moment, we are likely to misread large portions of the autobiography as megalomania. Actually, we should be less surprised at Mr. O'Casey's continual return to the crisis of *The Silver Tassie* than at the fact that his attitude to Yeats even after it was one of filial love.

Yeats was under no obligation to make a success story of Mr. O'Casey's career; he was under no obligation to like *The Silver Tassie*. But, all other questions aside, we may judge his famous rejection of it in terms of the consequences. Yeats did more than any other man to deflect from the theatre one of its two or three best playwrights. I am not sure that Mr. O'Casey's later plays are as good as his earlier ones; I am sure they would be better than they are had Yeats and Agate and the rest kept the playwright in the theatre. Though diffuse, and blemished by self-pity and proletarian snobbery, the autobiography, half the time, is as good as the blurbs say it is; one shakes one's head, not over what O'Casey has written, but over what he has been sidetracked from writing; the autobiography is *ersatz;* the best passages are scenes from plays that will never be written; scenes by a playwright without a theatre. If the plays Mr. O'Casey has been printing are increasingly "unproduceable" the reason (if I may be allowed an Irishism) is that they've been increasingly unproduced; a playwright without a theatre is far too free. And yet we don't really know whether *Cock-a-Doodle Dandy* is good theatre, bad, or indifferent, because we haven't tried it. There is also the question how good the theatre is in which it would be tried. A creative ensemble would be more interested in tackling a work that is not tied down by the habits of past performances, a work which demands, and will help to form, a new kind of performance. Where are the actors who will give us, not repetitions, nor even revivals, but discoveries? Do we reject O'Casey because as a communist he is beneath us or because as an artist he is beyond us?

Hitch Your Star to a Wagon

DR. JOHNSON said marriage wasn't unhappy except as life was unhappy, and we may add that the theatre isn't dead except as our culture in general is dead. I shall not follow the Sunday papers and call the theatre a fabulous invalid, because the phrase suggests debility without death; whereas there is a good deal in theatre now that is quite, quite dead; and, contrariwise, what is more fabulous than its usual debility is its occasional strength. Along with much mortality there is not a little vitality, and in the midst of death we are in life.

The recognized eras of theatrical greatness are those of the great playwrights; yet a theatre is not dead when there are no playwrights; it is dead only when there are no actors. In an age without playwrights the actors can still give us theatre, and that in at least three sorts of composition: revivals, vaudeville, and star vehicles. Of the three, revivals have had the highest prestige, because the tradition of "serious" acting since Betterton has largely been the tradition of acting Shakespeare. Shaw is now becoming as safe a standby as Shakespeare. What could be more symptomatic of our situation than the fact that the best performance of the 1951–2 season was a reading of a single Shavian scene ("Don Juan in Hell"), or that the best play on Broadway as I write is Shaw's very first effort at playwriting (*Widowers' Houses*)?

For lack of another term, I am using the word vaudeville to include cabaret, revues, variety, music hall, and, above all, musicals. In all of these the individual item is traditionally more important than the composition, if any, of which it is a part; and, within the individual item, the individual performance easily transcends the script and the score. Ideally, a vaudeville show should present one first-rate number after another. As a rule, however, even a musical is a desert of mediocrity with a single oasis.

> Fair as a star when only one
> Is shining in the sky.

Except for the star, everything else in the show is sheerest night. The remedy is to present the oasis without the desert; the star without the black sky; in short, Beatrice Lillie as she appears in her "Evening" without featured players, bit players, chorus, and orchestra.

The show without Beatrice Lillie would be nothing, Beatrice Lillie without the show is everything. It is the live part of contemporary theatre with the dead part cut away. Touching the very quick of theatrical art in Miss Lillie's work we realize how dead is not only the kind of show she herself has often been condemned to appear in but (more important) the kind of show that is thought to have higher status. The realization is forced upon us that standards of theatrical craftsmanship get lower as the intellectual pretensions of theatre people increase: it is an exact inverse ratio. In general, therefore, visitors to this country have to be advised against revivals and sent to night-clubs and musicals. Visiting directors will often find the talent they need for drama among the non-dramatic actors of this "lower" echelon.

Doubtless the speakers at a recent New York debate were right in saying that talent abounds and is being blocked; but it is being blocked at the source; it is not yet available; because it is untrained. Most actors are unemployed, yet the fact remains that it is hard to find a first-rate cast for any play. The only large group of actors who know how to do anything is the "hoofer" group. It is with this in mind that I am using so smiling a subject as Miss Lillie as theme for a sermon. *She can do things;* and the concept of the actor as one who does things is unhappily receding before the concept of the actor as folk hero (filmstar, covergirl) and the actor as common man (who doesn't know how to speak, sit, stand, or walk, let alone sing, dance, and turn cartwheels). Miss Lillie is an edifice of control and agility upon a foundation of humor.

As for "star vehicles," Uta Hagen is appearing in something called *In Any Language* by two authors whose names I feel no urge to look up. I hasten to add that I have nothing against "vehicles" as such, and I grant that the genre is to be judged by criteria less exacting than those of drama proper. A vehicle serves its purpose if you can ride in it; and, far from hitching my wagon to a star, I am eager to attach a star to any wagon that will carry her. In representing that this vehicle drops Uta Hagen rudely in the roadway, I had better drop the metaphor.

The writer of a vehicle play can fall short of drama only where it is possible for the actor to make the deficiency good. Actors have been known to suggest to audiences a depth of emotion and even a profundity of thought of which no trace is to be found in the script. If such cases are examined, however, it will be found, first, that at least the script didn't put too many obstacles in their way and, second, that it prompted and initiated what they realized and completed. The actor can make a moderately witty line sound very witty; with an un-witty line he is powerless. He can make a statement sound significant if the author has at least made clear *what* he is stating. In short he can make the purse if the writer provide him with silk and not a sow's ear.

The first minutes of *In Any Language,* as well as the advance publicity, give us the impression that we are in for a satirical treatment of Ingrid Bergman and Roberto Rossellini. It would have been perfectly legitimate for the authors to disappoint this expectation later; it would have been legitimate for them to depart, as they did, from satire itself, had they found any other path to comedy. Instead the evening is tense with the fight waged by actors and director against the play. I think George Abbott's directing as far above most directing of the "serious" variety as Beatrice Lillie's acting is above our Shakespeareonics. But if there's anything that cannot be forced it is light comedy. I am told that Uta Hagen's role is good in that it "frees" her from the straitjacket of classic austerity and/or neurotic intensity in which she is supposed to have been constricted. Let's hope it frees people of the illusion that she ever wore such a jacket. An actress of her accomplishment has no need to prove her versatility. Unversatile actors aren't actors, they are at best personalities.[1] We not only knew Uta Hagen could act. Her non-comic work couldn't possibly have been so good if she hadn't had the comedienne in her. As to bringing the comedienne out of her and placing it before the public, Miss Hagen wanted to do it and the authors of *In Any Language* couldn't entirely stop her; yet they do very seriously hamper her. After this, if she can't find a real play, she should, if possible, make sure that a vehicle is a vehicle is a vehicle.

[1] But see pp. 55, 87, 130, 156.

What Is Acting?

WHAT IS ACTING? If it is tossing your head, arching your back, sawing the air with your arms, sitting in grotesque positions, stamping across the stage, moving in rapid rotation from one chair to another, throwing yourself on the floor, falling off your seat, knocking people downstairs, Katharine Hepburn may be said to be acting the title role in Shaw's *Millionairess*. What is virtuosity in acting? If it is roaring instead of speaking, whining instead of whispering, if it embraces the abuse as well as the use of voice and gesture, if it permits the constant repetition of a single rhythmic and tonal pattern, Miss Hepburn is a virtuoso. What is the interpretation of a role? If it is not to discover what is in a role but to impose yourself upon it, if it is not to impose your true self upon it but a self you vamp up for the occasion, if it is not to find the accents and climaxes but to accent everything and make a climax of every speech, if it is not to establish relationships with other characters and other actors but to inhibit all relationship with other characters and other actors, if it is not to seek the author's meaning but to smother all meaning in rapid activity that is too mechanical or too neurasthenic to deserve the name of energy, Miss Hepburn is a great interpreter.

If London liked the show, London cannot distinguish between vital energy and the galvanic activity of a headless hen. Nor can one think so highly of those in London who, though perceptive enough to sense that something was wrong somewhere, deduced, without examining the facts of the case, that it must be because the octogenarian author's life was ebbing and even American monkey glands could not revive him. The performance does indeed give the impression that the play is uninteresting. "All this effort and the script still doesn't come to life!" say those who do not realize that all the effort has gone into killing it. The fact that Shaw so often succeeds with our public should not blind us to the fact that he succeeds at a price and sometimes does not succeed at all. Applying an artistic rather than a commercial criterion, we should have to say that the success is seldom more than partial—one actor in a dozen will have the tone and rhythm without which Shavian comedy does not properly exist. The memory of a Shavian playgoer is studded—not, unhappily, with great productions —but with individuals who transcended a general competence or incompetence: Stephen Haggard as Marchbanks, Claude Rains as Caesar, John Buckmaster as the Dauphin, Charles Laughton as the Devil. Mere competence is not enough for Shaw, though it is preferable to super-production by Michael Benthall. No one who saw the merely competent, rather down-at-heel Paris production of *The Millionairess* in 1938 left the theatre disliking the play. Competent production is only incomplete; super-production means perversion.

Now you can pervert a Shakespeare play and no one will notice, since no one knew what to make of the play in the first place, but in perverting Shaw you are perverting an author who has frequently been criticized for making his meaning all too clear in prefaces and stage-directions, not to mention dialogue. Well, our producers are forever proving that he is not too clear for *them*. He can explain his view that Joan's voices are real to her and to her only, and this won't stop Margaret Webster broadcasting angel voices to the whole audience over the PA system. He can spend half a lifetime explaining his view of leaders and can sum it up in the preface to this very play *The Millionairess,* and that won't stop Mr. Benthall and Miss Hepburn presenting their own view—or non-view—of the subject. Shaw believed in getting rid of rich and poor alike by socialism. Economic equality would permit those few of the ex-paupers and ex-millionaires who have ruling talent to come forward and rule. Our inequality provides no legitimate outlet for them. The millionairess is a frustrated ruler. Her frustrations are ugly, her nature is not; the cardinal error of Miss Hepburn's "interpretation" is to make Epifania absurd and repulsive. True, an effort is made in the last couple of minutes of the play to reverse all that has previously been said and done. It is too late. And in Shaw's script there is no reversal, nor could Shaw ever have countenanced the means by which Miss Hepburn tries to bring one about: feverishly and erotically acting against the lines and endeavoring to subordinate a whole paragraph of Shavian eloquence to her own false emphasis on one word ("nice"). This is not the only way in which the final, summing-up speeches of the play are confused in the Benthall-Hepburn production. Shaw printed two endings: one for the capitalist west, the other for communist countries where, in his view, the problem posed by the play has been solved. In the current production, *both* endings are drawn upon! America is the stronghold of capitalism, yet there are still those, no doubt, who think the communists may take over at any minute.

Sometime this play could be done right. Shaw gave the best hint in his prefatory mention of Ben Jonson. In merit *The Millionairess* is comparable neither to the best Jonson nor the best Shaw, yet in kind it is an attempt, like Pirandello's *Man, Beast, and Virtue,* to revive the Jonsonian kind of farce, which is both ferocious and meaningful. As such it requires a special kind of performance. Even Cyril Ritchard—the only actor in the present production with a style—is not right for it. Mr. Ritchard plays comedy of manners. What we have here is an intellectual Punch and Judy show. Miss Hepburn fails by going all out at the Punch-and-Judy *motif* and hoping that intellect will be added unto her. Robert Helpmann fails by ignoring the principal tip Shaw gives to the actor playing the Egyptian Doctor, namely, not to use a stagy, foreign accent; he speaks English, says Shaw, "too well to be mistaken for a native." Then there are two average, British drawing-room actors, and one, below average, who is sometimes heard to say "yahs" for "years" and "jahray" for "jury" but is in general inaudible because he tries to speak with tongue and teeth without recourse to his lungs and vocal cords.

After seeing half a dozen recent Broadway plays you might well wonder if you'll ever see anything but children and old maids on the stage any more. Though *The New York Times* singled out the word "mature" to describe one of the latest exhibitions of immaturity, and "senile" to describe *The Millionairess*, there are theatregoers who'd be glad to turn from today's version of maturity to the brains and verve of even minor Shaw, just as they'd be glad to turn from Miss Hepburn's St. Vitus Dance to a genuine Shavian vitality.

Charlie Chaplin's Mea Culpa

IT IS MORE THAN thirty years since Charlie Chaplin established himself as the master of a craft. For more than twenty years he has been faced with the question: where do I go from here? A question with two aspects. Technically, it is: how am I to adapt myself to the talkies? Spiritually, it is: how am I to adapt myself to a new age? For the classic silents are pre-1914 in mentality if not in date.

If we understand how special these questions are in the life of a film actor we are in a position to see how special everything about Mr. Chaplin is. The very fact that such questions arise for him betokens a consciousness of talent that is a far rarer phenomenon than talent itself. Adaptation to the talkies would have been no Herculean task except on his terms: that the talkies be a mold for greatness. Adaptation to a new age would only mean acquiescence in it if Mr. Chaplin had not been full of a desire to interpret and to lead. Just as special was the range of his mastery: he wasn't just a great actor, he made his name as the creator of a symbolic role with which he and half the world identified themselves, and so he was a sort of dramatist. The muse of history favored him: as soon as his education in pantomime was complete, the silent screen stood waiting to record and broadcast his prowess. Charlie not only accepted the screen's services. He enslaved it, exploited it, taught it to do things it had never done before.

All this happened naturally, rapidly, and in a very short time. He didn't have to think about it—until people told him what he had done and how great it was, until the movie industry went over to sound, until the bitch History—history personal and world-wide—inflicted a series of wounds. It is easy to say that, since then, he has done too much thinking, that he now uses all too many words and is over-intellectual, pretentious. It is harder to know what he should have done, what he should do. The inept thing is to wish he would "just stick to the Tramp" for this is to forget that an artist must develop—one cannot say he must improve, let alone that he must repeat himself. Critics, of course, cannot tell him where his future development lies. All they can do is discriminate between advancing and backtracking, between exploring and merely getting lost. It seems to me that Mr. Chaplin's two latest films represent a triumph and a failure, respectively.

In *Monsieur Verdoux* we found for the first time that Mr. Chaplin could use the sound film for all it is worth. And, granted that he probably cannot throw the Tramp off altogether, he brilliantly contrived to turn him upside down to suit the topsy-turvy world of the fascist epoch. If *City Lights*, for example, says all that the Chaplin of the early period had to say, *Monsieur Verdoux* sums up the Chaplin of the later period, the period when he had begun to think and to lose popularity, when his love of women, laughed at in the twenties, had come to be linked, by the logic of the intellectual underworld, with his political leanings. Coming after *Monsieur Verdoux, Limelight* is as much a *mea culpa* as any Soviet artist's return to the bosom of Stalin. It is a return to the bosom of the bourgeoisie, and it is expressed in the quintessentially bourgeois form of entertainment: sentimental domestic drama. This form doesn't stop an artist being pretentious—as students of Chaplin's late father-in-law know to their cost. And in *Limelight*, the high-flown sentimentality of Mr. Chaplin's drama has a lethal partner in the academicism of an Eglevsky ballet.

I saw *Monsieur Verdoux* half a dozen times and was still discovering fine details the last time. At a second viewing of *Limelight* I found myself chafing at the length of every "serious" passage. The film has neither the richness nor the precision of detail that we have learnt to expect from this great artist. Even the editing is faulty: if the heavy scenes are too long, the light ones are too short. Nor is the story at all points well told. When the prim landlady comes in rollicking drunk we feel that some preparatory scene must be missing. Occasionally—as in a lengthy passage about whores and syphilis—one wonders if different versions of the story are here jumbled as in some Elizabethan bad quarto. More certain is the fact that the real vitality of Mr. Chaplin is absent from most of the film and that instead we have at best a dazzle of dexterity, at worst a blur of sentiment—he can't see for crocodile tears. The sentimentality affects Mr. Chaplin's portrayal of bad people as well as good: instead of the big, lively villain of old we get the Hollywood cliché of a dear old bozo (well played by Nigel Bruce). The *mea culpa* attitude is not only morally repugnant; it is artistically deleterious.

All this is to judge of course by the incredibly high standard which Mr. Chaplin himself has set. The film is not only better than 999 out of 1000 films, it has passages of the real Chaplin. Outstanding among these, naturally, are the music hall turns: the appetite whetted by the song in *Modern Times* is here richly fed if by no means sated. It is worth sitting through the "serious" scenes with the Girl not only for Claire Bloom's remarkable beauty but because Charlie interrupts them to flirt briefly with the landlady across a banister. There are many (if not enough) characteristic details which illustrate Charlie's vivacity as a comedian and his intelligence as a dramatic realist. When a pungent smell offends his nostrils he quickly examines the sole of his shoe. He pulls out his pants—pressed! —from under the mattress. He makes his room seem a matter of habit and habitation by always knowing (as most actors don't) where the furniture is. By the way he sits in a particular chair he can tell you he is used to sitting in it and how.

The good things in *Limelight* are exceptional and peripheral. The film is a glorious failure about a glorious failure. The name of the protagonist is Calvero, but the portrait on his mantelpiece is that of Mr. Chaplin, young. Symbolic autobiography! What an amazing conception for a movie man! And in *Monsieur Verdoux* it was executed with genius. The picture had a sharp focus in the middle, even if it was fuzzy on the edges. In *Limelight* the fuzziness is all at the center. What analogy is there between a rich and famous movie star threatened by an Attorney General[1] and an impoverished old music hall singer begging in pubs? There wouldn't have to be one, of course—if Mr. Chaplin himself hadn't planted the biographical reference and fostered it with tears of self-pity. I don't claim to know in what direction Charlie should proceed. But we can all see various directions in which he should not proceed. One is that of a conciliation which can be no true conciliation. Charlie must follow his own star even if he loses the Attorney General's forty-eight.

[1] At the time these words were written, Mr. Chaplin was threatened with investigation by the Attorney General's office should he apply for re-entry to the U.S. He has now settled in Switzerland (1954).

The Poet in New York

THE OLD WORLD and the new have often met dramatically in New York. It is curious to think of Lorenzo Da Ponte, Mozart's librettist, teaching at Columbia University. Another European, Garcia Lorca, also on the Columbia campus for a while, found it curious to think of himself—the Spanish *poeta en Nueva York*. And now we have Jean-Louis Barrault producing *The False Secrets* at the Ziegfeld. Marivaux in the home of Billy Rose! King Arthur, as it were, at the court of a Yankee! Yet why not? Was Marivaux any less of a duck out of water in eighteenth-century France? No more than in the pictures of his contemporary Watteau can we look in Marivaux for the outer facts of life. Both men lived in a dream.

Grimm and Voltaire tried to dismiss Marivaux two hundred years ago; *The New York Times* reports today that his masterpiece "does not appear to be remarkably distinguished"; but the dream lives on. It is a dream, though, of reality—inner reality. Marivaux has a subject: the awakening of love, the recognition of its awakening, and, to some extent, the results of such recognition. The title of his first success—*Harlequin Refined by Love*—indicates the kind of result that interested him; whatever did not interest him he excluded with the ruthlessness and precision of a surgeon. His people may not have the various characteristics which a different tradition has led us to expect; they have what is essential to the drama on hand. Nothing in English is very close to him; our closest analogues, perhaps, are Jane Austen and Henry James. French writers in this tradition to whom we have granted the "distinction" Brooks Atkinson refuses to Marivaux include Musset and Giraudoux.

Marivaux' approach to theatre may be just as strange to us as his approach to human character. He was oddly placed. Though Adrienne Lecouvreur once played a part for him, he had success almost exclusively with Italian actors who at first didn't know French. Even total speechlessness may be a resource. The new Harlequin, Thomassin, made his debut in a scene without words. And, because his predecessor in the role had been a great acrobat, while he himself had been a tragedian, Thomassin created a new character: a quiet, quasi-naïve harlequin, spiritual, touching. One Autereau wrote him a couple of scripts in which he enacted the awakening of love in an innocent heart. This was where Marivaux took over, and where our thoughts leap forward to Deburau, Mr. Chaplin, and M. Barrault.

In *Harlequin Refined by Love* at the Comédie Française you can see the once new Harlequin in the spry impersonation of that fine comedian Jacques Charon. For New York, M. Barrault has modestly chosen a piece in which the clowns are neither melancholy nor conspicuous: *The False Secrets* rests principally on the shoulders of Madeleine Renaud and Jean Desailly. The work of these two superb artists suffers a little from the size of the Ziegfeld, from the audience's ignorance of French, and possibly, I suppose, from the prevalence of Mr. Atkinson's view of Marivaux. It remains for the connoisseur of literature the perfect embodiment of Marivaux' humanity, and for the student of acting a lesson in the handling of a script which offers none of the levers that the modern actor is taught to look for. (In self-defense, the latter calls this French work "stylized," the truth being that it has a style to which he has not found the clues. He finds it "unreal," thus unconsciously revealing both a narrow notion of reality and a failure to recognize the "unreality" of all technique, all art.)

We see Thomassin's new Harlequin—or is it Pierrot, and do historians derive him from Brighella?—in the second item on the program: *Baptiste*. Here we are in the nineteenth century, and almost ready for one of Charlie Chaplin's dream sequences. Pierrot dreams that the statue of Columbine has come to life and that Harlequin has run off with her. In order to follow the pair to the ball, Pierrot robs and murders an old-clothes-man. Since the ghost of the latter rises up to demand vengeance, Pierrot would be in a fix—if he didn't wake up. The best bits in the narrative are those that have Chaplinesque charm and point: for example, the rope Pierrot prepares to hang himself with he inadvertently lends to a little girl to skip with. Seeing *Baptiste* for the third time, I was surprised how well it wears. M. Barrault's own performance is perhaps less inventive and less dazzlingly comic than the Bip series of Marcel Marceau, the great mime whom America has yet to see. The reconstruction of a Deburau pantomime (for that is what *Baptiste* is) by M. Barrault and Jacques Prévert is less authentic without being more exciting than one I saw in Rome by another very gifted mime, Jacques Lecoq. M. Barrault is no specialist. If he has disappointed the apostles of pure mime, it is because he has exploited their specialty for the general good of theatre. It is his mission, not to do one thing supremely, but to do everything splendidly. If as Pierrot he lacks some final quality equivalent, say, to the profound dignity of Chaplin, he has created a fey sprite compact of energy and wit. M. Barrault's exemplary achievement is not in a single role, nor yet in all his roles: it is that he is the complete man of the theatre: actor of all types of roles, director of all types of plays (and non-plays), creator of a repertoire, builder and educator of a company.

A sense of all this makes each evening at the Ziegfeld a curiously festive one. I find in the audiences a relaxed joy and warm exhilaration quite unlike anything I have witnessed in a New York theatre before. The source of this delight may be partly the fascination of the unknown—there are gasps of pleasure at every move M. Barrault makes—yet it is even more the shock of recognition: recognition of the art of theatre in its many-sidedness, its fullness. Here is no exotic dish to give us a *nouveau frisson;* it is the wholesome food we have forgotten the taste of. As far as exoticism goes, New York—"the most sophisticated city in the world"—"the modern Babylon"—is well-enough provided. What Paris has brought us is a good old-fashioned evening of poetry, the poetry of words and the poetry of bodily movement: in sum, the poetry of the theatre.

It's All Greek To Me

THE SIMULTANEOUS appearance in New York of M. Barrault's French company and the Greek National Theatre has raised some nice problems of theory. The critic who said that he disliked *Electra* in all the English versions but liked it in modern Greek which he does not understand was making pretty bold assumptions about the nature of language—and of drama.

What do you like in language you do not understand? The

answer is generally held to be "the music," but for me the
musical theory was refuted once for all by I. A. Richards some
years ago when he showed that English has no music that is
detachable from its sense by imitating the sounds of a Miltonic
strophe in a piece of nonsense. The "music" of an unknown
tongue is illusory. The fact that one invents such a phenomenon and then proceeds to enjoy the invention must be attributed to naïve awe, snobbish xenophilia, or, more likely, to
certain romantic associations clustered around literature and
summer vacations. *Omne ignotum pro magnifico.* The zeal of
many people for opera "in the Italian original" is in direct
proportion to their ignorance of Italian, for while they readily
notice crudities of English, they take all the Italian librettist's
geese for swans.

To prefer incomprehensible Greek to comprehensible English is also to assume that words in drama don't much matter
anyway. Some New York critics begin by apologizing for their
lack of languages and end by judging the show, Greek or
French, precisely as if they had missed nothing. One of them
said he didn't know French but was sure Marivaux couldn't
interest even those who did. Others were cautious in their
remarks about writers but under no inhibitions when discussing acting.

Now can you discuss the acting of a performer whose words
you don't follow? You can say you were moved or were not
moved, but this is not criticism, it is data for your fever chart.
A critic has to know *what* moved him, and whether it is
related to the *intention* of a performance. If you consider what
one of our own actors does with a line—of Shakespeare or
Odets, it makes no difference—you can figure for yourself how
little that is relevant a foreigner could make of it. Why do we
assume that we know what Greek actors or Russians do with
their lines? True, the actor's work is not confined to the
handling of lines but, except when there are no lines at all,
even the non-verbal "business" is apt to have a relation to the
dialogue; not understanding the dialogue, you will misinter-
pret the business. What is over-acting? What is under-acting?
You cannot spot either of them at sight. It is a case of too
much or too little for the matter-in-hand, and the matter-in-

hand includes the words. In Greek tragedy, it is generally agreed, the dialogue is more than half the play.

A type of art which, in Aristotle's phrase, "reveals its power by mere reading," cannot reveal its power by mere seeing. The question is: to what extent are we helped out by knowing *Electra* or *Oedipus*—the two plays our guests brought us—in translation? The answer is that you have to know the English almost by heart so that you can follow line by line without fear of getting lost, and that even then the English version you memorize must have a line-to-line correspondence with the Greek (which, at the Mark Hellinger, would have meant with a modern Greek translation). I found that to know the English in outline was not enough. In the middle of many a two-page oration, I had no idea what was being said, and, since nothing was being done, I repeatedly found my mind wandering.

A friend said that if I'd been moved by Katina Paxinou's Electra I would have been convinced it was great acting and I'd have left it at that. I was not moved. But I know I am not entitled to blame this on the actress. On the contrary, the experience makes me skeptical of all those critical pieces on Duse that were written in entire innocence of the Italian language. There are many things a woman can put across without words; dramatic literature is not one of them; and unintelligible words are not better than no words at all.

I do not mean that the evening was one of uninterrupted boredom. My boredom was interrupted by Dmitri Mitropoulos' music which I rather liked, by the movements of the chorus which I often enjoyed, by an occasional "stage picture" which a knowledge of the story enabled me to interpret, perhaps also by the aura of the occasion, the psychological effect of thinking, "I am in the presence of Greek tragedy in Greek played by Greeks." But no: this last can't be counted: what is expected of you can never be equated with what you really feel. In any case, boredom with interludes is not the experience we ask of theatre; incomprehension with lucid moments is no basis for criticism.

I have been told that, to be consistent, I should regret the French and Greek visits altogether. Obviously not. For one thing there are crucial differences between the two enterprises. Modern Greek is a language known to even fewer of us than ancient Greek; whereas M. Barrault's audience at the Ziegfeld responded to jokes that depend on a very thorough knowledge of French. Even if this were not so, few or none of the French plays currently offered are as dependent on language as the two Greek tragedies, the special art of Barrault being pantomime. Surely all the foreign companies that have had success in New York have offered much more to the eyes than the Greeks are doing. If I have regrets, the chief is over my own ignorance of Greek. I should like to check my impression, at present ill-founded, that Alexis Minotis, Miss Paxinou, and their company are far from first-rate.

A man once told me he liked symphonic music because it started a chain of free associations in his mind—after the first minute it was no more than the accompaniment to a daydream. Conceivably the "music" of the Greek language could serve a similar purpose; and there would be a use for the ancient tragedy in Brave New World.

The Pink and the Black

IT OFTEN HAPPENS that a married man falls in love with a young girl, and that the wife intervenes and the girl goes away. There are many easy ways of "setting up" the story; to have the wife arrange for the girl to be seduced by the husband's best friend might be described as the hard way. It is the way either of a sensation-monger straining after effect or of an artist whose complex mind requires a complex vehicle, like Jean Anouilh who tells the story in *The Rehearsal or Love Punished* (the only new work in the Barrault repertory at the Ziegfeld) .

M. Anouilh is complex in that his real interest doesn't lie where we expect it to lie but somewhere else instead—or somewhere else as well. He was first introduced to New York as a playwright of the Resistance with a play allegedly written to defend a partisan Antigone against a collaborationist Creon. The allegation was not flatly erroneous; it was half true—and wholly misleading. The politics of the play are by no means so unambiguous; and the play is not, in the first instance, political. Admittedly, its real purport was not easy to grasp in isolation from the French background and particularly from the other works of M. Anouilh.

By the time you've seen three or four Anouilh plays, things begin to fall into place in your mind. They are all the same play, or perhaps it would be fairer to say they are one of two plays. The first we have seen under the titles of *Antigone, Legend of Lovers, Cry of the Peacock.* The second we have seen under the title of *Ring Round the Moon* or read under the title *Léocadia.* Anouilh had completed both plays when he himself was little over twenty. Their titles then were *Ermine* and *Thieves' Ball.* The event "Anouilh" occurred in 1932 with the opening of *Ermine* in Paris. *Thieves' Ball* was not produced for six years, but other plays were; and by 1942 Anouilh could publish all versions of both plays, one set under the title *Pièces Noires,* the other under the title *Pièces Roses.* Since the war Anouilh has become (I am told) the most popular playwright on the continent. He cannot really be said to have reached New York, however, till 1952, twenty years after the event; the unhappy affairs that took place under his name were simply not Anouilh.

The Rehearsal is the latest *pièce noire.*[1] Like *Ermine,* the first one, it is about two states of being: poverty and purity. Each state is brought into conflict with its opposite—poverty with wealth, purity with corruption—and the two conflicts are one because it is the poor who are pure, the wealthy who are corrupt.

> She was poor but she was honest.
> Victim of a rich man's crime . . .

[1]Since this review was written there has arrived from Paris a volume indicating that M. Anouilh is dissatisfied with his dichotomy and has put *Ring Round the Moon, The Rehearsal,* and *Colombe* in a third category: *Pièces Brillantes* (1954).

the lines of the old song sum up the heroine of *The Rehearsal*.
Reverse the sexes, and they go some way towards summing up
Anouilh's other recent play *Colombe*: in both plays we see a
virgin disillusioned and destroyed. Anouilh's virgins stand
alone in a world of debauchees. They yearn for the absolute in
the morass of the relative. His Antigone stands, not for virtue,
but for extremity. "We are people," she says, "who push
questions to the limit." Creon asks: "If it isn't for other
people, or for your brother, for whom then?" And this unorthodox revolutionary replies: "For no one. For myself." The
unvirginal Medea also longs for purity—and finds it in destructive energy; it is the more virtuous Jason who surrenders
to the "relative," and decides he must build a wall between
him and nothingness (*le néant*). . . .

In *The Rehearsal* we see the closed circle of rich, corrupt
society broken by a poor, pure teacher of orphans. The protagonist is neither the girl nor a representative of the other side
but Tigre, a man belonging to the other side, yet lured by the
absolute, by poverty and purity. When his wife goes into
action against him, she is actuated less by sexual jealousy than
by social snobbery, and less by social snobbery than by fear of
purity. His best friend Héro can be talked into deflowering the
young teacher because he too hates nothing so much as the
absolute. Héro repeatedly tells us "I like breaking things." He
is near enough to the villain of melodrama to tell us "I have to
be rather disgusting, it's in my part" yet it is a melodrama
colored by psychology—he is revenging himself on the world
for the failure of the great romance of his life—and salted with
Gallic sophistication and "existentialist" philosophy.

So much for the intellectual complexity of *The Rehearsal*.
The play is also complex as dramaturgy. It is a complication of
melodrama, and it is an inversion of a Marivaux comedy. M.
Anouilh's use of Marivaux is the most audacious technical
device of the play. All the characters are rehearsing Marivaux'
Double Inconstancy (the title of which is suggestive enough).
Many of Marivaux' words are found to express the real sentiments of our protagonist and the girl. More remarkable is the
way M. Anouilh stands Marivaux on his head, turns a *pièce
rose* into a *pièce noire*. Here, love is not active and beneficent,

it is passive and disastrous. (Subject for a treatise: "From *Harlequin poli par l'amour* to *l'Amour puni:* a chapter in French cultural history.")

Marivaux on his head is still Marivaux. As theatre, *The Rehearsal* is of the great French tradition, that is to say, the Italian one. I hesitate to mention *commedia dell'arte*—the term is used by drama critics to suggest any style they're sure is wonderful though they haven't a notion what it's like. By his ideas M. Anouilh is related to the existentialists, but perhaps the most important affiliation here is not M. Sartre (whom M. Anouilh antedates) but that Italian existentialist, Luigi Pirandello. The idea of M. Anouilh's *Traveler without Luggage* comes from Pirandello's *Late Mattia Pascal,* perhaps via Giraudoux' *Siegfried.* To join yourself to Pirandello is, luckily, to join yourself not only to his ideas but to the great tradition of comic Latin theatre which reaches back to the *commedia.* M. Anouilh will stand or fall in the degree to which he belongs to this tradition. I would not say his ideas are uninteresting—as yet. I would only record the impression that his special gift is an imagination that is histrionic, scenic, and musical. In a word, M. Anouilh is theatrical; and that is why—whether his is our preferred type of drama or not—we cannot do without him.

I Have a Bright Idea

THERE'S A GAME children love, or used to, that begins with the exclamation "I have a bright idea!" I forget exactly how it goes but I recall that whoever is on hand has to ask whether the idea is animal, vegetable, or mineral, and that when the answer is found it is rather an anti-climax. I wonder if the "ideas" of contemporary culture are prompted by any less childish impulse or can, when identified, be greeted with any greater satisfaction. To begin with, they are not really ideas. Ours is the age of substitutes: instead of language, we have jargon; instead of principles, slogans; and, instead of genuine ideas, Bright Ideas. Bright Ideas win elections, and a cluster of them constituted a "theory" which justified the slaughter of six million Jews. A Bright Idea is an invalid idea which has more appeal to the semi-literate mind than a valid one; a phenomenon of some importance in a culture whose diagnostic is semi-literacy. It is a thought which can't bear thinking about; but which is all the more influential on that account; it surprises or reassures, it flatters or inflames; if it cannot earn the simple epithet "true" it frequently receives the more characteristically modern eulogy of "intriguing" or at least "interesting." At the very worst it is praised as "cute." The modern person, engaged in that search for meaning in life which formerly was known as the religious and philosophic quest, marries one Bright Idea after another, divorce being as frequent in the ideal as in the real world. "I can't *tell* you what this book will do for you," a Los Angeles lady once sighed into my ear, "it's *so* semantic!" She had a Bright Idea.

Nearly sixty years ago, Shaw wrote: "If the world had no more ideas than the theatre has, how long would society hold together?" Today, one is tempted to retort, society teems with ideas but is holding together only by the skin of its teeth, while the theatre teems with the same ideas and, far from holding together, is losing out to films, fiction, and TV. The retort would be unjust because when Shaw said "ideas" he meant it, whereas what our theatre and our society teem with are the fads, or Bright Ideas, which he spent seven decades denouncing. There is a miniature, but perfect, example in Shaw's correspondence with Mrs. Patrick Campbell. After seeing the actress in *Macbeth,* Shaw wrote her: "I couldn't understand the sleepwalking until D.D. [unidentified] told me someone had told you that Lady Macbeth should be seen through a sheet of glass. I wish I had been there with a few bricks. . . ." That sheet of glass is the very archetype of theatrical Bright Ideas, and for every window-breaker, there are half a dozen glaziers, calling themselves directors or teachers of acting. Indeed, a director hesitates to stage Shakespeare today *unless* he has a Bright Idea. One of the simpler Bright Ideas is transferring your play to another period for no sufficient reason. *The Taming of the Shrew* is more "intriguing" as a Regency farce. This particular transfer (not an invented one) is arbitrary. We have recently witnessed some that are not, and they are even worse. Chekhov's Russia and Verdi's Africa have been transferred to the U.S. South, the idea being that domestic affairs are more real to an audience than foreign affairs. It may be a true idea: all that's wrong is that it doesn't apply to matter in hand. In context it is only a Bright Idea.

Marx and Freud had ideas; the theatre has Bright Ideas. Counsel for playwrights accused of Marxism should plead the *a priori* impossibility of guilt: a playwright with *no* ideas cannot be found to have Marxist ideas. What the "social" playwrights took up in the 'Thirties was a set of Bright Ideas whose purpose was to give us the feeling of heroism without enjoining on us the duty of being heroic. Such playwrights could be sincere in retreating when a feeling of heroism gave place to a feeling of fear. Today it is not Marx but Freud who turns in his grave every time a Drama of Ideas opens on Broadway or in the West End. The theatre which Shaw berated for its hedonism now lectures us on the sex problems of adolescents and the complexes of old maids. The "master-drama" of this generation is *A Streetcar Named Desire*. When a series of young actors auditioned for me not long ago I had the impression of seeing Blanche Dubois and Stanley Kowalsky over and over again, though my records indicated I had witnessed scenes from a dozen different plays. More than one of the young men even dressed like Stanley. Marlon Brando's T-shirt has attained the dignity of a Bright Idea.

Can't a man improve his plays by filling them with Improving Ideas? Can't he make them profounder by referring to profound subjects? That seems to be the logic of Messrs. Moss Hart and John van Druten in their latest offerings. Ideology is a great temptation. You imagine that all you need to do is refer to "schizophrenia" and you are exempt from the onerous duty of *creating* a schizoid character. You imagine that all you need to do is refer to religion many, many times and you have dramatized faith. On the first night of Mr. van Druten's *I've Got Sixpence* it was God who turned in His grave. The play is "religious" in the same sense as that Californian lady's book was "semantic." Salvation here is just as mechanically contrived as in any proletarian drama of the older generation. In the theatre it seems hard for a god not to come *ex machina*.

"Going Serious" has been, perhaps, the commonest Bright Idea of them all. In the thirties it meant communism or the Buchmanite movement. To Mr. van Druten today it means Californian religion. In nearly all instances it has entailed an artistic decline. Nor need we accept the moral earnestness of the gesture at face value. Among the people one has known most intimately, those who have gone serious have not always gone best. Most of us too easily admire the sudden dive into a Cause, *any* cause; there is sickness in our admiration; causes are Bright Ideas. In soberer moods we grant that *The Climate of Eden* is a bad play, *Once in a Lifetime* a good one. Better no ideas than Bright Ideas. Yet, to be sure, a cult of anti-intellectualism—"the peasants in Mexico are happier illiterate"— would be the ultimate Bright Idea. The corrective to Bright Ideas lies not in No Ideas (that is, in the idea of no ideas) but in—ideas.

Lillian Hellman's Indignation

NOBODY ASKED HER to be Shakespeare. The genre to which *The Children's Hour* belongs is an honorable, if not a major, one. Call it the publicist's drama, the drama of indignation. In such drama we shall not expect to feel the emotion of characters as strongly as the author's animus. We shan't ask what such a dramatist has created, we ask who is the enemy this time, and how the dramatist has made us see his importance.

The material from which *The Children's Hour* is made suggests two stories. The first is a story of heterosexual teachers accused of Lesbianism; the enemy is a society which punishes the innocent. The second is a story of Lesbian teachers accused of Lesbianism; the enemy is a society which punishes Lesbians. Now, since either one of these stories could make an accepta-

ble indignant play, one could scarcely be surprised if a playwright tried to tell them both at once. This is not quite what
Miss Hellman does. She spends the greater part of the evening
on the first story. In fact the indignation she arouses in us has
but one source—our impression that the charge of Lesbianism
is unfounded, an impression reinforced by everyone's holy
horror whenever the subject comes up. Then, in the last few
minutes, we learn that one of the teachers *is* Lesbian. But it is
too late for Miss Hellman to tell Story Two and spell out its
moral. The "guilty" teacher kills herself, and the curtain
comes down. Taking the play as a technical exercise, we could
praise this ending as clever, or damn it as clumsy, but if we are
interested in Miss Hellman's indignation, and especially if
during the evening she has induced us to share it, we are
bound to feel cheated. We are told that the play has been
revived because of the current red scare. Now suppose it had
been about teachers accused of communism, that for over two
acts we had been asked to boil with indignation at the wrongness of the accusation, only to find, towards the close of Act
Three, that one of the pair *did* harbor communist sympathies?
Of course, a play can favor communism; a non-communist
play can favor the toleration of communists; but these very
different plays cannot be squeezed into the last ten minutes of
a play protesting at the incrimination of non-communists. Or
can they? The political analogy suggests not only the logical
weakness of Miss Hellman's position but also the historical
and psychological path along which she reached it. Is it not in
politics, rather than the theatre, that we have witnessed this
drama before? Mr. A would say it was infantile to accuse Mr. B
of communism—"after all you're accused of communism nowadays if your hair is red"—and yet, later, when Mr. B did come
out with communist views, Mr. A was neither displeased nor
surprised. In the thirties, Mr. A would have said that of course
an Alger Hiss was not a spy and then, if the espionage had
been proved, he would have said, well, the Soviet Union was a
special case. *The Children's Hour* has nothing directly to do
with communism, but it was written in the thirties, and is the
product of the dubious idealism of that time. Commenting on
the play, Miss Hellman wrote: "I am a moral writer, often too

moral a writer." As our feeling of being moral increases, our awareness of moral issues declines. The "too moral" writer takes everything for granted.

For example, her antogonists. In *The Children's Hour* there are three: cowardice (Mrs. Mortar), credulity (Mrs. Tilford), and sheer evil (Mary). In each case, Miss Hellman counts on our having our response ready. Our hatred of cowardice is to put the flesh and blood on the skeleton from Broadway farce which is all the author provides. Our understanding of credulity is relied on to make plausible an old lady's believing the villain's implausible accusations: no character is created of whom we must say, "*she* of course would have believed." Finally, our being against sin is supposed to assure our hatred of a villain's unexplained villainy. I for one would not insist on a psychological explanation of evil (though such an explanation would be in place in drama of this sort) but if you don't explain it psychologically, you must either explain it some other way or *create* it as the Elizabethans did, making it live moment by moment in language that sprang from poetic vision and moral imagination. Miss Hellman's villain is a *diabolus ex machina* not simply lowered on stage at the end but smuggled in at the outset. What a playwright might fairly ask us to accept at the close we have to concede at the very beginning.

This villain is a child. Instead of the sweet little chee-ild done to death by the tyrannical teacher we have the sweet little teacher done to death by the tyrannical child—an inversion of orthodox melodrama which would be all very well if the values of melodrama, as well as the roles, were inverted. But Miss Hellman is a melodramatist, first, in seeing life as a melodrama insofar as she sees it at all and, second, in being less concerned to see life than to manipulate it. Her chief device is the purely mechanical inversion of stock melodramatic characters. A child is wicked, a grandmother (in *Autumn Garden,* say) cynical. The effect is one of sophistication —melodrama for a smart set. The pleasure in seeing such things resides in the titillation of cruelty twice removed from our own backs—once by the proscenium arch, a second time by the sophisticated style. . . . Admittedly, the audience at the

Coronet was not concerned with the moral ambiguities I find inherent in *The Children's Hour*. As far as I could observe, they were busy being delightedly shocked at two phenomena: Lesbianism and wickedness in a child.

Sometimes in the course of the evening one has the impression of an author let down by a director. The actors seem lost. Two of our leading realistic actresses (Patricia Neal and Kim Hunter) are on stage but have not been given anything to play. The whole apparatus of naturalistic stage-design is also there but it remains a background. You'd think the old lady (Katherine Emmet) was in a hotel rather than her own home; she doesn't care which chair she sits in or how much she marches around. One of the younger ladies agrees it's terribly cold but sits as far as possible from the stove. . . . The director was Miss Hellman herself, and the chief fault of the direction is that it shares the faults of the script instead of correcting them. Everything on stage seems unreal, inorganic, unrelated to everything else. To make matters worse, the director seems to know it, seems to be striving to galvanize a mechanical monster into life. Hence there is an absence of genuine passion not only in the individual characters but in the whole production, and nothing in its place but the hard humorless drive of the authoress's will-power. Since indignation is a genuine passion, I adjudge *The Children's Hour,* on its own terms, a failure.

Acting: Natural and Artificial

TRYING, SOME TIME AGO, to discover how Shakespeare was acted in his own time, I found that scholars classify acting as either *natural* or *artificial* and put Shakespeare into whichever category they prefer: Shakespeare's own principal utterance on the subject—Hamlet's advice to the players—lends itself equally well to either interpretation. Though my first impulse was to reject these categories altogether, I soon caught myself reintroducing them in disguise: *natural* reappeared as *realistic*, *artificial* reappeared as *stylized* when I disliked it and as *the grand manner* when I approved. And looking back over the history of theatre, I realized that critics have fallen into two classes: those who say acting has become so natural it lacks beauty and those who say it has become so fancy it lacks naturalness. The critic's plea is either for a return to the grand manner or for a return to reality. But this is not to say that we all stand either for one style or the other, simple or grand, natural or artificial. On the contrary, so soon as we think about it, we recognize that dramatic, like all other, art necessarily involves both imitation and selection, nature and artifice, truth and beauty. We want the right balance, so we put our own weight on the side which contemporary theatre is neglecting. To interpret Hamlet's advice correctly we would need to know whether Shakespeare's contemporaries were leaning too far toward the natural or toward the artificial; Hamlet was against the unbalance, whichever it was. *Natural* and *artificial* are not names of rival styles in acting; they are names for lack of style in acting. Acting is both natural and artificial, yet to the extent that it comes off, to the extent that it is *good* acting, it is not notably either. At this point, we seek more laudatory words. We replace *naturalness* with *reality*, *artifice* with *style*, nor would we grant that a performance had *reality* till we felt it had *style*, or *style* till we felt it had *reality*. Hence, though we can divide bad actors into two widely different schools—natural and artificial—we shall find that good actors have a great deal in common with each other. We must not be misled at finding a great actor of the past assigned by critics to the natural or to the artificial category. This, if it means anything, and if the actor was really great, means that he corrected the balance, was *natural* in counteracting excessive artifice, or *artificial* in counteracting excessive naturalness. The terms are relative. Forbes Robertson is often cited in pleas for the grand manner; he has also been called the most natural of actors. Much the same is true of Duse. Henry Irving has become a byword for rant and artifice, yet he shocked his Victorian public with his harsh, abrupt "realism." Betterton and Garrick were congratulated on their naturalness, but just compare their portraits with performances by actors of our current nose-picking school! To say that their naturalness had its limits is only to reiterate that they were actors.

Have good actors so much in common that we should not readily notice stylistic differences between them? Differences that can partly be described by words like *natural* and *artificial?* These are rhetorical questions, and I agree with the implied answer but think it less important than the fact that even the minimum requirements of good acting are so considerable that Burbage, Betterton, Garrick, Kean, and Forbes Robertson *must* have had more in common with each other than any one of them had with a defective, one-sided actor, natural or artificial. When a critic contrasts one actor's style with another's he is almost invariably saying that one is right, the other wrong, one a good actor, the other a bad. Thus, Leigh Hunt does not present Kemble and Kean as great actors who have little in common; he is telling us that Kemble is not great. So with Shaw on Bernhardt and Duse; he finds Bernhardt's acting faulty; those who think him prejudiced in favor of Duse's greater naturalness should read his good-natured demolition of one of the better natural actors of the time, John Hart. If you grant that good acting is neither "natural" nor "artificial" you will not find it very profitable to describe one good actor as "more natural" or "more artificial" than another: this will only be to say that good actors are not *wholly* good. Again, if you compare the relative "naturalness" of eighteenth- and twentieth-century acting, you will have to discuss what the two periods consider natural. Which in turn involves what *is* natural in the two periods. And naturalness is relative to place as well as time: a gesture that is natural to an Italian is unnatural to an Englishman. . . . In short, though the word *natural* may lead us into interesting speculations, it leads away from the subject of acting; it is not a convenience but a distraction. It follows that the same is true of *artificial,* its antithesis. In a given period, the tendency of bad acting (thus of the acting profession as a whole) is "natural" or "artificial"; and the critic will be busy deploring the tendency. As for good acting, its being both or neither forces the critic, if he is to come to grips with it at all, to more specific description. For, though in transcending the natural and artificial, good actors have a technique in common, what interests us is what they do with their technique. Having come out into the clear, where do they go? Classifications a good deal more helpful than natural and artificial are no doubt possible. But more interesting for the student of theatre than the generalities are the particulars. For once an actor has his technique (i.e., *is* an actor), his individuality shows itself. He has shed everything that passed for his personality in the days when personality meant the part of him that was accessible to his conscious mind and to the minds of fans and publicity men. He now has his personality [1] as an artist. The one *persona* is an obstacle, the other an instrument. The critic, for his part, if he has put bad acting in its place, and knows a false *persona* when he sees it, is free to forget about styles and talk of actors' personalities. The best recorded writing about acting is sheer description of performance, and amounts in each case—I am thinking of certain pages in Cibber and Lichtenberg, Hazlitt and Montague—to a portrait of the actor.

[1] See pp. 31, 87, 130, 156.

Acting vs. Reciting

PRAISING THE Drama Quartet, people are saying how nice it is to do without scenery. I do not share their implied disdain for stage design, but I am not surprised at it. What surprises me is the assumption that, when a play is read to us, nothing is missing but decor. Or does the fact that readers use gesture make them actors?

You can say yes to this, and cite the sages. Dr. Johnson wrote that we go to the theatre to "hear a certain number of lines recited with just gesture and elegant modulation." Dryden seems not to have demanded much more: "All passions may be lively represented on the stage if to the well-writing of them the actor supplies a good commanded voice and limbs that

move easily and without stiffness." And when Johnson says:
"A dramatic exhibition is a book recited with concomitants
that increase or diminish its effect," we know where we are.
This is the notorious "literary" view of theatre, bluntly restated by a Shakespearean scholar only the other day: "In the
theatre, as in the study, the poet's words are all that count." Of
more interest than the untruth of this statement (whatever
can be so flatly asserted can, I presume, be as flatly denied) is
its motivation and background: it has its origin in the study of
a theatre where the words did in fact play a much larger role.
Of this theatre Bernard Shaw once wrote: "In Shakespeare's
time the acting of plays was imperfectly differentiated from
the declamation of verses; and description or narrative recitation did what is now done by scenery, furniture, and stage
business." Anxious to restore the long speech and the "rhetorical" way of delivering it, Shaw preferred what he thought of as
the older method to the newer. And his special perspective
gave him special insights: his insistence that Shakespeare's
lines not be broken by "business" is still called for today. But
as usual—one should rather say, on principle—Shaw overstates
the case. A fair amount of "business" is to be inferred from
Elizabethan scripts, and the scantiness of stage directions cannot be taken to mean that the Elizabethans did not insert
"business" even where the scripts do not infer it. Nor was the
Elizabethan stage as bare of furniture and scenery as scholars
in Shaw's early days thought. As for acting, we know nothing,
really, of the style which Alleyn or Burbage practiced, though
the praise accorded these men in the roles we know they
played certainly suggests that they did more (for example,
with *character*) than a mere reader would. And this is to speak
of tragic acting only. The comedians, we know, were acrobats
and dancers; speaking was but one of their several accomplishments. (For that matter, the wary Dr. Johnson admits that the
"literary" view of the stage is inapplicable to comedy: "Familiar comedy is often more powerful in the theatre, than on the
page; imperial tragedy is always less. The humour of Petru-
chio may be heightened by grimace; but what voice or what
gesture can hope to add dignity or force to the soliloquy of
Cato?") To these empirical remarks I would even venture to

add a syllogism: all good acting has more to it than recitation, Alleyn and Burbage were good actors, therefore Alleyn and Burbage did more than recite.

The man who best helps us to see this is Constantin Stanislavsky. Many think of him primarily as the bringer of the new style—the style that works with scenery, furniture, and stage business, rather than with language; for a time, undeniably, a particular form of this style—naturalism—*was* what he stood for. What he stands for in the long run, however, will not be this style or any other. It will be his approach to acting—in any style. It will be what he has to teach *anyone* who wishes to act. He understood the minimum requirements of good acting, one of which is to put words in their place. This is not necessarily to make words less important; it is, rather, to make them more effective. The "place" of words is in the mouth of the speaker—and, beyond the mouth, in his body and mind. A stage director has to "sink" his author's words into the actors, and then help the actors, as it were, to hoist them out again. In short, words are, for actors, not statements but responses to stimuli, like gestures. We, the spectators, should not have the words simply handed to us—we should see them springing from a situation, from a character, from a query, a blow, or a snort. A minimum requirement for an actor is that he enable us to see them in this way. William Gillette called it giving "the illusion of the first time." I am not happy with this phrase, for it seems to me that much more is involved and that an actor should on occasion give the impression that a thing *has* been said before. But that the "gesture" of real speech is always necessary is certainly true. And with it goes gesture in the literal sense. Describing gesture as a "concomitant" of "recitation" may be accurate enough from an outsider's viewpoint, but anyone who learnt to act would, I think, have to approach it differently. Stanislavsky said this when it much needed saying. But actors, and teachers who trained actors, must surely have known it at all times. For the actor, it is more practical to consider the "book" as the "concomitant" and the "gesture" as the main thing, if we can a little stretch the meaning of the word "gesture" to include "posture," and the word "posture" to include the posture of the mind as well as the body. That we have to stretch the meaning of words is of course no accident. The art of theatre is poor in precise terminology; that must be one reason for confusion. But it surely makes sense to differentiate between the working actor's attitude to words and the spectator's. For the latter, the words will be predominant—if the play is of the type where words predominate. But, even with such a play, the words must become secondary for the actor as he works. He must subordinate them to the context from which they spring, or they will never gain the importance which their author wishes them to have.

Another element of confusion comes in because reciting is not the opposite of acting, it is half-way to acting. The Drama Quartet half-acted their play. Radio actors half-act their plays, as anyone knows who has watched them in the studio. Now half-acting is only successful when practiced by whole actors: what enables Charles Laughton to portray Shaw's devil is not his practice in reciting but his practice in acting. A generation trained in reciting would not recite well. It is therefore a mistake to regard the method of the Drama Quartet as a solution to our problems. We can settle for nothing less than acting, as it was, is, and ever shall be.

Guilding the Lilli

THE LOVE OF FOUR COLONELS by Peter Ustinov, produced by the Theatre Guild, is either too serious or not serious enough, too frivolous or not frivolous enough. And since the consistency with which it misses the mark is too great to be fortuitous, it may not be impertinent to discuss how such things can be.

We inherit from what might be called the puritan-philistine tradition a fatal separation of the funny and the serious; we are predisposed to believe that if a statement is amusing it probably isn't true and certainly isn't important; conversely, we admire gravity, and are slow to see the stupidity it usually conceals. To rebel against this tradition has seldom been to question the fatal separation itself. It has only been to champion the other side, to be the spokesman of unseriousness, to deny the importance of being earnest. This partial rebellion has become vocal again since the war, especially in England, where one of the younger dramatic critics has written: "I believe in superficiality, I believe in shallowness." [1] Today such a declaration is so uninteresting, one wonders how it could have rung with challenge when Wilde made it half a century ago. The main reason, I suppose, is precisely that *Wilde* made it: it's all right to say you're superficial if you're not. Then again, for a mere pose, fifty years is a ripe old age. But bad habits die hard, and it remains easier to get a reputation for sincerity if you have no sense of humor, just as it remains easier to "shine in the high esthetic line" if you have no sincerity. Our theatre—playwrights, directors, and designers—tends towards the extremes of the sordidly naturalistic and the vacuously esthetic. An increasing number of actors gravitates toward one of these poles or the other. You notice it in their dress and conversation: this one, dirty and unshaven, in T-shirt, leather jacket, and jeans, discourses about the new play he is in, all alcohol and abortion; that one, clean and dainty, in colored waistcoat, carrying an umbrella, talks of the eighteenth-century vases he has just seen in the antiquary's window.

Since Peter Ustinov has not moved irrevocably to one pole or the other, you may at first be tempted to hope that he will keep away from both. What he actually does is to oscillate disconcertingly between the two, finding no resting place anywhere in between, and furthermore finding himself much more at home at one pole than the other. This is the pole of frivolity. As a man has in the end to be himself or nothing, one cannot but recommend that Mr. Ustinov accept his destiny by embracing frivolity and sending seriousness on her way. In *The Love of Four Colonels,* every shred of explicit edification could be cut without loss. Phrases like a "man hypnotized by

[1] I am glad to record that, today, Kenneth Tynan disowns his earlier dictum (1954).

his own mediocrity" might pass in many plays; here there is no context to support them. The same is true of apothegms like: "The French genius is the genius of mistrust." As for: "Then would I taste of that better thing they call reality . . ." Why not: *then I would* or: *then I'd like to*? The word *reality* here, like the words *charity* and *perfection*, in the play's peroration, must go. Having got rid of the ballast of dull moralizing, Mr. Ustinov's ship of humor must fare as it can with whatever cargo of moral implication the humor carries with it. And here some really pleasant qualities emerge. Or rather they would emerge if the Theatre Guild production let them. Under the paraphernalia of production lies an agreeable jest about our disunited United Nations. At a Saturday night party—or perhaps at a cozy, old-fashioned London matinée where tea and cakes are brought in at intermission—this play, stripped of its generalizings, might be very funny; it would undoubtedly be relaxing. But not only is this production no joke; it is tense with effort. I suppose everyone knows how a play is prepared for Broadway, the prolonged agony of doctoring it goes through. All I am saying is that agony has after-effects. It shows. Whereas art, including theatre art, seems effortless.

You may say that a little play is lucky to get so big a production; in that case, the more gilt on the lily, the better. This show is neither lovely to look at, nor well acted. Rolf Gerard's sets are elaborate without beauty; if over-production was the aim, surely so gifted an artist could have made sure the show was gorgeous. Among the actors, there were no untalented people. It was all the more galling to see bad performances. Larry Gates and Robert Coote as the American and English colonels respectively are exceptions: lucky in having the humorous and not the philosophical lines, they provide most of the evening's fun. The reality these characters have, though on a "low" plane, is far preferable to the unreality of the Frenchman and the Russian who are seen on the "high" plane of ideology: inevitably perhaps, George Voskovec and Stefan Schnabel come to grief in these parts. I was curious to see Leueen MacGrath for the first time; her role of good fairy let me see precisely nothing. Reginald Mason's name I knew as that of the first American to play Pirandello's Laudisi; his director in *Love of Four Colonels* let him run the small, small gamut of clichés for the stage Old Man . . .

The director is also the leading man: Rex Harrison. I once saw a production in which a whole cast was kept stationary in a close circle throughout an act while the actor-manager, with complete freedom of movement, described a larger circle around them, doubled back, and darted between them. Mr. Harrison's directing is not quite like this, and even if it were one would forgive it—provided that he brought what all this pomp and circumstance leads us to expect: a great performance. Instead we have the shadow of a star without the substance; a manner, not a style. He breezes on, his role of bad fairy entitles him (perhaps) to a phony voice and a phony walk, he lies languidly on the table (trust actors to find uncomfortable places to lie on), and proceeds to manipulate a flexible wrist. Well, the audience knows who it is, the *mana* of kingship is in our midst, and when this our tribal monarch walks in later with a false beard on, the lady next to me says: "Isn't he marvellous?" Lilli Palmer does a version of eighteenth-century comedy that would do credit to a dramatic academy's best student of the year and one of an American floozy that she can improve by learning an American accent . . .

Mr. Harrison and Miss Palmer have both given first-rate performances in their time. But in what sort of drama? What sort of production? The best work of Mr. Harrison's that I've seen was in the film of *Major Barbara*. In those days his face was not that of a mere public figure or Man of Distinction; it had the vastly more heartening lineaments of a real man. Miss Palmer's best work over here is generally held to be her Cleopatra in Shaw's play: another part that requires only one sort of distinction, that of simplicity. What is the incentive that drives an actor from the art of acting, in its living simplicity, to sophistication without grace, bigness without grandeur, and death without dignity? Ambition should be made of sterner stuff.

The Innocence of Arthur Miller

THE THEATRE is provincial. Few events on Broadway have any importance whatsoever except to that small section of the community—neither an élite nor a cross section—that sees Broadway plays. A play by an Arthur Miller or a Tennessee Williams is an exception. Such a play is not only better than the majority; it belongs in the mainstream of our culture. Such an author has something to say about America that is worth discussing. In *The Crucible*, Mr. Miller says something that *has* to be discussed. Nor am I limiting my interest to the intellectual sphere. One sits before this play with anything but intellectual detachment. At a moment when we are all being "investigated," or imagining that we shall be, it is vastly disturbing to see indignant images of investigation on the other side of the footlights. Why, one wonders, aren't there dozens of plays each season offering such a critical account of the state of the nation—critical and *engagé?* The appearance of one such play by an author, like Mr. Miller, who is neither an infant, a fool, or a swindler, is enough to bring tears to the eyes.

"Great stones they lay upon his chest until he plead aye or nay. They say he give them but two words. 'More weight,' he says, and died." Mr. Miller's material is magnificent for narrative, poetry, drama. The fact that we sense its magnificence suggests that either he or his actors have in part realized it, yet our moments of emotion only make us the more aware of half-hours of indifference or dissatisfaction. For this is a story not quite told, a drama not quite realized. Pygmalion has labored hard at his statue and it has not come to life. There is a terrible inertness about the play. The individual characters, like the individual lines, lack fluidity and grace. There is an O'Neill-like striving after a poetry and an eloquence which the author does not achieve. "From Aeschylus to Arthur Miller," say the textbooks. The world has made this author important before he has made himself great; perhaps the reversal of the natural order of things weighs heavily upon him. It would be all too easy, script in hand, to point to weak spots. The inadequacy of particular lines, and characters, is of less interest, however, than the mentality from which they come. It is the mentality of the unreconstructed liberal.

There has been some debate as to whether this story of seventeenth-century Salem "really" refers to our current "witch hunt," yet since no one is interested in anything *but* this reference, I pass on to the real point at issue, which is: the validity of the parallel. It is true in that people today are being persecuted on quite chimerical grounds. It is untrue in that communism is not, to put it mildly, merely a chimera. The word communism is used to cover, first, the politics of Marx, second, the politics of the Soviet Union, and, third, the activities of all liberals as they seem to illiberal illiterates. Since Mr. Miller's argument bears only on the third use of the word, its scope is limited. Indeed, the analogy between "red-baiting" and witch hunting can seem complete only to communists, for only to them is the menace of communism as fictitious as the menace of witches. The non-communist will look for certain reservations and provisos. In *The Crucible,* there are none.

To accuse Mr. Miller of communism would of course be to fall into the trap of over-simplification which he himself has set. For all I know he may hate the Soviet state with all the ardor of Eisenhower. What I am maintaining is that his view of life is dictated by assumptions which liberals have to unlearn and which many liberals have rather publicly unlearned. Chief among these assumptions is that of general innocence. In Hebrew mythology, innocence was lost at the very beginning of things; in liberal, especially American liberal, folklore, it has not been lost yet; Arthur Miller is the playwright of American liberal folklore. It is as if the merely negative, and legal, definition of innocence were extended to the rest of life: you are innocent until proved guilty, you are innocent if you "didn't do it." Writers have a sort of double innocence: not only can they create innocent characters, they can also write from the viewpoint of innocence—we can speak today not only of the "omniscient" author but of the "guiltless" one.

Such indeed is the viewpoint of the dramatist of indignation, like Miss Hellman or Mr. Miller. And it follows that their plays are melodrama—a conflict between the wholly guilty and the wholly innocent. For a long time liberals were afraid to criticize the mentality behind this melodrama because they feared association with the guilty ("harboring reactionary sympathies"). But, though a more enlightened view would enjoin association with the guilty in the admission of a common humanity, it does not ask us to underestimate the guilt or to refuse to see "who done it." The guilty men are as black with guilt as Mr. Miller says—what we must ask is whether the innocent are as white with innocence. The drama of indignation is melodramatic not so much because it paints its villains too black as because it paints its heroes too white. *Othello* is not a melodrama, because, though its villain is wholly evil, its hero is not wholly virtuous. *The Crucible* is a melodrama because, though the hero has weaknesses, he has no faults. His innocence is unreal because it is total. His author has equipped him with what we might call Super-innocence, for the crime he is accused of not only hasn't been committed by him, it isn't even a possibility: it is the fiction of traffic with the devil. It goes without saying that the hero has all the minor accoutrements of innocence too: he belongs to the right social class (yeoman farmer), does the right kind of work (manual), and, somewhat contrary to historical probability, has the right philosophy (a distinct leaning towards skeptical empiricism) . . .

The innocence of his author is known to us from life as well as art. Elia Kazan made a public confession of having been a communist and, while doing so, mentioned the names of several of his former comrades. Mr. Miller then brought out a play about an accused man who refuses to name comrades (who indeed dies rather than make a confession at all), and of course decided to end his collaboration with the director who did so much to make him famous. The play has been directed by Jed Harris.

I think there is as much drama in this bit of history as in any Salem witch hunt. The "guilty" director was rejected. An "innocent" one was chosen in his place. There are two stories in this. The first derives from the fact that the better fellow (assuming, for the purpose of argument, that Mr. Harris is the better fellow) is not always the better worker. The awkwardness I find in Mr. Miller's script is duplicated in Mr. Harris's directing. Mr. Kazan would have taken this script up like clay and re-molded it. He would have struck fire from the individual actor, and he would have brought one actor into much livelier relationship with another. (Arthur Kennedy is not used up to half his full strength in this production; E. G. Marshall and Walter Hampden give fine performances but each in his own way, Mr. Hampden's way being a little too English, genteel and nineteenth century; the most successful performance, perhaps, is that of Beatrice Straight because here a certain rigidity belongs to the character and is in any case delicately checked by the performer's fine sensibility.) The second story is that of the interpenetration of good and evil. I am afraid that Mr. Miller needs a Kazan not merely at some superficial technical level. He needs not only the craftsmanship of a Kazan but also—his sense of guilt. Innocence is, for a mere human being, and especially for an artist, insufficient baggage. When we say that Mr. Kazan "added" to *Death of a Salesman*, we mean—if I am not saying more than I know—that he infused into this drama of social forces the pressure of what Freud called "the family romance," the pressure of guilt. *The Crucible* is *about* guilt yet nowhere in it is there any *sense* of guilt because the author and director have joined forces to dissociate themselves and their hero from evil. This is the theatre of two Dr. Jekylls. Mr. Miller and Mr. Kazan were Dr. Jekyll and Mr. Hyde.

Hans Andersen's Boomerang

THE EMPEROR'S CLOTHES, by George Tabori, is not a very good play but the labors of Harold Clurman and Lee J. Cobb made the evening at the Barrymore a tense one. The acting of the

Group Theatre tradition is probably, aside from musicals, the best kind of American theatre work, and it is a kind not, to my knowledge, found in Europe, despite its origin in Stanislavsky's "method." When Americans attempt an English manner (say for Shakespeare, Shaw, or Wilde), they most often come a cropper; in *The Emperor's Clothes* it is the one English actor (Esmond Knight) who seems gauche and helpless.

Lee J. Cobb is perhaps the leading exponent of this American way of acting; what is more important, he is one of our finest actors. I do not mean we have no misgivings about him. His besetting temptation is sentimentality. When in doubt, he thumps the table, screams his head off, or wallows in a fit of weeping. Like most actors of his school, he sometimes seems to mistake the jitters for creative energy. In *The Emperor's Clothes*, however, Mr. Cobb gives of his best. The degree of control and craftsmanship in his performance is so great that those who wish to see actors "being" their parts and not acting them begin to talk of overconscious actors, artifice, and excessive intellectuality; Stanislavskyites themselves begin to wonder if Mr. Cobb has stayed in line. For though he does carry you away with the violence of his emotions, and this to a degree very seldom known in the theatre today, he also engages your intellect and arouses your admiration of his skill. His performance has a double action: it draws you in and it holds you away. In the jargon of theatre esthetics, there is *empathy,* and there is *alienation.* I submit that this is the paradox—or, better, the dialectic—of first-rate acting.

Mr. Clurman is also a master of his craft. The plasticity of his scenes is in broad contrast with the ghastly stiffness of other directing jobs of the 1952–3 season—Miss Hellman's or even Jed Harris's. The Group Theatre's stress on the organic, the spontaneous, the inward, the "real," pays off. This is a production in which one can sit back and enjoy apt moves and groupings, smooth transitions, accurate punctuation, distinct articulation, well-built climaxes, well-timed anti-climaxes, lulls, and pauses. If there is anything in the direction to complain of, it is a certain softness of texture. In this play, as in *Time of the Cuckoo,* we find Mr. Clurman making too easy an appeal to sweet background music. To my mind, the heroic ending of

The Emperor's Clothes is softened by over-much sentiment in the performance. The weakest scenes of all are those where Maureen Stapleton speaks some pseudo-Chekhov with piano accompaniment.

Perhaps this last weakness is partly the actress's fault. If Mr. Cobb might be the cue for a eulogy of the Group tradition, Miss Stapleton forces us to see certain dangers in it. Already in *The Rose Tattoo* one wondered if, for all her fine talent, she mistook neurasthenia for vitality. Still, in that play, one at least took the fluttery, feathery movements as belonging to, and springing from, the part and the occasion. It is when Miss Stapleton repeats them all in so different a play as *The Emperor's Clothes* that they come to seem mere mannerism. Yesterday's inventions are today's clichés; syncopation can be as mechanical as a regular beat.

Is the actress herself to blame, or the director—or the author? Mr. Tabori is a controversial figure. *Flight into Egypt* had a cold reception here, and the reviews of *The Emperor's Clothes* are also unfavorable; yet on both occasions the theatre was much more highly charged with thought and feeling, particularly the latter, than I have found it to be when much more highly praised plays were brought before us. The theatre is always and rightly in search of a play for the times, a play that is a luminous theatrical image of our permanent crisis, a play which at the very least would be stirring journalism—in the way that Koestler's or Orwell's novels are stirring journalism. The theatre of George Tabori engages our attention because it is an earnest effort in this direction. If it fails for reasons other than sheer inadequacy, it is because Mr. Tabori's journalism is full of literary affectation and pretension. When he reaches after elegance (as in the portrayal of a baron) he is just corny.

If it is hard to apportion credit and blame as between actor and director, it is even harder, these days, to apportion it as between a script and a production. *Flight into Egypt* petered out in utter ambiguity of plot. One didn't know whether Mr. Tabori's people decided to stick to Europe or become refugees in America, though this was (as far as I could make out) the main point at issue. In *The Emperor's Clothes* there is also a broken link in the narrative chain. A Hungarian professor, as of 1930, has gone off to be investigated by the political police. His wife has every reason to believe he will crumple under their pressure. When an old wooer of hers offers to get her out of the country, she has every inducement to go. At this point, the dialogue has her say, No, "another name or place will not help us"; yet the action seems, on the contrary, to sweep her offstage to pack her bags . . . No doubt this short passage could be clarified. I mention it, however, as typical of the blot or blur that characterizes Mr. Tabori's two plays in the form in which they have been brought before us. I don't know if Mr. Tabori's friends blame the flaws in *The Emperor's Clothes* on Mr. Clurman; they did blame the flaws in *Flight into Egypt* on Mr. Kazan. No mere spectator could unravel this tangled skein, but a sense of theatre would suggest that Messrs. Kazan and Clurman gave much more to these plays than they took away. When you listen to Mr. Tabori's lines in isolation from the actors and the stage they sound either very flat or very fancy; it takes production to raise such writing above banal fiction and florid melodrama. It takes acting of the very highest order to give these people reality. Without Lee Cobb and Anthony Ross, the Hungarian professor and his doctor brother are the stereotypes of the anti-fascist literature of twenty years ago. This is a play we would only wish to see clothed in all the regalia of theatrical illusion. As a mere script, it puts us uncomfortably in mind of the emperor's new clothes.

On the Sublime

THE MANAGEMENT of *John Brown's Body* said there were no available seats at the opening and that anyway they would want to talk matters over before admitting me to their show as they thought there was a danger of my reviewing it unfavorably. They were wrong about the seats. I had no difficulty in buying tickets for the opening at the box office. And I was willing to do so because of my long-standing admiration for Charles Laughton, director of the presentation.

Though they were right about the unfavorable review, they were wrong about the grounds of it. Apparently a quotation from my piece on acting and reciting[1] had been circulated in *Theatre Digest.* I had said that the Drama Quartet's readings were not a solution to our principal problems in the theatre: that is all. Does the management feel that a favorable review is unsure unless a critic believes that reading *is* a solution to our principal problems? Strange, if they do: for in *John Brown's Body* the issue of acting vs. reading does not arise. Here is a poem to be read, not a play to be produced. One might claim that there is too much acting in the performance rather than too little. But this is to anticipate.

We all enjoy the reading aloud of poetry. What we find at the Century Theatre, however, is poetry that seldom manages to be poetry and reading that is seldom content to be reading.

In respect of Stephen Vincent Benét's poem, I can claim to have entered the theatre with that complete freedom from prejudice which total ignorance alone can confer. I have always postponed the task of tackling so long a piece of verse. If I shall now postpone it in perpetuity, it is because hardly a line I heard at the Century Theatre struck me as better than pleasant, straightforward, mildly amusing, or moderately forceful. Those whose knowledge of dramatic verse is limited to the dramas of Maxwell Anderson may find Benét sublime; any whose ears are attuned to the melody of Yeats or Eliot (to mention no greater names) will find it pedestrian. And though Benét is more successful with longer units than the line, and the cumulative effect of a page of narrative or character-revealing monologue is fairly considerable, he is excelled here by a dozen contemporary writers of prose fiction. Even so, this poetry might be accepted for what it is—if it did not pretend to be so much more. What might have been an entertainment proves an embarrassment because of the epic pretensions of form and content. Having looked back to Homer, Benét looks forward to Norman Corwin. It is not only with a

[1]See above, pp. 55–58.

Tolstoy's that his historical imagination cannot be compared. It cannot be compared with any good historical novel—say, Robert Penn Warren's *Night Rider* where some of the same problems are much more profoundly imaged.

Accompanied by a singing, speaking, and sound-effecting choir, Raymond Massey, Judith Anderson, and Tyrone Power speak what I assume to be a series of the better passages from Benét's poem. Miss Anderson has power; Mr. Massey and Mr. Power have real enough gifts of a smaller sort; individually and collectively the chorus functions with beautiful precision; Mr. Laughton's keen eye and yet keener ear have exercised a degree of control for which one cannot but feel a vast admiration. If our admiration remains abstract, and we do not enjoy ourselves, it is, as much as anything, because the actors assume a manner that tells us what attitude we are to take. Explicitly in the program and Mr. Power's introductory speech, implicitly in the style of the performance, we are told how to respond. A modern phenomenon! Our concert programs tell us that the symphony we are about to hear will "carry us away," lest otherwise we fail to be carried away; and the result is we do fail to be carried away; because we are thinking *about* being carried away. When a performance tells us what our response should be it thereby prevents us from having that response.

Now *John Brown's Body* is presented with such an air of sublimity as even a poem that deserved it could not support. The three speakers spend the evening posing for an imaginary photographer seated rather high in the balcony; when speaking they gaze misty-eyed at the camera; when silent, they gaze misty-eyed at their speaking colleague. In "Acting vs. Reciting," I described reciting as half-acting. Our Drama Trio inhabits a weird no-man's-land between acting and non-acting. As non-actors they come before us in evening dress. As actors they proceed to impersonate soldiers in uniform or maidens in distress. This is in itself an exciting feature, a tribute to the actor's true art. What is awkward is the transition back into non-acting—or, more precisely, the way Mr. Laughton has the trio act while not acting, kissing a hand, encircling a neck, sitting in pictorial attitudes under romantic lighting. Why, there is more artifice in this simplicity than in the complexities of regular theatre which it affects to eschew! No scenery, no action, just three speakers and a poem: yet Mr. Laughton so complicates the formula with lighting, grouping, and movement, that I again end wishing that this fine artist would accept the everyday complication of regular theatre. I know that one cannot dismiss experiments merely on grounds of *mélange des genres*. It would matter nothing that reciting is half-acting, half-reading, if its possibilities were as vast as those of the elements unmixed. It matters nothing that Mr. Laughton's work cannot be defined as good drama or good theatre— provided it be good something. My real complaint is that it is, for this artist, not good enough, and my hunch is that it is an evasion. An evasion of theatre. Mr. Laughton walks round and round theatre like a dog that cannot make up its mind to sit down. He tries the movies. He reads aloud in hospitals. He recites the Bible to schools. Or on TV. He invents the Drama Quartet. He trains a Drama Trio. Meanwhile he falls in love with literature and therefore with Thomas Wolfe. It is all an evasion.

One of the great moments in all my theatre-going was the moment when in a hotel room in Paris Charles Laughton read Bottom's first scene in *A Midsummer Night's Dream*. We write about jaws dropping, but that is the only time I actually saw a jaw drop for sheer surprise and delight; it was the jaw of Charles Dullin. The portrayal of Bottom, like certain passages in the *Galileo* of 1947, was sublime; and not just sublime reciting but sublime acting, sublime theatre.

Pathetic Phalluses

ON THE FACE OF IT you'd think a playwright would make an effort to conceal his borrowings. That William Inge parades them is not, however, a sign of naïveté, it is a declaration of allegiance. The torn shirt of Stanley Kowalski is no mere fact in another author's story, it is a symbol, a banner, an oriflamme. It stands for the new phallus worship.

There is of course no denying that a hero has a body and that it is a male body. What is remarkable in certain plays of Tennessee Williams and William Inge is that so much is made of the hero's body and that he has so little else. The rose that, for Mr. Eliot, is rooted in so deeply and broadly human a garden blooms, for Mr. Williams, on the bared chest of quasi-primitive man.

Admittedly, it may be impossible nowadays to sustain the attitude of the phallus worshipper in its purity. Kowalski is an impure phenomenon: if he is the full-blooded husband that every woman craves, he is also destructive and evil. In fact it is the cunning mixture of good and evil, health and sickness, that, for millions of spectators, has proved a fascination.

William Inge's *Picnic* may prove an equally effective piece of synthetic folklore—a folklore that is created, not *by*, but *for* the folk, the folklore of the age of mechanized mass media. Mr. Inge, too, gives his Priapus a bad character, but he is careful to stipulate that the badness is the kind the public sympathizes with: this Priapus is pathetic. To offer pity to the kind of man upon whom contemporary civilization has showered its praises might seem, from the utilitarian point of view, unnecessary: why stack cards that are already stacked? But from the point of view of synthetic folklore, it may well be a stroke of (synthetic) genius.

On the lowest estimate, it is a very happy accident. On the one hand, we have our alienated, homeless author, on the other our comfortable public, very much at home. How can the two meet to their mutual advantage? Well, for one thing, the indelicate public can decide it likes its authors delicate. For another, the authors can prove they aren't as delicate as all that, they can concede that indelicacy is a mighty fine thing. They can yearn for their opposite, they can indulge in orgies of overcompensation, they can flirt with the common man. A generation has passed since a movie star earned the title of the world's sweetheart. The Broadway public is not the world, nor is it composed of common men, but it is prepared to play the lover to any playwright-sweetheart who offers the right combination of coyness and compliance.

Second only in importance to the polarity of playwright and public is that of playwright and director. Until recently it seems to have been assumed that a director would merely reinforce an author's effects, accenting what was already accented, to A adding more A. Our more sophisticated theatre prefers to give a play "the treatment"—adding to quality A a directorial temperament or idea of quality B. If a script A is deficient, and B is precisely what was needed to make good the deficiency, the partnership of author and director is a triumph. Though one can criticize Mr. Kazan's directing on various grounds, there is no denying that he brought to *Death of a Salesman* something that Jed Harris failed to bring to *The Crucible,* notably the tension of personal, not to say neurotic, relations. To *Mister Roberts* it was the author, Thomas Heggen, who brought the guilt, the director, Joshua Logan, who brought the innocence. Reviewing the play several years ago, I defended Mr. Heggen at the expense of Mr. Logan; in retrospect, it seems only charitable to acknowledge that, without Mr. Logan, Mr. Heggen would probably not have been able to give us an evening of theatre at all.

Picnic, also, is directed by Joshua Logan, and those who find Mr. Inge a self-sufficient playwright have understandably complained of the B which the director adds to the author's A. For my part, I am not so sure that it is the writing which gives the evening its undoubted interest. Mr. Inge's main story seems to me tiresome in the extreme: that is why my comment on it has had to be solely sociological. I can accept it only as a libretto for Mr. Logan's directorial music and (what is closely connected) as material for his admirable actors. It is very lucky for Mr. Inge that his hero and heroine are not type cast. Mr. Logan was shrewd enough to allow for the fact that the phallus is much too featureless for drama. Ralph Meeker may have played Stanley Kowalski but (like Mr. Brando for that matter) he could never be *taken* for Stanley Kowalski: an actor can bring B to a character that is all A. With Mr. Inge's phallic hero goes a heroine of equal crudity and equal appeal: the dumbest and loveliest girl in town. Though, in a sense, it is her dumbness that makes her beauty irresistible (gives it "mass appeal," assures that it is "democratic"), I personally was glad that the actress (Janice Rule) did not humiliate herself that much but intruded a pleasantly human intelligence. Kim Stanley contrived to make the most brilliant performance of the evening out of one of those Hollywood-Broadway adolescents who are bookish because they are not beautiful.

The subplot of *Picnic* is quite a different matter. It is another of those rather patronizing tales of amorous old maids, yet I feel patronizing in calling it patronizing, for certainly I found myself drawn into the joke and thoroughly enjoying it. Here too the acting and directing are first rate. Eileen Heckart and Arthur O'Connell manage to be both very funny and very real in parts that encourage the actor to be simply one or the other. But, in this section of the play, the acting is strongly underpinned by a script. One cannot help asking why an author who can create the schoolteacher Miss Rosemary Sidney and her cheery colleagues who have seen life in New York (at Teachers College and elsewhere) need reach after literature and ideas? Why can't he see through the fallacies of the new cult of Priapus and give himself to his own impulse for genuine domestic comedy?

(Answers: if he did *not* reach out after ideas, Bright, Literary, and Edifying, he would lose that middle-brow approval without which there can be no "rave reviews" in the tonier press; and if he were not a priapist, there could have been no such poster on Times Square—showing a young man in his underwear carnally gazing at a girl—as stood over the movie theatre where *Come Back, Little Sheba* played, that is, there could be no "mass" interest in his work. In short, he would be a failure.)

Camino Unreal

THE STRANGE EXPERIENCE of seeing *Camino Real* divides itself into three: things you like, things you dislike, and things you are held by without knowing whether you like them or not.

The script, when I read it some time ago, I disliked—partly because it belongs to the current deliquescent-rococo type of theatre and even more because it seemed far from a brilliant example of the type. The genuine element in Tennessee Williams had always seemed to me to reside in his realism: his ability to make eloquent and expressive dialogue out of the real speech of men and his gift for portraiture, especially the portraiture of unhappy women. There is also a spurious element. Sometimes it's his style that is spurious, for when he is poetic he is often luscious and high-falutin'. Sometimes it's his thought; one day a critic will explain what Mr. Williams has made of D. H. Lawrence. Nor are Mr. Williams' reflections on art more convincing than his pseudo-Lawrentian hymns to life; and when he tells you his theory of the Awful, he is awful. Sometimes the trouble is with Mr. Williams' material: surely it would take more than a theory to justify the subject-matter of his novel or of, say, the short story of the man who likes being beaten and is finally *eaten* by a Negro masseur. . . . The spurious element seemed to me notably large in the script of *Camino Real.*

It would perhaps be an oversimplification to say I dislike the script and like the production. Mr. Williams may have contributed more to the production than a reader of his script would guess. Though the solemn speeches remain lifeless in the performance, the funny ones gain a good deal. Again, the reader is aware of very little besides dialogue; he is insufficiently aware of the scenario. Mr. Williams has argued in *The New York Times* that an action like throwing a bag out of a window may say more than words. True. And it may be the writer who thinks of such an action. Nevertheless, to think of it is very little. The action has of itself next to no meaning. It has meaning only as created by actor and director. In *Camino Real*, Mr. Williams is not a dramatist but a scenario writer.

To me the evening was of interest chiefly as the latest essay of Elia. We are told that Mr. Kazan was virtually co-author of *A Streetcar Named Desire* and *Death of a Salesman* even to the extent of changing the character of the leading persons; it is arguable that both plays would have failed without his changes. Still, in these cases, he had to regard a play as a mold into which his ideas could be poured. In *Camino Real* it all looks the other way round. The production seems to be the mold, the script to be fluid. At any rate, it is Mr. Kazan's presence we feel most strongly, Mr. Kazan's methods whose results we witness.

It is a disturbing presence, as of a man (if I may exaggerate) with an ego rather than an identity, a man with more notions than convictions, a man of tremors and palpitations rather than profound feelings. Mr. Kazan goes to work on the actors' nerves like an egg beater. His orgasmic organization of scenes has become a mannerism: time after time, the slow to-and-fro of dialogue works itself up to the frenetic climax. Yet it's no use knowing he is not a good director unless you can also see that he is almost a great one.

Mr. Kazan's most commendable quality is a simple one: he is a showman. This is partly a matter of sheer efficiency; in his productions, everything is taken care of, second by second. (The layman would think this would be true of all professional theatre; actually, the theatre is second only to international politics as a breeding ground for amateurism, stupidity, and sabotage.) But Mr. Kazan's showmanship goes beyond efficiency into legerdemain. He is a wizard. Even if I knew I was to witness a hateful interpretation of a hateful play, I would await any Kazan production with considerable eagerness. For Mr. Kazan's name in the program guarantees an evening of—at the very least—brilliant theatre work at a high emotional temperature.

Perhaps the most memorable things in *Camino Real* are choreographic, and yet they could not have been done for Mr. Kazan by a choreographer because they are worked out in the terms of acting, not dance. One of these things is just a presentation of people rushing to catch a plane. Mr. Williams made the episode symbolic by calling the plane *il fugitivo*, and having Marguerite Gautier and Jacques Casanova try to get aboard, but Mr. Kazan makes it symbolic in much finer fashion—by simple intensification of the event as we all know it. If we have sometimes to complain of neurasthenics and hysteria, there is no doubt that Mr. Kazan has found his own way of lifting a performance above the trivial and naturalistic. Conversely, when the action tends towards the artifice of dance or ceremony, he knows how to keep it anchored in everyday reality. When the others dance, Eli Wallach as Kilroy mixes dancing and boxing and embarrassed awkwardness quite magnificently. Crowned king of cuckolds, Joseph Anthony exploits the rite of coronation for an actor's purposes, and something beautiful is also something horrible.

Of the cast of *Camino Real* it is not enough to say it is a strong one; rather one should say in hushed tones that it is almost that un-American thing, an ensemble. Most of the performers are from the Actors' Studio,[1] and bring with them the happy results of five years' work together. An actor of the "British," elocutionary sort (like Hurd Hatfield) seems rather out of place among them. On the other hand, there are two "outsiders"—Jennie Goldstein and Ronne Aul—whose different flavor is a welcome addition. They remind us that there is a whole world of theatre outside the rather enervating regions of the Stanislavsky method as that is at present interpreted. Bringing Miss Goldstein to Broadway was a very happy idea. Ronne Aul, one of the liveliest presences on the American stage today, cannot be left to languish in the half-light of modern dance. If Mr. Kazan can enlarge his "company" with such astutely-chosen performers as these two he will always be able to procure twice as good a production for his author as anyone else in town.

Though *Camino Real* gives Mr. Kazan more power, I cannot agree with those who say it exacted from him a different style because it is a fantasy. Even when confronted with "realistic" plays like *A Streetcar Named Desire* and *Death of a Salesman,* he gave us a phantasmagoria. Blanche Dubois' background was diaphanous walls and voices disembodied as Saint Joan's. Willie Loman's life was shrouded in shadow and woodwinds and ghosts from Alaska. The only difference is that *Camino Real* doesn't even pretend to realism. The unreal which formerly crept up on us here meets us head on. Whether New York will prefer this I do not know. Possibly the escape into unreality was welcome in the former plays only because it

[1] See below, pp. 123–127.

was disguised as its opposite; and now that it is overt the public will either reject it or declare it unintelligible; in which case the play is done for. Possibly, on the other hand, there are many besides myself who cannot resist the wicked fascination of Elia Kazan.

A Major Musical

To PREFER *The Rake's Progress* to *Wonderful Town* is in my view snobbery; yet the opposite preference could easily be the merest inverted snobbery. For, in the age of the common man, we have, socially, the snobbery of the proletariat and, culturally, the snobbery of the lowbrows. Sound critical grounds for approving musicals have not yet been established. The public accepts them *un*critically. Critics who like them give wildly irrelevant reasons for doing so, the chief one being patriotism. I came at one time to detest the very mention of *Oklahoma!*, amusing as the evening had been in the theatre, because of the solemn pronouncements it brought forth. The term Grass Roots was always used—as if Messrs. Rodgers and Hammerstein were cowboys. Invited to accept *Oklahoma!* as an American, or rather Amurrican, *Magic Flute*, some of us could not resist the temptation to reject it as that and as anything else it might pretend to be. We would have done better to accept it as a major achievement in a minor genre. This is what *Wonderful Town* is. Whereas *The Rake's Progress* is a minor achievement in a major genre: it invites, if it does not easily survive, comparison with Mozart.

Distinctions of genre, and of major and minor, are "purely verbal," if you will. But they make a lot of difference. We all agree that *Porgy and Bess* is a great musical. What do we all mean? We cannot mean it is an opera—for that would be to say it is not a musical at all. It is curious that love of this work should lead critics to put it in a small niche beside Mozart and Wagner rather than a large one beside Sullivan and Johann

Strauss. On what Olympian heights do we think we stand that
we can pretend to look down on everything but the highest?
One of Arthur Mizener's early essays demonstrated that we fail
to know what are the first-rate qualities of Beaumont &
Fletcher because we will only see in them second-rate Shakespeare. The point has application over the whole field of
culture.

George Gershwin's *Porgy and Bess* is major work in a minor
genre. For an example of minor work in a major genre we
need go no further afield than the novel it is based on, DuBose
Heyward's *Porgy*. The bigness of Heyward's intentions is
shown not merely in his choice of the novel form but even
more in his style. The reader feels the presence of a mist of
fancy words between him and the subject. For fog lights, the
author offers him no moral vision but only a shy fascination
with the sordid and exotic that is at best juvenile and at worst
smug. Heyward's view of the Negro, for example, may be
kindly; it is certainly close to the traditional and dangerous
image of the Negro as primitive and the primitive as savage. In
this image we can find the reason *why* Heyward can be kindly:
it's "father forgive them, they know not what they do." When
Porgy commits murder, Heyward is not shocked. As a work of
American popular culture, his book is amazing in the indifference shown to the accepted code of poetic justice. And it is not
that Heyward is capable of "French" cynicism, it is simply that
his people are not quite human beings—they are likable, if not
house-broken, animals, among whom killing is not murder.

In folk-tale, pastoral, and idyll, we are familiar with conceptions of this sort. The primary contribution of Gershwin to
Heyward's libretto was that he raised it to the legendary level.
Which means, for example, that what was unconvincing in
prose became convincing through music. Take the ending.
Heyward's aspiration to myth is shown in the changes he
made when he went from novel to play. (He wrote three
versions in all: novel, play, libretto.) At the end of the novel,
Porgy simply looks older; he stays where he was. It is at the
end of the play that he sets out for New York, from Charleston, in a go-cart, 3 x 4, drawn by a goat. In a naturalistic
setting the incident is absurd; only with Gershwin's aid does it

acquire the other reality of myth.

I don't mean to define the reality either of myth or Gershwin's music as "other." There is a good deal of everyday reality in the novel which is also present in the musical. There is not a little everyday reality in the musical which had not been present in the novel: Sportin' Life, enlarged in the play, is both intensified and diversified by Gershwin's music. But Gershwin's most original act was to take Heyward's unreal picture of Negro life and give it the reality of fantasy. This is not Charleston, it is a modern Arcadia, a Negro never-neverland. Within this dream, murder can be passed over like a child's tantrums.

One of the critics described this tale of homicides, fornicators, and dope addicts as a story of "admirable people." The fact that he could think so is a tribute in the first place to the mythopoeic gift of Gershwin, but in the second to power of musical comedy as a convention. "Material seeks a form, as man woman." I envisage the Porgy material seeking not only the personal forms dictated by George Gershwin but also an established framework with established associations for its audience. It is worth stressing that *Porgy and Bess* is a musical, not an opera: the work of Heyward was to be salvaged by exploitation for "lower" not "higher" purposes. A musical is, *per se,* a kind of fairy tale (good or bad). Only in a musical could the Arcadia of Heyward's imagination find adequate and unpretentious realization.

I do not want to carry my inverted snobbery (if that's what it is) too far, and pretend that *Porgy and Bess* is beyond criticism. Heyward and Gershwin created a world, not an action; an idyll, not a drama; a series of numbers, not a tragic or comic whole. The tradition of the musical is not that of music drama, it is that of operetta, vaudeville, and revue; it has the defects of its qualities, and towards the end of *Porgy and Bess*—as I judge from three different productions—the cumulative effect is not more impressive than it is exhausting and benumbing.

If the production at the Ziegfeld is the most exhausting and benumbing of the three, that is partly because it is also the best; talent can be tiring. I found Mr. Breen's directing satis-

factory; if the above speculations are true, I should acknowledge that their truth was revealed to me by his production.

I do not know what racial characteristics Negroes have.
Seeing them on the stage it is tempting to believe that they
have more vitality than the rest of us, and that this vitality
shows itself in superior rhythm, agility, and litheness. At any
rate, that is my impression, seeing this production at the
Ziegfeld after the production by white actors in black face at
the Zurich opera house.

When, in addition, a colored player—like Cab Calloway—
has talent, the result is an astonishing combination of fantasy
and force. Mr. Calloway imposes himself on the imagination.
At any moment one can recall to the mind's eye the picture of
the quick body bending, the furtive eyes dancing, and the big
mouth wide, wide open.

From Leo X to Pius XII

POSSIBLY THE CONTRIBUTION of the Group Theatre was not a
particular production, nor even the sum of its productions; it
was a contribution to the theory and practice of theatrical
education. As a result, some of the most interesting theatre
work of today is done in the classrooms and studios of ex-
Groupers like Elia Kazan, Lee Strasberg, Robert Lewis, Stella
Adler, and Sanford Meisner.

I was recently privileged to see Mr. Meisner's production of
Mandragola at the Neighborhood Playhouse. I say "privileged" not only to acknowledge the school's hospitality but
because Machiavelli's masterpiece is so seldom seen. Though
Pope Leo X thought it worth while to build a theatre expressly to exhibit this play in, his successors have found its
anti-clericalism less congenial. I came upon a small production
of it in Florence in 1948, but three years later—on April Fool's
Day—the Demo-Christian government stamped it Non Appro-
vato.

Mandragola seems not to have been translated into English till Stark Young published his version in 1927. So far as I know it has still not had a professional production in our language. What passed for its "first appearance on the English stage" (in 1939) was actually the appearance of another play under the same name. Machiavelli's salty dish had been changed by Ashley Dukes into one of those nondescript desserts, only slightly obscene, that they serve in English hotels. It was synthetic Sheridan—or perhaps a compound of Bowdler and some minor disciple of Pinero. Nahum Tate's sentimentalization of *Lear* is tact itself in comparison. There is one consolation: Dukes' changes work out so badly that after reading him our love of Machiavelli's original is greatly increased: if Dukes is always wrong, Machiavelli is always right.

The action of the play consists simply in the accomplishing of adultery. How will our "hero" get into the (married) "heroine's" bed? The husband believes his wife to be sterile, but is persuaded she will become fertile if she partakes of the magic herb mandragola. Yet the first man she sleeps with after doing so will die. The husband must kidnap some lusty young fellow, thrust him into his wife's bed, and discard him. The truth, of course, is that the wife is not sterile, the herb is not magical, and the man is not "some lusty young fellow" but the same person who told the husband about mandragola and who at the end of the play is rewarded for his counsel by the present of a key to the married couple's house: namely, our hero. Not that he was clever enough to hatch the whole plot himself. His contribution is, not brains, but money, and he pays it out to three accomplices: an idea man to draft the plan of campaign and convince the husband, and a couple of moralists to win the cooperation of the wife. Who better for this last function than—her mother and her confessor? The cutting edge of Machiavelli's irony was never sharper than in the confessor's use of Catholic sophistry to justify adultery; Roman farce is transfigured to great drama by a fantastic intellect, an intellectual fantasy.

The crowning event of the plot is the crowning irony of the play: not merely that the hero arrives in the heroine's bed but that he is pushed into it by her husband, not merely that the heroine has a lover but that she has never seen him before he enters her bed, that she is fully reconciled to the situation and, after the first union, determined to perpetuate it. The limitations of modern gentility were never more manifest than in Ashley Dukes' inability to "take" Machiavelli's climax—and with it his view of his characters, his whole criticism of life. Mr. Dukes had hero and heroine meet and establish a romantic relationship *before* adultery took place.

It would not be worth harping on such misunderstandings except that they illustrate (if at an extreme) the kind of difficulty we all have as moderns, and as non-Italians, with such a play, a difficulty worth overcoming not only because *Mandragola* is a masterpiece but also because it belongs to a school of drama that we do ill to forget. In what probably remains the best essay on Machiavelli in English, Macaulay said that "tragedy is corrupted by eloquence and comedy by wit" and that *Mandragola* is a prime instance of uncorrupted comedy—a comedy in which character is defined, not by clever or graceful talk, but by plot. In short Macaulay uses Machiavelli as a stick to beat Congreve and Sheridan with—today we might be tempted to beat Wilde and Giraudoux with it. Whether or no it is fair to describe these four as corrupt, it is certainly salutary to look back at the classic—and could we not say realistic?—comedy of the Italian Renaissance, at Calmo, at Ruzzante, and, above all, at Machiavelli.

Many of the things that Machiavelli does well, Molière, it is true, does better. One realized that Mr. Meisner's students had seen Barrault in *Les Fourberies de Scapin* and had learnt how so crude a thing as farce could be exploited by so subtle a poet as Molière; the "diabolical" rhythm of farce is a fine instrument for the "diabolical" mind of Machiavelli. What distinguishes Machiavelli from Molière is a certain fanaticism.

Sheer fanaticism, to be sure, would never yield comedy. We know from *The Prince* that Machiavelli pretends to be the polar opposite of a fanatic—a cynic. Yet (a) he is fanatical in his advocacy of cynicism and (b) his cynicism is contradicted, modified, or transformed by certain ideal allegiances, notably patriotism; and his patriotism is part of a profound and revolutionary humanism.

More important than these *isms* is the spirit of Machiavelli. A clerical government, given a certain sophistication, might tolerate his cynicism and, given a certain liberalism, might tolerate his ideals; what it could never be happy with, unless it were positively stupid, is his restless and questing spirit. I should not wish to deny that his mind was full of ambiguities. Yet I should place him not with second-rate logicians but with first-rate poet-philosophers like Voltaire and Nietzsche—one might almost say: like Swift. In the realm of pure thought, ambiguity may be simply a fault, the fault of indecision or inconsistency. In the realm of the imagination, ambiguities, though not good in themselves, may be put to work. In *Mandragola* they function as comic tensions. The complexity of Machiavelli's personality is in this play, even though, under the control of his genius, complexity takes the form of an unexampled simplicity.

Personality

THE PHYSIQUE AND TECHNIQUE of Martha Graham have been brilliantly described by Robert Horan, Agnes De Mille, and other experts on the dance. If a theatre critic can add anything to the understanding of her work, it will not be because he knows more, or as much, about it, but because he sees it in another way. He sees it as theatre. He sees the dancer as actress and, yes, as dramatist.

The statement that the two best American dramatists are Charlie Chaplin and Martha Graham is not to be dismissed with the observation that one of them is English and neither is a dramatist, for the fact remains that this pair have worked for decades with American materials on American soil and that they have excelled in dramatic composition. It is true that this excellence has been overshadowed by the acknowledged originality of their performing; but I don't think anyone who took a second look at any of the major works would fail to see it; *City Lights* and *The Gold Rush, Letter to the World* and

Night Journey, are among the finest dramas ever produced in this country.

In the nineteenth century, drama became too exclusively dramatic—that is, too exclusive of epic and lyric. In the twentieth century the movies reminded us of the value of the epic element in dramatic entertainment, and the best movies were Mr. Chaplin's. The lyrical element was also farmed out to another medium—not the movies but opera and ballet. Of the poets who essayed drama, even the greatest were less dramatic in their plays than in their poems. It was an inspired idea of Martha Graham's to exploit the dramatic quality of non-dramatic modern verse as she does in *Letter to the World,* revived for Bethsabe de Rothschild's Festival of American Dance.

A double inspiration, for Emily Dickinson's phrases seem— if not a description of Martha Graham—at any rate a verbal equivalent of her dancing. Eat evanescence slowly, the postponeless creature, cornets of paradise, gay ghastly holiday, looking at death is dying—these are among the phrases which Martha Graham weaves into a pattern of action. Skilful patterning is the least of it. If I understand what has usually been meant by a tragic sense of life, it is something that our playwrights do not have and which Miss Graham does. She can express anguish and she can make it the companion of joy. She can put the elemental emotions to work like a symphonic composer. She opens wide sluices which our torpor and sophistication had shut. "The birth of tragedy from the spirit of music" is Nietzsche's fine formula: Martha Graham seems to lead us back to that musical beginning, a realm of Jungian archetypes, Goethean mothers, feelings purged of trivial and accidental contacts.

She can express anguish. "There is a pain so utter it swallows being up." She has shifted the dancer's center of gravity in order to seize and define pain. Her favorite arm-position is the elbow flexed, the fore-arm upright, the hand back and horizontal, almost clutching. The "pain" sequence of *Letter to the World* is the grandest and deepest, but

> After a great pain a formal feeling comes
> The nerves sit ceremonious like tombs

The feet mechanical go round a wooden way
This is the hour of lead.

Modern dance often has lines as straight as Mondrian. It is
especially good at giving an impression of weight—weight
pressing downwards into the earth.

She can make sorrow the companion of joy. "Mirth is the
mail (male?) of anguish." The humor of Martha Graham is
not abundant and all-embracing like Mr. Chaplin's, it is the
other face of her gloom, and that is *all* it is. So soon as Miss
Graham ventures out into pure humor she becomes a little
coy. To be true, her humor must remain tied to her solemnity
—if only by the rope of parody, as in the sequence with March
at the love seat. Her humor belongs to the dialectic of her
personality.

Which is integrated. She has two eyes but one vision. "Life
is a spell so exquisite that everything conspires to break it."
The universal conspiracy provides the antagonist, the conflict,
without which victory could not be exquisite. "Glory is that
bright tragic thing that for an instant means dominion." Here
Emily Dickinson's words soar so high they suggest what must
be an artist's ideal rather than his attainment; yet the bright
tragic thing is seldom far away when Miss Graham dances.

About *Night Journey*—Miss Graham's version of the Oedipus story—I should like to be more prosaic. When the Greek
National Theatre was here, I was disappointed to find them
presenting their Chorus in the staid, white neo-classic tradition that goes back through Reinhardt to Winckelmann and
perhaps no further. I believe we should have a more modern
version of Greek tragedy if we had a more ancient one, and I
hear that a living Greek director, Charles Konn, has actually
been trying a pre-classical style. For myself, the only time I
have felt that *this* must be what the Greeks meant by a chorus
was in *Night Journey*. The reason may be largely that there is
nothing literary, nothing of the Victorian nightshirt tradition
about it. This chorus dances with an absolute modernity; we
enjoy the twentieth century in them and at the same time we
feel swept back two and a half thousand years.

The individual performances in it are also very striking

(especially Stuart Hodes' staccato leaps as Tiresias). And, in general, not the least attraction of a Graham production is in the realm of sheer stage personality. Even a dancer with very small roles like Patricia Birsh is given the chance to project personality and, like several of her colleagues, seems to have as much to project as a whole cast of actors. I should not speak of mere quantity. The personality projected (this time I am thinking of Natanya Neumann) is of a lofty and subtle beauty not seen in a minor role since the Barraults were with us.

Graham is of course a supreme personality. The opposite of what generally passes for such in theatre circles. That is: Graham is not an ingratiating person without art but an austere, unprepossessing, forbidding person transfigured by art. Her personality is a creation. And it continues to be created during each performance: when we say it holds us, we mean we are in the grip of a concentrated will. Graham does not have to dance in order to win us. She doesn't even have to move. Such is concentration—otherwise known as personality. What I mean is: she is great.

On Being Read To

OUR NEW HABIT of being read to is good and bad. It is good insofar as it indicates an interest in the spoken language. It is bad insofar as it indicates our inability to read for ourselves, our fear of being alone, our lack of concentration, our preoccupation with that part of an author's personality that reveals itself less in his works than in his platform appearances.

I am referring to the less defensible of the two current types of reading aloud: reading by authors. Reading by actors seems to me more proper because reading is part of the actor's craft; a bad reader is (to that extent) a bad actor. Though authors may have an especially accurate knowledge of the tone and rhythm of their own work, they do not, as authors, have the ability to communicate that tone and rhythm to others by

means of the voice. As to their personalities being right for the
job, that will make no difference except insofar as they are
actors and can externalize their personalities in performance.
Until the art of presentation has been perfected in a man, his
personality can only function in his performances as an interference. It is true that such an interference may be of
interest; of more interest than some literature; to many people, of more interest than any literature. But this is not to say
it is good performing, good reading. When we hear a poet read
and call him terrific, we mean that we are impressed by him as
a person and that we are amazed to learn he has so loud and
enthusiastic (or soft and mellow) a vocal organ. When we
want his poems read to us, we send for an actor.

There are two current types of actor-readers: the reader of a
single role, whether on the radio or in a "drama quartet," and
the reader of many roles—the latter being half-way to the one
man—or woman—theatre of Ruth Draper. Emlyn Williams
has perfected this second type. Insofar as he stands at his little
table and reads a narrative in the third person, he is a pure
reader. But when he comes to dialogue, he reads the speeches
with full characterization in the voice and approximate characterization of posture, gesture, and facial expression. Not that
the text can be chopped in two quite so cleanly. Mr. Williams
will begin to take on a character's tone of voice when he is
described in the narrative. He will also embellish the narrative
passages with any noises and gestures that may be intimated in
them. The diagnostic of Mr. Williams, as of Mr. Laughton,
the reader, is that he has a complete actor's technique to draw
on. Where the amateur would use gestures of mere emphasis,
Mr. Williams will choose an action with a reference: a quick
movement of the hand to the face will tell us someone has
been splashed in the eye. Or he will build a whole scene by a
repeated turn of the head—to see if the speaker's companion is
listening. Abstract gestures can be added at more solemn moments: at the end of a chapter he will "freeze" under the
dimming lights with one arm outstretched.

To read fiction in this manner asks more of an actor than
taking a part in a play, and it is largely for his virtuosity that
Mr. Williams was praised; the public was asked to see in him a

brilliant freak. But since the New York public declined the
invitation, I want to urge that there was a better reason for
seeing either of Mr. Williams' programs, namely, that he was
presenting the work of Charles Dickens, and this with such
intensity as to make us see the novelist's work freshly, as after
reading a great critic. Like a great critic, Mr. Williams can
only bring certain qualities out at the expense of others. Two
hours of reading from a novel that would take sixty hours to
read entire cannot but be misleading and "unfair"; Dickens
not only needs many words for certain of his best effects, bulk
is with him an essential quality; one would not offer a friend a
thimbleful of beer, and Dickens never offered us a thimbleful
of fiction. On the other hand, to isolate certain portions of
Dickens is to find unsuspected felicities. What one appreciates
in Mr. Williams' Mixed Bill is, first, the mastery of the individual scene and, second, the force of the individual word and
phrase. By scene I intend, as it were, a scene from a play, with
its regular dramatic structure—the setting of the stage, the
warming up, the climax, the cooling off. Such are the episodes
Mr. Williams offers from *Our Mutual Friend* and *The Pickwick Papers.* As for phrases and particular words, it is only
when we see Williams that the comedy of Dickens' lines is
released—or at least, only then do we fully realize how much
fun and meaning a particular verb or adjective conceals. Or
how much fancy goes into a statement of fact: it is from
hearing Mr. Williams, not from reading for ourselves, that we
remember that Podsnap's face was like a face in a tablespoon
or that Chadband looked like a bear trying to stand on its
hind legs.

Which brings me to *Bleak House.* In trying to present this
novel as a whole Mr. Williams was undertaking something
much more risky than the selections on his Mixed Bill. Here
anyone who knows the book notes what is missing from the
reading, and the others regret trailing up hill and down dale
with a single, not always fascinating, story instead of jumping
from peak to peak of novel after novel. Mr. Williams cuts the
last two hundred pages of the book, ending with the murder of
Tulkinghorn. In three "acts" he tells the story of Lady Dedlock's secret with as many comical digressions as he has time

for. Some of the episodes have the same kind of merit as the items on the Mixed Bill. There is the perfectly theatrical use of the hand-screen by Lady Dedlock in the "scene" where Guppy starts revealing her past. There are scenes of Mrs. Jellyby at home (though her thoughts are never nearer than Africa) and Mrs. Pardiggle inflicting her ferocious philanthropy on the poor. There are characteristically devastating deflations of Chadband, the Turveydrops, the Badgers. . . . Other features are peculiar to *Bleak House*. Mr. Williams' editing (particularly his elimination of Esther as narrator) sharpens the satire and underscores Dickens' powers of sheer narration. I surely am not alone in having rather neglected Dickens' plots for his scenes and characters. When stripped of some of the moralistic rhetoric, the Gothic narrative in *Bleak House* comes to seem pretty impressive. And within our idea of narrative we must include not only the bare roster of incidents but the connection, as made by Dickens, between one set of events and another, between events and society, between society and the cosmos. One is impressed in Mr. Williams' reading with the way in which Dickens will let his story broaden out at the end of a chapter into the lament of a Greco-Victorian chorus or will start a chapter with the natural or social world to which the new group of characters belongs. "The town awakes: the great teetotum is set up for its daily spin and whirl. . . ." Though Bleak House remains a little vague for all that either Dickens or Williams can do, one had a strong sense at the reading of both London, "the great confused city," with its "mud and wheels, horses, whips, and umbrellas," and of Chesney Wold in the swamps of Lincolnshire; the two places are twin poles of the action. . . .

The points Mr. Williams managed to make are far too many to mention in a review. I hope my few examples suffice to indicate that he makes them, and that his performance is the fruit, not of dexterity only, but also of intelligence; not of intelligence only, but also of love. This might explain why some people aren't sinking their teeth in it. Perhaps *fruit* is an unhappy metaphor. Mouths have been dropping open readily enough. My complaint is that people haven't let Mr. Williams open their eyes.

Within This Wooden O

SINCE THEATRE is a visual, not to say a spectacular, art, nothing is more remarkable than the way the appearance of a play changes from age to age. We are shocked to see Garrick (on the famous print) performing *Richard III* in eighteenth-century breeches and hose, yet we may ask whether Shakespeare would be less shocked to see Richard, as we nowadays do, in his habit as he lived. Would he not be shocked at the baroque stage of the eighteenth, the naturalistic stage of the nineteenth, centuries? Would he prefer the modest curtains and cut-outs of Granville Barker?

I do not mean these rhetorical questions to suggest that presenting Shakespeare on a non-Elizabethan stage is always a mistake. The theatre's responsibilities are to the present, not the past. Garrick was right. And we shall be right when we have found a theatre that belongs as fully to our time as his did to his. Who can say we *have* found it? What we must complain of in current Shakespeare productions is not that they are in a style we don't like but that they have no style at all—and any ideas and interpretations they may embody are only the bright ideas and cute interpretations of our subintelligentsia.

We have to go back and look at the Elizabethan stage because it is the beginning and we have to go back to the beginning. At the very least we can re-learn from productions on an Elizabethan stage the ABC of Shakespearean stagecraft. And when we know what Shakespeare brought to the eyes of his public, we can decide to what extent the same things should be brought to the eyes of ours. Such innovations as are then resolved upon will be made deliberately. We shall have restored Shakespeare, and we shall have worked out step by step the problem of adapting him to our time. Our Shakespeare theatre will be a precision tool.

It was with all this in mind that I went out to Long Island on Shakespeare's birthday to see *Macbeth* on a replica of the Globe stage at Hofstra College. It was a most revealing production, and suggested even more than it revealed. I had seen the play several times before; each time the production had conformed pretty much with the visual image I had of it in my mind's eye; yet each time the play failed. It failed because, as I learned at Hofstra, the image we have of it is one the play as written will not support. The *Macbeth* of our imaginations could perhaps be written by Monk Lewis, staged by Gordon Craig, or filmed in the manner of *Caligari;* the *Macbeth* of Shakespeare demands, not murky corridors and pinpoints of moonshine, but diffused light and a large block of visible space embracing some seven playing areas. Someone said that the Hofstra production lacked suspense, and it occurred to me that suspense is the mess of pottage for which the Shakespearean birthright has been sold. Suspense drives everything else out of the mind and that's why it's so sorely needed by playwrights who have nothing else to offer. If our minds are occupied with other matters, the need for suspense is not felt. On the Elizabethan stage the intricate things Macbeth says can be actually presented to the audience instead of being swallowed up in darkness. Passages that in modern productions seem long-winded interruption and obscure irrelevance take their place on this stage as the drama itself. We forego the superficial excitements of the thriller to discover that, as we sit mildly watching, we are being more profoundly excited. Why is it that your ordinary modern *Macbeth* "falls off in the second part"? Because the crime story is over. The only kind of curiosity that has been aroused in us is satisfied as soon as Duncan is dead. The evening's play has been sacrificed in order that for thirty minutes or so Shakespeare might prove the equal of Agatha Christie.

We know a good deal about the Elizabethan stage from books. It is gratifying to find that its impact on the senses is even greater than the most informed student expects. We have read of the depth of this stage; it is actually less deep than many other stages; our *impression* of depth is the result of its shape and its relation to the auditorium. This deep-seeming stage is not only good to look at but useful in permitting the easy separation of one group of actors from another; the grouping of many a Shakespeare scene becomes both more pleasing and more plausible. We have read of inner stage and balcony, but I for one was not prepared for the effect they have. It is not true that the Elizabethans lacked a peepshow stage. They had two of them: study (or inner stage) and chamber (the inner portion of the balcony). Each is a complete "modern" stage with three walls and a ceiling and as much claustrophobic tension as you please. We had known that the apron lends itself to outdoor scenes, as no theatre since seems to have done, but we have to see the Globe stage in action to be convinced that it equals the modern stage in its presentation of interiors too.

So much for this stage as a static picture; it is still more wonderful—and still harder to judge from books—as that moving picture which is the action of a play. The force even of the various tableaux derives in large part from the sudden movement of their unveiling; they are framed not only in space (by the rest of the stage) but in time (by the scenes that precede and follow). While study and chamber give a very firm impression of locality (contrary to much that we have been told about abstract and unlocalized space) the most brilliant effect is that of movement from one locality to another; Shakespeare's scenic progressions have partly the character of medieval staging, partly that of cinematic montage. On his stage, even the soliloquy is seen in terms of space and movement. To speak an aside or a monologue, the actor can simply walk across to a pillar or down to the rail (often seeming as he does so to move from one reality to another).

It was lucky, since he had Macbeth's soliloquies to handle, that Ian Keith was the boldest of the Hofstra actors in his use of the space at his disposal. The others, though obviously helped by their capable director Bernard Beckerman, sometimes seemed afraid of departing from the usage of the modern stage.

It should be added that Mr. Keith has few equals in this country as a speaker of Shakespearean verse; he does not yield to Maurice Evans in his eagerness to render the music but he succeeds also in delivering the sense. Voice and carriage take us back to the days of heroic acting.

On Staging Yeats

THE ONLY PLAYS of Yeats I have ever staged are *The Player Queen, The Words upon the Window Pane,* and *Purgatory,* but that's enough to start a discussion with. And they are very different, one from another.

Studying *The Player Queen,* you ask yourself, not how you can stage it well, but whether you can stage it at all. It contains much prose that is bad by any standard and especially bad as material for speaking and projecting from a stage. Its story is not well-articulated and might not be very interesting even if it were. As for meaning, you realize that your audience won't even know if there's supposed to be any. If you go ahead, it is partly from sheer faith—you feel that Yeats couldn't have put in years of work to absolutely no avail—partly from some quality in the writing that is rather hard to define, though not, I believe, to feel: a sort of zany vitality. Anyone who considers the play a masterpiece would no doubt be shocked at a production that suggested Punch and Judy and Christmas Pantomime, yet I confess my own assumption that, if the show didn't have the rough, fantastic life of these humble forms, it would have none at all. I also formed the opinion that Yeats had deceived himself when he thought he had got away from the local setting and had done well to do so. I sought to keep the play close to earth by emphatically Irish accents, props, costumes, and music. I even ventured to frame the play in a narration sung to an accordion by a beggar. He sat at the side of the stage and provided harp accompaniment to the songs. The tunes were taken from Irish folksongs, particularly street ballads. The narration, for example, was all sung to the air of *Finnegan's Wake,* which proved an admirable tune for a dance at the end.

I suppose Yeats' plays stand outside ordinary categories, but, if *The Player Queen* can loosely be termed an extravaganza, *Words upon the Window Pane* could be called a conversation piece, a drawing-room drama, even a naturalistic tragedy. Yeats disliked naturalism and was no good at it. Yet after a creakingly conversational opening, the play becomes effectively, even showily, theatrical. It is perhaps the only play in which the austere Yeats invites the actor to virtuosity. It is also the only one that has its own virtuosity—of structure. The emotional center is a flash-back to the eighteenth century in the original form of voices speaking through a medium in the twentieth. The primary dramatic contrast is between the medium's vision and the outlook of a modern skeptic, but the twist that makes the action ironic and effective is that the medium *is* a venal fake—and is destroyed by the voices from the past, which are not. Once you have done some bold cutting in the early part of the play and have found an actress capable of speaking not only as a spiritualist but as Swift and as Stella, your production problem is solved. One part, that of Corney Patterson, is so dismal a joke it should be cut. The others lend themselves to standard modern performance. The darkness, the hymn-singing, the trance, the presence of spirits are sure-fire melodrama.

As, in the setting of a seance, Yeats had inserted the drama of Swift and Stella, and had related it to the history of modern intellect, so, in the setting of a haunted house, Yeats inserts a domestic tragedy which represents the decline of Ireland and perhaps the modern world generally. In both cases, *Words upon the Window Pane* and *Purgatory,* the donnée is magic, and the general effect in the theatre that of a Gothic thriller. The drama of the director's position is that while he will *need* to exploit the thrilling element (to hold his audience), he will *want* to anchor the thrills in the sea of history (not only to get some of Yeats' meaning across, but, stylistically, to balance the Gothic with the realistic, sensibility with sense). Inevitably, the necessity wins out over the wish. And the success the two plays had with audiences was never satisfying; it seemed to have been won on false pretenses. I suppose it could satisfy those who think, with Mr. Eliot, that audiences, generally and legitimately, miss the main purport of great plays. Anyone else is bound to be worried at the way Yeats assumes that theatre can, generally and legitimately, be a private, not a public, art. Write on this assumption, and you will not get an audience of supermen—merely one of snobs, bluestockings, and bohemians. Which is precisely the audience Sean O'Casey found at Yeats' house on Merrion Square when he went to see *At the Hawk's Well*. The moral he drew was fair enough: "A play poetical to be worthy of the theatre," he wrote in *Inishfallen Fare Thee Well*, "must be able to withstand the terror of Ta Ra Ra Boom Dee Ay, as a blue sky, or an apple tree in bloom, withstand any ugliness around or beneath them." I was always relieved when the applause after our Yeats' one-acter died down, and the curtain rose on a "regular play" by Mr. O'Casey or J. M. Synge.

It is also fair to add that the moral Mr. O'Casey drew he presumably learnt from Yeats, from whom the idea of a national theatre, close to the soil and the people, stems. The esotericism of his later plays is not the cause of his unpopularity in the theatre but the result; and the result of the general failure of the Abbey Theatre, not merely of the cold welcome it always accorded the plays of Yeats. "In the midst of the fume, the fighting, the stench, the shouting, Yeats, as mad as the maddest there, pranced on the stage, shouting out his scorn, his contempt, his anger making him an aged Cuchulain . . ." O'Casey's words record Yeats' anger at the Abbey's reception, not of any of his own plays, but of *The Plough and the Stars*. Purists will say that instead of trying to convert the theatre into a private institution he should have given it up altogether. Life is impure. Yeats' anti-popular works contain more vitally "popular" elements than the plays he intended for a national theatre. The plays he wrote for drawing rooms have more theatre in them than the plays he wrote for the Abbey. They are not theatrical through and through. And their omissions suggest a dramatist dead on one side. (Where is the plot? Where are the characters?) But this is an age, as Francis Fergusson has reminded us, of partial perspectives. A dramatist who is *alive* on one side is a rare enough phenomenon. In *Purgatory*, his last play (if we take *The Death of*

Cuchulain as an epilogue to the Cuchulain plays), whatever he does *not* do, Yeats has arrived at a style of dramatic utterance superior to anything he had written in his life before and therefore inferior to nothing in modern English drama. If, from some viewpoints, it is anti-theatrical, from the professional viewpoint it is pure theatre—a play, not to produce, but to act. And it calls for pure acting—not the burlesque technique that is required for *The Player Queen* or the virtuosity demanded of the leading role in *Words upon the Window Pane,* but the speaking of great words and the discovery of the positions, moves, and gestures that go with them.

Give My Regards to Broadway

When Walter Kerr, the drama critic of *The New York Herald Tribune,* wrote that Broadway was not for me and implied that I preferred coteries and cults, in short that I was a snob, I was tempted to retort that the Broadway public is itself a coterie of snobs and that Mr. Kerr belongs to that cult of pseudo-democracy—democracy as an applause-producing noise—which is one of the major swindles of modern culture. Had I done so, I would have forfeited the right to make a better point, namely, that the matter of popularity cannot rationally be discussed so long as each of us is busy insinuating that his opponent is an enemy of the people. When more intent on analyzing the situation than on winning the argument, Mr. Kerr, I am sure, would admit the deficiencies of our "popular" Broadway theatre, and I, for my part, would admit those of the theatre off Broadway.

I am even eager to do so—as, whenever an Off Broadway theatre is drowning, I (or so it seems to me) am the straw it clutches at. Now the idea that the theatre off Broadway is better than theatre on it is an illusion that will not stand the test of a single season's theatre-going. If the professional theatre fails because it is commercial, the non-commercial theatre

fails because it is non-professional. A professional, by definition, has a trained talent; amateurs have ideals, which are
much less entertaining. Nor, for all the claptrap about simplicity and the dangers of too much scenery, is lack of money a
recommendation.

Perhaps I am unduly under the influence of disappointment, but I will record, for what it is worth, the impression
that the Off Broadway theatre, as most of us have up to now
conceived it, is finished. Our conception followed the model of
the Provincetown Playhouse in its early days: a theatre of
young people coming forward with something of their own to
offer. Today, the Greenwich Village theatre offers plays by
established authors in productions that are barely competent,
let alone interesting. The few new plays they have put on have
not (with an exception or so) whetted the appetite for more.
It's not just that they aren't works of genius, which they don't
have to be, but that they have no real identity. True, the
homoerotic element is rather insistent; yet such a recurrent
theme doesn't give an intellectual identity to a generation,
even to the extent that, say, proletarianism did in the thirties.
An epidemic is not a movement.

I would not set down these melancholy facts, even as a
concession to Mr. Kerr, were it not that a recent enterprise in
Greenwich Village permits one to hope for—or at least dream
of—better things. This is Terese Hayden's season at the Theatre de Lys on Christopher Street. Not that Miss Hayden has
avoided all the pitfalls.

The first two shows were *Maya* by Simon Gantillon and *The
Scarecrow* by Percy MacKaye. *Maya* is a pretty good play. I
happened to see it in Paris a couple of years ago directed by
Gaston Baty and starring Marguerite Jamois; and I recall
leaving the theatre dazed by their virtuosity. The evening at
the de Lys seemed undirected, and the leading part was miscast. I question whether *Maya* was a good choice in the first
place—it is not a great play, and it has no interesting relation
to this place and time—but certainly it was a bad choice if the
leading lady (or her director) would not accept the spirit in
which it was written. What saves the play from pretentiousness
is the light, French irony; we should never find out if the

author is serious; Helen Craig's way of insisting on pathos dramatized only our Anglo-Saxon attitude to prostitutes, not Gantillon's. And Miss Hayden must learn to reject inadequate translations. Not long ago she used the ruinous Ashley Dukes version of *Parisienne* when, with Jacques Barzun's far superior version, she might have put the play across. With *Maya* she wrongly assumed she could turn the trick by leaving the translator's name out of the program and making unauthorized cuts.

The Scarecrow is a more defensible choice for a producer with the ambition of filling a niche in American theatrical history. Its author is a venerable figure who has devoted a long life to idealistic service of theatre. The play itself presents a far-reaching idea and, what is more remarkable, presents it in a peculiarly theatrical image—that of an automaton or doll learning to be human. Miss Hayden's program tells us that Louis Jouvet planned to produce the play; it seems right that he should have; one can think of no American play which would commend itself more strongly to an actor schooled in French classical theatre; perhaps the only actor now living who could squeeze all the juice from the leading role is Jean Louis Barrault.

The Scarecrow was worth writing if only to place this single moving image before an audience, but one can't help regretting that Mr. MacKaye hedged it around with the kind of verbiage that theatre people call literature. As a poet, Mr. MacKaye combines the pretensions of Goethe with the capabilities of Bayard Taylor. Miss Hayden would have been mistaken to choose such bad writing for exhibition if American dramatic literature abounded in great poetry or if her principal interest had to lie in plays. But her principal interest, I should judge, is in acting. This is her contribution and my reason for hopefulness. Even *Maya* is a justifiable choice: done right, it is a play for actors, if not for an (American) audience, a play in which every scene is a challenge to the performer— nine scenes, nine *études*. What finally bore down my resistance to the tedium of Mr. MacKaye's writing was the opportunity his story offers to director and actors. And here it should be said that perhaps Miss Hayden's great practical achievement was the rounding up of a good young director (Frank Corsaro) and many good young actors. The opportunities of the script were not missed. Except at Circle in the Square, I don't know that the Village has seen such careful work before. Essential to Miss Hayden's new version of Off Broadway is the complete avoidance of amateurism. Which means the abandonment of the merely philanthropic notion of using an actor because no one else wants to use him. Yet when Miss Hayden uses established actors she gives them new tasks. Patricia Neal and Eli Wallach have been good before; if they could have a year at this kind of experience they would be better. And I should like to credit that muggy evening of *Maya* with one bright discovery: Susan Strasberg who with a little more training could be the first American properly to play the great part of Isabel in *The Enchanted* ("Intermezzo") of Giraudoux.

Sir Laurence Macheath

THE LEAST OF MY WORRIES, seeing the film of *The Beggar's Opera,* is that Sir Laurence can't really sing. A worse singer could have done the part of Macheath greater justice. Olivier's singing is not only feeble but phony: he slows down the tempo and vainly attempts *bel canto* where a brisk, semi-musical "acting" would have been not only acceptable but preferable to a good, purely musical rendition. And it is his limitations as an actor which this film brings sharply to our attention.

Looking back over Sir Laurence's career, or on that part of it which I personally have witnessed, I recall that he has almost as often been bad as good. Among the failures I would list Hamlet, Romeo, Shaw's Caesar, and Fry's Duke of Altair; among the triumphs Henry V, Mercutio, Hotspur, Uncle Vanya, and, more doubtfully, Oedipus and Shallow. I have the impression that Olivier either leaves a character vague or plays a single trait. The vagueness of his Romeo, his Hamlet, and his Anthony was fatal, as was the reduction of Shaw's Caesar to the single trait of senescence. On the other hand, the vagueness of Henry V was providential, while a "single trait" is all that Hotspur—or perhaps any character part—possesses. Such parts sound one note apiece. Great major roles sound at least two notes which form a dissonance. Confronted with a great major role an actor needs more than a handsome physique and charm of personality; and he must be more than a character actor; he must be an actor.

The role of Macheath is a case in point. The dissonance here, to be sure, is not that of modern psychology (Macheath is not "a complicated person"), it is principally a dissonance as between manner and matter: the one is artificial, the other real. The form is that of musical comedy, the substance that of actual villainy. Olivier's failure in the realm of musical comedy would have mattered no more than his failure in the realm of musicianship had it not been redoubled by a failure in the realm of reality. His highwayman is not only no singer, he is not only no musical comedian; he is no highwayman. The lightness of John Gay's manner is in direct, not inverse, ratio to his seriousness as a satirist; if his *Beggar's Opera* says nothing, it *is* nothing.

The nullity of the film cannot be attributed to limitations in either Sir Laurence's technique or his powers of characterization. It must in great part be laid at the door of the adaptor, Christopher Fry, and the director, Peter Brook.

Let us not underestimate the difficulty of revivals. To exhume a work is not to revive it, however prettily you dress up the skeleton; to breathe life into it you must either recapture the spirit of the original or by new insight create new life. A revival should be either a return to the essentials of the original or a new departure on the wings of a new inspiration. To present *The Beggar's Opera* today you could either do a "primitive" production, an imaginative, though not antiquarian, version of the early eighteenth century, or a "modern" production, an imaginative, though not modish, re-casting of the whole story. Either way the procedure is simple and radical.

Bertolt Brecht and Kurt Weill tried the "modern" method and gave us the best of modern musical comedies, *The Three-*

penny Opera. The twentieth-century English stage has never quite dared either to go forward to any idea of its own or back to the idea of John Gay. We must be glad that Nigel Playfair did the play in 1920 even if he drew its teeth by taking literally the word opera in its title. We must be glad that (in 1939) John Gielgud redirected it, lifted the incubus of opera off it, and handed it back to the actors. It was for the next major artists who should take up the play to demonstrate that it was more than jolly good tunes and a naughty story.

By the standards of current English theatre, Christopher Fry and Peter Brook are certainly major artists, yet it would be foolish to pretend that the result of giving them *The Beggar's Opera* to play with was unpredictable: in these hands the swords of satire would inevitably be turned, not indeed to ploughshares, but to prunes and prisms. True, the naughty story is still there, and so are all the jolly good tunes—except those that are sung exclusively by Sir Laurence—for the other actors' songs are dubbed by real singers. The parts of Polly and Lucy, Peachum and Lockit are well acted; and interpolation, far from being impertinent, almost saves the show when it gives new lines and actions to that great character actress, Athene Seyler. Even translation to the screen is not always, as such, a degradation: there are moments—in Macheath's progress to the gallows, for instance—which are better than any staging could be. And though on the whole it is annoying to have actors singing to each other or to themselves rather than to the audience, there were times in the film when their quasi-naturalistic procedure almost became a style: Peachum and Lockit made an amiable ballet out of eating and passing their plates . . .

If the Brook-and-Fry *Beggar's Opera* were *all* prunes and prisms—were fully assimilated to the New Rococo—it would have a style throughout, though not one that would be congenial to John Gay or his admirers. The trouble with the film is that it is imbued with *no* convictions. Neither "primitive" nor "modern" it nods frequently in both these directions and all possible others. A Ph.D. thesis could, and probably will, be written on the influences that have gone to its making, from the opening à la Hogarth to the closing à la Bruegel, from a dwarf lifted from Cocteau's *Eternal Return* to a discourse on art and life lifted from Pirandello. All this and Technicolor too.

The challenge of Gay's masterpiece remains. *The Beggar's Opera* was a historic event in the eighteenth century—not because it made fun of opera but because it was at once a fulfilment of the Restoration idea of comedy and a corrective to it—and in the twentieth it continues to beckon because, alone in our tradition, it shows us the full power of a non-operatic, musical theatre.

Julius Caesar, 1953

MORE EXCLUSIVELY THAN most other artists, the dramatist is concerned with the definition of man. Poet and painter may take a sunset for subject; a playwright's primary job is always to send actors out onto a stage, each actor not only *being* a man, but also *representing* another man. The stage is a pedestal or showcase for the exhibition of *homo sapiens*, and the fact that our greatest playwright portrayed *men* has rightly been stressed by generations of critics. The only danger in such an emphasis would be that it might tempt us to take these magnificent creatures and, as critics or producers, have our own way with them. Which is to forget that Shakespeare—not as philosopher, it is true, but as dramatist—defined his own terms. The query: what is a man? underlies all his works and in some of them comes to the surface.

In no play are the men themselves more impressive and in no play is the definition of man more explicitly urged than in *Julius Caesar*. Both the men and the definition have special value for us today. For when we believe in heroes, we tend to be doctrinaire and hence only half-human (Catholic or Communist), and when we begin to criticize heroes, we tend to reject them out of hand, only to discover that we cannot reconstruct a man from a bundle of motives and drives. Shakespeare steers between the Scylla of doctrinaire heroism and the Charybdis of naturalistic fatality. You can admire his people but you can also understand them; you can pity but you can also censure. We respect these people even after we discover they are wrong. Brutus after all has been wrong throughout. Shakespeare goes much further than Plutarch in underlining his wrongness—about each problem as it arises—yet "this was the noblest Roman of them all . . . Nature might stand up/ And say to all the world 'This was a man.' " Brutus *is* Shakespeare's definition of manhood. The pertinence of the definition today is that its two sides, the nobility and the wrongness, the strength and the weakness, are, for Shakespeare, equally real. Our actors will destroy the drama for us to the extent that they play up one side at the expense of the other.

In the thirties, Orson Welles tried, I believe, to isolate the politics in *Julius Caesar* and play that alone. He no doubt would have acknowledged that there was a price to be paid in damage to the individual characters—clearly not everyone in the play as written is either a little liberal or else a little conservative. But what perhaps did not interest Mr. Welles at all is the main point today: namely that in Shakespeare, by contrast both with Machiavelli and modern pseudo-liberalism, politics are absolutely continuous with the personal and moral life of man. This means that by Marxist standards, Shakespeare's political studies are hopelessly unpolitical and subjective. It also means that by the anti-Marxist standards fashionable today, they are much too political and objective.

The film *Julius Caesar* is, in the sense just implied, anti-Marxist. It is produced by Orson Welles' ex-partner John Houseman, who has gone back on Welles' famous "anti-fascist" interpretation to the extent of cutting out all the politics except a dull little lesson on the vanity of dictators. I don't primarily mean that he and his director have cut lines or incidents—though the great political scene of Cinna the poet is missing and the battle of Philippi is reduced to the dimensions of a Western. I mean that the implied definition of man excludes politics, and hence that a great political character like Cassius, so concretely seen by Shakespeare, is reduced to the vulgar abstraction of personal jealousy. That the part is played by the leading Shakespearean actor of our day only confirms the point: had there been any intention of rendering Cassius' political sagacity and the way this sagacity melts in the warmth of his friendship for Brutus, Sir John Gielgud could presumably have rendered them. As it is, we enjoy his superb speaking of individual passages (notably his opening, expository scene), without ever feeling that the separate cells amount to that large organism which is Shakespearean man.

Roles that are compact and soon done with rather naturally fare better: Louis Calhern's Caesar and Edmund O'Brien's Casca are the best performances in these parts one is likely to see. The bigger the part the tougher the problem, and oddly enough the MGM casting has its central weakness in the central role of Brutus. *Julius Caesar* with James Mason in this part, one is tempted to assert, is *Hamlet* without the prince. Here at best is a sphinx without a secret, at worst the wise psychoanalyst of current mythology, a nice man with pipe and spectacles who will end not with a bang but a whimper.

If Mr. Mason is unfit for Brutus, Marlon Brando is unready for Antony. He is the most beautiful young man of the American stage, and in this film like enough to a classic statue. He is also as mettlesome as a race-horse, a magnificent theatrical presence and temperament. And whether or not he has intelligence as it is measured in the schools, he has the right intelligence for an artist, a form of keenness directly visible in his eyes and indirectly visible in all his work: it shows in the very unreadiness of his Antony. For no attempt is made to improvise a glossy and sophisticated front: Mr. Brando unashamedly struggles with the part before our very eyes. Take his speech, for example. He has not learnt to speak in blank verse. He gets none of his effects in normal, full voice: he must shriek, mutter, distort the tone, break the rhythm. Yet one always listens (as one does not to Mr. Mason) because Mr. Brando's peculiar temperament and keenness are in the lines. And when one approves, it's like saying "Isn't his English wonderful?" of a foreign actor. It's magnificent, but it's not war. For where technique is deficient, characterization cannot but suffer. And while star actors with no technique can get along nicely on personality, Shakespeare demands more; and Mr. Brando has more to give.

In so gallant a performance, one would not even grumble at the actor's unpreparedness were it not that his director (Joseph Mankiewicz) seems rather to welcome than oppose it. In order to give us the unpolitical, "purely human" Shakespeare, a director must ask that each principal in *Julius Caesar* fall short of a complete characterization. It would, for example, be well within Mr. Brando's present range to make the main point about Antony that is made in the early part of the play, namely, that he is a reveller. Instead, we were just shown his handsome body.

Some of the film's limitations stem from the medium as such. The now widespread notion that Shakespeare's plays are cinematic is true only to the extent that they are made up of an unbroken succession of short scenes. The actual filming of Shakespeare never fails to remind us how utterly he belongs to the stage. A Cassius who walks through a real street talking loudly to himself (as in the film) can only seem demented. Even full voice-projection—by which the verse gains in dignity —seems absurd in a movie—like all effects in art when the necessity for them has been removed.

This is not to say that Shakespeare movies should not be made. There is nothing to sneer at in the idea of taking the poet to a larger audience. Since the studios can afford a finer cast than almost any theatre, the possible advantage to anyone not a resident of Stratford-on-Avon is apparent.

Nor do my strictures on *Julius Caesar* amount to rejection. This is, arguably, the best Shakespeare film to date. It is certainly the least cluttered with irrelevant apparatus. It contains much good narrative, and many striking images. It is informed with intelligence. What I have against its makers I could have against most Shakespeare producers: that they rest content with a divided mentality instead of letting Shakespeare help them toward his own version of man, seen steadily and whole.

Folklore on Forty-seventh Street

I HAVE SEEN two plays within a week about shy boy virgins finding their manhood in the arms of alluring widows. I need not mention the other soulful and problem-full adolescents of recent stage history, or the heartwarming spinsters and benign bachelors; for it is well enough known by now that the bonnets of the grandmas and the blue-jeans of the bobby-soxers are but tokens of our playwrights' sad and startling incapacity to deal with the love of men and women.

While it took Freud to find "offence" in fairy tales, we should scarcely have needed his genius to spot neurotic fantasy in the folklore of the asphalt jungle around Times Square. Not that the American theatre is guiltier than others. The traditional function of entertainment everywhere has been to feed the appetite for consoling fantasy—exactly as the restaurant in the lucky European theatre addresses itself to the stomach. Dreams, drives, and yearnings dance before the theatre audience's eyes in disguises which may be pleasant or unpleasant in themselves but which at all events console and compensate. The image of an idealized mother caters to our lack of self-reliance. The image of a stage villain provides us with a scapegoat. The image of tenderness appeases our sense of isolation, the image of innocence our sense of guilt.

The great pioneers of modern drama presented these images only to smash them in the name of reality; other masters of the drama have begun by accepting the images and ended by transmuting them into something else. It would be folly to expect anything of either sort from the theatre as such. Great plays are miracles conferred with becoming infrequency, services rendered above and beyond the call of duty. The everyday theatre is nothing more than a daydream factory. Tenderness, innocence, and the rest have to be mere commodities or they couldn't be produced quickly enough. While the artist transforms neurotic fantasies into a higher reality, the journeyman playwright is doomed simply, like the neurotic himself, to live with them. He does nothing to his fantasies except hand them over to the public. The public is excited by the contact. And the degree of excitement is the criterion of the dramatic critics.

Theatre is an escape, and "realist" theatre is no longer an exception to the rule: it differs from non-realistic theatre only in pretending to be so. For the escape here is into pretended realities like ideologies and psychological notions and scientific fetishes. Or reality, being relative, turns unreal when placed before the Broadway public: *Tobacco Road* was not reality, the play was a very titillating bit of slumming, and one didn't know why those silly people weren't eating cake. In the thirties, realist escapism signalized the flight of the intellectual middle class into the fun-world of proletarian legend. Today it signalizes the flight of that same public into a variety of notions, chiefly psychological. In the thirties you felt the reassuring presence of the "real" at the mention of a Worker. Today you feel it at the mention of a Homosexual.

Tea and Sympathy by Robert Anderson is about a private-school boy who is to lose the feeling that he is a homosexual by proving his potency with the housemaster's wife. The subject matter suggests a whole roster of other plays (*The Green Bay Tree, The Children's Hour . . .*) but most of all *Tea and Sympathy* strikes me as the 1953 version of *Young Woodley*, not so much for its plot, or even its setting, as for its relation to the public's current view of what is scandalous. The formula for such a work is Daring as Calculated Caution. Or: Audacity, Audacity, But Not Too Much Audacity. Such a play must be "bannable" on grounds of what used to be considered immoral but also defensible on grounds of what is now considered moral. Sweet are the uses of perversity.

Tea and Sympathy is a highly superior specimen of the theatre of "realist" escape. Superior in craftsmanship, superior in its isolation, combination, and manipulation of the relevant impulses and motifs. Its organization of the folklore of current fashion is so skilful, it brings us to the frontier where this sort of theatre ends. But not beyond it. One doesn't ask the questions one would ask of a really serious play. Here, in the cuckoo land of folklore, one doesn't ask how the heroine knows the hero is innocent, one doesn't permit oneself the thought that he may not be innocent, for he has an innocence of a kind the real world never supplies: an innocence complete and certified. One doesn't ask how her husband could be so unloving and yet have got her to love him: one accepts her neat, fairy-tale explanation that, one night in Italy, he needed her. One doesn't ask just how the heroine's motives are mixed —to what extent her favors are kindness, to what extent self-indulgence—for, in this realm, the author enjoys the privilege of dreamer, neurotic, and politician to appeal to whatever motive is most attractive at the moment.

Instead, one drinks the tea of sentiment and eats the opium of sympathy, realizing more and more, as the evening at the Ethel Barrymore Theatre races on, that these memoirs of an opium eater are not so much a play by Mr. Anderson as another essay of Elia, the latest phantasmagoria of Mr. Kazan, the incarnate spirit of the age; I would call him a human seismograph if there were a seismograph which would not only record tremors but transmit them. At every moment in the evening, one can say: this *has* to be a hit, or men are not feckless dreamers, the theatre is not a fantasy factory, and this is not the age of anxiety.

Technically, the production is perfection: the stage at all times presents a dramatic picture, progression from moment to moment is precisely gauged, every instant has its special value, simultaneous action in three playing areas is beautifully counterpointed. If the craftsmanship is expert, the casting is inspired, for Mr. Kazan goes by what the actors will do under his tutelage, not by what they have done when misled by others. What Deborah Kerr has done in films I have forgotten; what she does in this play I know I shall not forget; if the role scarcely invites greatness, it certainly lets Miss Kerr display a supple naturalness and delicate ardor we did not know were hers. John Kerr, who last year in *Bernardine* was merely brilliant, has been guided into a timing and a subtlety of stance and movement worthy of a veteran. And each minor role is what a minor role should be and rarely is: a type, but alive and concrete enough to come at you with the shock of recognition. Perhaps the greatest single pleasure of this evening of many pleasures was to enjoy so much observation of American life in such minor roles as our hero's roommate at school and our hero's father (both of them confronted with the charge that our hero is a "queer"). Here Mr. Anderson and Mr. Kazan trespass in the realm of the really real.

Daydreams are of course full of real objects, yet the effect of the realities in *Tea and Sympathy* is strangely dual. At times it lifts the show out of the commodity theatre altogether—and into the theatre of the masters. At other times, Mr. Kazan seems to say, No, daydream it is, and daydream it shall remain; and he stylizes the action and has Miss Kerr stand like impatience on a monument with one hand between her breasts and the other outstretched, waiting for our hero to embrace her. The total impression is of double exposure: two scenes, two realms, blurred, not blended. The confusion is the greater in that, presumably, no one on Forty-seventh Street admitted the material was folklore in the first place, and attempts are made in the course of the evening to tell us it is not so, but that this is a demonstration of real evils and their real cure, heterosexuals shouldn't be accused of homosexuality, no one should be falsely accused of anything, manliness is not just bullying but also tenderness, we are all very lonely, especially at the age of seventeen, and so on.

Anyway, in the calculated caution of its audacity, it is a play for everyone in the family; the script is far better than most; folklore and daydream are scarcely less interesting than drama; and the work of Elia Kazan means more to the American theatre than that of any current writer whatsoever.

How Deep Are the Roots?

LADIES OF THE CORRIDOR by Dorothy Parker and Arnaud D'Usseau is a story about the derelict women who live in hotels. A young one, who has a husband that uses a whip and keeps the company of call girls, takes to drink, disgusts herself by sleeping with the desk clerk, and commits suicide. An old one, concealing behind her old lace the arsenic of maternal tyranny, forces her son into spending his life with her by threatening to expose the fact that he had given up his last job under suspicion of homosexuality. A middle-aged one has a pathetic love affair with a younger man. As a kind of chorus commenting on the three principals, there is, on the one side, a successful career woman and, on the other, a couple of hags whose life is death.

However much one might wish that our playwrights would present human beings neither senile nor adolescent, neither in menopause nor in rut, neither psychotic nor impotent nor homosexual, one cannot declare the subject matter of *Ladies of the Corridor* illegitimate. The ladies our authors had in mind are important because they exist. And if there is a scandal in their existence—or their situation—it should by all means be loudly denounced. The trouble with the play lies elsewhere.

One must assume that our authors were attempting the kind of theatre which "makes you laugh and cry at the same time." Except at rare moments they fail; and when this kind of theatre fails it fails catastrophically. You laugh when you should cry, you cry when you should laugh; or you sit there anaesthetized. The audience at *Ladies of the Corridor* is often in confusion. Betty Field falls on her face, dead drunk. Someone laughs. Others join in. Whereupon an opposing team forms, to hiss: Sh! Both teams are right; neither is happy.

This play by two authors is two plays—and, therefore, by the odd arithmetic of art, less than one. The first consists of traditional cruel jokes like how funny it is to see a woman drunk, or an old bitch who seems sweet as grandma, or an oldster making a fool of herself with a young man. In the second, these things are taken, not seriously—for the word "serious" implies a free and mature moral intelligence—but very, very earnestly. I refer to the dangerous earnestness of those who make a hobby (say, at Sardi's) or a profession (say, in "progressive" politics) of indignation.

Anyway, the two plays trip each other up. If you like the

jokes and hate mankind (for the humor is all misanthropic),
you will be bored by the titillations of philanthropy which the
story is meant to provide. Conversely, if you are one of the
indignant, you will be wafted on winds of righteous emotion
only, time after time, to be dropped abruptly into the mire of
misanthropy. Or you will just be confused. Take the ending of
the play. When the love affair with the younger man collapses,
the lady is ill. She then has to pick herself up out of bed in
order to tell the audience that the future is bright because
loneliness is no bogy if you aren't afraid of it, a point which
has no organic relation to the drama we have seen, and which
is credibly reported to have been added at the last moment
when the authors feared the critics and the public might find
them morbid. But what is more morbid than meaninglessness?
Or bad art?

By "bad" I don't mean "inferior"; it is no crime to write an
inferior play; I mean corrupt; and by "corrupt," I mean that
human life is handled here without respect—mechanically,
unscrupulously, tendentiously. The ending—whether inserted
at the last moment or not—is only an extreme example. The
stories are handled with no more sincerity. The dipsomaniac is
handed a flagellant husband as casually as she might be
handed a raincoat. And when the homosexual cries "But I
never touched him" we ask, When will there be a homosexual
on Broadway who'll say he did? [1] In short, the character belongs to a certain current chatter and pother, not to the
human race.

There would be little point in attacking a play which has
already been sufficiently attacked—except for the special character of its badness. *Ladies of the Corridor* is full of cultural
history; the title is from an early poem of T. S. Eliot. More to
the point, the authors' names symbolize the respective out-
looks of two decades that have recently become legends, Miss
Parker being a specialist in the misanthropic wit of the twenties, Mr. D'Usseau a loyal adherent of the social theatre of the
thirties. One might say Mr. D'Usseau keeps politics out of it,
unless the strategy nowadays is just to show the "rottenness of
bourgeois civilization" (or something). Many of Miss Parker's

[1] Answered in "Homosexuality," pp. 149–152 below.

sallies are very funny. "Were you in love with your wife?" "We both were, that was the trouble." "Is she any thinner?" "I imagine considerably; she's been dead two years." Even so you have to be a social historian to be more than a little interested in the play as a whole, and you'd have to be a necrophilist to be in love with it.

Harold Clurman and his actors struggle hard against a distasteful script and settings by Ralph Alswang (who has assumed that, to present a drab and boring subject, you have to be drab and boring). Only three of the performers, it seems to me, manage to snatch some sort of personal victory from the general defeat: Walter Matthau, Betty Field, and Edna Best. Any producer with a sure flop on his hands should hire Mr. Matthau,[2] for he has the ability to ignore the rubbish around him and establish on stage the fact of his own ingratiating manner and strong personality; he has become Broadway's leading stop-gap. Betty Field may also be said wisely to ignore the play in that she creates, as far as possible, the realistic style which presumably was to have been Mr. D'Usseau's contribution to the dipsomaniacal episode; whatever happens to Miss Field's face and figure in the next thirty years, her future as a dramatic actress is secure.

If Miss Field was supposed to save Mr. D'Usseau's lurid melodrama, Edna Best had the more complex—and indeed impossible—task of playing Parker and D'Usseau at one and the same time. Lulu Ames of Akron seems, in any case, an out-of-date and New Yorkish notion of a wealthy midwestern woman; hazy memories of *Main Street* will not enable a playwright in 1953 to describe the class to which Adlai Stevenson belongs: there is confusion and ignorance here, I suspect, as to both class and chronology. Of course one no more believes that Edna Best comes from Akron than one believed Jessica Tandy came from Louisiana (in *A Streetcar Named Desire*). If the play were a good one, we should have to complain that the leading part is hopelessly miscast. For it isn't just that Miss Best isn't from Akron, but that she never conveys the impression of being the sort of woman who would make a fool of

---

[2] My advice was taken by the Theatre Guild when preparing a flop early in 1954 (Charles Morgan's *The Burning Glass*).

herself and have the Dionysian emotions the authors wish to dramatize. In the circumstances, the complaint must be that Edna Best has not been provided with a part. *New Yorker* jokes and *New Masses* melodrama are no proper fare for one of the very few actresses we have left who know how to speak high comedy. It is sufficient comment on the whole evening that the drama, even when clever, never attains as much theatrical life as a walk across the stage by Miss Best, or of one of her grimaces, her saying "ooh" with a little break in the voice, or her making gurgling noises to her dog.

The Perfect Play

SAMUEL TAYLOR'S *Sabrina Fair* is perfect; the obvious intention is perfectly carried out, the means are perfectly adapted to the ends. *Tea and Sympathy* and *Sabrina Fair* represent respectively the two current forms of proficiency: quasi-realistic drama and quasi-romantic comedy; and the Playwrights Company, which produced them, must be credited as the most accurate students of perfection in the imperfect city of New York.

When I tried to describe the near perfection of *Tea and Sympathy*, some readers thought I did Mr. Anderson too much credit; they said he couldn't have been *aware* of his skill in manipulating, organizing, and balancing the impulses that make up the perfect daydream. Yet they must grant Mr. Taylor such an awareness, for his calculations are there to be shamelessly enjoyed, as Euclid's are. Like *Tea and Sympathy*, the production at the National Theatre is a recognizable hit. Yes, contrary to general opinion, a hit can be recognized. If it doesn't have a bloom like a fruit, it has something equivalent to icing on a cake or chrome on a Cadillac or neon lights on the corner drugstore. You can see at a glance that all those shows that open in September are not hits; hits are not sleazy and down-at-heel; they are gowned by Adrian and glamorized in the classic tradition of Culver City. The stage management must be efficient (directing is not an absolute necessity), the cast must be studded with stars (preferably from Hollywood), the setting should be gaudy (the usual drawing-room will do), and the writing . . . the writing must be perfect: it must enable the author always to have the best of all possible worlds and reconcile—as imperfect authors have seldom quite managed to do—illusion with reality.

Mr. Taylor chose for his voice (it isn't quite a style) a vein of banter which enables him to claim and disclaim as he pleases. Does he claim that his play means something? If you like, yes: there are edifying passages about the difference between wanting money and wanting power. At moments, the principal love story is made to symbolize the union of the urge to love the world with the urge to conquer it. But, if you don't like this, then no: it is all disowned the next line.

Having it both ways is . . . perfect. Your language may be blunt, your knowledge of the world extensive, but your heart is warm; your conversation may be flippant and sexy, but your views are conventional; you can refer to Freud and Lucretius, but you are not—perish the thought—an intellectual; and though you know all the things to say about the rich, you don't happen to know any of the poor except your chauffeur (and the chauffeur in *Sabrina Fair* is a millionaire).

In nothing is Mr. Taylor more adept at having-it-both-ways than in the matter of money. Many times during the evening you can say: "Hear that? He's making fun of the rich"; yet his hero's discovery is that you get even richer by being less interested in money than power; and this hero not only marries into the chauffeur's million but is the author's idea man, the man of the future.

The two opposing viewpoints could, of course, be the basis for a work of art. But art knows no perfection, the perfectionist had best stick to the business of calculating his effects. For example, the problem of illusion and reality, which at some point baffles the artist, can be very precisely adjusted by the dispenser of a hit play. Isn't drama for the audience? Well then, let them have illusion and reality as they want them; which is to say, let them chiefly have illusion, but let us keep them from knowing it by administering small doses of reality. In the fun-fair of the mind let there be a booth marked Reality Inc. (with subtitles of which Money should perhaps be the chief). Having been made to feel one with the wealthy— the drawing-room play always made us feel this—we are ready to hear about the simple virtues of the poor and weep a silent tear. After cynical laughter, we were ever the more vulnerable to sentiment; and, when due homage has been paid to culture (*Sabrina Fair* invokes not only Freud and Lucretius but Byron and Emerson, not to mention the Miltonic title), it pleases us to be pretty mindless.

Perfection is perfection; one must not pretend to find a flaw; yet if a critic of *Sabrina Fair* did so pretend he would probably cite the live quality of the joking; it prompts at least the suspicion that Mr. Taylor could be imperfect if he wanted. He has studied not only Philip Barry but Bernard Shaw and would be capable of truly Shavian jesting if he didn't find it necessary to confer upon it all the perfectionist's kiss of death. Shaw took the dead Victorian farce, the dead drawing-room comedy, and breathed life into it; Mr. Taylor takes the achieved Shavian comedy and breathes death into it. It is distressing to see the great Inverter inverted: to see his technique, which he put at the service of the spirit, placed at the service of his enemies. Samuel Taylor is the rich man's GBS.

Yet I must not permit my rationale to give the impression that the show is predominantly distressing. A great deal of what I say must be taken for granted; Broadway is Broadway; 1953 is 1953. Then again, though perfection is dead, it won't kill you. And, in the theatre, when an author takes life out through the window, the actors bring it in through the door. The real merit of *Sabrina Fair* is that it provides six good roles for six good actors. They are stock roles, but the actors have been able to put a little flesh on the bones; and, after all, there are many parts these days with no bones to put flesh on. Direction (H. C. Potter) and stage design (Donald Oenslager) are a little too much in the "perfect" vein of the script: the slow-deliberateness of the directing underscores the mechanical quality of Mr. Taylor's wit; so does the designer's way of rendering a settled handsomeness and a brazen brilliance without fresh beauty or sprightly humor—without life.

Margaret Sullavan's acting, though a little forced, now that youthfulness is something she has to affect and demonstrate, is still full of brio and breeze. Joseph Cotten has the movie-star habit of repeatedly placing his face, as it were, on display (particularly in profile); he has a movie-star's imperfect speech—he lisps and keeps getting a frog in his throat; yet his presence fills both the theatre and the vacuum in the script. Of the minor performers, I should like to single out Cathleen Nesbitt whose voice establishes the tone of the play in the first scene and holds it for most of the evening; it is the haw-haw, Oxford accent which always converts what might have been just a play into High Comedy if not into High Church ritual. How far, after all, could *The Cocktail Party* have got on mere Christianity? It needed those weird, women's voices. England is a country where—in 1926—civil war was avoided largely by the use of the Oxford accent.

New Playwright, New Actress

ONE KIND OF American playwright was characterized long ago by Stark Young: "bold without power and humility about the great forces of life, highly journalistic, and dipping regardless into the depths, advancing with notable facility into regions where only the progressively oblivious could ever be quite at home." Mr. Young's subject was *The Silver Cord;* a more recent instance is *Ladies of the Corridor.*

But the brash type is no longer dominant; it has given place to a shy type. A playwright of the new generation, when successful, seems modest, fastidious, compassionate, poetic; when unsuccessful, he may seem cagey, gauche, spineless, tongue-tied. Two recent plays, *American Gothic* by Victor Wolfson and *The Trip to Bountiful* by Horton Foote, were successful enough to be worth attention yet were kept from complete success by the defects of the new mode.

Mr. Wolfson recounts the events that lead to the murder of a second wife by the first. The setting is a New England that recalls *Ethan Frome.* The murderess is a poor, demented creature whom we do not hate but pity. As performed by a capable group of young players in Greenwich Village, the play has a liveliness and a reality not usually found in the plays that producers put on uptown. But then Mr. Wolfson shies back from his catastrophe like a horse approaching a precipice—not from the murder itself but from the meaning of the murder. The horse falls over the cliff—but it is not a real cliff, we learn with some dismay, not a real horse. This is just a Gothic Tale, Mr. Wolfson seems to say, take it or leave it. And we leave it.

I believe it was Tennessee Williams who brought the word Gothic into current discussion (in a sense that applies less to *The Castle of Otranto* than to *The Castle* of Franz Kafka). In fact Mr. Williams bids fair to become, theatrically speaking, the father of his country; the new playwrights derive from him, not from O'Neill, Wilder, Odets, or Miller (to name his only conceivable rivals). Mr. Wolfson is not exactly a new playwright—his *Excursion* was a hit before the war—but his new play would be inconceivable without *A Streetcar Named Desire* and *Summer and Smoke.* Neurotic woman is the chief exhibit of the contemporary American stage, and Mr. Wolfson does not forget to have her shouted at by a male ogre (Kowalski) and courted by a mild-mannered rival (Mitch).

Though neurotic woman is assigned only the second-largest role in *The Trip to Bountiful,* she has no trouble moving in and taking over the show. Some of the best comic writing of recent seasons goes into her lines, but the cumulative effect of so many naturalistic details turns out, by paradox, to be pure farce; and the author's evident intentions are thwarted by his own facility. Lillian Gish, who acts the largest role in the play with a beautiful concentration and intensity, seems at many points detached—by the farce—from the play she should dominate. More crucial still, Kowalski and Mitch are conspicuous, this time, by their absence. The man who stands between the two women—his wife and mother—is of straw. The plot, the theme, the exigencies of theatre all demand that he speak, that he explain himself, but he is maddeningly and fatally silent, pleading some fifth amendment of the dramatic constitution.

That Mr. Foote's neurotic woman is so funny and forceful must in part be attributed to Jo Van Fleet who plays her. The new playwright has brought the new actor—or, more precisely, the new actress—in his train. Before the new playwright speaks, the new actress has brought onstage her prime attribute: "a quality," a bizarre, neurasthenic quality. Not that it is entirely undefinable. It is defined by grimaces and quiverings of the lip, by frequent sidelong glances, by jerky, syncopated movements of as many parts of the body as will move. The new actress cannot or will not keep still. She walks backwards a good deal and, if she has nothing else to do, rubs her right hand against her left forearm. She is well-adapted to central staging because she keeps turning her head and looking in the other direction. Jo Van Fleet is only one of her names. She has also called herself Maureen Stapleton, Geraldine Page, and Clarice Blackburn.

(In fairness to Miss Van Fleet I should add that, unlike some of her colleagues, she is not a mere "personality," bringing only her "quality" to the footlights. An actor should not *be*, but *mean*: and we are not in doubt that Miss Van Fleet finds her meanings as an artist must find them—by craftsmanship. Nonetheless, she bears the mark of her generation, and there are many roles which—for all the craftsmanship—her personality will not, at present, let her play. I thought the role of Camille in *Camino Real* was one—unless Mr. Williams wanted to make Dumas' heroine over and this Indian summer of Marguerite Gautier was meant to be another Roman spring of Mrs. Stone.)

It is of course foolish for critics to tell writers of one school that they should go to another school. A bad writer will not turn good by change of address. A good writer is unlikely to need a critic's counsel. There is a futility about the criticism which offers a renascence of drama on condition that the dramatists adopt a certain method or a certain philosophy, and none of us who write criticism have always avoided this error. On the other hand, with the shy playwrights of today, one has the impression that there is something inside them that is prevented from coming out largely by the censorship of certain current attitudes to playwriting. If there is no such thing inside them, they are not very good writers, and should choose another profession. If there is, let us break down the obstructive attitudes, destroy the censor, and see what happens.

There is a recent play which, in one respect at least, affords a corrective to the current trend of shy, sensitive, atmospheric writing. This is T. S. Eliot's *The Confidential Clerk.* It has a plot. Not just a story but the old, arranged, constructed, wire-drawn, and infinitely maligned article. If you have conceded anything to the "new" drama—of which one of the cardinal shynesses is shyness of plot—you will quickly take it back again at the first reminder of what a real plot can be. If you can't stomach *The Confidential Clerk,* the last act of *A Doll's House* makes the point much better.

God Bless America

THE PROFOUNDEST ANALYST of American culture, Tocqueville, suggested that democracy was not conducive to dramatic art. And the twentieth century, without removing any of the obstacles to theatre which the French critic listed, has added a few more, notably the movies in its second decade, radio in its third, and TV in its fifth. This being so, the surprising fact is not that the theatre is harassed but that it exists at all. Nowhere have the substitutes for theatre been so developed and accepted as in America. Yet there is still an American theatre. Why?

One thing we have learned is that in the present phase of history one medium's gain is not always the other's loss: the phonograph record has enlarged, not reduced, the audience at symphony concerts. The theatre affords, perhaps, no precise analogy to this famous triumph in the musical field. The old "road" theatre *was* largely wiped out by the movies; the Broadway public *is* very small compared with the movie and

TV public. Nonetheless, the spread of community and university theatres goes some way toward replacing the road companies. And, in New York there is usually a wide response to a good play *when it has a good*—or even just a glossy—*production*. In short, the idea that the theatre is dying—like certain churches—because the public has lost interest and is busy elsewhere is simply not true.

Professionally, the theatre retains the primacy which many of us believe to be its natural right; it is by virtue of no empty traditionalism that the theatre page (or column) precedes movies, radio, and TV in the papers or takes precedence over them in the magazines. The three newer arts remain to a remarkable extent parasites: they draw talent from the theatre, not vice versa. When we hear of a movie actor appearing on the stage, we find either that he was stage-trained or that he is a bad actor. There is of course the third possibility: that he has had stage training *and* is a bad actor; he *had* to go to Hollywood.

We are reminded that, in the early days of film, an actor had to come from the stage, there being nowhere else for him to come from. Isn't it possible, we are asked, for some other medium to become the main source of supply? It is possible, we have to reply, but there is no sign of its happening. On the contrary, one has only to attend a few TV rehearsals to see how utterly TV producers depend upon a technique of acting that could never have been acquired—nor even, perhaps, maintained—under the conditions they impose. Some of these conditions could be changed, though they probably won't be. Others seem to be inherent. The stage alone offers the actor full play—allows him to give a performance in an unbroken curve and places him in direct emotional contact with his audience. That is why real actors are dissatisfied with the substitutes.

The theatre exists. The snag is that it does not exist spaciously and variously enough to satisfy any of those who have its interests at heart. The producer's point of view has been that entertainment the public doesn't pay for, the country can do without. There is common sense in this; and, even in art, the businessman often proves less of a fool than other people.

A show doesn't get to be a hit without meeting standards of showmanship. There is more fun, more craftsmanship, even more art in the average commercial show than in the average serious play. The serious play as currently known to Broadway is a bore and an imposition. The cry of pain that goes up when reviewers pan these plays is emitted either by interested parties or disinterested muddleheads. Why should a businessman invest in anything other than, say, *South Pacific*, when *South Pacific* has the artistic as well as the economic edge? The nest of serious theatre has been fouled by a foolish subintelligentsia.

Yet—we must convince our prospective investor—there *is* a need for a non-commercial, or less commercial, theatre. In part this need derives precisely from the theatre's primacy among the arts of entertainment: in order to make money in radio, movies, and TV, invest it in actors, invest it in theatre. Then again, the commercial theatre itself needs a non-commercial division. I believe I am uncovering no secret when I say that the impetus towards the creation of a professional experimental theatre at Columbia University is coming, not from "serious playwrights," but from the author and the composer of *South Pacific*, Richard Rodgers and Oscar Hammerstein. They know that workers in the theatre need a training ground, and that there is a public—if not always a large and wealthy one—for other shows besides *South Pacific*. I do not mean that the audience for a non-commercial show must always be small and poverty-stricken. The box office of a small art theatre often has occasion to rob the rich. And perhaps the strongest of all arguments in favor of a subsidy for theatre is that it opens the doors to millions who would otherwise never pass through them; by subsidy, we can lower the prices and admit the people who otherwise take their dollar to the movies. Hence, the subsidized theatre, far from being an attempt to force something down "the public's" throat, is a democratic institution, signalizing a refusal to limit the audience to the well-to-do. Nor is it a threat to the commercial theatre. In Paris, commercial and subsidized houses live side by side in reasonable amity. And one notes that, artistically, they do each other a lot of good.

It may be thought that in invoking the European idea of

subsidy I have wandered too far from the situation in America. Here we shall perhaps have to forego the word Subsidy (like the word Socialism) so as not to antagonize such cultural isolationists as might otherwise be our best friends. But the economics of theatre in America already includes much besides business enterprise. Help for the non-commercial effort is coming from at least three very considerable sources: individual philanthropists, local communities (which may mean philanthropists in a group), and the State legislatures. By philanthropists I mean men who are investing money with very little hope of getting it back (let alone with interest) in productions which they happen to like. The community theatre, though not yet as successful, perhaps, as English repertory, has its recognized triumphs in Dallas, Cleveland, Pasadena, and not a few other cities. The State legislatures, whatever they may think of Socialism in general or Subsidy in particular, pour money into the theatres of the State universities which—in Wisconsin, say, or Indiana—are among the chief theatres of the state.

In short, the fact that money does not come to our non-commercial theatre in the European way, should not delude us into believing that it cannot come at all. Under the Eisenhower administration, it may be vain to talk of a Federal Theatre in the sense of a *Comédie Américaine* yet it is not vain to recall that our actual Federal Theatre of the thirties was no such thing but rather an improvisation of a characteristically American sort—a triumphant piece of private enterprise in the public domain. The American way, I take it, is to seize your chances as they come up, for America is a country where you believe—most of the time—that they *will* come up.

End as a Yes-Man

THE HUMAN RACE—it is the theme of Freud's *Civilization and Its Discontents*—pays a high price for its institutions and organizations. This is also one of the traditional themes of comedy and, since the industrial revolution, has almost become the main theme of all literature and drama. The artist being, *per se*, a champion of the human, the modern artist has most typically been the enemy of institutions. And, when he has lacked the genius to write a *Resurrection* or a *Saint Joan*, he has honestly contributed *The Dreyfus Affair* or *Children in Uniform*.

In our time, however, many artists have gone over to the enemy. Their argument is that an institution is no longer an enemy when it's run by their friends: the Marxist writer withholds criticism once there is a Marxist government. There is a misunderstanding here. The artist's opposition is not to the party in power but to the facts of power as they will be under any régime. For him, therefore, to withhold criticism is to abdicate and go into exile—abroad or not. At this date, it is scarcely necessary to give instances.

What is necessary, rather, is to realize to what a large extent artists are withholding opposition even in America. Two well-known playwrights have intimated in *The New York Times* that they no longer feel opposition to be safe.[1] There are two answers to this. One is that opposition was never safe: Zola was not safe when he wrote *J'accuse!* The other is that America is not yet as unsafe and unfree as certain liberals like to think. ("Freedom in America is hanging by a thread," one of them said in 1948, hinting that by 1949, unless Wallace was elected, liberals would all be in concentration camps.) If our playwrights today are yes-men, it is not because it is impossible to say No.

These reflections are prompted by *End as a Man* by Calder Willingham which in play form was promoted from the Theatre de Lys to the Vanderbilt Theatre and from the Vanderbilt to the Lyceum. It is about the sadistic goings-on in a military academy. A generation ago, such happenings would have been taken as the material for an indictment of the military class and perhaps of the whole social "system" to which it belongs. Admittedly, that is a limited interpretation of the subject, and the resulting play would no doubt have been rather narrow, abstract, and doctrinaire. Had Mr. Willingham found a way to

[1]See *The Theatre of Commitment*, pp. 11–12.

broaden the theme, one wouldn't dream of defending the earlier approach against his. But he is not more inclusive; he just switches sides, being *for* the army and *against* the individuals. And because he can cloak a more or less craven conformism in tough, not to say foul, language, he may be said to be grooming himself admirably for a totalitarian age. In *Death of a Salesman*, the older attitude of revolt was the strange bedfellow of the New Conformism. Mr. Willingham seems just to drop the revolt and take a hint from Mr. Miller as to the form conformism should take—namely, a neurological fatalism. What does *End as a Man* prove? That, in the best of all possible worlds, where authorities are wise and everything is taken care of, a couple of young men flutter the dovecotes by being psychotic.

Perhaps, however, *End as a Man* belongs less importantly to the history of literature than to that of performance. It began, in fact, as a project of some young men of the Actors' Studio, a New York organization in which professional actors are enabled through private philanthropy to continue their training with the help of Elia Kazan or Lee Strasberg.

I have been Mr. Strasberg's guest at many sessions of the Actors' Studio when the members, as a class exercise, performed scenes from plays. My impressions, however superficial, were far too various to set down, even in summary, here. I will mention only how different the work is from the traditional English training I am familiar with. English training begins and ends with speech. This American training, influenced by Stanislavsky, concentrates, not on technique itself, but on a kind of truthfulness of feeling through which, it is hoped, the action on stage will come to life. Fair enough. On the just assumption that the art of acting has fallen on evil days, the Russo-American approach does seem called for. Before we demand fine elocution or elegant gesture, we have a prior demand to make: that the stage be alive from instant to instant and that each instant carry us on to the next; for, like music, drama is non-stop action; only by moving can it come into being.

In attending to this primary principle, the Studio actors serve their art well. Their limitation up to now, as it seems to me, is that movement, as they understand it, is too insistently movement of the nerves. Perhaps the plays they are given know no other dynamic. Or perhaps the playwrights limit themselves to what they know the actors can do. Whatever the explanation, where the principle of motion is sheer plot or where, say, evil is to be presented, and not just maladjustment, I have thought the Studio actors to be baffled and lost.

But *End as a Man*—even in its limitations—lends itself to their method: here is no vision of evil, just a glimpse of neurosis, no profound moral life, but a violent palpitation by which alone one instant is joined to the next. The actors render and sustain the palpitation with a remarkable skill, varying it—providentially—with the one hearteningly human feature of the play, which is humor. From the opening seconds of the performance, as with *Tea and Sympathy*, one senses that combination of energy and control which keeps a performance taut and an audience alert. The directing of Jack Garfein is full of good, "Kazan touches," such as a pause filled by a cracking of knuckles, a hymn accompanied by rhythmic bangs on a trash can, speeches accompanied by handstands on the floor and other physical jerks on the bed. There is not only Mr. Kazan's feverish rhythm but also his technical skill in timing a pause or building a climax. This is not a script well spoken to the accompaniment of pleasing gestures but a series of small "actions" rendered with emphasis on the tensions within each character and the tensions between one character and another. I remember no speeches, I remember Ben Gazzara kicking his wardrobe in a rage; not because the kick is remarkable in itself, but because it is skilfully prepared and timed. And I recall sequences of action, as when Mr. Gazzara pretends to be a green goblin in a football player's drunken imaginings and dances round him with a broom.

The publicity men, following up the broad hints of *A Streetcar Named Desire* and *Picnic*, are trying to offer up Mr. Gazzara on the altar of the new phallus worship. Joshua Logan had carried male nakedness as far as it could go from the head down; Mr. Garfein started at the other end of his hero-villain; and the ads display the latter in shorts and garters. It wasn't really necessary: Mr. Gazzara can act. There is in his performance a very live contrast between an almost feline femininity and a bestiality so gross we call it masculine. A little of the English training in speech would not hurt Mr. Gazzara if he wants to play parts less uncouth. But his success is deserved, and praise is only invidious if it passes over the fact that William Smithers, Arthur Storch, and Paul Richards are equally exact, passionate, and distinctive in their roles.

Tension is tense. The old-fashioned actors you are likely to see in, let us say, Margaret Webster or Guthrie McClintic productions have no equivalent to offer. The life of *End as a Man* may be of a constricted sort but it is life. The Old Guard achieves something decent, dignified and decorative—like a funeral.

The Ill-made Play

WHAT'S AN EXAMPLE of a good "well-made play"? Probably there isn't one; the term has so long been used to describe a kind of play which all the authors we like have rejected in favor of—well, sheer Truth, sheer Significance. Ibsen, said H. L. Mencken, just let the facts "tell themselves." Today, when Ibsen's plays seem to many a trifle too "well-made," it is *The Glass Menagerie* and *Member of the Wedding* that are considered utterly real. In his book *Playwright at Work* John van Druten tells us he saw both plays three times and asked himself how the latter

> achieved the things that made it so moving and so novel. Each time the method has escaped me. I can attribute this only to its total honesty, and to the author's absorption in what she was doing. She wrote nothing that was not of the deepest truth and significance to her . . .

One practical tip Mr. van Druten does vouchsafe us: leave out the plot. "A play that was all atmosphere, with no plot at all would be my preference." A recent play of this school is *In the Summer House* by Jane Bowles.

A young girl falls off a cliff—not altogether unaided, it seems, by a jealous friend—and is killed. That would be the central event of Mrs. Bowles' play, if current dramaturgy respected anything as old-fashioned as a center—or even an event. The jealous friend would be the main character (if we had to have a main character) and the author's moral concern (if there had to be moral concern) would be with the degree of aid she gave in the fatal fall (murder, manslaughter, suicide, or accident). But *nous avons changé tout cela.* The fall from the cliff, never being precisely defined factually, cannot be defined morally. The author is not interested in events and morals but in mood and psychology, that is, of course, in melancholy and neurosis.

I have already heard the unstressed, undefined fall from the cliff compared to the pistol shot at the end of *The Three Sisters*, and am reminded that Mr. van Druten regards Chekhov as the father of the new dramaturgy. To follow up these suggestions would be unfair to Mrs. Bowles. We should discover her limitations and Mr. van Druten's error, not the quality of her play. That quality—all too derivative, it is true—derives from Tennessee Williams, Carson McCullers, and Paul Bowles, in short, from Mrs. Bowles' immediate environment. It is its modishness—that which would have qualified *In the Summer House* for publication in a magazine like *Flair*—that makes people around Broadway say it is too literary for the commercial theatre. The truth is, it is a good deal too stagy for literature. And too long. Though people think of drama as a condensed form, the New Drama is an exception to that—as to many another—rule: the new plays are but short stories writ long. It is not quite true that they are structureless. They have the structure of a short story. And there is nothing to be said against this structure except that it has no room for the major matters of drama and the novel.

Looking at short stories, one would say that they cannot be blown up into plays. Yet, looking at our recent plays, one would think them all based on short stories. Some difficulty there is, of course. Even Mrs. Bowles has to pad characters out with jottings from her notes on psychoanalysis. And there is a problem of range. In a story, a phrase is enough to suggest

Mexicans in the offing; in a play, you have actually to present these Mexicans; and the audience may detect that your knowledge of the Latin race comes chiefly from sources like *The Rose Tattoo*. In a story, lyricism has to be created in words; in a play, the signal "this is lyrical" can be given by an orchestra placed in the wings . . .

A piece of theatre, however, doesn't have to be a play, any more than a play has to be a tragedy or a comedy. It only has to take place on stage and keep us interested. *Member of the Wedding* did this; so does *In the Summer House*; and in both cases an authoress of uncommon talent had contributed her quota. Mrs. Bowles' is a lesser talent than Mrs. McCullers', but she has a not dissimilar gift for evocative dialogue and delicate portraiture. Even the staginess that might keep her from first-rate fiction is not always bad—on the stage. "If you have trouble filling up Act Two," advises Mr. van Druten, "you will be tempted to a drunk scene," and Oscar Wilde said there was nothing to do with temptation but give way to it. Mrs. Bowles' best scene is a drunk scene; her best character is a drunk.

I *think* the character is hers. The possibility exists that it is Mildred Dunnock's. At any rate, a collaboration of writer and actress has produced in Mrs. Constable—mother of the child who fell from the cliff—one of the memorable figures of recent stage history, made up, you may say, of current commonplaces about dipsomania, spinsterhood-widowhood and lostness, yet coming together with the force of something new. The greatest pleasure of the evening is to be found in the varied details of this role: the little fan Miss Dunnock carries in her first scene and the way she wiggles it, the fishing rod she carries in a later scene and the timid way she holds it away from her body, the fine realistic twist she gives to the standard comic business of a drunk's handling of bottle and glass (not to mention the hotdog Mrs. Bowles throws in for good measure), the towering fury Miss Dunnock can alarmingly produce at an instant's notice, the mischievous humor she has not before (that I know of) had a chance to show us.

And then there is Judith Anderson. It would be a mistake to say that Miss Dunnock steals the show from her, because it isn't clear that the show was Miss Anderson's in the first place. And the contrast, anyway, is not between good and bad acting but between two different schools—Actors' Studio and Old Guard, school of Kazan and school of Guthrie McClintic. Perhaps a critic should simply declare his preference. Mine— though I find much in Studio procedure to object to—is not for the Old Guard. At times it is hard for me to regard what Miss Anderson does as acting at all: I get the impression that she has two or three stances, two or three gestures, that she takes up the desired position (as if for a camera), and simply holds forth. There is little or no characterization, and Miss Anderson's body seems not to have the suppleness a modern role requires. She is a "personality" without a doubt—and this not in the higher sense[1] but the lower one: she is not a Toscanini but a Stokowski. Her personality is not something defined by her acting. Rather we are invited to admire her acting because she is a personality—even as we are invited to see something out of the common in commonplace words if the person who speaks them is a queen. Alas, poor star actors —they are Public Figures, and wish to be treated as such! They get their wish. They give a line a comic reading, and a mechanical guffaw comes from the gallery. They change noisily into the high gear of tragedy, and "You were terrific, darling" wafts later towards the dressing room. Delightful, is it not, to be able to establish such easy contact with an audience? And to elicit so quick a response? Yet depressing, too, perhaps, to think how mechanical it all is, how little it has to do with dramatic art, how much with the starved emotions of masses, the impulse to lionize, the repressed desire for royalty, and I know not what perturbation of the modern ego! There is a Pirandello play about a poet who, becoming a Public Figure, dies and turns into a statue. Star actors turn into statues without dying.

Has Judith Anderson done so? Or does she wish to remind us that there is, so to say, a statuesque aspect to the art of acting? Does she wish to dramatize for us the plight of a tragedy queen in an age of untragic republicanism? Does she wish to register a sort of protest against the little, twitching

[1]As defined above, p. 87.

plays of today? Her grander manner was certainly effective in the long, opening speech of *In the Summer House* and also in the suddenly larger passion of her last scene. And perhaps, after all, it is Mrs. Bowles' fault that the character in that last scene seems, first, to change into someone else and, second—in her very last speeches—to become unintelligible.

In his settings, Oliver Smith found pretty accurate equivalents for Mrs. Bowles' writing; one should perhaps not complain if, *ipso facto*, the limitations of the New School were also reflected. One of Mr. Smith's assignments was too hard: to stage a beach scene. Our peepshow stage almost never gives any impression of the out-of-doors, and the complete, sunny openness of a beach is outside its range. Some of the atmosphere of a beach was suggested by the performance: the actors were languidly blowing bubbles. On the other hand, Miss Anderson was stalking around in high heels, and people were sitting reading on rocks in complete disregard of wind and sun.

Called in to direct after the show had been before an out-of-town audience, Jose Quintero nevertheless managed to bring the show up to his usual high technical standard. One almost had the impression that he had brought some of the cast from his own theatre, Circle in the Square. Whither Mr. Quintero goes, one thought, there goes the New Actress (named Elizabeth Ross this time), walking backwards, eyes popping, lips quivering, right hand sliding up the left forearm, tensely standing and staring wherever her director—too obviously—has placed her. (Slogan for the New Drama: inactions speak louder than words.)

Pessimism as a Pick-Me-Up

OPTIMISTIC PLAYS are very depressing. "Too bad reality is different," you say in the lobby. It takes a pessimistic play to cheer you up. When you say "Life isn't as bad as all that" you are half way to declaring that everything in the garden is lovely. The great tonic of the 1953–4 Broadway season was *Mademoiselle Colombe* by Jean Anouilh, a tale of the futility of boy's meeting girl.

It was a production of many pleasures. Boris Aronson's sets alone were worth the trip to the Longacre Theatre. This designer, whose reputation is for thoroughness and grandeur, showed himself, here as in *My Three Angels,* to have as light a touch as anyone in the profession; his joyous wit and controlled fantasy provide a desperately needed alternative to the excessive, over-sophisticated gorgeousness of, say, Oliver Messel or Lemuel Ayres. Mr. Aronson's principal exhibit in *Colombe* was a backstage scene in which M. Anouilh's peculiar blend of French reality with theatrical unreality was translated into color and shape.

The play is also a showcase for some of our finest acting talent—by which I do not merely mean that some of our best actors are in it, nor yet that it enables them to show themselves off. Edna Best had a better chance to show herself off in *Ladies of the Corridor;* the authors gave her nothing else to show. Since Miss Best has one of the most charming selves in our theatre, it is pleasant to have her display it—but it is astonishing to have her dispense with charm altogether and get along quite as well without. Miss Best's part in *Colombe* is that of an aging actress wholly shrewish and shrill. Miss Best wears a false nose, chalky make-up, and a red wig; struts, gesticulates wildly, and screams her head off; in fact, goes all out; all of which is remarkable at a time when she'd get higher marks for acting if she relaxed and was a bit of a bore. As it was, Miss Best showed the way to the rest of a cast which—except for two performers —M. Anouilh dresses up as caricatures, outrageous as Hogarth or the Keystone Cops: Sam Jaffe, Harry Bannister, Nehemiah Persoff and others contribute notable cartoon-portraits. (Mikhail Rasumny is unintelligible.)

The exceptions are the hero and heroine through whom a more inward reality is explored. The heroine is played by Julie Harris. If my delight over this actress is somewhat belated, I had better admit that I was in Europe at the time when she came to prominence. Astonishing what can happen when one's back is turned! That Miss Harris has the special "offbeat personality" of the newer generation of actresses is the least of it and might well have set me against her. Her personality has the larger strangeness and even (potentially) the grander glamour that go to the making of a Garbo (different as Garbo is). Nor does the final impression come from mere color or timbre of personality. It comes, rather, from Miss Harris' gift, a gift not yet, to be sure, at its fullest pitch of development, but nonetheless unspoiled by any of the myriad forces which must have been trying to spoil it. I am afraid for her! She is like one of Anouilh's young women, all sensitive life, while round about is the wicked, insensitive world eager to hurt, not to mention the awful examples of Misses X and Y, first ladies of our stage, fifty and forlorn.

Eli Wallach is a favorite actor of mine; yet casting him as the hero of *Colombe* was a rash bit of "off-casting" which has not succeeded. It is very well to ask a straight comedienne like Miss Best to do a character part, but to ask a character actor like Mr. Wallach to play a juvenile lead? The springy *élan* and homey vivacity that he has to offer he is compelled to save for one scene—the last. Before that we have to observe him grimly holding himself in or yet more grimly simulating qualities he cannot seem to possess, like arrogance and intellectuality. The actor who played the role in Paris was possibly a less accomplished artist; he didn't do very much with the part; but there was no complaint about him because he fell into place; it is one of those rather neutral roles. Mr. Wallach, though he works manfully, and always holds the attention (because he is an artist), is the Achilles' heel of the show; and the anti-European newspaper fraternity has aimed to kill.

Achilles is not all heel. Apart from one gamble that didn't come off, Harold Clurman has played a careful game and won a number of tricks. Even his over-emphasis on the hero's badness can broaden our notion of a play which—however we take it—is witty and moving. I came away from the Paris production thinking M. Anouilh had but reiterated his standard theme of desecrated innocence, the only difference this time being that the innocent was a man. The Clurman production makes it clear that *Colombe* is—with *Antigone*—one of those more interesting plays of M. Anouilh in which there is some guilt on both sides of the conflict. The young woman is a very ordinary young woman (to make so ordinary a person so extraordinary on stage being a great joint achievement of M. Anouilh and Miss Harris), but the young man's superiority is pharisaical. In fact *Colombe* brings to mind a play that those who dislike M. Anouilh would dislike even more: *Le Misanthrope.*

Like Giraudoux, like Brecht, like Goethe, like Racine, like all foreign playwrights, M. Anouilh has been called untranslatable. So there sets in that process called Adaptation, which commonly means the conquest and destruction of an author by a jealous would-be rival. If the British version of *Colombe* was not quite that, it was nevertheless full of changes by which the Adaptor vainly sought to justify having his name in the same size of type as M. Anouilh. It is a pleasure to report that the version used in New York—by Louis Kronenberger—is more faithful to the original without being less amusing in itself. Following the British precedent, and presumably under instructions from his producers, Mr. Kronenberger did tone down the nausea and pessimism which are most conspicuous in the Edna Best role. In the French she says, "I'm constipated and I've two hundred alexandrines to learn by tomorrow." In withholding the constipation from the play, I can only hope Mr. Kronenberger is saving it for his next piece (in *Time*) on Miss X or Miss Y.

There were other small things to grumble about, such as an awkward transition to the last scene in which the PA system is ineffectively and indistinctly used. But by and large, it is a splendid evening, and you leave the theatre full of the hope that M. Anouilh's hopelessness inevitably engenders.

Shakespeare's Politics

MELODRAMA PRESENTS the struggle of right and wrong; tragedy —on one famous view of it—the struggle of right and right;

Shakespeare's *Coriolanus* the struggle of wrong and wrong. That's what makes the play so hard to take. As one of Henry Luce's anonymous spokesmen recently indicated, the American theatre public insists on some characters being simply right and others simply wrong. He might have said the same of any other public, American or un-American, in the theatre or out of it. We all view life as melodrama, insofar as we are fools. Only to the extent that we are men can we see it as tragedy or comedy.

Now, though our folly is by no means confined inside theatre walls, our humanity is very easily left outside them. For we are wholly foolish when our individuality is lost in mob emotion, and any crowd of people—including an audience—can become a mob. Tragedy and comedy always tend, in the theatre, to decline into melodrama and farce; those critics who are the mob's representatives praise tragedy and comedy precisely in the degree that they do so decline: *Hamlet* is "as exciting as a who-done-it," *The Would-Be Gentleman* is "as funny as *Room Service.*" Etcetera.

If it is hard, then, for a producer to put across a tragedy or a comedy, how much harder for him to put across a play that combines the more forbidding features of both to the exclusion of every melodramatic and farcical possibility! Such a play is *Coriolanus;* it is absolutely nothing but a masterpiece; we almost have to feel sorry for it.

Except that it hurts our feelings, gets under our skin, affronts our prejudices, and corrects our convictions. It is the most modern of Shakespeare's works in the sense that modern writers have been trying to write it: no wonder that our greatest comedian, Shaw, called it the greatest of Shakespeare's comedies! Those who have attempted political tragedy in our time have achieved, at best, brilliant political melodramas like *Darkness at Noon.* At worst, they have excitedly informed us that fascism or communism or capitalism is wicked and that common folk (like you and me in the $7.80 orchestra) are models of heroic virtue and good sense.

It is true that you can't fully identify yourself with anyone in *Coriolanus.* From the Broadway viewpoint, that is bad. From the human viewpoint, it is good—because you are prevented from dissociating yourself from evil, from pushing evil away, from locating it exclusively in the other fellow, the other place, Moscow or Corioli. The evil is here in Rome, in Washington, in Coriolanus, in our classmate Alger Hiss, in me, and in you—*hypocrite lecteur*. The reference to Hiss will seem pretty callow to our Marxist friends, not only because he was quite right to be a spy for Moscow (or is it that he *wasn't* a spy? I forget), but also because they acknowledge no continuity between personal character and political action. The rest of us have been coming round from the Marxist position (if we ever held it) to the Shakespearean one and are willing to see treason—that of Alger Hiss or Benedict Arnold—as the other face of pride, first of the deadly sins. Some degree of identification with Coriolanus we have, perforce, to permit ourselves.

The dignity of John Houseman's production derives from taste, intelligence, and discretion—most of all, discretion. Mr. Houseman is a man of integrity, and has resisted the temptation to slant a masterpiece whose greatness is all vertical. The People—about whom Shakespeare is so "undemocratic"—are presented in all their moral ambiguity. No attempt is made to whitewash the enemy leader, Aufidius. If Mr. Houseman tips the scales at all, it is to overweight the badness of his hero. Perhaps this was the inevitable result of casting Robert Ryan for the role. Unable to suggest caste and the pride of caste, Mr. Ryan seems too simply a boor (and, hence, a bore). Not that one suspects this actor to be boorish by nature: he works all too hard and too obviously at it. It is only that, if Coriolanus is not an aristocrat, he is just a disgruntled gladiator.

Nor was Mildred Natwick the right choice for his mother. What she does, she does handsomely, and it is thrilling to learn how far from her comic character work this actress can go; one admires her attempts at the breadth of gesture and emotion. But what of that fatal rigidity of character which characterizes three generations of her family (even the little boy tortures butterflies)? Before Volumnia kneels, we should think: this woman's knees would never bend. With Miss Natwick, loving compliance seems entirely natural.

Mr. Houseman's is not pseudo-British Shakespeare. With perhaps two or three exceptions, the actors do not use the hooing and cooing Oxford voice. But, in avoiding the British gentility, Mr. Houseman falls into an American gentility, almost midwestern in its hominess. The author of *The Merry Wives* (owner of New Place, son of a butcher) would no doubt understand. Yet the material of early Roman history is the least genteel he ever used. Half-barbaric, half-aristocratic (or is it that aristocracy always *is* half-barbaric?), the stuff of this story is destroyed by being refined. Mr. Houseman has not destroyed his play; the refinement is only partial; but it is damaging enough. Both Coriolanus and his mother have become remarkably middle class; indeed, the former role has been drastically cut for the purpose. Or take stage "business." The 1623 Folio tells us that Aufidius *stands* on Coriolanus' corpse in angry triumph; Mr. Houseman's Aufidius stamps his foot once—on the floor. The rest follows. The setting is by Mr. Oenslager. Alvin Colt's costumes, though very becoming in their rich reds, browns, and greens, are far too picturesque, too *nice,* for the subject. The effect of the whole production is of Beethoven's Fifth played pianissimo upon muted instruments.

On the other hand, it must also be said that Mr. Houseman's method yields results, both general and of detail. The chief general merit of the production—beyond the competence we can happily take for granted—is the peculiar sense of movement it conveys. This is a play that—for all the Elizabethan bustle of the scenes taken separately—remains stationary for whole sequences; then, of a sudden, it turns, as on a hinge or pivot, like some majestic old door. The alternation of stillness and tremendous reversal is Greek and awe-inspiring in its majesty. I would say that Mr. Houseman's largest achievement is to communicate a sense of this ancient and alien grandeur.

Among the many admirable details, the one that stands out in my memory is a conversation of three Volscian servants. The clowning of Gene Saks, Jack Klugman, and Jerry Stiller might serve as a model for future Shakespeare productions. In its unpatronizing lightness and uncute fun, its sharp satire, its controlled yet violent movement, the scene is in direct contrast to clown scenes as we usually and yawningly see them played. Modern elements, notably a sort of deadpan Brooklyn humor, are used for an Elizabethan effect. Paula Laurence's little "solo" as Valeria is successful in a similar way: here is simplicity where we usually get fancy talk, immediate charm where we usually get "Shakespearean acting."

I saw the show twice and would be glad to go again. While I deplored the choice of *Madam Will You Walk* as the opening play for the efficient new enterprise which is the Phoenix Theatre, *Coriolanus* makes ample amends. One hopes this theatre will rapidly forget Sidney Howard (what, after all, could be easier?) and establish for itself *an intellectual identity*. I don't mean a reputation for intellectuality. I mean that the Phoenix should stand for something; something more than just a well-produced show. Mr. Houseman could tell the managers what I mean. The Welles-Houseman Mercury Theatre *had* an intellectual identity.

Captain Bligh's Revenge

I DON'T RECALL an American play that has provided a livelier evening in the theatre than *The Caine Mutiny Court Martial*. A fine cast of actors—outstandingly, Henry Fonda and Lloyd Nolan—help to make this so, but the largest contributions are those of the director and the author. Charles Laughton's directing is not only good, it is good in a particularly valuable way. One often tends to think that the alternative in directing styles is between the manner of the Group Theatre—nervous, slangy, plebeian, American—and the "Shakespearean manner" —statuesque, elocutionary, genteel, British. It has taken the Anglo-American Laughton, having the best of both hemispheres, to find a third way. He has worked with American actors using live American speech (not Stage Diction), and he has slapped and kneaded this speech like dough until it has assumed a pleasing shape. The production has both the raciness of the new school and the dignity of the old. Laughton has used his Englishness not to fatten up the play with orotund vowels but to keep it lean with irony. He has used his

Americanism not to "soup up" the emotions but to sustain the pace and keep the tone close to the audience. And the final effect of all his complicated work is a plain simplicity! I should need to see this acting at least twice more before I could write on it. The art of it flashed by me like conjuring tricks. I should like the chance to savor it at each instant like old wine.

Herman Wouk has contributed his quota. He has a gift for crisp dialogue unsurpassed by any of our regular writers for the theatre. He has an excellent story to tell, and, in the confrontation of counsel with witnesses, has an exactly appropriate vehicle for his story. We receive each new witness with keen expectancy, follow his replies greedily, laugh over his foibles, applaud at his exit, start over with renewed expectancy at the next arrival, hear with pleasure or indignation what counsel has to say. . . . The march of exits and entrances, questions and answers, attacks and counterattacks, is admirably theatrical. And there are characters which are dramatic in the sense that they are more vivid on the stage than they are in the book. I would especially commend the two psychiatrists— Molière doctors caught in the toils of their *déformations professionnelles*—and the common seaman at a loss to cope with the language of the law (very like the young Negro in the Hiss case) .

But if we like Mr. Wouk so much we should be unfair not to take him as seriously as he takes himself and consider the claim he made in *The New York Times,* through his director, that the play is no mere psychological thriller but a tract for the times telling us to respect authority: mutiny is unjustified even when the argument against a particular commander is a strong one because the important thing is not to save a particular ship but to preserve the authority of commanders; for they win wars while we sit reading Proust. There is a good point here, and there must surely be a good play in it—a play that would show up the sentimentality of our prejudice against commanders and in favor of mutineers. If, however, Mr. Wouk wanted to write such a play, he chose the wrong story and told it in the wrong way, for we spend three quarters of the evening pantingly hoping that Queeg—the commander —will be found insane and the mutineers vindicated. When, in the very last scene, Mr. Wouk explains that this is not the right way to take the story, it is too late. We don't believe him. At best we say that he is preaching at us a notion that ought to have been dramatized. And no amount of shock technique— not even the reiterated image of Jews melted down for soap— can conceal the flaw.

Of course, if you don't take the play seriously, none of this matters: the first part is a thriller, the last scene gives you a moral to take home to the kids. That the two sections are not organically related need disturb no one who is unalterably determined to eat his cake and have it. Others cannot but feel some disappointment at seeing the territory Mr. Wouk opens up to the view but does not touch.

Mr. Wouk's retort to sentimental radicalism is in order. Yet cannot the New Conservatism—for surely his play belongs in this current of opinion—be equally sentimental, equally ambiguous? It is true that on occasion we owe our lives to naval captains. It may also be true that I owe my life at this moment to the Irish cop on the corner. Must I feel more respect for this cop than for my more sedentary neighbor? It is Mr. Wouk, by the way, who says that the book my neighbor is reading is by Proust. That's so you'll say my neighbor is an egghead. In short, Mr. Wouk carefully stacks the cards. His villain—Keefer —reads highbrow books. His hero—Greenwald—is a Jew. In real life, defense counsel might just as easily have been "Aryan," the villain—like Proust whom he reads—Jewish. But an author who wrote the story this way would *certainly* be accused of stacking the cards; then someone would suggest that Herman Wouk was the pseudonym of Ezra Pound.

There are also technical criticisms one might make. The exposition is not all clear sailing. Without the 300 pages that precede the trial in the book, it is hard to figure who some of the people are, what they have done, why they did it. Willie Keith's place in the book is central: in the play it is none too obvious that we need him at all. The villain Keefer's relation to Maryk, the accused, is carefully shown in those 300 pages. In the play, though it is talked about, we do not see it, we are not even sure whom and what to believe.

This last point is not purely technical: the blurring of the

Keefer story entails the blurring of the Queeg story. And it is because we are not clear about Queeg and his state of mind on the day of the mutiny that we cannot form an opinion on the main issues of the play. Just how crazy does a captain have to be for Mr. Wouk to approve his removal by a subordinate? The answer seems to be: he has to be *plumb* crazy, raving, stark, staring mad. Just how crazy was Queeg? It is impossible to figure. And while precisely this impossibility might make a dramatic theme, it would yield a play with a message decidedly Pirandellian; it would not increase our respect for authority.

The first time most of us saw Charles Laughton was in *Mutiny on the Bounty* when he played the wicked captain against whom officers and crew rose in righteous indignation. Inasmuch as *The Caine Mutiny Court Martial* says that a wicked captain deserves a vote of thanks, it might well have been entitled *Captain Bligh's Revenge*. Luckily, Mr. Laughton and Mr. Wouk are artists and, as such, have not been able to resist the temptation to make their wicked captain as offensive in the modern (i.e. neurotic) way as Captain Bligh was in the old satanic-melodramatic way. The result is, they create a character, and unfold a tale, which no amount of conservatism, new or old, can quite spoil.

Old Possum at Play

THE THEATRE IS a place where it may be the supreme achievement of a T. S. Eliot to provide a good part for an Ina Claire. In *The Confidential Clerk,* Mr. Eliot has not given Miss Claire the funniest lines she ever spoke, or the most shrewdly characterized, but he has caught the speech rhythms of a rich lady with religious longings, and from these Miss Claire can make the highest of high comedy. Such precise timing, such delicate underlining, such subtle modulation from phrase to phrase and word to word are almost unknown to our stage today. Our younger actresses, whose hands creep so nervously about in so many directions, might watch the fewer but righter paths travelled by Miss Claire's. Our light comedians, who so regularly practice the double take and other tricks of the eye and turning head, might profitably watch the quickness of muscle and attention by which Miss Claire avoids having her devices identified as tricks at all.

The rest of the performance is also impressive. Claude Rains offsets Miss Claire's light comedy with a persuasive piece of Ibsenite acting, pathetic and dignified. Joan Greenwood, if she is in some trouble with her more serious speeches, establishes her own bright color at moments when all around seems a little gray. This actress will be a splendid comedienne if she can prevent her vocal peculiarity (an amusing croak, soft loud, loud soft) from becoming her chief interest in life. Douglas Watson gives what is inevitably called a "thoughtful performance" in the title role. He is slightly too elocutionary. One would be less conscious of his vowels and consonants if he would either perfect a British accent or rest content with his American one. And I doubt if the role, though pale, condemns him to be, as he is, less confidential than deferential. Still, this is the most fully molded of the half dozen persuasive and sturdy performances I have seen Mr. Watson give in the past couple of years.

It is probably obvious from my report that the actors in this show seem to go their own way—though there is one, Mr. Newton Blick, who seems to be exactly what the author conceived, neither more, like Miss Claire, nor less, like Mr. Watson. It is hard to gauge the director's work. One could praise E. Martin Browne for giving Miss Claire a free hand or blame him for failing to impose a single style on the whole performance. Possibly Mr. Browne tends to duplicate Mr. Eliot's old-maidishness rather than make up for it; yet the happy corollary of this is that the author suffers none of the betrayals he would have met with at the hands of almost any American director. (Paul Morrison, the designer, has solved the tough problem of presenting the conventionality of a drawing-room and at the same time taking the curse off it—chiefly by slight distortions of angle and outline.)

Is it a good play? I ask myself that question at the first

intermission and suspend judgment. Ditto at the second. Looking around for a taxi when the show is over, I think: "I've been enjoying myself, I've been following every line with interest, once or twice I was moved, several times I was touched, I laughed sometimes, smiled often, why should this be so hard an evening to sum up and appraise?"

That the play is grotesque is the least of it: the whole occasion is grotesque. T. S. Eliot's name is in lights on Broadway! Coriolanus asking the suffrage of the plebs is not a stranger spectacle than Mr. Eliot asking the suffrage of those whose "rave reviews" are reserved for *Dial M for Murder* and *The Seven Year Itch*. Not that Mr. Eliot is a Coriolanus: in some mad medley of humility and ambition he seeks to come to terms with his voters. There are even signs that he has overdone it: the word on Broadway is that Eliot has written an ordinary commercial play and that it is *too* ordinary.

That is Broadway's revenge. Or would be—if it were true. But if anyone should see *The Confidential Clerk* without knowing who wrote it, the last thing he would write in his diary that night would be: "Have just seen typical Broadway play." It is true that the play falls short of both its main objectives: it is neither a great poetic drama nor a great light comedy. It is completely *sui generis*—praiseworthy or not, according to your own position. My position being a reviewer's aisle seat, I must praise the play as more entertaining than 99 shows out of 100—and in a different way. If you like being talked to by an incurably didactic but suave, eloquent, and intelligent uncle, you will enjoy listening to *The Confidential Clerk*. And in fact the Broadway audience does seem to enjoy it. They buckle down most remarkably to the task of following the low-pitched voices of Mr. Browne's actors and the sinuous, melancholy periods of Mr. Eliot's verse.

The extreme didacticism of the dialogue suggests that Eliot had a third objective: to say something. And some of us would have been glad to overlook his shortcomings as poet and comedian, had he seemed at grips with life or even in the grip of an idea. His best dramatic writing was done in the decade of propagandist theatre—the thirties—and was by way of a counterblast at the Marxists. The trouble with *The Confiden-*

tial Clerk—once you are past the first enjoyment of it—is that, though ideas are incessantly talked, there is no energizing and overmastering Idea. If there was a main theme, I had decided by the time the play was over, it was the search for the tradition you are really in. (Since the hero's real father is a second-rate artist, the hero concludes he should resign himself to the same fate.) And I rather think my hesitancy in stating *the* theme is due, not to any sleepiness on my part or any reticence on Mr. Eliot's, but, first, to the fact that there are several themes and, second, to the fact that theme, in this play, scarcely seems to matter. The farcical apparatus seems not to bring it into high relief as in classic comedy but to rub it out. Conversely, the farce is kept from natural eruption into laughter by the avuncular speechmaking. If Mr. Eliot has a gift for thinking, and a gift for comedy, the two gifts, in this play, frustrate each other.

What will *The Confidential Clerk* look like in the list of Mr. Eliot's own writings? As dramaturgy, it marks an advance over the previous plays in one respect: Mr. Eliot has come to see that a play needs a plot. Unhappily, a comic plot fails to justify itself when unsupported by comic rhythm, which is a fast, not to say, diabolical one; and Mr. Eliot, for all his larger qualities, seems, like his more fanatical admirers, totally to lack vivacity. In other respects, the dramaturgy is as limited as before—most notably, the characters are still too dim, too tame. The dialogue might have been put together by an accurate student of the previous plays and poems. The only relationship I could see to the poems was that they are sometimes paraphrased and watered down: the famous garden image of *Ash Wednesday* is explicated as by some New Critic . . .

Am I saying that what Mr. Eliot has written is prose? And is a drama of ideas? Is he turning Shavian? He began his career as critic and dramatist in strong opposition to drama in prose, drama of ideas, and drama by Bernard Shaw; *The Confidential Clerk* has all the earmarks of Shavianism as described by the early Eliot without the merits of the real Bernard Shaw. Perhaps there is some confusion in Eliot's attitude to theatre? Does he like and despise it at the same time? The possibility reminds us less of Shaw than James, who said that in the theatre you always have to throw your cargo overboard to save the ship. What is happening to Mr. Eliot in these latter days? Is he throwing his cargo overboard? (And is that *really* necessary?) Or has he no cargo left to throw? Is he in decline? Or playing possum?

The Idea of a Theatre

IT IS, ALAS, only since his death in 1944 that many of us have come to see that Giraudoux is a man to reckon with. Sketching the development of recent French drama some years back, I picked out only the names of Apollinaire, Cocteau, Obey, and Sartre. Behrman's version of *Amphitryon 38* had given me the impression that Giraudoux could be ignored; I was unschooled then in the ways of adaptors. In Europe around 1950, Giraudoux confronted me wherever I went: I saw *The Trojan War* and *Siegfried* in Zurich, *Electra* in Munich, *Intermezzo* in Rome, and *Ondine* in Paris. My eyes were opened to many things. I saw, for example, how I had come to overestimate the originality of *The Flies;* the mythological plays of Sartre and Anouilh are inconceivable without Giraudoux. More important, I had to grant that here was a first-rank man of letters consecrating his maturity to the theatre, finding in Louis Jouvet at once a great interpreter and a great instructor, and writing plays which constitute a claim to vast originality, plays which, if we accept them, would give to drama itself a new definition. And this definition is one which many modern persons would accept; for it is the definition towards which a great part of modern drama tends. On the technical side, it is a drama in which thought is more important than action or character and in which words are more important than thought. On the philosophical side, it is anti-materialistic, metaphysical, a drama of magic and miracle. I suppose the nearest thing to Giraudoux in our language is Christopher Fry.

Even Mr. Fry is not very near. A more legitimate comparison is with the German Romanticists who gave Giraudoux
both his philosophy and his dramatic technique. In *Ondine*
the German derivation is avowed. The play began with the
theme Giraudoux wrote in college on Fouqué's *Undine*. But
while the German dwells on the narrative—how the water
sprite Undine can have a human soul only so long as her lover
is faithful—Giraudoux shifts the emphasis to love itself. His
sprite represents the pure essence of love; her beloved represents love enmeshed in the ordinary impurities of living. Man
—as defined by this knight—is unfaithful. The story requires
a second woman for him to be unfaithful with; Giraudoux
calls her Bertha. The end cannot but be unhappy.

Trying to summarize *Ondine* I find myself in as much
trouble as with *The Confidential Clerk* and for the same
reason: these plays have a huge periphery and no satisfactory
center, they are full of topics, but if there is a main topic, it is
buried beneath too many jewels of wit and wisdom. That is
what I meant by saying that, in the end, thought is less
important for Giraudoux than words. It is a paradox. There
are no words without thoughts. But where there are too many
thoughts, the effect is of none; the effect is of words, words,
words. We call such writing brilliant; we call the author
distinguished; but we are enjoying ourselves only intermittently and we don't altogether approve. Such at any rate is my
experience of *Ondine,* both in French and English.

Not that the two experiences had very much in common. In
Paris, a program note informed you that there is an obvious
connection between theatre and religious solemnity and that
theatre is in fact a form of divination. Jouvet, who attributed
Giraudoux' success to "the magic of incantation," was apparently going to prove it or have the audience die in his attempt.
Distinguished, like his author, he was also, in this play, an
insufferable bore; French critics told me I missed the wonderful nuances but the French friend who accompanied me
wanted to leave at the first intermission. For my money, an
incantation is no substitute for a play. As for Giraudoux'
contribution, I suspended judgment.

Presumably the New York producers had seen the same

performance and drawn the same conclusion: everything should be entirely different. For I suppose the furthest you can go from Jouvet is a standard leading man from Hollywood, pleasant and uninteresting, handsome and helpless; the only trouble being that at this point you realize what a lot there was to be said for Jouvet. If he scarcely bothered with characterization, Jouvet at least knew what kind of a play he was in. In a work where aroma is all, he may be said to have had, as it were, the right smell; while his counterpart in New York . . .

The failure of Mel Ferrer would not, perhaps, have been fatal, even though his part is a big one, were it not that the rest of the cast (with a single exception) seem to take their cue from him. Or did he and the others take their cue from the director, Alfred Lunt? One cannot but wonder if the latter didn't fall asleep at rehearsals (as I witnessed the French audience doing at Jouvet's production). How otherwise could he have permitted character work at the level of summer stock? And failed to find any "line" of style or meaning? I was also surprised that the designer, Peter Larkin, used—or was allowed to use?—so little imagination. For the Paris production Tchelitchev invented a world of his own; the fairy world of the New York show is pretty much what you'd expect in a children's show on TV. The costumier has reversed Polonius' advice and given us something gaudy not rich. And the three lesser ondines look like strippers from a nightclub act or Gabriel Pascal's idea of courtesans at the time of Androcles.

Amidst all the goings on, Maurice Valency's resolutely prosaic words often sound like a mildly-worded reproof. Mr. Valency has written in *Theatre Arts* that his view of translation is very different from mine. I must say I'd never have guessed it from *Ondine*. I might take exception to certain cuts, but surely what Mr. Valency principally does is to try and write in English what Giraudoux wrote in French? One might have to press the question: does he succeed? were it not undercut by a second: *could* he succeed? What of Giraudoux simply does not come through into English? And it is no fault of a particular translator if the answer is: the aroma; just as it is no fault of his if the aroma is the essence. One may, rather, believe that it is the fault of Giraudoux; for one may believe that, in drama, the aroma ought *not* to be the essence; the words ought not to take precedence of the thoughts, nor the thoughts of the characters and the action.

What is certain is that translation strips Giraudoux' structure rather pitifully naked, and that his second act stands revealed as a piece of desperate improvising. We see here Giraudoux' failure to dramatize the main situation of the play, Bertha not being clearly seen, let alone movingly presented. The text is strewn with indications that the tragic triangle is meant to be grandly moving on the scale, say, of the Tristan story (which is mentioned [1]); but one side of the triangle is missing.

Yet Giraudoux was a man of gifts. If most of them fail to shine through the New York production of *Ondine*, there is one that does not, and that is his gift for creating young girls—or perhaps I should say for providing roles for very young actresses, as it is not precisely the characterization that is remarkable. It is not the girl's personality Giraudoux renders but the sparks it throws off, the radiance that surrounds it. In practical terms, this means that if an actress *can* throw off sparks, if she *is* radiant, Giraudoux will hand her situations and lines to match; in the ideal performance, the actress's contribution might well be larger than his. Audrey Hepburn's Ondine is near enough to the ideal to impress us with this fact. There are technical flaws. An actress shouldn't stand like a *Harper's Bazaar* model—legs flung apart, chest out, arms akimbo, etc. In speaking poetic lines, the identical singsong shouldn't be so often repeated. Speech that calls so much attention to itself makes a weak *r* and overemphatic final consonants all too conspicuous. These are motes in the sun. *Ondine* was worth writing, translating, producing just to place Miss Hepburn on stage in such a role. No one, I think, would speak of great acting. The time to fix Miss Hepburn's rank as an actress hasn't yet arrived. For the moment it is enough to watch such grace and beauty light up the stage, light up the auditorium, and if anyone asks us: what is theatre? to point at this actress and say: *she* is.

---

[1] At any rate, in the French original.

Homosexuality

READERS OF André Gide have inevitably noticed that the play titled *The Immoralist* has precious little to do with the novel that suggested it. There is something immoral about the novel's hero not only in society's opinion but in Gide's: the young man is cruel and selfish, the dramatically interesting point being, perhaps, that his callous neglect of his wife in Africa is in some ways salutary—for his body, for instance; bad is sometimes good; life is complex, disorderly, and to a large extent disgusting. The book is not a likable one, perhaps not even a good one, but the mind and sensibility of Gide are in it; you can't shrug it off.

Since Ruth and Augustus Goetz, the authors of the play, were evidently none too interested in Gide's theme, his mind, or his sensibility, one might deduce that they could go to a novel of his only for its story. But *The Immoralist* has no story; none, at least, that is pushed to the point of drama, an art in which the complexities of the world have to be concentrated in the relations of a small group of individuals. Gide's hero has a roving eye, and we are privy to many of his thoughts as his eye roves. For stage purposes, the Goetzes find themselves forced to invent characters for the eye to rove *to*.

Why would anyone want to adapt a novel that doesn't lend itself to adaptation? Ask what characters the Goetzes have to invent, and you have the answer. The two chief ones are homosexual partners for the protagonist. The Goetzes wanted to write about homosexuality.

Who doesn't? It is the subject of the hour. Why? Is homosexuality spreading or are we simply more and more aware of it? Unanswerable questions! What we may more profitably ask is where any pronouncement on the subject stands in the evolution of a more rational attitude to it. For, surely, since the time when the prostitutes danced on the sidewalk to celebrate the conviction of Oscar Wilde, public opinion has changed considerably. The Goetzes' play seems to have been conceived to carry a message of tolerance; if it does not spring from an understanding of the original *Immoralist*, it springs from sympathy for the married homosexual who wrote it. The play is a portrait of Gide seen through the spectacles of a generous humanitarianism. The message is pretty explicit in the speeches of a family retainer who asks the angry brother-in-law to be kind and in utterances of the protagonist himself, like (I quote from memory): "We didn't invent this problem."

Humanitarianism is generous by definition; by tradition it is rather misty-eyed and thick-headed. The kindness of so many humanitarians is the sort that kills; they must be kind only to be cruel. The Goetzes' kindness to their protagonist is so great they finally take the dilemma on which he is impaled and saw off its horns. The question has been: what can a homosexual husband do—assuming that his wife loves him and that he needs her affection? The answer proffered in the last scene of the play is that he can do without homosexuality! Or can he? This is modern drama. We can end, if we like, with a question mark. What the Goetzes don't seem to have realized is that this is not to ask a question but to beg one—and that, the main question of their play. Perhaps the honest ending would have been to let the husband stay with the wife, both of them knowing that there would also be young men. Is this more than the public of 1954 would take? Possibly; but a humanitarian playwright would be interested in putting the matter to the test. To write a didactic play is to suppose yourself ahead of the public and to suppose the public in need of your advice. A didactic playwright can write *only* plays that are more than the public will take.

There is a kind of liberalism which is safely reactionary. It offers you all the soft and self-congratulatory emotion of reformism without demanding that you run the risks. The chief trick of the pseudo-liberal is to fare boldly forward toward the heroic goal, then to slink quietly off at the last moment in the hope that no one is looking. It is certainly a handy trick when you're writing for the New York theatre where the critics start deciding what to say in the intermission; many is the last act which escapes unobserved.

The goal the Goetzes were making for was the open presentation of homosexuality and the open advocacy of a humane attitude to it. Up to now, as Gide told them in an interview, homosexuality in the theatre has been an accusation. Its standard form at present is, in fact, the *unjust* accusation; for our public has reached the point where it will allow the subject of homosexuality to come up, provided that the stigma is removed before the end of the evening. Our public's motto is: tolerance—provided there is nothing to tolerate. The Goetzes could hardly turn *The Immoralist* into *Tea and Sympathy*, but if our hero can't say he didn't do it in the past, can't we ask him to try not to do it in the future? If we can't teach our audience, can't we teach our hero? *He* at least must do as we say.

In short, the Goetzes stuck on a final scene that recalls the final scene of *The Caine Mutiny Court Martial* in its impertinence and its last-minute conformism. It is not true that what precedes that scene is uniformly undramatic. There is a drama in the story, though I don't think the Goetzes have written it, and I know Gide hasn't written it for them. It is a triangle drama in which the third party is the husband's lover. The Goetzes, at one point, even suggest a possible approach: the young man is an immoralist, not in being homosexual, but in insisting on having both wife and lover, in refusing to choose between them. The idea is neither confirmed, controverted, nor otherwise developed.

Oddly enough, it is the hero's two male partners who come off best theatrically—perhaps because they are played by two very skilful young actors, David Stewart and James Dean. The two principals—Louis Jourdan and Geraldine Page—do not fill the yawning gaps of the script. Mr. Jourdan plays with discretion, even with beauty, but gives no impression of being a complicated person or even an intellectual: his archeological papers and books are the merest externals. Geraldine Page does her usual act, a good one in itself, syncopated and fluttery, but without relation to this play. She did not make us feel she was a very powerful counterattraction to the boys. And that the directing of Daniel Mann did not impose unity or even unbroken intensity on the material may or may not be a reflection on Mr. Mann; there were scenes (such as Miss Page's drunk scene) which did seem to have benefited from his presence.

Despite damaging reviews, the play is not a flop. It has shock value. In the intermission you hear dowagers asking if such things can be; the male prostitutes on Times Square are easy to overlook for those who see New York through taxi windows.

Reigen Comes Full Circle

REIGEN by Arthur Schnitzler—known to American readers as *Hands Around* or *Round Dance*—was privately printed in Vienna in the winter of 1896–7 and published at the turn of the century. In 1918 Max Reinhardt acquired the stage rights. In 1920 the world première took place—not, as it happened, under Reinhardt's direction—at the Kleines Schauspielhaus in Berlin. The Kulturministerium declared it illegal, but the play continued to run until certain Nazistic friends of morality let off stink bombs in the theatre. In November, 1921, the producers and performers found themselves on trial. They were well defended; and acquitted. *Reigen* began to be produced all over Germany. But the age of morality was not dead; the stink was spreading. Accused of being a dirty-minded Viennese Jew, Arthur Schnitzler decided that his play would never again be performed so long as it was protected by copyright. (It is of curious interest that the leader of the agitation against *Reigen*, one Karl Brunner, was awarded the Goethe Medal by Adolf Hitler in 1942.) Arthur Schnitzler died in 1931. His son and heir, now a professor at UCLA, still tries to keep the play off the boards.

Since, however, Arthur Schnitzler had parted with certain French rights to *Reigen* before he decided to veto performances, the work can be legally presented, not only in France, but all over the world *as a film*; and it is as a French film—*La Ronde*—that the world, including, by a decision of the Supreme Court, the State of New York, knows it. It is good that the friends of morality in New York should have received a defeat at the hands of the friends of *Reigen*. But it is unfortunate that America is permitted to see this film while being forbidden to see the play. Production of the play is, at this point, morally desirable—as a corrective to the distortions which the director Max Ophuls has imposed on the film.

It is the kind of film we call good when we mean "not utterly banal." It is better than that. There are real actors in it. There is a real sophistication in the showmanship. Late Saturday night, if you feel like seeing a little French bedroom comedy, and don't mind its not being one of the best, you can see *La Ronde* and like it. Go really late, so you'll be nearly as tired as Mr. Ophuls must have been when he made the scenario.

That, if you revive an older work, you must "do something" to it is an assumption by no means new to the entertainment business. The term "revival" itself embodies the fallacy. If a work were indeed dead, you couldn't bring it to life. If it is still alive, its life is its own; to ignore this fact, to try and give it another kind of life, will probably be to kill it. The intention is revival; what happens is murder. A recent example, in my view, is Marc Blitzstein's version of Bertolt Brecht's *Threepenny Opera*.[1] The attempt to give Brecht life of another sort has been to kill the sort of life he does have. (Since personal motives are sometimes imputed to my criticism—a story circulated recently that my praise of an actress had been written in her dressing-room with her assistance—I should not conceal from any reader that I collaborated on another English version of Brecht's play. I'm not satisfied with this version either.) The adaptor of *Reigen* has committed the same murder as the adaptor of *Threepenny Opera*—betraying his author by removing the style and meaning—but with a different weapon. The classic irony of a Brecht or a Schnitzler (I do not mean to equate them) can be destroyed either by sheer weight on the one hand or by sheer lack of it on the other—by crudity or by whimsicality, coarseness or cuteness, ugliness or prettiness, Mr. Blitzstein or Mr. Ophuls. *La Ronde* is flippant and effete.

[1] Itself an example of the opposite. See p. 101.

What's wrong with flippancy? Many movies would gain by
it. We are taken aback in *La Ronde* because Schnitzler had
been writing *about* flippancy and *against* it. *Reigen* embodies
a keen sense of life as both tragic and comic; life in *La Ronde*
is never more than a moment of pathos, a moment of absurdity, a juicy incident, a passing titillation, sour romance, wry
farce. . . . Does life matter? Does this film matter? Schnitzler's
serious sadness has shrunk to a cheap cynicism. One may justly
say of the film that it is not even pornographic, and sympathize—sincerely enough—with those who came to snigger and
remained to snore. In pornography you feel the pressure of
some human impulse, however juvenile or neurotic. Cheap
cynicism makes you feel absolutely nothing. Of all attitudes it
is the most dispensable. Leaves you cold? Not even that. It
leaves you at whatever temperature it finds you.

There are directors who get good work out of not very good
actors. Mr. Ophuls has managed to take very good actors and
get bad work out of them. In the case of Anton Walbrook, it
may not be that the acting is bad; he has a part, possibly, that
could under no circumstances seem good, the part of a master
of ceremonies who moves—isn't life a dream? in Vienna, I
mean, among the waltzes?—from 1950 back to 1900, turns the
crank of a carousel, and smirks at all the copulation. If you
want a really naughty film, Mr. Walbrook works hard to give
it to you.

This is an actor who gave one of the best performances I
have seen in English-speaking theatre as Gregers in *The Wild
Duck,* a part which demands a Schnitzlerian mingling of
thoughtful laughter and tears too deep for thoughts. That's
nothing; Mr. Ophuls can even break the spell cast by Jean
Louis Barrault. The means he adopts are a little crude: bad
lighting and the camera too far away. But no doubt the motive
was less to destroy Barrault than to do cute and continental
camera work. Gérard Philippe is lost in character make-up,
and, with him, Schnitzler's character.

Some of the other actors come off better. Serge Reggiani
contributes a racy bit of French realism as a common soldier.
As Wife and Student, Danielle Darrieux and Daniel Gelin
play one sequence with delicious humor but it is not to be

overlooked that this sequence is Schnitzler verbatim. (A play, we know, needs a lot of adapting to the screen; yet the best parts of this film—and some others?—are the dramatic dialogue unchanged.) What Fernand Gravet, no doubt under direction, does with the Husband is typical of the film as a whole: he ignores the character as written and substitutes a cliché. (The husband and wife scene opens with the husband going over his accounts in bed with his wife beside him.) Schnitzler's Young Gentleman is called here a Student (because he reads a book?) ; the Count is a hussar out of musical comedy. The waltzes are by Oscar Straus. In fact what Straus did long ago to Shaw's *Arms and the Man,* Max Ophuls has now done to Schnitzler's *Reigen:* he has converted a satire into the thing satirized. The legend of Gay Vienna—recently denounced by Schnitzler Jr. and denounced by implication in all the works of Schnitzler Sr.—has again carried the day.

Acting, Sex-appeal, Democracy

THEATRE, I SUPPOSE, is the most strongly and directly erotic of the arts. In a theatre you do not merely enjoy passionate images as in painting or "the imagination of love in sound" (W. J. Turner's definition of music) ; from your seat in the orchestra you can fall in love with an actual actress. And so kings have gone round to dressing rooms to find their mistresses, and Dr. Johnsons have had to stop going there because their "amorous propensities" were too much inflamed by "white bosoms and silk stockings." Even on celluloid Rudolph Valentino could enamour millions, and Mary Pickford become "America's sweetheart."

The case of Valentino is simple: he was attractive in the most immediate way. With him belong all the young persons of both sexes whose physical charms people will pay money to see. I do not think he would ever have been called America's lover; the land of the pilgrims' pride requires a "sweetheart"

to take home to mom; Miss Pickford was less the object of love
than a symbol of what ought to be loved. And, as the movies
have come more and more under the domination of ideology
(chiefly Catholic), the Valentinos and Jean Harlows have
given way to the "wholesome" types.

I shall plead the fifth amendment, as it were, and not name
names. My point is that the erotic content of movies became,
not less—just less direct. If movie actors weren't simply objects
of desire they still belonged more to the erotic than to the artistic realm. They became folk symbols. If possible, they symbolized something *above* the common level, like dashing
heroism, or marital fidelity. But more and more often they
have come to symbolize the common level itself. They mirror
the poverty of our spiritual life rather than reduce it. Isn't that
democracy?

In the legitimate theatre, we have a name for the kind of
performer who establishes an indirectly erotic relation with
the audience without offering anything much that we could
call Acting or a Performance. It is Personality. I have suggested alternative interpretations of the word; [1] but that is the
standard one. The great current example is Shirley Booth.

I don't mean she *cannot* act, I mean she doesn't have to.
Within a certain range, she happens also to be an actress of
diabolical accuracy. She can carry her body as such people
carry their bodies, look over her shoulder as such people look
over their shoulders, speak—in pronunciation, speech melody,
emphasis—as such people talk—such people, that is, as she
herself is (at least in her public personality, which is all I
know). This, along with the gift of projection, makes her a
stage personality and, for some parts—or perhaps just one part
—the right actress. What could be more satisfactory on occasions when a playwright has rewritten her several parts, her one
part? Miss Booth's appearance in *By the Beautiful Sea* is
something else. This work is a banal musical comedy made
interesting by Miss Booth's "personality." It works. That is to
say, it *is* interesting to sit at the side—I had a chair in the aisle
—with one eye on Miss Booth and the other on her lover, the
public. These days it is the woman who makes the advances,

[1] See above, pp. 31, 55, 87, 130.

and the man who responds—in proportion as he finds in the
woman, not a goddess, not even a female, but himself. Someone has said Miss Booth is the very symbol of democracy. If
democracy means that the common man is delighted with the
common man, this is true.

It is unfair to pick on Miss Booth. Danny Kaye is a more
glaring example. Making love in public has been done before;
Mr. Kaye manages to make love *with* the public—and this, so
to speak, in private: a theatre critic who enters here is disturbing the privacy of Mr. Kaye's amours. (On his last New York
appearance I was excluded—with perfect propriety, I have to
admit—by the Palace management.) If Mr. Kaye has his private experience in public, I once had occasion to note that the
converse is also true. In private he was very public; his eyes
were glazed; focussed, if at all, on a distant spot; on that
occasion, in fact, Mr. Kaye proved unable to perform before a
small, intimate audience, with all faces visible. He said he
needed a mass audience or he couldn't summon his energies.
Individual faces had to merge in the one, featureless physiog-
nomy of the Mass. That also sounds to me like democracy—
People's Democracy.

Of course it is unfair to pick on Mr. Kaye either. My grudge
is not against him or Miss Booth but only against those who
confuse these amorous carryings-on with theatre. Not to be
unfair yet again, the emotional relations of a stage personality
and his audience provide *a kind* of theatre. One can complain
only if it pushes out the other kinds, only if the idea of the
actor as doer, performer, craftsman disappears before the idea
of the actor as democratic personality; and this with the support of professional writers on the subject. That there is a
public which wouldn't know the difference between a Danny
Kaye and a Charlie Chaplin—or which might even prefer
Danny Kaye—is merely unfortunate; that those who write on
theatre should be equally undiscriminating is a scandal. One
suspects that fewer and fewer of the latter can tell the difference between personality and ability, between sex-appeal (direct or indirect) and acting.

When a New York theatre critic likes an actress, how does he
say so? He declares (I will not mimic the lingo of his enthu-

siasm in full) that he has "lost his heart" to her, that he "loves" her, "adores" her, and so on. This is primarily, I suppose, because he is more affected by Eros than by Thespis, by sex-appeal than by dramatic art. (No one wants to throw Eros out; but there are those who don't care whether Thespis ever gets in.) There is another reason for not saying anything about an actress except that she's Mahvellous and you Adaw Her and this is that it's hard to find any other words. Acting is hard to write about.

I should certainly include myself in a general complaint and admit that when I look back over my theatre reviews I am mortified to note how little I have said about the acting performances I have seen. How little dramatic criticism gets beyond the review of the school play in the school magazine with its pious list of names and the reward for each name a single epithet! And I am not merely regretting that good performances are so meagerly recognized. Badness in acting is often not spotted these days, and even oftener not mentioned. Because the press is much harsher with playwrights, it is a common occurrence in New York that a bad performance of a good play is called a good performance of a bad play. Even when an actor or actress ruins a play, there are critics to write that, though the play is poor, the enchanting Miss So-and-so almost redeems it. They don't say of course in what way she is enchanting unless some trait of her personality can be summed up in one of the other half-dozen stock adjectives.

I submit that any reviewer who proposes to judge an actor should ask the following questions. First, is his interpretation in line with the author's intention? This may seem rather an obvious question to ask, but in fact it is never asked in the case of new plays because the critics are not expected to have read the script; hence they cannot know what the author's intentions are. Second, if an actor's interpretation is not simply coterminous with the author's ideas, is this good or bad? If the actor has added or subtracted, was the result a happy one or not? Third, aside from all questions of interpretation, was tonight's performance alive? The role of Shylock can be newly, correctly, profoundly interpreted and still not be given a good performance. I don't only mean when it is played by a bad actor but also when it is played by a good actor whose performance tonight (maybe not last night) was lifeless. From these three main questions, we can proceed to others. Is the performance alive only in moments or continuously? If it is sustained throughout the evening, has it the right shape, the right curve, from the first scene to the last? (A critic cannot just say "monotonous"; he must know where the changes should have come by which monotony would have been avoided; and what changes they should have been.) And so forth.

Defending myself and others, I should add that to write meaningfully about actors requires more space than the journalist critic even on the weeklies has at his disposal. The only critic who seems to have enough room is Mr. Wolcott Gibbs of *The New Yorker*, and he evidently prefers telling the story of the play.

The Standard Story

I HAVE BEEN asked why I review only "smash hits or plays of unusual intellectual interest." The reason—if this definition of my coverage is correct—is that if I tried to do the opposite and mention all the shows, this chronicle would be little more than a catalog. Nor do I mean to imply that shows I did not review are beneath contempt. Take two from the 1953–4 season: *The Magic and the Loss* by Julian Funt and *The Girl on the Via Flaminia* by Alfred Hayes.

They are both good productions—and this remark is, in a sense, sufficient commendation, since we are talking about theatre, and since, too, we are talking about a theatre in which many, many productions are not good. It was worth the trip to the Booth Theatre to see how Uta Hagen and Robert Preston cope with Mr. Funt's play. It was worth the trip to see a gifted new actor, Charles Taylor, cast as the son of the older pair. Mr. Hayes' play is directed by Jose Quintero and was moved onto Broadway from Circle in the Square, when the latter, located in Greenwich Village, was condemned by the fire department. The Circle's choice of plays has not been enterprising; Mr. Quintero's directing often rubs me (for one) the wrong way; and yet I would not abstain from the general vote of confidence which the group has won, nor minimize Mr. Quintero's achievement in giving his productions the imprint of his own personality.

Presenting a close-up of middle-class life in Manhattan, *The Magic and the Loss* tells how a business-woman comes to be threatened with the simultaneous loss of a son, a lover, and a job. *The Girl on the Via Flaminia*, as novel readers will agree, tells how, in 1944–5, an Italian girl agrees to be the mistress of a GI she does not know, how she is made to feel a whore and a traitor, and how she kills herself. In *The Girl*, then, we have a conflict between conqueror and conquered, American and European, the theme, I suppose, being the failure of Americans to understand. In *The Magic*, the conflict is that between career woman and her men, also that between modern (i.e., divorced) parents and their children, also . . . but conflict and theme are all too manifold in this play. All I wish to prove is that, if these plays are neither smash hits nor satisfactory works of art, it cannot be from any frivolity of intention, any ignorance as to where stories are to be found, or any lack of judgment as to what is important in our world. The material both authors went to is excellent. We have to feel grateful to them for locating the quarry and going so manfully to work with spade, pick and—yes—dynamite. What fine stone! It is only later that we feel let down—when we see our authors either offering for sale the unhewn rock or hurriedly, with hammer and chisel, chipping out mechanical imitations of the sculpture on the bargain counter at the junk shop.

Raw material or non-art, manipulated material or pseudo-art: there is a good deal of both in *The Magic and the Loss*. For most of the evening, this play is so resolutely literal, we can hardly accept it as a play at all. What we think we are getting is one of those naturalistic documents which proceed, as it were, across a prairie of dreary troubles to the bare rocky mountain of death. Such a play has to end in death because, in life as presented, there really is nothing to do but die. True, this kind of drama cannot be profound or even highly entertaining, but it can have the dour virtues: common sense, consistency, sincerity, *et al.* In the last few minutes, however, Mr. Funt changes his mind, *ex*changes it, perhaps I should say, for a commercial substitute, replaces the child in his own cradle with a mechanical doll marked Made in Hollywood and answering with a mindless squeak to the name of Happy Ending. (Terence Rattigan did it—in the American version of *The Deep Blue Sea*—so why shouldn't Mr. Funt?) While conveniently offstage, a young boy undergoes a change of life; and, along with his character as presented while *on* stage, turns the plot around. In the New Brunswick depot, he drops his hate of his mother, picks love instead, and returns as the god from the New Jersey machine. It is curious that an author who for so long doggedly refuses to depart from the literal will plunge of a sudden deep into the absurd. A necessary compensation? A last-minute attempt to get some drama into the story, stemming from a last-minute realization that the little literal truths are undramatic? Yet if we swing from the small simple truths to big simple lies, the big complicated truths in which all drama is found are ignored. I do not think Mr. Funt wants to ignore them; he simply hasn't allowed himself to get at them. Yet he has achieved more than this brief and oversimplifying analysis discloses. The material is always impressing us with its possibilities, and sometimes it breaks the dam of Mr. Funt's naturalism, gushing out in a humor and a pathos that are genuine enough. Then again, this is an author full of bright remarks about New York life.

In *The Girl on the Via Flaminia,* Mr. Hayes faces some of the same problems and notably the same story—should one call it the standard story of modern drama?—the story of the girl who is being hounded to death. And he sees it through: no Happy Ending for him. What his play seems to need is a happy beginning: Mr. Hayes' girl is dead at the start and goes right on being dead for three acts. There is no development, or, if there is, just as it seems to begin, the girl jumps in the Tiber. Mr. Hayes has presented, not a drama, but a situation. It is, let me add, a truly touching situation, and we appreciate the respect and curiosity Mr. Hayes brings to his people—especially the GI lover (played with respect, curiosity, and fire by Leo Penn).

In denying his protagonist all development, Mr. Hayes gives his leading actress a practically insoluble problem. I sometimes think our naturalistic dramatists have a wrong approach not only to parts as characters but to parts as roles. We say an actor "builds" a role. The metaphor can be misleading. What an author provides is not a pile of loose bricks which an actor can put together as he chooses. Unless the author has done some building himself, the actor can achieve none of those effects which will make an audience feel that he is great. If building is the right metaphor, we should say that the actor adds an imposing façade to a building that must already be there.

These plays of the little depressing facts, especially when they are also the play about the hounded girl, are notoriously monotonous. There is no building; just a nicely levelled bit of land. What can an actress do? If she is a virtuoso, she can force variety into a play that lacks it, and we shall enjoy the *tour de force*. There was something of this about Miss Hagen's extraordinary display in *The Magic*. I gather that Peggy Ashcroft, when she played in *The Deep Blue Sea,* also was so effective she made you see the mirage of a façade of a building that wasn't there. (I didn't see Miss Hagen in this play; Margaret Sullavan, whom I saw, was . . . monotonous.) For Betty Miller, playing Mr. Hayes' "girl," I have nothing but sympathy. She is not a virtuoso, but just another of Mr. Quintero's gifted New Actresses with a sensitive soul and wandering fingers. Bringing to the role considerable talent, tact, and concentration, she has been oddly singled out for criticism in a production that includes several vastly inferior performances—even a couple of rank amateurish ones. At this point, it should be firmly said, the actress is a scapegoat for the author.

Tea, Sympathy, and the Noble Savage

THE ESTHETICISM that is currently prominent in English theatre differs from the estheticism of the eighteen-nineties in that it is directed at the whole educated middle class; it is in no sense *avant-garde*. It can therefore make no headway in America, for the middle class here is unashamedly sentimental and earnest; it likes even a musical (*South Pacific*) dosed with humanitarian ideas. Our lighter works do not smell of decay; they reek with sentiment. Our authors cannot see what fun it is to fly the trapeze through a vacuum like Cocteau and his English epigones. While the European esthete strenuously endeavors to mean nothing, in America every author wants to mean everything.

For example, the authors of *The Teahouse of the August Moon,* John Patrick and Vern Sneider. This play was heralded with a glum essay in *The New York Times* and is punctuated by solemn animadversions on the same theme, to wit, the failure of the West to understand the East. I remember feeling sorry for Thomas Heggen when Joshua Logan made of his melancholy reporting a histrionic romp that had everything of musical comedy except the music. I can say nothing for or against Mr. Sneider, not having read his book. What is clear from merely seeing the play is that it lives exactly as the final version of *Mister Roberts* lived—only as one very limited kind of theatre. It never gets outside the small world of vaudeville sketches, and inside that world it lives as powerfully as *Mister Roberts* only through one character, a *Mister Roberts* character, the bad captain—here re-incarnate as a colonel, splendidly played by Paul Ford, who makes you laugh every time he speaks and sometimes even when he doesn't. Of the other actors the only one who is (or has a chance to be?) more than adequate is David Wayne, and even he somewhat spoils his performance by excessive coyness. I hasten to agree that, if not taken seriously, it's a nice show, my objections to a nice show being only the normal objections to a nice girl.

But perhaps it should be taken seriously after all? Is it light entertainment? On a stomach that had imbibed Robert Anderson's tea and sympathy only a week earlier, it lay a little heavy. So much more of exactly the same diet is hard to digest. The tea is tolerable enough, it's the sympathy—and its correlative antipathies. Let me explain.

The sympathy is for the Okinawans. An Oriental friend tells

me he regards *Teahouse* less as a compliment to the East than as a perpetuation of "the *Mikado* tradition" according to which Orientals are cute and infantile. We of the West probably wouldn't place the play precisely in that context, but we certainly can see it in the tradition of the Noble Savage, always dear to our dramatists. The Noble Savage, nowadays, is usually Latin-American, Sicilian, or plain Italian. *Teahouse of the August Moon* puts him back in the Pacific Ocean which was his home in the days of *Mourning Becomes Electra* and *Mutiny on the Bounty*.

The point the playwrights always made about the Noble Savage was that he wasn't really a savage at all; it was our non-savage fellow citizens who were savage; the miscalled savage lived at peace with nature and himself. Applied to the current world situation in *Teahouse of the August Moon* and *The Girl on the Via Flaminia*, the idea is that Orientals and Latins are better than Americans. So far as I know, only Americans *have* applied the idea to the world situation; and, if Orientals and Latins applied it, I suppose they'd have to say that Americans are better than Orientals and Latins. For the intention, insofar as it is rational, is the noble one of blaming yourself and not the other fellow; the only trouble being that the pattern is not only a rational intention; it appeals to something in us that is sub- and even anti-rational. The notion that they "do these things better in France" is a dangerous illusion not only because it spreads a pleasant falsehood about France but because the implied attitude to one's own country is not at all limited to rational self-criticism. Part of its content is self-hatred; another part, sheer diffidence (surely not a virtue); and another motif involved is the impulse to dramatize and simplify which takes the form of arriving at your opinion by mere inversion of the enemy's opinion: rabid nationalists think foreigners are wicked, Americans noble, *ergo* . . .

On Broadway, Okinawans are sweet-natured and wise, Americans irate and stupid; Italians are passionate and sensitive, Americans coldly sensual and callous. "*You* may have Leonardo," says the American protagonist of *The Girl on the Via Flaminia*. "But we have U.S. Steel"; while his opposite number on the Latin side—a young Italian from Mussolini's African army—quotes Leopardi. At this point the Noble Savage has dropped the last remnant of his savagery and is a cultivated gentleman, heir of the ages.

It should hardly be necessary to say that implacable criticism of America is a perennial task of American liberalism. But if playwrights venture into politics—and *Teahouse* is to be performed on Okinawa itself in the name of international goodwill!—they lay themselves open to political criticism— that is, to criticism in terms of the present situation and not simply in terms of universal principle. To paint a romanticized picture of common people in other lands in order to contrast it with the crass behavior of American colonels and GI's who prate about U.S. Steel is a political act; a cultural historian could scarcely fail to link it with the picture presented in books, movies, magazines, newspapers, and plays issuing from the other side of the iron curtain.

I am not trying to tie our authors to Malenkov in the way in which they might be tempted to tie me to McCarthy. It is simply that our criticism of America is only good when its motives are healthy; when it doesn't take the form of rhetorical patterns and the merest folk-lore; in short, when it is truthful. As for foreigners, I return to my Oriental friend's remark. Messrs. Sneider and Patrick wanted to pay him a compliment. He took it—rightly, I think—as an insult. Our playwrights should place the whole question of patriotism and international goodwill under advisement.

Or make sure that we don't take them seriously.

Who Are You Rooting For?

AMERICAN WRITERS have more success with light comedy than with other forms of drama. In fact American light comedy has become one of the more vital elements of world theatre. Even in Europe the lively item in a current repertoire is not unlikely to be an American light comedy—perhaps one that the youngest generation here has never seen, such as *Three Men on a Horse* or *The Man Who Came to Dinner*. And anyone who read through the plays of the twenties and thirties would, I believe, be less inclined to exhume the problem plays of those problem decades than, say, *The Torchbearers* or *Boy Meets Girl*.

Reviewing American light comedies, however, I find myself continually remarking the same flaw: an intrusion of crass sentimentality. If the greatest of American comedies are Chaplin's films, it is to be noted that we find the flaw there too. We find it again in the two best light comedies of the 1953-4 season, *Oh, Men! Oh, Women!* by Edward Chodorov and *King of Hearts* by Jean Kerr and Eleanor Brooke. Are American authors unwilling to stay inside the boundaries of light merriment? Pursued by some notion of "adding a third dimension, that of feeling," they only succeed in pushing their fists through the perfectly satisfactory two-dimensionality of their canvases. That, at least, is my interpretation of the sudden eruption of the passions at various points in both plays, accompanied, as it is, with a sudden access of morality on the part of the authors. All of a sudden, the smile disappears, and we are invited to take a devout interest in the needs of children, the duties of parents, the responsibilities of spouses and psychoanalysts, not to mention the promptings of the heart and that Note of Hope which is the Broadway-Hollywood surrogate for a shot in the arm.

It is surprising, perhaps, to what an extent the two plays are the same old one: variants on that classic theme of comedy, the misadventures of a professional imposter. Mr. Chodorov's psychoanalyst and the Brooke-Kerr comic-strip artist both think they are gods. The plot in both cases is one long attempt, on the authors' part, to humanize them by humiliation. In *Oh, Men! Oh, Women!* the attempt is successful. In *King of Hearts*, it is not: the protagonist is beyond cure. In this respect, it is the Chodorov that is more characteristic of American light comedy, the Brooke-Kerr play that will come in for criticism as being heterodox and heartless, if not dangerous and un-American. Brooks Atkinson says so bad a man as this king of hearts weighs a light comedy down. Wolcott Gibbs says he arouses such loathing that the actor in the part runs the risk of assassination. From the first critic, I derive this principle: a monstrous character has no place in light comedy. From the second, this: a monstrous character has no place on stage. Both principles are an established part of Times Square folklore.

Should I rather say Times Square philosophy? For implicit in New York journalism is a whole philosophy of drama according to which it is good that characters in plays be good —or at least likable; it is good that the playwright's view of life be: People Are Nice. Sometimes this thought takes a political form and might be summed up as Democratic Good Will. At other times it seems to be a theory of audience psychology. "We must care about the characters." Well, that much is easy to agree to, but the New York theory of drama is that you only care when you also sympathize—or, in the jargon of the intellectual underworld, "empathize." With whom can you identify yourself? "Who are you rooting for?" Like football.

I suppose it is one of the philosophies or pseudo-philosophies that constitute the growing pains of democracy. It is wildly untraditional. The traditional way of telling the impostor story is exemplified in Carl Sternheim's *The Snob*. Sternheim wastes no more sympathy on his hero than Ben Jonson did on Morose or Molière on Tartuffe: he confronts us with a man who is completely dehumanized by snobbery, a non-man, a monster. Now *King of Hearts* is no classic, but what was generally written off as its weakness is classic enough and constitutes its strength: the protagonist is a bad man who, having no goodness in him at all, cannot conceivably turn into an angel in the last act. Such a character is not felt but seen; his authoresses see him and, with their abundant and admirably non-mechanical wit, enable us to see him too. Why should we want them to be sentimentalists, blinded by their own tears? (It was a possibility; there are sentimental moments.)

Both *Oh, Men! Oh, Women!* and *King of Hearts* are well performed. It is almost *de rigueur* on Broadway that a light comedy be well performed; it is only "serious plays" that are—too often anyway—left to the untender mercies of Passionate Sincerity or Ruthless Realism. Light comedy has to be acted. And it sets a director as hard a task as he will ever be asked to perform. Anyone can direct a mere play; it takes a George Abbott to direct light comedy; Edward Chodorov (directing his own play) and Walter Kerr (tackling *King of Hearts*) place themselves in the Abbott tradition in their devising of excellent "business," in their adroit manipulation of "props," and, above all, in their brisk pacing and hair's-breadth timing. Their casting was also extraordinary. If the leading part in the Chodorov didn't, so to speak, deserve Franchot Tone, it certainly needed him, for he can almost make sentimentality seem unsentimental and passivity seem active. The perfect work of the show has of course to be done in the perfect (though small) roles. Anne Jackson does a finely etched discontented wife (vintage 1953). Gig Young and Larry Blyden do such ironic and shaded, yet zany and extravagant, performances as would qualify them in France for great parts in classic plays. (I am thinking of the great character work M. Barrault's company showed us.) Walter Kerr did some inspired casting. Who would have thought of Jackie Cooper for the amiable but mousy suitor? How solve the problem of a heroine who must be stupid and not stupid at the same time—except by appealing to Cloris Leachman's looks and talent? And as for Donald Cook . . . It would have been very well for the critics to say their Christian charity, their democratic zeal, or their bad digestion prevented them from accepting a stage monster, had they gone on to remark that Mr. Cook has his own way of making the public swallow him. His own way? The classic way: he keeps the actor and the character separate and induces the audience to love one while hating the other—as actors of the part of Richard III or any other enjoyable (but not sympathetic) villain have done for centuries. In view of *Private Lives* and *The Moon is Blue,* the personality and technique of Mr. Cook should have been already familiar. I confess that, until now, I didn't quite "get" either. *King of Hearts* is his show. His feline walk, his funny drawl with its inordinate vowels, his sure-fire smile, along with whatever is less definable in an actor, though no less real, make of an ambivalent presentation an uncompromising performance and an unequivocal success.

Crafty Godliness

> *I love the stage*
> *And hate to see it made the prostitute*
> *Of crafty godliness.*
>
> —JOHN DAVIDSON

HERE IS A SENTENCE I never thought I should live to write: I have just seen a play by T. S. Eliot in summer stock. Never, at any rate, until the last couple of years. By now it is *The New York Daily News* that's convinced Mr. Eliot is a playwright, and only the highbrows of the *Times* and *Tribune* who aren't so sure. The paradox is one Eliot invited. He has stressed the point that dramatic poetry is unlike other poetry; he can hardly be surprised if some admire his dramas in proportion as they are unlike *all* poetry. This brings the wheel full circle, for Eliot's interest in the drama began with his complaint that, of late, it had become prosaic.

Among those who know all Eliot's writings, there is, I think, general agreement that his plays are his least successful achievement. Just because of this, there is now a danger of dismissing them too lightly—as for instance with the formula that they are *simply* an attempt at commercial playwriting. Actually, the commercial theatre knows of no plays that resemble them in more than externals. Nor can the plays be neatly amputated from the body of Eliot's *oeuvre*.

To take a technical and trivial example: the quotations and obscurities. For a commercial playwright it would certainly be odd to slip a chunk of Conan Doyle or Shelley into the dialogue and not say so or to bury the plot of the *Alcestis* so deep that it has to be exhumed in *Comparative Literature*, Vol. 5, No. 2. I am far from offering these instances in Eliot's defense; on the contrary they bring out the old (J. Donald) Adam (s) in me: such carrying-on strikes me as beside all possible points. And, while I do not agree that *The Cocktail Party* is unclear in its main drift, there are certainly passages in it that convey just about nothing, either to me or to certain Eliot experts whom I've consulted. I can only suppose that those who say "Drama, not Poetry" were busy with their own dramatic and unpoetic thoughts while these passages were being spoken.

If Eliot failed, it wasn't because he took it easy. The real cause is the opposite: over-ambition. Eliot is trying to write a kind of play he cannot write, and I don't mean a drawing-room play: I mean a play in which the *Oresteia*, the *Alcestis*, or the *Ion* is re-created in a drama of modern life. And you'd almost think Eliot intended to do it simply by the exclusion of poetry, for he has never created characters and only once a plot. (Even this plot—of *The Confidential Clerk*—considering its ingenuity and comic intention, remains surprisingly inert in performance.)

We should not complain of the lack of poetry if in his prose (printed as verse) Eliot had created characters. His only full-size character is Becket. Now any writer could fail in this field, but Eliot may be the only one who could succeed only in the face of his own philosophy of life: for he does not believe that relationships between human beings are possible. Perhaps the only playwright to agree with Eliot has been Pirandello. Yet Pirandello believed you at least had a relationship with an image of the other person; you at least had the illusion of a relationship; and he dramatized the illusion. In Eliot's plays there is really nothing between people, not even false relationships, not even illusions. The husband and wife in *The Confidential Clerk* sit side by side and it is not merely that they don't understand each other, it is as if they have never talked to each other before; they are not *like* strangers, they *are* strangers: they wouldn't know each other's favorite brand of cigarettes. And that is not all: for Eliot, human relationships are not even an ideal. "The soul," he quotes from St. John of the Cross, "cannot be possessed of the divine union until it has divested itself of the love of created beings." I am sure a Christian apologist would want to add that St. John is referring to a state of mind *beyond* earthly love, not just *without* it. But Mr. Eliot's religiousness has always seemed to me rather close to misanthropy, just as his politics is never far from snobbery and is at certain points anti-Semitic.

Well, the snobbery pays off in the plays to the extent that it suggests the drawing-room setting and Eliot's highly unusual attitude to it. This drawing room is part-historical (England as seen by the man from St. Louis), part-legendary (made up of images established in Eliot's mind by, say, Noel Coward, P. G. Wodehouse, or even Aubrey Smith and Nigel Bruce). But the philosophy of St. John of the Cross, as quoted, and, it would seem, taken rather literally, is about the most anti-dramatic view of life ever committed to paper: the aim of life is—to get rid of human relationships! "If they could exist in the first place"—adds Eliot, and assumes they couldn't.

Eliot's three "modern" plays (*The Family Reunion, The Cocktail Party,* and *The Confidential Clerk*) are three attempts at one play. Each is, as it were, full of quotations from the others. Characters and situations recur—most notably, the agonized young person who goes off and becomes a priest or missionary (Harry, Celia, Colby). You can see what he's driving at, and I tend to think there's a kind of play Eliot *could* write: it would be made out of his favorite material (hollow men, waste lands, a sense of sin) but the vehicle for it would have to be, not anti-poetic, but super-poetic. *Murder in the Cathedral* is still his best contribution to the theatre.

It would be mean-spirited not to mention that, though the "modern" plays fail of their intention, they abound in incidental felicities—more in fact than have yet been revealed to any audience. For up to now, the major productions have been directed by an elocution teacher, E. Martin Browne, who, I should judge, has held the actors in check.

The production I saw this summer was *The Cocktail Party* at Bucks County Playhouse in Pennsylvania. Directed by the elocution teacher's stage manager, it followed the fatally formalistic "blocking" of the Broadway show: the actor who speaks most takes center stage while the others gaze out to sea, etc. But Uta Hagen showed that the part of Celia can be played with genuine passion, and Edna Best showed that Eliot's dry smile—helped out by a fine comedienne—can become the laughter of a whole audience. In short, while the plays are second-rate Eliot, they are better than most plays, and it would be interesting to know just how good—if for the first time they were really acted and directed—they could be. I should like to make one recommendation: that the part of Reilly, in *The Cocktail Party,* not be played by the star. The play is about Alcestis and Admetus, Lavinia and Edward, and we have not seen it till we have seen these parts presented as the "leads."

The Presence of Mozart

THE GERMAN THEATRE was and is dominated by Goethe and Schiller, the French by Molière, and the English by Shakespeare. One corollary of this fact is that an actor is chiefly valued for his Mephistopheles, his Marquis Posa, his Alceste, his Hamlet . . . Another is that a new author may have to cock a snoot at the national idols before he can establish his own claim to a divine spark; Shaw and Brecht are examples.

Music being less national than words, a nation cannot so easily keep its musical theatre to itself, and the operatic stage —not only in German-speaking countries but in England and America—is coming, one might almost say, to be dominated by Mozart. In England he is a theatrical presence second only to Shakespeare; while in America—there being no Old Vic, no Stratford Memorial Theatre—he is a theatrical presence second to none. Without him we should—in more senses than one—be lost. Our debt to those at the Metropolitan and City Center who keep Mozart present among us is, accordingly, incalculable.

Those who tell me that this vote of thanks had better been offered to RCA Victor are overlooking the adjective *theatrical.* I trust it is not mere professional bias that makes me feel that a purely musical approach to Mozart is inadequate. I have in mind not merely that stage production "adds a lot." That might be a disadvantage. Rather, I have in mind that Mozart is all the time *applying* his music to the spectacle, the character, and the story. One of the most striking examples was recently cited by Joseph Kerman in *Opera News*. It is that moment near the end of *Figaro* when the Count asks the Countess to forgive him. How could anyone know what the music was up to except by considering the theatrical context? And those who say "oh well, you can always *imagine* the theatrical context" just do not know the theatre and the kind of appeal it has. John Gielgud's performance in *Hamlet* is not something you can "imagine" while reading the play.

The only words vouchsafed to Mozart's Count at that great moment are: "Countess, pardon!" It is the music that tells us what this pardon means in human weakness and contrition. And we are reminded of the great arias in Mozart's operas where—in every case, I believe—the words are pretty commonplace and it is the music that provides the "poetry." Has the purely musical approach to Mozart some justification then? Certainly, music critics constantly revert to it. Only the other day the London *Times* was speaking of *Don Giovanni* as a triumph of great music over bad writing.

It is also true that there have been critics to find sublimity in the most banal verses of *The Magic Flute*. They would have us believe that Mozart's librettists are sages and great poets. This is a mistaken line of defence. The right defence of the Mozart librettos would start, I think, with the observation that great poetry set to music is not an ideal recipe for opera, in fact that there is no great dramatic poetry yet written that operatic music would not ruin. It is true that the songs in Shakespeare's plays are better poetry than anything by Lorenzo Da Ponte. Even at that, their "goodness" would be lost in arias of anything like Mozartian elaboration.

I do not want to get off on the vexed question to what extent we shall ever hear the words in opera. Rather, I'd maintain that, in any event, what the librettist needs is a command, not of great poetry, but of operatic dramaturgy. He is less of a poet than a planner of scenarios, and this planning involves a great deal more than the art of story-telling in combination with music (though Heaven knows that is a lot). To take a single example: the Mozart finales. There is seldom much narrative in them. What we have is the whole cast coming on stage. The task of the librettist is the interweaving of threads and, in Mozart, what an intricate interweaving that is! At this point, it is true, it becomes impossible to tell where the librettist's work ends and the composer's begins. But the fact that Mozart is a "dramatist" of the first order cannot be offered as evidence that Da Ponte is not.

The crucial case is *Cosí fan tutte*. The libretto has suffered more than a century and a half of contempt, and all because it is not much of a dramatic poem, not supreme reading matter. But it was never meant to be read! And, as for the plot being "absurd," as all the music critics say it is (consult your record album), why, all comic plots are absurd; perhaps the music critics haven't read *Twelfth Night*. This little story is a very respectable chip off the old block of Italian theatre. It is quintessentially theatrical. By all means, it would take a Molière to add the "poetry," but then Da Ponte *had* a Molière: namely, Mozart. You can't take part of a thing and condemn it for its incompleteness. *Cosí fan tutte* is as near to perfection, if I'm any judge, as any single product of the human mind; there being no faults to ascribe, how can we ascribe some to poor Da Ponte?

Some will retort that my argument is old stuff, and that Mozart productions are much more theatrical nowadays than a generation ago. Some critics have even been longing for the days when we just had a row of great singers on what was virtually a decorated concert platform. And I don't know that their position is incompatible with mine. A row of great singers on a platform might give us more of the drama than groupings of mediocre singers *on a stage that is not the right stage for Mozart.*

The "newly directed" operas of the Met have been riddled with, for the most part, justified criticisms. We might sum up by saying that, though we give thanks for the presence of Mozart, we deplore the way our impresarios dress him up. Many of the shortcomings can't of course be helped. They are matters of money—or rather, lack of it. But I seem to have detected, especially at the Met, a certain lack of faith too, not in the music, but in the drama, the theatre, of it all. In comedy, lack of faith usually shows itself in a straining to be droll, a childish chucklesomeness; in tragedy, in a fear of solemnity. See *Don Giovanni*—greatest of tragi-comedies—at the Met and you must needs be offended by both kinds of evasion. One critic who well understands Mozart as theatre—Ernst Lert—has stressed the element of brutal realism in Almaviva; yet even so impressive a singing actor as George London descends at times to the usual puerilities. We have had in our own language a critic—W. J. Turner—who has fully understood the Shakespearean depth of drama beneath *Cosi fan tutte.* Yet when Alfred Lunt directs it at the Met he seems to be thinking of Sheridan. The singers have been given a lot of help, that is clear—but only in externals. Mr. Lunt ignores the message Mozart is signalling.

The City Center, more limited as its resources may be, often manages to provide a more enjoyable evening. Except at the top of the balcony you can see and hear; at the Met I have yet to learn if there is such a thing as a good seat. The Center's standards are, of course, very uneven; in the 1953–4 season I saw a *Figaro* that was as bad as their *Don Giovanni* was good. But even when the result is not right, there is always a sense that the occasion is theatre. Among the shows I saw, this theatrical sense was most resplendent, not in Mozart, but in Rossini's *Cinderella,* a fact which should probably be credited principally to Lincoln Kirstein—to my mind one of the great benefactors of New York theatre today. (The only large grumble I have—and it applies as much to the Met as to the Center —is at the use of the Martins' Broadwayish translations; adequate enough for Strauss operettas, they are death to Mozart.)

". . . And Chronicle Small Beer"

THERE FOLLOW some jottings about shows which I have not reviewed at length but should not wish to ignore.

The Italian drama is unknown in America, and would evidently remain so if Alfred Drake didn't honor the country of his origin by directing Goldoni, playing Pirandello, and—

currently—adapting a Betti play, *The Gambler,* with himself in the title role.

Since the death of Pirandello in 1936 there have been only two Italian playwrights of note: Eduardo De Filippo and Ugo Betti. De Filippo, when he is wise, keeps close to the popular Neapolitan tradition in which he was reared. Betti is bourgeois and European. Seeing his work today we think of Sartre's *La Nausée* or Neveux's *Plainte contre l'Inconnu* (though in fact his "existentialism" antedates theirs) ; we think of Expressionism and of Kafka. Like *The Trial, The Gambler* presents the moral life of modern man in terms of a tribunal situated between this world and the next. As in T. S. Eliot's *Family Reunion* the protagonist is resisting yet steadily approaching the admission that he is guilty of murder whether or not he actually did the deed. Like Eliot and unlike Kafka, Betti caps the admission of guilt with an offer of salvation.

Speaking of Betti one inevitably mentions other authors not because one is sure which of them influenced him but because he is inescapably a "literary," a derivative author. Amid all the echoes it is hard to be sure if Betti has a voice of his own. If he has I should guess that it's not a philosophical voice but one that cries out in pain and loathing. He is more convincing (also like Eliot) in depicting the struggle than in conferring the prize. The optimistic philosophy arrived at in *The Gambler* is either spurious or obscure.

The play is given a far better performance than such things usually are. The average standard is that of, say, the Theatre Guild's *Legend of Lovers* or Cornell's *Antigone:* the play is lost in a chaos of uncomprehending direction, bad acting, and vulgar adaptation. The Drake-Eager version of *The Gambler,* though occasionally ponderous, is something better than adaptation, it is faithful yet, on the whole, idiomatic translation; the general level of the acting is respectable and that of two individuals—Alfred Drake and E. G. Marshall—first rate; the physical production scheme devised by Messrs. Mielziner and Shumlin is both brilliant and simple. By and large this is a more expert show than the original Italian production of the play. On the other hand, what I saw in Rome two years ago makes me aware of a serious flaw in Mr. Shumlin's production:

it duplicates Betti's ponderosity with its own. Mr. Shumlin seems to have believed that by slowing down the dialogue and the action he could achieve style and suggest profundity. The Italians got their effects by speed and lightness. Crucial is the portrait of the dead wife. In Rome she was just a modern girl. In New York she was something out of the dream sequence in an old-fashioned musical comedy.

It is good to see Alfred Drake again, and it is good to see him at this stage in his career. He still has the exuberance of youth, his work still quivers with possibility, yet he is old enough now to give also the sense of difficulties overcome and technique achieved. Of course, his technique as a straight actor is not yet *completely* achieved. Thousands of appearances in musical comedy have dug rather noticeable grooves; one notices both body and voice falling into the same four or five patterns all the time. If he is going to be the fine straight actor he could be, Mr. Drake will have to work constantly on himself while making thousands of appearances in non-musical comedy. Alternatively he can simply relax and continue being the best leading man of our musical stage.

The Strong Are Lonely is a translation of a French translation of *Das heilige Experiment* by Fritz Hochwaelder. Like the same author's *The Public Prosecutor* which I saw in Vienna, it is a teasing play because, while the author is always stumbling on great themes, he is always stumbling. One respects Margaret Webster (the director) and Eva Le Gallienne (the retranslator) insofar as they wished to say something to a public that rarely has anything said to it. But the upshot of such an occasion is only that everyone exclaims: "You see? There's no public here for serious European drama." Why will backers squander money on second-raters like George Tabori and Fritz Hochwaelder when they couldn't lose any more on Sean O'Casey or Bertolt Brecht?

It has been remarked that Ethel Waters' place is not "at home"—as she currently pretends to be in her one-woman show—but in the theatre. Yet her producers could retort that their notion was based on a thorough study of modern mores.

We like poets more than we like poetry. Our interest in public men is chiefly in their private lives. If we depersonalize actresses by astronomical metaphor, we at once personalize them by wallowing in the details of their marital life. And there is a great modern principle which reads: everything should be everything else—Einstein should be a political pundit, movie stars should tell us about theology, and so forth. If the producers' notion failed, it must be that Miss Waters is not very good at this sort of thing.

To see *Oklahoma!* after ten years was, for one spectator, to feel quite differently—and much better—about it. One never "just sees" anything. One sees through spectacles which the world provides, and in 1943 the world provided us, as I said in my review of *Porgy and Bess,* with a lot of chatter about grass roots and an "American *Magic Flute.*" If you brought to the theatre a knowledge of the Austrian *Magic Flute,* you were bound to be let down. If, on the other hand, you bring a knowledge of the musical comedies of the period 1943–53, Hammerstein's—and, more especially, Rodgers'—name leads all the rest.

The Little Hut has suggested to many that American taste is *sui generis.* But there is no reason why it should. This is a very funny play on any continent. If Nancy Mitford, in her free adaptation, has assimilated it to a British tradition of humor, that humor has constantly appealed to Americans—in, for example, a whole succession of movies from the early Hitchcock to the most recent Alec Guinness. It isn't Miss Mitford's fault that her leading lady in New York has little English and less humor. At that, it isn't chiefly the acting that is wrong; apart from the leading lady, the playing is well above Broadway average. The chief blame for the failure must surely rest with the director, Peter Brook, who has done, not too little, but far, far too much: a very live little farce has been murdered by a massive production. I should also put Oliver Messel's set on the debit side. It is gorgeous and it is clever. But it strikes precisely that note of self-congratulation—of pompous whimsy, portentous cuteness—which is the ruin of the evening. André Roussin, the author, could only say of this event: a poor thing, but not mine own.

Many of the shows which Messrs. Brook and Messel have lent their names to in England bear the stamp of the new English estheticism, seriously unserious, profoundly unprofound, and ungaily gay. *L'Invitation au château* in Paris was a charming trifle; in London—as *Ring Round the Moon*—it acquired the sort of ponderosity which New York could subsequently witness in *The Little Hut;* it became the *idea* of a charming trifle, abstract and lifeless. Oh yes, in a sense, the charm and the triviality had each been multiplied by a hundred. That was the trouble. Not every six-tier wedding cake tastes better than a bun.

WHAT IS THEATRE?

The Family, 1954

THE 1954–55 SEASON has opened with a couple of plays which
neither arouse profound admiration nor incite a critic to that
scornful and humorous dismissal which is the usual alternative. I don't mean they are boring, either. My state of mind
during the greater part of both evenings wavered, rather,
between mild discomfort and acute distress. Some of the malaise may have derived from my heartfelt agreement with both
authors on one central idea: that family life is the most successful instrument of self-torture yet devised by an ingenious and
masochistic species, an exquisite compound of tedium, irritation, comic misunderstanding and tragic suffering. If I were of
a grateful disposition, I should doubtless tell them how truthful they are and how much I enjoy agreeing with them. As
things are, I am going to retort that, though life may consist in
an attempt not to get stuck in the mud, I do not think the aim
of art should be to go back to the bog and wallow in it. Nor
can I be conciliated by any talk of inoculation, a hair of the
dog that bit me, or fighting fire with fire. The petty reporting
of naturalism has got to be transformed and transcended either by a larger realism or by poetic fantasy. The failure of
Home Is the Hero by Walter Macken and *All Summer Long*
by Robert Anderson is that they stay so stubbornly in the
smaller world, untransformed, and one might almost say: un-
formed.

I could be wrong about the stubbornness. Possibly an attempt has been made by both playwrights to get beyond genre
painting and the notation of psychological traits to the great
and complex moral conflicts which are the proper subject
matter of drama. For one thing, if they are not to send us

home in the first intermission screaming our nausea to the sidewalks of New York, they have to take the curse off the family catastrophe by indicating an alternative. Ours is an age of infantile paganism, pinning its faith on children and animals; and Mr. Anderson (though not Mr. Macken) is in this respect a man of the age. Both authors resort to one of the crudest features of melodrama. You can take the curse off the family catastrophe, paradoxically enough, by running a steam roller over some younger member of the family's foot. "Spare the rod and spoil the child"? No: use the rod, cripple the child, and save your play. An instructive treatise could be written on *The Juvenile Cripple as Tear-Jerker: from Charles Dickens to Charles Chaplin*. The voice of righteousness, for both the Messrs. Macken and Anderson, speaks through the lips of a juvenile cripple who has no evil in him at all. I should like to write a play in which a cripple is a "son of a bitch"; but Shakespeare thought of it first. Naturally, *Richard III* is considered highly unrealistic these days.

Except in painting a picture of a hideous family, and indicating a virtuous alternative only through a crippled boy, Messrs. Macken and Anderson take a different tack. Mr. Anderson fails through staying in the groove of current American dramaturgic cliché, Mr. Macken through never getting into it. *All Summer Long* is another mood play, belonging to the succession that began with *Summer and Smoke* and *Member of the Wedding*. The aim is Chekhov's trigger effect: the releasing of large forces by tiny movements. The actual fact is a series of tiny movements, each ticketed, in at least one speech, with the author's intentions and even views. All sorts of motives and motifs hover about the play without quite getting into it. Or, if they do get in, it is in the form either of clumsy symbolism or overt mention. Under the former head, I would place the main incident of the action: the house in which our family lives is being undermined by a river and will collapse. Under the head of overt mention, I would place many of the cripple's speeches, especially one in which he lists and sums up the other characters and another in which he states the theme of Joseph Conrad's *The Shadow Line*. The general effect is not of large forces and tiny movements but of big intentions bogging down in small facts. The strivings after poetry and mood accentuate, rather than mitigate, the irritating factuality of Mr. Anderson's naturalistic method. Then, too, as in *Tea and Sympathy*, this author tends to substitute clinical information explaining people for dramatic action presenting them. In fairness it should be added that, when we are momentarily not oppressed by all the paraphernalia of the family mechanism, we enjoy his ingratiating humor.

When I say that Mr. Macken fails through avoiding cliché, I mean that he is so austerely indifferent to present Broadway mores that he could only surmount the obstacle he places in his own path by writing an undeniably great play. Compared with Mr. Anderson's sentimental contrivances, *Home Is the Hero* is astonishingly innocent. It is the story of a bully who returns from five years in jail for manslaughter with his joy and confidence gone but still a bully. Joshua Logan could have turned the show into a hit by making the bully an object of pity and "audience identification"; for American stage bullies, current vintage, have the hearts of children. So far from emulating Mr. Logan, Mr. Macken acts the part of his own protagonist mercilessly, turning sullenly upstage when he might have been ogling the gallery. His shrewdness, even in the choice of a theme, has not equalled his sincerity. Does a bully, if he is only a bully, make a good protagonist for a drama? It is doubtful. Nor is the problem solved by casting an intellectual in the part.

Home Is the Hero seemed to me very badly directed (by Worthington Miner). At least it would be hard for a mere spectator to place anywhere else the blame for bad "blocking" and timing and a forcing of the pace as by an amateur imitator of Mr. Kazan. (For while Mr. Kazan builds the rising action of a sequence carefully from a low point up, Mr. Miner would suddenly try to make a scene jump from nothing to the highest pitch of excitement.) Sometimes one seemed to be watching TV plus the part of the TV setting that is not shown on the screen: an effort was made suddenly to fix our attention on two actors holding hands and posing for a camera. One of the actors, playing the cripple, seemed to see the cameras approaching his face every time he smiled; and he showed surprising facility in dropping the character he was playing as if he had been switched to another TV program.

All Summer Long was, as it were, much better bred, and its cripple trailed clouds of private-school glory out of another play. The standard of production was higher, and the child actors seemed, as they always do, better than the adults. (Which proves . . . ?) There was good directing, somewhat imitative of Mr. Kazan, by Alan Schneider, and good designing, imitative of Mr. Mielziner, by Mr. Mielziner. One performance, however, was disenchanting: John Kerr's. When I praised Mr. Kerr in two earlier plays, I thought I was praising acting. I now wonder if I was really praising a certain sort of personality—perhaps only a certain sort of sex appeal emanating from a pouting, indolent, insolent sort of face and a helpless, dead voice. In the next role he undertakes, let Mr. Kerr prove me wrong.

Off Broadway

I WISH IT WERE possible to say that the Off Broadway theatre could offer us everything belonging to the theatre art except the trappings. But actors are not trappings, and the small, poverty-stricken theatre can seldom offer us the best actors. Nor, in an external, ostentatious affair like the theatre, can "trappings" be lightly dismissed. T. C. Worsley, my colleague on *The New Statesman,* writes:

> Is there anything more depressing than well-intentioned but ill-conducted theatre endeavors conducted in totally unsuitable surroundings by earnestly highminded persons? The very essence of the theatre is an extravagance of bright lights, red plush, golden cupids, and vulgar excitement; the very antithesis is an austerity of wooden seats and unheated cellars.

Mr. Worsley hastens to add that wonderful things have happened in the cellars all the same, and I am going to exploit his remarks to suggest, not that the underground theatre should not exist, but that it must needs offer a clear-cut alternative to the theatre above ground rather than a dim, if not ridiculous, duplication of it.

If you simply do not have at your disposal the leading actors, designers, directors, nor money enough for the finest stages and scenery, let alone for golden cupids, can you give me a good reason for buying a ticket at your theatre? It is no answer to state that the Off Broadway theatre is a showcase for young actors. No one except an agent takes a seat for a reason like that—and *he* probably doesn't have to pay for it. All I, as prospective spectator, want to know is: what kind of show is being offered?

Now what answers to this question have the Off Broadway theatres been giving? The feeblest one is: a re-staging of a Broadway show. However, it was a less feeble answer when Circle in the Square managed to do a couple of Broadway plays as well as, or better than, Broadway had done them. Only where did that lead? To Broadway, of course; producer, director, and leading actress are now there.[1] I am not saying that Greenwich Village should not be a steppingstone to Broadway for the individual artist. But while individuals come and go, the Off Broadway theatre is an institution, and as such it needs a stable character, however mobile its personnel.

And on the whole it has been acknowledged that a Village theatre should not devote its energies to re-staging Broadway plays, grabbing Broadway plays before the uptown producers find them, or producing Broadway-type plays which do not make the Broadway grade. Two distinct alternatives have been proposed: new plays of a non-Broadway type and old plays which Broadway ignores. The famous Village theatres of the twenties elected the first alternative. And I am writing this review because two new groups have just appeared—The Players Theatre and Proscenium Productions—that have elected the second.

Having reported on the opening Broadway season rather gloomily two weeks ago, I am delighted to have good news to

[1] Luckily, they were unlucky; and had to go back to Greenwich Village. [1956]

give of the Village. And let no one think I prejudged the issue. Having seen what I have seen in the past year or two, when I read that the Village would offer Garrick and Colman's *The Clandestine Marriage* and Congreve's *The Way of the World* I fully intended to absent myself from both productions. Can comedy of manners be acted by Americans? In the Village?? By youngsters???

And what youngsters? I had seen a valiant attempt (eighteen months ago at the De Lys on Christopher Street) to do *The School for Scandal.* There were several non-youngsters in it, professionals of name and, what is rarer, ability. And yet the evening was a squalid mixture of terrified hesitations and desperate aggressions, leaving in the mind, at eleven o'clock, just a gently unpleasant vibration, as after dramamine. (Etymologists: work on this word.) So what could be done by these nameless ones from Wellesley College and The Carnegie Institute of Technology?

I leave the loud negative of my answer unspoken—because I was wrong. Deciding to see part of one of the shows, I found myself staying for the full length of both. They were—it is the finest word in dramatic criticism—good; and the first sign of this goodness came, as it must in the theatre, in immediate pleasure. "I enjoyed every minute of it," as we say, "It kept me on the edge of my seat." And the immediate pleasure of the occasion gave place, afterwards, to some astonishment that, in a city where "Shakespeare" is the name of a dull monster, a group—two groups, rather—of young people have trained themselves to speak classic comedy. And not only to speak it. There is a word—gait—whose archaism betrays the loss of a thing as well as an idea. "Manner of walking," says Webster. And what is harder than to walk rightly in non-modern costume while speaking in high comic style? The actor, we think nowadays, does not *act*, he *is;* and, in my last review, I was giving the example of John Kerr who has his successes in parts where *none* of the old attributes of a great actor—heroic physique and bearing, richness of voice—are required; while, as for gait, in his latest part he goes on crutches.

Our two groups have been learning to speak, stand, walk, make gestures, but I should not give the impression that the two evenings have the air of classroom exercises. For one thing, there are some very striking actor-personalities in both groups; personality, on the stage, being what takes the curse off technique. Frederic Warriner, though an old stager compared with some of his colleagues, has never appeared to better advantage than as the senile amorist of Garrick's play. Not every personality is so right for its role: Jacqueline Brooks' romantic languor, for example, will not take a comic rhythm. Sometimes the various personalities do not have the right relative weight. For instance, though Gerry Fleming's Millamant has a kind of beauty unusual in the theatre, Miss Fleming has not quite the force to be the cynosure of all eyes when Nancy Wickwire is on stage; for Miss Wickwire brings with youth and beauty a remarkable degree of vocal vehemence and control. For a youthful company, there were surprisingly few cases of vehemence *without* control. Once or twice, Sylvia Short errs in that direction, but I mention her chiefly to praise a crackling opening scene, a triumph of complexity for so young an actress, in which, gloating and ecstasizing over a box of jewels, she uses her abundant vitality to best advantage. Thayer David is to be congratulated on a make-up that turned him into a Hogarth, and Jerry Stiller on being Jerry Stiller, the frog-faced clown of last year's *Coriolanus*. If I am least grateful to the handsome young men of both plays, it is because the parts are the ungrateful ones (except when villainous: as Fainall, played with dark and feline fervor by Fritz Weaver). Louis Edmonds does manly battle with Mirabell; one would have cast him for the role after seeing his bearing alone. Yet a certain indistinctness of what is miscalled diction interfered with no part so much as his, and here I cannot resist raising the general point: must our American actors acquire a British accent in order to act English plays? If the acting coaches answer this question in the affirmative (as I do not), then may I submit that some actors think they have a British accent when they only have asthma? The simulation of a British accent is often only a simulation of certain common abuses of the voice among British actors, particularly a tightening of the throat with its resultant tight, "throaty"—and at the back of the house, inaudible—tone. Also, if American productions are going to be British, my ears demand that they be consistently so.

Comparisons are odious but interesting. The two shows are of approximately equal quality. Neither director, thank Heaven, has jazzed the play up by setting it in 1920 or providing a Freudian interpretation of the heroine, and if I give a slightly higher mark to Warren Enters (*The Way of the World*) than to the versatile Jack Landau (*The Clandestine Marriage*), it may only be because he does not burlesque the asides or have the actors bow on entering; or because he has put across a much harder play. (For once the plays themselves are squeezed out of a review of mine; the curious reader may turn to a couple of centuries' criticism on the subject.)

The American Musical

THE AMERICAN MUSICAL has become a byword, but a byword for what? At a recent press conference in Paris, a poet from behind the Iron Curtain was asked if there was anything of value in American theatre: he replied that there had been the Federal Theatre and there were still the musicals. His grounds for approving the Federal Theatre being presumably political, musicals were evidently the only kind of American theatre in which he found any artistic merit. The idea was that while the serious drama was monopolized by a decadent and reactionary intelligentsia, in the musicals the vitality of the masses found expression. Not, of course, that the musical was truly progressive; it was largely without content, "formalistic"; but the form was lively and interesting and, if taken over by the right people. . . .

Now the odd thing is that, though most of us disagree with the form of this very argument, we agree to its content. We feel that more could some day be done with the musical than has been done up to now, that the music and the book could both be raised to a higher power.

And yet the best musicals at present are not those which

indicate an effort to transform the musical, such as, to take a recent example, *The Golden Apple* by John Latouche and Jerome Moross. I found these men at their best when they stayed well within the convention, as they did in their fooling, and at their worst when they tried to transcend it, as they did in repeated attempts at poetry and social significance.

It is true that the musical does, at some points, break down the barriers between highbrow and lowbrow. A triumphant example was to be found in the scenery of *The Golden Apple* (designed by William and Jean Eckart) which in its spare, Mondrian lines and light, bright (not gaudy) colors was perhaps the loveliest sight of the 1953–54 season. But the idea of calling in the High Artist doesn't always have such happy consequences. When Oliver Smith's sophisticated cleverness adorns a George Abbott show, you tend to say: Oh dear, couldn't they have hired someone with less education?

The best musicals at present are not those with the biggest intentions behind them but those with the simple virtues in them of singable tunes and sheer showmanship. If I had to say what single man could do most to give us a good musical, I would reply: Richard Rodgers. I would place George Abbott second; and third, say, Michael Kidd or Jerome Robbins. A great designer is not an absolute necessity. Nor is a star actor, especially not if we have Mr. Abbott to find new talent for us. But excellent featured players are indispensable. In fact they are the life and soul of the party. During the past two years, I have not seen many first-rate musicals, but to every second—or even tenth—rate musical, featured players contributed first-rate items. All I can recall of *Hazel Flagg* is Jack Whiting, with his smart, soft-shoe rhythm, his suave, grave way of speaking his songs, his comical, cockeyed dignity. From *Golden Apple*, I retain Jonathan Lucas woozily dancing "Lazy Afternoon" and Portia Nelson jigging up and down, with voice and body alike, for "Doomed, Doomed"; from *Show Boat*, Helena Bliss leaning against the proscenium arch and dreamily singing till we forgot the time; from *Can Can*, Gwen Verdon's homey smile un-homey body and high, high kicks; from *The Threepenny Opera*, Charlotte Rae, savagely grimacing and lewdly hitching her stocking up. . . .

To admit that Rodgers' name leads all the rest is not necessarily to approve the direction that the Rodgers-Hammerstein musicals have recently been taking. On the contrary, I think Hammerstein is one of those whose soul is in greatest peril: he, more than anyone, is out to make the-musical-that-is-more-than-a-musical. His success with the public has been enormous, but is this always because his shows are good? Or could it sometimes have been because they fell in with a new trend in public feeling?

James Thurber says that America no longer wants comedy, and he blames this on McCarthyism: we are too scared to laugh. But surely the anti-humorous trend in popular culture began before McCarthy did? And has much broader than political causes? Take the difference between early and late Hitchcock movies. The public ceased to want the spry comicality of *The Lady Vanishes* and was given Ingrid Bergman ravenously chewing Cary Grant's ear. Or compare the Myrna Loy of around 1930 with the same actress in *The Best Years of Our Lives:* she had been rewritten, as it were, by Oscar Hammerstein.

No wonder that *On Your Toes* by Richard Rodgers and Lorenz Hart (revived at the Forty-sixth Street Theatre) strikes the newspapermen as old-fashioned. But anyone *except* a newspaperman will prefer it that way. The breath of a less stuffy generation is in the piece. I agree with Mr. Thurber that something was lost during the forties and early fifties—and here, in this musical of the thirties, it is: namely, a cocky, satirical, devil-may-care philosophy that is certainly very attractive and possibly rather useful. Anyhow, it is good light theatre, whereas, for example, the last scene of *Carousel* is an impertinence: I refuse to be lectured by a musical comedy scriptwriter on the education of children, the nature of the good life, and the contribution of the American small town to the salvation of souls. I regard such a *gaffe* simply as an opportunity to get out of the theatre before the crowd. I deplore the death of the king in *The King and I;* it was definitely his duty to stay alive and amuse us. But *On Your Toes* is true musical comedy, ending in a bracing "Slaughter on Tenth Avenue" in which no one is really slaughtered.

The new show is not beyond reproach. There are some quite

loathsome fruity-spangly costumes by Irene Sharaff; and the delicate Vera Zorina is badly miscast as a sort of Tallulah of the dance. But George Abbott cannot only get along without stars: he can get along *with* stars who don't quite fit. *On Your Toes* is not a setting for a leading lady, it is an ensemble show in which the two great motive-forces are Abbott and Balanchine. I sometimes think the classic choreographers do better work for Broadway than for City Center or the Metropolitan. Jerome Robbins, for example, is a much freer spirit when he is frivolous than when he is trying to interpret W. H. Auden. And I intend no slur on Balanchine's past when I say that his presence on Broadway is no anticlimax. How the "serious" theatre would come alive if anything ever happened there like that lovely moving pattern of limbs and umbrellas in fading light which is the dance in the rain from *On Your Toes!*

The find of the show (as far as I am concerned: others doubtless found her before) is Elaine Stritch who combines an assured and taut technique with an enormous and relaxed warmth of personality.

Who is the great exponent of what the American theatre does with most gaiety and zest? It would be hard to name anyone other than Mr. Abbott.

A Whole Theory of the Drama

THE AIM OF A writer who set out to imitate *War and Peace* might be described as Trying to Get Everything In. The aim of a writer who set out to imitate *Phèdre* or *Ghosts* might be described as Trying to Leave Everything Out. It is a paradox of art that Tolstoy does not include anything he does not need, nor do Racine and Ibsen exclude anything they do need; his maximum is also a minimum, their minimum is also a maximum.

How does a dramatist's minimum become a maximum? Leaving nearly everything out, the dramatist necessarily gives to the few things he puts in a peculiar prominence. In bad drama, this is only the prominence of isolation, insulation, sheer unconnectedness. The diagnostic of good drama is that the little it actually displays suggests, like the visible part of an iceberg, larger bulk beneath. A play may have a very large subject but can only present a few small clues to it. Nothing in a play is more than a clue. Dramatic dialogue is a form of shorthand, and dramatic characterization a form (if the word can be stretched a little) of caricature. Behind the few things the characters say, the few things they do, and the few things they are, we sense the reality of many things—indeed, in great plays, the whole of a civilization.

If this much is accepted, a whole theory of the drama unfolds which would justify the "absurdity" of Molière's plots and the "unreality" of Shakespeare's characters. Contrariwise, the "reality" of our modern characters and the non-absurdity of modern plots (or non-plots) stand condemned as a failure to meet the rudimentary requirements of dramatic art. Season after season the dramatic critic has to complain that the serious plays are mere tape recordings of actual conversations, mechanically-taken photographs of actual persons, particularly "little" persons (children, morons, cripples, old maids, *et al.*) . If all art stands at a remove from life, if, indeed, the artist's "art" is precisely his way of setting life at a remove, of bringing it into relief, the drama may be, in some ways, a crude or an extreme case, but it is in no other way an exceptional one. . . . *The Dybbuk* by S. Ansky, currently on stage at the Fourth Street Theatre, strikes me as a very happy example of a modern playwright's having found the clues to a big subject.

For, obviously, our lesser playwrights are not dully naturalistic from conviction or sheer wilfulness, but only from not knowing any better, from not finding a workable alternative. "A dramatic poet," writes Ramon Fernandez in his extraordinary *Vie de Molière*, "must base his creations upon creations which are collective and anonymous." The converse of this principle is that dramatic poetry cannot exist if the right collective and anonymous creations are unavailable—cannot exist, either, if the poet is such an individualist that he refuses to use such collective and anonymous creations as are available.

Where, today, can the poet find such creations? T. S. Eliot
has thought to find them in the Anglican church—and also in
the Broadway-West End drawing-room convention. He has
had his troubles. Writing *The Dybbuk* in the Russia of a
generation ago, Ansky was not so hard put to it—though one
might remark that what he did has been done only once with
such signal success. He used certain existing cultural patterns
which did not have to be "made dramatic" but which were of
themselves theatrical, and this by virtue not only of their
liveliness but also of their significance. Great art, we know, is
universal, but, before it is universal, it has to be thoroughly
local, it has to bear the signature of a people and a way of life.
The point has been proved by an artist rather close in nearly
all respects to Ansky—namely, Chagall. Sholom Aleichem I
should judge to be less close, for, unless the English translation
has misled me, Ansky's achievement is visual and aural, that is,
theatrical, rather than literary. Great theatrical work being
even rarer than great writing as such, *The Dybbuk* is the more
welcome on this account.

Such work labors under the handicap that it can only be
communicated in great performance, whereas great literature
is within your grasp as soon as you pick up the book. It is not
within the means of an Off Broadway group to create great
spectacular theatre of the sort Stark Young described when
reviewing *The Dybbuk* in *The New Republic* nearly thirty
years ago. Yet the production on Fourth Street is not so
opaque that the light of Ansky's genius does not come blazing
through. There is a relaxed air about the performance, a lack
of fuss and high pressure, that you would never find *on* Broadway; only once or twice did I find myself wishing the actors
would get a move on. More important, Broadway is, of its very
nature, irreligious; religion there is a self-proclaimed imposture, the merest neon-lit religiosity, asking the "angels" not to
give all they have to feed the poor, and reversing that unhappy
gaffe about the needle's eye. I've no idea whether Ansky was
theologically minded, and I am sure there are experts to tell
me that *The Dybbuk* is not at all a pious play; at the same
time there is something in it that is religious in a broader, and
perhaps deeper, sense. Ansky makes real to us people whose
religious tradition is perhaps the main thing in their lives and,

like Chagall, he seems to tell us that we can be happy in the universe even if we are miserable in the world. There is a fine Dickensian mixture, in this Hasidism, of mysticism and jollity.

The American adaptor of the play, Henry Alsberg, has maintained in *The New York Times* that it is a study of split personality and a demonstration of the indivisibility of body and spirit. Perhaps one has to talk in these terms to impress a certain type of modern person, but it would be wiser not to, as, in fact, the heroine's character is left undefined. If the dybbuk symbolizes a second soul within her breast, one would have to ask: what is the nature of her first soul? a question Ansky doesn't answer. The only "modern" character in the play—and he is also a classic character—is a young man who is at once spiritual and sensual to the highest possible degree: a conception with endless dramatic possibilities. Otherwise, you have to judge this play from a viewpoint not psychological but either religious or esthetic. You have to be a child before it, for it is above all a story. It differs from other good stories chiefly in releasing its power in theatrical images, even in what, given another context, could be cheap theatrical effects. The biggest moment is when the voice of another speaks out of the heroine —the voice of the dybbuk.

Rachel Armour, who plays Leah, has the loveliest face to be seen in any New York theatre at this time. Jacob expected Rachel and got Leah; the Fourth Street audience expects Leah and gets Rachel.

I do not know if Ansky shows us "the way to do it," but undoubtedly he shows us the way it can—or once could—be done.

Joshua Logan

WHEN I HEARD that Marcel Pagnol's movie trilogy *Marius-Fanny-César* has been transmogrified into a musical comedy called *Fanny* by Joshua Logan, S. N. Behrman, and Harold Rome, I thought of James Agate's avowal:

I am no transmogrifier. I do *not* want to see *Gerontius* danced, hear the *Eroica* arranged for string quartet or *Das Lied von der Erde* transcribed for piano accordion; I do *not* want to read *Tartuffe* as a novel. . . .

On the other hand, the best American plays of recent seasons —*A Member of the Wedding* and *The Caine Mutiny Court Martial*—are adapted from fiction, and one might point out that dramatic art as such has an epic source. Agate meant, of course, to express his distaste for what happens when a living masterpiece falls into the hands of merely commercial craftsmen. M. Pagnol's trilogy being no masterpiece, one doesn't care so much what is done to it: couldn't it even be improved? Were we all really so eager to see the touching little tragi-comedy of Marius reproduced in all its touching littleness? Let us, rather, grant Mr. Logan his premise: M. Pagnol's work *can* be regarded as source material for a supercolossal, musical spectacle. Touching little stories surely do not deserve a higher status than the sight of a ship in full sail (presented by Mr. Logan in a gigantic moving projection) or the sight of a pretty Arab dancing girl (presented by Mr. Logan with next to no clothes on). On the contrary, we have been deluged with touching little stories; they lost their interest long ago; lovely ships and lovely girls are forever new.[1]

I am not, I know, expressing Mr. Logan's own view of the matter. He has tried not to get rid of the touching little story but rather to make of it a touching big story, and *Fanny* is open to the same criticism as Oscar Hammerstein's recent work: it is both too literary and too maudlin. As such, it perhaps reflects the mood of the decade; though the reviewers aren't enthusiastic; and, at that, the mood of a decade is not

---

[1] It was Goethe, not the director of the Folies Bergère, who said of the stage: "It is Corporeal Man who plays the leading role there—a handsome man, a beautiful woman!" And, one might add, it is fear of this fact that so often turns Literary Man away from the stage. Thomas Mann wrote: "I realize more and more that my whole complaint against the theatre can be traced to its essential sensuality." I take these quotations from an important and highly provocative recent book: *Theater der Gegenwart* by Siegfried Melchinger (Frankfurt and Hamburg, 1956).

beyond criticism. Then again, Mr. Logan has the defects of his qualities: he is so aware of the audience that it is very hard for him to be aware of anything else. He is like a man who wonders so hard if a girl will kiss him back that he forgets to kiss her. The response cannot happen because the-thing-to-re-spond-to has been neglected; or (which may be the same thing) we are so definitely told how to respond that we can't do it. When the emotions, as in Logan productions, have been thrown to the other side of the footlights, the people on stage seem deprived and emotionless; if you wear your heart on your sleeve, you necessarily leave a cold and empty place in your chest. . . .

I overstate for the sake of clarity. Actually, many scenes *are* touching. There is a case not only for the supercolossal show, as Mr. Logan does it, but also for sentimental melodrama. Critics are rightly on guard against both. Mr. Michael Bent-hall's supercolossal shows (*Antony and Cleopatra* at the Zieg-feld, *A Midsummer Night's Dream* at the Metropolitan) are bad, because that is not the way to do Shakespeare. Many supercolossal musical plays are bad, because there is no trace in them of musical, visual, or dramatic taste. Sentimental melodrama is bad when it pretends to be more (for example, when it poses as social drama) or when it fails to be as much (that is, when it is dull). But, in Mr. Logan's hands, the supercolossal show is skilful, grand, and thrilling entertain-ment in the best nineteenth-century tradition (suggesting also at times the visual glamour and mechanical ingenuity of Ka-buki). To that same tradition belongs sentimental melodrama viewed as a legitimate genre and not as "serious" drama gone wrong. The Victorian actors did not burlesque sentimental melodrama as we do, for Victorian audiences did not take an ironical view of sentiment: they sat with handkerchief in hand, not with tongue in cheek. And I suspect that anyone who cannot in some measure recapture the Victorian attitude does not relish theatricality. Of course, that attitude exists in many who would not admit it. In the twentieth century we mistrust our emotions. Reading Dickens' sob stuff, we feel the catch in our throat but immediately disown it. Twentieth-cen-tury sentimentality comes to us in disguise, the British disguise being sophisticated chatter (Noel Coward), the American disguise being "tough talk" (Eugene O'Neill). . . .

A few weeks ago I was defending *On Your Toes* against *Carousel* and *The King and I*. This is only to say that a musical shouldn't try to be literary, educational, or tragic, not that it shouldn't be melodramatic. Now if the master of musical comedy is George Abbott, the master of musical melodrama is Joshua Logan, and only if you refuse to accept this latter genre will you reject *Fanny*. Only by disowning your own feelings can you totally reject the admittedly "thick" sentiment of the show. Only if you close the eyes and ears of your body and your mind can you totally reject these sights and sounds.

A boy loves the sea more than women. His girl, left pregnant by him, marries an older man. The boy returns, and tries to get the girl back. . . . The story is a sound one, and Mr. Logan takes a sound interest in it. Champions of our Mood Plays may regret that the psychology of his characters is so crude, but his work serves as a reminder that drama is a narrative art: if you have told your story, you have put over your play. And though Mr. Logan makes too many calculations about his public's responses, one cannot but admire his knowledge of that public, his use of it, so to speak, as a musical instrument. To reduce M. Pagnol's triple-length narrative to a compact plot is in itself a merely technical job, but Messrs. Logan and Behrman have picked from the long tale just those elements which have resonance at this different moment and in this different place. They have selected the American sentiments, or perhaps I should say the elements which would most appeal to Americans, who, in general, are men of sentiment.

Mr. Logan's casting is continuous with his dramaturgy. He has concentrated M. Pagnol's story in the personality of a handful of American actors—outstandingly, Ezio Pinza, Florence Henderson, and Walter Slezak. Technically, Pinza goes rather unused; he doesn't sing enough; but it is his temperament, his radiant warmth, that enables Mr. Logan to bring César to the vast audience in the Majestic Theatre. Florence Henderson is an actress of some ability; what is more important is that she brings great beauty to *Fanny* and that it is beauty of a type that speaks to the public in their present mood, that brings M. Pagnol's heroine all the way home to them. In one light, Miss Henderson is any American home-body, in another, pure youthful loveliness. For the purposes of a musical, that combination is unbeatable. The trick that Mr. Logan has pulled is to tell a "scandalous" French story while giving the impression that we're all sitting pretty in Our Town, demurely celebrating our own homey virtues.

Looking back over this review, I realize that I have given no impression of all the impish and florid fun that is in the show. The fat and fastidious Mr. Slezak plays Panisse, the older man whom Fanny marries to give her son a name. If this subtle comedian comes across the most forcefully of all the actors it is partly because he employs the least forceful methods, and partly because, in this adaptation, the comical Panisse—though not mentioned in any of Pagnol's three titles or in the present one—is the protagonist. It is also in the field of pure frolic that many other players make an admirable contribution; Gerald Price and Edna Preston deserve special praise for the particular color they bring to their roles and to the whole festive event.

A Real Writer

GRAHAM GREENE'S *The Living Room* will have died on Broadway before this review appears in print, but I think an autopsy is justified partly because the play was truly alive and partly because the circumstances of its death were dubious, if not incriminating.

The play is about a young Catholic girl who has fallen in love with a married man. If the story were told by an old-fashioned Broadway liberal, the couple could elope, and, after a few verbal thrusts at stuffy, illiberal views of sex, live happily ever after. But the plays nowadays are not about emancipation and escape; they are about the return to the cage or the failure ever to get out of the cage—a vain beating of wings against the bars for two Acts and three quarters and, at the end of Act Three, a dead canary lying on its side. Mr. Greene's tale of adultery is the standard story of present-day theatre: that of the highly-strung girl hounded to death. His protagonist, Rose Pemberton, kills herself.

Why? Mr. Greene gives his own reasons, and permits the audience to think of others. One cheery suggestion that I overheard was that the death is sacrificial: the girl is returning the husband to his wife. Which reminds me of the lady at *The Cocktail Party* who whispered when an actor turned down his glass: "He's emptying his life away!" Our more literary plays provide a field day for interpretative chitchat. . . .

What leads to the suicide scene is a scene between Rose and the wife. The latter pretends she wants to kill herself and scatters sleeping pills on the carpet before rushing wildly out into the night. What distresses Rose is the discovery that the husband is still solicitous for his wife's welfare. He says: "I wish I knew where she'd gone. She hasn't many friends." In her pain and isolation, Rose swallows the pills. She is no heroine. As she dies, she mutters a schoolgirl prayer that school may never start again.

Such are the fruits of adultery in the view of a Catholic author. But this author is a liberal Catholic; he wishes to criticize his own side. So, by way of family background, Rose is presented with three bad Catholics: two hags whose fear of death reaches psychotic proportions and a priest who is no more capable of real prayer than was Hamlet's Uncle Claudius. The moral is drawn: if any of these three had loved Rose sufficiently, she would not have committed suicide.

All of this is so meaningful and interesting a variant on the standard story that it exposes the standard treatment of it (say, in *The Deep Blue Sea*) as the threadbare nonsense that it is. For the first half hour of *The Living Room,* you positively bask in the pleasure of hearing words that have been put together by a real writer to define the lives of people with moral, and not just psychological, problems; for the proper stuff of the drama is not neurosis but immorality. How good it is to see religion shown on stage as, for better or worse, a substantial part of people's lives! How pleasant to encounter a religious playwright who is not naive or inhibited about sexual passion!

If, at the end of the evening, we are disappointed, it is because unusually high hopes have been raised. The confrontation of sensuality and religion is a great dramatic archetype, and as our minds turn to great examples, we realize that we are being unfair to Mr. Greene. *The Living Room* not only fails to be great, as, say, *The Dybbuk* is great, it does not quite match certain plays by similar authors with a similar degree of talent: for example, François Mauriac's *Asmodée,* which is another Catholic account of non-Catholic intrusion into a Catholic home. Mauriac's play is complete: these are his people, this is their plight, this is what would happen. But, with Mr. Greene, the minute you begin to discuss his characters, you become acutely conscious that you don't know them. "Would Rose actually have killed herself?" That depends upon what Rose is like. "Would she actually have had so little feeling for the wife's position?" That too depends. . . . Mr. Greene leaves his characters unfinished, and the girl's suicide is his failure more than hers. For when a playwright can't imagine what anyone says or what comes next, he substitutes sobbing for dialogue and, for action, death. Mr. Greene can also help out with a little macabre melodrama, however incongruous; he never quite manages to make his old hags seem part of the same play. And even in intellectual debate—which, for a brilliant author like this one, is easier to write—Mr. Greene is surprisingly gauche. He perpetrates what is, in this field, a cardinal error: to give the author's spokesman all the good lines. (Bernard Shaw knew better when he gave the knockdown arguments, not to Joan, but to the Inquisitor.) For the priest who turns out to be a flawed human being has through most of the play been the voice of Catholic wisdom, while his antagonist, the husband, spouts what Mr. Greene evidently believes to be "modern ideas." When the priest says: "I thought Freud said there was no such thing as guilt," there is no one on stage to retort: "Then you thought wrong." If Mr. Greene wants to do public battle with modern ideas, he should at least find out what they are.

I do not suggest that it is his duty to do such battle. If the situation in this play were clearer, one might be able to say that ideology has nothing whatever to do with it. Possibly Mr. Greene's strongest point against adultery is a strictly common-sense one which any good pagan can accept: that adultery doesn't seem to make people any happier but on the contrary. . . . Yet at this point I am assailed with doubts. Possibly Mr. Greene doesn't want us to be happy—but to sin our way to Jesus? Possibly he has loaded the dice: we should have to ask him to show us sexual passion which is *not* adulterous. Are there even married people who love each other carnally? One has many questions to ask Mr. Greene.

Meanwhile, he has our condolences. His play, well received in London and Paris, has been shockingly treated in New York not only by the critics but also by its producers. The Gilbert Miller management went to the trouble of importing from England a director, Hugh Hunt, whose work, so far as I know, has never been better than "deestahngay"—much like that of the Miller management. Perhaps someone told Mr. Hunt that the play was too quiet for Broadway, for he ruined Mr. Greene's quiet intensity (the best thing about the play perhaps) by having the actors shout, sob, bite their lips, grit their teeth, clench their fists, and in general convey the idea of Oh God What Shall I Do?—a question only asked when it is too late to do anything.

And then there was the miscasting, most notably of the main role. I liked Barbara Bel Geddes and the sincerity with which she was working on herself; Rose seemed in love, and love was given a quiet, un-Broadwayish dignity. But Miss Bel Geddes rendered no degree of spirituality, of religiousness, at all. It was impossible to believe she was connected by any bond to the Catholic culture which is Mr. Greene's subject matter. Nor is her technique adequate. What place is there in this living (no, dying) room for an affected little drawl out of *The Moon Is Blue*?

Eileen Heckart and Others

---

*"In mildest sunshine Jacob Apfelböck
Murdered his father—mother too withal—
And shut them both up in the laundry chest
And had to sit alone there in the hall. . . ."*

ON MY WAY to see Maxwell Anderson's *The Bad Seed,* I
found myself muttering Bertolt Brecht's famous ballad. The
theme of the homicidal child is a traditional source of quiet
fun; and, arriving at the Forty-sixth Street Theatre, I found
that the director, Reginald Denham, was willing and able to
continue the tradition. The lighting points up an open window through which someone is—or is not?—listening. The
action is full of odd little lulls, one of them broken by a man
screaming as he catches fire and burns to death, another by the
slight sound of the falling curtain as we gaze appalled (well,
almost) on the devilish child who sits angelically reading her
story book.

Little Rhoda Penmark is distinctly pushy: she pushes an old
lady downstairs, and a little boy off the wharf. She it is, too,
who set fire to the screaming hired man. And her mother, not
wanting to turn over the child to the law, has become her
accomplice. A Big Situation! Can it be resolved by having
mother murder little Rhoda and then commit suicide? The
idea seems to promise further innocent merriment. Rhoda
takes the overdose of pills. A shot rings out; mother's a goner.
When the lights go up again, we are all set for a double
funeral. But suddenly the piano starts up in the next room.
The touch is Rhoda's, the tune too. Enter Rhoda. Second and
last Big Situation! None of the survivors know anything of
Rhoda's misdeeds. She is a girl most likely to succeed—in
repeating them *ad infinitum.*

Now, I like that sort of thing, especially the trick ending in
which the audience is misled into believing that Rhoda is

dead. This is to toy with human affairs with an outrageousness that might yield farce as good as a Marx Brothers film or melodrama as good as a Humphrey Bogart—if ever the day should come when the commercial stage might aspire to the rank of screen at its best. Most of *The Bad Seed* is good theatre. One bit, indeed, is so good that it almost damages the rest. I refer to a couple of scenes played by Eileen Heckart as the mother of the murdered little boy.

One of the nicest things in theatre is the way in which a superb performance in a small role can momentarily transfigure a whole production. To act a bereaved mother is easy, and the actress does not live who wouldn't—or even who couldn't —do it like a shot. To act a bereaved mother *in a play that isn't serious* is something else again. Here, it will be important not, as it were, to be too bereaved; and yet to be bereaved; it is *not* easy. This bereaved mother, the script dictates, has taken to drink. Now, "doing a drunk scene" is easy too, so easy that it is seldom well done by men and, by women, almost never, as it would seem that, outside the theatre, actresses either don't get drunk or don't remember it, and, if they see other people drunk, turn away. . . . Well, Miss Heckart solves her problems. Whether by painstaking calculation or lightning intuition, she has worked out a series of stances and movements, of accents and intonations, which are right for this character in this play. Her bereavement is made real enough; it is also left unreal enough. Her drunkenness is funny enough; it is also ugly and sad enough. There are plenty of actors to give us sheer quantity—of pathos or anything else: vehemence goes naturally with the actor's temperament. But those with the art to balance this against that and to leave off when the "enough" point is reached are very few. Miss Heckart being one of them, she not only stops the show for a moment, but reminds us poignantly how far beyond our present profession of actors the possibilities of acting go.

That some of the other actors in *The Bad Seed* do not hold the balance so finely between seriousness and frivolity may not, however, be their own fault. I know nothing of the novel this play is based on, but, taking the play for what it is, I have the impression of an author intermittently and mistakenly trying to be serious. Heaven knows there is a serious play in this material! "What should a mother do?" Shades of Mrs. Alving! The moment the playwright points with any earnestness at a real mother who became the accomplice of her homicidal daughter he is giving himself a problem play to write. Though, in general, Mr. Anderson resisted this temptation, he had an occasional twinge of earnestness and, in effect, asked the actors kindly to practice another style for a few moments. For example, the actor playing Rhoda's father has suddenly to create the emotion a man really feels when his wife kills herself; luckily, he fails; but we are embarrassed at his embarrassment. The father's is a tiny role, but Nancy Kelly, playing the mother, was on the spot. The twinges of earnestness were written, mainly, into her part. What could she do? Shuttle constantly between one style—that is, one world—and another? The evening I saw her, Miss Kelly seemed to be—not desperately but still nervously—trying to keep up appearances. When an actor is uncertain about a part as a whole, he falls back on his "technique" and "personality" and hopes that, if he applies these to all the details taken separately, he can blind the audience to that central uncertainty, that fundamental flaw. I have no means of knowing for sure if Miss Kelly was working somewhat on these lines; I certainly had the impression she was; and so the details she did work on struck me as mannered and actressy; there was even a disturbing echo of another actress—Uta Hagen—in some of the movements and, even more, in the break in the voice, here without meaning. But this is the first time I have seen Miss Kelly; undoubtedly I have not yet found out what she is capable of.

I have heard it said that Mr. Denham's directing is cheap and old-fashioned, but, in the present context, the remark is no derogation. This kind of show is by rights a little cheap, and our real complaint, if we have one, should be against the Playwrights Company for trying excessively to uncheapen it with a physical production that, figuratively and perhaps literally, is too expensive by half. It is as if they wanted to create another *Sabrina Fair* when what was indicated was another *The Bat*—or should we simply say another Reginald Denham spine chiller? So much for the charge of cheapness. As for old-fashionedness, in melodrama there is strong case for it. In modernizing melodrama with psychology and sophistication, we are forgetting about the real guts of the beast.

A word of praise should go to Evelyn Varden for the bright color of her playing in the part of a landlady to whom, by the way, Mr. Anderson gave some very amusing lines of quasi-intellectual chatter—about Freud, inevitably.

Poetry of the Theatre

CLIFFORD ODETS' new play about Noah—entitled *The Flowering Peach*—is the best American play I have reviewed for *The New Republic* up to this time, and, just in case I am suspected of a preference for European plays, let me add that it knocks André Obey's *Noah* into a cocked hat. For Obey's theatricality, though amiable, is empty—it is Cocteau, as it were, relieved of his dazzle and adjusted to the mild light of a ladies' club or junior college. Obey's poetry, though pleasing, has no great significance; anchored in no recognizable reality, it floats rudderless as the ark itself and without divine guidance.

It can be retorted, I know, that Mr. Odets' ark carries all too heavy a freight of meanings. One theme, derived, perhaps, less from Noah than Job, is the humbling of human pride by divine discipline. But this Job is not alone. His youngest son stands up against him and against God and represents a modern point of view: the Divine Disciplinarian being too savage for him, he expresses the hope that even God can improve. No doubt Mr. Odets has read his Shaw. Then again, what God did with his flood suggests what America or Russia might do with the atom bomb. . . .

Granted that no playwright can really handle all this in a single play, one must admire what Mr. Odets has done instead, which is to anchor the Ark in Philadelphia: the Noah family are Jewish immigrants to the United States. The drama of ideas constitutes a kind of subplot which, in being rather a nuisance, only resembles most other subplots. The main plot is what Freud called a family romance, and through this romance Mr. Odets is able to create an image of man in his littleness and his largeness, his ugliness and his beauty, amid the circumstances of such a cosmic catastrophe as today seems no fairy tale.

I will not say that even the family romance is all of a piece. There is too much argufying about marriage and divorce. Driven by some irrelevant compulsion, Mr. Odets tries to force into his play more material concerning marriage and divorce than—by its own logic—it requires. Now there are two subjects on which Mr. Odets has always been more an ideologist than an artist: one is politics and the other is sex. That is why the marital squabbles in *The Flowering Peach* belong, paradoxically, less to the family romance than to the over-obtrusive subplot of ideas. The relationships to which the word Romance applies are those of Noah and his wife and of Noah and his youngest son. It would seem that while Mr. Odets tends to see young lovers in terms of schmaltz or brutality, for an old man who loves wife and child he can find the very language of the heart.

That is not all. Though the orthodox, Jewish or Christian, may be irritated by the ideas of the subplot, they cannot accuse Mr. Odets of doing what they probably expected him to do; namely, to belittle Noah's Faith. If religion is to be found, not in creeds and avowals but in reverence for life, in humility before the mystery of things, in a man's spontaneous and pervasive spirituality, then this Noah is a religious man, and so is his author. In fact Mr. Odets has shown our fumbling theological playwrights how to put religion—or rather, religiousness—on stage. The perfect instance and symbol of this accomplishment is Menasha Skulnik, as Noah, delicately holding a singing mouse (the mythical gitka) in his huge and horny hands.

Mr. Skulnik is three quarters of the performance, as Noah is three quarters of the play. He stands center stage—figuratively and often literally—and we, like the actors, sit at his feet while in a voice that nature meant to be ugly—a bassoon played by a Marx Brother—he beautifully tells us, as he phrases it, "a mystery." We have here the most lyrical of actors, but also one of the most powerful. I doubt if any such Atlas has carried a playwright's world on his shoulders since Lee Cobb worked for Arthur Miller in *Death of a Salesman.* But, while Mr. Cobb grunted, groaned, and screamed at the weight, Mr. Skulnik roars you as gently as any sucking dove, as sweetly as any nightingale. Of all our actors, he is the finest in repose, his modesty has most dignity, his smallness the largest largeness. He sits there, shoulders drooping, hands folded, knees together, toes turned slightly in—or he stands and shambles across the deck with his pants sagging from his backside and bunched up over his shoes—and the stage is lit as brightly as by . . . but why compare Mr. Skulnik to his inferiors? Let me remark, inadequately, that it is a wonderfully quiet and slow-moving play, and that Mr. Skulnik demonstrates what the Broadway public is loath to believe: that drama, like music, need not be either fast-moving or loud.

The supporting cast ranges between competence and distinction. Janice Rule's eyes make a very special contribution, though in the simplest of ways: they are lovely and sad and well able to evoke the whole succession of Old Testament heroines from Rachel to Ruth. Mario Alcalde is a markedly less developed actor than his colleagues. Physically, he has not yet outgrown an adolescent awkwardness; as for his mind, he has some trouble convincing us he knows what the ideological Mr. Odets is talking about. Yet immaturity has its likable side in anyone, not least in a young actor with looks and a good deal of spirit. Martin Ritt, on the other hand, seems almost too knowing for Mr. Odets' Shem, who is a crude profiteer; but his highly-nerved, vigorously paced performance is of great value to the show. Berta Gersten plays Noah's wife and, along with Mr. Skulnik, supplies the Jewish gestures and vocal patterns with which most of the humor is pointed up; she, too, is lovely in repose.

The play sets the designer at the Belasco Theatre an unusual problem, for he has to give physical definiteness to a story that belongs to two distinct eras: the remote past and the living present. Mordecai Gorelik tried to suggest the "unreality" of it by framing his sets in an arch, placed just inside the curtain. The "reality" of Noah's home was rendered in a sort of elementally simple and timeless style of architecture and furniture—for my taste, too abstract. The outdoor scenes were better. There were trees whose freshness spread to the play; and there was an ark that seemed eminently suited to the actors' uses. If one complains of some designers that they are painters who do not know stagecraft or the drama, one might make the opposite complaint of Mr. Gorelik; perhaps he retains the "social theatre's" hostility to the "esthetic," i.e., to beauty. . . . Abe Feder enjoyed himself at the switchboard, but I do not enjoy myself when I can't see the actors' faces—an occasional offence in this show. Rainclouds were so effectively simulated that the ghost of David Belasco was heard clapping.

I left the theatre in a glow of pleasure and admiration; that perhaps is the main thing to say. And the source of the pleasure? In some degree, it is just that a play has been *written* —that is to say, set down in living language. Modern plays in general are set down in dead language; the dialogue is something our directors have to drown in a sea of action. In American drama especially, the note of living language is seldom struck. It is heard for an hour or so in *Anna Christie*. It is heard in certain scenes of Tennessee Williams—when, for example, the mother speaks in *The Glass Menagerie* or Blanche in *A Streetcar Named Desire*. Yet Clifford Odets suggests comparison less with these compatriots than with two European contemporaries—Sean O'Casey and Eduardo De Filippo. These three poets of the urban masses are subject to similar temptations (especially the temptation of Culture) while their real talent is all, as it were, on the wrong side of the tracks. In the thirties, Mr. Odets was admired as the Voice of Protest. That no longer seems such a great thing to be. *Awake and Sing* has been admired, too, for the accuracy of its idiom; but this is the talent of the parrot and the tape recorder. The real merit of this author, as of O'Casey and De Filippo, is a matter of the *imaginative use* of dialect, which in turn is a matter of the poet's inner identification with the people who speak that dialect.

I call these writers poets with only one poetic genre in mind: the poetry of the theatre, a poetry of the spoken word, the acted word, the word held up to the light to be stared at by a crowd, the word flung across footlights by actor-marksmen aiming straight at the heart of an audience. And I have in mind that when Mr. Odets' plays were presented in London during the Marxist decade "a well-known English novelist and playwright" [1] dared to question the reality in Mr. Odets' realism. "Practically every scene is jazzed up, given more punch and excitement and noise than it should have, without reference to reality at all." If he had added "and a good thing too," I should have agreed with him. Not that I want to defend "noise," which, for that matter, Mr. Odets, in his new play, does without. But there was always more jazz and punch in Mr. Odets than there was "socialist realism," less of Karl, than of Harpo, Marx.

All of which is to repeat that he is a poet and of the theatre.

[1] As quoted, though not named, by James Agate in his review of Odets' *Paradise Lost,* later reprinted in *Red Letter Nights.*

There Is Charm and Charm

JEAN ANOUILH is at last enjoying something of a success in New York: his *Thieves' Carnival* received "rave notices" from Brooks Atkinson in *The New York Times* and Walter Kerr in *The New York Herald Tribune.*

The play tells the story of three rascals—pickpockets and burglars—who prey on the home of a Lord Edgard and Lady Hurf in Vichy. It is the quintessence of Anouilh: in this short, slight masterpiece that he wrote at the age of twenty-one, the French playwright seems to have prefigured everything he would write later. The world into which the burglars irrupt is one of almost amiable yet entirely despicable decadent aristocracy. The *dramatis personae* are a gallery of freaks—that is to say, a group of people who are one and all incapable of love.

One and almost all. The essential story is that just one lady and just one burglar fall in love. Their love, of course, can come to nothing—class difference constitutes a fatal gap and symbolizes the impossibility of loving in general—except that we are here in that land of pleasant (which Anouilh calls "pink") surmise where, because pretence is real, the impossible is possible. Is the amorous burglar really of humble birth?

> LORD EDGARD: You are twenty years old, are you not?
> BURGLAR: Yes.
> LORD EDGARD: Right. (*Takes out a photograph.*) Fine. Open your shirt. Fine. Now, the mark behind the ear. Fine. (*Takes out a medal.*) You recognize this medal?
> BURGLAR: No.
> LORD EDGARD: Never mind. You are my son who was stolen from me at a tender age! (*He falls on his neck.*)

With the help of the *fiancée* everything is patched up. Only, to be sure, Lord Edgard was lying. When the lovers leave, Lady Hurf says, "You never had a son stolen from you at a tender age," and that pillar of the peerage answers: "No, it's a picture I cut out of a magazine." The imposture seems to have been the one good act of his life, and the ending of the little entertainment is a happy one for the young couple. "For those," it concludes, "who have played the escapade with the zest of youth, the comedy is a success, for they played their youth, a thing which succeeds always; they weren't even aware of the comedy."

If the moral reminds us of Pirandello, the manner of the play takes us back through Musset to Marivaux. These are, indeed, not so much diverse influences as a single tradition, the tradition of a comic theatre in which masquerade is a symbol of human life—"all the men and women merely players." Out of the game of play acting, M. Anouilh creates an image of the game of life, and, conversely, out of the game of life, he creates a game for actors which for charm, wit, and sprightliness constitutes one of the best plays of the past quarter century.

But where are the actors, today, who know the rules of such a game or, if they do, can play it with any delicacy or aplomb? On our Anglo-American stage, Reality is limited to realism, and realism is limited to naturalism, and naturalism is limited to neurasthenics: while Style, in general, means a British deportment—stiff upper lip, stiff limbs, and stiffer backbone—and an elocutionary, Oxonian delivery. Proscenium Productions at the Cherry Lane Theatre achieved Style in this sense with their commendable production of *The Way of the World* in the fall. *Thieves' Carnival* is nothing like so great a piece of literature, yet it is much more deeply rooted in the life and tradition of theatre and for that reason it sets our actors a more important task: for them it is more important to be able to create the special life of theatrical art (including words but not consisting of words) than it is to be able to speak literature.

The production at the Cherry Lane has its points. The costumes, for example, give a surprising amount of pleasure: more than any other element in the show they suggest M. Anouilh's characteristic blend of humor with charm, caricature with wistful grace. I take it (for lack of other indication in the program) that they are to be credited to the designer, Don Crawford, whose sets also (if not equally) make a contribution. In the acting, as one would expect from young Americans, the humor is a hundred times better projected than the charm. William Le Massena—equally effective as old woman and Spanish grandee—is an actor whose comedy belongs to the world of Groucho Marx. Admirable in a more restrained manner is Tom Bosley who plays the Andrew Aguecheek of the evening and looks admirably droll in pink-and-white-barred burglar's undershirt. As to the two young leading ladies, the program pointedly remarks that one of them (Frances Sternhagen) has had her hair and make-up done by Helena Rubinstein; and indeed, she seems to walk, not out of a picture by Fragonard, but off a page of *Vogue*. That is a limitation. There is charm and Charm; the femininity of this show is in capitals. Dolores Mann (the other comely young person) probably isn't imitating either Barbara Bel Geddes in *The Moon Is Blue* or Audrey Hepburn in *Ondine,* but the spectator is bound to think her synthetic, mannered delivery an imitation of something or other. I wouldn't deny that, after a good spanking, Miss Mann might be able to act, and even speak, very well indeed.

One of the Proscenium producers, Warren Enters, again directed. Perhaps he is not as deft in the handling of action as of speech; or perhaps the task was too hard; at any rate, one cannot pay him quite the same tribute as last time. Though assisted by a choreographer, Mr. Enters has given this show less of the lissom elegance of ballet and pantomime than of the jollity of collegiate high jinks. There is too much coyness and self-congratulation in this fun.

One of the most theatrical, and not least effective, features of the play is a musician who plays the clarinet on stage. I do not know just how M. Anouilh visualized the role, but his stage directions simply specify a solitary musician in a bandstand when the show opens. The image of an actual bandsman seems to me much stronger than the one Mr. Enters invoked, which is that of a harlequin in diamond tights. Even if the harlequin reference must be overt, should the actor indulge in so much chucklesome cavorting?

If I have said that when Anouilh is charming this show tends to be glamorous *à la* Rubinstein, I should add that, when he is ironic, the show tends to be frightfully jolly and that, when he is wistful, it tends to be in deadly earnest.

But Junk Is Junk

I PREFER MOVIE THRILLERS to stage thrillers; is it because the latter are so much damaged by intermissions? Strong is the suspense that can survive two ten-minute interruptions. Joseph Hayes' *The Desperate Hours* succeeds, I think. The situation is interesting enough: an American family is held captive by gunmen in its own home. And Mr. Hayes knows how to keep us on tenterhooks as to whether anyone in the family will get hurt. For a moment, it seems that a clever father has maneuvered the crooks out of the house. But Junior has chosen this moment to leave too, and the crooks get back by using him as a hostage. "Crowded with incident" is the expression, I believe.

Junior's schoolmarm comes to visit and sees one of the crooks; the alarm is a false one, though; she doesn't realize what manner of man he is. There are crosscurrents. The three crooks can't agree among themselves; their one gun changes hands rather ominously. The family, too, though resolutely typical, contains different elements: while mamma has a steady head, papa and the son and daughter have dangerous leanings towards heroism. All this and a revenge drama too. The chief crook is out to "get" a certain cop, and the cop is afraid he'll have to "get" the crook instead. On stage, we see the cops in small, inset scenes between the main scenes in the house; they are busy, most of the time, keeping track of a car driven by a certain young lady who is coming to meet the crooks. In general, she gets steadily nearer, but here too Mr. Hayes can be relied on to provide some amusing contretemps.

That's the play. That's the kind of thing that gives the play whatever life it has in the theatre. The rest is either performance or junk. The performance is efficient; and so I have little to say about it. To prompt a discussion, a show must be less than efficient or more; *The Desperate Hours*, directed by Robert Montgomery, is summed up in the one word. The director presses a button, the set appears, the actors go through their motions, Brooks Atkinson writes a rave review, the box office drawer starts to jingle, the backers order new Cadillacs, *ce n'est pas magnifique, mais c'est la guerre.*

Among the actors, Paul Newman, perhaps, has more than efficiency to offer. I was impressed with the way he could go from his complaisant part in *Picnic* to the roughneck in the new play, though I hope he will watch some real roughnecks and stop watching (though, after all, this is impossible) Marlon Brando. The father is played by Karl Malden, an actor who bids fair to be permanently frustrated by the type-casting which is the bane of American theatre; that he is able to act the solid citizen correctly seems to deter producers from offering him roles which would release his full talent. I know what Mr. Malden can do from seeing him play that terror of a father in *Desire under the Elms.*

The Desperate Hours is, of course, "more than a thriller"; it is a thriller plus junk, and solemn, moralistic, pseudo-intellectual junk at that. The audience identifies itself with father Malden, the average American whose equipment is $15,000 a year and the wisdom of the ages—a 1955 version of the Common Man. The inner drama of the play is found in the growing rage of this righteous man who turns out to have a beast in him; but reason conquers passion; and the play culminates in his refusal to take revenge on the gangster who had tried to kill his son. (I wouldn't have made this summary satirical if the play didn't deserve it. Calculated hokum or natural naïveté? Or does it really matter which? Junk is junk.)

Isn't it strange? If anyone says the theatre ought to be edifying, a hundred Broadwayites rise to remind him that the theatre provides commercial entertainment. Then you pay your $4.80 for commercial entertainment, and are subjected to such harangues and exhortations as the churches have for centuries been offering at an optional charge. Or am I out of date about the churches? And have church and theatre swapped roles? Is the modern preacher just as eager to make an entertainment out of his sermon as the modern playwright is to make a sermon out of his entertainment?

I have often had occasion to point out that American farce is marred by moralism. The American *farceur* may begin by thumbing his nose; he will certainly insist on saluting the flag in the last act. A current example is Sidney Kingsley with his *Lunatics and Lovers*. For nine-tenths of the evening he gives the American household gods a terrible beating, but in the last minute we find him on his knees before them. It is too late. Since Mr. Kingsley has made us feel that the joke against respectability and sentiment is such a good one, we are not heartened at the discovery that he himself is respectable and sentimental. *Lunatics and Lovers* has been described as a "dirty show." But it is also a clean show. And personally I found the dirt—so handily flung around by Buddy Hackett—a good deal cleaner than the cleanliness.

The odor of earnestness is not good for melodrama either. True, there has always been some solemnity in this genre, and an unsophisticated audience could always be very moral about it. What is new about our melodramas today is not their virtuousness *per se* but their earnestness and their intellectual pretensions. They are full of notions, psycho- and sociological, which we are supposed to take seriously (as against the old sort, in *Dracula* for example, which we took playfully) . Hence, it is not enough for Maxwell Anderson that a child be a villain: the villainy has to be "explained" as a fact of heredity, an explanation as phony as anything in *Dracula* but *not admitted to be so.* It is not enough for Alfred Hayes that his heroes be heroes, his villains villains. We must have dull psychological "explanations" of villainy; and virtue must be given overtones of a pep-talk on "the American way of life" or a class in civics.

Pondering this problem a couple of years ago,[1] I suggested that the alternative to these pseudo-ideas was ideas. If the aim is a "higher" drama, this is true. But if the aim is farce or melodrama, we can do without all theories and notions except the most rudimentary moral distinctions which need no elaboration and can be taken for granted. In the realm of farce, I know of no good current example. But there is a current melodrama with many farcical elements and totally without moral or philosophic pretension. This is Agatha Christie's *Witness for the Prosecution.* If our society considers that writers like Mr. Hayes make a larger contribution than writers like Mrs. Christie, our society cannot distinguish between earnestness and seriousness, intellectuality and intelligence. To be as playful as Mrs. Christie presupposes a certain poised and mature worldliness; her play, like *The Importance of Being Earnest,* is a "trivial comedy for serious people." Was it Wilde, too, who said that only superficial people despise superficiality? Certainly none has known better than he that such contempt goes with gracelessness, cant, and unction.

If the theatre were that home of frivolity which it is supposed to be—a place where Pierrot pirouettes and Harlequin cracks his slender jokes—it would be a much nicer place than at present it customarily is.

[1] See above, page 49.

Wild Duck and Tame Phoenix

WE DEFINE THE greatness of playwrights variously, yet I sometimes think you can spot the supremely great ones in the first
scene of almost any of their plays. I am not thinking of their
skill in exposition or any purely technical feature but of that
quality of imagination by which they establish their own
atmosphere, create their own world. My sense of the greatness
of Chekhov does not date from my analytic study of his structures but from the moment, much earlier in life, when the first
few lines of *The Seagull* came to me across the footlights. My
sense of the greatness of Strindberg dates from a similar experience with *The Father;* no sooner was the curtain up than
the unseen hand of the author had me by the throat. It was
somewhat the same with Pirandello, Shaw, and above all
Ibsen. "Excitement" is a poor word, and mere excitation is not
necessarily good, but there is an excitement of the theatre
which is a lure to all of us who are stage-struck; and the great
moderns provide more of it, not less, than the non-great ones.
Our journalists who think of such dramatists as "coldly intellectual" naturally assume that what you or I enjoy in modern
drama is its "cold intellectuality." No doubt Beethoven's last
quartets seem coldly intellectual to those who don't really like
music.

There is also the difference between a twitching of the
nerves and an excitement that is grand and noble. Before the
curtain has been up five minutes on *The Master Builder* at the
Phoenix Theatre you know which it is that the author and the
designer have in mind. Boris Aronson's set is lofty in conception and clever in execution. American stage design is usually
competent and often brilliant, but Aronson (alone?) is an
explorer—an explorer of the stage as a medium and of the
play as a mystery to be guessed. His sets for *The Master
Builder* amount to the largest single contribution made to the

show. His interpretation of Ibsen is more sure-footed and more suggestive than anything else that happens. In three settings (which could only be described by photography) he contrives to have the best of both the worlds, the abstract and the representational, the symbolic and the actual, very much like the Norwegian master himself.

The acting in those first five minutes, or even the first twenty, is equally impressive. The previous evening I had been seeing that pompous exhibition of dull acting which is the Cornell-McClintic production of Christopher Fry's *The Dark Is Light Enough.* This evening, I say to myself as soon as the actors start, we are back in the living theatre: Muriel Berkson, Art Smith, Gene Saks, and Margaret Barker are all doing better work in small parts than anyone last night did in big parts. . . . The New York theatre is extraordinarily uneven; there is no ratio between talent and fame, perhaps not even an inverse ratio; and in Oscar Homolka we have a real star, not another of those much-publicized bores. His entrance is quiet, unshowy. In a few small, quick movements, he has established the character. We see the bigness of Solness, the susceptibility to young women; here the weariness is indicated, there the humor, in another place the fear, in another the hauntedness; and all these nuances (school of Geraldine Page, as it were) from an actor of massive presence and fine sleepy strength. I respect Mr. Homolka and could and did watch him intently for hours; because he is every inch an artist, he couldn't be dull if he tried.

Then why does he try? Why does he try so very hard? A performance that starts out as a masterpiece *tout court* ends as a masterpiece of disastrous understatement. The massive presence has the inertia of massivity, the sleepy strength never wakes up. There is "build-up" after "build-up"; and no climax. Let no one say Mr. Homolka couldn't do it if he wanted to. One would never be angry with an incapable actor. One is angry at the sight of capacities unused. Here is one of our most powerful performers declining to show his power.

The failure can be explained away as an "interpretation" of Ibsen. The script has been rather drastically cut, and indeed everything (always excepting the work of Aronson) has been reduced in scale, just as *The Seagull, Coriolanus,* and *Doctor's Dilemma* were reduced in scale at this same theatre. Is it the ambition of the Phoenix to be the last stronghold of ultranaturalistic acting? This management has intelligence, knowledgeability, and taste but, apparently, no daring whatsover; and without daring there can be no vital theatricality. But I have no means of knowing if Mr. Homolka was influenced by his management. Perhaps he had everything his own way? This is indeed an alternative explanation. Ought he to have directed the show? It is noteworthy that a crucial scene in which Solness does not appear is quite abominably directed. The death of Solness is announced before we are ready for it, and then the actress playing Hilda Wangel performs some inept gymnastics by way of indicating I don't know what about her acceptance of Solness' death.

Hilda is played by Mr. Homolka's wife, Joan Tetzel. It is not flatly a bad performance, for Miss Tetzel is not without charm, but it is rather a thin performance and a very wrong one. When Miss Tetzel has given us her smile, she seems to have all too little left to bestow. Directed by her canny husband, she boldly tries to make do with girlishness, pleasant looks, and sincerity. No doubt, the "interpretation" is that Hilda can be played with a minimum of reference to Ibsen's notorious symbolism and a maximum of simple femininity. The result of the "interpretation," however, is that the rich material of the Hilda-Solness relationship is reduced to an almost Hollywoodian banality. At best this Hilda is a Bennington girl with a crush on the professor.

I get the impression—this is not "inside dope," but an outsider's intuition, right or wrong—that Mr. Homolka has worked very hard on Miss Tetzel's performance somewhat at the expense of his own, that he defers to her in a way that makes for happy marriage rather than good art. At the second performance he seemed tired throughout; played all three acts on the same note; and spoke an unnecessarily sloppy English (granted his right to a strong Austrian accent). He needs a director.

The production does a disservice to the reputation of Ibsen in New York. If you emasculate an author, you can scarcely be surprised if ignorant persons declare him a eunuch from way back. Too much of Ibsen's poetry, his passion, and his meaning is missing from the show. At the same time, the evening is an exceptional one. If this is Ibsen and water, many theatre evenings are water without Ibsen. For all that I have said against him, Mr. Homolka is an actor of the first rank. And there's always Aronson.

What Is Beauty, Saith My Sufferings, Then?

CHRISTOPHER FRY has for years been trying to write beautiful plays, and, on the side, he has conducted a polemic against what he believes to be the great obstacle to beauty in the theatre—realism. Yet the fact is that the beauty of Mr. Fry's plays, when they are beautiful, is too calculated an effect, an effect which the author seems to be forever congratulating himself on; whereas the modern playwright who has achieved beauty with least strain and most abundance is the last of the great Russian realists, Anton Chekhov.

There is no more beautiful modern play than *The Three Sisters*. It is curious that this should be so. The subject matter suggests neither celestial loveliness nor infernal grandeur, nothing that might make up a Shakespearean drama, comic or tragic. Middle-class life is boring, and traditionally it entered the drama only to be made fun of. Ibsen took a different tack. His idea was that suburbia only *seemed* boring; the house behind the façade was haunted; the man behind the stolid brow was neurotic. Ibsen's is a dramatic idea, while Chekhov's seems not to be so: it is to place the very boresomeness of lower-middle-class culture on the stage. Not content with being a great playwright, he wished, it would seem, to give himself the greatest possible handicap—to fight, as it were, with his right hand tied behind his back. But this is only a manner of speaking. Great artists like to be trussed up. "In der Beschraenkung zeigt sich erst der Meister." It is the Chekhov characters, not their author, who are inhibited and constricted. It may be said of Chekhov as of Shakespeare that he was "of an open and free nature," [1] a phrase no one would apply to our minor playwrights, nor even to Ibsen and Strindberg. Chekhov seems to me the only democrat among the major modern dramatists, or perhaps I mean the only Christian: the only one, at any rate, who can depict the "little" people around him with a deeply romantic and passionate love and hence without direct contempt on the one hand or, on the other, the indirect contempt of abstract, doctrinaire admiration. This may be the fundamental reason why his plays are beautiful. It is not an intended beauty. It is a beauty that radiates from a beautiful spirit, and its radiance is an irreducibly real love of his fellow men.

Such love is simple in that it is not neurotic and compulsive, but spontaneous and flowing; it springs, not from fear and need, but from joy and plenitude. But it is also complex, in being an integral part of a rich and many-sided mind. Genius, surely, implies an unusually subtle and successful organization of the personality—everything being more closely related to everything else than in the rest of us. Now one of the crucial relationships in Chekhov is that between his love and his humor. Perhaps there is always a connection between these. Without humor, an intelligent man fails to love himself; clearly, then, he cannot "love his neighbor *as himself*"; nor, without humor, can he "place" the faults in other people which intelligence makes him aware of. Chekhov was able to set his love and his humor to work in constant, and constantly fruitful, interplay. And, if he had a genius for loving, he is also one of the great humorists. He learnt not only from Tolstoy but from Gogol.

The Fourth Street Theatre has not the resources, personal or economic, to present a great production of so hard a play as *The Three Sisters*. And the presence of certain veteran profes-

---

[1] I speak of his artistic personality. In his relations with people, he sometimes showed himself as inhibited and constricted as his characters.

sionals in the cast calls the more attention to the limitations of younger players; nor are the seasoned professionals all of equal caliber. Unevenness in the acting is the chief fault of the show. The only other thing that seriously bothered me is the theatre itself. The play is done arena style in the middle of a long, narrow room. The arena is square—from wall to wall one way, and up to the spectators' feet the other way. If you sit towards the back of either bank of seats, you feel you are peering into a tunnel. As for the "stage" you feel you're at the side of it, and you keep wanting to move round in front. In short, the "blocking" always seems wrong and is always calling attention to itself. What a sensible invention the proscenium stage was!

These reservations made, I have to report that the evening is one of the most enjoyable of the season. After all, a Beethoven sonata can be enjoyed even when it isn't played by Schnabel on a Steinway. This is a great and lovely play, and its greatness and loveliness come through instead of being obstructed and whittled away as I remember them to have been in the grandiose Broadway production of a dozen years ago. For one thing, the play is correctly interpreted by its director, David Ross. He has managed to get rid, not only of the grandiosity (which, at the Fourth Street, is rather easy), but also of all that mooning and swooning around that passes for Chekhovian acting in the Anglo-American theatre. It is made clear that the sisters are small-town girls, not Park Avenue hostesses in disguise. It is made clear that the orations on the glorious future reflect, not the author's optimism, but the sad futility of Vershinin and Tusenbach who speak them.

The outstanding individual performances are three, and one of them is turned in by a youngster, Peggy Maurer, as Irina, who brings with beauty and intensity a capacity for stillness and repose which most of her colleagues miss. (Many young people today think they are practicing the Stanislavsky "method" when they're only fidgeting and pulling faces.) When Miss Maurer loses the last trace of physical rigidity, she will give a first-rate performance. If it seemed odd to have cast one of the oldest actors as the young Andrei, Morris Carnovsky more or less justified the choice. If he was not fully credible as a boyish fiancé, and his "Yiddish theatre" gesticulation conveyed more embarrassment than character, he portrayed the pains of modern cuckoldom later with a combination of respect and intensity thoroughly Chekhovian. For me, the perfect gem of acting in this not ignoble tiara was Philip Loeb's portrayal of the Doctor. Thinking of the rather shameless way in which Edmund Gwenn, playing the part on Broadway, was allowed to ruin the Doctor's pathetic drunk scene with ribald antics, I am very grateful to Mr. Loeb for restoring that episode to its true dignity. He gets all his effects gently, but completely and firmly; this, too, is a Chekhovian formula.

I also liked George Ebeling's comical, soft Tusenbach, and several other performances, but the main merit of the show lies less in individual assertion than in the evident devotion of each to the good of all. Devotion is yet another Chekhovian virtue and, obviously, my main point is that the production is one to cherish because it stays so close to a great playwright. Stark Young's text is close to him, too, so far as I, with a little Russian, can judge, both in the letter and the spirit.

Tennessee Williams and New York Kazan

Jo MIELZINER's setting for *Cat on a Hot Tin Roof* consists of a square and sloping platform with one of its corners, not one of its sides, jutting out towards the audience. A corner of a ceiling is above, pointing upstage. On the platform are minimum furnishings for a bed-sitting-room. Around the room, steps and space suggest the out-of-doors. The whole stage is swathed in ever-changing light and shade; at the outset ribbed light and shade projected on the front curtain suggest sunlight filtering through Venetian blinds.

Such is the world of Elia Kazan, as we know it from his work on plays by more authors than one. The general scheme is that not only of *A Streetcar Named Desire* but also of *Death of a Salesman:* an exterior that is also an interior—but, more important, a view of *man's* exterior that is also a view of his interior, the habitat of his body and the country of his memories and dreams. A theatre historian would probably call this world a combination of naturalism and expressionism, yet one has no impression that it was arrived at by mixture, or even by choice, of styles: it is a by-product, or perhaps end product, of a certain sort of work which has its own history and identity. It is one of the distinctive creations of American theatre.

It is re-created, for the new production, with a difference. One might say, changing the metaphor, that the objective of Mr. Kazan's campaign was, without abandoning any of the old positions, to advance to new ones, above all to reach and conquer that far outpost of the imagination which we call Grandeur. (If only he had directed *The Master Builder!*) He has departed further from naturalism: just as there is less furniture and less scenery, so there is a less natural handling of actors, a more conscious concern with stagecraft, with pattern, with form. Attention is constantly called to the tableau, to what, in movies, is called the individual "frame." You feel that Burl Ives has been *placed* center stage, not merely that he *is* there; in the absence of most of the furniture, a man's body is furnishing the room. When the man lifts his crippled son off the floor, the position is held a long moment as for a time exposure. My neighbor nudges me at this point, and whispers, "Why, it's a Michelangelo." I suspect she has Burl Ives curiously confused with the Virgin Mary, but I appreciate the fact that she was called upon to whisper *something.*

All the groupings are formalized. My review should probably be accompanied by diagrams showing where Mr. Kazan put everybody, by twos, by threes, this one over here moon-gazing through the imaginary window, this one over there ego-gazing at the imaginary mirror, all fixed to the spot until the director's signal is given to move. (*"You* roll into a ball," said one of the great Russian directors to a recalcitrant actor, "*I* throw you.") When Mr. Ives has a funny story to tell, Mr. Kazan lines up the other actors in a row to listen to him. When Mr. Ives wishes to be more intimate, an actress steps to the left and makes a space for him in the row, as if the performance were a dance or a military drill. The lights are handled with equal formality. A follow-spot from the back of the balcony chases the actors around, picking out the center of the action for a kind of emphasis resembling a movie close-up; one is often reminded that this stage director is also a movie director.

Another aspect of Mr. Kazan's formality is the repeating of features of former shows—as if he is trying to establish symbols or at least fixed patterns. He did remarkable things with the Requiem that closes *Death of a Salesman.* I have the impression he tries to repeat them in *Cat on a Hot Tin Roof,* and I was rather disturbed by the identical use of Mildred Dunnock's plaintive vein as a final "shattering" effect. Another recurrence, partly effective, partly just disturbing, is that of the final scene from *Tea and Sympathy.* The play, in each case, is all but over; it only remains to say that the man and woman do make love. For this statement Mr. Kazan pulls out all his stops, or rather all those that are tender and tremulous. And the soft music would be all right if he didn't also, as it were, add the words of a hymn: it is not the lyricism but the moralism of these endings that seems to me unconvincing. Doubtless it is but the traditional moralism of melodrama— the idea of Virtue Triumphant. What I find unacceptable is the justification of this idea as provided in the two plays concerned. But this is to anticipate. Here I wish only to indicate that all of Mr. Kazan, what we admire more, what we admire less, is in the show.

And with the means of the new American theatre (school of Lee Strasberg and Harold Clurman) it does reach the most cherished end of the older theatre—true grandeur of performance—at a time when the older theatre itself (school of Guthrie McClintic, shall we say) is failing to do so. *Cat on a Hot Tin Roof* is grander theatre than *The Dark Is Light Enough,* or than the Jeffers-Anderson *Medea,* or than any American Shakespeare production that I remember.

I do not think the reason for this resides in the formality itself. The effectiveness of this grandeur results, in my opinion, from the interaction between formality in the setting, lighting, and grouping and an opposite quality—informality is hardly the word—in the individual performances. The externals of the physical production belong, as it were, to the old theatre, but the acting is internal, "Stanislavskyite." Within the formal setting, from the fixed positions in which they are made to stand, the actors live their roles with that vigilant, concentrated, uninterrupted nervous intensity which Mr. Kazan always manages to give. I say he gives it to them, since clearly they do not find it unaided. Directed by Jed Harris in *The Crucible,* Madeleine Sherwood seemed cut off from her own emotions. Directed by Mr. Kazan, she is able to find and release feelings which surely were far less readily accessible. Another kind of directorial feat is represented by Burl Ives' performance. Mr. Ives is not first and foremost an actor. If he comes across as such in the new play, a lot of the credit must go to the director who so skilfully exploits and guides his personality and physique.

Yet another distinction of Mr. Kazan's shows is the work done in the small roles. There is a part in *Cat on a Hot Tin Roof* with almost no lines at all, but what Mr. Kazan is able to do with a bald head, a rumpled suit, and trousers that sit rather low on the hips, might almost, were the word not so inflammatory, be called co-authorship. Last, there is a sort of triumph that is completely uncontroversial: it occurs when the work of the Actors' Studio pays off in what is both an excellent characterization and a piece of excellent workmanship. The compliment is for Pat Hingle who, as the tame duck of a brother, demonstrates that to a real actor there is no such thing as an ungrateful part. You have only to see Mr. Hingle clap hands—he does it once, the act is over as soon as begun— to see that he is the real thing.

(2)

Yet something is terribly wrong. To say there is no unity of effect is the understatement of the century. After first seeing *Cat on a Hot Tin Roof* I felt that such different things had been done to me that I couldn't possibly gather my responses together and write a review. It is only after a second visit that I venture to piece together a tentative analysis.

The cat of the title is the heroine, the roof her marriage; her husband would like her to jump off, that is, find a lover. Driven by passions he neither understands nor controls, he takes to drink and envies the moon, the hot cat and the cool moon being the two chief symbols and points of reference in the play. The boy says he has taken to drink because "mendacity is the system we live in." His father, however, explains that this is an evasion: the real reason is that he is running away from homosexuality. At this point, the author abruptly changes the subject (to the father's mortal illness) and never really gets back to it. One does not, of course, demand that he "cure" the boy, only that he present him: he should tell the audience, even if he doesn't tell the boy himself, whether a "cure" is possible, and, if not, whether homosexuality is something this individual can accept as the irrevocable truth about himself. At present, one can only agree with his father that the story is fatally incomplete. *Cat on a Hot Tin Roof* was heralded by some as the play in which homosexuality was at last to be presented without evasions on the author's part. The miracle has still not happened.

If some things in Mr. Williams' story are too vaguely defined, others are defined in a manner far too summary and definite. The characters, for example, are pushed around by an obsessively and mechanically sexual interpretation of life. "How good is he (or she) in bed?" is what everyone asks of everyone else. Now it seems to me that there are people, even in the world of Tennessee Williams, who would not ask this question, especially not of those who are near and dear. And what does the query mean? A girl seems good in bed if you like *her;* otherwise, she seems bad in bed; and for most of us that is the heart of the matter. Mr. Williams, who apparently disagrees, sends his people to bed rather arbitrarily. The husband's friend, in the new play, goes there with the wife to prove he is not homosexual. And she must have been seeing *Tea and Sympathy,* for she co-operates. In the circumstances we can hardly be surprised that he proves impotent; yet he reaches the startlingly excessive conclusion that he is homosexual; and

kills himself. Surely the author can't be assuming that a man is
either a hundred per cent heterosexual or a hundred per cent
homosexual? One wouldn't know: the whole thing is disposed
of so grandly in quick, if lengthy, narratives. It is characteristic
that the plot depends for its plausibility upon our not questioning that if a man and a woman come together *once*, a child
will result.

Not all the characters are credible. If a girl has a hunch that
her husband is homosexual, does she simply clamor for him to
sleep with her? Not, certainly, if she is the kind of girl portrayed at the Morosco Theatre by Barbara Bel Geddes. Which
brings me to the relation of play and production. It seems to
be a relation of exact antithesis. When the curtain first goes
up, Mr. Williams sends on stage a girl whose dress has been
spilled on at dinner; but, so far as the audience can see, the
dress is as spotless as it is golden and sparkling. It is the same
with her personality and character. From the author: a rather
ordinary girl, *bornée*, perhaps stupid, shabby-genteel. From
the production: Barbara Bel Geddes, the very type of non-
shabby, upper-class gentility, wholesome as a soap ad. It is the
same with other characters. Burl Ives may not be right for
Williams' shocking vulgarian of a father but his pleasantness
certainly keeps the audience (to use his own vocabulary) from
puking. Ben Gazzara may not seem Southern, or a football
player, or a TV announcer (the problem husband is all three)
but he is handsome and he can act neurotic intensity. It is the
same with the whole evening: the script is what is called dirty,
but the production—starting with the Mielziner set and its
chiefly golden lighting—is aggressively clean.

So what is the function of Mr. Kazan's directing—to mislead? Reviewing *The Dramatic Event* in *The New Leader*,
Molly Day Thacher (Mrs. Kazan) said that I attribute Machiavellian motives to unmotivated, intuitive acts. That is why
I speak here of the *function* of the directing and not its
intention, the result and not the motive. I would grant, in any
case, that the motive is to "make the most of the play"; but the
most has been made of *Cat on a Hot Tin Roof* at the cost, it
seems to me, of conflict with the script. Some directors are
content to subordinate themselves to an author and simply try

to make his meaning clear. Others bring in extra meanings at the cost of understressing or even obscuring some of the author's meanings, so that mystifications and obfuscations enter in without Machiavellian intention. No one, I believe, would deny that Mr. Kazan belongs to the second school. Giving a "clean" production to a "dirty" script he has persuaded people that the dirt is unimportant. The show *looks* wholesome; therefore, it *is*.

Not that one would prefer to see all this moral squalor spelled out in full natural detail, but that one shouldn't expect uncoordinated double vision to provide a clear picture. In the last act, while the script is resolutely noncommittal, the production strains for commitment to some sort of edifying conclusion. While nothing is actually concluded, images of edification are offered to our eyes. Barbara Bel Geddes is given an Annunciation scene (made of more golden light and a kneeling posture). At the very end, as I said, comes the outward form of that *Tea and Sympathy* scene without its content. And, in many places throughout, a kind of mutually frustrating activity has the effect of muting the emotions that are supposed to sound out loud and clear. On the other hand, there are places where director and author stand together. These include all the comic bits. It should not escape notice that Mr. Williams is a very gifted humorist. Author and director join forces to help Mildred Dunnock, Pat Hingle, and Madeleine Sherwood create three of those superb tragic-comic portraits in secondary roles which are one of the chief attractions of current New York theatre. (I am thinking back to Eileen Heckart in *Picnic* and *The Bad Seed*, Elaine Stritch and Phyllis Love in *Bus Stop*, etcetera.) Author and director are together, too, in the best scene of the play—a masterly piece of construction both as writing and as performance—a scene between father (Burl Ives) and son (Ben Gazzara) in which a new and better theme for the play is almost arrived at: that the simple old family relationships still mean something, that, in the midst of all the filth and incoherence and impossibility, people, clumsily, inconsistently, gropingly, try to be nice to each other. In that old goat of a father, there is even some residue of a real Southern gentleman. He is Mr. Williams' best male character to date.

Though I believe the new script is sometimes too naturalistically sordid for theatre, and therefore has to suffer changes Kazanian or otherwise, it is also true that in many passages the writing has its own flamboyant theatricality. The humor, though compulsively "dirty," is, by that token, pungent and, in its effect, decidedly original. The more serious dialogue, though rhetorical, is unashamedly and often successfully so; the chief rhetorical device, that of a repetition of phrases somewhat *à la* Gertrude Stein, is almost always effective. There is no one in the English-speaking theatre today who can outdo Mr. Williams' dialogue at its best: it is supple, sinuous, hard-hitting and—in cases like the young wife and the father—highly "characterized" in a finely fruity Southern vein. Mr. Williams' besetting sin is fake poeticizing, fake philosophizing, a straining after big statements. He has said that he only feels and does not think; but the reader's or spectator's impression is too often that he only thinks he feels, that he is an acute case of what D. H. Lawrence called "sex in the head." And not only sex. Sincerity and Truth, of which he *speaks* and *thinks,* tend to remain in the head too—mere abstractions with initial capitals.

Mr. Williams' problem is not lack of talent. It is, perhaps, an ambiguity of aim: he seems to want to kick the world in the pants and yet be the world's sweetheart, to combine the glories of martyrdom with the comforts of success. When I say that his problem is to take the initial capitals off Sincerity and Truth, I do not infer that this is easy—only that it is essential if ever his talent is to find a full and pure expression.

Homage to Scribe

A LADY SHELTERS an escaped prisoner-of-war, and shields him from the military police by disguising him as a servant. As the policeman-in-chief is an old foe of hers, she "hugely" enjoys fooling him. But all is not fun. The lady and her niece have both fallen in love with the fugitive. Which of the two will win him? And what qualities of nobility or meanness will the rivalry show forth? The lady is a heroine, and never even lets her rival know she is interested in the man. Having saved him from the police, the heroine magnanimously hands him over to her niece.

No story, I suppose, is impressive in the form of a summary, though anyone with a nose for it might scent out a drama even in the meager information just provided. Very dramatic in possibility is the fact that on so small a battlefield no less than two battles are indicated and that both are being fought for the same prize: the two women are competing for the man's hand and they are joining forces against a villain who wants the man's head. And, in fact, the play I am summarizing was once a very famous drama: *Bataille des Dames* by Eugène Scribe and Ernest Legouvé. How many present-day theatre-goers have even heard of it? Eugène Scribe has been praised as effusively, and damned as blackly, as any playwright that ever lived. How many present-day theatre-goers have ever heard of *him?*

The subject, indeed, might never have confronted even a dramatic critic had Mr. Milton Smith not revived the play in the Brander Matthews Theatre at Columbia University. What a task! If the revival of a celebrated masterpiece presents problems, what about the revival of a forgotten play written in a forgotten style? One possibility, of course, is to have the script reconceived and rewritten till it is something completely new and in the swim. A recent instance is Alexandre Dumas' *Kean,* as revised by Jean-Paul Sartre. Dumas' *Kean* tells us that the make-believe of the stage is a higher reality than life outside. Sartre's *Kean* tells us that the swindle on stage is pretty much the same as the swindle off it: all life is make-believe, and make-believe is make-believe squared. In such a case, as with Bertolt Brecht's version of *The Beggar's Opera,* the old play is but a pretext for a new one. Alternatively, we may be historians and wish to have the old play presented just as it was, the question being whether, in its pristine state, the play still preserves its theatricality. *Bataille des Dames* was translated by an English contemporary almost as famous as Scribe himself, Tom Robertson. The heroine of

the Robertson version speaks in this vein: "No! True tenderness, real, deep, profound love can stimulate our sex to laugh
in face of peril, to smile while death drags at our heartstrings,
and, when danger is past our courage leaves us, our woman-
hood returns to us in—tears." To which our hero returns:
"Every hour, every instant reveals to me some fresh charm.
Oh! angel, fairy, enchantress, teach me how I can repay you!"
Unnecessary to denounce this style of writing; it denounces
itself. The interesting question is why such a rhetoric ever had
currency and why, once current, it fell into desuetude and
contempt. After all, for great stretches of the time, it was good
enough for Dickens and at least one generation of his readers.
And, as late as 1905, a gifted playwright, Clyde Fitch, could
end an act of *The Girl with the Green Eyes* with this stage
direction: "Throwing herself down on the floor, her head
resting on her arms in the armchair, she sobs hysterically,
wildly, 'What have I done? Dear God, what have I done?'"
The fact that this last query has become a byword should not
blind us to the positive qualities of melodramatic rhetoric.
The phony tough talk of today's popular writing is not superior; and we laugh at those inflated periods partly because we
fear that, if we didn't, we might prove susceptible to their
emotionality. Yet the fact remains—whether the reasons are
creditable or not—that the old rhetoric, along with the afflatus
of conscious virtue in heroines and conscious vice in villains, is
no longer negotiable.

   In adjusting *Bataille des Dames* to the modern stage as *The
Queen's Gambit,* Maurice Valency has steered a middle course
between literal translation and the total reconceptions of Sartre and Brecht. Giving up the melodramatic rhetoric and its
dramaturgical accoutrements (asides and the like), he has not
imposed a philosophy of his own, but has been content to
subject the material to stylistic revision. In effect, he has made
over a romance into a comedy, for he takes a satirical attitude
to incidents and characters which Scribe accepted with some
degree of earnestness. Occasionally the new comic matter is too
perceptibly extraneous. These dragoons have been inserted by
someone who knows his Gilbert and Sullivan and frequents
American musical comedies. The jokes approach the New

York wisecrack. (Young man on seeing Leda and the swan depicted in embroidery: "I can't quite fathom the swan." Embroideress: "Neither could Leda.") But on the whole Mr. Valency's strategy is remarkably successful: his play is a play and, in a large measure, it is Scribe too. Even the parody is of that best sort: the parody which increases your respect for the thing parodied. Try and read Scribe and you will be bored; see him as presented on the Columbia campus and not only will you be amused but you will even begin to comprehend how the man could be so influential. Ibsen himself, we are told, directed no less than twenty-one Scribe plays in Bergen; an American scholar has said that every innovation in nineteenth-century drama originated with Scribe and that the high point in every main dramatic genre was also reached in his work.

This last is not true, of course. But at a time when the phrase "well-made play" is little more than an emotive noise signalling disapproval (ask any dramatic critic what a well-made play *is*), the practice of Scribe is a reminder that plot without much else makes better drama than much else without plot. The moderns have the advantage, perhaps, in their openings; having no further end in view, they can simply write an interesting scene. Plots as good as Scribe's require elaborate preparation; at the first intermission, the Columbia audience was only partly convinced. It was in the second and third acts that the preparations paid off, and a fine series of big scenes, punctuated by big moments, unfolded before us.

A few weeks ago a dramatic critic was praising a playwright for getting rid of dramaturgic machinery and just letting the truth speak. What a pity it is that such a thing as dramaturgy ever existed, since truth can hold forth unassisted! What a lot of fools there have been in the theatre—from Aeschylus to Ibsen! Except that if we want all the news that's fit to print, there is this item: since the onset of naturalism half a century ago, we have had a spate of "truth," and by now we are again willing to acknowledge that life is not art for the reason that chaos is not cosmos. Which means, among other things, that we are willing to recognize the merit of that greatest non-genius of the drama, Eugène Scribe.

Orson Welles and Two Othellos

To MENTION Orson Welles in any company, literary or theatrical, is to call forth tired jokes about his alleged decline and fall. Yet, to my mind, this man who bids fair to be only another of the disasters of the American theatre, could have been one of its chief glories. At a time when indignation about social evils and fascination with mental abnormality have been accepted as substitutes for the dramatic sense, Orson Welles has that rare gift—a specifically theatrical imagination. Someone has said that the actor's task is not to live on stage but to make the stage live, and none has known this better than Orson Welles, or known better what, as stage director, to do about it. By consequence, his best work stands out not merely as meritorious, but as potentially epoch-making—as work that might have given the history of theatre a different turn. "But yet the pity of it, Iago, oh Iago, the pity of it, Iago." Here is only, it would seem, yet another American story of self-destruction; Orson Welles seems as thoroughly lost as any member of the lost generation. From the Boy Wonder, the wonder seems to have gone, if not the boyhood.

And so we get these pathetically puerile entertainments: the movie *Macbeth* with Scotch accents affected by assorted amateurs from Utah, Marlowe's *Faustus* in Paris with excruciating interpolations by the Boy Wonder, only accepted because the audience didn't understand English. And now *Othello*, a film bad from every point of view and for every public. Technically, it is gauche, the dialogue being all too obviously dubbed. It lacks popular appeal, as the story is neither simply nor skilfully told. To connoisseurs of Shakespeare, it can only be torture. And to the dwindling number of Welles-admirers, the unhappy few among whom I count myself, it is another disappointment. One is tempted to say that, while Shakespeare turned a sensational tale into high tragedy, Orson Welles has turned the tragedy back into a sensational tale. But this is to flatter Mr. Welles, who apparently has no sense of narrative, that is, of the procession of incidents, but only an interest in the incidents themselves—no, not even that, but only an interest in separate moments within the incidents, and this just for the opportunity they offer for arbitrary effects, visual and auditory. Many of these effects are superb. Who but Welles would have given the curtain rings such a strident sound? Who but he would have set the opening of the temptation scene (Act 3, scene 3) to the clump of the actors' shoes on stone? If there were a real mind in charge of the production as a whole, Orson Welles would be the greatest assistant director of all time.

Yet if Mr. Welles' failure as director is partial, as actor it is complete. Is Othello fat? Does he look as if he had a hangover? I am sure there are fat actors who could play the part. And Kean himself used to fortify his performances with brandy. But must not the fat actor seem to lose his fatness? And, as to alcohol, for all I know, Mr. Welles was dead sober when the shots were taken. An actor has to look sober when he is drunk; if Mr. Welles looks drunk when he is sober, he is all the less an actor. At any rate, the Othello we meet at the outset should be soldierly, not to say heroic, and happy, not to say romantically ecstatic, whereas Orson Welles, on the screen, looks pudgy, sleepy, self-indulged, and miserable. On top of which, he never acts, he is photographed—from near, from far, from above, from below, right side up, upside down, against battlements, through gratings, before landscape, before seascape; and the difference of angle and background only emphasizes the flatness of that profile, the rigidity of those lips, the dullness of those eyes, the utter inexpressiveness and anti-theatricality of a man who, God save the mark! was born a theatrical genius. I don't know what *The Daily Worker* said, but it missed a trick if it didn't hold up Mr. Welles as a prize example of individualistic, bourgeois culture in decay. To which I suggest adding that the whole film is a precise example of formalistic decadence. Very much an Art Film, *Othello* is a rag bag of the ideas of yesterday's avant-garde. In 1955 Orson Welles has caught up with the Cocteau of 1920—or should one say with the Gordon Craig of 1910—or the Henry Irving of 1880, for the musical processionals with which the film opens and closes seem positively Victorian compared, say, with the Hollywood *Julius Caesar* of two years ago. Even a Wellesite like myself, interested in each image as it impinges on the retina, realizes poignantly at the close that all these images— lively and dashing as so many of them are—add up to nothing.

It is very different with the *Othello* that has just been staged at City Center. Here we forego the splendors of Italy, the ingenuities of the camera, and a list of famous names in the cast, but the drama as Shakespeare wrote it is communicated to us tolerably complete. There are some obvious limitations, notably an Othello (William Marshall) who has not yet learned the trade of Shakespearean acting. Mr. Marshall looks like Othello, and hurls himself at the part with great vehemence. It is the craft which, as yet, is lacking, and he might start by learning how many syllables there are in a blank-verse line and where the accents fall. (Not that Orson Welles can teach him. Unless I'm mistaken, the film contains the line: "It is the cause, it is the cause, *O* my soul.") And it may have been Mr. Marshall who led the director (John Stix) into neglecting the poetry of the play and trying to make up for the loss with a plethora of props and the "business" they call for. Instead of a song, we are given a harp. Ladies spread cloths over benches for no reason, and gentlemen sit and write letters we know nothing about. Such is the madness of naturalism. But, by and large, the play moves along with a simplicity and swing that are a fine achievement in a young company. Certain individual performances stand out from a general competence. Michael Wager gives what I imagine is the finest performance of his career so far as Roderigo. In future he should play character parts, not juveniles; he has the command of language so lacking in Mr. Marshall plus a real sense of the weak and grotesque. Paul Sparer brings to Cassio some of the dignity of tragic acting with a good deal of the ambiguity, irony, and pathos of the modern manner. Cavada Humphrey's Emilia is the most perfect creation of the evening: a fully-rounded character, just right at each individual moment, but also moving in a single curve from the first instant to the last. Of Jerome

Kilty's Iago, which has been criticized for a lack of grandeur, I would say this. A Shakespearean part is made up of speeches, and each speech contains a series of points. If it is the mark of the good actor that he makes all these points, and of the average actor that he lets the words simply tumble off his lips as they may, then Mr. Kilty is a very good actor. Every point is made, and, when appropriate, with finesse and wit. One of the worst features of the Welles film is humorlessness; tragedy is extraordinarily dependent on humor, and, most of all, the tragedy of *Othello,* in which the villain is comic. Knowing this, Mr. Kilty is able to keep not only his part but the play itself crisp and crackling. The whole production, steering a middle course between the older and newer fashioned (between singsong on the one hand and mumbling on the other, between empty pageantry and irrelevant gimmicks), makes one feel that something is being done for Shakespeare in New York without importations either from Hollywood or London.

A Great Bronze Gong

In *Tiger at the Gates,* Hector fails—and this is the gist of the action—to keep the Trojans out of war. Jean Giraudoux wrote the play to explain, as far as possible, why. At no point does Hector tell himself, as we tell ourselves whenever danger arises, that war is morally and materially necessary. The immediate causes of Giraudoux' Trojan War are as trivial and accidental as the murder of an archduke at Sarajevo. The underlying cause is larger but so mysterious that it can only be hinted at—in the cryptic word Destiny. It is not long since historians spoke scornfully of such "mystical" conceptions, but today there are signs that they are returning to them. "Our fight," says Herbert Butterfield, "is against some devilry that lies in the very process of things, against something that we might even call demonic forces existing in the air. The forces get men into their grip, so that the men themselves are victims, in a sense, even if it is by some fault of their own nature—they are victims of a sort of possession." Which is exactly what Giraudoux demonstrates in his play. If the fight between Hector and Destiny is an unequal one, we do not admire him the less because he cannot, and even knows he cannot, succeed. On the contrary, in a universe so malign, defiance is the supremely—perhaps the uniquely—admirable quality. Such, at any rate, is the view stated by Giraudoux and restated in later plays by Sartre, Camus, and other Frenchmen.

The play is open to criticism. If decadence means that individual cells have developed at the expense of the organism as a whole, the art of Giraudoux cannot escape the charge of decadence. In all his plays, language descends in such a torrent that the speeches, as it were, jump the banks of the drama. In *Tiger at the Gates,* for example, the logic and eloquence of one passage make Andromache say that she and Hector live in constant conflict; the action of the play suggests quite the contrary. As for Giraudoux' novels, surely they carry the famous *preciosité* far into the realm of the insufferable. I tried to re-read *Bella* recently and gave up.

Giraudoux' peculiarities make him the harder to translate. What are we to say to this description of love making, "When they disentangled themselves they licked each other with the tips of their tongues because they found they were tasting salty"? The line was wisely cut in the New York production, but I hasten to add that the translator—Christopher Fry—has done much less cutting than is usual on these occasions. He modestly and, to a degree, correctly describes his script as a translation, not an adaptation. It "speaks" beautifully throughout. My reservations have chiefly to do with a certain upper-class British gush that occasionally weakens the style. When Giraudoux had Helen say of men, "it's nice to rub them against you like great cakes of soap," Mr. Fry substitutes: "They're as pleasant as soap and a sponge and warm water." [1] He translates the quite plain "vous le savez bien" with the

[1] The same weakening is to be observed in the rejection of Giraudoux' austere, ironic title *The Trojan War Will Not Take Place* for Fry's florid, obvious one. The reiteration of the phrase in the dialogue itself is also largely lost as an effect because Mr. Fry translates it in several different ways. [1956]

modish "you know *only too* well"; and in one place the ultra-simple "belle" is rendered as "ravishing."

These are peripheral points. Central is the fact that the show provides one of the finest evenings of theatre that I have experienced in New York; and, though I have seen Giraudoux in several countries and on many occasions, this is the first time that I have been completely captivated. For one thing, the play is among his very best. Secondly, solutions were found to the problem of performing him which I preferred even to Louis Jouvet's (though I have not seen Jouvet's production of this particular play). Accustomed to a type of drama in which dialogue is subordinated to character, the director, Harold Clurman, has made his actors fill in what the author left vague. Occasionally, perhaps, there is a little embarrassment, for Mr. Clurman has insisted that an actor sustain the character in passages where Giraudoux has forgotten everything except that actors are standing there reciting. But, upon the whole, the Clurman production succeeds in adding a good deal of drama to the show without forfeiting one jot of dignity or eloquence. I enjoyed the Clurman production of *Mademoiselle Colombe* two years ago, but could scarcely help being bothered by the varieties of style and non-style in the cast. The matter has been attended to this time. The solution was: English actors. And the few Americans who had to be added to please Equity have been what Hitler would have called "co-ordinated" (except for an awkward Ajax).

Half the play is Hector, and half the cast is Michael Redgrave who plays him. The time has come to stop underrating this not merely intellectual but also intelligent man, this not merely handsome but also heroic actor. Though in *Tiger at the Gates,* he underscores the witticisms too heavily (English actors are always told to regard the American audience as slow-witted), the body and soul of the part are there, and one can scarcely think of another actor in English-speaking theatre who could have put them there. It would be too much to hope that the rest of the cast might be on this level: if Mr. Redgrave is rather more than a match for Jouvet, Walter Fitzgerald, though sound enough in his slightly soporific, singsong way, as Ulysses, is no match for the great actor for whom the part was written (Pierre Renoir). On the other hand, I cannot imagine even a French production's outdoing Diane Cilento's witty comment on Helen or Leueen MacGrath's pointed portrayal of Cassandra.

What is great theatre? The component parts are brains, good taste, fine craftsmanship, high purpose, and so forth and so on, but the whole is greater than the sum of the parts and comes to us as a single impression which is at once intellectual satisfaction and emotional entrancement. Our theatre is a place where, normally, the silence is broken by nothing more coherent or congenial than the clatter of dishes in a sink, but once in a long while something like a great bronze gong is heard, reminding us that reality and the art that transposes it in the theatre are not banalities beneath our contempt but mysteries worthy of our reverent attention. I think I have heard this solemn note a few times, of which the second night of *Tiger at the Gates* was one.

Incidentally, most of *Tiger at the Gates* could have been written last week (though I don't know by whom). This passage, for instance:

> It's usual on the eve of every war for the two leaders of the peoples concerned to meet privately at some innocent village on a terrace in a garden overlooking a lake. And they decide together that war is the world's worst scourge, and as they watch the rippling reflections in the water, with magnolia petals dropping on their shoulders, they are both of them peace-loving, modest, and friendly. . . . And warmed by the sun and mellowed by the claret, they can't find anything in the other man's face to justify hatred. . . .

This description—as it seems just now—of the Geneva Conference of 1955 was written before Chamberlain went to Berchtesgaden in 1938. It has taken the play twenty years to cross the Atlantic, a fact which prompts a further reflection. The nineteen thirties was the decade of political art, and anti-war drama flourished: it was mainly Popular Front melodrama heralding the final victory. How strange, then, that the two best anti-war plays of the decade were pessimistic and that neither of them reached the American stage until 1955! The other, Brecht's *Mother Courage,* has still not arrived.

Two Hundred Years of Mowing

FOREIGN ACTORS, even when they are not better than native ones, by their proficiency in another style make us acutely conscious of our limitations, a state of mind which is the beginning of all improvement. To see the actors of the Comédie Française, now playing at the Broadway Theatre in Manhattan, is to become conscious of limitation in that tradition of acting which we may call naturalistic. Our actors chiefly sit, and when they sit, they lounge. These actors chiefly stand, though, when they sit, they sit well. When our actors do stand, they look for a raised surface to place one foot on; then they lean sagely forward and place an elbow on the raised knee. The French actors stand erect. There is a similar story to tell about arms. To our actors, an arm is an instrument to lean on things with, and the things leaned on are not always inanimate: some of our actors find it hard to keep their hands off their colleagues or even off themselves, for one arm can keep the other busy, and of course our modern costume is provided with an escape from the whole problem—the trouser pocket, the naturalistic actor's first and last refuge. The French actors never seem to lean on anything, and as for clinging to each other's bodies, they hardly ever even touch hands. They have taught their arms to cope with the circumambient air. One of our leading actors, faced with a classic script, once asked me: "But what is there for an actor to do?" He had noted the absence of cigarettes, drinks, food, spittoons . . . for of such is the kingdom of naturalism. The implicit answer in the work of the Comédie Française is: when there is nothing to do, do nothing. For example, there is a "meal" in *Le Bourgeois Gentilhomme* in which the actors neither eat nor pretend to. They just sit. For the focus of the action is elsewhere. Again, the American actor will say: "I can't stand there propping up the wall, give me something to do," while these fine French actors, when the focus is not on them, will contentedly stand to one side doing nothing, and their doing so would never raise a question in any spectator's mind; it is part of the game.

When an actor exercises a much higher degree of selectivity, he inevitably throws a heavier stress on the things he does do. And to justify its omission of certain kinds of detail, the Comédie Française exhibits proficiency in certain forms of action as far removed from common behavior as playing the piano is from ringing a doorbell. Reading the first scene of *Le Bourgeois Gentilhomme* we think we exhaust in a moment the content of the stage direction: "takes his hand and makes him dance." Actually, the phrase is only related to performance as a signpost is to landscape. What we get is Lulli's music, and two carefully related dances: the dancing master's correct and attractive one, and Mr. Jourdain's bad, but carefully bad, imitation of it. In passages like this—and the play is made of them—the French actors do things which our actors could not even learn during the longest rehearsal period. For they attain a style which is the product of a whole career in this sort of work; and behind the individual career is the career of the institution. It is the story of the Oxford lawns—"just mow them for two hundred years, sir"—all over again.

Among the many performances of the Comédie Française that I have seen, this one is among the best-looking and (thanks to Lulli) among the best-sounding. There is a gasp from the audience when the curtain rises on Suzanne Lalique's dazzling white salon with its gilded balcony and spiral stairway, and further murmurs of delight greet all the dances of the show, which have their climax in the comic nightmare of the Turkish episode. I would judge the director of this and many other Comédie productions, Jean Meyer, to be one of the supreme directors of our time. His work does not call overmuch attention to directing itself, but each part of the show has been so perfectly molded, and the parts united in so expressive a whole, that one knows a master hand has been at work. No director has a lighter touch. Meyer makes Molière move with the delicate, darting rhythm of Mozart; which is precisely right.

The acting affords an example of French ensemble work at

its best but not quite of great individual performance where it is definitely called for—namely, in the role of M. Jourdain. Whatever theorists say in favor of ensembles, the old playwrights wrote for stars. Molière went even further: he wrote for himself. And I think that particularly Molière's own roles call for an actor with two qualities which even the perfected ensemble actor need not have: the authority or magnetism of a great star and the human substance of a representative man. These qualities are hard to define. But when one reads that the Comédie invited the late Raimu to play Jourdain, one feels that they recognized the need. In addition to the theatrical glamour of a star, Raimu carried with him so much of the very substance of non-aristocratic French life. The play is not ruined for lack of a Raimu, but its possibilities can only be realized, I suspect, through such a man. Louis Seigner who plays the part at the Broadway Theatre is an actor of ability and charm, but he is either too delicate or too much a formalist to give us the ugly and shocking thrust of Jourdain's mania. In the English sense, at least, he is too much of a gentleman.

With this single reservation, my response to the show was jubilant. It is superb performing, and it is Molière. This author, it is true, is ignored by our theatre. Even some French critics have levelled criticisms at him which, if taken seriously, would wipe him off the map. It has been said, for example, that his style is bad. I have also read that *Le Bourgeois Gentilhomme* is carelessly constructed. This last opinion is a careless construction if ever there was one. I defy anybody to attend the current performance and not notice that the form is as elegant and firm as that of a Bach suite. And, as to action, the play simmers, rises to a boil, and then positively boils over: if that is not organic form, what is? The fact is that here is a genius too huge, irregular, and, as it were, Gothic to be contained in those schoolmaster's categories on which so much French commentary depends. It may be that, as to method, Molière improvised some of his forms, but, once finished, they were no more improvisations than is the last movement of Beethoven's Ninth or any other masterpiece which may have begun in caprice. The comic sense of life was more highly developed in Molière, it would seem, than in any other human being that ever existed, and he gave this sense the purest expression one can ever imagine its having. When we recall that he is fully accessible only in performance, and only in excellent performance at that, we realize how much we owe to our French visitors and to the French government which sent them over.

The Example of the Comédie Française

(A speech made to the Friends of the Columbia University Library in the presence of the actors of the Comédie Française.)

IN OUR New York weekly magazine *The Nation*, the issue dated July 31, 1879, appears a dispatch from London above the initials XX:

> The Comédie Française gives to-night the last representation of its extraordinarily successful series, and I am reminded that I am on the point of losing my opportunity for carrying out an intention long deferred, and making a few remarks upon this very interesting episode of the visit to London of the children of Molière. The first remark to be made is that this visit has been a brilliant, a complete, an unclouded success. It is saying little for it to say that it is incomparably the most noteworthy event that has occurred for many a long year in the theatrical annals of London. . . . But what I may say is that the episode will have been a memorable one in the annals of the house of Molière itself. Its members, individually, have refreshed their laurels and renewed their fame, and the beauty and power of the best French acting have affirmed themselves under circumstances which give added value to the triumph. The appeal has been made to a foreign audience, an audience whose artistic perceptions are the reverse of

lively, whose ear does not respond quickly to the magic French utterance, and whose mind does not easily find its way among the intricacies of French sentiment; and yet the triumph has been perfect, and the Comédie Française and the London public have been thoroughly pleased with each other.

Mr. XX—who was Henry James—goes on to say that there had been opposition in France to the idea of sending the Comédie abroad. "In this view," James says, "the Comédie Française has no right to detach itself from French soil; it is beneath its dignity to wander off to foreign lands like a troupe of common strollers, to fill its cashbox and make barbarians stare." And he adds that they never would have gone travelling except that the House of Richelieu was closed for repairs.

I don't know if there was opposition to the idea of an American visit in 1955. If there was, I can hardly imagine that it was on the same grounds. The huge enterprise of bringing five productions across the Atlantic seems calculated rather to empty the cashbox than fill it. Neither the Salle Richelieu nor the Salle Luxembourg is closed for repairs. And, indeed, looking more closely at the situation, one may ask in some bewilderment: why *did* they come? I have no inside information on the point. I assume that the wishes of Mr. Sol Hurok, their sponsor and impresario, had something to do with it. But why did he have such wishes? In the seventy-six years between the company's first visit to England and its first visit to the United States, the world has changed so much that even the theatre has had to change a little. Among the innovations, air transportation across the Atlantic is not more important than the fact that transportation by boat has been brought within the reach of a much larger section of the population. New conditions bring a new psychology. People think no more of crossing the Atlantic today than Henry James' generation thought of crossing the Channel. It is done. It is one of the things that are done. And perhaps the ultimate reason why the Comédie Française has crossed the Atlantic is that today one does cross the Atlantic. I don't mean there are political grounds for it, though there are. I don't mean that public relations men are for it, though they should be. The motive is at once less rational and more immediate. It is a matter of living the life of one's own time.

Everyone is going everywhere. Martha Graham has gone to Japan with Marcel Marceau on her heels. The iron curtain itself lifts when the theatre's velvet curtain calls: Bertolt Brecht's East German company goes to Paris, and the American *Porgy and Bess* will go to Moscow.[1] In short, though in politics the national antagonisms are today as sharp as ever, in culture we are getting a first taste of a new cosmopolitanism. A cultural pattern which we were not wise enough to adopt because it was reasonable is being imposed upon us by the very conditions of life. And the going is hard for those nationalists who try to extend their politics into the cultural field. When Hitler shut his country off from the world for twelve years, there was no new German literature except abroad. The nationalism of Stalin has also been sterile, and the Russians are beginning to talk again of cultural exchange. I don't know how much the "Geneva spirit" means in international politics, but it has at least enabled us to find out that the Russians have started to feel out of things. They too would like passports, and by next year, who knows? the caves of St. Germain des Près may be full of bebopping Bolsheviks.

It is possible, of course, to talk nonsense about our travels. Some folk even imagine that we can abolish war by buying our students steamship tickets. Now wars cannot be avoided by the removal of prejudices between peoples, because wars are not caused by prejudices between peoples. As Giraudoux points out in a play that is now running in New York, no one hates war or loves his enemy more than the statesmen who take tea together at Berchtesgaden or Geneva just before wars start. In any case, it is not goodwill that sends us abroad but curiosity. And our interest is not in a foreign country in general—much less in its political relation to our own—but in our own profession or hobby and the way it is practiced somewhere else. And so, with due respect to ambassadors, consuls, and others who help us on our way, the interest which we of the

---

[1] It did. [1956]

American theatre feel in the Comédie Française is a theatrical interest, and at that no unselfish one. They interest us for what we can learn from them. If our eyes are admiring they are also envious and acquisitive.

The general impression that the Comédie Française makes on a sympathetic foreigner was also described by Henry James:

> The *traditions* of the Comédie Française—that is the sovereign word, and that is the charm of the places—the charm that one never ceases to feel, however often one may sit beneath the classic, dusky dome. One feels this charm with peculiar intensity as a foreigner newly arrived. The Théatre Français has had the good fortune to be able to allow its traditions to accumulate. They have been preserved, transmitted, respected, cherished, until at last they form the very atmosphere, the vital air, of the establishment. A stranger feels their superior influence the first time he sees the great curtain go up; he feels that he is in a theatre that is not as other theatres are. It is not only better, it is different. It has a peculiar perfection—something consecrated, historical, academic. This impression is delicious, and he watches the performance in a sort of tranquil ecstasy.
>
> Never has he seen anything so smooth and harmonious, so artistic and completed. He has heard all his life of attention to detail, and now, for the first time, he sees something that deserves that name. He sees dramatic effort refined to a point with which the English stage is unacquainted. He sees that there are no limits to possible "finish," and that so trivial an act as taking a letter from a servant or placing one's hat on a chair may be made a suggestive and interesting incident. He sees these things and a great many more besides; but at first he does not analyze them, he gives himself up to sympathetic contemplation. It is in an ideal and exemplary world—a world that has managed to attain all the felicities that the world we live in misses. The people do the things that we should like to do; they are gifted as we should like to be; they have mastered the accomplishments that we have had to give up. . . .

Much of what James says would still hold today (though perhaps not the remark about attention to detail, for, in comparison with our naturalistic American acting, the French players seem happy to leave a great many details out) .[2] But there is also a danger in the enthusiasm we share with James —that we be lured into advocating sheer imitation. Let us rather, in our very admission that the Comédie is inimitable, agree not to try to imitate it. When we admire what the other man can do, we must hope that our admiration provides us with the energy, not to do likewise, but to do differently. We can steal trinkets and ornaments, we can even steal the furniture, but we inescapably need a house of our own to accommodate the loot. Only a strong culture can afford foreign influences, just as only a strong stomach can assimilate strange foods.

So I am not asking that we attempt the same style as the Comédie Française but only that, in paying tribute to the achievement of that great theatre, we be inspired by its example. Its example in point of organization is overpowering; and I almost decided to devote my few minutes to the topic of a national theatre: we hear a lot of twaddle in America about state-aided theatre which the sheer facts of the Comédie Française utterly refute—as, for example, that a state theatre is inevitably the cat's-paw of politicians. In the end I didn't think I should inflict a lecture about such twaddle either on our French visitors or upon the rest of this distinguished gathering, yet Matthew Arnold's slogan "The theatre is irresistible: organize the theatre" is still pertinent; and I will permit myself one observation on the problem of organization.

When the Comédie Française went to England in 1879, they took with them the leading dramatic critic of the time, Francisque Sarcey. Asked why England couldn't have a Comédie Française, Sarcey replied (in substance) : "Because when you transplant a tree you have to carry with it the soil the roots are sunk in; the roots of the Comédie Française are in French history which cannot be lifted." For one thing, we might add, the Comédie Française has its origin in monarchical government, as does the subsidized theatre of Europe generally. The

[2] Cf. pages 242–243 above.

American experience has been different, and this means that, if ever we organize our theatre, we shall organize it differently. I cannot agree, however, with those who are content to leave the American theatre to competitive enterprise and who say that nothing ever was or ever will be done to organize it. During the past thirty years, especially, there have been numerous attempts at a broader type of organization from the early Theatre Guild to the Federal Theatre. If most of them individually have declined and fallen, the degree of interest and support is larger every time, and in 1955 we may say that Organized Theatre is an accepted idea, even if it is not yet an established fact.

This university has announced its firm intention of playing a part in the organizing of the American theatre by way of building new theatres, enlarging its staff, extending its dramatic and theatrical studies, and perhaps even by setting up a professional repertory company. If the actors of the Comédie Française will come back in ten years' time, we may be able to show them something and not merely tell them something. In the meantime their example is before us, and I call it a triumph of organization not because of the size of the subsidy they receive, or because they have handsome buildings, or because they have kept going for a long time, or because the bureaucratic machinery is well oiled, nor even because they keep the national repertoire before the nation, though all these things are important: the triumph consists in the fact that the end-product is great theatre. And so I return from a brief excursion into sociology back home onto artistic territory. I have spent some of the happiest evenings of my life in the Salle Richelieu and the Salle Luxembourg. They were not social evenings. I was usually quite alone, and had just about enough money to pay for my favorite *strapontin*. If theatre is good enough, you can even bear to be alone. I was carried for those two hours into the world of Racine, Corneille, Marivaux, Labiche, Claudel, and above all Molière. So, you see, I have my own reasons for wishing students to go to Paris, even if they don't manage to abolish war.

It has been a thrilling experience to see some of the same actors in New York. It would be invidious in the presence of

our guests to do much picking and choosing among performances. If I do mention two names, let them be taken as representative and not exclusive. The work of these two has been a
revelation to me. I refer to the comic acting of M. Jacques
Charon and the comic directing of M. Jean Meyer. We hear a
great deal in our time of the *commedia dell'arte,* and we
imagine that that theatre was possessed of an unequalled
dexterity, lightness, grace, and speed. These are, perhaps, the
characteristics of great comic theatre of any place or time. At
any rate, such is the great comic theatre which our friends
have been showing us. And I cannot but think that, beyond
the delight of the moment, such theatre will have a fruitful
effect on the theatrical life of this country.

Inaccuracy

To MY MIND, Chekhov's supreme achievement is *The Three
Sisters,* but the fact that *The Cherry Orchard* is more famous
indicates that it has made easier contact with the public, which
takes from an author what it craves and leaves the rest alone.
What we call the influence of an author is likely to be the
influence of one famous fragment of him. Ibsen, for example,
had very little influence by virtue of his interest in individuals,
which preoccupied him, but much by virtue of his social
conscience, which he was scarcely aware of possessing; in
schoolbooks he survives as the father of the social drama.
Anton Chekhov survives in journalistic criticism as the
founder of a type of drama in which "nothing happens" and
little people drift in and out remarking that their lives are
empty, a drama in which plot has been replaced by mood, and
chiefly a sunset mood of nostalgia and defeat. Now, though I
wouldn't say that this notion of Chekhov derives from an
adequate reading of *The Cherry Orchard,* I would say that it
derives from a non-reading of all his other works, and that
The Cherry Orchard provokes, if it doesn't quite justify, such

a notion. When Chekhov composed it, he not only *wrote* about dying, he *was* dying, and neither his emotions nor his imagination, it may be, retained their full force. His intellect he has preserved intact, and he is consequently able to carry his special dramaturgy to its furthest reach. The delicacy of his sensibility is unimpaired, and that marvelous sense of humor which was, so to speak, his sword in the struggle for existence is all the more gallantly employed as death approaches. Obviously, then, *The Cherry Orchard* is a masterpiece, but, lacking the fullness of *The Three Sisters,* it is a masterpiece more in the mode of Chekhovism as popularly understood—a Chekhovism of nuance and innuendo, muted lyricism, gentle pathos and gentler humor. And the success of a performance will depend upon an accurate subtlety.

Because the production at the Fourth Street Theatre is both inaccurate and unsubtle, I adjudge it, in the main, a failure. It has its points, of course. The whole text is there in another of Stark Young's straightforward versions (this one not so markedly different from other English renderings of the play). And the technical standard of the show is higher than one is used to Off Broadway; the axe sounds like an axe, the sound-effect of the breaking string is authentically strange and well-timed.

There are several good individual performances, of which the best is the most unobtrusive—Gerald Hiken as Trofimov. Though none too richly endowed with the physical attributes of an actor, and none too highly developed, as yet, in his craft, Mr. Hiken imposes himself by an intensity born of concentration and an intelligence that has given him the character as Chekhov wrote it, no more, no less. Nancy Wickwire was, so to speak, groomed to give the star performance of the show as Varya, but sometimes the grooming is a little more evident than the performance. But, then again, the fact that Varya comes to seem the main part in the play is a tribute to Miss Wickwire's power. (In nothing, by the way, are the soundness and thoroughness of Chekhov's dramaturgy more manifest than in the fact that *any* part becomes luminous and prominent by being well performed.)

If self-assertion is a slight blemish on the otherwise smooth surface of Miss Wickwire's portrait, it completely disfigures the

Yasha of Leonardo Cimino. Here is a gifted young actor (and I have seen him in several roles) who is unable to stop when he has made his statement but is constrained to underscore, capitalize, italicize, and over-punctuate, using especially the exclamation mark, till his manuscript is unreadable. He pulls faces. He strikes attitudes. And, if anyone remarks: "So does Yasha," I shall retort that Mr. Cimino has not convinced me of the fact.

And where are the two leading characters in the play? *The Cherry Orchard* may be a small play by comparison with *The Three Sisters*. At the Fourth Street, it is smaller still, being deprived of its two strongest presences: Mme. Ranevsky and Lopakin. Strong, in a moral sense, Mme. Ranevsky is not—rather, a classic study, *à la* Turgenev, of feminine, elegant, "romantic" weakness, a weakness that falls before the strength of the self-made man, Lopakin. She is the cherry blossom, and he the axe. Lopakin, it is true, is not the villain of a Marxist melodrama; his author was at pains to stress his humanity. Did this stress mislead George Ebeling, at the Fourth Street, into forgetting the role's original premise and its part in the story? This Lopakin brings on stage at the outset all the warmth of a Methodist minister at a mothers' meeting; so, naturally, by the time he goes so far as to take over the cherry orchard, he is overwhelmed by his own audacity and suffering from heartbreak. Heartbreak! How many heart-whole characters in the older drama are being interpreted by our actors as heartbroken! The age of anxiety is the age of self-pity. Now David Ross, the director of the play, had intimated in *The New York Times* that he was going to disencumber Chekhov of all the accumulated lies and evasions of two generations of "Chekhovism." This was very misleading of him, for there is a very portentous air about the show, a complete lack of simplicity. When Mme. Ranevsky makes big claims for the orchard, Lopakin snaps back: "The only remarkable thing about this cherry orchard is that it's very big." Such a rejoinder is shockingly reductive, and nothing if not prosaic. It reminds me of Hemingway's remark that the only difference between the rich and the poor is that the rich are richer. Yet, at the Fourth Street, they try to make something wistful, inspiring, and "poetic" out of it. If Mr. Ebeling reaches out towards a romance that is not there, Elizabeth Farrar fails to take hold of one that is. Certainly, Mme. Ranevsky is a failure but as what? As a mistress in a villa in Mentone—that is, in a role with considerable social and, in a sense, spiritual pretension. When she pours scorn on Trofimov for having reached twenty-six without taking a mistress, we hear the echo of the pride she must once have felt in her femininity. . . . But why run on about characteristics when none of them has been presented on stage?

I enjoyed *The Three Sisters* last year at this theatre. At a second visit one enjoys Mr. Ross's use of his cramped central stage a good deal less. One becomes too aware of unnatural, unreal positions, moves, and groupings. One comes to feel that, after all, Chekhov requires something like a real room for works in which walls and furniture play so significant a part. Then again, if I may repeat myself,[1] a strong wind of emotion blows through even a rough-and-ready performance of *The Three Sisters*, as through a Beethoven sonata played by a capable amateur. *The Cherry Orchard*, it seems to me, is like some exquisite and exact bit of tone-painting by Debussy that makes no impression at all unless it receives from the performer an equal exquisiteness and exactitude.

[1]See pages 222–223 above.

The Road from Rouen to New York

Joan of Arc lived that Julie Harris might do this play.
—COMMENT ON *The Lark* IN THE NEW YORK PRESS

You don't mean to say that girl really lived?
—COMMENT OVERHEARD IN THE THEATRE LOBBY AFTER A PERFORMANCE OF *The Lark*

IN 1890 BERNARD SHAW complained of Sarah Bernhardt as Joan of Arc: "she intones her lines and poses like a saint." At the time, Jeanne d'Arc was hovering uncomfortably between heaven and earth. Subsequently she was split in two: one half sent to heaven by the church and called, indeed, a saint, the other half brought rudely down to earth by our playwrights. It is this second Joan—named "natural man" by Lillian Hellman's inquisitor—which Julie Harris has been called upon to play in *The* Anouilh-Hellman *Lark*. Who is better qualified? She is the very idea of a modern actress. *The New York Times* recently published a photograph to demonstrate that, on Forty-second Street, Miss Harris looks like one of the crowd. Imagine what Sarah would have said to that! But she would, at least partly, be wrong. In the first place, being the ordinary person has its decided advantages. No intoning, no posing. Julie Harris can convince you that this girl is indeed the daughter of the rustic couple of Domremy. In the second place, the ordinariness is only a mask. When Miss Harris takes it off, you see that she is beautiful, glamorous, and powerfully attractive. And she has learned to make use of a supple wiry body and the stage-space surrounding it. Her performance as Joan has many lovely and touching moments from the first tableau where she sits in despair with her head in her hands to the last where she stands erect and smiles her homey, oval, midwestern smile. Presumably with the help of her director, Joseph Anthony, than whom no one on Broadway has a more daring sense of movement, she is able to say more with her body than one would have believed possible in so very verbal a play. No actress' Joan is likely to be complete. Under any director, speaking any script, Miss Harris' otherworldliness would always be more elfin than saintly, her belligerency rather that of Peter Pan than of a grown-up patriot and capable strategist. But the greatest limitation—a lack of range, of variety—is imposed by the script.

Like Shaw, Anouilh has come to the life of Joan of Arc from a feeling that here was all that he had been trying to say in his previous plays. Shaw was right: the confrontation here of individual and society, intuition and philosophy, conscience and convention, vitality and system is Shavian theatre in a nutshell. And, prima facie, the Anouilh pattern also fits: here is another of those clear-eyed virgins whom a world of weary or wicked men takes and destroys. Well and good—provided that the playwright is interested in this kind of virgin and this kind of destroyer—is interested, that is to say, in religion and politics. Shaw fills Joan with his own religious sense, and interprets her career according to his own view of history: she was the first nationalist and the first protestant. Anouilh's lack of interest in history is total. In the program to the Paris production he tells us that the Joan of history was a big, healthy girl but that he "couldn't care less" and his Joan is going to be weary, undernourished, and haggard. We are meant to understand, no doubt, that this author is after dramatic essences, not factual externals. But what is undramatic about a big, rawboned peasant lass? Is it not the emaciation that is abstract and unreal, the child, not of truth, but of Anouilh's philosophic system? As Miss Harris did not play the emaciation but seemed very full of beans and red corpuscles, I will not press the point.

Admittedly, Shaw also gave us a highly personal view of Joan, which departs from the facts in at least one essential point, namely, in representing the trial as scrupulously fair. To this end, Shaw gave an inquisitor arguments such as no inquisitor would (I think) ever have approved, let alone employed, and made Bishop Cauchon amiable and rational. Anouilh not only presents another highly personal interpretation, however, he also follows the Shavian version of the facts as if it were established history. Indeed, one of the New York reviewers excused his following in Shaw's footsteps on the grounds that it all really happened that way. At this point it is high time—if Catholic critics are too polite to speak out about Anouilh—that a Catholic dramatist should write a Joan play and remind the public, first, that the trial was as shameless and corrupt a frame-up as anything in Soviet annals and that, as for character, Bishop Cauchon was in all probability about as likable, enlightened, and high-minded as Senator Joseph McCarthy. We allow Shaw a certain license, partly because he came up with a fine play, partly because what he said has general application even if it is not specifically true of Joan. Anouilh can claim no such indulgence. Rather, one has the right to complain that in this the least imaginative of his works he also displays so little interest in the truth—the truth about Catholicism, for example. His inquisitor says: "love of man excludes the love of God." It is true that a priest protests, but he is sent out of the room for his pains. It is true an attempt is made to make the inquisitor symbolize all who fanatically put an Idea before people. My point stands, a fortiori, that the play moves all the time away from concrete truth to abstract theory. And the theory is not very good theory. As a thinker, Anouilh has the narrow-mindedness we traditionally associate with the religious, only in his case it's the fact that his mind contains *no* religion that makes him narrow. In vain that he tries in this play suddenly to be "positive" and celebrate human goodness. The enthusiasm is *voulu* and unfelt. Real is only the old, comfortless, nauseated atheism. Despite his intentions, his Joan is a character *reduced* to his pattern, and (in the French original) dies chiefly to avoid the coming of middle age.

This last feature was more than Miss Hellman could stomach. By a brief deletion, she desperately tries, in the last scene, to rescue Joan from Anouilh. She inserts a little speech of her own to guarantee that Joan, lost to sainthood, may be at least a good girl. She goes back into the body of the text and slashes the inquisitor's speeches so that our audiences will never find out what Anouilh meant to convey. Meanwhile, the producer has Leonard Bernstein turn on the phonograph at awkward moments (hark the metallic angels sing), otherwise chiefly relying on a director whose whole talent lies in what may be called the choreography of the thing. Anouilh's conception was scenically very simple: his play is a discussion, and that's that. The New York production is a really grand show—visually much finer than *Tiger at the Gates,* for example—a show which, with Julie Harris in the midst of it, all playgoers will enjoy, especially those who are not interested in Joan of Arc, history in particular, or truth in general.

On the Waterfront

NOT LONG AGO Elia Kazan made a movie about the New York waterfront, and now Arthur Miller has brought out a play about the New York waterfront. The climax of both movie and play is reached when the protagonist gives information to the police which leads to the arrest of some of his associates.

These facts bring abruptly to mind that not long ago Mr. Kazan took the position that Communist affiliations should be publicly declared, while Mr. Miller did not take that position but broke with Mr. Kazan and, with the help of another director, put on a play with a hero whose heroism consists in refusing to "talk." Of course it is not the strained personal relations of Messrs. Miller and Kazan that have public interest but the position which these strained personal relations (along with much else, no doubt) have driven them to adopt. It will surprise no one that, in Mr. Kazan's movie, the act of informing is virtuous, whereas, in Mr. Miller's new play, it is evil. What is surprising, or at any rate appalling, is that both stories seem to have been created in the first place largely to point up this virtue and that evil, respectively. Now it is easy enough to end by winning the game if you begin by stacking the cards, only you then have to concede that the game loses all its interest as a game. In Whittaker Chambers' *Witness*, informing is dramatic because Chambers has so much to say on both sides: he senses the infamy of the act *and* its necessity, its utter wrongness *and* (in certain circumstances) its ultimate rightness. Now obviously both Mr. Kazan and Mr. Miller come to the informer theme because (to put it mildly) it is one of the great issues of the day. What a pity, then, that both men empty it of all content and give us, instead of the conflict that life offers and that dramatic art demands, mere melodramatic preachment! At that, I insult the fine arts of melodrama and preaching, for these works lack the verve and unpreten-

tiousness of melodrama, just as they lack the purity and profundity of good preaching. In both *On the Waterfront* and *A
View from the Bridge,* truth—life in its concreteness—is obscured by a fog of false rhetoric. Observe, for example, how
music is used in the film: to inflate, not to define. And observe,
in *A View from the Bridge* the use of . . . Poetry.

Actually, when I received a printed copy of *A View from the
Bridge,* and found that a lot of the dialogue was in verse, you
could have knocked me over with a feather. When I saw the
play acted, I suspected Mr. Miller of many things, but never
this. The gravity of the deed must not be exaggerated, of
course: some of this verse would make acceptable prose, if
typed up differently. But some of it, like much of the work of
Maxwell Anderson, suggests that poetry is a writer's Sunday
clothes, party manners, or assumed Oxford accent. What is too
silly to be said can be sung, and what is too pretentious for
prose is poetry. The accent in Mr. Miller's case isn't Oxford,
it's Graeco-Latin. A town that for centuries has been known to
us as Syracuse is called Siracusa. Mr. Miller's notion of Italians
is strictly operatic ("In my country you would already be
dead," says the Sicilian avenger), and, as for Greek tragedy,
insisted upon in preface and play alike, he would have been
well-advised to let his story become Greek by its own poignancy and grandeur and not by choral tips to the audience.

As published by the Viking Press, the play is prefaced by an
essay in which Mr. Miller says that prose is the language of
private life, dramatic verse "the most public of public speech."
But in what way is Fry more public than O'Casey, Yeats than
Shaw? I know that my rhetorical question does not close the
discussion. My point, rather, is that Mr. Miller never opens it,
never, indeed, opens *any* discussion, but seems to live in a
surprising degree of isolation from the great debates which are
the intellectual life of our time. Sometimes he will state a
generally accepted truth as if it were a personal discovery of
his own. Sometimes he will show himself unaware that others
have gone much further along the same path as himself. Indeed, in his current preface, in order to make Arthur Miller
sound broad, he is not above making out that Ibsen, Chekhov,
and Shaw are narrow. The closer he gets to the crux of a

matter, the stronger is his tendency to substitute oratory for inquiry. For example, it is either a trick or a blunder, when defending a given genre, to make the definition so wide as to include other genres. In his new preface, Mr. Miller's defense of the "social" play takes the form of claiming that *every* good play is social. To such poor argumentation, one should add, as the next largest fault of Mr. Miller's articles and prefaces, a clumsiness of style that often approaches unpublishability. "The debilitation of the tragic drama, I believe, is commensurate with the fracturing and aborting of the need of man to maintain. . . ." It sounds like the victory of Teachers College over the English language; when prose has sunk so low, there is, no doubt, nothing left but poetry.

On the other hand, one seems to detect a positive element in the new preface by way of an effort to transcend the philosophy on which this author was, so to speak, raised. The only single word for that outlook is "Stalinism" but it should only be used if we understand that its adherents weren't usually Communists but only "progressives" whose feelings were hurt whenever anyone said anything against Russia. This form of progressivism has lingered in the theatre long after being discredited in other sections of the community. But, if the new preface is any indication, Mr. Miller is no longer helping it to linger.

A View from the Bridge has had a curious fate in the theatre. A tremendous hit on the road, it had a cool reception from the Manhattan papers; yet the advance sale was considerable, and it will have a run of several months. No importance should be attached either to the out-of-town hullabaloo or the local disappointment. The play is fairly representative Miller, neither better nor worse; your opinion of him will go neither up nor down after you've seen it. The famous hard-hitting dialogue is often effective. There are several well-devised scenes, and there is one well-drawn character: as usual with this author, a father; Van Heflin plays the role with great skill, though he was miscast in it. Boris Aronson contributed a set which finds the common factor as between modern Brooklyn and ancient Greece in a way that would have been wonderful, had the play been written by a poet. Though the directing of

Martin Ritt is too busy and sometimes a little vulgar, the
supporting cast is strong and well-varied.

I should add, perhaps, that there is another way of taking
the whole thing. Mr. Miller says he is attempting a synthesis of
the social and the psychological, and, though one may not see
any synthesis, one certainly sees the thesis and the antithesis.
In fact, one never knows what a Miller play is about: politics
or sex. If *Death of a Salesman* is political, the key scene is the
one with the tape recorder; if it is sexual, the key scene is the
one in the Boston hotel. You may say of *The Crucible* that it
isn't about McCarthy, it's about love in the seventeenth century. And you may say of *A View from the Bridge* that it isn't
about informing, it's about incest and homosexuality. Strange
how this argument always constitutes a sort of alibi for the
author (as, in effect, Robert Warshow said in the best analysis
of Mr. Miller yet written) ! [1] Nor is the sex story in *A View
from the Bridge* as performed, satisfactory in itself. The ambiguity of "Is he or isn't he?" is inherited from *The Children's
Hour* and *Cat on a Hot Tin Roof:* much is made of false
accusation, yet we don't feel sure that the accusation is false.

A View from the Bridge is preceded by a shorter play called
A Memory of Two Mondays. Alone among Mr. Miller's plays,
it is something less than shattering in intended effect, something less than cosmic in intended scope. I had the impression
that, had certain gaps been filled (or certain bits not omitted?), there might have been half an hour of unforced and
touching drama in it, and not just evocations of Odets and
Saroyan.

[1] In *Commentary*, March, 1953.

Marriage, 1955

I was praised recently for having intimated that there was
too much homosexuality in current plays, but what I meant to
imply was that there was not enough. Having gone so far, our

playwrights will have to go further; having inflicted the subject on us, they will have to say something about it, and not
snatch it back out of our hands in the last scene with a speech
or two about the wickedness of false accusation. *Third Person*
by Andrew Rosenthal comes as a partial answer to my prayer.

The story is this. It is 1947. In a house in the East Sixties
live an architect and his wife and little daughter. A younger
man who had been the architect's buddy in the Marines has
settled in as an uninvited but not unwelcome house guest. An
aging homosexual, waspish and witty, is attracted by the
young man but, getting nowhere, decides to "fix" him by
telling the architect's wife that she has in Kip (the younger
man) a rival for her husband's love and that this rival is a
neurotic from way back. There follow the three necessary
scenes (wife and Kip; wife and husband; husband and Kip) in
which we learn that Kip is indeed a rival and, if the wife
insists on having it that way, a conscious and aggressive one;
that the husband, however, has not had sexual relations with
the boy and denies to his wife and himself that there is
anything "like that" in the friendship; he accordingly slaps
Kip's face and tells him to get out. I wonder if my readers can
guess how the play ends? It is easy to think up one of those
morally ambiguous and theatrically sure-fire endings that
make people feel something has been said that is both important and respectable. For example (lest anyone suspect me of
bluff): we can get Kip in bed with the wife and "cure" him.
Or (more subtle, this one) we can rename the play Close
Shave, send Kip packing, and bring down the curtain on the
marriage bed, which is once again to be put to its proper use
in this, after all, one hundred per cent American home. Or
again . . . but let me report what Mr. Rosenthal does. When
Kip reappears with his overcoat on, the husband suddenly
doesn't want him to leave any more; apologizes; cajoles. Kip
leaves, but only just. He says he may be weak enough to phone
soon asking to come back. He tells the husband not to take the
phone off the hook. The wife is pretty decent about things,
wants her husband, her child, her home, and suggests a snack
in the kitchen. The phone rings. Exit wife to kitchen. The
phone keeps ringing. Will the husband pick it up? Yes. Yes,

he's just going to. He stops. No. No, he's going down to the kitchen. Curtain.

Summaries cut plays down so; a fact from which some dramatic critics have derived their theory and practice. Let me make it clear that I admire Mr. Rosenthal's ending. The use of the telephone, to be sure, is too much of a trick, but on stage that never greatly matters if the point being made is humanly sound. And this one is. The crude device gives a subtle definition to the husband's state of mind. He has just admitted to his wife and himself that Kip is the one great love of his life, so, actually, Mr. Rosenthal's chance of a corny ending was not the marriage bed but romantic, homosexual elopement. It is out of respect for truth, rather than dramatic critics, that he sends the husband to the kitchen.

The style Mr. Rosenthal has adopted is a fairly plain, uninflated prose, concise and witty. One admires above all else in the show the sustaining of a low-pitched yet intense and intelligent dialogue. I liked it best in the serious scenes, particularly in Kip's speeches, but I wouldn't discount the attempt to set the drama against a background of upper-class tittle tattle, somewhat on the lines of Somerset Maugham's *The Circle*. If I could remember any of the wisecracks, I would quote them; but a wisecrack is, by definition, an unmemorable epigram; and I can only report that the jokes are dry, keen, and bitter.

At times, the dramaturgy creaks. The wife has to have a confidant, and Mr. Rosenthal hasn't been able to provide anything but a cliché for the purpose: one of those sassy, well-dressed old maids that are so dear to the Broadway audience. More important, when one accepts the play as the serious document that it is, one cannot but wish that it were even more serious. Too many crucial questions are left unanswered. A play in which we are told (and need to know) that a married couple haven't slept together in six months should make much clearer to us the sexual constitution of all its leading characters. It seems that the husband has had intercourse with no one for six months; Kip for a matter of years. The only thing that would make these facts credible is explanation; and none is provided. In this respect the play is not "too clinical," as has been alleged; it isn't clinical enough.

Though going much further in honesty than other Broadway treatments of the homosexual theme, it does not go the whole way, and, in fact, through lack of candor about the primitive sexual needs of human beings, ends up—quite unintentionally, I imagine—as a defence of platonic friendship against sex. Such a notion is an evasion of the issue: homosexuality is validated on condition that it isn't sexual! Now, though I have been authoritatively tipped off that this is the moral of *Cat on a Hot Tin Roof,* I feel sure that it shouldn't have been the moral of *Third Person.*

On the other hand, there *is* something to the charge of "too clinical" if it means that the view of human beings taken by Mr. Rosenthal is too narrowly psychiatric. His subject, it is true, invites such narrowness: our friends of the East Sixties, being all too often without serious religion, art, or politics, may well have nothing to occupy them but their neuroses. But this is no alibi for an author, who can only portray people by standing at a distance from them—at a distance and, I would say, on an eminence. His richer sense of life must be implicit in his picture of their spiritual poverty.

I think Mr. Rosenthal makes something of an effort in this regard through Kip, yet, though this is the title role, the identification of the audience is, rather, with the husband; and, as is the way with such characters, the husband remains both too rudimentary and too vague. He says he loves Kip because Kip is the only person who ever needed him (which is too pat an explanation), while the character of his longing for the boy is only rendered in inadequate symbols, such as Rupert Brooke's poetry and talks on mountain tops. . . .

The play was directed by Bill Butler, who showed taste and skill in keeping the show clear of any possible charge of scurrility or even cheapness. Mr. Butler is ably abetted by his cast, particularly Murray Matheson who paints a subtly and sharply correct portrait of a dangerous male spinster and Bradford Dillman (Kip), virtually the star of the show, who solves the problem of "playing a homosexual" the right way—that is, by ignoring it.

A Funny Sort of Red

WHAT AN ANTICLIMAX! For years, in quite unprecedented fashion, the dramatic critic of *The New York Times* has been clamoring for an O'Casey production on Broadway. Here is an O'Casey production on Broadway, and the dramatic critic of *The New York Times* is just about the only person who thinks it is great. The cause of Sean O'Casey, if it is a cause, has been set back years, perhaps decades, by the performance of *Red Roses for Me* that Gordon W. Pollock has produced and John O'Shaughnessy has directed. But is it a cause? Molly Day Thacher has written in *The New Leader:*

> The truth is that if one can forget the agitation—and forget, as well, the picture of the thin little Irishman with the thick-lensed glasses—if one can simply read O'Casey's later plays, one finds them to be sad, muddled, and minor echoes of his great ones. The deep and serious issue with O'Casey is not: Has a certain senator prevented production of his plays throughout the world? It is, rather: How has the Communist doctrine, which is so alien to the nature of his talent, affected a playwright of great endowment and previous achievement? Is it an accident that the power and spontaneity of his writing deteriorated after his "political awakening"?

Sunset and Evening Star, the last volume of his autobiography, does indicate that Communism has blunted Mr. O'Casey's sensitivity to two things that many still cherish: truth and freedom. In a chapter called "The Dree Dames," he takes the position that ladies who wish to tell him that their relatives have been liquidated by Stalin are impertinent intruders in the O'Casey home, "marring the serenity of a summer day." Why should Mr. O'Casey have to listen to such stuff? In the following chapter, he refuses a fair hearing even to George Orwell. . . .

Even by all this cantankerousness and inhumanity, however, one should not be jockeyed into assuming that there is a simple and direct relation between talent and political rectitude. Bertolt Brecht has written better than Mr. O'Casey in the past two decades, and is a much more knowing Communist, not to speak of Pound and Hamsun and the rest on what used to be considered the other side. Come to think of it, it was the Communists who first sold us the notion that our political opponents can't write well, and it is writers who have been over-influenced by the Communists who continue to give the notion currency—Arthur Miller, for example, who in 1955 challenged his opponents to write a scenario for him in these words: "Now let us see whether fanaticism can do what it never could do in the history of the world . . . let it take its club in hand and write. . . ." I propose to let Mr. O'Casey have not only his Communism but also the possibility of greatness as a Communist writer—or, which is not the same thing, of greatness as a writer who, incidentally, supports Communism.

Red Roses for Me is about the death of a proletarian hero in the Dublin strike of 1913. It is proper that a Communist author should choose that phase of Irish social conflict, rather than the nationalist rising of 1916 which has been immortalized by Yeats. In addition, O'Casey takes the curse off the proletarianism by the method Odets used in this country: by a poetry of dialect, which is the poetry of a people. In fact, the simple story, not very well told, occupies but a small part of the evening. The time is taken up by what I can only call dramaturgic decoration, some of which is so good that it almost redeems the play and certainly makes the show worth seeing, some of it so bad that at best one is bored and at worst resorts to Miss Thacher's diagnosis. The good part is nearly all comedy, and this of the zaniest sort. Incomparable, except that one has the early O'Casey plays to compare it to, is a little scene in which a Catholic, a Protestant, and an atheist discuss their differences while sheltering from bullets under tables and behind chairs. Utterly charming is the tale of the Protestant who steals the Virgin's statue with the result that a miracle is proclaimed by his Catholic neighbors when he returns her, washed and shining, to her niche. Mr. O'Casey is neither anti-Protestant nor anti-Catholic, and is able to play one faction off against the other in a riot of loving fun. It is the capitalists he hates; and is unable to portray; instead, the ruling class is "symbolized" by a police inspector—a cartoon, as it were, by one of *The Daily Worker's* less gifted collaborators. In the symbolic and abstract character of this figure one descries the origin of Mr. O'Casey's "expressionism," which represents an attempt, not to imitate Kaiser and Toller, but to thrust onto the stage, somehow, people whom Mr. O'Casey was absolutely incapable of creating. Intellectually, this is no doubt an honest effort to grapple with what is "objectively" important; dramaturgically, it is nothing more nor less than cheating.

To be fair, the "expressionism" of *Red Roses for Me* goes beyond the portrait of a single man. Accused in his early days of merely stringing scenes and skits and songs together, as in a revue, Mr. O'Casey tries in the later plays to build the music, dancing, and incidental fun, into the structure of the whole— to the point, indeed, where these elements impose and *are* the structure, and it is the narrative which is incidental. I do not know whether such an attempt could ever succeed: plot, says Aristotle, is the soul of the drama. Even if Aristotle were wrong, one would have to complain that, though Irish speech, music, and pantomime are fine things, Mr. O'Casey is too abjectly dependent on them. He sings the Irish melody till his voice goes flat; a good deal of the Hibernianism in the later plays is farfetched and phony. Folk tunes are nice, but deciding to have actors sing them is temptingly easy. Pantomime is excellent, but is composed by performers: all the writer has to do is provide the merest externals of it in stage directions.

If writing of this sort could scarcely be great drama, it would nonetheless be the book and basis of great theatre, the deciding factor, in that case, being the staging of it. Believing, no doubt, that *Red Roses for Me* is great drama, which it is not, Mr. O'Shaughnessy has not made of it the great theatre which it could be. Trying to tell the story, he only underscores the fact that his author is *not* trying to tell the story. Using an imaginative choreographer (Anna Sokolow) in one fine, lyrical scene, he only underscores the fact that the whole entertainment should have been choreographic. Having a respect for Mr. O'Casey's dialogue, he decides that ingenious rhetoric is great poetry and slows down to a snail's pace sentences that could be effective only if thrown off with an air of insouciance. In every department equally, Mr. O'Shaughnessy knows How Not To Do It. The "blocking" of a scene in which a girl writhes on the ground in her death agonies while the actors look on *from a distance* has the awkwardness of a beginning directors' class at Yale.

Mr. O'Casey's heroine could be gracefully tossed into our lap by any good-looking Irish lass with a touch of acting talent, but is thrown headlong at us in the Booth Theatre by an actress (Joyce Sullivan) with all manner of grander intentions, none of which is realized. The hero is played by Kevin MacCarthy. This actor is hard to write about because an air of unrealized potentiality hangs about him. I am always tempted to postpone writing on him till the next time. He has both intelligence and charm, yet goes, with each role, thus far and no farther; a mysterious rigidity or inhibition holds him back. And so it is in *Red Roses for Me*.

Mr. O'Casey's later plays are themselves so schematic, so inorganic, that the actors' work has to be doubly alive, doubly flexible and flowing. In a large cast, only E. G. Marshall was fully equal to the challenge. In the combined impishness and fire of his fooling—as well as in such details as a beautifully composed old man's "mask" and bearing—he gave us an indication how O'Casey might one day be successfully performed.

For Communism will pass, but Mr. O'Casey's clowns will endure forever. And his childish attitude to "The Dree Dames" will come to seem only the defect of a quality which all can admire. His talent, too, belongs to a realm which is childish—perhaps one should say childlike—in the best sense. In his plays, amid the realities of naturalism and the abstractions of politics, he has created a dream world of sublime infantility: the funny men to whom he justly owes most of his fame—Fluther Good, Joxer Daly, and the rest—are a gallery of charming children.

A Directors' Theatre

THOUGH OUR AGE notoriously lacks direction, it does not lack directors: boards of them in business or hordes of them in the theatre. The Victorian theatre was an actors' theatre; the era of Shaw, Barker, and O'Neill tried to substitute an authors' theatre; but, now that we have no Shaws, Barkers, and O'Neills, it is not the actors who have filled the vacuum, it is the directors. Their contribution to a show is so large that they are not only virtual co-authors but co-designers, co-composers, co-choreographers, co-everything. And they are not just partners but senior partners. If the impress of a single personality is on a show these days, you may be pretty sure that that personality is the director's; to speak of Shakespeare's *Hamlet* will soon be as unusual and eccentric as to speak of Schikaneder's *Magic Flute*. The playwright is just a librettist; the composer's name is Reinhardt, Meyerhold, Piscator, Baty, Logan, or Kazan.

The British stage has, on the whole, resisted this modern tendency, resting content with good individual performances roughly-and-readily integrated by a fellow actor or a "producer" who was often little more than a stage manager. But, today, the directorial showmen of America and the Continent have at least two rivals in England: the Russian-born Peter Brook and the Irishman Tyrone Guthrie.

The 1955–56 season will go down in stage history as the one in which Mr. Guthrie took Broadway by what can accurately be called storm. In less than the time of three rehearsal and tryout periods, he has brought three productions up to a standard of technical proficiency unsurpassed in our theatre. All three—Wilder's *The Matchmaker*, Marlowe's *Tamburlaine the Great*, and Pirandello's *Six Characters in Search of an Author*—have a verve and a shimmer that betoken a tremendous theatrical gift in their director. All three are full of movement well conceived and well controlled, of groups well grouped, of masses well massed, of ingenuity, of surprising "ideas." . . . All three this, and all three that: my point is best made by citing the fact that three plays which are so different that they would prompt no comparisons at all, the one with the other, have blended, in my memory of the three productions, into a single impression. For example, one of the memorably theatrical "moves" is that of an actor's popping up between another actor's legs. *Tamburlaine? Six Characters?* Both! What can be done in one play can be done in another. Three plays can become one. The not only divergent but incommensurable personalities of Wilder, Marlowe, and Pirandello can be subordinated to the one personality of Tyrone Guthrie. This circumstance guarantees that each evening will indeed be an entertainment, for Mr. Guthrie's personality as it comes through to us in his work (obviously, I am not concerned with his private personality) is wholly that of the showman. We still have the right to ask: What kind of showman? and also: How satisfactorily can Wilder, Marlowe, and Pirandello, respectively, be subordinated to the mind and art of Mr. Guthrie?

Personality being unique, each case is different. The results are most satisfactory where the author's personality is least strong. Of *The Matchmaker,* my complaint is only that Mr. Guthrie stands too close to the rather chi-chi semiculture of more highbrow British theatre; a George Abbott production would have been funnier for being less fancily facetious. Mr. Guthrie and Marlowe might seem to have in common the cynicism inherent in "sheer theatricality," yet further consideration suggests that, while *Tamburlaine the Great* is immoral, being, as C. S. Lewis says, "the story of giant the Jack killer," Mr. Guthrie is only amoral, and lightheartedly so, again as partaking of the effete insincerity of the West End. Where Marlowe was defiant, Mr. Guthrie is only amused; where Marlowe, in his colossal error, was at least spunky, Mr. Guthrie, behind all the external false energy, is tired and perhaps even bored. The cries of Bravo when one of Tamburlaine's victims is hoisted in air and transfixed by arrows are a true index to Mr. Guthrie's interpretation. Brooks Atkinson gets the impression that Marlowe (the bow and arrow man) was unsophisticated! In truth, Marlowe and Guthrie are both as sophisticated as men can be, but while Marlowe's sophistication is youthful, nihilistic, and intellectual, Mr. Guthrie's is blasé, apolitical, and trivial.

Pirandello has twice depicted directors of Mr. Guthrie's tendency (if not with his talent), and it is an irony that Mr. Guthrie should have to place one of them on stage: the director in *Six Characters in Search of an Author*. On the face of it, this event constitutes Mr. Guthrie's revenge, for his production inverts Pirandello's main thesis and proves, instead, that directors and actors are more real than a writer's characters. But, with Pirandello, you always have irony within irony, and, by the end of the evening, what Pirandello says about directors has been amply demonstrated—namely and simply that they come between the audience and the experience the author wished to communicate. Before creating the Guthrie-like director of *Tonight We Improvise*, Pirandello had been in Berlin; to his praise of the "miracles" of Reinhardt and Piscator, he added (in a press interview) the observation that, nonetheless, the work of the new directors could be "a crime committed against the spirit of an artistic creation." Those who go to Guthrie's *Six Characters* in a state of primal innocence will quite rightly enjoy a "marvellous show," but those who know what Pirandello's sense of tragedy can mean in poignancy and beauty, not to speak of insight, must feel cheated of the main content of the piece. It was good to turn the attention of our public from mere philosophy and to bring out the humor of the script; but Mr. Guthrie brought out much humor that is not in the script at the expense of the searing tragedy that is, so that, fantastic as it sounds, his untragic *Six Characters* is continuous with his unserious *Tamburlaine,* just as that *Tamburlaine* was continuous with a farce, *The Matchmaker.*

Now while we may be prepared to have directors take up small scripts and make them large, it is a question whether we want them to take up large scripts and make them small. And if, like Pirandello, we do not, we must, like him, impugn the whole idea of a directors' theatre. In the drama schools today the advent of the director ("circa 1900") is presented as a giant step in the march of progress, and for some reason it is assumed that the history of theatre *is* progressive, even though it is obvious that the history of other arts is not. How did the poor benighted Kean, Garrick, Burbage get along without their Reinhardts and Guthries? Having seen what Mr. Guthrie does about, and with, actors, we should be almost ready, by now, to answer that the situation of the older actors had its advantages. For it is not only the dramatist whom Mr. Guthrie maltreats. In theory, as I judge from articles he has written, he is all for the actor, but in practice he is often against him—in the straightforward sense that he binds him, instead of stretching him, that he does not draw from him the best work he is capable of. In Mr. Guthrie's productions we see star actors doing just what they have done in other shows or lesser actors being shepherded about in droves by the most expert sheepdog that ever came out of Ireland. Here one should distinguish Mr. Guthrie radically from some of the other crack directors I have just listed, and especially from Mr. Kazan, whose gift it is to discover a certain quality inside a young actor, and then to make sure it emerges. Has Mr. Guthrie ever done that? *Tamburlaine* and *Six Characters in Search of an Author* leave an impression—which I honestly hope will not prove justified over the years—that he has a weakness for bad actors.

How Not to Write an Audience

ONE OF THE CURRENT topics of conversation in New York is Paddy Chayefsky, the first writer, I imagine, whose works have been adapted, not *to,* but *from,* TV. Nor is this fact all that is remarkable about the film *Marty* and the play *Middle of the Night.* Mr. Chayefsky draws on the everyday life of New York with so much ease and eager interest, you could believe for a moment that no one had ever been familiar with New York before. He has his eyes and ears open, he enjoys a lot of what he sees and hears, and he has the talent to communicate some of the enjoyment and many of the facts. Some of his humorous sallies—such as when the young husband in *Marty* bawls out his wife for her lunches out, of cans and cellophane—are worthy of Clifford Odets. Nor, any more than Odets', are they merely literal transcripts of life. At their best they are poetical reworkings of the vernacular. At their worst they are slick reductions of it to comic stereotype. If a man says once: "That Mickey Spillane, boy, he sure can write," you can rest assured he'll say it three times. In a weak moment, Mr. Chayefsky will give a character a tag-line like: "Oh sure, what the hell?" to say over and over and over.

It is, perhaps, in the nature of the case that the film should be far superior to the play, for the talent of Mr. Chayefsky is journalistic, and the camera is a better reporter of external facts than the stage will ever be. If Mr. Chayefsky's mentality is not to bother us, we need the constantly busy camera to keep our attention fixed on the streets, bars, kitchens, and bedrooms of Manhattan. In the role of a John Gunther "inside New York," Mr. Chayefsky is smoothly and sometimes charmingly successful. Another possible comparison would be with Vittorio De Sica, for *Marty* conveys a similar sense of relaxed identification with lower-class metropolitan life, not without a similar romanticism about it. Enjoying these things, you are prepared not to probe beneath the surface—until you see *Middle of the Night*.

Even then you will like what you find, provided only that your demands on the theatre are quite different from mine. What do you go to the theatre for? To recognize things out of the life you left behind you? To say of this actor: "He's just like Mr. Jones across the way," and of that: "Just like *my* husband?" and of this speech or the other one: "Just what mother always says!"? It is true that our theatre expends an inordinate amount of energy engineering such recognitions; and perhaps one day—1984?—drama will consist of absolutely nothing else. If so, Mr. Chayefsky is riding the wave of the future.

That he is certainly riding the wave of the present is clear enough from the themes he chooses. Are you lonely? Plain? A little old, now, for marriage? Have you fallen in love with a man old enough to be your father? Is your potency on the wane now you've passed fifty? Do you find call girls sordid yet fail to find a satisfying alternative? As I think back to *Middle of the Night,* I have it all mixed up, somehow, with memories of "Mr. Anthony" on the radio years ago or Norman Vincent Peale in a magazine I was leafing through the other day. "Now tell me: do you think it'd be right for me to break with my husband?" "My dear, that is a question only you can answer." But this Shakespearean retort was uttered—I believe—by Edward G. Robinson in reply to his leading lady. The whole play is like that. This author doesn't even bother to write characters; he writes audiences; the program almost tells you as much, announcing no names but just The Girl, The Manufacturer, etcetera. (Shades of expressionism!) The plot and persons are the most threadbare of improvisations; the author's concern is not with his own creations but with you and me.

Anyone who has not yet experienced this sort of thing will object that, nonetheless, an author can only reach you and me through his creations. No: *nous avons changé tout cela.* What happens in business these days? It has been discovered that the quality of the product is less important than the quality of the salesmanship; we don't sell products any more, we sell a customer "on" a product. And so the art of selling can be reduced to the injunction: concentrate on the customer. In the theatre, customers are called The Audience, and in concentrating on the audience Mr. Chayefsky is the playwright not only of the hour but of the age.

Isn't it good that a playwright should respect his audience? But if Mr. Chayefsky respected it more, he would bear down on it less; he would also talk down to it less. He has very little to say, but he will keep saying it at considerable length, with considerable unction, in language of considerable banality. I, too, am audience and must report that never have I been treated as a smaller or stupider child than by this author.

When a dramatist writes with his audience, not his characters, in mind, his writing is necessarily all contrivance, it is all, as it were, malice aforethought. This is why Mr. Chayefsky's intended eulogy to average humanity doesn't work out. Or rather the averageness works out, but not the humanity.

Which perhaps is as it should be for the playwright of the age
—this age of salesmanship and conformity. The idea of an
"average man" is valid enough in certain fields—"the average
man fills so many cans of garbage a day" and so forth. But
much as we all love our average man, none of us will confess to
being him. Whatever our weakness, we feel too full of freedom
and possibility to accept the definition; and the artist, preoccupied with such feelings, is interested precisely in the non-aver-
ageness even of the person stigmatized as average. Perhaps,
outside his plays, Mr. Chayefsky would be unmodern enough
to support the artist in this (for one deplores in him the abuse,
not the absence, of intelligence). But, inside the plays, we
truly get the average and not the unique, the preachment and
not the truth, the facts and not the life of the facts.

The relation of play to performance is an annoying one. It
is true that fine actors always did appear in false and rubbishy
plays. But the falsehood of, say, Sarah Bernhardt's vehicles by
Sardou and the rest was overt and involved no deception: the
falsehood of melodrama is even enjoyed as such. Since the rise
of realism, human falsity can be wrapped up in facts and
offered as genuine, realism, in this instance, being the vehicle
of unreality. So here, with Edward G. Robinson in *Middle of
the Night*. Delmore Schwartz has observed that the acted
emotions of Julie Harris in *East of Eden* went far beyond the
written emotions of John Steinbeck. And Paddy Chayefsky
owes it to Mr. Robinson that some people will think there is a
real man in his play.

There is a more cheerful way of looking at it: the stage play
is a form in which some of an author's deficiencies may be
made good by actors. With very few lines to speak, Anne
Jackson and Martin Balsam miraculously manage to compose
the portrait of a young woman with a quite unconscious father
fixation and her, in general, self-effacing, though not unaware,
husband. I shall not easily forget the energy that is in Miss
Jackson's long silences, or how she can make the hammiest
joke about a Freudian error sound like the wit of Oscar Wilde.

Mr. Logan directed the actors painstakingly, though he had
a leading lady with whom no director, I imagine, could do
very much. And this author brings out Mr. Logan's weakness

as much as his strength, for Mr. Logan too tends to make a fetish of the audience, and consequently to insult it with corny contrivances—such as, in this case, imitation-TV captions and imitation-TV background music.

Whimsy and the Cultured Classes

THE PONDER HEART, adapted by Joseph Fields and Jerome Chodorov from the story by Eudora Welty, is about . . . to tell the truth, when I left the theatre, I was very unsure *what* it was about. There had been a murder trial, and the accused had been acquitted, but the telling of the story had been so whimsical that I hadn't known what or whom to believe. It seemed to me quite possible that Uncle Daniel *had* murdered his wife Bonnie Dee, but that one wouldn't hold this against him for various reasons—first, he was crazy; second, he was such a nice man; and third, like Miss Madrigal in *The Chalk Garden,* he seemed vaguely to symbolize something rather grand and religious and therefore to be entitled, *ex hypothesi,* to a few murders. When I got home, however, and read the story, I was surprised to find not only that Miss Welty had not left this possibility open but that she had made it clear that Bonnie Dee had dropped dead while Uncle Daniel, in his friendly fashion, was tickling her to keep her mind off a thunderstorm.

This fact is handed straight to the reader by Miss Welty's narrator, Uncle Daniel's niece, Edna Earle, and indeed the position of the niece was the toughest problem the adaptors had to face. What happens to a novelist's spectator-narrator in a play? He (in this case, she) becomes a minor character— with perhaps only a doubtful title to be even that. Meanwhile, the main characters in the drama, previously seen only through the narrator's eyes, have wheeled off into space, like planets released from all gravitational pull. Uncle Daniel, in the play *The Ponder Heart,* is such a planet-without-an-orbit.

In the story, Miss Welty lays it down through Edna Earle exactly how we are to take him: though this lady makes a brave show of defending him, she also lets drop that he has been in a mental home. On stage, two things go wrong. First, for a very long time, we don't know how to take Uncle Daniel's strangeness; only later on (and I cannot say at what point) do we realize he is crazy. Second, when we do realize, there is nothing to stop us from identifying ourselves with him —on the assumption, naturally, that our insanity is worth double the sanity of the vulgar. In the story, the presence of Edna Earle as narrator ensures that the point of view is consistently that of sanity. We know where we're at.

I suppose any story suffers a sea-change, though not necessarily into something rich or strange, when it migrates to the stage. In the present case, a story that is fundamentally realistic, however funny, poetic, and odd, has been cut down to the size of an accepted sort of theatrical zaniness. Comparisons have already, and rightly, been made with another current show, *No Time for Sergeants,* which stakes out no claim to be more than a roistering farce. However, the rank insanity of Uncle Daniel is less close to the rustic simplicity of the hero in *No Time for Sergeants* than it is to the flights of fancy of Mary Chase in *Harvey.* Possibly, all three plays have the same importance for the student of American (or modern) culture: the glorification of the simpleton is the obverse of hostility to intellect, while the acceptance of imbecility as wisdom is an unconscious confession of intellectual bankruptcy.

That the lunatic should be regarded with religious awe is no new thing, and already in the nineteenth century Dickens touched the old awe with the new sentimentality. But it was left to the twentieth century to make of infantility its master ideal. Even in the thirties, all that social indignation would melt before the amiable imbeciles of *You Can't Take It With You,* and it has been the pleasure of a later generation to become again like little children at the behest of Richard Rodgers' tum-titty-tum and Oscar Hammerstein's Sunday School addresses. . . .

I don't want to give the impression that all this modern wickedness and heresy is concentrated in *The Ponder Heart,* to which the word *concentrated* is in all respects inapplicable. Though in the second instance I may be complaining, in the first I am merely reporting that, for example, when Miss Welty has Bonnie Dee leave the washing machine on the porch, Messrs. Fields and Chodorov have her station a *dish*-washing machine in the middle of the drawing-room floor and then have water pipes installed to feed it. In the story, it's a big day when a telephone is brought in; on Broadway, there's a TV set and a huge icebox filled with things that belong in closets. . . . And in this way, the world of *Room Service,* rather than Southern fiction, is re-created. On the other hand, a great deal of Miss Welty's own wit is preserved, not least because a great many of her lines are quoted. Taken moment by moment, rather than as a total experience, the evening is an amusing and lively one.

The performance has the Broadway virtue of efficiency: technically, nothing ever goes wrong, and everything on stage looks as bright as a new pin. In the American theatre the decisive process is casting, and our producers and directors are good at it. David Wayne was a decisive and fortunate choice for Uncle Daniel. Having criticized Mr. Wayne for his cuteness in *Teahouse of the August Moon,* I am glad to say that he reappears in *The Ponder Heart* purged and purified. Now that he relaxes more, his warmth and sparkle spread themselves much more easily around the theatre. Though he is younger, better-scrubbed, and blander than my mental image of Miss Welty's character, there is no doubt that his personality carries the show. As Bonnie Dee, Sarah Marshall proves herself a remarkable and welcome new presence in our theatre, but one wishes her director (Robert Douglas) could have helped her to join together, as it were, the ends of the part, for at present there is no connection between the nicely defined silent urchin of the beginning and the screaming wife of the end. Also, Miss Marshall's natural English accent sometimes shows through her assumed southern one.

Pondering *The Ponder Heart* in general—Fields, Chodorov, or even Welty—one senses some sort of frustration of the comic sense that has causes going far beyond these three individuals. The idea that American (or, again, modern) culture

is lacking in tragic sense, percolating through from philosophers to editorial writers on *Life* magazine, has become a commonplace but what about the hostility of American (or
modern) culture to the comic spirit? All of us enjoy slapstick;
the middle classes make a fetish of backslapping good humor;
the cultured classes (especially through their official organ
The New Yorker in which *The Ponder Heart* first appeared)
are dedicated to that species of spiritual winking and shrug-
ging of the shoulders that we call whimsy. Meanwhile, where
is comedy—with its diabolical energy, its taut intellectuality,
its moral severity? Whimsy is so innocuous. The writer of true
comedies would have to have followed the advice which
Joseph Conrad provided for the development of the tragic
sense: "in the destructive element immerse."

The Last Drawing-Room Comedy

IN THE COMMERCIAL THEATRE, first impressions are taken to
be all that matters. The reviews that determine the fate of a
show are written one hour after the first performance. The
whole effort of producers and directors is to excite your interest in the first five seconds and then to prolong the excitement
for two hours; after which the experience is over, and all that
can be hoped for is that you tell your friends: I Was Excited.
And so there are many shows which rouse one to tears and
laughter so long as they are in progress and which, after they
are done, leave no residue at all, not even a little uneasiness.
For me, *The Diary of Anne Frank* was rather like this. It was
good while it lasted, but I have almost nothing to say about it
because almost nothing of it stayed with me. It is one of those
plays which depend on what the audience brings with them;
the author doesn't give them anything to take home. It is a
commercial product, too, rather than a work of art, in that all
the roughnesses of individuality have been smoothed away
from it. Commercial art is as smooth, rounded, and unexcep-

tionable as an egg, while true art by contrast has something offensive about it, something imperfect and, possibly, maddening. That is why one's dislike of a play by Arthur Miller is much more of a compliment than one's inability to dislike the latest little commercial comedy.

If first impressions are all, let the management of *The Chalk Garden* take note that I fled their show in dismay after one act. But what is more stimulating than irritation? I have since seen the show in its entirety at my own expense, and have read the script twice slowly through. I believe that, all in all, *The Chalk Garden*, by Enid Bagnold, is the best new play (*Tiger at the Gates* not being new) of the 1955–56 season,[1] a very brilliant piece of composition, one of the most skilfully *built* plays of recent years, with a good subject, and an honorable theme.

Miss Madrigal, the protagonist, seemed guilty of the murder of her stepsister, even though she wasn't; the element of doubt saved her from the gallows, but not from jail. In presenting an episode of this lady's subsequent life, Miss Bagnold adroitly uses a double action. The first action of her play consists of the progressive revelation, to the others on stage and to the spectators out front, of Miss Madrigal's past; it is this action which gives the play its primary contact with the audience, for it has the interest of a murder mystery. The inner action is the story of a young girl whom Miss Madrigal saves from a fate similar to her own; it is on this action that the play's claim to meaning and distinction mainly rests. I state forthrightly that Miss Madrigal committed no murder, because this is what she herself definitely implies, and because the whole thing otherwise makes no sense. She tells how the case against her had plausibility, but not truth. She also intimates that she had been such a liar that when she eventually told the truth it wasn't believed. ("When she told the truth it didn't save her." "I learned in nine days that innocence is not enough.") In a sense, it seems, she had made herself a murderess by sheer

---

[1] A competitor arrived later in *Waiting for Godot*, but at this point I regret ever having started the game of picking winners, much less having begun to list all the horses in the order they came in. [Summer, 1956]

mendacity; the law being concerned with justice and not with pity, with the weighing of statements and not with charity, could only reach the negative conclusion. Having taken her punishment, and having been reborn through suffering, Miss Madrigal extends to a young girl in distress the pity and charity that had been withheld from herself. The distress is just such a self-destructive mendacity as her own. Laurel (whose governess she has been appointed) likes to think that she was raped at the age of twelve and that she hates her mother. So she languishes in her grandmother's chalk garden, in which nothing can grow, until Miss Madrigal does battle both with the girl's neurosis and her grandmother; and wins. Laurel at last sees that truth is more interesting than fiction and goes off with her mother. Miss Madrigal stays with the grandmother, who must now face solitude and not being loved.

A somber play then, with a moral more or less Pirandellian: the true meaning of life is to be sought, not in fact-finding, but in compassion and the domestic pieties. Yet, as also with Pirandello, if there is heartbreak underneath, there are para-doxes on the surface. And Miss Bagnold's paradoxes—that is, her comic images, tricks, and phrases—are so striking that for many they obscure the rest of the play. *The Chalk Garden* is prima facie a sort of drawing-room play to end all drawing-room plays. To symbolize that fact, the old butler Mr. Pink-bell is dying all through and does die in the last scene: while the new butler belongs to the time when servants are recruited from "the sick, the mad, and those who can't take their places in the outside world." Mrs. St. Maugham, the grandmother, is the last lady: "I don't entertain any more. The fight's over. Even the table is laid with fragments of forgotten ritual"—for she doesn't know why she's ordered two wine glasses each for one bottle of wine or whether knives are to be placed inside or outside spoons.

Why is the show so hard to take? To begin with, for many people it isn't, or it wouldn't still be running on Broadway after nearly five months.[2] Its history on the road suggests, moreover, that it might not have succeeded unless it had been

[2] It ran, in all, from October 26, 1955, to March 31, 1956.

given just the treatment the director (Albert Marre) has given it. Yet even if Mr. Marre is to be given fullest credit for saving the occasion, I am still somewhat put out by the production because it stresses what to me is already overemphatic in the script: that Miss Bagnold is a bizarre "character," given to headlong movements and cockeyed ejaculations. Hence, one doesn't take hold of the story, let alone the theme.

I walked out the first time because the performance was so full of effort and strain. Gladys Cooper (the grandmother) was hamming it up, and Siobhan McKenna (Miss Madrigal) kept pointing her head at the balcony and booming. The performance I saw a couple of months later was better, though not without the same clumsiness and mechanical drive. The vocal quirk must be one Miss McKenna always has trouble with, as it is present in her Juno on the new recording of O'Casey's play. Nonetheless, my second visit made me see how much the show depends on her unactressy beauty and strangely fine combination of the delicate and the solid. As the new butler Fritz Weaver shows as surprising a gift for the grotesque comic here as he did last year for the grotesque tragic when he played Flamineo in *The White Devil*. However, the imperfection of his Cockney accent disturbed me, and he followed his elders and non-betters in making his comic points too broadly.

The fact that the play seems obscure is due as much as anything to the casting of Betsy von Furstenberg as Laurel and of Marian Seldes as her mother. Miss von Furstenberg has a body and a personality to which I am as susceptible as anyone, but her lack of interest in a *role* is also considerable. The role of Laurel develops; Miss von Furstenberg ambles in and out. The mother has been regarded as the off-horse of the family, "plain, shy, obstinate, silent . . . even your wedding dress you wore like wrapping paper"—none of which seems to apply, even inaccurately, to Marian Seldes; and so a connecting link in this carefully concatenated family scheme is missing.

Even for the script, and even now, my admiration has limits. The wit descends to cleverness, the elegance to preciosity, the originality to eccentricity, the intelligence to exhibitionism. "For a phrase she would make capital of anything," as someone says of someone in the play. And, finally, Miss Bagnold does not have what it takes—emotion, love, imagination, genius?—to give her main conception the form and force that it deserves. Where Pirandello reinforces his paradoxes with Sicilian passion, and Giraudoux redeems his preciosity with a flood of Gallic melancholy, Miss Bagnold, while commending to others fertility and richer soil, is somehow stuck, finally, in her own garden of chalk.

A Directly Sensuous Pleasure

THE EXISTENCE of *My Fair Lady*—after Shaw's *Pygmalion*, book and lyrics by Alan Jay Lerner, music by Frederick Loewe —would be fully justified even if the new musical were only a showcase for its three leading performers: Rex Harrison, Stanley Holloway, and Julie Andrews. To say that Mr. Harrison "makes the adjustment" to musical comedy is to understate the case. The fact is that only musical comedy permits him to show what he can do without inviting him to attempt what he cannot do. In his serious roles, like Henry VIII or the leading man of *The Love of Four Colonels*, Mr. Harrison tried to make up in puffy pretension for what his characterization lacked in substance. In *My Fair Lady*, he provides just as much characterization as musical comedy can stand (and in fact is one of the few actors not to underplay Higgins' ill-nature) while at the same time proving equal to the special and extra demands of the genre, notably the ability to perform the songs. I say perform, because, in this genre, it is of no earthly use to be able to sing and not perform a song, while if you can perform a song, without being able to sing it, all criticism of your musicianship is beside the point. Mr. Harrison speaks and acts his songs admirably.

"Musical comedy" is a misnomer because, actually, its tradition is less comic than sentimental. Though it seems to have driven vaudeville out of business, it has not taken over the comedians, who, after all, were the chief glory of the older form. It is a great and exceptional thing when a musical features a Bert Lahr or a Phil Silvers, and I for one particularly welcome the introduction to the genre of Stanley Holloway who plays Doolittle. Mr. Holloway brings with him the atmosphere of the old music hall, and Messrs. Lerner and Loewe have risen to the occasion by capturing that atmosphere in the two numbers they have assigned to Mr. Holloway, "With a Little Bit" and "Get Me to the Church on Time." Very much of the old and true tradition is the way in which Mr. Holloway, when he sings, holds his trousers in front as if they were skirts. Loud, gusty, and full-blooded, he is at the same time ironic, precise, and almost dainty.

It is a star's job to twinkle, and, even more than they are actors, the three stars of this show are personalities of quite extraordinary radiance. Almost any nice smile, these days, is called winning, but Julie Andrews' smile beats everything; it is lucky for Mr. Eisenhower that Miss Andrews is British and can't run against him in November. And, except with Cheshire cats, a smile is no isolated mechanism, but an index to the soul. Miss Andrews has a very pretty soul, and in her simplicity, which "gets across" without any superimposed glamour, there is the real glamour which is of the essence of theatre. She also fits exquisitely into the pattern of the show, offsetting Mr. Harrison's unmusicality with a tuneful voice, and Mr. Holloway's robustiousness with a natural delicacy. If she is not quite able to bring off the final coup of the role of Eliza— the achieving of independence (in the last act of Shaw's play) —that is only because Messrs. Lerner and Loewe haven't given her the chance.

Ought they to have? The query leads to a discussion of the whole undertaking. Unless we deny the initial premise—that a Broadway musical can and should be made from *Pygmalion*— it may be impossible not to grant Messrs. Lerner and Loewe all the inferences they have drawn. But actually there is only one change I seriously jib at: the utter sentimentalizing of the end. Shaw reluctantly allowed Mrs. Campbell to end the play with a hint that all was not over between Eliza and Higgins, and, in the movie, Pascal had Wendy Hiller follow Mrs.

Campbell's precedent. In *My Fair Lady,* what had been a hint stuck on at the end becomes the main theme of the second half of the show and involves having Higgins turn into the standard leading man of musical comedy and at that as cornily lovelorn as they come. Even earlier in the evening Higgins painstakingly explains that he's "an ordinary man" in order to remove the difficulty which the ordinary man of New York in 1956 might have in identifying himself with a British genius of a phonetician, vintage 1912. It has been assumed, I take it, that a musical comedy has to present the meeting and mating of the common man with the common woman. The assumption can be questioned. And it is certainly true that the second half of the show—the part invented by Messrs. Lerner and Loewe in honor of the common man—is far inferior to the first half; it is one long anticlimax rendered tolerable only by the musical numbers.

Even of the first half, it cannot be said that the new material has been perfectly fused with the old, for Mr. Lerner's writing is on one plane, and Bernard Shaw's is on another. Anyone familiar with the Shavian text, and fond of it, is bound to feel jolted from time to time. On the other hand, Mr. Lerner has been shrewd enough to be reverential. A vast amount of Shaw's dialogue has been retained. And, since the non-Shavian words, except for a couple of corny love songs, do not fall below Shaw as far as they rise above the average musical comedy, one could easily be so impressed by the latter fact as to overlook or forgive the former. Mr. Loewe's music and Hanya Holm's choreography are also something distinctly better than "in good taste." Oliver Smith (sets) and Cecil Beaton (costumes) have shared the general respect for the Shavian original while cooperating in the creation of a musical comedy variant. (At the moment I have only one quarrel with Mr. Beaton: I believe that clothes exist to show off women, and not vice versa.)

Though I have questioned one of the adaptors' evident assumptions, I am not questioning the necessity of all changes, even all drastic ones. The introduction of music of itself gives a play not only a different frame but a different atmosphere. Music constitutes a different order of experience, and musical comedy creates a world of its own—most characteristically, I believe, a Never Never Land of fantasy. Reviewing *Porgy and Bess*, I pointed out how, at the hands of Gershwin, Dubose Heyward's spurious realistic document became a genuine fairy tale. As it happens, Shaw took his story from legend in the first place; in *My Fair Lady* it goes back where it came from. A lot of the immediate pleasure which the show so abundantly provides derives from the fairy-tale charm and nostalgia created by the ensemble of stage design, costumes, choreography, music, and actors' personalities (credit for the masterly coordination of these elements going to the director, Moss Hart).

Theatre is more of a directly sensuous pleasure than theatre criticism would suggest, and it is therefore proper to stress that, for all the flaws that may reveal themselves to analysis, this show presents to the senses an appearance of flawlessness and touching beauty. Undoubtedly, this is the kind of thing Broadway does best, and undoubtedly Broadway has acted, in this instance, with a degree of restraint and even positive taste, for which it is not yet famous. One can bestow upon *My Fair Lady* ungrudging, if not unqualified, praise.

Inaccuracy Again

THE *Uncle Vanya* production has won a much greater public response than *The Cherry Orchard* and *The Three Sisters*, which preceded it at the Fourth Street Theatre, because Franchot Tone is in it. So much the better for the prestige of Off Broadway theatre. The show reaches a higher general standard than the preceding ones. Yet I found it unmoving, and I cannot agree to the now widespread notion that Chekhov's major plays are supposed to be uniformly cool and funny. They are punctuated with superb jokes, they are informed with a profound comic sense, but they are also suffused in emotion. This suffusion was somehow rendered in that much clumsier Fourth Street production, *The Three Sisters;* and one forgave the faults. In the *Uncle Vanya,* it is not rendered, so that I, for one, feel rather unappreciative of the other attainments of the show.

Franchot Tone is something better than ingratiating as Dr. Astrov. It is a delight to follow his careful shaping of a speech, his precise pointing of a line. He has a rare plasticity, charm, and virility. He is, in fact, an out and out man of the theatre, and the shortcomings of this particular performance stem from his being all too much at ease on the Fourth Street stage. The assured way he takes the hand of a woman, the professional way he kisses her, suggest rather the Franchot Tone of the tabloid headlines than the shy and fumbling Dr. Astrov of Chekhov's story.

As Vanya, George Voskovec is more venturesome and spirited, yet his free, not to say vehement, gestures set him too far apart from the Anglo-American style of his colleagues and give the impression of an aimless thrashing about, as if he were afraid that when he stopped the flailing he would drown. He seems to me all over the part, but never in it.

Starting with these two leading roles and going down the list, one has to complain (as with *The Cherry Orchard* at this same theatre) of inaccuracy. Chekhov's Sonya suffers from not being a beauty, but it is a mistake for the actress in the role simply to stand there being extremely unappetizing. Joyce Redman found a finer solution in the 1946 production of the play: she indicated that what Sonya lacked in movie-star looks she made up in womanliness; and so one felt that Dr. Astrov was missing something; which is an excellent and utterly Chekhovian point. Chekhov's Professor Serebriakov is inept, but it is a mistake for an actor to play the role ineptly. Clarence Derwent shows an awareness of the Professor's silliness, which is precisely what the poor fellow lacked. From the indication of such an awareness comes ham acting.

As a result of some or all these things, that exquisitely touching final scene—one of the "beauties" of modern literature—was neither exquisite nor touching. The externals were there; "es fehlte nur der geistige Band." Then there is the crisis of the action at the end of Act Three. An all-too-clever directorial line was provided: the scene was to be handled as "comedy." But how the concept of comedy has dwindled in modern America! It has shrunk to the little measure of the poster outside the movie theatre. Comedy means laughs, and laughs mean jokes, and jokes mean flippancy. . . . Error compounded with error yields results, of course; and one of them is a "comic" Chekhov with the juice strained away, the juice of urgent emotion and serious significance.

In *Miss Julie,* as produced at the Phoenix Theatre, there were interesting things. For instance, in the pantomimic interlude there was an attempt at a theatricality which would at the same time be bold and delicate: a girl, left without partner, picked up the hatstand and danced with it. There are possibilities in little items of this sort which our stage has scarcely begun to exploit. But then the curtain fell; there was an intermission (in this play which was written to abolish intermissions) ; and afterwards, Viveca Lindfors was back on stage renewing her claim to be Miss Julie.

One can guess why she wanted to make such a claim. Not only is she Swedish, a part of the role itself is plain sailing for her, since she has a lovely face and a noble presence. The loveliness gives her a measure of theatricality; the presence gives her a portion of the character. But, it has to be said, she is *too* beautiful—for this role and for first-rate acting. For, while all fine actresses are beautiful, including Marie Dressler and Julie Harris, none of them *is* a beauty. As Miss Lindfors is nothing if *not* a beauty, what I have to say about her Miss Julie is already said.

The evening starts with a shorter Strindberg play, *The Stronger*. In this, Miss Lindfors had no lines. But when did a beauty need lines? Certainly not when, as in this case, her play is directed by her husband (George Tabori). The play is a monologue, and all the lines were spoken by Ruth Ford. But Walter Kerr says Miss Lindfors has the finest profile in America, and the profile is placed stage center. In fact, both profiles, the left and the right, are placed stage center, one for the first part of the play, one for the second, while Miss Ford is placed behind a barricade of tables far out at stage left, almost in the wings. Even at that, Miss Ford once or twice is on the point of winning our attention, but at this crisis Miss Lindfors puts her foot down. Or rather lifts her hand up. Or clasps a doll to her bosom. Or merely smiles her mildly mysterious Swedish smile.

A bad time was had by all, but of course it was *Miss Julie* that took the blame, not the actors. Some of the newspapermen even said that the theme of class conflict was now obsolete, though they did not add that many of the comments on this theme had been contributed by its adaptor, George Tabori. In fact Strindberg's ending was travestied, and resembles the rewrite of a classic by Bertolt Brecht without being as much fun. Strindberg's Jean very understandably hypnotizes Miss Julie and sends her out to kill herself. Mr. Tabori's Jean turns unaccountably into a proletarian rebel, and rushes off into the unknown, renouncing bosses.

It is true that the audience as a whole doesn't grasp this last point because, dramaturgically speaking, it isn't properly handled. When Jean says his piece, we aren't listening, any more than we were listening to Ruth Ford in the other play. For Miss Lindfors is on stage, preparing to attack the prettiest wrist in America with a razor.

To those who want star actresses to remain the sacred, untouchable cows of our theatre, and who therefore want the critic to blame their failures on playwrights, let me explain that I would not criticize Miss Lindfors' work so severely if I considered it totally beyond redemption. As she gets older there is hope that she may become less of a beauty and more of a performer. Even now, it is possible that she is not so much incapable as misled; she tries, under whatever impulsion, for effects which are simply not in her range or "of her sort." Sometimes one can say: "that is rather interesting," but even then one is too aware of the fact. Miss Lindfors' hands and arms perform large gestures; one watches them perhaps with surprise, perhaps with incredulity, but hardly with pleasure. Passion, with her, is never convincing. She suddenly yells. She uses a sweeping movement of hand or arm. But we hear the yell and see the movement in isolation from the context. There is no connection, no cohesion, let alone liquefaction and flow. And so for all the physical beauty, the effect can be that, at times, of a Falstaffian weight to the exclusion of

Falstaffian wit. What is the opposite of soaring? It would be a verb that the critic of Miss Lindfors could often use.

Chekhov And Strindberg Off Broadway: there was a time when the headline would have seemed almost heartwarming. *On* Broadway there was only one thing worse than their ignoring the classics, and that was their performing the classics. Walter Kerr cites the "all star" Broadway production of *The Three Sisters* as evidence that Chekhov can't be popular whatever is done for him. Those of us who saw that show know what it did for him: it wrung his neck. Or rather it put him and us gently to sleep. It was a triumph of euthanasia. With that triumph in my memory I welcomed the Fourth Street production of the play with open arms. But, in this world, *plus ça change, plus c'est la même chose*. Whatever medical science may say, euthanasia is infectious.

I like to hear the words of the masters spoken on the Off Broadway stage, but not to the exclusion of their souls. The task of dramatic critics, from now on, is not to pat the Off Broadway people on the back for the marvellous headway they have made since grammar school, but to hold them to a high standard, beginning with a high standard of accuracy. *Uncle Vanya* and *Miss Julie* are scandalously inaccurate productions. To tell us how much their producers love the classics is only to remind us of Oscar Wilde's dictum that "each man kills the thing he loves."

A Liquid Grace

ONE OF THE SUCCESSFUL playwrights of our day told me that all good playwrights write for their own day and succeed in their own day. He gave some examples from the first half of the twentieth century and even later.

In the first half of the nineteenth century, things must have been different. For among the very few interesting plays of the period, three—*The Prince of Homburg, Danton's Death,* and

A Month in the Country—were not even *un*successfully performed. The first two did not reach the stage till long after their respective authors died, the third not for a couple of decades after it was written, and even then only as adapted by a second hand.

Theatre people blame authors for their inability to write theatrically, but there are many authors who could justly blame the people of the theatre for not knowing dramatic literature when they see it. Not that it occurred to Ivan Turgenev to cast the first stone. After completing *A Month in the Country*, he concluded that he was no playwright and—with what shining consequences the whole world knows—devoted his energies to the novel. Mr. Magarshack, his biographer, does not tell us what Turgenev thought of the play as adapted for the stage. It seems likely that there was no way of doing justice to it in the theatre until Stanislavsky had trained a generation of Russians to perform the plays of one of Turgenev's admirers, Anton Chekhov. "The lacework of the psychology of love which Turgenev weaves . . . demands a special sort of playing," Stanislavsky has written. "It could not be solved with hands and feet or any of the accepted methods. . . . One needed to suggest unseen radiations of will, emotion, yearning; one needed looks, stage business and pantomime, imperceptible variations in the tone of voice, psychological pauses. . . . It was necessary to remove everything that made it hard for the spectator to enter into the actors' souls. . . ." But this "special sort of playing" was simply the sort that Stanislavsky had already done more than any other single man to create and which, under various influences, would spread westwards and find its way into the Phoenix Theatre, Second Avenue, New York, in 1956.

"*A Month in the Country*," Stanislavsky says, "is built on the most delicate curves of love experience." *Curves* is indeed an apt word to help describe this elusive masterpiece. The action of the play might be imaged as a set of beautifully drawn and related curves. Love seems to come curving at the characters through the air, like some dangerous, but deft, missile. Now, though sexual passion is the subject of many mediocre plays, it is, I believe, the subject of relatively few great ones. And from any of these few—*Phèdre* or even *A Month in the Country*—one can see pretty clearly what the difficulty is, namely: in that "two hours' traffic" which is a play to render both the directness of love and its indirectness, its single impact and its mixed motives, its frontal attack and its manifold devious strategies. *Phèdre* is, of course, the supreme instance in this kind; Proust himself, in a thousand pages, could not have shown the movements of our amorous feelings —forward and back, upwards and downwards, quick and slow, large and small—either with more precision or with a fuller sense of identification.

Phèdre is a classic product of French culture, and a model of structure. Turgenev saw himself as burdened with a Slavic will-lessness and phlegm, and used to admit to faulty architecture in his work, his method of composition being to invent characters and then ask himself what to do with them. The admission helps to explain why he too readily pooh-poohed his playwriting. In actual fact, *A Month in the Country* is superbly constructed, as anyone who wishes to list the scenes and note their bold yet subtle interrelationships can verify. There is an element of "Chekhovism" in the general scheme: the country house, the kind of men and women who live there, the arrival-and-departure pattern of the story, the way people seem to be drifting in and out, the way various persons are going their various ways (a great deal of fun and pathos accruing from the variety). But in his dramaturgy Turgenev is traditional, it seems to me, to the point of being classic. There is something very like main plot and subplot in the juxtaposition of the romantic love story of Natalia Petrovna and the comic courtship of the Doctor. The two plots are significantly connected by the Doctor's marrying off of Natalia's rival (Vera) to a rich neighbor (Bolshintsov). And a frame for both plots is suggested by brief but vivid scenes among the servants. We see, not just a family, but a society. In this play in which Turgenev, as is well known, anticipated modern psychological drama, he also retained the ingenious plot and strict, intricate structure of the older theatre. (How Ben Jonson or Molière would have enjoyed his version of the "cuckold's" deception! The final sequence shows a masterly handling of cross purposes.) For our time, *A Month in the Country* is more than praiseworthy: it is exemplary.

The Phoenix Theatre, where the play is running, has been in the habit of inviting just about anybody with a Name to come down to Second Avenue and run amok among the classics. The place seemed destined to become a graveyard for mangled masterpieces. But now the dull fizzle of damp squibs has been followed by the sparkling and awe-inspiring flight of a genuine rocket. *A Month in the Country* is a beautiful show, and not by accident.

Michael Redgrave had a double qualification as director: he knew the play backwards and he was able to bring to it his unusual combination of practical and theoretical understanding. Polish is better than gloss, and Mr. Redgrave's production has something which is better than polish—an airy and consistent lightness, a liquid grace.

What I feel to be the limitations of the show derive less from the direction than from the text, which is, for America, much too British, and, for any place, a little too stagey. Mr. Redgrave says that Emlyn Williams, the adaptor, "compressed" the Turgenev script, but the truth is that while Mr. Williams makes some large cuts he often takes more and fancier words to render a Russian phrase than does, for example, Constance Garnett. Granting that most of Turgenev's play still comes through, and that many parts are serviceably spruced up to smarten the pace or "point" a joke, I think that an adaptor who is not above padding many lines *out* might certainly have left *in* lines that are invaluable keys to character—such as the line stating that Islaev, Natalia's husband, once had his dreams, or the lines revealing that Natalia herself had no youth because she had to play Antigone to a blind father. On the one hand, Mr. Williams Anglicizes and, as best he is able, Dickensifies; on the other, he pushes theatrical know-how beyond the point of diminishing returns, and much of the dialogue is so "well-adapted to the stage" that the sap of real Russia, real life, has had to be drained off. Then again, there is a reckless sort of inaccuracy, which I can illustrate from one example among many. Natalia calls the Doctor a small-town Talleyrand. The theatre-wise Mr. Williams, deciding to substitute a name his audience will know, chooses that of Machia-velli! But Turgenev's Doctor was a *Talleyrand,* crawling igno-bly from one régime, as it were, to another, avoiding notice for a while, hanging on, and then turning up again large as life.

The acting—except for two of the small roles—is on a very high plane. Here again, the Phoenix is to be congratulated on breaking with its bad old traditions and choosing performers qualified, not by Name only (or, in some cases, at all), but by talent and by the spirit in which they come to their task. "Type casting" would not lead to the choice of Uta Hagen as Natalia, but she gives us the character as completely as we could ever hope to have it, and thereby makes the action of this difficult drama absolutely transparent. What a pleasure it is to watch Miss Hagen at work on a scene! Particularly thrilling to me were her moments alone with the audience. (Why were monologues abolished?) She sweeps down towards the footlights exclaiming: "For the first time in my life I am in love!" and our hearts jump at the fine, free audacity of it. Like Turgenev himself, this actress is able to be both modern and traditional, subtle and broad, turned-in-toward-herself and turned-out-toward-the-public. Apart from these brief solos, we see Miss Hagen—and this, really, is her specialty—in relation-ship, fluid, quicksilver relationship, with others; that ebb and flow, that constant subtle fluctuation, is what carries us along.

Now here is something the stage can do which the novel cannot do: record, and offer to the senses, the immediacies of personal exchange—the glance as it meets the eye of another, and as it withdraws again—the smile as it produces an answer-ing smile, or fails to. Such things are the actor's materials. But we only see their nature and recognize their potentiality when they are exploited to the hilt. *A Month in the Country* is full of intimate scenes between two people. Those between Miss Hagen and Alexander Scourby (Rakitin) and those between Miss Hagen and Olga Bielenska (Vera) best exemplify the marvellous reciprocity I am speaking of.

Where, by the way, has Mr. Scourby been hiding all this assured and persuasive elegance? He gives a gleaming perform-ance of a role that might easily have seemed tarnished, or even rusty. Miss Bielenska's voice is, perhaps, not quite ready for a theatre as big as the Phoenix, but she has composed a very accurate and rounded portrait of Vera. What is even harder, she has known how to prepare, without seeming to prepare, the surprises in the role, and how to let Vera mature in the course of the action till, a full-grown woman, she can cry: "You are my rival!"

Not strongly supported by his partner in courtship, Luther Adler as the Doctor does enough for two. Even the expression to "take stage" does not say what happens when this actor comes on. *Take* the stage, indeed! He picks it up and throws it to the back of the balcony. An actor of the good old school, he makes big stuff out of everything. An entrance, an exit, a sitting down, a standing up, a taking of snuff—they are Events, like a presidential address or the announcement of a new invention. Physically there isn't very much of Mr. Adler, but what there is, is all actor; and, in the old European (or should I say Jewish?) way, he uses all of it—literally, from top to toe, the body stooping or swaying, the hands, the whole arm, busy, busy, busy—to say or do the least "little" thing. He is full of all the excess energy of the comic tradition—like Dickens or Dickens' creations. His Doctor is a whirlwind of a performance. Were ever so many of an author's comic points made in such rapid succession? With so many added that the author never dreamed of? I end cursing New York that has scarcely let me see this comedian before in four years of reviewing, but blessing the Phoenix for letting me see him now in this great part in this great play.

Undramatic Theatricality

---

(1)

IN SOME WAYS the most interesting thing that has appeared in *The New Republic* during 1956 is an item that probably should never have been published at all: a letter from Dore

Schary asking who was Delmore Schwartz. Assuming that Mr. Schary really didn't know, it was interesting that he should be so anxious to find out or at least that he should pretend to be so anxious to find out. A few years ago, some of the same movie people who had boasted an ignorance of William Faulkner's identity were prepared to do an about-face and boast that "America's leading writer" was "naturally" working for them. The highbrow is not the only man with a sense of guilt.

The Broadway approach to serious writers is pretty much that of Hollywood to its Faulkners: buy them or boycott them. And behind a pretense of lighthearted indifference lurks a resentment which, being so dubiously grounded, generates guilt feelings. As the latter are usually unconscious, the resultant disorder, emotional and intellectual, could scarcely be greater.

Of course, since the highbrow is not, *qua* highbrow, a saint or a hero or a genius, there is plenty to say against him which is based, not on irrational fears, but on solid fact and well-reasoned argument. And anyone who tries to be as honest a critic as possible is hard put to it to steer through the various crosscurrents of snobbery and counter-snobbery. More than one newspaper critic has dismissed my work, for example, as precious to the point of unreadability, yet the most insulting communication I have received in my professional capacity— as a matter of fact, the only one that contained not only denunciation but insult—came from the Off Broadway producer of a poetic play which, apparently, I was not to be allowed to dislike. Such are the conflicts that go on behind the bland façade of dramatic criticism. It is no longer, if it ever was, a single conflict of highbrows against lowbrows. Any one of us can be attacked as either highbrow or lowbrow according to the wishes of the aggressor. The technique of aggression resolves itself into this: the choice of a stance which appeals to the group of readers or listeners you wish to appeal to and the assumption that the Enemy has taken the opposite stance. Such an arrangement confers the joys of battle upon all, even if at the end of the struggle nothing true, or even very sincere, has been said.

When a play like Samuel Beckett's *Waiting for Godot*

appears on the horizon, general mobilization is ordered, the guerillas leave for the hills, and the population at large receives instructions for civil defense. Before one can enquire what the issues are, someone has thrust a weapon in one's hands, and one may have fired and led one's men to victory before discovering what it was all about. The minute I saw, in *The New York Times,* the producer's statement that the play was not for casual theatre-goers but for intellectuals, I could have written Walter Kerr's review for him. And I felt myself being propelled into writing a defense of the play as if by its success or failure civilization would stand or fall. Such is dramatic criticism.

Or is it? Walter Kerr's attitude—the anti-intellectualism of an intellectual—is unusual on Broadway. For, in general, the Broadway critics are not intellectuals and, as to whether they are *for* intellectuality or *against* it, are, like the American people, divided about fifty/fifty. The division was very noticeable in the reviews of *Godot.* The group as a whole (always excepting Mr. Kerr) admitted, in effect, that Beckett was beyond their ken. But while one team was prepared to be respectful towards what was not fully understood, the second joined Mr. Kerr in finding something of a scandal in the very existence of difficulty. And there emerged, in his review and theirs, an explicit espousal of an opinion which up to now I have only come across as an unacknowledged, and even disowned, preconception: the opinion that it is best to be a simple soul because we live in a simple universe. Here are three statements of one of the big ideas of the twentieth century:

> Thinking is a simple, elementary process. *Godot* is merely a stunt. . . .
>
> —John Chapman, *The Daily News*

> The author was once secretary to that master of obfuscation, James Joyce. Beckett appears to have absorbed some of his employer's ability to make the simple complex. . . .
>
> —Robert Coleman, *The Daily Mirror*

(In fairness, one should add that in order to get in another dig at Mr. Beckett, Mr. Coleman went on to contradict himself:

"Waiting for Godot is . . . an attempt to oversimplify eternal philosophical concepts. . . .")

. . . the rhythms of an artist [Bert Lahr] with an eye to God's own truth. All of them, I think, are the rhythms of musical comedy, or revue, of tanbark entertainment—and they suggest that Mr. Lahr has, all along in his own lowbrow career, been in touch with what goes on in the minds and hearts of the folk out front. I wish that Mr. Beckett were as intimately in touch with the texture of things. *Waiting for Godot* is not a real carrot; it is a patiently painted, painstakingly formed plastic job for the intellectual fruitbowl.

—Walter Kerr, *The New York Herald Tribune*

God's own truth . . . the folk out front . . . in touch with the texture of things. . . . The superior insight of genius is unnecessary. All we need, to take upon us the non-mystery of things, is constant communion with the man of non-distinction.

Speaking of obfuscation, what could obfuscate our experience of Beckett's play more than the cloud of conflict between highbrow and lowbrow, highbrow and highbrow, lowbrow and lowbrow? This conflict is, of course, anterior to the play. The play itself presents a problem for our audiences too, and that is the problem of nausea as a playwright's conscious attitude to life.

Though it is permissible to be nauseated by existence, and even to say so, it seems doubtful whether one should expect to be paid for saying so, at any rate by a crowd of people in search of an amusing evening. Yet, since the humor which provides amusement is precisely, as Nietzsche observed, a victory over nausea, it would be hard to stage the victory without at least suggesting the identity and character of the foe. The suggestion, it is true, may be made with great or small emphasis, yet it is always there, and the emphasis, in fact, is invariably stronger than the reader or audience wishes at first to acknowledge. It has taken Krafft-Ebing and Freud to force a general admission of the importance of nausea even, say, in the work of Swift, where it is most prominent. That the gossamer of *The Importance of Being Earnest* conceals the dynamite

that would send its author to Reading Gaol was clear to none
of the dramatic critics of the day (though Bernard Shaw had,
perhaps, an inkling of it) ; and that is to be expected, because
another function of humor is that of camouflage: dynamite is
being concealed under gossamer. In this way, the humorist
staves off the punishment for his aggressions. But he receives a
substitute punishment: to be discounted as unimportant. Important is—to be earnest. The only way a general audience
could accept, say, W. C. Fields is by kidding itself he didn't
mean a word of it: in "reality," he must love nothing so much
as the wee home i'the suburbs, the patter of little feet, dogs,
Mother's Day, the medical profession, and the total abstinence
union.

American optimism drives American nausea a little more
deeply underground: that is the difference between America
and Europe. For, if the conscious "thought" of "serious" literature and drama becomes more insistently "positive," a nation's
humor, arising from the depths of discomfort, repression and
guilt, will become more and more destructive. Even now, if
there is nothing quite so happy-drunk as American confidence,
there is also nothing quite so blackly despondent as American
cynicism, the "hardboiledness" of the "tough guy." But the
ranks of the community close in order to hide the fact. Hence
the great loathing and fear of any more conscious type of
pessimism, such as that which flows in a steady stream from
France. For Broadway use, the professional pessimism of
Anouilh is made over into professional idealism. The professional pessimism of Tennessee Williams, an avant-garde writer,
is converted into its opposite by a Broadway director: when the
curtain falls, the Mississippi equivalent of Godot is undoubtedly about to arrive, promising us and Mr. Williams prizes
and potency and, if come it must, a grave in Forest Lawn, with
an angel choir singing: Ah, sweet mystery of life, at last I've
found thee.

(2)

Samuel Beckett's point of view seems pretty close to that of
Anouilh or Sartre. *Waiting for Godot* is a play that one of

them ought to have written. It is the quintessence of "existentialism" in the popular, and most relevant, sense of the term —a philosophy which underscores the incomprehensibility, and therefore the meaninglessness, of the universe, the nausea which man feels upon being confronted with the fact of existence, the praiseworthiness of the acts of defiance man may perform—acts which are taken, on faith, as self-justifying, while, rationally speaking, they have no justification because they have no possibility of success.

Like many modern plays, *Waiting for Godot* is undramatic but highly theatrical. Essential to drama, surely, is not merely situation but situation in movement, even in beautifully shaped movement. A *curve* is the most natural symbol for a dramatic action, while, as Aristotle said, beginning, middle, and end are three of its necessary features. Deliberately antidramatic, Mr. Beckett's play has a shape of non-dramatic sort: two strips of action are laid side by side like railway tracks. The strips are One Day and the Following Day in the lives of a couple of bums. There *cannot* be any drama because the author's conclusion is that the two days are the same. That there are also things that change is indicated by a play-within-this-play, which also is in two parts. The first time that the characters of the inner play come on they are a brutal Master and his pitiful Man; the second time they are both equally pitiful because the Master has gone blind.

What has brought the play before audiences in so many countries—aside from snobberies and phony advertising—is its theatricality. "Highbrow" writers have been enthusiastic about clowns and vaudeville for decades, but this impresses me as the first time that anything has been successfully done about the matter. (Prokoviev's *Love for Three Oranges*, at least as City Center presented it, was a ponderous blunder.) Mr. Kerr gave Bert Lahr all the credit for a traditional yet rich clown characterization, which, however, had been skilfully put together by Mr. Beckett, as any reader may verify.

Mr. Beckett has not only been able to define the "existentialist" point of view more sharply than those who are more famously associated with it, he has also found for its expression a vehicle of a sort that people have been recommending without following their own recommendation. *Waiting for*

Godot is, therefore, an important play. Whether it is more important than these two achievements suggest is the question. To me, the play did not come over with the force of revelation, nor with that of sheer greatness. Mr. Beckett's voice is interesting, but it does not quite seem individual, because it does not quite seem new. "Haven't I heard that before?" one continually asks oneself, and one is surely not exploiting an external fact unfairly in saying that Mr. Beckett is excessively —if quite inevitably—over-influenced by Joyce. If Russian literature is cut from Gogol's *Overcoat,* one is tempted to think that Irish literature, even when it is written in French, as Beckett's play was, is cut from those coats of many colors, *Ulysses* and *Finnegan's Wake.*

I do not think the play is obscure except as any rich piece of writing is obscure. No doubt there are meanings that will disengage themselves in time as one lives with such a work, yet enough is clear from the first not only to arouse interest but to communicate the sense of a unified and intelligible image of life. I take it that Mr. Beckett belongs to that extensive group of modern writers who have had a religious upbringing, retain religious impulses and longings, but have lost all religious belief. I should differentiate him from, say, Sartre in that he does not write from the standpoint of atheism but, theologically speaking, from that of skepticism. People who have seen *Godot* are able to suggest this or that solution—Christian, anti-Christian, etcetera—precisely because Beckett has left the door open for them to do so. They are wrong only if they intimate that the author himself passed through the door and closed it behind him.

Rough words have been spoken about the allegedly excessive symbolism of the play. This is unjust. Mr. Beckett's finest achievement is to have made the chief relationships, which are many, so concrete that abstract interpretations are wholly relegated to the theatre lobby. He gives us, not tenets, but alternatives seen as human relationships (between bum and bum, master and man); also as ordinary human attitudes to God, Nature, and Death on the one hand, and, on the other, to the "trivialities," such as clothes, defecation, smells. . . .[1] There is

[1] Philip H. Bagby says this better in a note to *The Times Literary Supplement*: "It seems likely that Godot will never come, but it is by

a lot of life to the play, and there is a lot of life *in* the play.

The New York production is so good that I can dispose of the only serious shortcomings in a few lines. The lighting is of that "modern" sort which is now old-fashioned and was always awful: you don't see the actors' faces properly, and every time an actor moves he is either moving into much less light or much more. One of the actors seems miscast. This is Kurt Kasznar as Pozzo, the Master, who gave us a playful stage villain instead of a stomach-turning real one; Mr. Kasznar was so brilliant as the Director in *Six Characters in Search of an Author* that he has been lured into repeating part of the characterization in a very different role.

On the first night, Alvin Epstein as Lucky, the Man, threw away the most effective speech in the play, into which Beckett seems to have poured all his training in Catholic philosophy. At the second performance, which I also attended, the fault had largely been corrected, without detriment to the pantomime, which is Mr. Epstein's specialty. E. G. Marshall, as Vladimir, the cleverer of the bums, was overshadowed by his partner. His acting seemed to me defensive—and therefore, as things work out on the stage, a little self-destructive. The part was underacted sometimes almost to the point of inaudibility. Long speeches were attacked diffidently with the usual result: that they constantly seemed to be over before they were, and one thought: Heavens, is he starting up again? Yet all this is by no means as disastrous as spelling it out makes it sound. In any part, Mr. Marshall is interesting; if I am disappointed, it is because this is the first time he has been no more than that.

Estragon, the less philosophical bum, the *dummer August* of this particular circus, is played by Bert Lahr. If to Mr. Kerr this fact just means the saving of a highbrow play by a low-

no means certain. His messengers (or messenger) may or may not be false prophets. Numerous alternatives are presented: the mutual affection of Vladimir and Estragon, Vladimir's longing for death, Estragon's reliance on Godot's promises, Lucky's dependence on his master and Pozzo's dependence on his slave, waiting and journeying or, if we must find an allegory, Christian consolation and existentialist action by virtue of the absurd. Very likely still other possible courses are offered us in the dense texture of the play, but we are never told whether we should choose one or all or none of these alternatives."

brow actor, it is just as fair to look upon it as the perfect execution by a lowbrow actor of a highbrow writer's intentions. If the perfection of it is bound to hurt the less perfect impersonations by contrast, it has the merit of enabling us to visualize a perfect production of the play as a whole and even, by extension, a perfect play of this type perfectly produced.

We sentimentalize vaudeville now, and overrate it; go back to the reports of William Archer and Bernard Shaw, and you'll find it was usually atrocious. I shall not insult Mr. Lahr by giving the credit for his work to an institution that did not in fact have very high standards. That he acquired certain habits is all to the good, though there are plenty of actors with those habits who would have failed in *Godot*. The triumph here is partly due to his bringing to the script a respect which has not been shared by all the commentators on it. One does see the advantage of his training, for, while Mr. Marshall has to *create* a clown and constantly work at it, Mr. Lahr did his creating in that line so long ago that he settles and relaxes into a clown personality as others do into carpet slippers and a smoking jacket. He reminds me strongly of Menasha Skulnik in *The Flowering Peach*. On both occasions, literature and popular comedianship met. But it was a matter of marriage, not lifesaving. Both actors showed respect for the words they spoke, while the words, gratefully, but with a proper pride, gave something to the actor that made him larger and richer than he had been, perhaps ever, before. "Like leaves" is a simple conjuncture of words, and Mr. Lahr adds beautifully to its content by the care and ardor of his rendering. But Mr. Beckett's context helped too, since it is only by preparation in the dialogue itself that such simplicity can become poetic.

Herbert Berghof directed. I have less reverence for this play than he, and would have lopped off the last bit of the first act. I would also have been tempted to make cuts at several points where the dialogue stumbles. (The rhythm is very firm for longish stretches and then from time to time goes to pieces.) But reverence towards a script is a good fault and, on Broadway, an unusual, almost exemplary one.

Though many directors have their characteristic tricks, or their famous and much-publicized manner, very few give to their shows the imprint of an individual human being. This imprint Mr. Berghof—in the quietest way in the world—imparts. In a brief commentary, one has to point to particular touches—such as the delicate way one bum takes the other's thumb out of his mouth while he sleeps, or the soft and stealthy way in which Mr. Lahr would curl up and doze off, or the confident way in which one actor or the other would undertake moves which the realistic directors don't use (such as walking in a circle). But Mr. Berghof's personality—gentle, sensitive, youthful, fanciful—is not to be found in the "blocking" and stage business alone; it is far more subtly interfused and, with the cooperation of the actors, gives the evening its special aroma and dignity.

A remark—perhaps irrelevant—about the title. "Godot" is the person you are waiting for who, presumably, will set things to rights when he arrives. I assume that Mr. Beckett made up the French word from the English one, God. But, as someone will no doubt inform *The Times Literary Supplement*, there is a once well-known play of Balzac's in which we spend the whole evening waiting for a character called Godeau, who has still not come on stage when his arrival is announced just before the final curtain falls.

The Other Orson Welles

THE *King Lear* production at City Center could be said to have become a *succès de scandale*, except that it wasn't really a success of any kind. But Orson Welles, its director and star, did make headlines by playing Lear in ancient costume and a modern wheel chair. He hurt one ankle at rehearsals and the other on opening night, after which he missed a single performance and played, for the rest of the run, sitting down. That, as far as the public record is concerned, was that. If I now go behind that record, it is because the important Welles is precisely the Welles that does not make the headlines.

Not that Being a Headliner is not a job in itself. On the contrary, it is a job which has attracted Mr. Welles for a quarter of a century now. As a boy, he aimed at headlines out of juvenile high spirits and sheer ambition. And now that his spirits are not so high, and many of his ambitions have been satisfied (if any ambition is ever really satisfied), he is capable of aiming at headlines from sheer wilfulness or sheer habit. He is even capable of not consciously aiming at headlines at all ("You know I can't stand publicity," I heard him shout to his stage manager not very secretively), but just relying on his unconscious to make sure that he gets them, even if the unconscious has to resort to its own special and vindictive methods, creating a state of affairs in which Mr. Welles will happen to fall not once, but twice. If Mr. Welles had had three legs, he would have tripped three times.

All the world has reached the opinion that Mr. Welles is self-destructive in the grand manner of the Jazz Age, and it is always hard not to agree with all the world. I publicly did agree with it in my last comments on the subject.[1] But I realize now that part of my motive for writing as I did was to provoke Mr. Welles into proving me wrong—as a man shouts: "You're unfaithful" at his wife, just to make her provide him with a watertight alibi. And, though the public story of this *Lear* production would tend, rather, to prove me right, there was a private story which renewed in me the hopes which Mr. Welles used to arouse in all who know a theatre from the back of a bus.

Having been permitted to sit in at some of Mr. Welles's rehearsals, I saw at work the theatrical imagination whose fruits had been shown to the world in the modern-dress *Julius Caesar,* the Negro *Macbeth,* and the film *Citizen Kane.* When I saw the map that Mr. Welles had procured for the first scene —six feet by fifteen it must have been, unrolling from two poles—I recognized the famous and magnificent Wellesian audacity. The map was audaciously used too. At one point it was stretched out on the floor, and Lear marched up and down on it. At another, when it was being held upright, Lear strode

[1] See above, pages 235–238.

clear through it, tearing it right across. This was a Lear who, when he knocked his throne over (and inevitably this Lear would knock his throne over) would seem to be hurling it into an abyss. This was a Lear (to mention what some nitwit critic might call a "mere" detail) who carried no ordinary sword, nor even just a superior one, but a weapon of double the usual size, a giant crucifix of a sword, majestic and awe-inspiring.

While the audacity came to me with the shock of recognition, I had a shock of real surprise at the discovery that Mr. Welles also has the gift of control. In these rehearsals, I saw nothing of the Welles of popular mythology, undisciplined, perverse, or just plain drunken. He was punctual, and he was punctilious. In fact, when he is seriously a twork directing, he stands at the other extreme from either the old-fashioned, romantically "inspired" director with his head in clouds of rhetoric or the new-fashioned, "dynamic" director with his head, so to speak, in his own viscera. Neither grandiose nor feverish, he spoke the language of common sense, and gave the actors tips based on a veteran's know-how and a theatre-poet's intuition. He had done his homework, and come to rehearsal with a clear outline. At the same time, he had not made the mistake of filling in the outline with a content imagined at home in isolation both from the particular actors concerned and from the creative state established in rehearsals whenever the morale is good. The director who does his work at home is a sculptor modelling with hard clay. It takes rehearsal—and rehearsal with the proper psychological adjustment—to soften the clay and present him with a really malleable medium. And the creativity of rehearsals consists in the way in which one thing leads to another. The director receives his "inspirations" out of things that happen there. His spur is the spur of the moment. A fine production comes into being as a chain reaction starting with the first rehearsal. Now I doubt if there is anyone who understands all this better than Orson Welles, or who can act more skilfully upon such an understanding. The results are remarkable. And I felt that Mr. Welles got a good deal less than his deserts from the newspaper critics.

But why aren't the results more remarkable yet? Not wishing to return to the theme of Mr. Welles's personal problems, I shall suggest two reasons of a technical and artistic nature. Or rather I shall stress the technical and artistic side of what may be *purely* a personal problem. In the first place, Mr. Welles should not both act and direct. True, Garrick did it; most of the old heroic actors did it; but this is not to say that Mr. Welles should do it. For one thing, he is not a heroic actor (though he has *some* of the qualifications, notably a heavy build and a deep, resonant voice) ; in leading parts, he is not even, I believe, a first-rate actor; nor, of course, does he give the best performance he is capable of, for he is busy directing the other actors. Not that the other actors feel this: they inevitably feel, rather, that, because he is playing the lead himself, he is grossly neglecting them. It's the two sides of the same coin: the leading actor can't work enough with the others, and the others can't work enough with him. Through nearly all the rehearsal time, another actor replaced Mr. Welles on stage, while Mr. Welles sat out front at the director's table. The stand-in read the lines, if at all, without characterization, "walked through" the moves perfunctorily, without gestures, without looking at anyone. The first previews were upon us before Mr. Welles had gone on stage with his colleagues. Necessarily, then, the scenes Lear appears in got reduced to two things: recitation of speeches as learned at home (not as growing from the relation between Lear and the actor addressing him or being addressed by him) and production ideas, also planned at home, and now simply imposed on the actors like someone else's clothes.

Mention of production ideas brings me to the second criticism of Mr. Welles. Just because he works so well on the spur of the moment—which in the theatre, despite the slighting connotations of the phrase, is one of the great ways of working —he should be warned off big "production ideas." Theatre people should not have "ideas" at all unless they are prepared to take the full responsibility, as Granville-Barker did, and become masters of ideas, masters of their field in the fullest theoretical way, real scholars of the subject. Otherwise, they simply thrust on Shakespeare silly notions that will stand up neither under critical cross-questioning nor scholarly investigation. Mr. Welles has always been tempted to turn the theatre into a Notion and Novelty Store. "The essential," he is quoted as having said, "is to excite the spectators. If that means playing *Hamlet* on a flying trapeze or in an aquarium, you do it." How many confusions can be compressed into how few words? In the first place, exciting the spectators does *not* mean playing *Hamlet* on a flying trapeze and, in the second, mere excitation is not the final end for which works like *Hamlet* were written. What Mr. Welles means is that he is strongly subject to crazy temptations to do things like playing Hamlet on a flying trapeze or at least to say that he will. But this is the cheap and childish side of Mr. Welles. His real talent is not even in that direction, but, as I have hinted, starting from sober and sound craftsmanship, culminates in effects which, while they are audacious, can also be dignified and grand. There was a grandeur in the best moments of his *King Lear* far surpassing anything in Guthrie's *Tamburlaine*. The latter was more highly praised only because it was so full of flying trapezes and aquariums.

I do not insist that Mr. Welles become a Granville-Barker. Shakespeare has been greatly mounted by performers who had no intellectual grasp of him at all. There may be a moral for Mr. Welles in this story from Maurice Baring's *Sarah Bernhardt:*

> A friend of mine . . . was present at some of the rehearsals of *Hamlet* and he told me that once or twice Sarah Bernhardt consulted him as to the meaning of a passage. He said what he thought, and she answered in a way which showed she had completely misunderstood him and had perhaps not even listened. The process was repeated two or three times running, the misunderstanding growing deeper and wider. Then, he said, she went on to the stage and played the passage in question not only as if she had understood the words he had explained, but as if she had had access to the inner secrets of the poet's mind.

The Missing Communist

WHILE THE COMMUNISTS have never been numerous in this country, it is a commonplace that their influence anywhere is out of all proportion to their numbers. It is also true that, while the failure of the Communists to attract the American "proletariat" has been abysmal, they have been distinctly more successful with the professional classes. And with no group whatsoever, it seems to me, have they done so well as with the theatrical profession.

There are various reasons for this. One, obviously, is that theatrical people are very easily carried away with enthusiasm. And, though there are other things to be enthusiastic about in this life besides Communism, few of these can combine, as Communism does, the appeal to enthusiastic generosity with an appeal to precisely the opposite impulse. For if we shout with joy at the idea of shaking our chains off, we sigh with relief at the idea of having them clamped on again. The double appeal corresponds to the double nature of men in general and theatre people in particular. The latter tend, even more than the rest of the population, to combine a vast quantity of "democratic" goodwill with an equally vast ambition to have prestige and be in cahoots with those who have even more. Most actors wish to be "stars," and what happens when they get their wish? On the one hand, they express a dogmatic faith in their public (the public which elects them and keeps them in office, as it were), and on the other they are *arrivistes*, patronizing the best hotels, eating at the best restaurants, riding only in taxis, living behind squads of agents and secretaries. On the one hand, then, the impulse to kiss everybody and burst out crying from sheer love of mankind; on the other, the impulse to exact from the world a preposterous over-valuation of their own importance; this doubleness is evident not

just in "left-wing"[1] actors and producers but also in many of
the famous "left-wing" playwrights of the period. From which
we may conclude that if the Stalinist brand of pseudo-radical-
ism had not existed, someone with a shrewd grasp of theatre
psychology would have had to invent it. I am reliably informed that when Ilya Ehrenburg was in New York he would
eat only at the Chambord, and I doubt if that was because it
was near the Third Avenue El. It was more likely his historic
mission to prove that the International and the International
Set are not only compatible but identical.

However this may be, on Broadway, over the past quarter
century, Communism has been the only political force with
any real spread or any real staying power. Not that this is ever
admitted, least of all by the Communists. Few production
outfits wear their party card on their sleeve; few plays openly
confess to a Communist author or a definitely Communist
idea. But the Party has been, and remains, much more active
on Broadway than most people assume. A visitor to this country
just recently might have gathered from at least one liberal
journal that none of the theatre people then being questioned
about their politics had ever had anything to do with Communism except in the fevered imaginations of "witch hunters."
Little jokes were made about the absurdity of suspecting the
funny men of the entertainment world of such ideas and
activities. But the joke was really on the liberal journals, as
anyone acquainted with the facts well knew.[2]

A stranger to New York might take a little time to find
professed Communists in the theatre. And this was the case

---

[1] "Left-wing," in quotation marks, means "calling themselves left-
wing but actually in the Communist orbit and, therefore, consciously
or not, dominated by Communism." (Howard Fast, as quoted below
[page 463], speaks of "us on the left.") This is not to deny that the
term, without quotation marks, legitimately covers a lot of non-
Communist and even anti-Communist territory. The tragi-comedy is
complex. Am I myself left-wing? Are the magazines that rejected this
piece, "The Missing Communist"? An FBI investigator visited Columbia
University to ask about my left-wing tendencies at the same time as I
was vainly trying to sell the piece to one left-wing journal after another.

[2] The only reason why this passage is vague is that I have not written
it to bring an accusation against particular individuals. If the truth of
it were questioned, however, I could always change my tune.

long before the Smith Act may be said to have driven Communism underground. What he would have found then, and
could without much trouble find today, are Communists professing to be progressives, anti-fascists, or possibly even sympathizers. How far the "line" has drifted from the *Communist
Manifesto* may be gauged from the fact that some of these
people will explain at length why the explicitly pro-Communist utterances of Brecht are today much less *à propos* than
many a piece of non-Communist writing which contains, say, a
word against war or in favor of the "common people." If such
writing has a great established name attached to it—anyone
from Jefferson to Sholem Aleichem—so much the better, but
even a bit of *kitsch* will do, for the requirements, after all, are
"warmth" and "love of humanity" which, in the implied definition, are found more abundantly in Edgar Guest than in
Baudelaire. Sentimentality has always served to fog all the
issues, and was therefore denounced by earlier Marxists as
"petty bourgeois," but sentimentality is the characteristic
weapon of Marxist culture in its Stalinist phase, as the most
cursory glance at Stalinist literature will confirm. At this
point, *kitsch* becomes, for the rest of us, doubly suspect; even
the names of Jefferson and Sholem Aleichem become suspect
when they are the merest *aliases*.

First, there are professed Communists; second, Communists
professing progressivism and many other nice-sounding isms;
third, and most numerous of all in the theatre, there are the
unconscious sympathizers. In the nineteen thirties, it was possible for unconscious sympathizers to sympathize with *all* aspects of Communism. A shocked silence would descend upon
gatherings of "non-Communists" if some intruder referred to
the Moscow trials as a frame-up. The Soviets today cannot
command such wholehearted support, but nothing better illustrates the continued power of their propaganda than the fact
of its influence upon persons who not only are not Communists but quite consciously dissent from Communism. For example, the Communists' insistence on social injustice in the
United States, their methodical reiteration and exaggeration
of the same facts and allegations, creates even in Americans
pretty much the mentality of the Russian in the story who,

when he heard an American criticize the Moscow subways, replied: "Well, what about the negroes in the South?" The sting is taken out of every criticism of Russia by an appeal to what is in itself a fine impulse—the impulse to set our own house in order rather than scold other people. At the very same time that the Communists admitted having framed Rajk and many others, I received an ad for John Wexley's book on the Rosenbergs in which much more scrupulous treatment than Rajk ever got is represented as among the foulest barbarities of our era. And Arthur Miller, apparently desiring to break free from a Stalinism which he had never admitted being in bondage to in the first place, can only condemn Soviet policy as "cultural barbarism" if he quickly adds that America isn't very much better, the evidence for the equation being that Mr. Miller's own liberty has been "suppressed." [3] What is here flatly defined as the suppression of liberty was actually the refusal of a single employer to let Mr. Miller go through with a single assignment. Mr. Miller had a play running on Broadway during the very season when he said his liberty had been suppressed; his income as a playwright must obviously be far beyond what most writers have earned in any country in any age.

There is no better evidence of the continued influence of popular-front mentality among non-Communists than in Broadway plays about politics. There was one this winter (1955–56), for example, in which, though a sympathetic portrayal of a refugee *from* Communism indicated the author's feeling of independence, one of the principal assumptions of the story was squarely in the Stalinist tradition. This was the assumption that American life is currently poisoned by persecution mania. If a government employee's wife, long before she married him, indeed as a schoolgirl, joined the Communists for a very short time and then rebelled, he is nevertheless ruthlessly dismissed from his job today: such is America, 1956. But, in sober fact, one of the reasons the play (*The Innkeepers* by Theodore Apstein) failed is that the author's assumption

[3] "More, when my liberty was in effect suppressed in America, no American writer . . . raised a protesting voice. . . ." Letter released to the press, February 7, 1956.

about life in America today was news that had not yet reached his American audience. It is only behind the Iron Curtain that audiences believe Howard Fast's play *Thirty Pieces of Silver*,[4] with its American Judas, to be a representative picture of American life. It was there that I myself was asked how many fascist parades I see in Manhattan *per month* and also when I last saw a lynching (presumably from my windows on Riverside Drive).

A character is missing from American plays that touch on Communism: the Communist hero. All and sundry are suspected of Communism, but only villains and clowns are guilty of it. Communists on stage—in *The Love of Four Colonels, The Prescott Proposals, Silk Stockings, The Great Sebastians* —are always (a) foreigners and (b) cut out of cardboard. The feeling of being falsely accused being the archetypal sentiment of living in the twentieth century (classically imaged by Kafka), the false accusation of Communism has become the stereotype of political drama—from *The Crucible* (by implication) to the current hit *Time Limit*.

On two occasions, I felt the temptation to rewrite a play, putting the missing Communist in the niche that plot and theme seemed to leave for him. His absence was the principal flaw in the structure of both. In Robert Ardrey's *Sing Me No Lullaby* we were asked to believe that things are made so hot in America for citizens who were once popular-fronters that the very heat forces them to become out and out Communists: life having become impossible for this young man in witch-hunting America, he feels compelled to flee to Red China. The author could have avoided talking a lot of nonsense by making the young man a Communist.

The other example is *Anastasia* by Marcelle Maurette and Guy Bolton. Anastasia *is* the Czar's daughter, but obviously that doesn't make either her or the authors happy, for the latter have depicted the White *emigrés* as a corrupt and repulsive lot. Where is she off to at the end? And why can't she have that nice young man who has loved her so long and so well? A neat solution is at hand if only we are permitted, through the

---

[4] The Blue Heron Press, New York, 1954.

young man's torn trench coat, to descry a Party card. Why should she be the missing princess if he can't be the missing Communist? Ilya Ehrenburg would approve, for Anastasia and her Communist lover could now enter Moscow in triumph and continue the great work from the Muscovite equivalent of Chambord.

I leave it to sociologists to figure out why something a good deal less coherent was actually put before us. Students of dramaturgy may perhaps conclude that a new, though somewhat Pirandellian, pattern is evolving. In the new drama, the missing Communist will resemble Signora Ponza in that you will spend the first part of the evening wondering who he is and the second discovering that he isn't. He isn't who you thought he was and he isn't anyone else and he obviously couldn't have done the things he was accused of doing because, well, if you must know, he doesn't exist. The man who exists has quite a different name and isn't a Communist at all. He's progressive, of course, and a good anti-fascist, and, yes, if you insist—we're among friends here after all—he's, well, let's say a sympathizer. The term fellow-traveller is not in my vocabulary.

In all of which, art and life are one. For the Communist hero is missing from American life too. If Alger Hiss had been a Communist, and had courageously kept his secret through all the vicissitudes we know, what a hero he would be! But the man has hardly even heard of Communism, and take a look at him: how *could* he be a Communist? If Julius and Ethel Rosenberg had been Communists, how their comrades would have to admire the heroism of their keeping silent! Everything for the Cause! But, instead of heroes, they are victims, and Communist authors will only be able to compare them with other victims like Dreyfus, not with heroes like Zola. And, since some kind of Zola can always be cooked up, and he also was no Communist hero, I predict some attempts in the near future at a revival of interest in the Dreyfus case. But my main point here is that the Hiss and Rosenberg cases are also dramas *manqué,* the *manqué* element being the same as in Broadway plays that touch on the Communist theme.

Is this all very arbitrary and baffling? Or is there a pattern which we can get the hang of? I incline to the second conclusion. If there is an element of the mysterious to the story, we at least cannot assume that it is wholly fortuitous. In this realm mystification is a method, a fine art practiced for definite ends and on a gigantic scale. In a famous speech expressing a view which another hand later made the basis for the most outspoken Communist play ever written, Lenin said: "We must be able to . . . resort to various stratagems, artifices, illegal methods, to evasion and subterfuges. . . ." Do we prefer to think he didn't mean it? That the Russian has been mistranslated? That I have torn the remark from a context which actually says just the opposite? Or was Lenin really in favor of evasion, and did certain evasions multiply in geometric progression, until for millions of men, *Communist or not,* they became standard practice. I italicize *Communist or not* because the ultimate triumph of Leninism lies in the mystification of non-Communists.

So I hope no one supposes I am writing all this to make it seem that the playwrights I mentioned are Communists or even fellow-travellers. My argument has much more force on the assumption that they are not.

Thirty-two Non-Reviews

The show must go on.—PROVERB

Je n'en vois pas la nécessité.—VOLTAIRE

ONE OF THE PRIVILEGES of my position as the dramatic critic of a liberal weekly is that I am not required to cover all the shows. Nor am I held to any "objective" principle of selection. Although I do not write up a show which I think would not interest our readers (if only, sometimes, because it will have closed before my review is out), from the shows which I think would have general interest I select the ones that have most interested me. It is therefore not to be expected that my choices should seem the right ones to any other human being; in retrospect, they don't all seem right even to me.

And only one class of play has an agreed status. I think of it as the idiot child of playwriting. Every season there are at least several plays in which no one, not Brooks Atkinson, not Walter Winchell, no, not even the poor sailors whom the management lets in free to fill the empty seats, finds rhyme or reason. Nobody even knows how they happen, though they are sometimes sponsored by the large "conservative" producing firms, such as the Theatre Guild. While a serious playwright is told to wait a year or two, even a decade or two, for his first Broadway production, the idiot playwrights, some of them anyway, have an inside track. One hopes there is a good solid reason for this, such as that they are subsidized by Moscow, or are enjoying love affairs with producers. Otherwise the irrationality of the phenomenon would give one the creeps. The idiot playwrights' subject, if they have a subject, is usually Sex, though when Mr. Atkinson calls them pornographic, as he usually does, he does them too much honor. Pornography is active; there is a living impulse behind it. It is human; the lower animals find dirty pictures boring. The idiot playwright is a lower animal. His soul is not a cesspool, it is a zero. But why limit our interest to the human race? Crawling things are of interest too. At least it is interesting to speculate what they are there for. Idiot plays stimulate an interest in metaphysics. For if it is hard to know why the universe exists, surely it is much harder to account for the existence of (to give only three examples) *Black-eyed Susan, Little Glass Clock,* or *Affair of Honor.*

At any higher level than these, there is difference of opinion, even in principle. About the Vehicle Play, for example. I met someone who had just seen *The Great Sebastians* and had no complaints whatsoever. Yet conversation revealed that he had no higher an opinion of that play than I had myself. But he had an idea to excuse its shortcomings with—namely, that a Vehicle Play is not a play but a vehicle. So far, so good, I rejoined, but was *The Great Sebastians* a good vehicle? Was it swift, handsome, comfortable? Who looks at the vehicle, countered my friend, when the Lunts are in it? Then you're not saying this one *is* a good vehicle? I asked. When the Lunts are in it, he said, any vehicle is good.

In short, my friend doesn't care what the Lunts do or say as long as they go out on stage. Is not Sarah Bernhardt said to have been able to reduce audiences to tears by reciting the alphabet? Nonetheless, I propose to go on believing that there are worser vehicles, so that I can keep my confidence in the better ones. For example, *Camille*, though not a good play in its own right, seems to me a supreme vehicle for a certain kind of acting talent. As it stares you in the face from a book, Dumas' prose is wretched. But, in the theatre, it disappears. It hides behind Marguerite Gautier's smile or under her bed. A real acting vehicle is a fairy-tale coach: at a certain point it vanishes. *The Great Sebastians* refused to budge. There it stood, all evening, getting in the Lunts' way; and ours.

I did not review *The Great Sebastians*. I did not even review the slightly better vehicle of the Lunts' previous performance in New York, *Quadrille*. And when people tell me I should "just review the acting," I shake my head. For though there is nothing that I, in my capacity as dramatic critic, would rather do than describe and discuss the Lunts, I must wait for an occasion when my response to them will not be held in check by displeasure at their play. Displeasure that constitutes so strong a barrier may, no doubt, be called prejudice. And, though I concede the validity of a good vehicle, it is true that I am not easily convinced that a given vehicle is good. I have made a large emotional investment in dramaturgy. Whatever I may *think*, I *feel* that the play's the thing; this feeling—as a few minutes' investigation will confirm—underlies nearly all the reviews in this book. I have never been coaxed out of it by outstanding performers who appear in bad plays, not even by Geraldine Page in *The Rainmaker* or Paul Muni and Ed Begley in *Inherit the Wind*,[1] but only by some few who can do without plays altogether, such as Charlie Chaplin and Martha Graham—whom it is also possible, incidentally, to regard as playwrights.

[1] I would add here Kim Stanley in *Travelling Lady* except that "bad" is both too strong and too crude a word to describe an over-extended one-acter with some graceful scenes and several freshly observed characters.

During the two seasons 1954–55 and 1955–56, I reviewed neither idiot plays nor vehicle plays. But there was at least one play which I expected to find interesting, and thought I ought to find interesting, but which, in the event, I did not find interesting, and that is Christopher Fry's *The Dark Is Light Enough.* I had read it with interest, and would have felt no reluctance about doing a book review. But theatre is theatre. And a Guthrie McClintic production is *not* theatre. It is not even bad theatre. Our greatest talents—such as John Gielgud and Orson Welles—occasionally give us bad theatre—messy, misconceived, exaggerated, preposterous theatre. Not one of these epithets could be applied to *The Dark Is Light Enough* in its New York production. It was tidy, correct, discreet, sensible. The decencies were preserved. The tone of the proceedings was dignified. In short the atmosphere was less that of a Dionysian revel than of parents' day at a private school. And while gentility is bad enough in any of the arts, in the theatre it is freakish, like the presence of an English vicar in a Venetian bordello.

These comments on shows I have not so far commented on constitute what E. E. Cummings, who gave a set of Non-Lectures at Harvard, must let me call Non-Reviews. Twenty-three other snap judgments follow.

The Boy Friend, a musical by Sandy Wilson, is a fine exhibition of British, deadpan comic acting, especially on the part of Julie Andrews and Eric Berry. But the joke against the generation immediately preceding one's own is vulgar, provincial, second-rate. First-rate jokes are against one's own generation.

Reclining Figure, a light comedy by Harry Kurnitz, has been roughly criticized because it doesn't rattle along at the famous Broadway tempo. What does it matter? It is entertaining; if you don't laugh without interruption (which is all but impossible) you laugh loudly and often. I think Martin Gabel—producer of this and other similar plays—is to be congratulated on keeping Broadway acquainted with sharp, unsentimental humor, when he knows he could get higher marks in *The New York Times* (and elsewhere) for telling "democratic" lies about people.

.

The Tender Trap, by Max Shulman and Robert Paul Smith, is yet another American farce that bogs down in sentimentality and moral pretension. There are dozens of good jokes in the dialogue, and sometimes, for a short while, there is even a thread to join the small pearls together. But in the end the authors are less interested in the plot ("the soul of the drama") than in lecturing us on wholesomeness in girls, the duties of bachelors, and the problems of the unmarried woman of thirty-three.

Peter Pan AS A MUSICAL. Out of Los Angeles comes the worst musical score I have ever heard (even out of Los Angeles), yet the occasion, to a large extent, is saved by Jerome Robbins (director) and his two stars, Mary Martin and Cyril Ritchard. That a whole musical should be choreographically directed and yet not hinder the stars from giving liberally of themselves is a more original achievement than is being admitted. (Sidelight on Mr. Ritchard's performance as Captain Hook: one views with apprehension the tendency of modern actors to give a new touch to the old villains by intimating that the latter are effeminate.)

THE PHOENIX THEATRE, interim report, Spring 1955. All in all, the enterprise on Second Avenue has been a letdown to those of us who originally had high hopes for it. We know it is a kind of achievement even to keep the doors of such a theatre open for more than one season. We know that several good plays have been put on and that a number of talented performers have been employed. We know that Norris Houghton and T. Edward Hambleton are producers of more than average taste and intelligence. In fact it is because we know all this that we are disappointed.

A phoenix is a phoenix, but the producers this season have offered us three turkeys: Robert Ardrey's *Sing Me No Lullaby,*

Sandhog by Waldo Salt and Earl Robinson, and a rather dull
revival. The first two could be described as evocative of the
spirit of the Red thirties except that nothing was really evoked
and the word *spirit* had better be kept out of it. The "revival"
is Shaw's *Doctor's Dilemma*. It is worth seeing because it
contains several first-rate Shavian scenes. It was a bad choice
for the Phoenix because it is one of Shaw's faultier plays, as
has always been acknowledged since Desmond McCarthy enu-
merated the faults after the first performance half a century
ago. But, admittedly, the choice of play is enlightenment itself
compared with the choice of director and leading man. The
director (Sidney Lumet) shows an understanding neither of
Shaw nor the stage; the actor of Sir Colenso Ridgeon (Shepherd Strudwick) can't get his tongue round Shaw's lines, let
alone make Sir Colenso's tailcoat and pin-stripe trousers seem
to be his own. All of which is something of an insult to
Geraldine Fitzgerald, who is the first actress I've seen to enact
the country girl who needs a great man—which is the Jennifer
Dubedat Shaw describes. (Miss Cornell just played her usual
grande dame.) As Louis Dubedat, Roddy McDowell acts well
but wrongly. The director should have insisted that he play
the death scene as a deliberate plot to fix a romantic image in
the head of his widow. In portraying Dubedat, Shaw had in
mind not only Karl Marx's rascally son-in-law but also a
young criminal who had said in court: "I am a disciple of
Bernard Shaw," a line spoken by Dubedat (except at the
Phoenix). Then, too, Shaw parodies a passage from Wagner
that begins: "I believe in God, Mozart, and Beethoven." At
the Phoenix, this passage is so reverently rendered that the
newspapermen have congratulated Shaw on its sincerity. Luckily, large pieces of the play are production-proof, and a gifted
actor like Frederick Worlock can simply take over.

THE CITY CENTER, 1955. If the Phoenix has been rather a
disappointment, the City Center's drama season this year has
been decidedly pleasant. True, it opened with *What Every
Woman Knows*, but none of us is perfect; and I bear no
grudge, as I slipped out in the dark quite a while before the
end; the last half hour was probably superb. Like *The Four*

Poster, which came next. Possibly I was the only critic to whom it came as a shock; I'd never seen it before. The shock was of . . . well, what is the biggest shock for anyone who sees all the shows? The shock of delight. It is seldom that we see comic performances worked out in so much fine detail by so fine an intelligence as that of the Cronyns. And Jessica Tandy has a great voice.

What, in the theatre, is a great voice? An organ tone? Cordelia's mellifluous pianissimo? Great actors have so often been criticized for their ugly voices that I am almost ready to state that a great theatrical voice is always an ugly one. Listen to Edith Evans. Or Miss Tandy. The high, bizarre tone reminds one of Mrs. Roosevelt—rather than the Voice Beautiful of radio announcers. And don't they project rather oddly, rather excessively, throwing their voices rather calculatingly to some friend in the top gallery, amusedly watching it settle in his lap? A great voice is a voice that will do great things. We are told that Henry Irving's voice rasped and snarled—but with great power and variety. So with some of our actresses today . . . Miss Tandy, for instance.

The latest City Center show is *The Time of Your Life*. Was the director, Sanford Meisner, bent on replacing Mr. Saroyan's champagne with a dry sherry of his own? In place of the author's wacky and woozy dream, some Group Theatre "reality"? In any event, most of the old play is still there, and most of it is still good; it provides one of the most memorable of American entertainments.

The Saint of Bleecker Street, by Gian-Carlo Menotti. This work is a by no means mute appeal to which the blurb-like reviews in *The New York Times* read like the desired and expected answer. Interesting that Brooks Atkinson and Olin Downes (both men reviewed it) had little but good to say when they spoke in general, little but bad when they deigned to be specific. The music is so near to Puccini that you often wish it would go the whole way. The subject seems all too cunningly chosen; too nearly what any shrewd author's agent would suggest to his Italian-American clients. Several scenes are good theatre, though, and the whole show is quite brilliantly staged. If only Mr. Menotti could write and compose as well as he directs!

Bus Stop, by William Inge. William Inge's new play at the Music Box left me speechless; I didn't know what to make of it. The stage bristled with talent. Kim Stanley turned in another of her fine characterizations of provincial girls. Elaine Stritch did just as well as the girl behind the lunch counter as she has done as the hard-boiled gal in musical comedy. Albert Salmi, playing a cowboy, emerged as one of the chief youthful talents in New York, and Phyllis Love as an adolescent made sure we noticed that hers is really the main part in the play. Harold Clurman's directing is not only superb in itself but welcome at the moment for its quiet thoughtfulness and modesty. Mr. Inge has contributed some of his best lines, and also seems to have followed the advice given in *The Dramatic Event* two years ago: that he stay within the confines of good-natured, satirical, light comedy. Then why? Why did the laughter out front seem so mechanical and vulgar? Why did the sentiment on stage seem so remote and unimportant? At any particular moment the show is pleasant enough: why did the evening as a whole seem an expanse of nothingness? Is it just that Mr. Inge's emphasis on sex, sex, sex shocks me? (It does.) I still can't help reading Mr. Inge's plays as a homeless man's fantasies of home, an alienated man's fantasies of "belonging"—hence the curiously morbid overemphasis on healthy instinct.

Twenty-seven Wagons Full of Cotton is Tennessee Williams at his best and worst: at his best in portraying another Southern woman (this one by no means identical with the others but a fat slob of a giggling gal), at his worst in portraying the two men of the case (they are merely ideas—and, of course, nasty ideas). The plot exemplifies that "abuse of the terrible," that unscrupulous exploitation of the obscene, which, in a perceptive essay in *The Avon Book of Modern Writing*, Hilton Kramer has shown to be the hallmark of the Bowles, McCullers, Williams school of writing. I would add to Mr. Kramer's statement that the success of this phenomenon in the

theatre depends on the horror's not being received as the
author presumably intended it. At The Playhouse, the mention of flagellation produces knowing chuckles, delighted gur-
gles, and even outright belly laughs. No wonder the director
(Vincent Donahue) was in doubt what to do! The play had
been tried out in New Orleans and found by many too repulsive. For New York, a lighter touch was advocated; the terrible
was to be stripped of its terrors. With the result that the
sniggerers are encouraged in their sniggering, and that one of
the actors, Myron McCormick, is not "with" the play but
seems to wish to rewrite it as a farce. On the other hand,
Maureen Stapleton—in the leading role—is the quintessence
of Williamsism; her personality, her background, her training,
and her talent combine to make her the perfect performer for
the New Drama.

Guys and Dolls, after Damon Runyon, by Jo Swerling, Abe
Burrows, and Frank Loesser. How pleasant to go from the
fashionable psychopaths of Broadway's "serious" drama to the
nice old-fashioned delinquents of *Guys and Dolls,* as currently
revived at the City Center. (If I begin to sound like J. Donald
Adams, or even Cardinal Spellman, I should add that I can
face it. By this time people are on the side of "daring frankness" only by force of habit. Because Zola, Ibsen *et al.* were
daringly frank in order to liberate us, we have come to assume
that daring frankness is *per se* liberating. And we are slow to
admit being repelled by what is repellent for fear someone will
say we are the ones that would have banned *Ulysses.*) Anyway,
Guys and Dolls is so glorious a piece of entertainment that it
almost makes me fall down, like Mr. Inge, and worship solid,
fleshy, lowbrow America. One has to admit that as a piece of
art it far surpasses all Broadway's deliberate attempts at the
artistic. Most of the "serious" plays one sees give the impression of an art form dying on its feet. The only thought
prompted by one I saw just the other day (*The Champagne
Complex* by Leslie Stevens) was: can it really keep going for
two hours? And even this query had so little life in it that I
didn't stay to find out the answer. Plays! They start late, they
end early, and two long intermissions offer poignant invita-

tions to go home. Plays! A trickle of dialogue, the plot of a
short story or a one-acter, a touch of dark lighting and a tinkle
of sound effects for atmosphere, a sitting room or a back porch
for scenery! There is a Russian proverb, "where it is thin, it
breaks." Dramaturgy, right now, is where the theatre is thin.
But the musicals start early, end late, and have a single intermission which is over before you can get to the men's room.
The dialogue is seldom fine but often racy; there is enough
plot for half a dozen "plays"; and the action goes ahead in
great leaps and bounds from setting to setting, interior, exterior, New York, Havana, all points east or west. If you proposed to do in a "serious" play the things that are done all the
time in musicals, your producers would dismiss half of them as
impossible, the other half as arty and avant-garde. Under the
latter head I'm not just thinking of musicals like *Allegro* in
which avant-garde elements are consciously used (projections,
speaking choruses, bare stage, PA system) but, for example,
of the way in which a journey is indicated in *Guys and Dolls*:
in the middle of a bare stage appears an illuminated sign
FASTEN YOUR SEAT BELTS. Musical comedy is a very free form.
You can try anything, and it will not be dismissed with gibes
about Piscator and Germany in the twenties. You can try
anything; and you *must* try many things. A musical is a
veritable club-sandwich of a show with dances and songs between layers of dialogue-bread. I'm thinking not only of quantity but of texture. "Make the gruel thick and slab." The
musical is significantly American not because of its famous
tempo, nor the mechanical efficiency that is the basis of that
tempo, but rather because of its texture: here is the thick and
slab gruel of American life (not the most delicate of dishes,
but a nourishing and tasty one) served up by chefs with
shrewd heads and open hearts, for all the world to relish.

The Diary of Anne Frank, dramatized by Frances Goodrich
and Albert Hackett, contrary to most people's expectation,
including mine, proves to be a moving but not at all harrow-
ing piece of theatre,[2] though it weakly ends with Anne reflect-

---

[2] But see page 279 above.

ing on the goodness of human nature—a principle which her story is so far from confirming. Susan Strasberg, as Anne, is nearly as good as everyone says. The night I saw the play, there was a touch of actressiness and/or precocity in her opening scenes (and, in general, the Anne of the play seems less mature than the Anne of the book), but Miss Strasberg grows on you as the evening proceeds. She has not only the radiance which producers call "star quality" but an uncommon range for even a very talented actress of her age. The achievement of the other actors is to conceal the fact that all the characters except Anne are stock and might easily become tiresome. Even conceding that the Diary did not provide the Hacketts with ready-made characters, one wonders why (a) they didn't try to invent more and (b) why they left alone certain very dramatic *motifs,* such as the young boy's resolve to conceal his Jewish identity after the war, a resolve which could introduce a much-needed element of conflict into the romance.

The Young and Beautiful by Sally Benson, based on stories by F. Scott Fitzgerald, contains some very witty scenes; and the humor throughout is far superior to the standard Broadway article. Marshall Jamison's direction is deliberately, if not always successfully, mannered; and I felt that another director might have guided the star, Lois Smith, from that fault of overemphasis which alone kept her charming and varied performance from being first-rate. Someone seemed to have told her—and in so many places—"that's good, keep it," and she kept it, oh how she kept it.

Will Success Spoil Rock Hunter? by George Axelrod, provides an amusing evening for the many who, like myself, found the same author's *Seven Year Itch* a great bore. Or rather, an amusing three-quarters of an evening: for the ending is moralistic junk (on which Louis Kronenberger made the perfect comment in *Time* magazine: "Integrity in Hollywood writers should be seen and not heard"). The management is guilty of fraud in its advertising, which displays a large bosom that plays but a small part in the evening's fun, as it belongs to an actress (Jayne Mansfield) who can't act and who really doesn't

have to, because the elegant Martin Gabel and the droll Orson
Bean effectively take charge of things.

The Cradle Song by Gregorio and Maria Martinez Sierra.
English version by John Garrett Underhill. At Circle in the
Square, Jose Quintero does nearly all that could be done to
make me like a play which I do not like. The production is, I
think, by far the best work of this young director. He has more
skill with actresses than with actors; and the cast this time is
almost exclusively female. When a playwright gives him half a
chance, he tends towards the frantic; but this playwright never
gives him half a chance. Two things he can always do very well
indeed: one is to establish a lively, ever-changing flow of
feeling between two performers who are speaking to each
other. The other is to give to a scene as a whole a lyric quality
and a lyric curve. Both accomplishments are on display in this
show. I still don't like the play. There is charm and humor in
it. There is also diffuseness, and dullness of mind. And the
English version is often ponderous and awkward.

A Hatful of Rain by Michael V. Gazzo. As a production *A
Hatful of Rain* represents the present-day American theatre at
its best, and even the script contains some of the most interesting American writing in recent drama. No praise could be too
high for Shelley Winters as the young New York wife, and
Anthony Franciosa as her brother-in-law. I would hold up this
work as showing what the Actors' Studio has—or should have
—really been trying to do: not wallowing in sordid details, or
merely reproducing the facts of life, but seizing the essence of
those facts, and having seized it, not fearing large, expansive
emotion but letting it come out when it must. Our young
actors chatter a lot about the "real"; they should all go to this
show and *see* the real. Mr. Gazzo, the author, is to be com-
mended for the quality of his dialogue. Without being feebly
naturalistic he has managed to avoid that inflation with which
even the best American playwrights, from Eugene O'Neill to
Arthur Miller, simulate poetry. But the drama *A Hatful of
Rain* has not only not been written yet, it has not even been
thought through. Though good dialogue and superb acting
make a dozen little dramas of a dozen separate sequences, no

attempt, even the most external and calculated, seems to have been made at integration. I should report that I saw a draft of the play performed at the Studio a year earlier. The changes made in the meantime seem to me to serve the interests of public relations rather than dramatic art. For example, Shelley Winters is given some virtuous twaddle at the end that is calculated, I suppose, to forestall attacks on the author's moral character, but what she says makes hay of scenes and relationships that had been among the best things in the show. If other people imposed these changes on Mr. Gazzo, he has to learn to say no to other people; if he imposed them on himself, he has to learn to say no to part of himself.

Pipe Dream by Richard Rodgers and Oscar Hammerstein, based on John Steinbeck's *Sweet Thursday*. Why can't Rodgers and Hammerstein forget about literature, realize that they are not the bearers of great tidings, and settle down to writing musical comedies?

The Matchmaker by Thornton Wilder. Obviously, this script proceeds from a finer intelligence and sensibility than is commonly at work in our theatre, but I find the theatricality self-conscious, and the core of the drama sentimental. As for the humor (and most of the play is funny), I agree for once in my life with the dramatic critic of *The New York Post* who spoke of Mr. Wilder as teacher being jolly with the class. This impression may, however, stem largely from Tyrone Guthrie's production which is so facetious that it sometimes fails to be funny. And I hate to see a superb comedienne like Ruth Gordon "camping" all over the stage that way, and shouting so, and repeating the same gestures.

Mr. Wilder's friends and admirers tell me that *The Matchmaker* is not to be regarded as a major effort but just a trifle which he wrote with one hand tied behind his back. I recall being told much the same about *The Skin of Our Teeth* years ago. And of *Our Town* years before that. Since Mr. Wilder hasn't written any other full-length plays, the captious might be starting to wonder if the hand behind his back is his writing hand.

Questioned about his views on the drama not long ago, Mr.

Wilder's principal contribution was: "get rid of that proscenium arch." [3] Surely one needn't be a fellow-traveller to cry: formalist! Getting rid of proscenium arches is all very well in its way, and I never met anyone who had anything against it, but no play will succeed on an open stage for which it *was* written unless it has qualities that would make it a success on all the types of stage for which it was *not* written. Nor is the proscenium arch as black as, in a manner of speaking, it has been painted. Direct address to the audience, as used in *The Matchmaker,* charmed me as much as anyone, but, if we follow out the idea of Mr. Wilder's formalism to its conclusion, it ought *not* to have charmed us in a Broadway theatre: the proscenium arch, that fatal barrier between actor and spectator (and so on and so forth), should have spoiled everything. But it didn't.

Mister Johnson, after Joyce Cary, by Norman Rosten, makes two authors seem two too many, as it is a pure product (if pure is the word) of Broadway mythology, and but for the danger of libel suits I should probably suggest that the whole story came to the director Robert Lewis in a dream. He had been directing *Teahouse of the August Moon,* and naturally it got on his nerves; but the neurotic repeats his mistakes, and Mr. Lewis dreamed *Teahouse* in the only slightly disguised form of *Mister Johnson.* Your analyst can unravel it for you. Africa is an established dream symbol for Okinawa, Englishmen in khaki for the American army. The dreamer is "trying for" an image of bliss: naked bodies swaying to the beat of drums and glistening in the tropical sun, sexual customs that combine the maximum of opportunity with the maximum of rationality, crimes that are exciting while they last but which you haven't really committed partly because you were provoked by a white man and partly because, as a black man, you are incapable of crime (you weren't around when the Fall took place, and anyway Adam was white) . . . . Yes, Mr. Lewis

[3] Asked by *The Saturday Review,* "What in your opinion are the most important trends in American playwriting and how do you relate your own work to these trends?" Mr. Wilder's answer, in full, was: "Breaking down that box-set, abolishing that curtain, getting rid of that museum-visit that is suggested by the proscenium."

is black, and not by inheritance. Inherited color is like inherited wealth; in a democratic country you can't take the credit
for it. Mr. Lewis is black by choice. He earned that blackness.
At any rate, he dreamed it, and put all the nice, cuddly,
childish part of himself into the black figure he paraded as in
his dream. And the other part of himself? Well, the analyst says
—but then you can't always believe these analysts—that the
other part of himself is concentrated in the white men of the
dream. And how "other" they are! They are as unpleasing as
the protagonist is pleasing: starchy, snobbish, prejudiced,
often stupid, and above all guilt-ridden. In short, they are an
inferior race. That was why, when he woke up, Mr. Lewis
found he had broken out all over in a cold sweat. For he was
white now. Even when he turned the lights out he was white.
And it is a terrible thing to belong to an inferior race. When
he switched the lights on again, his eyes fell on the newspaper.
In the headlines, that Southern business again. He started to
hunt for the theatre page. Wait a minute. That Southern
business. Down there, they consider Negroes the inferior race.
What a ghastly mistake! When just the opposite is true! I have
an idea. I'll make my dream into a play. Demonstrating, for all
to see, that just the opposite is true. That should help a lot.
That will show the Negroes who their friends are, show the
whites who their, well, critics are. In its own small way, this
should promote understanding and improve race relations
quite a lot, shouldn't it? Or should it?

A single technical point. The law of diminishing returns
applies to theatrical effects. An effect may be good the first ten
times, become boring the eleventh time, and infuriating the
twelfth. You have to watch it. And the most ticklish of effects,
I believe, have to do with laughing (or smiling) and weeping
(or sobbing). More than enough is worse than no feast.

Now the leading actor (Earle Hyman) in this show didn't
know this, and Mr. Lewis must have forgotten it, for Mr.
Hyman grinned and giggled till you felt like shaking him, and
in his last scene, by weeping too much, prevented his audience
from weeping at all. In real life, a man and, more especially, a
woman can go on sobbing indefinitely; the monotony may
annoy you, but has this degree of justification, that it was
probably intended to. On stage, anything more than a single

brief sob is apt to get in the way of the emotion the actor is trying to communicate. Pervasive sobbing renders the words indistinct. The careful placing of sobs at the end of phrases tends to be comic. The actor of the Stanislavsky school may work himself up to real sobbing, but it does not follow that he will take the audience with him. On the contrary, such a peculiar sound as sobbing often tends to push people away, rather than arouse their sympathy. Someone is sobbing his heart out, and your only thought may be: what an awful noise! Beginning actresses are great offenders. Sobbing gives them no trouble at all. They just inhale with hideous violence after every few words. Which instead of making an audience sympathetic makes it indifferent or irritable. . . .

Mr. Hyman has what ought to be a very touching last scene in which, learning that he is to be executed, he asks that he not be hanged by the soldiers but shot by his judge. In real life, there's no knowing how a young man might handle such a terrible plea. Certainly, his words might be incoherent, just as his delivery of them might be inaudible and impossibly phrased. But how is the intended emotion to be created in an audience? I suggest that it is, among other things, by an artful repression of part of the actual experience—namely, the part that, technically speaking, only makes a mess, blurring the outline, clouding the meaning. I suggest that, whatever men really do at such moments, a stage character might assume a strange and improbable calm. Then we can listen to him. A skilful actor can always suggest that there are all kinds of things *behind* such a calm.

Olivier on Disk

IT IS obvious that, as entertainment, mere recordings from poetic drama cannot begin to compete with the stage, the screen, or even TV. The short excerpt is too short to satisfy, and the long excerpt is too long to enthrall. The value of dramatic recordings is not to the general public but to the student, the connoisseur, the expert; and it can be a high value, largely, I believe, as a record (in the other sense) of what leading performers did with a given text. What would any student of theatre not give to know how Burbage, Betterton, Garrick, and Kean spoke To Be Or Not To Be? Not only were there no phonographs in those times; to this day there exists no satisfactory notation by which vocal performance (tone, tempo, volume, phrasing, cadence, timbre, et cetera) can be represented and preserved on paper. But, now that we have the phonograph, we can say with precision and certitude of John Gielgud, Maurice Evans, Laurence Olivier: this is how they said it.

It follows that music, in recordings of drama, is simply a nuisance. No doubt, the record makers think that by adding music they are taking the curse off the "educationality" of the thing. They are wrong; they are only appealing to a fallacy, succumbing to a fad, and perpetuating a pest. I refer to the assumption that silence is a bad thing, that mere human speech is not enough to break silence, and that, therefore, a noise known as music has been invented to fill the interstices between words and to present humankind with the anxious alternative: be inaudible or shout. As an alternative to this alternative I offer the following formula. *Silence, not music, is the proper background of speech and, second only to speech itself, is the finest of dramatic effects.* And I italicize it so that the FBI won't miss it; for it is deeply subversive; carried into effect it would rapidly destroy the American way of life, perhaps by violence. For on the day when all the cables have been cut to all the juke boxes in all the bars, luncheonettes, and restaurants in America, the American streets will be found littered with the corpses of men who for the very first time have heard the sound of their own voices; and the notion that they have committed suicide will be discounted as Communist propaganda.

Actually, except for the pleasant purposes of argument, I shouldn't deny to film or TV the use of incidental music (though I should be happy to point out many abuses of it). I have in mind, rather, the unfortunate spread of movie meth-

ods to the stage (how unnecessary was the harpsichord in
Orson Welles's *King Lear* at City Center!) , and, more particularly, the spoiling of dramatic phonograph records by such
non-dramatic elements. The instance before me—*Richard III*
as distributed by RCA-Victor—is an extreme case. This is not
a recording "influenced by the movies." It is nothing more nor
less than the sound track of a movie, unedited and uncut.
Which is to say that, as a work offered as phonography alone,
it is highly unaccepable—to every sort of listener and for
every sort of reason. Those who can see the film instead will
obviously do so. Those who wish to be reminded of the film
will see the film again. In any case, a recording could be no
vivid reminder, since movies are primarily a visual medium. As
for those who, for reasons personal or geographical, cannot get
to the film, they either know Shakespeare's *Richard III* or they
do not. If they do not, they will find this recording impossible to
follow. There are so many characters, it will be impossible for
them to know who is speaking; there are so many incidents, it
will be impossible to know what is happening. Small comfort
for them to reflect, during one of the interminable stretches of
William Walton music: on the screen such interesting things
must be going on now! Nor does RCA-Victor make any effort
to guide the helpless listener through this maze. The booklet
accompanying the album contains only a list of the cast and
some chatty remarks on the play by a critic (Walter Kerr)
who evidently hadn't seen the film or heard the sound track.
You might expect that the listener who knows the text would
be more happily placed. Actually, he is kept so busy tracing
the cuts, interpolations, and splicings-together that he hasn't
time to follow the story in its own terms; he is just confused.

I feel I know what I'm talking about because I played these
six sides, and did my best to listen to them, before I saw the
film. Only misanthropy could prompt me to advise any fellow
man to do likewise. Even now that I have seen the film, I can
only advise RCA-Victor to withdraw the album and substitute
two sides of excerpts with a minimum of music. For my readers
should be warned that the music is not confined to the background. Quite often there are no words at all but just the kind
of music that is not interesting enough to listen to, blaring

symphonically away. Later, when you see the film, this music falls into proper insignificance behind the spectacle and pantomime which it was composed to accompany.

Anyone concerned with the relation of sound track to film might be interested in the fact that, after hearing these records, I expected very little of the film; and yet, when I saw the film, I found it to be an extraordinary beautiful piece of work, perhaps the best achievement of Olivier in any field. The general principle involved has already been implied: good sounds might make a bad sound track, while it is unlikely that a good sound track will constitute in itself a good work of art. It is also a matter of Olivier's particular talent—which is not for radio and phonography but for acting and film-directing.

There is a good deal to be said against Olivier's voice. It is not grand, it is not rich, it is not warm. It fails, therefore, in most cases, to meet the demands of tragic drama and/or of a large auditorium, as anyone can vouch who saw this actor as Antony at the Ziegfeld Theatre. He had to do a lot of experimenting with the kind of voice he does have before its true uses were revealed. As late as 1946, Stark Young was complaining of jerkiness and a discontinuity of tone. For a long time Olivier was learning by trial and error what effects can be got with a voice that by its very thinness is extremely incisive and clear. I recall how, before the war, he would conduct an assault on blank verse in order to demonstrate the possibilities of rubato and staccato. While John Gielgud swept his incomparably graceful scythe, Olivier jabbed away, as it were, with a sharp and fine-pointed dagger. And today he can play any part except that of a tragic hero like Antony or a mellow, full-blooded soldier like Caesar. As Richard III—granted the premise of the style [1] chosen for the film as a whole—he is

---

[1] About which I am silent from having, not too little, but too much to say. But it could all be inferred from my "Doing Shakespeare Wrong" in *In Search of Theatre. Richard III* may not be based on the facts as a modern historian knows them but, for all that, it is not the fairy tale Sir Laurence chooses to believe it is. British directors these days want their drama exquisite to the verge of effeminacy. I find myself praising that exquisiteness from time to time—after all it isn't, in itself, a fault—but even in the best exhibits—*Richard III* or the Williams-Redgrave *A Month in the Country*—there is also much to be on guard against.

superb. Even vocally the performance is first-rate in the movie theatre; but not being principally a vocal perfomance, it is not quite compelling on the phonograph. Here our attention is called to the extreme lightness of the voice, and the solutions to the various problems assigned may seem too special. Only as convinced by Olivier's appearance and acting can we agree to Richard's having so delicate a vocal organ. The records often give the impression of a feeble falsetto and hence of a character who is not villain enough.

The listener must not be dazzled by the list of names in the cast: Pamela Brown, though often on view in the film, contributes less than half a dozen words to its sound track. And, aside from Olivier, only three actors make their presence felt when heard and not seen. They are Alec Clunes, Ralph Richardson, and John Gielgud. Gielgud's reading of "Clarence's dream" is the one gem of the album and should undoubtedly be distributed on a separate record as a model of Shakespearean speaking. The assignment was a very hard one: to tell the story of a dream, keeping all the values of the story itself, though the teller of it is a man distraught and near death. Perhaps none of our actors but Sir John could realize both sets of values so fully: he gives us all the elegance of the rhetoric plus all the poignancy of the drama, all the flamboyance of the narrative plus all the inwardness of the character. Here is a great actor who has much that Olivier has and much that Olivier has not, including warmth, richness, and grandeur of utterance.

Further comments on *Richard III* had best be left to critics of the film; I'll rest content with the remark that the editing and cutting that on the disk are merely confusing (to those who know their Shakespeare) seemed to me largely justified in the film. One thing still mystifies me, though. While the intention of many small changes in the text (like "chop off his head" for "raze his helm") is obvious enough, I jotted down many others that seemed pointless—such as "dabbled with blood" for "dabbled in blood" and "will not appease thee" for "cannot appease thee." The movie makers give themselves an alibi by stating that they have drawn on the texts of "Colley Cibber, Garrick, et cetera," though what "et cetera" means I don't know. Ninety-nine per cent of the script is Shakespeare, with a clever editor (Alan Dent) jumping adroitly between the folio and the various quartos. One scene and one speech from *Henry VI*, Part Three, are also included. The latter being Richard's "Aye, Edward will use women honorably," the phonograph listener can compare Olivier's rendering with John Barrymore's (Audio Rarities 2203: the speech is wrongly described, at least in *The Long Player*, as being from *Richard III*).

Olivier's excerpts from *Henry V* and *Hamlet* are currently available on a single RCA-Victor record. The presentation of both plays is open to most of the criticisms just made of the new *Richard III*. Though in neither case is a complete movie sound track inflicted upon us, even the *Henry V* passages, which are not excerpted from a sound track, have been fixed up to simulate one with lots of fanfares and William Walton. When will Sir Laurence learn that we love him for himself alone?

De Filippo on the Screen

I CANNOT HELP being amused at the embarrassment of certain movie critics over the film of *Romeo and Juliet*. Afraid, perhaps, of being accused of not appreciating Shakespeare, they were not ready to admit that what is better as Shakespeare may be worse as cinema, and vice versa, the reason being that, on the stage, the sound track takes precedence over the visual track, while, on the screen, the opposite is the case. What Shakespeare left us is dialogue, and we fit the rest of our stage production to that; what the movie maker gives us is a series of images, and he must fit the dialogue to that.

A purist would therefore hold that plays should probably not be filmed at all and, if they are, should be completely assimilated to the cinematic art, so that, in the end the question to be asked would be: "Is it a good film?" while: "Is it faithful to the play?" would be a question *not* to be asked. But, though purism is of its nature very sound and convincing, few of us, in this unsound and unconvincing world of ours, are purists. We don't much care what category works of art belong to provided that we like them, nor do we mind if they are inferior as this, provided that they are superior as that. Consider the Shaw films. They are ersatz. Shaw himself welcomed them as simply a way of reaching a wider public *with his plays*. Why not? As examples of cinematic art, they are inferior to *The Maltese Falcon* or any other memorable Hollywood product. But we seldom pay our dollar to see an *example* of something. Nothing in the cinematics of the Shaw films makes us miserable, and what we are enjoying is—the play, better rehearsed and better acted than we are likely to see it in the ordinary circumstances of commercial theatre.

This is, of course, not wholly true. Had the camera photographed an actual stage performance—say, from a fixed position in the mezzanine—the play, oddly enough, would not seem to have been rendered at all. Concessions have to be made to the cinematic principle. A Shaw film—let us say, any dramatic film—will differ from a "pure" film only in refusing to let the camera detract from the dialogue. All plays, of course, contain much dialogue that is there for dramaturgic reasons which, on the screen, will no longer obtain; it must be cut. The dialogue that cannot be cut is the part which is either crucial to the drama or commendable in itself. (I should place under the latter head the Queen Mab speech in *Romeo* which some of the movie critics—logically enough from their special standpoint—gladly let go.) As non-purists, we shall accept the fact that the dramatic film is full of those long speeches, or long passages of talk in short speeches, which the purist will reject. Tension between the dramatic and cinematic principles cannot always be avoided. Sometimes the camera will try to carry the emphasis where the script does not wish it to go. For example, the film of *Pygmalion* tends to make a climax of the reception scene, which is not in the play at all. Life is imperfect.

All this is by way of preface to some remarks about a couple of remarkable Italian films which have escaped general attention, presumably because they are not remarkable examples of cinematic art and because the plays they are based on—like the players in them—are unknown here. They are *Sidestreet Story* ("Napoli Milionaria") and *Filumena Marturano*. One man wrote the plays, adapted them to the screen, directed, and starred in, both movies: Eduardo De Filippo.

I have written of the art of De Filippo at length in *In Search of Theatre*. Making the journey to Canal Street to see *Filumena Marturano* without subtitles or dubbing at the Cinema Giglio, I am forcibly reminded how small a dent he has made in non-Italian culture. In these days of theoretical internationalism, one is reluctant to admit how utterly *local* is so much of theatrical art. How can a dialect theatre—the theatre of Eduardo is Neapolitan—pass the boundaries of its dialect? And that is not the only problem. Eduardo is one of those stage actors whose magic cannot penetrate celluloid: on the screen it is impossible to see much more than competence in this man whom Gordon Craig, as report has it, considers the finest living actor.

There are compensations. The largest, and title, role in *Filumena Marturano* is played by Titina De Filippo, Eduardo's sister, who has more luck with the screen, it seems to me, than he does. Filumena is a woman from the slums of Naples who, starting as a mere prostitute, manages to become the mistress of a wealthy playboy whom she loves and expects to marry. When, however, after a quarter of a century, the playboy pays court to a fair young socialite, Filumena forces the issue by pretending to be dead and exacting what seems a death-bed marriage. The man has this marriage annulled later, but in the meanwhile he has found that Filumena has had three children by various fathers and that they have been raised on his money. The second act curtain of the stage version occurs with her disclosure that he is one of these fathers. She won't tell him which of the boys is his son. She will never tell—not even when, at the end of the play, he remarries her of his own free will because he is bored with the socialite and knows who his real friend is.

A plot summary could hardly suggest the kind of fun and pathos Eduardo gives to his story. The introduction of the sons (to him and the audience) is a very big scene. An amusing motif of more scenes than one is his attempt to find out which son is his. Filumena's mock death scene sounds like something from classic comedy. The effect of it is somewhat spoiled in the play by its being almost over before the curtain goes up, but in the film it is presented fully and tellingly. Another place where the film is an improvement over the play is after the annulment. While the play simply jumps to the remarriage, the film fills the gap in, showing the man's getting bored with his floozy and feeling the need of his old friend. . . .

A dramatic, not a pure, film, *Filumena Marturano* leaves intact certain long narrative speeches which, in Italy, are already famous set pieces—notably, one in which Filumena tells the whole story of her upbringing. In America, such a speech would have been cut not only from the film but from the play. Naples is a different place, and Neapolitan folk drama is a different art; one enjoys it not least for its difference. One enjoys the Neapolitan gestures: Eduardo pressing his palms together and shaking them to express exasperation, or Titina digging her fingers in her eyes and flinging her hands sideways to tell us she cannot weep. One enjoys, above all, the fine blend of comedy and drama, the naive pathos, the almost noble seriousness of what might easily be ludicrous. Some non-Italians are surprised, even displeased, by this last feature. "Why don't they play comedy as comedy?" Fully to answer the question would be to explain and justify a simpler, but also more delicate, realism than our own stage at present has to show.

Martha Graham

WHEN A MANAGEMENT compresses "eighteen premières, five important revivals, fifteen repertory favorites" into three weeks, people who have other things to do besides watching dances must pick and choose. Yet within the scope of a single

review I cannot do justice to the five evenings I did devote to
Bethsabee de Rothschild's presentation of Modern Dance at
the ANTA Theatre. I will limit myself to the work of a single
choreographer—Martha Graham—and my comments even on
her will be fragmentary.

I treasure things in her work that to a dance expert might
seem secondary—notably, her stagecraft, starting with stage
design. The designs for all Graham's dances are among the
most original in the modern theatre, and a large part of the
credit must surely go to Graham herself, who knows so well
what she wants. But at least one of her designers—Noguchi—is
a genius in his own right. (I call him "hers" because she alone
in our theatre has a use for him.) One of the triumphs of the
festival is a structure of copper tubing which is Noguchi's
setting for the story of Jeanne D'Arc. By a miracle of the
imagination he has created a medieval quality without imitating medieval art and a modern quality which enhances the
medievality instead of negating it. Even aside from such particular inspirations, I like Graham's idea of scenery as consisting of a few objects placed on a platform; it would have given
Belasco rather a shock, but would have been less of a surprise
to Shakespeare. (Designers for the dance have to keep most of
the stage floor free; it would do stage designers a lot of good to
work under a similar compulsion.) These few objects may
constitute a setting (landscape, architecture, furniture), or
they may consist of portable properties. Graham makes original use of both. More precisely, she is original in that she does
use them: settings and props are not a passive background but
are employed in the action on stage. A gateway of wood is also
a horizontal bar for a gymnast (in *Theatre for a Voyage*). Or
what begins as part of the setting may be dislodged and
become a prop (as happens with a sort of burning bush in
Cave of the Heart).

The modern theatre boasts about the skillfully realistic use
of props which it has learned from Stanislavsky. But there is
also a non-real, or surreal, use of them, which was never so
vividly illustrated as when Graham as Emily Brontë plays
chess or holds a goblet. Are trinkets and jewels props or
costume? Nowhere in modern theatre are personal ornaments

—a flower or a pin in the hair, a bangle on the arm—more important than in the art of Graham. It is partly a matter of the choice of ornament, partly of its placing on the body, and partly of the ability of the dancer to wear it: Graham has mastered all three departments. In the study of her art, we pass from setting, to props, to adornments, to clothes—an unbroken chain. As to clothes, I should say that the ballet exploits only a small part of their theatricality. The purpose of ballet costume is exhausted if the shape of the body is indicated and a touch of glamour added. Graham's interest in clothes is more wholehearted. Where the ballet features the outline of the leg, she features the full skirt, and many of the patterns of her dancing are simply (if it were simple!) undulations of skirting —what Herrick called the "liquefaction" of women's clothes. Where ballet costume frees the body for "sheer" movement, a Graham dance imposes deliberate limits to movement in the form of numerous props and copious folds of dress. (Even hair is a prop when worn long and especially when let fall over the face and down over the chest as with Helen McGehee in one of the new dances.) As dancers, Graham's company must surely feel encumbered and inhibited at times. In *Ardent Song*, Patricia Birsh carries a large sea-shell and is wrapped up as tight as a mummy; yet it is in this very episode that Miss Birsh proves herself one of the outstanding members of the group; in limitation lay her opportunity.

If I'm making the art of Graham seem a matter of objects, obstacles, and devices, I'd like to correct the error by calling attention to more elemental kinds of theatricality. First, the sheer thoroughness of it all. What we usually see in the New York theatre is work, good or bad, that has been knocked together in a tremendous hurry by a group of people who have never even met before. It should hardly be necessary to add that *this shows*. The opposite shows, too. A production of the Berlin Ensemble that has been quietly rehearsed for three months with actors who are working together year in and year out is quite a different thing. The resulting thoroughness is not merely a matter of added stage "business" but of the ripeness of unforced fruit, of organic growth. Such a ripeness is to be seen in the works which Graham has labored on, not months, but years, like *Appalachian Spring, Night Journey, Deaths and Entrances,* and *Diversion of Angels.* Second, the direct creation of visual beauty. There was a time when modern dance was thought to be all contractions, distortions, sharp angles, miscellaneous grotesqueries. Today, some of the younger dancers have raised the cry that Graham is reactionary and *vieux jeu.* The fact is, obviously, that we have here an art at full maturity. Too modern for the oldsters, too conservative for the youngsters, the phenomenon is simply that of a fully realized style. One might go on to reflect that some of the older crowd will yet learn to like it, while more and more of the younger crowd will clamor for something different. My point here is that this older Graham can give us certain rare satisfactions. She has won through to that special simplicity which, in the life of an artist who develops for decades, comes after complexity. For all the famous eccentricities, Graham, I feel, has always striven towards such a simplicity. You can see it in the way each particular piece develops. In the beginning it is lumpy like dough; the work Graham does on it is a kind of kneading till all is smooth.

The part of Graham that I resist, and find impure, is sometimes prominent in titles and program notes. Too much anthropology (or too little). Too much psychoanalysis (or too much Jung). Too much literature (or too much advice from Bennington College). And this part is prominent in works not yet developed to their final pitch. But from *Diversion of Angels,* a masterpiece, I can at any moment recall two simple images. One is of Pearl Lang darting and quivering through the air, the other of Mary Hinkson standing quite, quite still. Two statues, if you will, with Miss Lang caught, as by some baroque sculptor, in mid-flight. Images! Graham creates images of an exquisite loveliness. Perhaps this is not one of the main things she does? Let the dance critics tell us what is; I have been reading them, and I find that in general they say absolutely nothing. . . . I feel grateful for such loveliness, and cannot help feeling that it is of the essence—if not of dance, then of theatre.

Marcel Marceau

EVERYONE KNOWS that pantomime means acting without speaking but which of us, invited to see "some pantomime," would know what to expect? The lights come up on a bare stage. Silence. Before the dark curtains stands a single figure in a plain, white costume and ballet slippers. He walks; but never reaches the side of the stage; never advances a step, in fact. It is a trick of *seeming* to walk; *marcher sur place* is its name. A small thing? Yet the audience is agog. We who have acquired a certain proficiency in interpreting those faint gasps and murmurs, those audible smiles, those shiftings in the seat, those turnings of neighbor to neighbor, which are the response of an audience detect a most unusual degree of delight. And of interest: for if originality in art consists in a new mingling of illusion and reality, here it is. A walk is defined as a certain sequence of movements; yet here are the movements and no movement; here is a walk which is not a walk.

Such is the most rudimentary of the pantomimic exercises of Marcel Marceau, the supreme product of the youngest generation in world theatre, who has just made his first New York appearance. Actually, any student of mime can *marcher sur place*. It is the mark of M. Marceau's personal magnetism that he can fascinate our audiences nightly with so elementary an exercise. But I am speaking only of the first half-minute of his program. There follows a series of items, lasting anything from a matter of seconds to a matter of minutes, and varying in complexity as from the average night-club skit to a poem of Wallace Stevens.

When T. S. Eliot's Sweeney says: "I gotta use words when I talk to you," he is admitting that words can be pretty unsatisfactory, and M. Marceau shows us that doing without words can be, instead of a deprivation, a liberation—as the more knowing movie critics realized, with a pang, when the "talkies" were invented. The language of pantomime surely has its limits (though I can't say I know where), yet within its own frontiers it can speak with a purity reached in words only by the masters. To this it might be retorted that I have in mind only the masters of pantomime. But I don't think so. In the Keystone Comedies there were only one or two individual masters, yet whole films spoke with a purity never achieved by any genre of "talkie."

To the purity of the genre, M. Marceau adds his own genius, which one can hardly help comparing to Charlie Chaplin's. Half M. Marceau's program depicts a character called Bip who is first cousin to Charlie the Tramp—the common man as romantic bum and lovable bungler seen through laughter and tears, that is, through funny absurdity and pathetic absurdity. In fact I heard Faubion Bowers, the Orientalist, complaining that all our Western mime is limited to these two elements whereas the Oriental mime runs the whole gamut of the dramatic and tragic modes.

If the art of Chaplin and Marceau has common boundaries, the differences within those boundaries are so large that one comes to question the value of the comparison. How, for example, can one reasonably say that Marceau is better (or worse) than Chaplin? Essential to M. Marceau's art is the absence of props; half the fascination of watching him is to see how he conjures up imaginary objects. In Chaplin, on the other hand, we admire the choice of props to use and the way he uses them. Again, when we praise Chaplin, we praise not only the soloist but the actor with other actors, the screen-director, the screen-writer; in Marceau, we admire the economy —what he can do without props, without camera, without colleagues. To all of which one must add the difference between the stage and the screen as such. Essential to M. Marceau's art is the constantly rippling flow of feeling from him to the audience and back from the audience to him. Watching his work develop over the last half-dozen years (I claim the distinction of having first introduced him—in Schloss Leopoldskron, Salzburg—to the Anglo-Saxon audience) I have had the opportunity to see grow what we vaguely call authority. (It is one thing to play a sonata brilliantly in a drawing room;

another to hold all Carnegie Hall spellbound; this last demands authority.)

I wish that words of mine could give a vivid impression of M. Marceau to those who have not seen him. Do not imagine that he deals chiefly in dumb show, like Harpo Marx "speaking" to Chico. To M. Marceau bodily movement is not a substitute for words but a direct way of depicting the human scene and indicating an attitude to it. One of his most charming numbers is called *The Public Garden,* and in it he portrays over a dozen different people for no more than a few seconds each. Part of the game is that the audience is kept guessing for a moment whom he is portraying now. He seems to be holding something above his head, then taking hold of a string. Ah, yes, he is the balloon seller. And, look, the little boy he's sold a balloon to must have been rude to him, he seems insulted. . . . A park-full of people is described with incredible dispatch, exactitude, delicacy, affection, and, of course, abundant humor.

One of the most ambitious numbers is called *Bip and the Butterfly.* Here M. Marceau enters the higher realm of poetry, not by way of big statement, but by way of a shimmering and shifting of meanings all connected (insofar as words can say it) with the strangeness of the desire to seize a kind of beauty which, when seized, will die. The means adopted are darting looks, flickering fingers, and a slender, lithe body under perfect rhythmic control.

In some of its finest moments, the pantomime of Marceau is lyrical, and in one number, called *Youth, Maturity, Old Age, and Death,* the lyrical is raised to the power of the sublime. The whole thing lasts perhaps half a minute during which M. Marceau remains rooted to the spot. As the lights go up, he is curled up like a foetus. Slowly he uncurls, gradually rises, at the same time making a roughly circular movement of the whole body. At last he is erect, his arms high above his head, and he is walking (without walking) forward, upward. Imperceptibly, with a slight twitch perhaps, a shrinking takes place. The chest caves in, the shoulders grow rounded, the arms drop and come forward and inward, the whole body sinks, and the aged corpse with which the action ends resembles the foetus with which it began.

I have spoken chiefly of the stories and the body-movements that go with them. There is a great deal more to say. An essay might be written on M. Marceau's use of his face. The idea of white clown make-up is old and familiar; what M. Marceau does with it is not. For him, the whiteness is not a mask, replacing mobility with fixity; it is, rather, a way of making movement more easily visible; some details are eliminated in order that others may be underlined.

And I should like to congratulate M. Marceau on the great improvements he has made in mere showmanship. In Paris, some of his items used to be rather awkwardly introduced, and were sometimes accompanied by a rather ineffective sound. Today, the phonograph music is wonderfully appropriate, and the items are introduced by two young colleagues of M. Marceau's who make up charming *tableaux vivants* in the spirit of the item in question.

"The foundation of drama," wrote Arthur Symons in his important essay "A Theory of the Stage," "is that part of the action which can be represented in dumb show. Only the essential part of action can be represented without words, and you would set the puppets vainly to work on any material but that which is common to humanity. . . ." And so Symons, and Gordon Craig later, championed marionettes. And, later still, Craig had to explain that he had intended, not to insult the actor, but only to isolate and define a certain part of the actor's work, namely, its foundation.

In one respect, our generation is luckier than that of Symons and Craig. Instead of the dim theory of the *Übermarionette*, we have the vivid reality of Marcel Marceau.

James Agate

MUCH OF THE GREAT dramatic criticism—William Hazlitt's or Bernard Shaw's—was a rather incidental part of a great career in literature, but there are also instances of a whole lifetime principally and profitably dedicated to dramatic criticism. In our day the leading example on this side of the water is

George Jean Nathan and, on the other, James Agate. The fact that the latter is almost unknown in this country—*Rachel* and *The Later Ego* are the only things of his to find an American publisher—would be sufficient reason for calling attention to him. Yet I bring the name of Agate forward less because his merit has been overlooked than because his *kind* of merit seems, unhappily, to require, as well as deserve, an apologia.

I can say this in all modesty because I myself have long underrated this critic. I first read him in the thirties when I was a boy and he was a critic of *The Sunday Times* and, in my view, a fogey. He had all the standard opinions and attitudes, it seemed to me, of a crusty old codger. He was no great shakes in the analysis of plays, which I had decided was my specialty. He was very inhospitable to all that I regarded as important in the new drama—continental expressionism, the homemade expressionism of Sean O'Casey, the poetic drama of Eliot and Auden. In fact, intellectuals, Bohemians, and leftists—the three at the time were one—were his pet hates. And it was doubtful if he knew the difference between a real intellectual like Eliot and a semi-intellectual like J. B. Priestley. Of the newest names on the continent, like that of Brecht, I suppose he had never even heard.

Can it be that the real merits of a dramatic critic—as has been alleged of other artists—reveal themselves only after death? A curious irony, indeed, if this seemingly most fugitive and ephemeral of the arts should actually show its true face under the aspect, if not of eternity, at least of history! Yet, certainly, what the dramatic critic's reviews "add up to" when they are collected is the measure of his achievement. Together, they constitute his "view"—short or long—of the stage. True enough, very few people will ever share this "view" with him. For, if any class of books has a small public, it is books of collected theatre reviews. As Agate once said: "Anybody can write dramatic criticism; it takes a very clever fellow to get it reprinted." He was a very clever fellow. His whole career was planned. He made up his mind that the English theatre during the period of his labors should not go unchronicled. And, today, anyone who wanted to know about theatre in London over the quarter century 1922–1947 would above all need the collected works of James Agate.

Though theatrical reporting is not as easy as those who have not practiced it might imagine—and there have only been a few first-rate practitioners in the field—it is not chiefly as a reporter that Agate should be known. What does his proper title—that of dramatic critic—comprise? I attempted an answer in *The Dramatic Event,* stressing the grasp of facts and the gift of appraisal. Agate's work is a reminder that a dramatic critic should be above all—a writer. We may put it less pretentiously still and say: an entertainer. His column must, above all, be something that readers turn to—and read through to the end. Assuming that his readers are intelligent, this means that the critic must have two things: personality and an axe to grind.

In his later years, Agate doubtless became all too much of a "personality." (It's all very well to become a "character" in the world's eyes; to become one in your own eyes is a fate not even an Oscar Wilde can face with impunity.) Yet had Agate not been a personality all his life long—and this in a sense that we ought to regard as legitimate and fine—I should not be writing about him now. As for the axes a critic grinds, I mean that a man cannot keep our interest from week to week unless, in addition to "writing well" and "being very bright," he seems to be "getting at" something, to have an end in view. Disapprove as much as you like of *what* he is getting at, provided you realize that he wouldn't have interested you in the first place, had he not been getting at it. Demonstrate to the world that his personal involvement has led him into this, that, and the other error, provided you grant that it also made him worth refuting. A critic not only has the right to the "ulterior motive," the *arrière pensée,* the "personal prejudice," he has to have them as a matter, so to say, of biological necessity. It is not the slightest use his having a lot *in* his mind, if he has nothing *on* his mind, even if it is only a nagging worry, an undefined hunch, or a passionate yearning. In the thirties, we would have been brief and said he must be a propagandist. And Agate, who was against the propaganda of the thirties, had, providentially, a propaganda of his own, a philosophy of theatre which it was pleasure to propagate.

We find it finely and fully stated in his very first volume of dramatic criticism published in 1918. *"Buzz Buzz,"* the title page reads, "by Captain James E. Agate." The book is a defence of "the nursery sense of theatre," the child's willing acceptance of the whole histrionic fairy tale. "To Charles Lamb," he writes, "I owe my extravagant 'idea' of the theatre," placing himself squarely in the romantic tradition. Behind the figures of the actors he has seen loom the shadows of some he has not seen—Rachel (whose life he wrote), Garrick, Kemble, and, above all, Edmund Kean. After that of Lamb and Hazlitt, the most important generation to Agate was that of his youth—the generation of Ibsen, Shaw, and Wilde. He saw Réjane and Sarah act, and he sat at the feet of the great dramatic critic of *The Manchester Guardian*, C. E. Montague.

Buzz Buzz is full of Montague. If today the book seems a trifle "nineties-ish" in the strained decorativeness of its prose and its rather juvenile insistence on the amorality of the artist, yet Manchester is in it too, by way of hardheadedness and pride in a job well done. There is a great deal to be said against defining any man's character in terms of a single antithesis, yet I cannot resist doing just that to James Agate, for he was masculine and feminine, prosaic and poetic, commonsensical and fastidious, downright and delicate, Mancunian and Wildean.

In *Buzz Buzz*, Agate scolded Arthur Symons for speaking of "the intrusive little personality of the actor" and preferring puppets, and we find him a couple of decades later scolding Tyrone Guthrie for losing the actors in physical production. He wasn't for Gordon Craig. "The settings and costumes," he wrote on one occasion, "are so good that one does not notice them, and the same goes for the production." He pointed out that in what he considered the best theatre review ever written —Montague on Benson in *Richard II*—we hear nothing of directing or scenery or "production ideas." *Theatre consists of two great arts, playwriting and acting, and there is no third art coordinating them:* this is Agate's doctrine and, finding himself less gifted as a critic of literature than as a critic of performance, he takes for his chosen sphere: acting. We should read him above all for what he says about Réjane, Sarah,

Forbes-Robertson, Marie Lloyd, Sybil Thorndike, Edith
Evans, John Gielgud, Laurence Olivier. I do not mean to
disparage his remarks on other subjects. To print one's review
of *The Family Reunion* in verse is itself a most pertinent
criticism of the play. And Agate's works abound in *aperçus* on
a wide range of topics. For a sampling:

> *The Constant Nymph* must always be happy in three
> themes which no amount of good writing could ever
> defeat. First there is the "heart-of-a-child" theme. . . .
> Tessa is flowerlike, and it will be a sorry age when we are
> not moved by the spectacle of virgin purity and fineness of
> mind going hand in hand with a sense of fun and a
> healthy knowledge of life. . . . I am less sure of the
> validity of the second theme—the early dying. There
> never was any reason why the naughty heroines of Pré-
> vost, Mürger, and Dumas should find Heaven by the
> consumptive route except that death pays all and secures
> the moral ending. . . . The third theme is the age-long
> one of the conflict between respectability and the artistic
> temperament. . . . We are expected to forgive in the artist
> conduct which we should not tolerate in the electrician.
> . . . The public which is most obedient to Mrs. Grundy at
> home and most likes to flout her in the theatre is the
> Great English Public which provides ninety-nine percent
> of playgoers. In view of these three themes—child-heroine,
> early demise, and the artistic clash—how could *The Con-
> stant Nymph* be a failure?

> This play [Peter Ustinov's *The Banbury Nose*] may be
> full of sedition, false doctrine, heresy, and schism. That
> doesn't matter. I find it entrancing. . . .

> The divination and discovery of the good in [the] com-
> monplace, the making of distinctions on low levels, is, in
> point of actual practice, ninety-nine hundredths of the
> critic's job on this matter-of-fact planet.

> All plays are too long. . . . The average West End com-
> edy contains the sketch of an idea some half an hour long,
> which has then got to be stretched to such a length that
> 10/6 may reasonably be demanded for it.

Show the spectator an action, and you will have his whole mind; speculate and theorise for him, and he will begin speculating and theorising for himself.

A play is not a novel coarsened to delight a serried mob breathing down the back of each other's necks. The remark of the American to the English butler—"To whom do you, beautifully, belong?"—sets the novelist's page a-tinkle with mischief and irony; spoken on the stage, it is a knell.

Pure emotion is so exhausting that without interest you would be done up in a single act.

Critic: Galsworthy is ten times the draw Shaw is because there is not an intellectual idea in him from first to last.
Playwright: Shaw is ten times as big a draw as Galsworthy.

Cecil Beaton, who ravishes the eye while making hay of the realities. . . .

Oliver Messel, who in the theatre has Nature beaten to a frazzle. . . .

Now one of the most curious things about that quaintest of countries [the United States] is that Uplift goes hand in hand with a sentimentality which would make a rhinoceros vomit.

These characters [Clifford Odets'] have no background. They are unaware that anybody has had feelings like theirs before.

But he is happiest when "the actors are come." I dare not begin to quote his comments on actors or this tribute would swell to an anthology. "The actors are come": on this line James Agate's comment, like Hamlet's, was "Buzz Buzz," which, as the commentators are almost prepared to admit, means: "Don't teach your grandmother."

OTHER REVIEWS

1944–1967

Drama Now

This piece was commissioned in 1944 by The
Nation. *When their literary editor refused to
print it, it appeared in* Partisan Review *(Spring
1945). In modified form it re-appeared as the
Foreword to the first edition of* The Playwright
as Thinker *(1946). As such it attracted far too
much attention, and accordingly was dropped
from later editions.*

WITH THE HELP of a sheaf of recently printed plays [1] I shall
try in this review to identify and characterise several different
levels of dramatic art as it now exists.

There are some of course who believe that plays are not
meant to be silently read any more than musical scores. Unlike
music, however, drama is conceived and recorded in words.
The theatrical director is simply an interpreter of the dramatist's words. Since every reader of a play is a self-appointed
director with a theatre in his own mind I propose to assume
that the well-equipped reader can experience and appraise the
play in his study and that a play which is bad to read is a bad
play. Good literature may be bad drama *but the converse does
not hold.* It is a pity Charles Lamb did not see the philistine
inference which would be drawn from his assertion that much

---

[1] S.R.O.: *The Most Successful Plays in the History of the American
Stage,* compiled by Bennett Cerf and Van H. Cartmell; Doubleday,
Doran. *One Touch of Venus,* by S. J. Perelman and Ogden Nash; Little,
Brown. *Anna Lucasta,* by Philip Yordan; Random House. *Jacobowsky and
the Colonel,* by Franz Werfel; Viking. *Get Away Old Man,* by William
Saroyan; Harcourt, Brace. *Four Plays,* by J. B. Priestley; Harper's. *Red
Roses for Me,* by Sean O'Casey; Macmillan.

great dramatic literature was not theatre: it was that great theatre is not literature. Hence the unfavorable overtones in the word "theatrical" and in the word "literary." Actually, to call plays "too theatrical," as we do, is like calling sugar too sweet; but so is calling plays "too literary."

The proof that the anti-literary drama pundits do not mean what they say is that they print plays. A printed play may of course be used as a memento of a pleasurable evening in the theatre—*used* but scarcely *evaluated*. This is hard on the critic. Confronted with a printed play he has little excuse for airing his knowledge of actors, electricians, designers, directors, producers and box-office managers. The only man to be praised or blamed is the man who on Broadway is happily protected or unhappily buried by all these: the author. Let us consider some current authors in inverse order of merit.

(2)

Oscar Hammerstein deserves first place on any such list. His work *Oklahoma!* (the exclamation mark is his own) has been "hailed" as a new genre, praised in at least one literary quarterly, awarded a Pulitzer Prize by special dispensation, and not unfavorably compared with *The Magic Flute*. It is probably the outstanding theatrical success of the war; and it is entirely representative of current trends. In fact it belongs with the new Americanism in being folksy and so damned wholesome; and also in being trite, cocksure, sentimental and vacuous. On the stage the thing is decked out in gay color and from time to time enlivened by tricky dancing. But in all drama, including musical drama, color and dancing are only embellishment; in this case the embellishment of a scarecrow. (Unlike James Agee I saw *Oklahoma!* on the stage. Anyway what Agee said about it was true. You don't have to visit the Sahara to know what it's like.)

But perhaps it is beside the point to apply any critical criteria. *Oklahoma!* came to me in an anthology edited by Bennett Cerf and Van H. Cartmell who in their foreword endorse Lee Schubert's remark that "the box office never lies."

They continue as follows: "It is fashionable to poke fun at public taste, and to hold that no really good play can be a financial success. The record, spread out on the following pages, does not support such a theory." Spread out on the following pages are the worst plays I have ever read, such as *East Lynne, Rip Van Winkle,* and *The Bat.* Of their three most recent choices—*Life with Father, Arsenic and Old Lace,* and *Oklahoma!*—the editors write: "That they are, from any viewpoint, the soundest and most thoroughly representative of their type is an encouraging augury to lovers of the theatre." Consequently: "American playwrights and American audiences can face the future with high hopes and light hearts." No voice more authentically philistine has been heard since Matthew Arnold cited a Victorian's prayer that "our unrivalled happiness may last." With light hearts and heavy purses the 100% American playwrights and the 100% American audiences are to enjoy the best of all possible theatres. The box office never lies, and when asked how good these three plays were it replied with aplomb: Two million dollars apiece.

(3)

To move from Hammerstein to S. J. Perelman and Ogden Nash is to move one rung up the cultural ladder. But only one. If *Oklahoma!* is Broadway's idea of folk art, *One Touch of Venus* is Broadway being oh so sophisticated. If the word folksy connotes the adulteration of the folk spirit, our current understanding of sophistication implies an adulteration of the comic spirit. The sophistication of *One Touch of Venus* is the cleverness of the half-educated. It is crudity ill-concealed by quasi-refinement. It is a guffaw suppressed to a snigger. *One Touch of Venus,* as the title alluringly hints, deals with sex or rather, to retain the original metaphor, it touches on sex, and nothing reveals its character more than than the way it fingers Venus without coming to grips with her. Nothing in the realm of humor is more acceptable than bawdry; nothing to my mind is less acceptable than the Broadway sophistication which pleases old ladies by avoiding outspokenness and at the same time titillates young ladies by cowardly insinuations. You may find it funny to hear a woman sing:

> *Venus found she was a goddess*
> *In a world controlled by gods*
> *So she opened up her bodice*
> *And equalized the odds.*

But the very next stanza tells us:

> *Look what Beatrice did to Dante*
> *What Dubarry did to France*
> *Venus showed them that the pantie*
> *Is mightier than the pants.*

And after that there are forty more lines of it. As to Mr. Perelman's prose, it consists of humor on this order:

RODNEY: *You're practically naked! I can see your—*form!
VENUS: *Don't you like my—*form?

The idea is to mention sex as often as possible because sex is very funny but not to call anything by its name because that wouldn't be very nice. Perelman, Nash, and their audiences (not forgetting Kurt Weill who used to be a musician) are nothing if not knowing. Why, they even know who Dante and Beatrice were.

Which brings me to a second point about *One Touch of Venus*—the nature of its burlesque. Burlesque and parody may be aimed at the most august object, but they must imply an understanding of the object. Unhappily we get the impression that Perelman and Nash and the kind of audience they address do not. The humor of

> *Giotto and Watteau*
> *Were obviously blotto . . .*
> *Cezanne and Modigliani*
> *De-glamorized the human fanny*

betrays, not quite intentionally perhaps, that hostility to culture which is a leading theme, overtly or not, of New York wit. The audience recalls having heard those queer French and Italian names in college (this audience is very collegiate) and how silly they sound when shown up by artists whom the veracious box office approves! The burlesque humor of Perelman and Nash is polysyllabic and allusive in form; its gist, its ground base, is a bronx cheer to culture.

(4)

On the next rung of the ladder we find plays in which some attention is paid to certain perennial tasks of the drama such as telling the the truth about people's lives and problems. My specimen is a play which has been called "the most important event in our native American drama in twenty years," *Anna Lucasta* by "an extremely successful writer in Hollywood," Philip Yordan. Mr. Yordan doesn't always tell the truth (he isn't a box office) but he does take a look at people and their problems. A Harlem family plans to get the money of a young Negro just arrived from the South by marrying him off to one of their number who has hitherto been a prostitute. Being one of those soulful whores she falls in love with the boy in earnest. The wedding day arrives but before nightfall the father has revealed the whole story of Anna to the boy's family. In despair Anna returns to her whoring without waiting to consult her bridegroom. A tragic ending is indicated. But Mr. Yordan learnt all about endings in Hollywood. The public, which after all is barely one remove from the box office, demands happy ones. Clearly the hero of the play has to be soulful too. He must still want to marry Anna in spite of everything, and her attempts at suicide must fail. The play ends on the proverbial note of hope.

It would be no use telling Mr. Yordan it won't do. He knows it will. He knows the truth from the one who never lies. A critic called the play "a combination of *Anna Christie* and *You Can't Take It With You.*" And what a combination that is! All the pleasures of the sordid with no morbid, mournful, modernistic, conclusion. And can Mr. Yordan write slick dialogue? A machine couldn't do it better. And does Mr. Yordan love the Negro people? His original choice was a Polish-American milieu but, says the jacket, "eventually he was persuaded to shift the locale to Harlem." And can Mr. Yordan see the importance of persuasion? Negroes are lovable. They're nasty too, and you can put coarser words in their mouths than

Broadway would otherwise accept. And they're always marrying prostitutes. Oh yes, Mr. Yordan knows the truth.

(5)

On the next rung is Franz Werfel. He knows more about life than Mr. Yordan and probably wouldn't tell so many deliberate lies about it; his specialty is not deceiving others but deceiving himself. Werfel is therefore the first author so far mentioned who might conceivably be considered highbrow. By some he is still considered an artist. He is one of the few living writers whom professors in German Departments have heard of. A long time ago he wrote a play about a monster, which, being unrealistic, invited highbrow attention and settings by arty designers. Werfel was once known for such lyrics as the one that opens: "My only wish is to be related to Thee, O Man!" Today he is known for *Song of Bernadette, Embezzled Heaven*, and a philosophical work which *The Nation* did not allow me to ignore last fall.

The Werfel play of the times is *Jacobowsky and the Colonel*, adapted to Broadway by Mr. Behrman, who is obviously cut out for the job, and now published in a professorial translation which shows that Werfel is not much worse than Behrman. The printed play adds to the Broadway version, if my memory serves me, a symbolic interpolation of St. Francis and the Wandering Jew, two gentlemen whom Mr. Werfel loves to pose as. Adapted or restored, acted or printed, it is a dreadful play. Only the subtitle—*Comedy of a Tragedy*—is apt, for one is embarrassed throughout by all this fooling and footling in the midst of death. I never would have thought—till I witnessed it—that an audience could so enjoy the fall of France.

(6)

On the next rung—if I may blaspheme against the box office—come two writers whose most recent works have either failed on Broadway or have not appeared there at all: William

Saroyan and J. B. Priestley. For all the evident differences between them these two playwrights are fundamentally of the same caliber. Equally energetic, talented, missionary, they are faced by the same dilemmas, the dilemmas of the middlebrow, the dilemmas of the writer who is gifted but not supremely gifted, the man who, being a small artist, knows he might be a large entertainer, the man whose seriousness is all too easily compromised by his knowledge that he will reach a broader public if he is not *too* serious.

Saroyan tries to sell his stuff by direct self-advertisement and by disclaiming high intentions. "*Get Away Old Man*," he writes, "is an American play and nothing else. It was conceived, written, and produced solely to entertain." It closed after thirteen nights on Broadway. In presenting to the American public four recent plays, none of which Broadway has produced, J. B. Priestley takes the opposite line of protesting that "New York deliberately prefers to produce what is left of our [i.e. British] drawing-room stuff instead of bolder and more original work." Obviously both Saroyan and Priestley wish to be at once entertaining and artistic, and nothing could be more laudable if, in their desire to please everybody, they were not ignoring the cultural stratification of modern society —the rungs of our ladder. This is no mere error in their publicity. It is a mistake that vitiates most of their work. If a certain earnestness prevents them from stepping down to the lowest rungs of the ladder, a fear of minority culture, a yearning to be taken to the bosom of the public, limits their thinking and their sensibility. Occasionally, as in the movie *The Human Comedy*, Saroyan does step down to the lowest rungs. And when he hops back into place he is bewildered and unsure: his latest play even has a bitter ending! But all Saroyan's work is flabby inside, sentimental at the center, because he is in his work a moral and aesthetic coward. Choices are refused. Distinctions are obliterated. All substance melts into the ocean of sentiment. "The whole world's gone mad," says the protagonist in *Get Away Old Man*, "and no man knows who is innocent or guilty." What a staggering lie! To know nothing, according to Saroyan, is also to forgive everything.

Priestley finds what may be the only exit into speculation

that is open to this class of philosophers: occultism. In the early thirties he wrote phoney plays about eternal recurrence as expounded by the egregious J. W. Dunne. Today he offers us a play about "an extra-sensory or second-sight relationship" and three socio-political plays calculated to make you what New Yorkers are now calling "PM happy." They lack a dialectic of ideas and of artistic structure. They might almost be by J. Donald Adams. Priestley also is the kind of man who has his picture taken with a pipe in his hand.

Saroyan and Priestley are the two prime instances in the dramatic world of highbrows trying to be lowbrows without losing caste. Hence their exaggerated hominess, their forced simplicity, their patriotism and insistent local color, their chronic fear of the esoteric. It is interesting to note what comes of their attempt to speak to everybody on everybody's behalf: they speak to the lower middle classes (socially *and* culturally speaking) and they express the lower middle class mentality.

(7)

Sean O'Casey's proper place is on the top rung of the ladder. Today, however, his foothold is not so sure and occasionally he lowers at least one foot to a rung below. Lest anyone suspect that I consider O'Casey corrupted by "Stalinism," I had better admit that his reported editorship of the London *Daily Worker* is to me neither here nor there. Indeed it is regrettable that his American publishers have too timorously omitted to bring out *The Star Turns Red* (London, 1940), O'Casey's best play since *Within the Gates* and probably the best Communist play in English. Instead they have given us *Purple Dust* (1942) and *Red Roses for Me* (1944).

Both plays are full of good things. The former abounds in an unforced humor that puts to shame both the folksy and the sophisticated schools of Broadway. Even the somber *Red Roses for Me* contains such exquisite characters as little Eeada who comes in carrying a statue of the Virgin Mary and quietly asks: "Could you spare a pinch or two of your Hudson's Soap, Mrs. Breydon, dear, to give the Blessed Virgin a bit of a wash?" For the rest, the play is another projection of O'Casey's staple subject: Dublin. This statement is the key to its strength and its weakness. Its strength lies in familiar O'Casey virtues—rich dialogue, strong situation, deeply-felt characters, stark contrasts of mood and texture. The weakness of the piece is its failure to exist in its own right: it is made up of pieces of the O'Casey we already know.

In fact it might be said of all O'Casey's later plays that they indicate no clear line of development, only the occasional introduction of a new technic, new plots, a re-grouping of elements, a more emphatic doctrine. The bad judgment of W. B. Yeats, known to all who consult *The Oxford Book of Modern Verse*, was also responsible for O'Casey's rejection by the Abbey Theatre. In England he has found Communism but not a new art. One cannot welcome his turning to autobiography. His *recherche du temps perdu* is inhibiting his development. In this vein he is not a Proust; the sentimentalist, always latent in him, comes to the fore; in *Red Roses for Me* his prose poetry becomes verbiage.

Or do I pick on O'Casey unfairly? What has *any* dramatist achieved since 1939? The artistic theatre has always led a dog's life, but for some time now it has hardly existed at all, except possibly in Ireland where O'Casey is no longer welcome.

(8)

Devotees of the drama probably have a pretty clear notion of the course of dramatic history in recent decades. The years 1880–1914 saw the most significant crop of plays since Schiller if not since Molière. In the years 1919–1933 these plays were splendidly produced, especially in Germany and Russia, along with new plays along lines which the earlier generation had laid down. The last dozen years have not been so creative. Fascism has swept the continent; Socialist Realism produced no important dramatist in Russia; in England and America there were minor experiments in social drama and poetic drama. Of course the cry of a theatrical renascence was raised. It always is. But where is Clifford Odets today? Where is the

Federal Theatre? The last war, someone will say, introduced a lively decade of theatre, why shouldn't this one? The answer, I feel, is that the last war was immediately preceded by Ibsen and Strindberg on whose steam the next generation could forge ahead. Between the generations such a man as Max Reinhardt was an essential link. This time the links, or most of them, have been broken. The most one can say is that the theatre at present fulfills the first pre-condition of renascence. It is dead.

The Old Vic, the Old Critics, and the New Generation

When the Old Vic visited New York in 1946,
VIEW *commissioned this review.*

THE "RAVE NOTICES" of *Henry V* in *Time* and *Life* and a pompous publicity campaign conducted by Theatre Incorporated invited us to expect everything of the Old Vic. But after the scramble for tickets came the evenings in the huge, ugly, foetid theatre. The building which Theatre Incorporated chose contained all too many seats, for even on row three one couldn't hear everything. One associates discomfort, inconvenience, and every sort of embarrassment with "highbrow" theatre; and Theatre Incorporated was not going to disturb one's preconceptions.

Performances prepared for an intimate London theatre could not be wholly successful in that barn. Especially if the performances were not perfect in the first place. The Old Vic Company has intelligence, seriousness, honesty, and two of the best actors of our current stage. What it lacks is training as an ensemble. Some of the supporting cast will never be good enough; one must attribute their inclusion in the company to manpower shortage. Others need years of discipline. More than any other single thing the Old Vic needs a directorial genius—a Stanislavsky, a Reinhardt, or rather a man who will have the same relation to our generation as Stanislavsky and Reinhardt had to theirs. For the chief lack in all the Old Vic productions is coordination. This is not simply a technical lack, something that could be made good by altruism and drill. It is a hiatus at once personal and intellectual: a lack of a leader and a lack of a philosophy. Of course an absence of overall interpretation might be considered a merit in an age when interpretation means finding the class-war in Schiller or the *front populaire* in Shakespeare. Certainly there is something fine in the naturalness of these British actors; nothing they do can ruin the play for us; and in these days that is a lot to be grateful for. But obviously it is not everything. One craves a more complete theatrical experience. Some critics have located the deficiency in a particular spot—in the feeble music, the characterless decor, the merely decent costumes. All these are part of the same trouble. Richardson and Olivier are playing a double concerto for a middling orchestra with no conductor.

This must be admitted. But there is a great deal more to be said about the visit of the Old Vic to these shores. For one thing the secret leaked out that *dramatic criticism no longer exists.*

Earlier in the year Irwin Shaw, Maxwell Anderson, and their friends had established without much difficulty that the theatre reporters of the dailies know nothing about drama. That has been obvious for a long time and is not what I mean. One looks for dramatic criticism not to the dailies but to the weeklies and monthlies. And twenty years ago one would have found good stuff there from the pens of Stark Young, Joseph Wood Krutch, and George Jean Nathan. Today the same names appear in the same magazines but they have obviously been inherited by other people, weary, bored people. (Who would not be weary and bored after twenty-five years of Broadway?) The spryness and verve of the critics of the twenties has fled into the brains of the anonymous philistines of *Time* and the egregious Mr. Wolcott Gibbs of *The New Yorker*. Now if to be civilized were only to cloak one's barbarism in the sheep's clothing of a dilettante, Mr. Gibbs would be a better critic than Walter Winchell or Burton Rascoe. Some people like Mr. Gibbs because he ridicules many bad plays. The trouble is that he ridicules good ones too. In fact his special contribution is an attempt to legitimize philistine prejudice. "Why pretend to like what even the smartest critic of the smartest magazine doesn't pretend to like?" Sophocles, Shakespeare, Chekhov, the kings of stageland? Who's frightened of *them?* The middlebrow shares with the middle-class a passion for regicide.

So far as I could discover, the only accounts of the Old Vic that were thoroughly worth reading were Stark Young's. Mr. Young has standards and he describes acting better, perhaps, than any other critic of this century. It is hardly necessary to say he likes Chekhov. The point is that he brushes off the Old Vic's Chekhov in a couple of paragraphs. The point is he seems bored nowadays not only by bad performance but by the theatre itself. Now a critic is not entitled to dislike his medium. Nor to be wholly reminiscent and nostalgic. "Things were different in my day" is the unwritten corollary—well, not always unwritten—of nearly every statement Mr. Young makes about the theatre. Let us grant Mr. Young's corollary. What follows? That every performance is to be matched against the Moscow Art Theatre, every actress against Duse? By no means. A dead actress is very dead and should be left to rest in peace. One must see present-day performances in the context of the present day. One must be interested in the future more than in the past of acting. The theatre is a very contemporary institution, and the theatre critic must be a very contemporary person. In a sense he must be more a propagandist than a sage, more a journalist than a philosopher. He is not primarily interested in distributing the prizes among the actors, in evaluating their work under the aspect of eternity. He is concerned to encourage what is best in the present in the hope that in the future it will be yet better. Better than Duse, better than Garrick, better than Burbage? These are questions one must leave to God.

The Old Vic performances were the most important event on Broadway for some years; and upon our recognition of the importance of such things depends the immediate future of

New York theatre. To listen to the "critics," however, you would suppose they were in the habit of seeing better productions every day of the week. Mr. Gibbs is patronising about Shakespeare though respectful towards *State of the Union:* and is there not a similar contradiction in better critics? They grumble at the fact that so much theatre is fourth-rate and are accordingly willing to praise the third-rate. When, however, something second-rate comes along they remember all they learnt at school and attack it for not being first-rate. Now, if, as I believe, theatre criticism should be politics, not metaphysics, this is very bad politics indeed. Those who carp at the Old Vic to the point of making them appear inferior to ordinary Broadway are actually discouraging one of the best current efforts to raise the theatre above the moronic level. And theatre criticism has no more urgent function than to encourage the good.

Someone will retort that my own position is also dubious, being a defence of the second-rate. This is a misunderstanding. I defend the second-rate not as something to which I am reconciled but as a necessary step from the third-rate. If we are again to have in the world theatre as good as Stanislavsky's it will come only through such groups as the Old Vic Company. Mr. Olivier has done much third-rate work—witness his Hollywood movies. He is now doing work which is next door to the very best. Whether he and his colleagues stay on their present track depends largely on the reception they get and, since they are artists, not only on the public reception but on the critical reception. For an artist needs reputation among the expert even more than flattery from the ignorant. Encouragement is surely in order.

What went wrong? For some years the theatre has been (except commercially) dormant. As dramatic art declined, dramatic criticism—necessarily perhaps—disappeared. And today it is a lost art. The Old Vic walked into a vacuum: no theatrical culture, no trained audience, no critics. They were saved partly by commercial advertising and partly by the as yet unshaped, undirected desire which a new generation has for drama. In this desire lies a possible future. No doubt Theatre Incorporated, The American Repertory Company, and the

National Theatre Conference all have their eyes on it. I wish them luck; and hope that all three of them will become a hundred times more adventurous than they are at present. Of these non-commercial ventures of today one has to fear not so much that they will be small and weak as that they will be large and vulgar and hard to distinguish from the highbrow end of Broadway (consider, for instance, The Theatre Guild and The Playwrights' Company).

But this is to extend my theme beyond the critic's powers to mend or mar. Within my own sphere what I am asking for is a "new criticism" of the theatre. And as to its newness I want to stress here not so much new principles (which I have elsewhere adumbrated) as a new climate, the climate of a new generation. Doubtless we are the poorer for not having seen Duse, as our fathers were the poorer for not having seen Macready; but we must spend no time regretting it. There can be no *continuous* criticism of acting in that sense, since each generation is limited to its own exhibits. The task of the critic of acting is to recognise the *contemporary* best, and that only.

It remains to credit the Old Vic in America with several good deeds. They gave the young generation the chance to see several great plays for the first time. They proved Yeats' version of *King Oedipus* to be a stage-masterpiece that communicates the full tragic experience to a modern audience. (It is of curious interest that this, the messiest of the Old Vic productions, was not English in inspiration, as some complained, but French, being directed by Copeau's pupil, Michel Saint-Denis.) They revived one of the finest of many forgotten modern masterpieces, *Uncle Vanya*, and gave a performance that was at least better than the usual Broadway Chekhov. (Miss Cornell will never consent to be anything less than a princess in any role, thus glamorizing, vulgarizing, destroying Chekhov's "scenes from country life.") Although the Old Vic did not quite present Chekhov's play (nearly every main character was slightly wrong) they presented *a* play that, unlike most Chekhov productions, had other qualities besides a wistful atmosphere, that, in fact, had both delicacy and force.

The Old Vic's production of *Henry IV*, I and II, along with Mr. Olivier's film of *Henry V*, suggests a final note on the quality, the limitation, and the promise of the present Company. Both play and film are mainly meritorious. Theirs are the sterling, primary virtues—the virtues of forth-rightness and respect for the playwright. As for the film in particular, it is legitimate to point, as Delmore Schwartz has done, to the conflict between a medium primarily auditory and a medium primarily visual. Yet a more meanacing thing seems to me to be that Mr. Olivier found a method for the filming of this play that cannot wisely be applied to any other work of Shakespeare: the fooling, the vaudeville, the picture-post-card effects that are delightful in *Henry V* would be offensive in any play that we regard more seriously. Taken as a pattern, this will be a disastrous move. Taken as something enjoyable in itself, taken as a *jeu d'esprit,* it is very acceptable. Is not the same true of the stage *Henry IV?* It is a great experience to see both parts of this play performed competently by the many and brilliantly by the two virtuosi. But the play feels as badly as any the Old Vic's lack of mature and comprehensive interpretation. They made nothing of the civil war, which after all is a chief subject of the play. They spoke their lines and left the rest to Shakespeare. In short the Company is still in an inchoate state as an artistic ensemble. Its achievement has been to re-create a serious interest in drama under the extraordinarily difficult conditions of wartime London. Whether this achievement is to be merely a tiny chapter in the history of the Second World War or a creative page in the history of dramatic art depends not only on the Company but on the new postwar generation.

The war is over. Whatever is in store for us next year or the year after, this year is ours. The theatre is active again; here and there, creatively active. These are the more pertinent facts. The additional fact that the critics of the lost generation have now so little to say will dismay us only if we lack the courage to accept it as a challenge.

Barrault: A Dialogue

Though I had resigned as dramatic critic of The New Republic *in 1956, I agreed to review the New York visit of the Barrault-Renaud Company in the following year.*

A. . . . . Even the choice of plays for the New York visit was not the happiest. The only masterpiece on the list—*The Misanthrope*—is pure dialogue and, as such, accessible only to those who respond to every nuance of the French—

B. The *only* masterpiece?

A. *Volpone* was a masterpiece till Zweig and Romains got hold of it. This French version—

B. But all translations—

A. They didn't have to bring us translations. In any case, this isn't one. Romains was quoted in a press-release as saying that it was left to the modern playwright to complete what Ben Jonson had merely begun. Zweig and Romains ruined *Volpone* by presuming to improve on it.

B. Yet you enjoyed the movie.

A. It was a good movie; and I take the Word to be less important in movies than in theatre; certainly, one was able to accept it on its own terms, and one of the chief holes in the script was filled by the awesome presence of Louis Jouvet.

B. The character of Mosca a hole?

A. In the modern version, yes. At any rate he is unintelligible. The adaptors seem forever on the brink of releasing some secret about him. It was Jouvet's achievement to conceal the fact that they had no secret to release. This Mosca always seemed to be having his own thoughts, and even misgivings, though actually all that was involved was that Zweig and Romains couldn't take Ben Jonson's moral severity. They wished to be sophisticated and replace the accusing finger by a shrug of the shoulders. Though the worser villain, Volpone, is bundled off into beggary, the lesser one, Mosca, remains to enjoy a perpetual carnival! This surely is Viennese whipped cream instead of the full Mermaid wine, Parisian pinchbeck instead of Jonsonian gold—

B. One of Romains' own plays would have made a much better choice, to be sure. But contemporary French drama *was* represented—with *Nights of Wrath*. Salacrou's arrival on Broadway is surely overdue.

A. They should have done his *Unknown Woman of Arras*— earlier Salacrou but less dated. *Nights of Wrath*, after all, is standard Front Populaire melodrama—with the hero, *of course,* on our side, and the coward, *of course,* dickering with the enemy.

B. Why not say it is a play about a brave man and a coward? And surely there is drama in the fact that two seemingly "grey" average men turn out, in a crisis, to be, respectively white and black? One can't extend one's disapproval of fel- low-travelling into a veto on all political plays of the familiar pattern. Besides, that pattern is not the main thing here. The little scene between husband and wife, when they try to face the appalling situation of having a violent Résistant in their house, is exquisite macabre comedy. . . .

A. One little scene, yes. But in many big scenes, Salacrou is lost in a fog of Germanic Expressionism. Actors step to the footlights and appeal oracularly to the gallery. Walls come and go like ghosts. Lights flash unexpectedly on and not so unexpectedly off. Barrault gets his modern political hero mixed up with the ghost in *Hamlet:* look where he strides!—

B. A greater contemporary was also represented: Claudel.

A. A greater lyric poet, but hardly any sort of dramatist. The absence of poetry from the modern stage in general enables every poet who tries the drama to get much more credit than he deserves. Eliot is one example, and Claudel is another. And Barrault chose perhaps the worst of all the latter's plays: *Christopher Columbus.* As a compliment to America, natu- rally. I don't suppose Spanish-Americans have ever been paid such a compliment before, as Claudel assumes that it was the Aztecs who behaved barbarically to the Spaniards and not vice versa. The master idea of the play—that Columbus' motive for

exploration was religious in general and Catholic in particular
—is not only inaccurate but ridiculous. It also has no drama in
it, as witness the silly scene between Columbus and his men
when, in effect, he tells them not to worry about starving to
death as, several centuries later, there'll be a Cardinal Spellman.

B. The form is interesting.

A. The form, again, is Germanic, and Expressionistic. Yes:
and dated. Cinematic interludes—the orchestra wandering
across the stage—spoken choruses—sung choruses—bare stage
—Rodgers and Hammerstein did it all in a musical.

B. Is that bad?

A. These things were interesting as novelties, and now the
novelty has worn off.

B. I enjoyed the show—not because this or that device was
used—I enjoyed the way the actors—

A. Let's finish, first, with the writers.

B. You will tolerate Lope de Vega?

A. Gladly. But "George Neveux, *after* Lope de Vega" is
another matter. And that is how the author of *Dog in the
Manger* is billed. This was Lope de Vega romanticized, moder-
nized, Gallicized, Parisianized.

B. Lope's play presents problems.

A. Which were not solved but side-stepped. It seems to me
that the interesting things in Lope are precisely the baffling and
outrageous things which in this production have been removed. Particularly outrageous are classic Spanish morals.
The heroine of this play proposes dropping the hero's servant
down a well once he has served his turn; and the hero makes
no comment. Such are classic Spanish morals. The passage, of
course, has been cut by M. Neveux. He has softened Lope
more than Zweig and Romains softened Jonson. Even the
main plot is not left intact: Lope's hero plays fast and loose
with a girl who loves him, whereas M. Neveux' girl does not
love him. And again—

B. And again I had the time of my life.

A. You liked the acting.

B. It is time to speak of that. But that is not all I mean.
Though I agree that Lope's play, performed in its integrity,

would be outrageous, I am not sure it would be enjoyable. Audiences—unlike some readers—do not like being baffled; and if a director has been baffled by a script, it is hard to believe he will put anything on stage but incoherence. Granted that something is lost whenever you "adapt," this is a script that would never reach the boards unadapted. I agree that the result was utterly French. But even faithful translations become utterly French when staged by Frenchmen. If by temperament, my dear A, you are a purist, you would undoubtedly be happier away from the theater.

A. The commercial theatre—

B. Any theatre. Lope's, for instance. No man committed himself more wholeheartedly to the impurity of theatre than Lope. He would gladly have made his two thousand and first play out of Neveux' adaptation of *Dog in a Manger*.

A. Let me attack one more play on M. Barrault's list: Giraudoux' *Intermezzo*.

B. Is *that* Germanic and Expressionistic?!

A. It certainly has some of the faults of German Expressionism: when we think we have to do with persons, we find we have principles on our hands. The character of Isabelle is nice as an idea, but turns out to be *merely* an idea. And the chief "dramatic situation" of the play is her choosing between two other ideas—also parading as characters.

B. True character, surely, is achieved in certain scenes. I find the Supervisor a well-defined and amusing character—

A. Again: certain scenes. Again: one character. Such achievements only make matters worse, for, instead of being consistently abstract and allegorical, the play wobbles disastrously between two modes, two worlds.

B. That would not be so if the role of Isabelle were rightly cast.

A. Then why is the role *never* rightly cast? I have seen the play in French, English, and Italian, and each time saw Isabelle "miscast." I conclude there is something wrong with the role itself: namely, that, though the idea is clear and sounds theatrical, the lines and situations do not permit an actress actually to give it theatrical expression.

B. I found the Barrault production successful wherever the

individual actor showed sufficient talent: Barrault as the Ghost, Desailly as the Supervisor, Bertin as the Inspector . . .

A. As we are now discussing performance, let me say that the weakness of the Barrault ensemble, as an ensemble, was nowhere more apparent than in *Intermezzo*. There simply weren't enough good actors to go around. The Mayor and the Druggist would have been much better played by a dozen American actors I could mention—not only On, but Off, Broadway.

B. You must concede the method of repertory: which is to give everyone a chance. The star sometimes takes a smaller role, the supporting actor a larger one . . .

A. With calamitous consequences. Mlle. Valère is little more than a well-trained pupil, she has neither the radiance nor the talent for a leading role. And though there must be leading roles which M. Bertin could play to perfection, Volpone is not one of them. He lacks the violence, the crude sexuality, the vulgarity. Nor was M. Desailly able, like Jouvet in the film, to make the modern Mosca interesting.

B. But then, most of the leads were played by M. Barrault and Mme. Renaud.

A. If only that thought were more reassuring! But M. Barrault is an unorthodox actor rather than a great one. Sometimes, as in his Hamlet of the last visit, he is, more than anything else, eccentric. Other times—in straight roles, as in movies and the modern, more realistic plays—he is straightforward but negative almost to the point of dullness. He is cold, and he is unspontaneous; as a result, you never sense a live relationship between him and another actor, for live relationships are warm, and—

B. Now you go too far. And, in fact, your whole analysis seems rather that of a prosecutor than a critic: you have listed all possible grounds of complaint to the total exclusion of everything else. To start where you ended—

A. Where I was interrupted.

B. I grant a high degree of idiosyncrasy in M. Barrault, a coolness of temper, and a limitation in range. But within his limits, he is superb—and his best parts in the present repertoire do not require him to transcend those limits. The word

cool is misleading. Though I don't care for M. Barrault's way
with the tender emotions—he merely descants on them—he
can render the heat of Alceste's irascibility admirably and
make you realize to what an extent Molière was presenting the
traditional Choleric Man, though in the untraditional character of an intellectual. It remains possible to find something
noble and heroic in Alceste, as Eliante puts it, precisely because he makes his mistakes, not in chill, calculating, Pharisaic
pride, but in transports of rage. In the cause of rationality he
is forever losing his reason.

A. He is also supposed to feel tender emotion for Célimène.

B. You wisely say: supposed to. How tender the emotion
really is I don't know. Barrault did contrive to suggest a
tenderness at moments—squeezed in, as it were, between the
lines. And isn't that all the text would justify? The words
themselves are chiefly railing, which is Célimène's just complaint. The erotic undercurrent in that railing is something
Barrault *was* able to suggest. The particular kind of love scene
which is Act Four, Scene Three, *was* his kind of thing, for the
tenderness is held at arm's length, while the emotions in the
center are such as he can fully express: fury, bafflement, suspicion, woundedness, forlornness . . . I don't recall any other
production in which this scene became, as it should, a full
emotional climax.

A. Barrault is not one of the great Alcestes. At the outset, it
is not the melancholy *homme aux rubans verts* one sees, it is a
famous mime and mannequin who proceeds to jump a foot in
the air to show he is angry. Aimé Clariond at the Comédie
Française—

B. That leap is almost the only "eccentricity" of a performance remarkable for its seriousness and restraint, a performance, too, in which Barrault does what you say he cannot do—

A. I deny it.

B. Namely, enacts a live relationship with a partner. Critics
have said what a stroke of genius it was to confront a "misanthrope" with a coquette. The confrontation of M. Barrault with
Mme. Renaud—whom, by the way, you have studiously avoided
mentioning—is a phenomenon scarcely less felicitous.

A. Madeleine Renaud is a different matter.

B. Exactly. And the difference constitutes a polarity that animates that whole magnetic field which is the stage. Their qualities are complementary: the one cool, if you will, the other warm, the one reserved, self-contained, making people, as it were, come to him, the other frank, dependent, going to people to help or to be helped.

A. You mean he is a man and she is a woman.

B. I mean·they give to maleness and femaleness, and the polar relation between them, theatrical expression. I mean that, when he works with Mme. Renaud, M. Barrault's limitation is no disadvantage. On the contrary, it serves to give his acting sharper definition. And what he does not have is supplied by her. To see such a partnership is one of the rarest pleasures of theatre-going. And there is no substitute for it. For while such a pair may "simply be interpreting" the lines of Molière the life of their relationship as it exists on stage cannot be found in the book. It begins and ends with this glance, that smile, a sudden turn on the heel, a touch on the shoulder; it can be prolonged only in the shadow-world of memory.

A. I've said nothing against *The Misanthrope* except that you'd have to know French to follow it.

B. But *Dog in the Manger* was also "carried" by the great partnership. You see the aim of Neveux as being to ruin Lope. I see it as being to provide great scenes for Barrault and Renaud—a high enough ideal for any playwright. What is more delightful than the sense of a current flowing between two actors, now in a trickle, now in flood, and never the same for two seconds together? The Lunts have given us such experiences. But I suppose no actors who came together just for three weeks' rehearsal could ever do it. Necessary, perhaps, is a subtlety of relationship, as established off stage, and then, on top of it, the greatest power to externalize and project that subtlety on stage. The matter deserves looking into, for, while The Great Actors have been given a good deal of study, The Great Partners have scarcely been identified . . .

A. You proceed from the defence of two individuals to a general speculation in theatre history! Let me sum up my own position in a single statement: if one had hoped to be astonished by the Barrault visit, if one had hoped for a revelation of greatness or novelty such as the Berlin Ensemble has been providing all over Europe, one cannot but profess oneself disappointed.

B. The Company is in a position comparable to that of a Little Magazine some years after its inception. The contributors are no longer breathless with things they have been saving up to say. What they have to say is now familiar, because they have said it. So they go out of business. Or become big business. Barrault has become big business.

A. That is what is wrong. He stands for nothing any more. When he wants to give his audience something a little daring and novel, what does he do? He revives something he did before the war—such as his pantomimic representation of a horse! That the latter was also the best single item in the whole New York repertory is the clearest proof of M. Barrault's spiritual bankruptcy.

B. I see that the facts lend themselves to your interpretation, but I don't know what alternative Barrault had, or whether your terms—"standing for something," being "daring" and "novel"—really embrace the reality of the situation. Are you really saying more than that Barrault has grown older? Surely the new "daring" and "novelty," the new "standing for something," will have to come from those who are now where Barrault was twenty years ago? Or do you expect art to be progressive?

A. I don't expect at all. I report.

B. No. Your reporting is wholly dictated by expectation— disappointed expectation. I can make better claim to be a reporter because I am grateful for what I see—in proportion, that is, as it gives me pleasure. For example, *Christopher Columbus*. The script may be as inane as you say; the entertainment was entrancing. Take as small an example as the representation of waves by means of a rope across the stage which someone in the wings cracks like a whip. That has the combined subtlety and simplicity of ju jitsu. One isn't accustomed to such ingenuities. One is startled, thrilled, enchanted.

A. Then *you* go by expectation too: your expectation that this would be just another Broadway show. And you overpraise it because it isn't.

B. Some kind of touchstone is indispensable. I find mine more legitimate than yours. For isn't the point precisely that the Barraults show us a kind of work our theatre lamentably lacks?

A. You are about to preach a sermon in favor of repertory.

B. Yes—if repertory entails all that the Barraults bring us: the sense of dedication and *esprit de corps*, for instance, with which the actors in *Christopher Columbus* went to their acting, their songs, their pantomimes. It did seem to me notably preferable to the craftily imposed zest which, say, our musical comedy actors are taught to bring on stage. It is more than skin deep. On their faces one does not read a grin that has been put there by a director but expressions, sad or gay, that come from a certain corporate life, a certain faith. Some people were surprised that their productions were not more sophisticated—

A. The lighting never worked right. The scenery was not only lightweight but, at times, inadequate to so large a theatre, dingy. Many scenes had a loose, improvised quality, as if the actors were free to move as they wished.

B. To me it is a relief to get away, for once, from our chrome-plated super-showmanship. In the Barraults' work, the relation between modern performance and, say, some Spanish or Italian actors on a platform in an inn-yard is still agreeably visible. Within that unsophistication, there was room for more virtuosity than you have let me mention in this discussion. *Madam's Late Mother*, for example, which was on the same bill with the Salacrou, is a very great farce and received masterly treatment not only from Mme. Renaud, who is capable of any feminine characterization from the most noble to the most vulgar, but from a supporting player of superlative talent whom also you have not mentioned: M. Beauchamp. I overheard the comment that this farce, while wholly successful with the public, was slowly paced. *Slowly-paced yet successful:* if the Broadway approach to farce is right, how would that be possible? I do not think any merely technical explanation will suffice, unless one include under the heading of technique the fact of training and working together for years on end. This, so to say, spiritual fact of the group's togetherness amply compensates for the individual flaws you have mentioned.

A. But you can't *see* their togetherness. You can't *see* their spirit.

B. That perhaps is the fundamental issue between us—a quasi-theological one. I believe God is visible; you do not.

A. So it's a real sermon you're going to preach me. Not about repertory but about God.

B. It's a real sermon I'm going to preach you. Not about repertory but about community.

Playwright of the Fifties

This discussion of Ionesco was commissioned by the Columbia Spectator *in 1958.*

WRITING OF Charlie Chaplin and Ferdinand the Bull, the psychoanalyst Martin Grotjahn comments: "Each steadfastly refuses to accept defeat by reality . . . Reality is overcome by a denial of its existence." This helps to explain why Chaplin's attempt at a kind of social drama of the screen could never be wholly successful: it required an acknowledgment of, if not an obsession with, precisely that reality which humor denies the existence of. When, in his early films, Chaplin remained a pure humorist, the idea was: "objectively, life is dreadful, but it doesn't matter, one can triumph over its dreadfulness by becoming again like a somewhat smaller child than Christ had in mind—namely, an infant at the stage of unqualified narcissism." If one expected people to be simple, one might find it strange that such a man would turn to Marxism which, before all other philosophies, teaches that reality cannot only be confronted but transformed.

The humorist who believes that reality cannot be transformed is involved in no such contradiction, but does he do more than add to our already considerable stock of narcissistic fantasies? This depends how "good" a humorist he is, that is to say, how good an artist. Private fantasy becomes both public and artistic through the mastery of the forms. These are, of course, traditional—that is, they are public already—and in learning to use them the artist is joining himself to his ancestors. The "experimental" artist is usually the one who chooses more remote ancestors: the modernist sculptor is neo-African, and the modernist playwright imitates the *commedia dell'arte* or even Aristophanes.

In an essay in *The Evergreen Review*, Eugene Ionesco distinguishes between two kinds of advance-guards. One, by being up-to-the-minute right now, will be out-of-date by tomorrow morning; the other aims at rediscovering timeless truth and reintegrating it with what is of our time. In short, one would add, the second kind of advance-guard consists of artists; and what I have been describing in terms of form is described here by Ionesco in terms of content (which is fair enough in a realm where form and content are one). The artist delves down in the history of mankind (much as he delves down in himself and his personal history) in search of the content *and* the form—the power, as it were, and the glory. And one agrees with Ionesco that there is a particular need in our time to scrape back (as a painter might say) to the design or (as M. Ionesco does say) to find the foundations, to rediscover the pure and permanent forms. The language of painters suggests itself because in painting such things have been going on these fifty years; and, in the dance, Martha Graham has devoted her life to such rediscovery.

Now you cannot reach for the elements if you are afraid to be elementary; nor must you be surprised if, when you are very simple, you are called obscure, precious, devious, and super-subtle. The newspaper reviews of, say, *Waiting for Godot* were exactly what should have been expected. It was only when the play was done at San Quentin last fall that it was honestly listened to—and therefore understood without difficulty. (I should like to say: "See *The San Quentin News*, November 28, 1957," but should criticism be provocative?) And the New York reviews of Ionesco have run true to type.

But we should not make a martyr of him. As he says, if an

advance-guard theatre (of the right sort) has an audience of fifty a night, its necessity is demonstarted, for what could bring into being so unprofitable a little event but the supreme cause of all—spiritual need? Nor are we paying Ionesco the right sort of compliment if we suppress our doubts and reservations. When a man goes back to the beginnings, it is hard for him not to stay there. His work may well be rudimentary rather than elemental, simplistic rather than simple. In any case, all qualities have their defects, all strategies their disadvantages . . . The fragmentariness of Ionesco's work to date is not the less disappointing for being (very likely) quite inevitable. It is not that his plays *are* short but that they could not be long: they are like the first airplanes that couldn't stay in the air more than a matter of minutes.

Like a plane, a play needs the right sort of motor. Sometimes, one fears that both Ionesco and Beckett prefer the wrong sort, that they imagine their despair is itself a motor— that they do not despair of their despair. Beckett, at least, becomes a little tiresome—when (let us say) he has cried out that the world is a terrible place for the seventeen hundredth time. The impulse to retort: "Kill yourself and get it over with" is checked only by the realization that seventeen hundred cries of Help! prove that the crier isn't sinking any too rapidly. To feel despair is one thing; to say so is another; to keep on saying so yet another; while to make a reputation by saying so, to be promoted by public relations men for saying so, is to become rather a bore. And to reply that this is appropriate is only to put the cart before the horse. The aim of placing one's boredom on stage is that it might become amusing. Although both Beckett and Ionesco are opposed to doctrinaire theatre, even this opposition can be given doctrinaire expression, and *Endgame,* certainly, is limited by its author's love of his own one idea.

A comparable limitation is, I think, to be found in a couple of Ionesco's works, and notably in his play, *The New Tenant.* All that happens in this play is that a lot of furniture is brought on stage. At the end, the protagonist is completely walled in by it. This rudimentary fable would make a good nightmare, but, as an expression of Ionesco's quite remarkable mind it is notably inadequate. It is little more than a scenario for a pantomime. *But at times it is very funny.* As for instance when we are told that the protagonist's furniture is blocking not only the stairway but all the streets of Paris, not to mention the River Seine.

I have argued that the humorist who believes that reality cannot be transformed escapes the contradictions in which Charlie Chaplin is involved. The next step in the argument is that humor is the weapon par excellence of the artist who sees reality as unalterable.

Unalterable and monstrous. "The world as a whole," says one of the younger playwrights of today, "escapes my grasp. I refuse to pretend to find it in a doctrine; rather, I submit to it as pure chaos. The world—and with it the stage that presents it—confronts me as a monstrosity, a piece of riddling mischief, which must be put up with though not surrendered to." A grim statement but one which takes shape in the drama, not as tragedy (for there are no heroes and the world makes no sense), but as comedy, and not really as comedy either (for there is no civilization, no agreed set of standards, no social norm) but as farce. In farce the irrational has freer sway than anywhere else except in the Id itself where all is irrational. Reason enters into farce only insofar as the forms of a play are themselves touched with rationality and insofar, too, as humor —a release for the irrational—employs intellect as one of its tools.

Ionesco has himself used the designation Tragic Farce. That is becoming one of the key terms of contemporary drama. It is the comedy of the atomic age, the age when man sees himself as a dwarf cowering beneath the mushroom of a nuclear explosion. It was preparing itself considerably before the first such explosion did occur. What is Pirandello's *Henry IV* but such a tragic farce? The many misinterpretations of the play were provoked by the author's calling it "a tragedy" when in fact such grandeur as the play attains derives from the image of the little sufferer standing in the colossal shadow, and not from heroism struggling towards the light.

Then there is the chapter entitled: Michel de Ghelderode. This Belgian playwright, just now beginning to be known in the U.S., wrote some of the most remarkable plays of the century—most of them tragic farces—back in the twenties . . .

"Slowly I drew from my pockets my two pistols, and in silence, for two seconds, held them aimed at him. He did not flinch. I lowered them, let my arms fall. I felt myself disarmed, desperate: what could bullets—any more than my feeble strength—do against the cold hate and obstinacy, against the infinite energy of this absolute cruelty, without reason and mercy?" This is the ending of Ionesco's story "The Photograph of the Colonel." The "hero" has the chance to kill the "villain," who is a homicidal maniac, but his finger refuses to pull the trigger. A parable of the helplessness of man in a hostile universe, the story as a whole is but a minor example of Kafkaesque fiction. Such is Ionesco when his view of life is the only motor in the machine. Changing the metaphor, one might call it stillborn tragedy. A live baby is born when the sense of humor starts to play; the baby's name is Farce.

I shall not use quotation to prove the point because, though there are funny remarks in Ionesco, his fun is not essentially that of the individual remark nor yet of the brief exchange. But he has the first gift of the comic artist in the theatre— which is to create a state of euphoria in the audience. Only after that state of mind is created does theatrical fun begin.

And after it begins, in an Ionesco play, what then? When I say that humor is his salvation, I am not implying that, after failing in an important way, he succeeds in a trivial way. I believe that Ionesco's humor says more than his solemnity. It becomes a kind of theatrical poetry giving to his feelings a form and a life. His feelings and everyone else's. If you insist, you can be as baffled by *The Chairs* as by *Waiting for Godot*, and, certainly, some people have their reasons for insisting. But, in each case, if you ask simple questions of the play, you will get a simple answer. What are we confronted with? Words. What are the words about? Universal and everyday facts of human life. Almost no elemental experience does not enter in, if only by the poignancy of its felt absence.

Nor am I saying that it has been left for Ionesco to give to farce a tragic element. Farce always had a tragic element—was always, indeed, closer to tragedy than it was to "realistic

drama" or even to certain kinds of comedy. Recently I translated a farce that Courteline wrote in 1898 and was told by
friends that it "anticipates Ionesco." Farce in general anticipates Ionesco. In other words, Ionesco writes farces. Which is
no small achievement. It means that he has had the creative
force to revive a lost art. True: Ionesco's farces are tinged—
perhaps more than tinged—with the nihilism which is common to most contemporary French writing. But that may not
be without its advantages even from a non-nihilistic viewpoint. Nihilism may well have sharpened Ionesco's wits, and
thereby heightened his conflicts and produced a more dramatic result.

At any rate, Ionesco is an event in an uneventful milieu.
The theatre's doors are always open, but usually nothing of
note is going on inside. The curtain goes up every night, and it
goes up on much the same thing every night, except for one
night in ten thousand when there is a surprise, no surprise
being more surprising than a new arrival, a genuine new
talent. The nineteen twenties were lucky: Brecht, Lorca, Cocteau, O'Neill . . . In the thirties came Giraudoux and Anouilh, in the forties (less interesting theatrically) Sartre and
Camus. Ionesco is the playwright of the fifties.

The Peking Opera

*This is a newspaper article, commissioned by
Nathan Cohen for* The Toronto Star *in 1960. I
sent a copy to Adlai Stevenson at the United Nations, asking him: how about it? His answer,
signed by a secretary, had a polite form but no
content.*

THE STATE DEPARTMENT may one day explain to me why it
recognizes the existence of Franco and Khrushchev and not
that of Mao Tse-Tung. Also why it forbids the Peking Opera

to come, so to speak, and see me in New York, while permitting me to go and see it in Toronto. Well, as Brendan Behan was saying the other day: "I'll never be a politician, I've only got one face."

To Toronto, then, I came. And when I opened my program at 8.25 p.m. I was dismayed to be told that I was about to see the "visage" of the New China, the image of "the great transformations for which 650 million Chinese are working." But the Canadian tour of the "Company of Chinese Classical Theatre" had obviously been arranged by people with more than one face. To my relief, the performance did not live down to the program.

It's an old story. In Russia, there was always a lot of talk of the New Soviet Art, but what Stalin actually liked and insisted on was the Imperial Ballet. That situation bore a negative aspect because Stalin waged a cruel war on the avant garde. What happens to the avant garde in Chinese theatre—if there is one—I don't know. The Peking Opera is their Imperial Ballet, so to speak, and one that one cannot but wish preserved as long as possible.

Why? Because only by "preservation"—a better word would be Tradition—can such a form of theatre exist at all. There is little here that could be done by scratch companies such as we have in the West. It's like those English lawns that have to be rolled daily for 500 years. This is a craft which is handed down from generation to generation. Each actor must be trained from early childhood. Once such a theatre was closed, it is inconceivable that it could ever be got going again.

Why do we want it kept going? The theatre man's answer to this is that the Peking Opera is pretty much the theatre of his dreams—here become a reality. Western theatre men have dreamed of the *commedia dell'arte* ever since the decline and fall of that type of theatre in the 18th century. When we see De Filippo or Marcel Marceau we say, a little wanly: the Commedia lives again! But "wanly"—because a theatre can hardly live again in a couple of individuals! No: if *commedia dell'arte* means Total Theatre—a theatre in which the actor is not only speaker and gesticulator but singer and acrobat—the nearest that we shall ever get to it is to see the Peking Opera.

The acrobatics are amazing. But, as far as that goes, all good acrobatics are amazing. What is significant is the context of these acrobatics—the context of acting, of drama. Here is a vision—no, an actuality—of an utterly different kind of theatre from what we are familiar with. Here the actor's instrument—his own body—has been developed to the full.

So it is a thrilling experience to see these shows. And one learns a lot. Can one also say that the Peking Opera is relevant? Can any of this art be brought over onto our own stages?

It is doubtful. Is theatre really international? Oh yes, we are all full of internationalism. And good will. That's something else. The art of theatre is always rooted in a particular soil. It is transported and exported with difficulty, if at all. Even from relatively close countries. How much even of European theatre can be brought over to New York or Toronto? And both in the Kabuki Theatre and Peking Opera there are elements which one knows one never makes contact with—not just the language itself but the weirdly stylized delivery—all that shrill falsetto!

Is there anything we *can* take over? It seems to me that a certain influence may be felt, not by actors, but by writers. Which is paradoxical since the writing is the least impressive part of Chinese theatre. Nonetheless, I can't see much point in our actors studying Kabuki for a few weeks, as some are about to do in New York at the Institute for Advanced Studies in Theatre Arts. Whereas it is already a fact that Western writers have borrowed elements both of Japanese and Chinese drama and with profit. W. B. Yeats wrote Noh Plays a generation ago, and a little later Bertolt Brecht wrote both "Japanese" and "Chinese" plays.

Brecht's theatre company—the Berlin Ensemble—has shared with the Peking Opera Company what are without doubt the highest plaudits of the Paris critics and audiences at the Théâtre des Nations. Is there anything more in common between the two groups, other than their allegiance to communist governments? In view of such "Chinese" works as *The Good Woman of Setzuan* and *The Caucasian Chalk Circle*, it might be tempting to think so. Yet I *don't* think so. At no time did Brecht try to become an Oriental playwright. He merely used any feature of Oriental theatre that he could turn to use in quite a different context. Far from trying to enter into the Oriental spirit, he welcomed Oriental elements expressly for their foreignness . . .

This is another story. The conclusion of the present story should be a strong representation to the U.S. Secretary of State —Mr. Herter or his successor—to follow Canada's lead and allow the Peking Opera Company to appear in New York.

Opera in New York

This comment on the Met was commissioned by Gordon Rogoff during his brief term as editor of Theatre Arts *in 1962.*

SOMEHOW YOU MUST get there by eight, for, whatever else they are, they are not unpunctual. If it's your chauffeur's night off (it is usually my chauffeur's night off), and if there's a taxi strike, you have a sufficient excuse for taking the subway, and the subway brings you almost under the awning at Seventh Avenue and Fortieth Street. The lobby is large, and it is full: in the outside world a baby is born every minute, and here a dowager is delivered every five seconds by Bentley or Rolls-Royce. Receding chins, bulbous necks, gilded dresses on elderly harridans, and, over and about, the uniform of the nineteenth-century gentleman, black and boiled-white. Surprising how many people at the Met are too fat to walk. You see them being propelled through the lobby by solicitous relatives. If the lobby is plain and rectangular, the auditorium is glamorous, perhaps the only really glamorous auditorium left in New York. Gilding and red plush and little yellow lights on five tiers of horseshoe. One likes to look at the auditorium and it is what the designer seems to have intended one would like to look at. For sh! the curtain is going up, and the stage is hard to see. One of those bulbous necks is directly in front, bald head shining above it. So is a pillar. Or a piece of another gallery. Or one is too far to the side and can only see the wings opposite. Or one is too high up and can only see the floor, and only the front part of that. Is this also the only auditorium in New York in which every seat is a bad seat? But sh! this is the Metropolitan Opera House, it is a privilege and a pleasure to be here, the experience is talked of the world over, and anyhow, paying for the seats has just about broken the bank. Perhaps operas should be heard and not seen? But even this question rapidly becomes academic. One can hear the orchestra, oh yes, can one hear the orchestra—often all too well, and sometimes out of proportion, since one is sitting just above the brasses, but where are those golden voices (the standard here is universally a gold standard), voices that certainly sounded golden at home on the high-fi? Many of the voices really don't "come through." The auditorium is too big. The vast expanse between stage and balconies seems rather a barrier to sound than a conductor of it. Silver threads among the gold! Some voices even sound tinny. More are just faint. One has a sensation of witnessing a performance through a window—if indeed one is near enough the stage to avoid the feeling of being on another planet. Well, all this is too disconcerting to be boring —for twenty minutes or so: it takes that long to adjust to all the maladjustment. It is after that that the rot sets in. And not only into me. Also into the gilded dowagers and the fat-necked swains. Into everyone. The noise of the orchestra sweeps on, steady as that of the traffic on Seventh Avenue outside; the singers steadily if vainly strive to compete. Absurd, but you accept it. Everyone accepts it. From a cushioned chair, homo sapiens will accept anything. Homo sapiens sinks into a mood that is neither sleep nor wake, that is certainly not interest or involvement but is perhaps not utter rejection or conscious boredom. Yes, after a few minutes of latecoming and irritability, the Met audience reaches the dead center of indifference and stays there. You can feel it. You can see it. A psychiatrist might explain if this is good or bad. Is it perhaps what people need—after a hard day at the office or an easy one trying on the gilded dress or clipping the coupon? Is this state of mind perhaps the contribution of the Metropolitan Opera House to mental health? Is it not also, in all likelihood, entirely traditional? Is this not how the Emperor Joseph II felt when he heard *Don Giovanni* and told Mozart there were too many notes in it? Perhaps the Met is the last bastion of aristocratic culture. I wouldn't be surprised.

It is just conceivable, of course, that my description is slightly unfair. Let me put the case for the other side. The sleepy mood of this audience—glumly withdrawn as at most moments you can see it to be—is interrupted at almost regular intervals by the cries of a group of persons with voices louder than the singers but with vocabularies limited to a single Italian word, of which, however, they know both the masculine and the feminine form. To shout Brava! in an American theatre is a grammatical feat of some magnitude, and it is interesting to be in the audience at those moments, at least the first few times. Dowagers and swains usually seem surprised yet they don't take it amiss. They clap their hands, sometimes rather heartily. The provocation for these little interruptions is commonly an extremely high note sung very loudly, preferably (this season) by a soprano. The loudness is defensible as being in the interests of audibility, but the spontaneity of the Italian outcries is suspect, as prima donnas have been known to hire their own help. To each, her mafia. This too, however, might be justified: perhaps, even, these leading ladies wish to suggest that theatre should be a place of excitement.

The other side has an argument yet more cogent. An evening at the Met is enlivened not only by very high notes sung very loudly but by very long intermissions very amply provided for. If one attains a truly philosophic detachment, one can even regard the opera as an interruption of the intermissions, especially as these could be held to start with the two-hour dinner period, six to eight p.m., the Met being the only theatre in New York that is equipped with a restaurant. If for example one decides on *Dinner and Turandot,* one can establish the ascendancy of intermission over opera in the proportion three to two—a clear-cut victory if ever there was one—because there is less than two hours of opera, and the Met makes a break of thirty minutes between acts one and two, plus twenty-five minutes between acts two and three. The thought of operas in four acts is, in every sense, intoxicating, as the Met is the only theatre in New York that is equipped with a bar. True, the prices at this bar are double what they charge in other bars around Times Square, but what do you want? Communism? The prices of Fall Out Shelters are high too; they too are chiefly, well, for those who occupy the boxes and the orchestra at the Metropolitan . . .

As the reader will guess, I have been going to the Met this winter. If on the whole I haven't been enjoying it, who am I among so many? The Met has its clientele. Not the least of the inconveniences attendant on going there is the difficulty of finding a purchasable seat. When a theatre attracts more people than it can seat it can afford to ignore the others. Or can it? The Met runs at a loss anyway. And it does not take amiss the suggestion of Secretary Arthur Goldberg that it has a positively national significance—what it signifies having to do with the nation's spiritual life. Mr. Goldberg apparently assumes that the Met signifies spiritual strength. I challenge him to produce the evidence. Not that evidence in a field like this can have the character of courtroom facts. Still, one can explain oneself. As I myself shall try to—forthwith.

It would be surprising if one found no enjoyment at all in the Met's productions, after all the effort and expenditure that has gone into them; nor is it the case. Great music is played, after all, and the orchestra's playing nearly always gives pleasure. Some of the voices do come through. *La Forza del Destino,* for instance, is sustained largely by the voice of Richard Tucker which rises beautifully into the air (of which, at the Met, there is so much) . And precisely because of the obstacles to be overcome, one values there a majestic voice like that of Birgit Nilsson even though it is rather blankly majestic or a ringing one like that of Sandor Konya even though it rings too insistently. If I do not pursue this topic, it is not for lack of interest in the special qualities of each singer, but because this is not the issue. The issue for me is the art of opera. Singers would sing had opera never been invented. The question of opera is the question of musical drama.

I am not referring to Musik-Drama in the narrow sense, but to a conception that includes Mozart as well as Wagner, Gluck as well as Mozart. Though the composer might be imagined to be the foe of dramatist and librettist, it will be found that, in fact, the great operatic composers have all conceived opera dramatically. It is only necessary to add that they have also conceived dramas which it takes music to create. Those who think Mozart's *Figaro* better than the play of Beaumarchais should grant that Mozart, for example, fills in the Countess's character by musical means. Music has been called "the imagination of love in sound." Be that as it may, music can communicate the feeling of romantic love with a sudden power and glory not possible even to Shakespeare in *Romeo*. Some of Beaumarchais's people say they love: Mozart's people give off love in sound. So do Puccini's people, perhaps too monotonously. (As a young lady was saying at the Met the other night, he's always quoting the most romantic bits of Gian Carlo Menotti.) Still, Puccini's gift leads logically to a re-casting of the Turandot story which gives that story an organic, dramatic life which in the previous versions it had lacked. There had been no reason for the princess to change her ways from those of cruelty to those of love. In the Puccini opera, she sees another woman sacrifice herself for the same man who loves *her*. What woman could fail to respond? The happy resolution springs naturally from the unhappy contretemps. Which is dramatic.

According to a convention which serves no purpose but to stultify the operatic stage, operas consist of silly stories and lovely arias. Actually, some satisfactory operas consist of only adequate song and rather good narrative. An example from the current Met repertoire is *The Girl of the Golden West*. Others disclose their musical value when you have granted the melodramatic premise: *Il Trovatore* is a mad, splendid opera, founded on a mad, splendid story. The current exhibit of this sort is *La Forza del Destino*. Nowhere is the self-defeating character of the Met's methods more apparent. The key to this sort of story is movement. Granted that the need for rapid movement is counteracted by the need of singers to stay put when they complete some long arias, an impression of much movement must still be given. It *was* given in the not very distinguished Italian movie of the opera a couple of years ago. But the Met employs singers, not actors: it provides a dog-show for soprano-fanciers.

Some people will tell you the dramatic problem has been solved by the hiring of regular stage directors like Tyrone Guthrie and Margaret Webster. But they make no difference. Or rather, they make a difference that is not the needed one. These directors come into a few rehearsals and have everyone stand somewhere other than where they have been standing these fifty years. This is merely putting a good face on a bad body. Singing becomes operatic performance, not when the singer is moved to stage left or is forbidden to face front when embracing her lover, but when every moment in the opera is acted out as meticulously as every moment in a play is acted out. Naturally, operatic acting is going to be different, since gestures and moves have to be found for situations that never happen except in opera, especially for one situation that never happens except in opera, that the actor is singing.

In a brief exchange of letters with Mr. Leopold Stokowski, Mr. Rudolf Bing has recently declared that the Met does rehearse its operas enough. If the singers were not together with the orchestra, he went on, it was NOT for lack of rehearsal . . . But enough rehearsal for what? When I was at the Met this winter, the singers and the orchestra were together quite often, and it really didn't help much. I assume Mr. Bing is right when he says they don't rehearse any more at various other celebrated spots. The only opera house that has managed to rouse me from the Metropolitan blues (since the Glyndebourne of the thirties) is the Komische Oper in East Berlin. The Berliners apologize because the Komische cannot offer the leading singers of the operatic international set. But if they could, that would be that: Mr. Bing would be saying they don't rehearse any more than at the Met and the particular achievement of the Komische Oper would be cancelled out. This achievement is nothing less than the acting out of each moment of stage time. It entails rehearsing as a play is rehearsed: daily for many weeks, going over each tiny bit of action countless times. I do not mean to minimize the genius of the man who has led the project, Walter Felsenstein, but merely to mention a prosaic prerequisite of his enterprise.

I have been told that the Met is "at least an alternative to Broadway." There, the ornery, the brassy, the outright commercial; here, the aristocratic, the classic, the artistic. I am attracted by the idea; not by the facts. In "commercialism" are some sound principles of theatre which our operatic friends neglect at their peril. Whatever a Broadway producer does not concede, he does concede that each moment in a show has to be a live moment. Indeed, most of the faults of commercialized showmanship come from the hysterical over-charging of each moment, an attempt to make each instant a climax, an attempt that must fail since Mount Everest cannot be itself if its summit is obscured by a hundred surrounding Mount Everests. Often, those super-charged moments go dead. Still, the intention was right. Broadway producers are admirable as theoreticians; it is only in practice that they go astray. The Met has not conceded the point of principle. The drama implicit in many moments—many half-hours—is left unrealized. *La Forza del Destino,* for example, opens with a rather swift scene in which a young man tries to abduct a young woman but is discovered by her father. Forced to defend himself, he draws a revolver, and in the scuffle that ensues, the older man is killed. Enough action, in all conscience, to sustain one scene! Yet, at the Met, one is only aware of people standing around, mostly quite still and oblivious, and at a certain point the older fellow adopts a recumbent posture. No wonder the psychology of the Met audience is one of *settling back.*

I'm so glad Felsenstein employs bad singers. Actually, they aren't bad, they're just un-great enough to drive the soprano fanciers from the temple, un-great enough not to completely overshadow those colleagues who sing small roles. The effect is of a play sung, which is what the great operatic men, Mozart, Wagner, Bizet, Offenbach, Verdi, Puccini, Alban Berg, all have wanted.

East Berlin also has its Met, the Staatsoper. Perhaps there will always and everywhere be a public for this sort of thing. The oldest profession in the world, after all, is that of the soprano. But when Mr. Goldberg wishes to be very grand about the arts and the nation, he really should get to know as much about the former as I suppose he does about the latter. Why *help* the Met? Let it last just as long as there are people who wish to spend their money on it. And if that is to be the whole definition of opera in the United States, let the retreat to the phonograph and the tape-recorder continue. There is a lot to be said for high-fi. Many a singer who sounds quite horrible at the Met reveals himself as an artist with a voice on the phonograph. Even the drama can be followed better when you have libretto and translation in hand than when you vainly try in the theatre to keep up with recitative in a foreign tongue. (That's all I'll say here on the question of opera in English, except that only the Met would put *Cosi fan tutte* into English, while leaving *Tales of Hoffman* in French, considering that the latter lends itself to translation, while Da Ponte's Italian definitely does not.)

I didn't like the Martins' Broadwayish translation of *Cosi fan tutte*, but, on the whole, one can say of Met productions: the closer they come to Broadway—the supercolossal Broadway musical, actually—the more effective they prove to be. *La Perichole* may come to us stripped of real romance and also of real satire; lacking both naiveté and sophistication this is not Offenbach but it is something, and that something is produced; it is directed; it sustains interest; it amuses at all times, and at moments it delights.

The simple pleasures of the rich? Yes, and, as such, preferable to the simple boredoms of the lower middle class. If Offenbach owes little to the Met, the Met owes a lot to Offenbach. He forces these people (people on stage and off) out of their rut. If it's good that Felsenstein's singers are not the best, it may even be good that Offenbach's music is not the best: the show has to be good. And there is another factor. The incredulous contempt of modern persons for the plots of Verdi's melodramas has providentially not been extended to fantasy. The conviction which the performers totally lack in *La Forza del Destino* they possess in *Tales of Hoffman*. And, of course, the operatic stage lends itself no less to fantasy than to melodrama. As I did not see *La Perichole* this season, *Tales of Hoffman* provided the most entertaining evening I spent at the Met. If George London's voice sounds considerably less rich there than on his records, he makes up for it with a commanding actor's presence and much corporeal gusto. (Not that the director, Cyril Ritchard, is content to stop there: he must add the footling facetiousness of Mr. Alessio De Paolis— only Met audiences would accept such things as genuine comedianship.)

It is good to achieve the theatrical, and here the Met can learn, and has learned, from the Broadway theatre. But this is not to achieve the dramatic. The turning point in *Turandot* is only there in the Met production to the extent that Puccini imposes it by purely musical means. The director didn't bother about it. What is bothered about in *Turandot,* and in all Met productions which one hears spoken of in awed tones, is stage design and costume. In a recent press conference, Mr. Bing explained that he has been willing to spend from $50,000 to $100,000 on stage design and costume to improve a single production. The improvements are real. But how far can they take us? True, the bigness of the Met stage is an opportunity for a fine artist like Eugene Berman to implement his grandiose vision on an unparalleled scale, and I enjoyed gawking at the Bermanic wonders (in *La Forza del Destino*) every time the lights went up. But they got less and less interesting as each Act proceeded. They even proved to be in the way, for they dwarfed the performers.

And Berman is the best of what the Met can offer that is perfectly in line with its new intentions in visual art. It is quite a step down to Cecil Beaton. And usually (when I went) the set was by Rolf Gerard. Don't these two names say it all? The Met has had its face lifted. It has a new look. Everything is magnificent, glorious, stunning, and, more especially, gorgeous, delicious, luscious, and cute. The Met has gone in for Style, and this is Style, as we all know from the pages of *Harper's Bazaar* and the windows of Bonwit Teller. One might say of the Met managers that they think they've bought art when they've only bought *haute couture.*

(Not long ago a counter-current in stage-design was represented by Caspar Neher and Teo Otto. Otto was attacked in the *Times'* letter column as old-fashioned. The writer's more modern alternative was the style of Appia—Appia who died in 1928!—and who, with all his talent, fathered the present-day frou-frou.

I have been speaking of two things at the Met: the public and the performance. Together they make up a perfect specimen of the effete. The public: overprivileged, overfed, overconfident, exclusive, uncommitted, uninvolved. The performance: overdecorative, overinflated, overcharged, chi-chi, lush, a mere exhibition, whether of coloratura or chiaroscuro. It's the familiar phenomenon of the jaded palate and the over-spiced condiments that are used to please it. It is possible that nothing can be done except exactly what Mr. Bing is doing, in which case one can either admire him for his sense of reality, or pity him for his helplessness. But if it is inevitable that the Met be what it is, it is not inevitable that one continue to go there. Nor is it so sure that I shall lose my belief that any great theatre would have to be all that the Met is not.

A Touch of the Adolescent

O'Neill was once described by his publishers as the most widely-read dramatist after Shakespeare. However this may be, this is not the first play of his to be reviewed here as a book. The review appeared in The New Leader *in 1964.*

MORE STATELY MANSIONS [1] is a four-hour play put together by the Swedish theater man Karl Ragnar Gierow from an O'Neill manuscript which was about twice as long as that. So far as one can tell without seeing the manuscript, Mr. Gierow has done an excellent job, for one cannot tell that he has done a job at

[1] *More Stately Mansions*, by Eugene O'Neill; shortened from the author's partly revised script by Karl Ragnar Gierow, edited by Donald Gallup; Yale University Press.

all: *More Stately Mansions* seems a finished O'Neill play. In the cycle of plays which O'Neill was busy with in the '30s, it comes immediately after *A Touch of the Poet,* and resembles that play in style and substance. This is to rank *More Stately Mansions* with the finer works of its author, for in the '30s he became a better writer, less pretentious, more sincere. He drops the grandiose *kitsch* of *Strange Interlude* and *Mourning Becomes Electra* and lets his own voice be heard. It is a flat voice at times, but it has character, and in one play, *Long Day's Journey into Night,* it becomes the voice of suffering humanity, the voice of tragic drama.

More Stately Mansions is about a young man, Simon Harford, and the battle for possession of his heart that is fought by his mother and his wife. There is a corresponding battle within Simon, who is also divided in his professional aims. Having "a touch of the poet" about him, he would like to pursue the life of the spirit, and the spirit for him is directed toward the creation of the good society. But when he is challenged to show his family that he can succeed in business where they are failing, he rises to this challenge and gives up his poetry and its social ideals. Ultimately his mother withdraws into a crazy illusion of living in a pre-business civilization, while his wife accepts the cash-nexus in full knowledge of what it is, and also becomes a mother to Simon in place of his actual mother.

As O'Neill tells it, it is a haunting, blood-curdling tale. The drama is pre-eminently the art of human extremes, and O'Neill enjoys depicting extremities and piling on the agony. Conflict in his plays is invariably conflict *à outrance,* so we are not surprised that the rivalries of the wife and mother, like the resentment of Simon against now one, now the other, produce the desire, even the resolve, to kill. All of which makes for "good theater." The question is whether it makes for more than that. I would say that, like much of the work of Arthur Miller and Tennessee Williams, *More Stately Mansions* succeeds quite well as psycho-philosophic melodrama, and it is better than Miller and Williams precisely in what the Broadway crowd would find worse: it is not slick, it is not adjusted to the clientele of Sardi's and the Algonquin. If the dialogue is occasionally awkward and more than occasionally ponderous, it earns these defects by an unhurried thoroughness, an evident preoccupation with something more than the moment. O'Neill is no poet, but one can read almost any passage from *More Stately Mansions* and take pleasure in the honesty, the dignity.

So ingratiating is this dignity that for a good deal of the way O'Neill can convince us that he has more than a melodrama on his hands. There is, for example, a highly interesting element of social realism in the play. The setting is the America of Andrew Jackson's time, and O'Neill's interpretation is on the lines of some of that time's great social critics—Carlyle, Engels and Marx. Brecht himself would have admired the little scene in which a capitalist's wife, to demonstrate her new-won belief in the system, blackmails and browbeats into acceptance of the cash-nexus a representative of the pre-capitalist ideal of honor. But if *More Stately Mansions* is a thoughtful play, there are contradictions at the base of the thinking. America, it seems, is blamed for having missed the opportunity of giving humanity a fresh start and creating an earthly paradise. Yet the fact of this failure is also presented as proof that human nature is perverse and evil, in which case the opportunity to make a fresh start never existed.

The logically minded will ask which of the two mutually exclusive propositions—that man is good, that man is bad— O'Neill really believed. But the psychologically minded will be quick to observe that he believed both without knowing it, and appealed to one view or the other according to context. That he does not wish to thrash the matter out and expose his own confusion reveals itself, at times, in the dramatic structure of *More Stately Mansions*. For example, since the protagonist is to pass in the course of the play from the optimistic view of human possibility to the pessimistic one, you would expect the reversal to be a climax. Actually, it is not dramatized. The play jumps from one point to the other without presenting the change. And it does this early on, so that the hopeful attitude is hardly created at all, whereas the voice of disenchantment is heard so often it gets monotonous. (It is such an achievement for an American to overcome the official optimism of the country that he tends to think his hard-won pessimism must sound original and daring. In Europe pessimism is taken for granted, and optimism—as when a European writer joins the Communist party—is a "daring" gesture.) In other words, O'Neill's failure to "thrash the matter out" is not just a philosophic limitation but also a dramatic one. Thesis clashes with antithesis, but then there is no development forward to synthesis, only a continuation of the same clash, whence the notorious O'Neillian monotony. Some such criticism of O'Neill used to be offered in the '30s, when the critic meant that O'Neill ought to have moved forward to Communism. But dramatically speaking the forward development would not have to be any particular philosophy. A development of the plot would do, provided that the dramatist refuses to develop that plot arbitrarily, "melodramatically," and only presents such developments as he can "feel" to be truly implicit. What we come to, finally, in O'Neill is a blockage, not of thought per se, but of feeling.

It also becomes apparent *why* the positive and hopeful side of *More Stately Mansions* is too weak to sustain a fully dramatic dialectic. What is offered as a Utopia ahead was really only the image of an Eden in the rear. What is offered as a Might Have Been is actually a mere Has Been. In this play, as in so many others, O'Neill constantly recurs to the theme of the loss of specifically *adolescent* romance and optimism. The theme is an excellent one in itself, as Conrad's *Shadow Line* and a thousand other works testify. If it does not work out excellently in O'Neill it is because of this confusion between a goal that is ahead and a starting point that is behind. This confusion is itself far from arbitrary. It happens because O'Neill can *find* no goal other than the starting point. That also could be an excellent theme to treat—if it were a theme, and were treated, instead of being just a fact which the author cannot treat because he cannot stand back and look at it. In *More Stately Mansions* the protagonist, giving up political progressivism, *re*gresses instead to childlike dependence upon the mother-woman, but the sense of loss is not dramatized because the political progressivism had belonged to the same phase of being as the dependence: progress was itself regress.

The life of men and women exists on the other side of two crises, the crisis of infancy and the crisis of adolescence. Both times it is a matter of going out into a cold world, of discovering that there *is* a world to go out into, a nest to be left behind. In our society, at least, it would seem that no one surmounts these two crises with complete success, and the failure to surmount them can even be made a virtue. Particularly in art. For childhood remains more vividly alive in the artist than in anyone else. This does not prevent the great artist from also being the most "mature" (highly developed) of men at the same time. But the less than great artist may see fit to wallow in immaturity. There have been actors, praised in all sorts of other terms, whose actual appeal is their durable infantility. If they are female, their spiritual age is generally about 12, sexlessness being a part of the act. If they are male, the spiritual age is a little older than that since physical toughness is a part of the act.

By calling this sort of thing an "act" I imply that it is done to please—that there is a demand for it, an audience for it. And indeed immaturity is less important as existing in artists than as demanded by their audience. Immaturity is a cult of modern civilization as a whole—Western and, more particularly, American. From the boyish charm of actors, the mind runs on to the fact that Boyish Charm is all a man needs these days to pursue a profession—any profession. It even unites the professions, and enemies within the same profession: it is the one thing John F. Kennedy had in common with Barry Goldwater. In short, we live in a culture that does not believe in men and women but in Boys and Girls; the fashion pages of any paper or magazine are enough to prove it.

Or take Marilyn Monroe. It is true enough that she was not a traditionally glamorous woman. Her originality consisted in her not being a woman at all but a child. There was a piquancy about the asexual innocence behind the sexual provocation. And she was a child with large breasts, those much photographed breasts which almost came to replace the stars and stripes as emblems of the national allegiance. They meant sex maybe. Certainly they meant Mom. For the sweetheart of American men, taken collectively, must offer a combination of a sexless relationship with a kid sister and an incestuous relationship with Momma. And, American playwrights being as responsive to time and place as they are, Arthur Miller could hardly have been the only one who saw in Marilyn Monroe exactly what he had been looking for. Her emotional age seemed well under 20 and, most important of all perhaps, she was a misfit.

Wondering where tragedy has gone, people gravely ask if Willy Loman of *Death of a Salesman* is an adequate hero, if the little man of democracy has the requisite dignity, etc. But actually heroes have not been replaced by quiet, little businessmen, they have been replaced by big, noisy adolescents. The Teen-Ager (an American invention) is the current culture hero, and the archetypal dramatic situation of the culture is the adolescent misfit who is cutting loose a bit and is sorry for himself a whole lot. Therein lies the essence of even pseudo-American works, like *Look Back in Anger*, which contains no adult anger whatsoever, but is one long adolescent tantrum. What else can be said of Arthur Miller's actual stage presentation of himself and Miss Monroe? What *After the Fall* really shows is the adolescent male discovering sex: at first it is absolutely yummy but a little later on, girls turn out to be awful bitches, and one needs to let the world know it—loudly. A wonderfully adolescent touch in the stage production (hence perhaps Kazan's adolescence rather than Miller's) was a tableau showing the protagonist surrounded by young women all of whom want him—while he sits and suffers! Rewritten by Terry Southern and renamed *Before the Fall*, Miller's latest could become a real play for an audience of men and women.

The cult of immaturity is an admirable subject for art when seen from the viewpoint of maturity, as in Southern's novel, *Candy*. But our dramatists, with Eugene O'Neill at the head, have taken their Candys at face value: they have really *believed* those men needed her. And they are convinced that she suffered terribly when satisfying their needs. They are wrong, and *Strange Interlude* has as one of its many faults that it is untrue from beginning to end. Perhaps only in the Broadway theater, whither so many Candys are escorted on their free evenings, could such stuff ever have been taken for truth, and one can hear the repeated exclamation as the characters of *Mourning Becomes Electra* bounce from fornication to homicide and back again: "Good grief!" Even perhaps: "Good grief, it's daddy!"

The crisis of infancy cannot be dealt with in a play, so in drama we get a double dose of the crisis of adolescence, the infantile character of which is not to be underestimated. The typical O'Neill protagonist cannot bear to part with Mom, and if he has to, there is nothing for it but Death. Human happiness is known only in moments of floating passivity that presumably recall life in the womb; and these moments are experienced in adolescence. Hence, for men and women, happiness is in the past, a few luminous moments remembered. Period. The life of men and women, as we have encountered it in literature or even in life, does not exist for the greatest American dramatist. His adults are only projections of adolescent nightmare. And, in that nightmare, experience is thinned down to a mere syndrome of unhappy adolescence: nostalgia, deprivation, and, in one's rage, the wish to kill oneself and others. It is this last feature that makes O'Neill's *Electra* ludicrous: to this merely puerile murderousness he would reduce the majestic plot of the *Oresteia*. If he is not exactly Aeschylean, does O'Neill manage to be Strindbergian? At one time he was swept off his feet by reading Strindberg, which has caused some to think he wrote Strindbergian plays. But what might be called the archetypal situation in Strindberg is one in which the romance of falling in love has given way, perhaps long ago, to cold hate. His bad women are not even Lady Macbeths who collapse under the burden of guilt, they are Gonerils and Regans who rage coldly on to the end. His men do not need love: they need respect, so they can keep their old patriarchal status. Even Miss Julie is not seeking love: she is seeking degradation.

O'Neill's characters, on the other hand, being American adolescents, want to be loved, and they don't really want anything else. They only misbehave when they don't get love. Hatred itself seems only the product of this failure. (This bit of current dogma is appealed to by O'Neill's distinguished son-in-law, Charles Chaplin, in the *ex cathedra* declaration that closes *The Great Dictator*.) And when the young American doesn't love, or isn't loved, or both, he has two flags with which to signal his message to the world: the bottle and the whore (of which recent variations are the needle and the boy) . In O'Neill's plays both of these flags are waved *ad nauseam*.

Now, if no one fully solves the problems of infancy and adolescence, at least these problems are later complicated by a growing awareness of the reality outside oneself, and the knowledge that the world was not built for ME—was not even built exclusively for LOVE—is no longer totally overwhelming. But for O'Neill's characters it is. They take very personally indeed the discovery that the world was not built for them, and are likely to seize the occasion to disburden themselves of all their ideals. And it is not simply that they only want to be loved. All too often they only want to be loved by Mom. How can I possibly give up Mom for a wife? the protagonist of *More Stately Mansions* has to ask himself. After long years of cogitation he finds the answer: by making sure my wife *is* a Mom. It takes this to save him from seizing his actual Mom and making her his wife, so close do we come to the crime of Oedipus in a play written, as it were, by Oedipus himself, and not by Sophocles. From which it can be seen how near O'Neill's life-worship comes to death-worship: sex leads back to the womb.

There is too much talk about sex in *More Stately Mansions*. Which might also be said about modern life in general: not that there is too much sex, but that there is too much talk about it—perhaps indeed because there is too little sex. Our literature is as sex-obsessed as the chatter of "college boys," and presumably for the same reason. Such chatter gets boring after a while. Sex has to be mixed with other things to be really interesting. The art of the drama illustrates this, time and time again. How much sex does Shakespeare exhibit or talk about in the greatest tale of passion that he told, *Antony and Cleopatra?* It is just as much a war play as a love story, and to *Romeo and Juliet* the feud of the families is an essential element, as are the humors of Mercutio and Tybalt, as is the botany of Friar Laurence.

I have mentioned that in *More Stately Mansions* O'Neill verges at times on social-historical drama. The same could be said of *A Streetcar Named Desire* and *Sweet Bird of Youth*— the theme of the decaying gentry of the South has considerable life in both. But the adolescent obsession with sex enters in not only to hold such material down to a minimum but also to subordinate it very strictly to the "love interest," and it ends up as either background or symbolism or both. The decaying gentry of the South are, for example, an appropriate symbol for the inner life of Blanche Dubois-Tennessee Williams.

Harold Clurman has made a gallant attempt to prove something like the opposite of the point I am making. He says that the story of *Desire Under the Elms,* sexual as it seems, is really about the disposition of the soil of this North American continent. It is true that O'Neill was very consciously concerned with this latter subject. He wanted it to be the subject of the famous Cycle. But the question whether it is the subject of *Desire Under the Elms* or the Cycle can hardly be settled with reference to O'Neill's intentions. It is a question of the impression given—granted that the person "impressed" be reasonably responsive. It seems to me that Mr. Clurman's idea might arise from a discussion around *Desire Under the Elms,* but would never, never come spontaneously from a reading or seeing of the play. In modern conversation, A is so frequently said to symbolize B when all that is meant is that A *could* symbolize B. In art, whether it *does* symbolize B depends upon whether the artist *made* it symbolize B, and to make it symbolize B surely means to call the symbol to the attention of any audience not hostile, stupid, or ignorant.

I cannot believe that a qualified audience would take *Desire Under the Elms* to be primarily about the ownership of the soil. Rather, in a ranking established by the work itself, the question of land ownership is subordinated to the sexual question. Consequently, economics often symbolizes sex, and not vice versa; and it is O'Neill's doing that it is thus, and not vice versa.

Similarly, as I see it, *More Stately Mansions* is no more about Jacksonian America than *Mourning Becomes Electra* is about the Reconstruction. In both cases, history is the merest backdrop for the O'Neill family neurosis of around 1900–1915 as seen in terms of the popularized psychoanalysis of 1915–1930. In the case of *More Stately Mansions* and the cycle it belonged to, this was obviously not intended to be the case. O'Neill had it in mind to give some impression in drama of the whole sweep of American history from the Revolution to the present. So one wonders if one of the factors bringing him to abandon the cycle and burn parts of what he had already written was the realization that he could not break out of the closed circle of his own adolescence, and that therefore his dramatic history of his country would turn out to be only an unbroken series of disguised portraits of his parents, his brother and himself. *More Stately Mansions* would support such a conjecture, and since it survived destruction, we are told, only by accident, we have in it a clear-cut instance of the kind of work O'Neill wished to destroy.

Long Day's Journey into Night is a much less disguised picture of the family neurosis, and O'Neill did not try to destroy it. Is it not precisely *because* the picture is less disguised? No pretense, here, that the real subject is American history! And what a relief it must have been to throw away most of the camouflage and "come right out with it"! Whether or not *Long Day's Journey into Night* provides a catharsis for its audience, which has been argued about, it must surely have provided one for its author. Even such disguises as remain serve to reinforce the main point I am making. For example, Eugene O'Neill was not an adolescent in 1912, which is the time of the action of the play, but Edmund Tyrone, the character corresponding to him, is. In making the shift, O'Neill acknowledges what both his real interest and real competence were.

At that, the portrayal of Edmund is the least satisfying feature of *Long Day's Journey*. To portray one's family is one thing, to portray oneself is another, and O'Neill resorts to the desperate device of characterization by quotation: we are asked to believe Edmund is a bit of a poet because he quotes quite a bit of poetry. And there is a paradox in the success of *Long Day's Journey* as a whole. In the act of acknowledging his utter identification with the adolescent, and the adolescent's viewpoint, Eugene O'Neill transcends that adolescent and his viewpoint to give a dramatic account of three men and women.

Such a transcendence is not achieved in *More Stately Mansions*. There is no breakthrough to what might fairly be called either tragedy or critical realism. We get—melodrama. Well, melodrama is a good genre too, and its appeal to the adolescent in each of us is fair and above board—*if* it is above board. Melodrama is thoroughly satisfactory when it is intended as melodrama: there is an awkwardness about it, and much waste motion in the writing, if it is intended as more. For in art, as in morals, noble intentions have no particular merit: *More Stately Mansions* could have been a better play had the author's intention been *less* noble. I speak in principle. In actuality, artists as serious as Eugene O'Neill do what they have to do and pay the price.

Comedy and the Comic Spirit in America

*This is the text of a talk commissioned by **Alan Downer** and the Voice of America during the winter of 1964–5.*

IT CAN BE acknowledged from the outset that the play does not flourish in America as the novel and poem do. With the possible exception of Eugene O'Neill, the leading American dramatists do not rank with Melville, Twain, James, Faulkner, and Hemingway, Emily Dickinson, Robert Frost, T. S. Eliot, Wallace Stevens, Robert Lowell.

And so it is that a writer who was spoken of at one time as America's Bernard Shaw—S. N. Behrman—is already almost forgotten. He has in fact none of the qualifications of Shaw: is not a writer of first-class prose, is not a man of many or of interesting ideas, let alone a maker of first-class plays. One might as easily speak of Noël Coward as the English Bernard Shaw, though passages in *Private Lives* are more scintillating than anything Behrman has written. The character of the American theatre has been such—the American theatre has been commercial to such an extent—that any writer with a modicum of Shaw's subtlety and seriousness would have turned to the novel to express himself. There is delightful comedy in many of the stories of Henry James, but when James's *Washington Square* was made into a play by other hands it became something less than either comedy or tragedy.

To speak only of the Bernard Shaws and Henry Jameses is to set our sights high. How many such writers are there anywhere at anytime? If America has produced little that is noteworthy in the way of drawingroom comedy, it has produced very many comic plays of other kinds that have delighted audiences not only in America but all around the world. Half a century ago comedy meant French comedy. Even when the author was not Labiche, or Feydeau, or one of their many French imitators, it was a non-French writer of their school. Are we today approaching a point where something of the sort could be said of American comedy? I don't think any single figure stands out like an American Labiche, but rather that a whole genre has imposed itself, so that almost any comic play that succeeds in New York goes on to succeed in the rest of the world. A play at present on the boards, *Luv* by Murray Schisgal, would be an example. There is something about the American comedies that tends to make the European ones seem a little staid and old-fashioned. The public flocks to American comedies to hear, as it were, a "new small talk," to dance to a new and more exciting rhythm.

One is reminded of the difference between operetta and American musical comedy. Masterpieces of operetta remain masterpieces whatever happens, but the operetta theatre, in general, comes to seem faded and boring to a public that has seen *Oklahoma!* properly performed, though *Oklahoma!* is not a masterpiece. It's a case of the victory of the genre, and of a change in fashion. Not a season's change in fashion, either, but one of those radical changes, as from crinolines to short skirts, that set one era off from another.

Some of the better American comedies *are* musical comedies. I say this without having that prejudice in favor of the musical comedy which makes some of our New York newspaper critics rejoice at half a dozen examples of the genre every season. If you only see the shows that in some form or other reach England and continental Europe, then you are not seeing a representative but a superior selection. One season as a critic in New York would teach you that most musical comedies, though they may cost half a million dollars apiece, are very dull rubbish indeed. You emerge from them cursing the genre, not hailing it as the greatest American invention since federal democracy. So much effort, you cry, and so little result! Never did mankind owe so little to so many. But the best are good, and in a way that specially concerns the student of the comic spirit in America. Take *Guys and Dolls* or *Kiss Me Kate*. What's good about it? I don't think the merit of such a show can be localized in the script. Read the script, and you won't think of Oscar Wilde. I don't think the merit of such a show can be localized in the score: listen to the music, and you won't think of mentioning it in the same breath as Offenbach or *The Threepenny Opera*. But when all the parts are put together, the finished show has *pep, zing, zip,* and maybe even *oomph.* You can usually tell in the first few minutes if a musical comedy has this particular kind of aliveness. If it hasn't, it is alive in no fashion, and the half million dollars have been thrown away.

While on the subject of *Guys and Dolls,* let me tell a story. A few years ago I edited an anthology entitled *From the American Drama.* It put many people's backs up because all the serious playwrights from O'Neill to Arthur Miller were omitted. I was toying with the notion that serious American playwrights were generally second-rate Europeans, whereas the specially American contribution lay in the so-called lighter plays. And in musical comedies. This explains the inclusion of the book of *Guys and Dolls,* a musical comedy, which, I said, embodied "the American quality" very well. Now one of my most serious reviewers—too serious, maybe, to be the right man to review this book—observed that in representing *Guys and Dolls* to be especially American I was confusing America with New York City. Now it is true that I am not a native American, and I might be presumed to cherish a few European fallacies about the United States. But I had not implied, or thought, either, that New York could be equated with America as a whole, as this critic supposed. However, New York is America in that it is certainly not Europe and does not resemble any European city any more than it resembles New Orleans or Minneapolis. And something of the character of New York is caught in the lingo of *Guys and Dolls*. The habitat of the lingo is in many spots unmistakable. Even that, though, is not what I had meant by "the American quality" of *Guys and Dolls*. This work has little or no value as a document. As a naturalistic study of milieu it is non-existent. For that matter, Damon Runyon, who wrote the story it is based on, and perfected this type of humor, was not a New Yorker at all, but a Southerner. In speaking of the American quality of this work, I am speaking of what sets it off from anything English or European—or Chinese. And so a non-American would fail to know just what I mean—or fail to agree that *Guys and Dolls* is inalienably American. So clearly so, as I said, that it is hard to get a plausible performance out of a non-American cast. It is a matter—one might put it—of how bottoms wiggle, or fail to wiggle. National character is in the behind. At any rate, it can most readily be spotted there. Ask an actor to walk across the stage: when he has done so, you know if he could appear in *Guys and Dolls*.

(In this respect Negro shows are only extreme instances of American shows. I have never seen anything more ludicrous than a European production of *Porgy and Bess*, done by white singers in black face. You knew their behinds weren't black. Perhaps Sir Laurence Olivier, in *Othello*, is the only European actor who ever seemed black all over, and he consumed so much energy in achieving this effect that some aspects of the role had to be sacrificed.)

As for *Guys and Dolls*, it draws upon the rhythm of American life—or, to be more precise, upon certain rhythms *in* American life—in order to create living theatre. This is not at all the same as *describing* America. *Guys and Dolls* is in fact at several removes from the actual appearances of American life. But it is by no means unrelated to the reality. On the contrary, certain features of the reality have been seized and brilliantly exploited. True, it is superficial, this *Guys and Dolls*. If indeed it were ever *not* superficial, it would tumble into bathos, as many musical comedies tumble into bathos when their creators sound off on race relations, education, or God. To forget God, and work with surfaces, can be a duty at times. Or as I think Humphrey Bogart once put it, leave messages to Western Union.

In what sense is musical comedy comedy? George Jean Nathan used to say the term was a misnomer, in that the typical musical comedy is not comic at all, but, on the contrary, highly lachrymose. What statistics would show I have no idea. Certainly the Rodgers and Hammerstein musical comedies could be cited in support of Nathan's view. But, of good musical comedies—good in Nathan's opinion or mine—a great many *are* in the comic tradition, especially if one grants that much non-musical comedy has been in some degree sentimental. Oscar Hammerstein seems to me to represent, not so much a permanent genre, as a phase in American history, the same phase as Norman Vincent Peale and President Eisenhower, a phase of humorless highmindedness, a phase of philistine goodwill and conformism. His predecessor as collaborator with Rodgers, Lorenz Hart, had been another kettle of fish. Hart wrote comic lyrics, hard-hitting, free-wheeling comments on the more outrageous features of American life. That's *another* phase of American history, of course, and not necessarily more characteristic of musical comedy. But the name of Lorenz Hart can be used as the cue for a discussion of the social commentary in American comedy, musical or otherwise.

Comedy written within the framework of commercial America, Broadway or Hollywood, tends to pull its punches. Devastating accusations are made along the way, but in the end are withdrawn. The traditional happy ending of comedy, when assimilated by this pattern, tends to signify a kind of capitulation. Here is a satirist who started out in act one as a radical critic of society and then got scared in act three; the happy ending is a convention that enables him to creep, so to speak, to the cross. A thousand examples of this pattern could be given, and only a slightly less large number of dramatic critics failing to see any such pattern. What such critics record is that Dramatist A, while seemingly a bit subversive and unsavory in the first act, turns out, along about 11 p.m. to have his heart in the right place.

Confronted with this phenomenon, the stern European critic can think of nothing but to rebuke the American dramatist for not keeping it up to the end. He assumes that a revision of the last twenty minutes of each play would set everything to rights. But a whole culture is involved, of which "commercial" writers are selling the standard product. They are perfectly adjusted to things as they are and could no more afford to revise the last twenty minutes than they could afford to know that the last twenty minutes needed revising. The purely commercial artist in American society has a position like that of the purely official artist, the Party artist, in a totalitarian society. He is an example of *Gleichschaltung* or, if you prefer a Shakespearean image, of the dyer's hand taking on the color of the dye.

Better artists are *im*purely commercial or not commercial at all. Let me, in relation to comedy, and in relation to comedy that is satirical and makes a comment on society, mention responses of some better artists.

One kind of writer meets commercialism halfway. He expresses a willingness to work within the system, and this willingness is expressed in an acceptance of certain conventions. If there is satire against this or that, it may be presented as just the point of view of a single character; if it is more than that, it can be retracted in the happy ending. So far this better writer is indistinguishable from the inferior or totally adjusted writer. The difference emerges in the malaise everywhere perceptible in the better writer's work. Sometimes this is so great that a sentimental ending is insufficient as a counterweight. Think of such plays as *You Can't Take It with You*. It was the Marxist criticism of them that the unrest they embody and communicate is dissipated by a phony reconciliation at the end. The question is whether this criticism is merely doctrinaire. It looks right. It seems to fit. But when you go back to those plays—I don't want my argument to depend on my being right about *You Can't Take It with You,* in particular —you often find that the sentimental ending falls into place as an ironic insincere bow to conservatism, while the spirit of rebellion in the body of the play rings true.

That is one pattern. There is another, that the European more readily understands, because it is "consequent" and of a piece. Marc Blitzstein's *Cradle Will Rock* is an American musical comedy and at the same time a consistently Marxist study of society. No reconciliation at the end of this one—on the contrary! Now Blitzstein's piece is certainly one of the better American musicals. If it is no masterpiece, that is because all too many compromises are made, not—in this case— on the political, but on the artistic front. The writing, especially, is limited by being wholly in a vulgar commercial mode. Perhaps the intention was to exploit cliches and transcend them. But to my mind, the transcendence is very incomplete. And this has to do with the fact that Blitzstein's attitude, though it can be called extreme by those who think in political terms, was conventional and conformist in cultural, and so ultimately in human, terms. He did not rebel except politically, i.e., on the surface. On the contrary, he accepted most of what a real rebel would be rebelling against: the way of life, the way of feeling and thinking and behaving, of the established regime.

Marc Blitzstein was a Communist, but it is not Communism I am objecting to. No; I can give an example of deeper rebellion in one who also has been inclined to Communist opinions, namely, Charlie Chaplin. And I make no apology for bringing Chaplin into the discussion, even though some people will have it that he is neither a dramatist nor an American. His work was done in America, and a large part of it was the creating of (cinematic) dramas. Are not the Chaplin films the supreme American comedies?

Chaplin represents, among many other things, rather thoroughgoing rebellion. Of the sentimental pseudo-solution of things he definitely makes a joke. If Americans have not understood his hankering after Communism, they have understood even less—in my opinion—what precedes it and explains it: that this successful man rejects the world which embraces him. Granted that he wanted the homage; one must concede also that he does not return it.

What I am alleging of Charlie Chaplin is more obviously true of W. C. Fields. And he too should be brought into the discussion, not so much because he often wrote his own scenarios, as because the discussion can justifiably pass from comedy to comedianship and even from comedianship to the comic spirit in America.

It has often been said of Fields that he is misanthropic, but, more specifically, he is a critic of what passes for the American way of life. Not even a critic. He is just against it. He thumbs his nose at it. He gives it a Bronx cheer. He takes up each idol of popular Americanism and breaks it—the baby and the child, the wife and the mother—everything that makes a house a home. And the American retreat and refuge from these—the whisky bottle—which in "square" American works has so often been shown as pathetic is here held up, in bravado, as a solution. Thus the most radical writer of American comedy— or, at any rate, the writer of the most radical American comedy —in the Nineteen Thirties was not Marc Blitzstein but W. C. Fields.

Similarly, if one would name a "first lady" of American comedy, one should not pick a real lady like Katharine Cornell, nor yet a beautiful actress of drawingroom drama like Ina Claire, but rather Mae West. Miss West has not been seen on stage all that often, but on the strength of her film appearances alone, she was for a while the first lady of American comedy, just as, a little earlier, was Marie Dressler. Margaret Dumont, the dowager of the Marx Brothers films, is a lady of that same comic world, the principal comic world, probably, that America has created outside the novel.

When I praise Chaplin or Fields I am not praising their personal and special achievements alone. In that generation, there existed, if chiefly in the movies, an American comedy: the Marx Brothers afford another excellent example. Though not radical in the usual political sense, they are far more radical critics of society than the recognized radicals. The

"American way of life" is rejected point by point. It is the bad joke from which they make their good jokes.

Today, *Doctor Strangelove* provides a Marx Brothers' view of the atomic age. At least what is good about it does. *Strangelove* has a weakness. It has something of the self-congratulatory cleverness of Private Eye and the current English school of the Devastating. The upshot of these sick jokes is that they cancel themselves out. There is such a thing as becoming so radical you find yourself a conservative again: you have rejected so much in theory that you accept everything in practice. Such is cynicism. *Strangelove* has the makings of a radical film but dwindles into a conformist one. It communicates the suspicion that its makers might in actuality decide that since our generals are NOT crazy they are entitled to drop the bomb. One could call this the spirit of appeasability. Whereas, W. C. Fields, though he is unpolitical, is unappeasable, implacable—"incorrigible," if you will.

I am speaking of the makers of the Strangelove film in the abstract, as if they were a harmonious team, and as if accident played no role. The novel *Candy* is better comedy, and consistently embodies the non-political radicalism I am talking about. It is the best American comedy of recent years in any genre. And it makes the most pertinent of comments on the current state of the American soul.

A final point. The comic element is often the best part of plays that, as a whole, are not considered comedies. This is particularly true of American plays, and most particularly, of those of the two most prominent American playwrights of the present moment, Tennessee Williams and Edward Albee. Williams has often been admired for other, supposedly profounder elements, and when he has been condemned it has been on the grounds that the profundity was spurious. Those who do the condemning should, however, hasten to add that Williams has a fine comic sense and knows how to use it. The Father in *Cat on a Hot Tin Roof* is a comic figure in far more than the fact that he uses scandalous language. Comedy is here used for its classic purpose: to place people in their society, to define them as what Karl Marx said they are: the sum of their social relationships.

Is it not largely wit and humor that prevent both *Streetcar* and *The Glass Menagerie* from being unbearably sentimental? The confrontation of Blanche DuBois and Stanley Kowalski is a brilliant comic *idea*, worked out, to be sure, to a pathetic conclusion. Even so, the pathetic conclusion is, artistically speaking, the least valuable part of the story. Of the Mother in *The Glass Menagerie*, the same may be said as of the Father in *Cat on a Hot Tin Roof*: she constitutes a splendid social portrait. The same forthright method is used too—monologue, virtually—a torrent of characteristic words which define the character socially—by jokes. Conversely, the bad plays of Williams have good passages, *and these passages are all very funny*.

Of *Who's Afraid of Virginia Woolf?* and *Tiny Alice*, this much is relevant here. To both evenings in the theatre, there is a good deal of fun, and there is also an attempt to be deep about modern life. The attempt to be deep, in both cases, fails, *but the fun in both cases*, IS *fun*. And of course there must be more to fun that works on such a grand scale than tricks of phrase or adroitness with quips and gags. And there is. If Mr. Albee can't define what he feels to be the tragedy of modern people, while groping for such a definition he does write an effective comedy of modern life. It has been said that the dialogue of the man and wife in *Who's Afraid of Virginia Woolf?* is really the dialogue of two catty homosexuals. Those who say this apparently think that it disposes of Mr. Albee and his play. But no: what amuses and interests us is that a married couple talk with the sick-slick cleverness of "fairies." This is finally a comment, not on Albee, and not on "fairies," but on married couples—there lies the social substance, and there too the fun. Mr. Albee is holding up the mirror to nature, and showing something that was always funny: inversion of natural function. His comment is valid, I think, as a kind of social realism, and I think it achieves a kind of symbolism, if not always the kind the playwright seems to be after. The confusion in sexuality symbolizes the American and modern confusion of identities. Anyhow, the first act of *Virginia Woolf* is the funniest bit of playwriting in many years, and that must be my excuse for including it in a discussion of

American comedy. The man in the street's definition of comedies is "plays that are funny." I was taught in school that this was a very poor definition. But I have remembered it. I have not remembered what they taught me was a good definition.

The German Theatre Today

This report on theatre in Germany, where I was living at the time, was commissioned by Show *in 1965.*

IN THE ERA before Hitler, the Germans made an extraordinary contribution to the theatre of the world. Specifically, three movements were launched, one after the other: Naturalism in the Nineties; Expressionism, between 1910 and 1925; and Epic Theatre between 1923 and 1933. In each movement German dramatists were among the leaders, if indeed the whole movement, as with Epic Theatre, was not German. The roster of names, from Hauptmann through Wedekind and Sternheim to Brecht was an impressive one, and to each movement belonged characteristic directors—Brahm for Naturalism, Jessner and Fehling for Expressionism, Piscator for Epic Theatre. Then there was Max Reinhardt—too big, too eclectic to pin to any particular school—and the extraordinary roster of German actors of that time, from Moissi to Pallenberg, from Werner Krauss to Fritz Kortner, from Gustav Gruendgens to Peter Lorre.

During the Hitler years, this theatre was, outwardly, less changed than you might suppose. Jews and Communists had been removed, but Jews and Communists had never amounted to a majority. Even the programs could remain the same to a surprising degree, since a large part of the German program is always devoted to classics and another large part to unpolitical light entertainment. Nor was the market suddenly flooded with Nazi plays. The Nazi regime movement was genuinely anti-intellectual and did not produce many plays. There was a great deal more propaganda in the theatre of the Twenties: propagandist theatre has generally been leftwing theatre.

But there were no more "movements," and there were no more great men. Any notable figure of the theatre 1933–45 had been a notable figure of the theatre 1918–33. Just what it means to have a regime that makes war upon the human spirit itself is very clearly seen in the outcome. When we angrily talked in the years of 1933–45 of Hitler's destruction of culture, we did not know how right we were. And in the year 1945 it seemed there were no German writers at all. It even seemed that way in 1950 and almost that bad in 1955. But in the past ten years a new generation has come of age which has its own point of view and a lot of talent. The names of Guenter Grass and Heinrich Böll are only the best-known of a gifted group.

As for the drama, it seemed for a while that the German theatre had emigrated to Switzerland. During the war, the Zurich Schauspielhaus had been a refuge for German actors and directors, and so it was not entirely accidental that the principal German-language playwrights of the decade after the war (1945–55) were Swiss whose plays were first done at the Schauspielhaus: Max Frisch and Friedrich Dürrenmatt. It is not without interest that the leading playwright of German Expressionism, Georg Kaiser, lived in Zurich till his death in 1945. Brecht, though not present in the flesh, had his plays premiered in Zurich—his *Mother Courage* was done there as early as 1941, his *Galileo* shortly thereafter.

I mention this because it is probably necessary for German playwrights today to be post-Brecht, that is, *to have had the Brecht experience,* and this Frisch and Dürrenmatt could and did have, years ahead of their colleagues in Germany: hence their head start in the drama of the post-war era.

Among purely German playwrights who have come to the front since 1955 let me mention five: Rolf Hochhuth, Heinar Kipphardt, Martin Walser, Peter Weiss and Peter Hacks. Of these, only Hochhuth is a familiar name in America. But, on the basis of the Herman Shumlin production, it can hardly be said that his work is known here. *The Deputy* will have to be done again in something much closer to its integrity. I believe it will be, for while its limitations were all too mercilessly noted from the outset, it has merits that will come with the shock of surprise to many. It is by far the most important *act* of the German theatre after Brecht. (Funnily enough Mr. Hochhuth says he has avoided contact with Brecht, but he can scarcely have avoided it altogether or he could not have made the comments he has on *Galileo* and other works.)

Hochhuth is not, of course, the only German writer to remember the Nazis. His whole generation is remembering them, to the infinite embarrassment of their fathers—i.e. the Nazis themselves. During the nineteen sixties, the German press has been full of items about the Nazis. When last I lived in Germany—some fifteen years ago—it was said you couldn't find a German who had been a Nazi. Today, other Germans are finding them all the time. Television dramas take up the theme, as do regular movies and novels. Hence the plays on the theme are part of a larger context. A favorite subject in this discussion is the pliable and conformist German who was a Communist or Socialist in the twenties, a Nazi in the thirties, and a Christian Democrat in the fifties. Martin Walser has written the tragi-comedy of this subject in his *Eiche und Angora,* which was tried out at Edinburgh in 1963 under the title *The Rabbit Race.* In his latest play, *The Black Swan,* Walser treats the subject of the doctors of Hitler's extermination camps. Although they cover up their past in a largely successful and wholly astonishing way, one of them is found out by his own son who (at the end of the play) commits suicide. (Reading Walser and the others, one realizes that *The Deputy* itself was a play about the generations, Pius standing for the fathers, Fontana for the sons. Young Germans today are looking back with an anger such as John Osborne never knew.)

Second only in fame to *The Deputy* is Heinar Kipphardt's *In the Matter of J. Robert Oppenheimer,* which has now been done in Berlin, Munich, and Paris. Kipphardt was Dramaturg in the East Berlin Deutsches Theater till he broke with the regime in 1959. He has dropped the Communist Anti-Ameri-

canism but has not shed some of the Communist clichés about
American life. His play will have to be a good deal different
before it can be offered to Americans as a picture of America.
Conspicuously, he is far too sorry for Oppenheimer who, after
all, is not a ruined man. Defenders of Oppenheimer (including the man himself) have protested. It should be added that
critics of Oppenheimer will wish to do likewise. Would he not
in fact be a more dramatic character if he were less the noble,
pathetic, blameless persecuted professor of leftwing tradition
and more the man who told his questioners that he was willing
to do anything the government might order him to do? Persons who know Oppenheimer have spoken of a pride and a
tendency to hubris in him which strongly suggest Greek tragedy—but which are no part of Herr Kipphardt's liberal docu-
mentary.

At the moment the "hottest" name of all among German
playwrights in the West is that of Peter Weiss. I just saw him
interviewed on television by the editor of *Theater Heute,* the
leading German theatre magazine. He uttered the magic word:
Artaud, so far the only alternative proposed, in Germany or
perhaps anywhere, to Brecht. The TV cameras were offering
us a one-act of his, *Night with Guests.* A black-bearded bandit
with a knife breaks in on a family and makes the father go out
to fetch his treasure-chest. He then takes the father's place in
the family and lies down to sleep next to the wife. A night-
watchman comes in to say there are thieves around. At this
point the father returns dragging a chest and is taken for a
thief by the watchman who stabs him. The bandit stabs the
wife. The children murmur nursery rhymes. Finis.

Mr. Weiss was very unpretentious when talking about *Night
with Guests,* as well he might be. Far more important is his
also far longer and bigger *Marat-Sade—The Persecution and
Assassination of Marat as Performed by the Inmates of the
Asylum of Charenton under the Direction of the Marquis de
Sade.* Who could say that the idea for this play is not original
and is not stated imaginatively? The contrast Marat/De Sade
is full of human interest and dramatic possibility. Weiss's
problem is with action. He camouflages it somewhat with
showy, if scintillating, theatricality, and tries to cover a lack of

commitment with an alibi about being against the pointing of morals and attaching of labels.[1] At that, Weiss is an inspiriting new presence in the theatre, and his play provided the most notable premiere in Germany since that of *The Deputy*.

Peter Hacks is a Munich Communist who has gone to live in East Berlin. He has had a number of plays done in the East, one of which had him in trouble with the authorities there: it seems he likes to criticize what goes on even in the socialist East.

Hacks is "post-Brecht" in a different way from his Western colleagues. In the East there seems to be a question whether Brecht should be an influence at all. I do not note his influence in most of the plays to be found in the fortnightly *Theater der Zeit* under the heading "socialist dramaturgy." I find plain old-fashioned dramaturgy—with Communist propaganda as the content. Hacks has undergone the Brecht experience, and in the past has perhaps suffered from the temptation to be an imitator. Today he is hoping to develop forward on his own, leaving the conservation of Brecht to the latter's widow and her famous theatre-museum, the Berlin Ensemble.

I saw two of Hacks' adaptations, as performed in the Kammerspiele of the Deutsches Theater: Aristophanes' *Peace* and Offenbach's *Helena*. Since they were directed by another graduate (so to say) of the school of Brecht, Benno Besson, it was hard to judge how much of the Brechtianizing of the Hellenic and the Gallic works was the adaptor's doing. In any case, it is only one side of Brecht that is seen in these works at the Kammerspiele, while quite another side is shown by Manfred Wegwerth at the Ensemble. Wegwerth tends to be the ponderous dogmatist and demonstrator. Besson and Hacks are so in love with Brecht's elegance and humor that they do not always stop short of the cute and coy. It is interesting that a kind of aestheticism is possible within the frame of Communist, political theatre. And *possible* it evidently is: for, the night I saw *Helena*, Walter Ulbricht was there, clapping very respectfully.

---

[1] The point is based on the Peter Brook production. That Weiss had written another ending I did not then know. When I found out, I passed the information on—see *PL*, October–November 1966. (Footnote added 1967).

One play in the Deutsches Theater repertoire I will mention here though I have not listed its author (Rolf Schneider) among the notabilities and I did not see the play on stage but on the TV screen. This is *The Case of Richard Waverley*. Richard Waverley turned out to be none other than Claud Eatherly, and since W. B. Huie's book had come out, claiming to show that Eatherly was far from a worthy character, Mr. Schneider was summoned to the TV Studio to denounce Huie as a member of the Radical Right and to quote Guenter Anders re-endorsing Eatherly. Since there were good actors in the production, it may possibly have seemed to viewers who have never been to America to give a good picture of America. To anyone else, it is grotesque, and has only been matched, so far as my TV viewing here goes, by an East German reconstruction of the Kennedy murder in which the actors took their cue from Brecht's *Mahagonny* and Hollywood pictures of the Scarface era. I make no apology for mentioning this program here for it constitutes by all odds the most *original* drama I have seen in Germany.

For what theatre do these dramatists write? The answer given by my colleague Kenneth Tynan in a recent issue of *Holiday* is: a very enviable theatre indeed. In Germany, theatre is an accepted part of the community and its culture. This, whether in socialist or capitalist Germany, means that it is a subsidized theatre—how very heavily subsidized one realizes when one sees lavish productions not closing even if the audiences are small. Mr. Tynan notes how devoted the German theatre public is: arriving punctually, behaving itself, remaining in its seats at the end to applaud. Generally, too, a German theatre is a nice place to be in. The seats are comfortable, and there is plenty of knee room. There is space for an indoor stroll during the intermission. There is a bar, and you can even eat between acts or before the show. Prices are low, even in relation to the German standard of living. In Berlin the top can be as low as 10 marks ($2.50), and I haven't known it be higher than 15 marks: either of these figures is less than the price of most hardbound books. Also, the top price generally applies only to two or three front rows of the orchestra: as one moves back, the price drops a mark or two every few rows.

Other economies are possible through block booking, which is widely organized.

The standard of performance remains high. A provincial German company can be expected to do Shakespeare (not to mention *German* classics) far better than a British Repertory Company could, were a British Repertory Company (which would be unusual) to try. And in Germany one would apply the word "provincial," anyway, only to the theatres of smaller towns and not to those of Hamburg, Frankfurt, Stuttgart, or Munich, each of which has theatres worthy of a metropolis.

Perhaps I should add Leipzig, Dresden, Weimar, and Rostock to this list, but I have not yet been able to travel through what in the West is called "the zone" and what in the place itself is called the German Democratic Republic. I have, however, seen a good deal, recently, of theatre in that great showcase of Communist culture: East Berlin. "Are the East Berlin theatres better than those of West Berlin?" I am often asked this question. I find it unanswerable, since standards vary so much from one theatre to another in both parts of the city. Some productions in the West are first-rate. (An example is the Schiller Theater's production of the *Marat/Sade*, though the director is a Pole). But it does seem to me that two of the East Berlin theatres, the Komische Oper and the Berlin Ensemble, more often produce absolutely dazzling shows than any theatres, not only of West Berlin, but of our modern world generally.

This is not to say that either one of them maintains the same standard in all, or even most, of its presentations. Each tends to have in its current repertoire two or three great showpieces alongside four or five other items of considerably less brilliance. This explains why people who pay a short visit to Berlin, or who catch the Ensemble in London or Paris, receive such a favorable impression—and also why an East Berliner is often surprised just *how* favorable this impression is, since he has seen shows which are routine or even bad in the same theatres.

I myself had never been in Berlin long enough before the present season to see more than the two or three great showpieces, and so a certain amount of disappointment has attended the experience of seeing the whole repertoire. It's the first time I've seen quite a bad play at this theatre: *Frau Flinz* by Helmut Baierl, secretary of their own unit of the Communist Party—and wouldn't you know it. (This is the play Helene Weigel thought appropriate to a guest appearance in Warsaw, but it seems that the bigwigs of the Polish CP thought otherwise and walked out before the end.) It's also the first time I've seen a really bad production at this theatre. *The Threepenny Opera* has been put on, not for fun, but to demonstrate the intimate link between capitalism and prostitution. (The point is elaborated in the program by a lengthy quote from Ed Murrow's TV program on call girls: I only hope Murrow is collecting a royalty on this, even if Frau Weigel assumes he will invest it in the white slave traffic.) Well, it wouldn't matter what was in the program, or what the dialecticians think the play meant, if anyone in the cast played with zest and humor and could sing.

What future for the Berlin Ensemble? They have performed a historic task: to establish Brecht as a great dramatist. Have they a further function, or will they now just do Brecht over and over and over and become boring?

What future for German theatre as a whole, East and West? This depends, obviously, on whether Germany will *be* a whole or whether the split is permanent.

As far as the West German theatre is concerned, I find Mr. Tynan's account one-sided. What I have said of the theatre of 1933–1945 seems to me still pretty much the case: that its glories are vestigial, relics of a more truly creative time. It is nice that Erwin Piscator is still directing in Berlin, but where are the young Piscators? It is splendid that a Kortner is still active, and a Trude Hesterberg, but their merits only bring into higher relief that no equally talented younger generation has shown itself.

Or should one say: been allowed to show itself? Part of the problem is what a Berlin newspaper has called the "closed society" of German—and especially Berlin—theatre. A good many refugees have not chosen to return, and others have tried to return, only to find themselves far from welcome. There are very few Jews around, and Jews were the life and soul of

German theatre in its great period (1900–1933). There are very many Nazis around, and while they were able to keep up appearances to a certain extent in the Nazi period, they are finding that harder now.

The rejuvenation that artists like Grass and Böll, Walser and Weiss, have brought to German writing has not been attended by a corresponding rejuvenation of institutions—including the institution of theatre.

Are things as bad in the East? As I say, I have less first-hand knowledge. The Communists, clearly, are less averse to getting rid of incumbent officials—in order to replace them with Communists. Is that always an improvement? The "thaw" has not gone so far in East Germany that you can hope to see there much of the more important current drama.

There is one institution that didn't need rejuvenating because it is new. This is German television. And it is only right to end this report with a reference to TV because the little screen is actually replacing the stage to a certain degree. There is a play on German television from about eight to nearly ten every evening. Sometimes there are plays at that hour on all of the several channels serving Berlin "viewers." Generally, they are good plays, done by good people, and they are broadcast without commercials and in extenso. (I can even feel I've begun to know the theatre of East Germany outside Berlin since I saw the Landestheater Halle's production of Brecht's *Round Heads* on television. It took up nearly three hours.) Since East productions are seen in the West, and vice versa, both sides are under pressure to do the best possible job: in this respect the division of Germany is productive. And now the playwrights are beginning to write directly for television, not for commercial reasons, but because it may be the best way to get a script well performed and placed before an audience. The prejudice against television which I brought with me from America has completely evaporated, and I am now much more inclined to stay at home of an evening and turn on television than to make the often rather long trip to a theatre.

Eight German Productions

Productions from all over West Germany were exhibited at a Festival in West Berlin in the spring of 1965. The following coverage of the event was commissioned by the magazine Theater Heute *and published by them in a German translation. The original appeared in* The New Leader.

HAMLET (HARRY BUCKWITZ: FRANKFURT): There were possibilities. The idea was not to present a static portrait of a dreamer prince, illustrated with melodious poetic arias, but to tell a story, a rather barbaric story. At first glimpse of the leather raincoats (on soldiers), and of Michael Degen's Prince, this seemed to be working, and one's appetite for the great enigmatic masterpiece was aroused all over again. But, alas, not satisfied. No story tells itself, least of all this one. If a driving, male energy, a feeling for the emotionally substantial and active, is enough to carry Degen through a scene or two, we soon begin to ask for more. Whatever the character of Hamlet is (and on this there will never be agreement), the role of Hamlet makes one very clear demand on the actor: variety. For one thing, it is written in half a dozen different styles, from the elegant, balanced prose of "What a piece of work . . ." to the syncopated verses of "Oh what a rogue. . . ." Sometimes there is a stylistic leap within the very same scene —as from elegiac prose in the Yorick speeches to the extravagant rhetorical verse outburst in the grave. Degen reduced all styles to one, which thereby after a while became no style at all but an amorphous outpouring.

And certainly Degen's acting was the best we saw. Frank Kutschera as Polonius seemed to have been told not to be funny: he reduced the old man to nullity. There was a praise-worthy effort to show him and his two children *as a family,* contrasted with the Hamlet family much as Gloster's family is with Lear's. This effort was thwarted by lack of characteriza-tion—lack of acting—in all three parties. Renate Schroeter, one felt, was capable of a good Ophelia, but "no man is an island," one cannot play without a partner. The final blow was dealt this production when Siegfried Wischnewski as the King had to be replaced at the last moment. Did he have to be replaced by an actor who not only couldn't act the part but couldn't even look it—was wrong even as to type? One saw a Claudius whom one couldn't imagine doing *any* of the things he does—even drinking too much, or making love too cloy-ingly, let alone committing murder and being a "cutpurse of the empire." A little, dried-up post-office official with a grey crew-cut! Well, to this I owe the one realization this produc-tion brought me: the play of *Hamlet* hinges on Claudius, in the sense that unless he has the prominence Shakespeare gave him, and unless he is exactly the kind of man Shakespeare made him, the whole action crumbles. Given a great actor, all Hamlets seem to be equally valid, but Claudius is one and indivisible and must be cast and played "right."

Now how could all this happen to Harry Buckwitz? I have been hearing for years of his achievements in Frankfurt, and looked forward to seeing him let loose with this director's dream of a play. He made a mistake in allowing such a *lapsus* to be seen in a national theater contest. Another radical mis-take had been made much earlier: to accept the designs of Michel Raffaelli which were not only bad in themselves but, to paraphrase Falstaff, the cause that badness is in other men. They hobbled the play. Seldom have any designs influenced any play for the better as much as these influenced *Hamlet* for the worse. They consisted of little huts and stairways and turrets half-made with a giant meccano set and never finished. They prevented each scene from looking like itself. They made odd irrelevant noises, and failed to function (the doors didn't close, and so on). But then I think the German stage has to learn that Shakespeare plays should not be presented as a sequence of half a dozen tableaux but in a single setting: Only

then will the action be articulated properly and the total structure be revealed.

THE BEDBUG (KONRAD SWINARSKI: BERLIN) and MARAT/SADE
(HANSGUENTHER HEYME: WIESBADEN). Both these plays
have been *causes célèbres* this season in a way that is possibly
novel and certainly bizarre. There is nothing new about a
political play causing a flurry; it is meant to. But the flurries
caused by Vladimir Mayakovsky's *The Bedbug* and Peter
Weiss' *Marat/Sade* have to do, in both cases, with their politics
being so unclear. Or, if you prefer, so flexible. In the middle of
the current dust-storm is the young Polish director Konrad
Swinarski. He is presumed to be a Communist because a
Communist regime lets him travel around and bring glory to
it, yet in the Communist press of Germany (see *Theater der
Zeit*) he is presented as the Communist press presents its
enemies a few months before the axe falls. The "charge" (that
would be the word) against Swinarski is that he sympathizes
with the petty bourgeois enemy in the latter's two classic
forms, that of the *Spiessbürger* in Mayakovsky and that of the
decadent, over-individualistic intellectual in Weiss.

It is, of course, hard to sort out the elements that went into
the making of *The Bedbug* production at the Schiller Theater.
The place is West Berlin's (generally most inadequate) rejoinder to Helene Weigel's remarkable outfit in East Berlin. It is
"in politics" even when it does unpolitical plays—perhaps
most of all then, as giving its own definition of cultural freedom. So why does it announce a play by Stalin's favorite poet?
Presumably because he committed suicide, possibly from dissatisfaction with Stalinist Russia. Such dissatisfaction—broad-
ening out into a dissatisfaction with modern society generally
—is present in the play to such an extent that one would not
produce the play at all if one did not wish such dissatisfaction
to be spread. The ultimate defense of Swinarski's view would
be that the play could hardly be put across at all if the director
took another view. And I suppose his enemies don't want the
play produced at all. This position is also defensible. It is not a
good play. To sympathize with the *bourgeoisie* in West Berlin

is the reverse of a daring act: the place is dominated by them. Understandably, then, a haze of dullness hung over the proceedings at the Schiller. Swinarski seemed to know that it might. And indeed the hand of the director is seen much less in the politics of the piece than in the effort to make it entertaining in spite of itself, an effort that at times seemed based on the formula: when in doubt bring on the *corps de ballet*. A certain febrile energy on the periphery is used to hide a lack of energy at the center—which also is legitimate when a play does lack energy at the center.

Other questions arise: *Why* did the Schiller Theater want a director from Warsaw for its West Berlin showcase? Why did the director wish to accept the invitation? Why was his government—strict in such matters—interested in having him accept? Did the disapproval of East Berlin come as a surprise or was it part of the calculation? By consequence, was the Warsaw government gratified by the acclaim the show got in the West or upset by the criticism it received in the East? Are either Poland or Swinarski going all the way to "Formalism" in their efforts at de-Stalinization? And so forth. But all these questions lead away from the theatrical arena into that of world politics.

Marat/Sade was presented at the festival, not in Swinarski's Schiller Theater production, but in a Wiesbaden production directed by Hansguenther Heyme. Yet Swinarski is at the center of this storm too since, once again, his production has been attacked as one-sided, incorrect, and anti-Communist. Weiss' play presents the contrast of the social revolutionary (Marat) and the individualistic intellectual (De Sade). The audience's sympathy can go to the one or to the other. When the Communists do the play—and in Rostock they have—they will obviously champion Marat against De Sade. Did Swinarski champion De Sade against Marat? This question is really two questions. Was De Sade "championed" in Swinarski's production? And if so, was Swinarski responsible for this, or can the responsibility be pinned on the author, Peter Weiss? The second question is made all the more difficult because this is an author who talks out of both sides of his mouth. The Swinarski production grew out of an intimate collaboration of author and director. Weiss could hardly not be behind it. Yet he appeared before the East German TV cameras to endorse (if not in exclusive or conclusive terms) the Rostock production. And he told an American interviewer (Henry Popkin) that the play is Marxist.

The Heyme production is either very sly or very naive. For it either slyly bypasses all this *Problematik* in the hope that a synthesis of interpretations may result, or it naively ignores the *Problematik* and fares blithely forward just hoping for the best that youthful enthusiasm without intellectual grasp might achieve. One hesitates to say which production comes closest to Weiss' intentions—since it is not clear that his intentions are clear—but it is *possible* that Heyme's show is the more Weissian precisely in its lack of clarity, precisely in the fact that it forges ferociously forward, looking neither to Right (De Sade) nor to Left (Marat). That Heyme did not have actors of the first rank to play De Sade or Marat also had a result not entirely negative. This play is pre-Aeschylean in the sense that the choruses carry more weight than the principals. In the Swinarski production, De Sade got more weight because the part was played by the leading actor of the company (Ernst Schroeder), while the choruses were indistinct, both literally and figuratively. Though the choruses were not really more distinct in the Heyme production, here they were part of a general and—one might charitably judge—intentional indistinctness, the indistinctness of the revel and the orgy. Behind the Swinarski lay the theater of Sartre and even, maybe, of Shaw. Heyme's, I suppose, was an attempt at theater of cruelty.

I can't say I respond to it particularly; I don't know if others do. Unless one is further gone than I am in the neurosis of voyeurism, the orgiastic is quite boring to look at: for the eyes and ears, nothing but repetitious bustle, priority always given to quantity over quality. Excitation can be very unexciting.

As to the problem of who is right about this play, it can never be solved till Herr Weiss comes clean and publishes all variants of his script. At present, he is always pulling unpublished bits out of his back pocket and saying that such and such a director didn't use them. His TV pronouncements, like any prefatorial ones, can be ignored; for so often an author says his play says what in fact it does not say.

THE BLACK SWAN (PETER PALITZSCH: STUTTGART). Palitzsch has undercut criticism of his directing of this play by explaining in a public discussion that the author (Martin Walser) collaborated with him and (apparently) gave him all needed directives. Anyhow, the production is very well directed; the directing is the best thing about it, in conjunction, that is, with the designs of Gerd Richter. Modern design in general has been going nowhere for so long. The bankruptcy of modernist stage design is to be seen in a catastrophe like the Raffaelli *Hamlet* designs as infallibly as the bankruptcy of modernist architecture is exhibited in the ugliness of rebuilt Berlin. This bankrupt *Modernismus* is characterized by pointlessness: its very functionalism is all show, though ugly show. That is why it is so heartening to find a designer like Richter doing something "modern," "experimental," *for a reason.* I'm thinking of the room without any walls in which the *Swan* opens. Here an effect of the claustrophobic was achieved on a huge, open stage, by the device of outlining a little room with floor and ceiling only. (The ceiling hung from the flies, the floor consisted of a platform about a foot high.) A meaningful contrast of indoors and outdoors was also possible within this scheme: photographs of the surroundings were hung in front of the cyclorama, and it helped greatly that they hung in a curve, not in the usual movie-screen format. The small platform forced the actors to be "falling over each other," and falling over the furniture. That, so close together physically, they failed to communicate was thereby dramatized.

That is one detail, or group of details, which made this production a very distinguished one. The play is weak, and one wouldn't be able to sit through it if the director did not exercise considerable discretion and skill. There is, for example, a scene in which lunatics perform a sort of combined Mousetrap and *Walpurgisnacht*. I should hate to see what Heyme's young Dionysians would do with it, but Palitzsch reduces both sound and movement to a minimum, thus increasing, instead of dissipating, the gruesomeness. One sees that Palitzsch's Brechtian training does after all prove of use outside the Brechtian *oeuvre,* and also that it need not have the result of converting all plays into Brecht plays.

But this directing is not of the kind that makes second-rate writing seem first-rate, and so one has to hope that Palitzsch will get some better plays to work on than *The Black Swan.*

DONA ROSITA (HANS BAUER: DARMSTADT), MUSIC (HANS JOACHIM HEYSE: BOCHUM), THE SNOB (RUDOLF NOELTE: BERLIN), THREE SISTERS (NOELTE: STUTTGART). The early 20th century was the Festival's "special period." That, perhaps, is hardly an accident. The present is not offering very much. The Nazi period, within Germany at least, offers nothing. The search for roots leads back to the grandparents.

Doña Rosita is perhaps *too* hard to get at. Or perhaps a German rendering of something so extremely Spanish is only tolerable to a German spectator. Even in the original the question suggests itself as to whether Federico García Lorca didn't lay on the local color too thick, didn't draw too exclusively on the charms of local tradition both in language and mores—a question suggested also by the Irish writers from Synge on, with whom García Lorca has rightly enough been compared. How much more obtrusive, then, the effort to be ultra-Spanish, when it is an effort made against the grain, an effort made in despite of a language with another grammar, another rhythm, another prosody, and in despite of bodies that look and move differently! Bauer made a gallant effort to solve the problem, and seemed to be succeeding better with most of the audience at the Freie Volksbuehne than with me. With an exception to be noted in a moment, he accepted the play on its own terms, a Spanish *genre* painting, and worked out the lyrical values of the scenes, instead of trying to force dramatic values upon them. A nice quietness hovered over the scene, if not quite the breathless hush which Juergen Fehling contrived to get (in an exquisite production of this play in Munich about 15 years ago). The play was done with taste and *con amore.* The moment where, in my judgment, it broke through the frame of García Lorca's convention was the moment near the end when Rosita realizes she will never marry. Here the actress suddenly made a leap from the lyric to the dramatic mode and sobbed and yowled like the pathetic women of other authors. And it was the cliché of the dramatic mode, according to which incoherence and blur are permitted to the performer, if only he shake and sob enough. I think Miss Mikulicz (Rosita) hoped the play was by Tennessee Williams after all.

Music, by Frank Wedekind, though German to the core, is also hard to salvage, and I got the impression that possibly the Bochum theater didn't have the human resources of most of those that contributed to the Festival. There was a faintly collegiate air to some of the jesting; the actors were tempted to giggle, it would seem, but *we* were not. If a certain awkwardness characterized the evening at the Theater am Kurfuerstendamm, I think this was partly the fault of us, the audience: We lacked the imagination which Wedekind asked from us. But partly it was the fault of the folk on stage who did not do everything possible to put us in the right frame of mind. Just a little, it may have been the fault of Wedekind too, since there seems to be a degree of uncertainty of direction and convention in the script itself. Pathos and sentiment, or parody of pathos and sentiment? Most of *Music* is parodistic, and was played as such, but occasionally Wedekind seems to think he can make the jump into the real thing and take us with him. Roswitha Rieger in the leading role began to shed real tears and ask that we do likewise. The invitation was rejected—with embarrassment. And the evening ended on a note of uncertainty. The reviewers, I gather, mostly went home and wrote that it was terrible. But it wasn't. The Wedekindian world is still fascinating to enter, and this production was good enough to permit us to enter it.

What is stylization and when is it successful? What Heyse offered in his production of *Music* was a burlesque of melodrama: a formula that has often yielded laughs, heaven knows, but which was not adequate to the present occasion, at least as applied by less than brilliant performers. Noelte's approach was far more sophisticated. He holds, I would guess, that stylization is successful when it is not stylization at all. For he took the acknowledged master of stylized comic theater in German, Carl Sternheim, and de-stylized him. He brought Sternheim's figures in *The Snob* out of that realm of almost surrealistic fantasy in which many previous directors had placed them and made it clear that the painting was from life: this was Wilhelminian Germany. There is a gain in humanity. Theobald and Luise Maske are no longer idiots but have a point of view. One can feel sorry for them at times. One can feel that Theobald has a lot of right on his side when he protests at what Christian is doing to him. Yet, on the basis of *The Snob,* I cannot say that Noelte's work represents a net gain on the productions I used to see years ago, such as *The Strongbox* in East Berlin in 1949. I read in his program of "new ideas," but I was not convinced that what I read is valid, nor did I perceive that it was communicated by what I saw on stage. What was gained in sympathy for each character was lost in sharpness of outline. This was a vague interpretation, and in the end what really succeeded was not the new "realism" of the theory but the most farcical element in the script. In his desire to innovate, Noelte introduced more beds than Sternheim ever thought of. There was a theory behind this: Christian's road is through the bed. But what the theater audience, says to itself is: Hooray, lots of bedroom scenes! So, what may have been intended to make Molière of Sternheim ends making him a Feydeau. Feydeau was also a great writer in his way; but Sternheim should be Sternheim.

Noelte obtrudes too much. He is the kind of director who won't let you forget his presence for a moment. He even had the audacity to tamper with the script of Chekhov's *Three Sisters.* "Didn't Brecht tamper with Shakespeare?" someone asked me when I mentioned this. But Noelte isn't Brecht, and in any case this *Three Sisters* was not offered as a new play based on Chekhov, or even an adaptation, but as Chekhov *pur sang.* In this case, it is not legitimate to cut anything out, let alone such a splendid passage as Olga's final speech. Such things are impermissible, not merely because one reveres Chekhov, and would always want him to have his own way, but even more because all passages in a Chekhov script are absolutely necessary to the total structure and vision. To cut, as Noelte did, the Doctor's singing in the final scene is like cutting the bits of low-life in Shakespeare's tragedies, as used to be done in the 18th century. The Doctor sings a banal little song of the time. That has immense value, not just as characterizing him and his insensibility, but as belonging to an intricate pattern of composition. It contradicts and corrects and puts in the right perspective the immense sadness of the sisters. What did Noelte do? He cut out the repeated singing and, in one place, inserted instead the chimes of a delicate little watch. That is not Chekhov. That is not Russian realism. That is something more refined, more *con*fined. It reminds me, as did the rest of this *Three Sisters,* of *A Month in the Country* as I once saw it at the *Comédie Française,* thoroughly Frenchified, with all the unclassic "irrelevancies" and "digressions" eliminated, until it became neat and well-scrubbed and of a (small) piece: all that has stayed distinctly in memory is the image of a single room, white and very symmetrical.

Maybe Noelte saw it too, for the single room has taken over the *Three Sisters.* He eliminated all changes of scene. One of the classical unities can be imposed on Chekhov, he seems to say, even if the others have to be foregone. And, even if the others have to be foregone, there is a fourth unity that can be added: unity of mood. For this (to him) basic idea of the essentially Chekhovian, Noelte has recourse to the hoariest of exploded fallacies: that Chekhov's plays are nothing but vignettes of depression and defeat.

These are very straightforward, unconfusing errors, of course, and offer a solid base for a production, good or bad. Noelte's production is better than good: it is astonishing in its goodness, and the astonishments, instead of exhausting themselves, like most theatrical astonishments, in the first few minutes, keep happening right up to the final curtain. Had *Three Sisters* actually been this kind of a play, this would have been the definitive production, and one would never have dared to look at another for fear of disappointment.

Though everyone used to see Chekhov in the same terms as Noelte still sees him, no one till him ever dared to stick to those terms in actual performance. There was always a lot of cheating. Notably, actors, those arch-individualists, were always allowed their outbursts of temperament, and these broke the notorious mood. Noelte doesn't cheat. If the idea is isolation and talking-past-each-other, then he puts his actors as far apart as his spacious set allows, and they talk past each other. If they should be almost inaudible, then they *are* almost inaudible. (In the Hebbel Theater, this sometimes means *totally* inaudible: the seats creak as the people at the sides strain to see better.) And talk of "ensemble playing"! In several decades of playgoing, I have never seen more sensitive exchanges between actors. They seemed to be equipped with spiritual radar.

Though Noelte leaves a lot of Chekhov out, what he presents *is* in Chekhov; thus certain Chekhovian values are realized as perhaps never before. If much is lost by the exclusions, something also is gained by the very separation of elements: we see certain of the ingredients in a chemically pure state. So it is, for example, with the Masha-Kulygin-Vershinin relationship. Each of the three actors obviously saw his "problem" as many-sided. And one saw the results out front. For instance, no one laughed when Kulygin put on the false moustache; and, seconds later, when he took it off, he was able to make a big effect (if this isn't too vulgar a way to put it) with what had happened to his face during the "comic" incident: it had turned from merely confused to absolutely devastated. Often Noelte disclosed an underlying doubleness or dialectic where most directors have only found a single thread. An example is in the Irina-Tusenbach relation. Usually she is all sweetness and light, and he, rather a jackass. Let certain negative signs show in her, let her be not quite so pretty, not quite so Christian, and let Tusenbach be equal to his own lines and actions, instead of a little beneath them, and the scales are evened up, and a bigger drama is under way.

Having stated what is un-Chekhovian about Noelte's work, we should in fairness give him credit for fidelity to one of the most Chekhovian "principles": that the dramatic in this material will also best release itself through what seems most undramatic, the quietest will in the end prove loudest, the gentlest approach will have the most violent effect. He consistently

denied his actors "self-expression" in outbursts of temperament, but by the end of the evening each had been enabled to
express himself as fully as he could ever expect to.

This production should be kept in the repertoire as long as
may be possible, so that the lesson can be learned by many.
But meanwhile the gifted Rudolf Noelte should attempt to do
a Chekhov production in which he not only includes every
line but accepts the vision which made every line and every
stage direction so vitally necessary.

Charlie Chaplin and Peggy Hopkins Joyce

*This piece is what came of a commission to re-
view Chaplin's autobiography in 1964. It came
out in* Moviegoer *in 1966.*

CHARLIE CHAPLIN'S AUTOBIOGRAPHY is two books, a good one
and a bad. It could even be issued in two volumes, one good,
one bad, since the good book consists of the early chapters, the
bad book of the later chapters. The story of Chaplin's childhood makes a good book—even in *his* prose. This prose is that
of an auto-didact whose auto-didacticism never went more
than just so far. The prose is an aspect of the phenomenon
Chaplin and one would not for anything be deprived of it by a
Gerold Frank. The story of Chaplin's adulthood, on the other
hand, would only make a good book if written by a Scott
Fitzgerald. Chaplin's prose cannot take hold of it. Chaplin the
writer cannot see it. So he hands it over to Chaplin the
public-relations man: the interest is in listing the celebrities
our Hero met and in defending him against the Villains.
Hence the second half of the book gives no impression of what
it means to be a man and have a life, let alone of what it
means to be Charlie Chaplin and have *his* life. We believe

Charlie when he offers evidence that he was not a scoundrel, a
spy, or a functionary of the Communist Party, but he never
helps us to understand the remarkable circumstance that the
protégé of Mack Sennett became the buddy of John Howard
Lawson. The result is that many who wish to join Chaplin in
defending Chaplin are inclined to write off the later part of his
career altogether and to deplore what is generally called his
more serious side. A mistake. *Monsieur Verdoux* is not a
failure. Just the contrary: when did Lawson or any of the
American Communists ever manage so successfully to get
Marxism into art?

Such, at any rate, were the thoughts that crossed my mind
when reading Chaplin's book. It was at this point that I saw
an ad for a showing of *A Woman of Paris*, a film I have heard
talked about for years but never seen. I knew in advance that
it was unique in being directed by Chaplin without Chaplin
playing in it, also that it was unique among his films in not
being a comedy.

I followed up the ad, and have now seen the film, but only
once, and with distractions: the subtitles were in Russian, and
the voice that read them aloud on the soundtrack read them in
German. I know from experience that plot summaries are apt
to be inaccurate if one doesn't check back with the source, but
in this case no such check was possible. What I saw, as well as I
can remember, was as follows.

A cottage in the country. Evening. A young woman is having trouble with an oldish man whom we guess to be her
father. He locks her in her room. A little later she slips out of
the window and is helped over the tiles and down to the
ground by a young man. They exchange lovers' gestures, and
she climbs the tiles again. But father has locked the window
now. The young man says she can go along to *his* home. She
goes. But her arrival precipitates a second family crisis. The
young man's father wants none of her, so the young couple
decide to run away together to Paris. They get as far as the
local station, when the young man tells her to hold on a few
minutes while he goes back home for something. But when he
gets back home his father is taken ill. The girl phones from the
station to see what has happened. He is about to tell her when

his father drops dead. Which makes him drop the phone. At this moment the train pulls into the station. Thinking she is abandoned, the girl climbs on to the train.

We meet her next a year later. The scene is a very gay night club—girls fly through the air on wires, as in the circus. She is now an established courtesan called Marie St. Clair, and makes her entrance on the arm of an established man about town, Pierre Rebel (accent on the second). She is not just his friend for the evening but his mistress until—next step in the narrative—she reads in the paper that he has got engaged to be married. He assures her rather convincingly that it is only a *mariage de convenance* but, after a display of indifference, she proves hard hit and proposes to drop the relationship. Monsieur Rebel isn't at all affronted but merely bids her call him up sometime when she is of a different mind.

One evening she is sitting sad and lonely in the whorehouse —or whatever more elegant name the rather grand establishment should bear where she and her girl friends live—when one of these friends calls up to say she is at a delightful party: why doesn't Marie come on over? She gives the street address but can't recall if the apartment is on the left or right of the stairs. We glimpse a gathering of middle-aged persons cavorting like Victorian undergraduates on a Saturday night: a pillow fight is in progress. But the door that opens to Marie must be that of the apartment on the other side of the stairs, and who stands in the doorway but her young man, young as ever, though bearing the marks of sorrow, and wearing the uniform of an artist: a smock. He is now a struggling Parisian painter, living with Mama, whom he has brought with him from the cottage. He is so poor, his table napkins have holes in them, which he vainly tries to conceal. She is in evening finery, including furs and jewels. He does not guess the source of all this wealth, but she is embarrassed anyway.

She asks him to paint her portrait. For this he must come over to her place next day to help her choose the right dress. At her place he sees a good deal: her girl friends and a man's collar that slips out of a drawer with her own clothes. He is sad but goes ahead with the portrait.

And so he should, for he loves her in spite of all, tells her so, and asks her to marry him. She says yes, for she still loves him. All would be well; except that Mother is against it. He weakly tells her that he wasn't marrying Marie but only having an affair. Unhappily Marie turns up, unheard, just before he says this. She decides to make that phone call to Pierre. He is delighted, and they arrange to meet for supper. The young man, crushed, takes out a revolver, loads it, and rushes out to find the pair. He has an impulse to shoot one or both as they climb into their cab. Instead he follows them to their night club, sits down between them, and starts a fist fight with Rebel. The management throws him out of the main hall, but in the anteroom he shoots himself and falls on the balustrade against the fountain.

A plainclothesman brings Mother the news, and her son's body is borne in. Also his revolver. She is livid, grabs the gun, and stalks out in search of Marie St. Clair. Meanwhile Marie is en route for the old lady's apartment to see the body. When the mother gets back home, revolver still in hand, Marie is kneeling before the corpse in tears. The mother stops, takes in the scene and its significance, lets the gun fall, seizes the nearest hand of Marie. Her warm handclasp is returned: a look of reconciliation and love passes between the women. The end.

Such is the story of *A Woman of Paris*. Making a summary, one can hardly help having a little fun with it. But the film itself, though touched with comedy here and there, is in deadly earnest. That is to say, the convention the author adopts is at no point burlesqued. He assumes it is viable, and gives himself to it heart and soul.

The story has four turning points: first, the girl's going to Paris alone; second, her meeting the young man again; third, her hearing him say he won't marry her; and fourth, the mother finding her weeping on his corpse. Each turning point is achieved through outrageous coincidence. For the first, the father has to die during the phone call, and the train has to draw in seconds later. For the second, the young man has to happen to find an apartment on the same landing as Marie's friend's friend; Marie's friend has to forget which her friend's door is; and Marie has to pick the wrong one—not to mention that the young man has to be home and answering the door. For the third turning point, eavesdropping has to be resorted to, yet if Marie must hear the crucial statement, it is equally important that she not hear what precedes it or she would guess that the young man didn't mean what he was driven to say. The fourth turning point is a matter of the timing of exits and entrances. The mother has to leave the apartment so Marie can enter it and then the mother must return while Marie is still in a posture that will produce the right impression: were she drying her eyes and enjoying a little light refreshment she would get shot.

All this is *so* extravagant that to burlesque it would be to fall into the labored, bathetic facetiousness that indeed so many burlesqued versions of Victorian melodrama have fallen into over the years. Such an extravagant mode has too many of the elements of burlesque in it already for it to take any more. And if it be retorted that it lacks the most important element of burlesque—the funny—the answer is that this is just the element it must at all costs exclude. You can easily kill melodrama by making fun of it—and you have no guarantee that your fun will itself be funny.

What is our greatest comedian, and greatest composer of comic scenarios, doing with a film that is so unfunny? Actually there is a good deal of incidental fun, and there is no mistaking the signature on it. When Pierre Rebel's imperviousness to feminine distress is to be dramatized, Chaplin has him pick up a saxophone (of which we previously knew nothing but which just happens to be around) and tootle on it. (The film is silent but the sight gag makes the point audaciously enough, perhaps all the more audaciously for being so obviously a substitute for a sound effect.) And where comic realism is in place in this otherwise so unrealistic a work, it is used with a master hand. At the height of her worst spat with Rebel, Marie suddenly throws the diamond necklace he had given her out of the window—a gesture worthy of the author's friend Peggy Hopkins Joyce! But through the window can be seen the bum who picks the necklace up and makes off with it. No real lady, Marie races downstairs and up the street and grabs it from the thief. Final Chaplin touch: she hunts for a small piece of money and gives it to the poor fellow.

Only for the necessary few moments does the film pick up the characteristic rhythm of Chaplin comedy, a rhythm quick but unhurried like that of the old *opera buffa.* The tread of the film as a whole is slow, weighted. Whereas in the comedies the principle is that of rapid change, each image being only that which leads to each succeeding image, in this melodrama we get a series of tableaux which the eye dwells on. They are extravagant, as befits the occasion. They are the pictures that hung upon Grandma's wall if Grandma had a rather representative collection of Victorian story pictures. Chaplin puts his tableaux together expertly, lovingly, and of course without cracking a smile.

These considerations are rather technical and abstract. One cannot leave a Chaplin work there. Chaplin's films are uniquely personal. I mean this literally: no other filmmaker, so far as has become public, has ever used the medium so autobiographically. From a photograph in the new autobiographical book one learns, for example, that the setting of *Easy Street* is modeled on one of the London streets the Chaplins lived on. And surely the main reason Charlie has always played one role is that this one role was himself. Actually he has played two roles: the Tramp and his opposite the Masher. Verdoux is the Masher become monstrous; and so is Hinkel. The weakness of *The Great Dictator* arises partly from the fact that even a monstrous Masher is no adequate image for Hitler. The scene of Charlie toying with the globe is great pantomime but it diagnoses Hitler's trouble as peacock vanity: we look in vain there for the destructive energy that threatened millions of people.

Of the personal "character" of *A Woman of Paris,* the autobiography has this to say:

About this time Peggy Hopkins Joyce, the celebrated matrimonial beauty, appeared on the Hollywood scene, bedecked in jewels and with a bankroll of three million dollars collected from her five husbands—so she told me.

Peggy was of humble origin: a barber's daughter who became a Ziegfeld chorus girl and had married five millionaires. Although Peggy was still a beauty, she was a little tired-looking. She came direct from Paris, attractively gowned in black, for a young man had recently committed suicide over her. In this funereal chic, she invaded Hollywood.

During a quiet dinner together, she confided to me that she hated notoriety. "All I want is to marry and have babies. At heart I'm a simple woman," she said, adjusting the twenty-carat diamond and emerald bracelets that mounted up her arm. When not in a serious mood, Peggy referred to them as "my service stripes."

Chaplin then tells how Peggy had let one husband into the bedroom on the wedding night only after he slipped a check for a half a million dollars under the door. Without having reported any intimacies between himself and her, he does report that at a certain point her interest turns from him to another man. When she threatens to hit him with a champagne bottle, Charlie threatens to throw her off the yacht they are on.

During our bizarre, though brief, relationship, Peggy told me several anecdotes about her association with a well-known French publisher. These inspired me to write the story *A Woman of Paris* for Edna Purviance to star in. I had no intention of appearing in the film but I directed it.

Some critics declared that psychology could not be expressed on the silent screen, that obvious action, such as heroes bending ladies over tree trunks and breathing fervently down into their tonsils, or chair-swinging, knockout rough stuff, was its only means of expression. *A Woman of Paris* was a challenge. I intended to convey psychology by subtle action. For example, Edna plays a *demimondaine;* her girl friend enters and shows her a society magazine which announces the marriage of Edna's lover. Edna nonchalantly takes the magazine, looks at it, then quickly casts it aside, acting with indifference, and lights a cigarette. But the audience can see that she has been shocked. After smilingly bidding her friend adieu at the door, she quickly goes back to the magazine and reads it with dramatic intensity. The film was full of subtle suggestion. In a scene in Edna's bedroom, a maid opens a chest of drawers and a man's collar accidentally falls on the floor, which reveals her relationship with the leading man (played by Adolphe Menjou).

The film was a great success with discriminating audiences. It was the first of the silent pictures to articulate irony and psychology.

This analysis is very silly, of course. One thing we learn from the autobiography is that Chaplin can tell us nothing of his own art. *A Woman of Paris* is so *un*subtle that those who insist on subtlety in art will reject it altogether. Its appeal is wholly to those who can accept melodrama as melodrama. Nonetheless the word "psychological" is called for, if not quite in the way Charlie had in mind.

Being a melodrama, *A Woman of Paris* is, on the face of it, not psychological, but moral: it is about the transcendence of hate by forgiveness. But the convention of melodrama, while dictating the use of such a theme, also, by its character, bids us not to take it seriously. If a melodrama has any substance, that substance is not moral but psychological; it is also not stated and explicit as theme, but embodied and implicit as plot and character. So the work as a whole has an ostensible and a concealed meaning, a manifest and a latent content.

As the basis of a melodrama in praise of forgiveness, Charlie proposed to use the experiences of Peggy Hopkins Joyce. "I had no intention of appearing in the film but I directed it." In other words, he was not to be found in a single role of the film but distributed among all three main roles. Earlier perhaps he might have played the Adolphe Menjou role himself. It is after all that of a Masher. But by this time (1923) Charlie was at the height of his fame as the Tramp, and that he had ever been the Masher was forgotten. He obviously could not play the heroine's role, but that should not stop us from remembering how readily he could identify himself with any only apparently fallen angel. Yet if we look more closely at the plot we shall find that its central figure is really the third figure, the young man, and that this is so because his author is identified with him even more intensely than with the others.

In the ostensible scheme, *a young woman seeks love and finds it* at last outside sex—in pure affection for a sometime foe. That is a lesson in Christian ethics, if not one we are induced to pay any attention to. In the psychological, hidden scheme, *a young man seeks love and fails to find it.* His parents stand in the way. His father drops dead at his first attempt to fly the parental nest. His mother dominates him to the point where he belies his own feelings and loses the girl a second time. This second loss is given a significance in the film which my summary did not try to take in. Though Marie St. Clair posed for her artist-sweetheart in the clothes of a courtesan, the portrait, when unveiled, showed her exactly as she had been in the country cottage, clothes and all. For he did not love the courtesan, and by marrying her would restore, as it were, the country girl's virginity. Per contra, by driving Marie away, he drives her back to Rebel and confirms her identity as courtesan with presumable finality. That is the point at which he kills himself.

The story would have struck a responsive chord in the breast of Chaplin's father-in-law, Eugene O'Neill, for this is the kind of subject *he* always chose: the boy who cannot really break away from his parents into adult love; the girl who as soon as she is not all virgin is all whore; the dialectical opposites of simple home and wicked world.

Does a film like *A Woman of Paris* really rank with plays like *Strange Interlude* and *Mourning Becomes Electra?* That depends where these plays really rank. I don't think O'Neill had sufficiently emerged from the crisis of adolescence to present it fully in art. *A Woman of Paris* doesn't "present it fully in art" either. But it doesn't set out to. *A Woman of Paris* is framed in a convention—that of Victorian melodrama—which it at no point challenges. Here we see indeed how naiveté pays off. Chaplin can accept melodrama so wholeheartedly that he is not tempted to go beyond it—into tragedy any more than into comedy. Hence the fantasies that lurk in it *merely* lurk in it: they do not jump out of it. They do not burst the frame. Perhaps Charlie Chaplin emerged no further from the crisis of adolescence than O'Neill—or less far. But it doesn't matter, for melodrama is an adolescent art anyway. In it, neurotic and immature fantasies do not have to be worked through, but need only be re-created. At the end no hard truth is learned, no catharsis of the soul is experienced. On the other hand, melodrama remains thin and boring if there is nothing but a mechanical retelling of the tale with a mechanical repetition of its moral. It becomes "thick" and fascinating in the degree that it does express an artist's anxieties, provided these are also your anxieties and mine.

So what does *A Woman of Paris* prove about Chaplin? Not that he was just as capable of "serious" work as of unserious work, but that he was gifted for melodrama as well as for farce. This is actually not proving very much, since melodrama and farce are brother and sister. But it is good to recognize the melodramatic gift of Chaplin since it is not abeyant in any of his full-length comic features: it contributes some of their richness both in pure narrative and in human implication. It forces us to realize, as we seem reluctant to do, that Chaplin's films are not mere vehicles for acting but are dramatic creations, and dramatic creations of his own. A melodramatist *is* a dramatist. And if a comparison of Chaplin and O'Neill does not wholly or necessarily favor the latter, then Chaplin must rate as, in a sense, a *serious* dramatist into the bargain.

The Civil Obedience of Galileo Galilei

This review was commissioned by Seymour Peck for The New York Times *in 1967.*

SOME TWENTY YEARS AGO Harold Clurman saw Joseph Losey's production of *Galileo* and my production of *The Caucasian Chalk Circle* and reported in *The New Republic* that we in America had not yet learned how to present Brecht's plays. He was right. And, on the evidence of *Galileo* at the Vivian Beaumont today, one could only conclude that, even now, the lesson has not been learned.

Not that the new show doesn't have its points—possibly, as many have been saying, more points than any previous production in that theatre. One understands how the directing of John Hirsch gets to be praised for firmness. His show is what it is, and one is not left in doubt. One is tempted to describe it as highly *audible*—except that, in fact, if you sit at the side, the actors' voices reverberate as in a cathedral every time they turn away from you (which is often, since the play is done on an apron stage). That one does not so readily think of warmer epithets than *audible* has its reasons.

Not flawless, by any means, as Galileo, Charles Laughton brought far more to the role than Anthony Quayle ever will. First, he could effortlessly portray a self-indulgent guzzler; second, he was able to seem an intellectual, and even a genius. The *combination* of physical grossness with intellectual finesse was theatrical in itself and of the essence of Brecht's drama. In regard to playing the intellectual, this too should be said. It is not done by playing intellect itself. It is done by making the characteristic attitudes of the intellectual live—emotionally. For instance, Laughton would always bristle when he talked with bureaucrats or businessmen: his Galileo was allergic to them. Conversely, when talking to his students he made it clear how much he got from their admiration of him: the classroom was his element. Mr. Quayle, on the other hand, treats everyone else on stage as a stranger, and even likes to have them at a distance so he can address them as a public meeting. The question why a British actor had to be hired for this role is all the more relevant since the British way of reducing people to their voices is highly inappropriate to this German representation of a great Italian. Mr. Quayle is convincing neither as the guzzler nor as the thinker. For the first he substitutes extravert heartiness; for the second, schoolmasterishness. In the final scene he consents to play emotion, but it is the comparatively uninteresting emotion of self-pity that comes through. He sobs. This time his isolation from the others is to the point. But self-pity is only self-pity.

One comment on the show has been that what the ecclesiastics argue with Galileo about is treated somewhat pedantically. This is partly the fault of Mr. Quayle and the production, but probably Bertolt Brecht shares the blame. The debating scenes are not in the class of those in *Saint Joan,* certainly—what debating scenes are?—and perhaps, in depicting a lecturer, Brecht becomes a lecturer himself to an undue extent. Still, to leave the matter there and conclude that the *play* is a lecture is to miss the most interesting—and dramatic—things in it.

The replacement of Ptolemaic by Copernican theories of the universe is described in the play but is not the subject of the play. All credit to the playwright—and in this case to Mr. Quayle too—that they lend to the description a certain poetry that produces, at moments, a quickening of the spectator's pulse. However, the emphasis given to this aspect by Mr. Quayle and the director threw the drama as a whole badly off. The struggle of ideologies is the background or, at most, the premise. The drama itself has to do with the human confrontation of this struggle and, specifically—in the version presented at Lincoln Center—with human inadequacy to it.

In a play, it is true, sheer inadequacy is none too interesting. But this inadequacy is not sheer. It is the inadequacy of a man from whom we would have expected better things. It is the inadequacy of a man who is also great and who has been shown to us *exclusively*—up to the point where he caves in—as a great man. The moral would (at the very least) be: what good is it to have great qualities A, B and C, if at the testing time, you fail, like any little poltroon. But Brecht was after bigger game than even that. His subject might even be called tragic, since he makes the bad not just a contrast with the good but the complement of it—its shadow. His Galileo is a "slave of his passions," as one of his antagonists puts it; but even his love of science was an addiction, like his love of wine and good food. This man felt, like Oscar Wilde, that there was nothing to do with temptation but give way to it. One thing that tempted him was the Copernican theory: he succumbed, hook, line and sinker. He *always* acted spontaneously, did just what he felt like doing. And what he felt like doing when he was shown the instruments of torture by the Inquisition was—saying whatever was necessary to avoid being tortured. So he said that the sun went round the earth, though it was his own unique contribution to human history to prove that the earth went round the sun.

At this point, however, something snapped inside him. Giving way to temptation suddenly ceased to be an unalloyed pleasure. Why? Because he sensed what less hedonistic souls also sense: that the Inquisition's demand called for some other response. Galileo's favorite pupil formulated it thus: "Unhappy is the land that breeds no hero." The scientist takes that in; is obviously "hit"; but manages to find a formulation to strike back with. It is this: "Unhappy is the land that *needs* a hero." I think the author of *A Man for All Seasons* took this formula to be Brecht's summing up: his own play seems intended as a riposte. The riposte, however, is in Brecht's own play already, but is provided in Brecht's own way, not in that of the conventional theatre.

First we have to concede that a land that needs heroes *is* unhappy. The good society will not make such demands on its citizens, and Brecht's Galileo feels this the more keenly because he suffers for it: after all he is a man who has always tried to shun suffering and have fun. That ever *he* was born to put it right! On the other hand, given that the land *is* unhappy, one must not, as Galileo had done, blithely ignore the fact, but proceed to ask: what follows? And what follows is precisely the pupil's conclusion: Unhappy is the land that breeds no hero.

Which Galileo, in the enforced seclusion of house arrest, recognises readily enough. Defect of intelligence was hardly his problem: on the contrary. It was the assumption that he could blithely ignore social reality which he had to give up, even if it meant that he would come to loathe himself in the process. He who had been such a plucky and confident fellow in so many a tight spot proved a coward on the day of reckoning.

That this sounds rather vague and general—"universal" is the word in academic circles—is perhaps what seemed to permit John Hirsch to present the main action of this play so blandly. It is all a little too obvious to be interesting. So the boaster is a coward, eh? But isn't that usually so? Perhaps it is, yet this is not where Bertolt Brecht rested his case. "Cowardice" is not, ultimately, the right word. "Passivity" would come closer, or "submissiveness." All Germans who think about Germany become somewhat preoccupied with submissiveness —for evident reasons. Very many Brecht characters are studies in submissiveness, and they are perhaps the most interesting characters in all his work: Schweyk and Mother Courage, Macheath and Azdak and Galy Gay . . . In Galileo's case, submissiveness has a kind of tragic inevitability, as I have hinted, because it is bound up with his very virtues, his receptivity to all impulses, his great gift for acceptance and enjoyment. How *could* such a man suddenly stop embracing the world—and hit out at it?

He doesn't. But because Brecht then seems to make the demand that he should have, and that future Galileos *must,* we are perhaps less convinced than distressed by the conclusion—the conclusion, that is, as presented at Lincoln Center. Actually, Brecht added another scene which modifies the main thesis. In this scene the onus for hitting out at the world is shifted from Galileo, the individual genius, to his principal pupil, and hence to helpers and servers generally, to "the people."

Mr. Hirsch is not the only director who has omitted the scene, but the others (those I know about, anyway) had spotted that its thematic content is present in an earlier scene which is never cut, the carnival scene. Alas, this is being presented at Lincoln Center amateurishly, frantically, all hither and thither, all buzz and blur. Mr. Hirsch seems to have thought it was the comic—or maybe spectacular?—relief, where in fact it is the poetic and thematic center. Its main feature is a long and splendid ballad by Brecht and Eisler much of which is cut in Mr. Hirsch's production and the rest of which is rendered unintelligible by busy romping and stomping. Since the climactic lines are thrown away by being given to the mob to sing let me tell those who are seeing the show what they should also be hearing, namely:

> Good people who have trouble here below
> In serving cruel lords and gentle Jesus
> Who bids you turn the other cheek like so [gesture]
> While they prepare to strike the second blow:
> OBEDIENCE WILL NEVER CURE YOUR WOE . . .

Speaking with the wisdom of the folk tradition, the balladeer who sings these lines has just been praising the rebelliousness of Galileo. The people will need to share it, if they're going to get anywhere. Now at this time, of course, Galileo has not recanted. When he does, what will the ballad come to mean? That we, the people, cannot hide behind our great men. They may let us down. If disobedience is to be learned, it will have to be learned by us.

This (arguably) is the main idea of Bertolt Brecht's *Galileo,* and it would readily emerge as such if the last scene were *not* omitted. It is (certainly) the idea that has most life and pertinence in the United States today. We have here a play written to urge not Galileo but us—us!—to disobedience, civil and less civil. The week it opened in New York, Martin Luther King also opened up a drama—with his demand for conscientious objection to the war in Vietnam.

Brecht's plays naturally attach themselves to such issues, and Brecht himself always was concerned that the attachment should be firm and visible. His is a theatre of commitment, and in fact his plays seldom get across at all unless they carry some of the appropriate activist fervor. Well, "get across" is a loose phrase. Brecht's plays could be said to "get across" in some fashion as *objets d'art,* as instances of *avant garde* theatre, as formal experiments. Only, if that is what they are, I for one would begin to believe that his detractors are right and that after all "there isn't very much to him." The Hirsch production is handsome and carefully designed, but even if it were even handsomer, even if the design were brilliant as well as careful, the result would still be insufficient to convince an audience that it is face to face with a major playwright.

Perhaps I exaggerate. I think the Lincoln Center production does hint at a certain grandeur. The story is lucidly enacted; the lines are, for the most part, clearly read; Brecht and his translators are permitted to make an impact. (How many translators, by the way, and who are they? The socalled Laughton version was already the work of many hands and has been much changed for the present occasion.) But the grandeur fans out into grandiosity. If not dull, the show is a little formal and inert. And the reason—beyond the reasons already given, such as the limitations of Mr. Quayle's acting (and he is the best of the actors) —is a complete lack of urgency. The show has nothing to say because Mr. Hirsch assumed that what Mr. Brecht had to say was that the earth goes round the sun or that a scientist's life is picturesque (model: Don Ameche as Alexander Bell) .

What goes on at Lincoln Center? Last year people were complaining that Herbert Blau made propaganda—and from a radical viewpoint—in flamboyant press releases and programs. *Galileo* was chosen as a play for him to direct; he leaves; and the play is done as if its issues belonged to the 17th century or the Hollywood view thereof. As for poor BB, he is handed over, in the program, to the tender mercies of Hannah Arendt. And she, who has so successfully disposed of so many, has little trouble disposing of *him*. Oh, she loves his poetry, but as to his point of view she finds it in sore need of correction—by her. So Brecht is set right in the program to his own show. No use to say, I suppose, that the fishmonger does not cry stinking fish. No fishmongers, we: since the departure of Mr. Blau we are—well, what?—aesthetes? Students of Hannah Arendt? Whatever the answer, an author who is apologized for, if not positively debunked, in the program, is also presented evasively on stage. But as it happens, that is not an artistic gain. To vindicate this author as an artist, you have to present his point of view sympathetically, passionately, aggressively. Only then will the lines begin to crackle, the characters to light up, and the themes to burn.

AFTERTHOUGHTS
AND
INDEX

Afterthoughts (1952–1956)

CUSTOM PERMITS THE dramatic critic, when he reprints his notices in a book, to dot the i's and cross the t's which the pressure of journalistic routine had prevented him dotting and crossing before. Each notice remains, however, a record of the response which was in fact his in the theatre. To "correct" this response later would be to fail to give a truthful eye-witness account without succeeding in giving anything decisively better—for even the most conceited of us cannot hope that his report will be complete and authoritative. Subsequent reflections have the status, not of godlike objectivity and definitive revision, but simply of . . . subsequent reflections. Hence the title of this appendix to my book.

page 64. HAS WEAKNESSES, HE HAS NO FAULTS. Since these words were written, it has been urged that Mr. Miller's hero is shown not to be faultless in that he has committed adultery. A fault indeed by seventeenth-century standards, adultery in the context of Mr. Miller's play is but a weakness, that is to say, a "fault" which author and audience forgive him—for the good reason that they're aren't sure it is a fault: it is an endearing bit of weakness. Some months after the opening reviewed above, Mr. Miller personally redirected the play in such a way as to minimize its politics and maximize the personal story of husband, wife, and girl friend. If his intention was to prove his play not to be about McCarthyism, he failed. If any part of my original review would not apply to the later production, it is the phrase NOWHERE IS THERE ANY SENSE OF GUILT. When E. G. Marshall and Maureen Stapleton played the husband and wife, one had the sense of another impulse seeking—if not quite finding—utterance. Is it perhaps an impulse that will find utterance in another play—on the subject of the tensions of unhappy marriage?

page 74. YOUNG MAN IN HIS UNDERWEAR. Mr. Inge thinks I stooped pretty low in making him responsible for an advertiser's handiwork. But my point was, rather, that it is the *destiny* of a work like *Come Back, Little Sheba* to be advertised in this way; the ad is an accurate index of the play's primary appeal. That the works of Faulkner, or even the Holy Bible, also have such an appeal seems to me not relevant; for that appeal seems to me in these cases peripheral and perverse, in the case of Mr. Inge central and legitimate. Mr. Inge tells me that the choice of a protagonist like the hero of *Picnic* is to be explained by the prevalence of the phenomenon in the United States and not by the character of the author. But many phenomena which Mr. Inge ignores are prevalent in the United States. Mr. Inge is a human being: we must regard his choices as significant.

page 75. KAZAN . . . VIRTUALLY CO-AUTHOR. This sentence brought me a friendly but firm note from Mr. Kazan, stating that he had not written one line either of *Streetcar* or *Salesman*. I take it Mr. Kazan includes under the heading of authorship only the dialogue. But it seems to me that if a director helps to create the very idea of a character—changing it from what it was in the author's original script—he is co-author—even though the creating and changing has been done without recourse to new dialogue. Dialogue after all is only one of a playwright's means of communication.

SEQUEL, 1954–1955. The paragraph from which this sentence comes, despite the elaborations above, gave trouble. I received a letter from Mr. Tennessee Williams' lawyer threatening legal proceedings if *The Dramatic Event* were not withdrawn from the bookstores and the offending paragraph deleted. The legal adviser of Horizon Press (my then publisher) demurred. No copies were withdrawn. No words were deleted. Then Mr. Tennessee Williams' lawyer turned out to be Mr. Arthur

Miller's lawyer too. By coincidence Mr. Miller also wanted the book immediately withdrawn from the bookstores, pending the deletion of a certain paragraph. No copies were withdrawn. No words were deleted. Instead, a letter from Mr. Williams and Mr. Miller appeared in Bert McCord's column in *The New York Herald Tribune*. It ended with the words: "Mr. Bentley's statement is a lie."

In relation to my analysis of Mr. Miller's daring (now reprinted in *The Theatre of Commitment*, p. 38), the sequel is full of interest. A radio station asked Mr. Miller to discuss my book with me on the air. He said he would do so if he could bring a friend along. The friend would be Mr. Williams. But then Mr. Miller inspected a copy of *The Dramatic Event*. It seems that, at the time when he demanded the suppression of the book, he had not read it; a fact full of interest for the student of mid-century liberalism. When Mr. Miller finally did read the book, he refused to discuss it publicly, and set down his reasons in a letter marked Not For Publication. The broadcast took place. Mr. Williams and Mr. Miller were absent, but the paragraph beginning at the foot of page 75 was duly transmitted to the attendant millions, and I replied to the implied arraignment with an admirably accurate paraphrase of the note above.

Mr. Kazan was asked to sign the Williams-Miller note but refused. Miss Molly Day Thacher (Mrs. Kazan) gave *The Dramatic Event* a favorable review in *The New Leader*. Mr. Williams was reported in the New York press as saying that, without Mr. Kazan, his new play, *Cat on a Hot Tin Roof*, would not have been a hit.

page 76. COULD NOT HAVE BEEN DONE . . . BY A CHOREOGRAPHER. A correspondent calls my attention to the fact that in the program Anna Sokolow is listed as Assistant Director. If part of what I attribute to Mr. Kazan should have been attributed to Miss Sokolow, then she was here less of a choreographer in the accepted sense than a director of actors. Also noteworthy is the fact that the style of the "choreographic" episodes did not differ from Mr. Kazan's style as we know it elsewhere.

page 78. THE PLAY IS DONE FOR. And so it proved. Only a small public is interested in a director's work as such. Only a small public goes to see a play because it is "interesting." And, as a matter of fact, the small audience at *Camino Real* did *not* profess to attend for this reason but, on the contrary, adhered to the usual Broadway pattern of extremes: if a play isn't the worst ever written, it's the best; if you aren't bored to tears, you are thrilled to the marrow. The effect was that of a clique, if not a claque. Because illiterates have to sneer at Mr. Williams for being literate, his literate admirers band together to hail him as a model not only of literacy but of literature.

page 125. CRAVEN CONFORMISM. A letter published in *The New Republic* declared that Mr. Willingham's novel was just what I said that his play was not: an *exposé* of a military academy. So I read the novel. Unlike the play, it does seem to belong to the tradition of the *exposé:* the reader's main response is "What a terrible place!" Yet the play still seems to me to have been what I said it was, the interesting question being: how did it happen? For the change does not seem to have been wholly intentional. Comparing passage with passage you would generally exclaim: "But that's in the novel too!" For example: A crucial question in the plot is whether the army authorities are corrupt—whether they will kowtow to a cadet whose father gives the school money. And the army proves just as incorruptible in the novel as in the play. The reason the novel gives a different general impression is that its method is different. It is a naturalistic panorama of life in a military academy. The author is saying: "I'm just telling you how things are." The facts pile up so horribly that you say: "Never will any son of mine go to . . ." etc. But the author could add: "Read it again. You'll see that I don't blame the army. It's just life."

This kind of naturalism seems to me rather disingenuous, and there is a parallel disingenuousness in the foul language of the book. If we object to it, the author will say we're the kind of people who wanted *Ulysses* banned in 1920; he may also remind us that this is how cadets *really* talk and act. We needn't be impressed. The brutalities of *End as a Man* are too quick and easy a way to a reader's nervous system; the fact that you or I may be a prude is not a sufficient justification for their use; nor is the fact that they are facts—"art is art because it is not life." It is time to acknowledge that while the generation of Zola was genuinely audacious and, so to say, earned its right to ugliness, "Zolaism" now requires no audacity at all and is practiced, unearned, by many conventional and dull minds . . .

We associate the accumulation of sordid details (it is perhaps rather comic that we do) with social conscience; *ergo, End as a Man* is a novel of social conscience. But, though there are actors nowadays who are willing to urinate on stage, audiences are not so "broadminded" as to accept such a performance and time is short; so that, when *End as a Man* is adapted to the stage, it undergoes a change whether the author wishes it to or not. In becoming less "dirty," it becomes less of a document; and in becoming less of a document, it loses something in indignation; less urine, less adrenalin.

A play perforce presents characters and little else. In the nature of things characters on a stage tend not to be presented naturalistically—as part of a milieu—but morally; which means that, unless the author is subtle, they are villains or heroes. Evil is as evil does. If the stage shows you doing something bad, you are a bad man; whereas if the audience finds itself muttering "you have a point there," you are a good man.

I describe the process of "dramatizing" in the most primitive terms because the theatre is commonly a rather primitive place and *End as a Man* is certainly a rather primitive play. Placed on stage, the Gazzara character (Jocko de Paris) becomes far more of a monster than he was in the pages of a book. Conversely, the General, for whom the reader feels no affection whatsoever, when he walks on stage with such upright things to say becomes, *ipso facto,* a nice man, your uncle or mine.

The book *End as a Man* was published in 1947, is about the year 1940, and belongs, by mentality, to the progressive literature of the thirties. The play was produced in 1953, seems to be about the army in 1953, and certainly belongs to the New

Conservatism of 1953. Yet the changes could all have happened automatically—in the process of dramatization.

page 132. NOTABLE CARTOON PORTRAITS. Notable but not, unhappily, harmonized, one with another. The production of *Mademoiselle Colombe* was marred by a certain disorder which came from heterogeneity of styles which, in turn, came from uncertainty in the producers' minds: they didn't know what they wanted the play to be like. This is not mentioned in my review because it wasn't immediately apparent to me. I was worried about something and, being unable to define it, was silent. Behind both the silence and the worry was no doubt my desire that the show be good and my annoyance with the people who won't see M. Anouilh's talent. I realize that I am here exposing pure prejudice on my part. I like to think that most of my reviews are less prejudiced than this one. I would rather be prejudiced in favor of a show than against it, yet I hasten to add that I never consciously suppress my reservations in order to help a show along, any more than I consciously exaggerate my dislike in order to be "devastating" or consciously moderate my enthusiasm in order to seem superior. This means that my faults as a critic are real ones and not assumed for the occasion.

page 239. MY RESERVATIONS . . . CHIEFLY. I.e., at the time; after brooding on the event, I had more, though I have no means of knowing whom to hold responsible, the translator, the producers, the director, or the actors. My second thoughts on the show were that Giraudoux' play had been, in certain ways, slicked up and, in others, mismanaged. The humor was slicked up by an overemphasis on sex that brought the delicate Giraudoux pretty close to that Broadway world in which sex is such a whale of a joke that the audience is given a signal to snigger every time it is mentioned. What I have called mismanagement marred the whole visual plan of the production, everything, that is to say, that would remain if the dialogue were removed. The setting was one of those unconvincing, uninspired, nondescript affairs, all space and levels, reminding us that the steps and platforms that were once an Innovation and Art can now, without any trouble at all, be Old Hat and a Damn Nuisance. In this setting, actors did unconvincing, uninspired, nondescript things, like climbing a platform to strike an imposing attitude, taking two steps to the right to relieve the monotony, or getting the hell over to the left so as not to be in the way. Thinking back, I even seem to recall that several of the actors—Morris Carnovsky, for instance, and Walter Fitzgerald—had a look in their eye that suggested they wished they were (a) dressed in slacks and smoking jacket instead of classical full dress and (b) at home.

Another show I had misgivings about only afterwards was *The Flowering Peach*. Carried away by the best of the writing, and by Menasha Skulnik's acting, I scarcely bothered to notice, for example, what the directing was like—namely, pretty dull and defensive. The production would have gained another dimension if, say, Mr. Kazan had worked on it.

"I scarcely bothered to notice," yet I must have noticed, for it all came to me quite clearly afterwards, rather long afterwards as a matter of fact, and I am mentioning all this now, not to vent my belated spleen, or demonstrate a capacity for seeing both sides of every question, but for the interest such data has in the analysis of the whole theatre experience. Reviewing *The Chalk Garden*,[1] I challenged the idea that first impressions are all. That was a play I at first disliked and later liked. Am I now simply illustrating the opposite possibility? No. I have not come to dislike either *The Flowering Peach* or *Tiger at the Gates*. The two evenings remain in the memory what they were at the time: two of the most passionate and beautiful experiences of theatre I have known in New York. The passion and the beauty carried so much immediate emotion that various faults and shortcomings made no conscious impression at the time, though it was proved later that I had tucked them away in some cupboard of the mind for future use. So I am restating, rather than recanting, the thought that was behind my remarks on *The Chalk Garden:* that the theatre experience is indeed larger and more subtle than our first impressions suggest. But there is this to add. While a first

[1]Above, pages 279–280.

impression of annoyance can for the time being cut off all further responses, a first impression of delight and enthrall- ment can be so powerful as for the time being to absorb and cancel all annoyances and every inclination to be cooly judi- cial. Here would be a reason, as far as it goes, for producers to concentrate on creating a strong first impression, even if they were *not* dependent on reviewers who hand in their notices right after the show. Not just because of our reviewers' haste, or our own frivolity, but for reasons inherent in the theatre experience—crowd psychology, the "electrical" contact with the live actor, etcetera—the first impression, the immediate contact, assumes an importance in this art which it has, per- haps, in no other. If one were not quite a human being, one could happily contemplate the possibility of simply revelling in those impressions, in that contact, as in a hot tub, or the downward rush of a roller-coaster, and never giving the experi- ence a moment's thought afterwards. The Broadway philoso- phy—now not confined to Broadway but gravely announced from platforms at Princeton, Yale, and all points west—is, of course, perfectly adapted to not-quite-human beings.

page 256. CATHOLIC CRITICS ARE TOO POLITE. Except for Richard Hayes in *Commonweal*, who wrote:

> . . . There is still a small irony in the fact that it was Jean Bréhat, the Grand Inquisitor of France, who spent five years collating the testimony which could release Joan's name from its ignominy. . . . Or consider the false abjuration (one witness tells us that Joan signed smiling in mockery); or the "arranged" relapse (how, for in- stance, may an excommunicated heretic be permitted to receive Communion? detail not mentioned by Anouilh or Shaw); or Joan's constant appeals to have audience of the Pope (again omitted), or the squalid matter of the secu- lar prison in which Joan was kept. . . .

As both Mr. Hayes' and my own review occasioned surprise in circles where Shaw and Anouilh were assumed to have given a fair and complete account of Jeanne D'Arc, it may be well to recall that the facts in the case are, after all, a matter of public record: see *The Trial of Jeanne D'Arc, A Complete Translation of the Text of the Original Documents,* edited by W. P. Barrett, London, 1931, and *The Retrial of Joan of Arc,* by Régine Pernoud, New York, 1955.

page 256. CAUCHON. . . HIGH-MINDED AS SENATOR JOSEPH MC-CARTHY. This statement is unfair . . . to Senator McCarthy. The historical Cauchon more closely resembled Shakespeare's fictitious Richard III. A sadist, a bully, and a careerist who would stop at nothing, he saw himself as the brilliant prosecuting attorney who by getting a young woman violently killed would become Archbishop of Rouen. In addition, he was, in modern French terminology, a collaborator with the enemy, and his immediate "boss" across the Channel was the infamous Cardinal of Winchester who used to charge his enemies with witchcraft much as Stalin would charge them with Trotskyism, if possible with the same results—a point by no means irrelevant to the trial of Joan. Mme. Pernoud makes it pretty clear not only that Cauchon had it in for Joan, which was clear before, but that he "framed" her—tricking her into the abjuration so that later he could "get" her as a *relapsed* heretic, a much worse thing to be than a heretic. When Joan fell into one of his many traps, this monster is reported to have laughed and said: "Now we have her" (*"Elle est prise"*).

page 258. THE INFORMER THEME. Just how important that theme is in the play has been discussed by many, including Mr. Miller himself who, in an exchange with Murray Kempton in *The New York Post,* insisted that, had he wanted to write about political informing, he would have openly done so. Now I believe Mr. Miller does himself a disservice if he implies that there is nothing more to his plays than meets the eye. Surely any play of substance has all kinds of significance, including some which were no part of the author's conscious intention. Even Hollywood movies are full of symbols and significances which critics like James Agee and Parker Tyler have illuminatingly unravelled. So Mr. Miller stands accused of no disingenuousness—except when he denies the possibility of his plays' meaning what at the moment he wishes them not to mean. If *The Crucible* was set in the seventeenth century so that, on convenient occasions, its twentieth-century reference could be denied, then its author *was* disingenuous.

People come to me and exclaim: "How can you say that *A View from the Bridge* is about Mr. Kazan? I happen to know that the manuscript was finished years ago." But I do not say the play was "about" Mr. Kazan. And what I did say would have to be only partially recast if the play were found to have been written earlier. Even if not one word of it was written since 1952 (and this has not been alleged), the choice of 1955 as the production date retains its significance. However much the smaller facts may have to be reshuffled, the large fact is that here are two men who have lived within the orbit of Stalinism, and here are their guilt feelings about it, outcropping in gigantic fantasies of self-justification.

Sometimes the public realizes what an author means before he does himself. Also, his work will *take on* meanings which he may not have anticipated: nor can all the meanings which works take on later be brushed aside as irrelevancies. Then again, how can political interpretations of his work come as a surprise to Mr. Miller? His plays do strike people as political. *Death of a Salesman* struck Eleanor Clark that way (*Partisan Review*, June, 1949). *The Crucible* struck the editors of *The New York Post* that way (witness their editorial, February 1, 1953). And both *The Crucible* and *A View from the Bridge* struck Howard Fast that way (*The Daily Worker*, November 8, 1955):

. . . how is it that so few have noticed that in his second play of the evening, *A View from the Bridge*, Arthur Miller deals directly and heroically with the problem of betrayal? This is a play about an informer, and all else is secondary to that fact; and just as in *The Crucible*, Miller sought for and found a classic American setting in which to tell the parable of the Rosenbergs, so here does he take out of ancient Italian and human tradition—remember Matteo Falcone—the awesome and frightened situation of that man, who by becoming an informer, lays upon himself an irrevocable curse?

Now possibly *The Crucible*, too, was conceived before the events which this political critic connects it with. Nonetheless, putting the play out in 1953, Mr. Miller must surely take some of the responsibility for its highly predictable reverberations; by now, the play is famous throughout Europe as a picture of the American way of life; while, here in New York, Howard Fast writes: "To us on the left, he has given beauty and tribute."

page 261. THE SEX STORY. Studying the printed text of the play I conclude that the confusion was created by wrong casting and direction. In the script, the suggestion that the young man may be homosexual is much less strong, if indeed it exists at all. Disconcerted by mistakes in the production, I failed, moreover, to note in the theatre a point of psychology which is pretty clear in the script: that there is unconscious homosexuality in the father. That is the real reason, as it turns out, that he kisses the boy, and it provides the underlying motif of the eloquent and expressive scene—Miller at his best —where the father goes to the lawyer's office for advice. How- ard Fast implies that Miller uses psychology only as a kind of protective smoke-screen, because one cannot be a frank social dramatist in this place at this time:

> I know full well the chains Arthur Miller wears, for working on Broadway in the cold war, he must fight with all the wit and skill at his command for his survival as an artist; and it is less his weakness than the interdictions of the times in America that have forced him to depend so much on the inner neurotic conflict of his protagonist.

I have to admit that I too had the impression for a long time that Mr. Miller's interest was much more in the social than in the psychological side of things, and I concluded that—from lack either of interest or talent—he left Mr. Kazan to handle the latter. Later, as I reported in *The Dramatic Event*, I sensed in *The Crucible*, especially as Mr. Miller himself redirected it, a degree of inwardness, of concern, if not with the secrets of the heart, at any rate with the tensions of the nervous system. The directing of *A View from the Bridge,* however, was such as to underline the social drama and confuse the psychological issues. Howard Fast was delighted ("all other practicing Broadway directors appear to pale into mediocrity by comparison" with Martin Ritt) but the injustice done to the script was reflected in nearly all the reviews of the production, including my own. *A View from the Bridge* was, I believe, the best American play of the 1955–56 season, unless, possibly, that title should have gone to its companion piece, *A Memory of Two Mondays,* also roughhandled in production.

page 264. SHARPLY CORRECT PORTRAIT. Reviewing *A Month in the Country,* Walter Kerr called Emlyn Williams' translation "crisp and sure," though, unless "sure" is just a pleasant sound signifying approval, it cannot correctly be applied to such a free, arbitrary, *un*sure handling of the original. In characterizing Mr. Matheson's work as correct have I, too, said more than I knew? Have I, too, guessed wrong? Correct though the portrait was in relation to the social type Mr. Matheson aimed at, it was not, I discovered, a correct rendering of the author's intention. And the deviation affected the whole story, for it suggested to me the Matheson character's interest in Kip, whereas the author, as he informed me, intended an interest in the husband. These particulars suggest that a dramatic critic should be more cautious than I had been in judging an actor's correctness of interpretation. Lessing says that a prime task of the critic is to distinguish between script and performance, and, unlike most present-day dramatic critics, I agree with him. At the same time, both actor and critic of *Third Person* could defend themselves by retorting that Mr. Rosenthal's intentions were not clearly enough embodied in his text. In conversation, Mr. Rosenthal was able to answer most of the questions raised in my review. The play *was* intended as a sympathetic account of purely platonic friendship, though both men, according to Mr. Rosenthal, could have been having sexual relations with others. I couldn't help being interested in the explanations but had to remark that such data belong in the play itself. On the other hand, I was disappointed to learn that the play Mr. Rosenthal intended to write was closer to *Cat on a Hot Tin Roof,* and other unresolved fantasies of homosexual life and false accusation, than the play I thought he was trying to write and even than the play he did write.

page 272.   WHAT MR. GUTHRIE DOES ABOUT ACTORS.   This passage drew upon me the comment that, after all, I don't make very explicit what Mr. Guthrie does do about actors.

It was the plethora, not the lack, of evidence that stood in my way. I also thought there was a certain consensus of opinion on the subject. The late James Agate complained for years of Mr. Guthrie's cleverness; he made the point that when we see all these minor characters ingeniously, though pointlessly, differentiated from each other in the name of modernity and ensemble work, we only long for the old actor-manager who simply grouped his colleagues around him and told them to shut up. Stephen Spender was making a similar point in *The New Republic* in 1953: "The lords and knights in Shakespeare's historic plays ought to represent the barons who terrified the kings—they oughtn't to be either the beard-wagging, arted-up dummies they usually are, nor the hotted-up, interpreted characters, each acting a little play of his own, whom Tyrone Guthrie is inclined to develop them into." A Canadian critic, Nathan Cohen, reports, in *Queen's Quarterly,* that it takes Mr. Guthrie to render the most moving play ever written —*Oedipus Rex*—completely *un*moving. "Poetry and passion concern him not at all. That is why the abler actors at Stratford [Ontario] have failed to improve in their craft; he really has nothing to teach them. That too is why he called back for a second and third season a great many inept actors. As long as they look right and move well, he is satisfied. . . ."

The danger of beginning to cite all the evidence against Mr. Guthrie's actors and his use of them is that it tends to overwhelm the evidence on the other side, which does exist. Kurt Kasznar gave a virtuoso performance as the Director in *Six Characters,* even if the balance of the play was the more upset thereby. Ruth Gordon gave a virtuoso performance in *The Matchmaker,* even if Mr. Guthrie did not stop her overdoing it all. Such coruscating solo performances as these do come through in Guthrie productions and do "get across." In comedy, anyway—comedy leaning far over towards farce. The same is not true of tragedy, for the reason given by Mr. Cohen. I did not see the *Oedipus Rex*, but I saw *Tamburlaine*. Anthony Quayle, who played the title role, is a good actor, and it is right that he should have received a lot of credit for playing the role at all. (Such a feat reminds one of Dr. Johnson's being asked if women preached well. He compared them to performing dogs, and remarked that you marvel, not at their doing it well, but at their doing it at all.) Mr. Quayle has a fine body, and a fine voice, and is fully trained in the speaking of poetry, but never for one moment did his characterization resemble Tamburlaine. The good breeding in his voice simply refused to disappear. The words roared at us that he was a savage, but the accent gently reminded us in every vowel and inflection that he was every inch an English gentleman.

I said some of these things in *In Search of Theatre*,[2] and am repeating myself to some extent, because gentility and estheticism are what, time and again, prevent British theatre from being entirely great. In *Tamburlaine* I found Mr. Quayle genteel, and Mr. Guthrie "esthetic." What degree of talent can surmount obstacles imposed by such character and background?

page 282. PUT OUT BY THE PRODUCTION. That what struck me as faults in the Broadway production really were so seems to me proved by the London production which I saw in June, 1956. Instead of wise-cracking aplomb, Dame Edith Evans, as the grandmother, used subtle shading and delicate underlining; and she was surely just what Miss Bagnold had in mind— a little birdlike and high-pitched and remote, a cross between a Dowager Duchess and your homely old aunt in the country. To see Peggy Ashcroft as Miss Madrigal was to realize how much Miss McKenna had tried to be the play instead of the character in the play—had tried to enact her idea of the Bagnold manner and aura—had tried to take hold of the

[2] See also above, the footnote on page 333.

whole play, as it were, and say to the audience: well, here it is, I like it and, by Jove, I'll make you like it! The effect, inevitably, was of recitation. But Miss Ashcroft found the "inside" of the character, and played her feelings, and the development of her feelings. Miss Bagnold's lines gave very little assistance, it is true, but especially the "drunk scene" provided this great actress with the opportunity to turn the character—I mean it in a complimentary sense—inside out . . . A less gifted actor than Mr. Weaver played the Butler much better: the part falls into place smoothly enough, provided much less is done with it. There was a partial misfire in the casting of Laurel, as the nice English girl chosen for it never gave the impression of wickedness. But I'm afraid that, in this part and that of the mother, Miss Bagnold set herself impossible tasks: emotional situations and developments are indicated which the poor player is given no chance to act out. And so this exquisite production of Sir John Gielgud's confirmed me in my opinion of the play too.

page 293.   LESS FROM THE DIRECTION.   But still partly from it. What Mr. Williams began, Mr. Redgrave continued. For example, Mr. Williams took quite a lot away from the character of Belyayev, the tutor. Turgenev's biographer tells us there was something of the famous critic Belinsky in the role. There was also something of Turgenev himself, who had entered Mme. Viardot's household as a penniless young man. To make Belyayev non-intellectual, almost anti-intellectual, as Mr. Williams does, was an impertinence. In the original, when Rakitin asks Belyayev if he reads poetry, the young man replies, No, he prefers criticism. In the Williams adaptation, he answers that he only likes "funny rhymes"! Instead of trying to redress the balance, Mr. Redgrave gave the role to an actor whose chief attribute is charm, and physical charm at that. As is the way with actors of that type, the young fellow had no clue to the inner life of the part. We saw dignity, grace, embarrassment, but not the passion that must finally burst forth, if only for an instant.

Mr. Redgrave played up the funny side of the play so much that the sad side suffered. Surely what happens to Vera should have an impact on the audience? The Doctor sells her for three horses to an unsavory older man! It is one of few decisive things that happen in the play, perhaps the *only* one that is importantly decisive; and in the Redgrave production it had no emphasis at all because the Doctor was such a dear that one couldn't take his actions seriously. . . .

Should I then retract my praise of Mr. Adler's performance? It is foolish to pretend to direct a play from an aisle-seat, but I may be permitted to state my conviction that the essential comedy of the Doctor (and Mr. Adler) could be retained even when the pathetic and ugly parts of the drama are fully expressed. Mr. Redgrave has publicly defended his "comic" interpretations against the straw man of a "romantic" interpretation. The essence of Russian realism, as it seems to me, is that this terminology breaks down before it: and everything —every single thing—that we call either comic or romantic has to be *there* on stage. Neither must be sacrificed to the other.

I state the ideal. Meanwhile, I remain thankful that one side of the picture was so beautifully painted, and I am not sorry, even some time afterwards, that my review chiefly conveys the immediate and real delight of the moment.

page 304. MR. BERGHOF'S PERSONALITY . . . SUBTLY INTER-FUSED. This fact became even clearer to me when, in June 1956, I saw a revival of the original French production in Paris. Some would say the French production was closer to Mr. Beckett's intention: not only was Mr. Beckett present at rehearsals, but the personality of the director (Roger Blin) was, by the stranger at least, not felt to be there at all. And the gravity of the proceedings gave, certainly, greater emphasis to the author's thoughts, one after the other . . . I preferred the New York production. Though, in theatre, the best director is not the most obtrusive one, neither is he the most self-effacing one: in the performing arts, the personality of the interpreter is a legitimate presence, and when we say that Toscanini effaces himself and we hear nothing but Mozart, we speak enthusiastically rather than accurately—we mean, or should mean, that there is no clash between Mozart's personality and Toscanini's. I think Mr. Berghof's participation legitimate and, indeed, called for. And I think the play greatly gains by comedianship like Bert Lahr's, which the French production lacked. It is not a matter of "gagging up" a dull piece. Whatever Mr. Beckett's taste in acting and directing, he has written a script with infinitely greater comic possibilities than were realized in Paris, where Estragon (Bert Lahr's part) was played by a straight actor. The night I attended there wasn't a laugh before Lucky's entrance, and even after that there weren't many. It was avant-garde and existentialist theatre with a vengeance: everyone was having a marvellous time being miserable. On the other hand, the point I made about E. G. Marshall was reinforced. The balance of the play is upset if a star—*the* star—plays Estragon, for Vladimir (Marshall) is just as weighty a role. And I thought the effect of having Vladimir older than Estragon, as in Paris (rather than vice versa, as in New York) was a happy one, for then Vladimir's philosophizings can be characterized as a little senile, which prevents them being solemn and tendencious.

page 313. THE NICHE THAT PLOT AND THEME SEEMED TO LEAVE. I had no notion of implying that they seemed *to their authors* to leave such a niche, much less that, in earlier drafts than those performed, the niche was actually filled by a Communist. But, in one of the two cases, this proved, upon enquiry, to be the case: Marcelle Maurette wrote me that, in her French original, Anastasia's lover *was* a Communist, and Anastasia did return with him to Russia. Robert Ardrey wrote me, on the other hand, that in no draft was his persecuted leftwinger a Communist.

No one who accepts the general point of my chapter will be surprised to learn, further, that the absence of the Communist from the final version of *Anastasia* and from Mr. Ardrey's play has more political significance than his presence in the earlier *Anastasia*. Miss Maurette says—and I believe her—that she is not interested in politics, and made the lover a Communist for dramaturgic reasons—as a foil to the Prince, his rival and opposite number. It is the reasons for suppressing this feature and damaging the dramaturgy in New York that must surely have been political: America is the place where one must not be candid about Communism. Mr Ardrey, for his part, had no conscious impulse to create a Communist at all. Quite the contrary. He was trying to live out the American myth of innocence *à la* Miller. The reality, as he saw it, was unjust suspicion. (And in the garden of Eden all suspicion is unjust.) But finding, as he must, that there *is* some Communism around too, he blames this on the suspicion. Lillian Hellman's Lesbian (in *The Children's Hour*) is not a Lesbian till anti-Lesbianism "makes" her one, and Mr. Ardrey's Communist is not a Communist till anti-Communism "makes" him one. Guilt, then, rests wholly with Senator McCarthy and such, and playwrights linger in Eden quite a while after Adam's departure.

Index

Abbey Theatre, 96, 361
Abbott, George, 31, 168, 191, 192, 199
Acting, 28–34, 52–58, 295
  American compared with foreign, 188–90, 240, 242
  critics of, 365–67
  in films and television, 121
  in foreign languages, 41–43
  Hamlet's advice on, 52–53
  "the New Actress," 119, 131
  paradox of, 66
  in Shakespeare, 56, 93–94, 237–38
  in Shaw, 32–33
  traditions of, 28–29, 38–39, 46, 66, 138, 321, 383
  See also Actors' Studio; Stanislavsky, Constantin
Actors' Studio, 77, 125–26, 130, 227, 326
Adams, J. Donald, 169, 323, 360
Adler, Luther, 295, 468
Adler, Stella, 81
Affair of Honor, 316
After the Fall, 399
Agate, James, 7n, 26, 197, 211n, 345–50, 465
Agee, James, 354, 461
Albee, Edward, 413
Alcalde, Mario, 209
Alcestis, use of in *The Cocktail Party*, 169–70

Aleichem, Sholom, 195
All Summer Long, 183–86
Allegro, 324
Alleyn, Edward, 56–57
Alsberg, Henry, 196
Alswang, Ralph, 113
American Gothic, 117–18
American Repertory Company, 365
Amphitryon 38, 145
Anastasia, 313–14, 469
Anders, Guenter, 419
Anderson, Judith, 70, 129–31, 226
Anderson, Maxwell, 69, 204–7, 217, 259, 363
Anderson, Robert, 109–10, 114, 183–85
Andrews, Julie, 283–84, 318
Anna Christie, 17, 210, 357
Anna Lucasta, 353n, 357–58
Anouilh, Jean, 7, 10, 44–45, 145, 299
  Antigone, 44, 45, 133–34, 176
  The Lark, 254–57, 460–61
  Legend of Lovers, 44, 176
  Léocadia (*Time Remembered*), 44
  Mademoiselle Colombe, 7, 44n, 132–34, 240, 458
  Marivaux and, 45–46
  Pirandello and, 46, 212
  The Rehearsal (*Love Punished*), 43–46

Anouilh, Jean (*continued*)
Thieves' Carnival (*Thieves'* Ball), 44, 211–14
Ansky, S., 194–96
Anthony, Joseph, 77, 255, 257
Antigone (Anouilh), 44, 45, 133–34, 176
Anthony and Cleopatra, 198, 401
Apollinaire, Guillaume, 145
Appalachian Spring, 341
Apstein, Theodore, 312
Archer, William, 303
Ardent Song, 340
Ardrey, Robert, 313, 319, 469–70
Arendt, Hannah, 449
Aristophanes, 418
Aristotle, 267
Armour, Rachel, 196
Arms and the Man, 155
Arnold, Matthew, 249, 355
Aronson, Boris, 131, 218–21, 260
Arsenic and Old Lace, 355
Artaud, Antonin, 417
Ashcroft, Peggy, 162, 466
Asmodée, 202
Atkinson, Brooks, xl, 3, 12, 13, 166–67, 211, 215, 316
  on Marivaux, 38, 39
  on Marlowe, 270
  O'Casey and, 25, 265
  on *The Saint of Bleecker Street*, 321
  See also: New York Times, The
Auden, W. H., 193, 346
Aul, Ronne, 77
Austen, Jane, 38
Autereau, 38
Avon Book of Modern Writing, The, 322
Awake and Sing, 210
Axelrod, George, 325
Ayres, Lemuel, 132

Bad Seed, The, 204–7, 230
Bagby, Phillip H., 301–2*n*
Bagnold, Enid, 280–83, 466
Baierl, Helmut, 421
Balanchine, George, 193
Balsam, Martin, 275
Banbury, Nose, The, 349
Bannister, Harry, 132
Baptiste, 39
Baring, Maurice, 308
Barker, Margaret, 219
Barrault, Jean-Louis, 38–40, 43, 83, 99, 154, 167, 368–77
  critique of, 372–73
Barrett, W. P., 461
Barry, Philip, 116
Barrymore, John, 335
Barzun, Jacques, 99
Bat, The, 355
Bataille des Dames, 232–34
Baty, Gaston, 98
Bauer, Hans, 429
Bean, Orson, 326
Beaton, Cecil, 10, 26, 285, 350, 393
Beauchamp, 376
Beaumarchais, Pierre de, 389
Beaumont, Francis, 79
Beckerman, Bernard, 93
Beckett, Samuel, 296–304, 379, 468–69
Bedbug, The, 425
Beggar's Opera, The, 100–3
Begley, Ed, 317
Behrman, S. N., 145, 196, 199, 358, 404–5
Belasco, David, 210
Bel Geddes, Barbara, 203, 213, 229, 230
Benét, Stephen Vincent, 69–70
Bennington College, 341
Benson, Frank, 348
Benson, Sally, 325
Benthall, Michael, 32, 33, 198
Beolco, Angelo (Ruzzante), 83
Bérard, Christian, 10
Berghof, Herbert, 303, 468–69

Bergman, Ingrid, 30, 192
Berkson, Muriel, 219
Berlin Ensemble, 340, 375, 384, 420, 421
Berman, Eugene, 393
Bernardine, 109
Bernhardt, Sarah, 54, 254, 308, 317, 348
Bernstein, Leonard, 257
Berry, Eric, 318
Bertin, Pierre, 373
Besson, Benno, 418
Best, Edna, 113–14, 132, 171
Best Years of Our Lives, The, 192
Betterton, Thomas, 28, 54
Betti, Ugo, 176
Bielenska, Olga, 294
Bing, Rudolf, 390, 393, 394
Bip and the Butterfly, 344
Birsh, Patricia, 87, 340
Black Swan, The, 416, 428–29
Blackburn, Clarice, 119
Black-eyed Susan, 316
Blau, Herbert, 449
Bleak House, 89–90
Blick, Newton, 142
Blin, Roger, 468
Bliss, Helena, 191
Blitzstein, Marc, 153, 410, 411
Bloom, Claire, 36
Blyden, Larry, 168
Bogart, Humphrey, 205, 408
Böll, Heinrich, 415, 421
Bolton, Guy, 313
Booth, Shirley, 156–57
Bosley, Tom, 213
Bourgeois Gentilhomme, Le, 242–45
Bowles, Jane, 128–31
Bowles, Paul, 128
Boy Friend, The, 318
Boy Meets Girl, 166
Brahm, Otto, 414
Brando, Marlon, 48, 73, 215
  as Marc Antony, 105–6

Brecht, Bertolt, *xxxvii–xxxviii*, 117, 266, 346, 396, 415, 421
  The Caucasian Chalk Circle, 384–85, 443
  Edward II, 21
  Galileo, 71, 415, 416, 443–49
  The Good Woman of Setzuan, 384
  influence of on German theatre, 415–16, 418
  Mahagonny, 419
  Mother Courage, 242, 415
  political views of, 25–26, 266, 311
  Round Heads, 422
  The Threepenny Opera, 101–2, 153, 191, 421
  use of oriental theatre by, 384–85
Breen, Robert, 80–81
Broadway, *xxxiv*, 97
  Off Broadway and, 97, 187
  Shakespeare on, *xxxv*, 362–67
  treatment of serious writers on, 295–99
Brook, Peter, 101–2, 178–79, 269, 418*n*
Brooke, Eleanor, 166
Brooks, Jacqueline, 189
Brown, Pamela, 334
Browne, E. Martin, 142, 171
Bruce, Nigel, 36
Brunner, Karl, 152
Buckmaster, John, 32
Buckwitz, Peter, 423–25
Burbage, Richard, 54, 56–57
Burke, Georgia, 9
Burning Glass, The, 113*n*
Burrell, John, 23
Burrows, Abe, 323
Bus Stop, 230, 322
Butler, Bill, 264
Butterfield, Herbert, 238–39
Buzz Buzz, 7*n*, 348
By the Beautiful Sea, 156–57

Cabinet of Dr. Caligari, The,
    92
Caesar and Cleopatra, 61
Caine Mutiny Court Martial,
    The, 138–41, 151, 197
Calhern, Louis, 105
Calloway, Cab, 81
Calmo, Andrea, 83
Camille, xxxvi, 317
Camino Real, 74–78, 119
Campbell, Mrs. Patrick, 47,
    284–85
Can Can, 191
Candy, 399
Capote, Truman, 8–12
Carlyle, Thomas, 396
Carnegie Institute of Tech-
    nology, 188
Carnovsky, Morris, 223–24, 459
Carousel, 192, 199
Cartmell, Van H., 353*n*, 354–55
Cary, Joyce, 328
Castle, The, 118
Cat on a Hot Tin Roof, xxxvi,
    224–31, 261, 264, 412,
    413, 455
Caucasian Chalk Circle, The,
    384–85, 443
Cave of the Heart, 339
Cerf, Bennett, 353*n*, 354–55
Chagall, Marc, 195, 196
Chairs, The, 381
Chalk Garden, The, 276, 279–
    83, 459, 466–67
Chambers, Whittaker, 258
Champagne Complex, The, 323
Chaplin, Charles, 25, 38, 86,
    157, 317, 377, 380
  autobiography of, 434–43
  compared to Marcel Marceau,
    343
  films of, 35–37, 84–85, 166,
    377, 401, 410, 435–43
  political views of, 37, 410–11,
    435
Chapman, John, 298
Charon, Jacques, 39, 251

Chase, Mary, 277
Chayefsky, Paddy, 272–76
Chekhov, Anton, *xl,* 184, 218,
    291
  The Cherry Orchard, 251–54,
    286
  The Three Sisters, 128, 218,
    221–24, 251–54, 286, 287,
    290, 429, 431–34
  Uncle Vanya, 286–87, 366
Cherry Orchard, The, 251–54,
    286
Children in Uniform, 124
Children's Hour, The, 49–52,
    261, 470
Chodorov, Edward, 166, 168
Chodorov, Jerome, 276, 278
Christie, Agatha, 92, 217
Christopher Columbus, 369–70,
    375–76
Cibber, Colley, 55
Cilento, Diane, 241
Ciminio, Leonardo, 253
Cinderella, 176
Circle, The, 263
Circle in the Square, 100, 131,
    159–60, 187, 326
City Center, opera company,
    172, 175, 193
City Lights, 25, 35, 84
Civilization and Its Discontents,
    123
Claire, Ina, 141, 411
Clandestine Marriage, The, 188–
    90
Clark, Eleanor, 462
Claudel, Paul, 369
Clean, Well Lighted Place, A,
    17
Climate of Eden, The, 49
Clunes, Alec, 334
Clurman, Harold, 65–8, 113,
    226, 322, 443
  as director of *Mademoiselle
    Colombe,* 133
  as director of *Tiger at the
    Gates,* 240

Clurman, Harold (*continued*)
  on *Desire Under the Elms*,
    402
Cobb, Lee J., 65–68, 209
Cock-a-Doodle Dandy, 28
Cocktail Party, The, 10, 17, 117
  reviewed, 169–72
  symbolism in, 201
Cocteau, Jean, 103, 145, 162,
  236
Cohen, Nathan, 382, 465, 466
Coleman, Robert, 297
Collins, Russell, 9
Colman, George, 188
Colt, Alvin, 137
Columbia Daily Spectator, 377
Columbia University, 37, 122,
  232
Come Back, Little Sheba, 74,
  454
Comédie Française, 39, 242–51
Commedia dell'arte, 38–39, 46,
  383
Commentary, 261
Commonweal, 460
Communism, 49, 63, 260, 309–
  14, 361, 410, 462, 469
  Brecht and, 25–26, 266, 311
  in East Germany, 414, 416,
    418–19, 422
  under Hitler, 414
  O'Casey and, 26–28, 265–66
  Shaw and, 25
  See also Politics—theatre and
Confidential Clerk, The, 120,
  170, 171
  reviewed, 141–45
Congreve, William, 83, 188
Conrad, Joseph, 184, 279, 397
Constant Nymph, The, 349
Cook, Donald, 168
Cooper, Gladys, 282
Cooper, Jackie, 168
Coote, Robert, 60
Copeau, Jacques, *xxxvii*, 366
Coriolan, 21
Coriolanus, 135–38, 189, 220

Cornell, Katharine, 176, 219,
  320, 366, 411
Corsaro, Frank, 100
Corwin, Norman, 69
Cosí fan tutte, 174, 175, 392
Cotten, Joseph, 117
Courteline, George, 382
Coward, Noel, 405
Cradle Song, The, 326
Cradle Will Rock, The, 410
Craig, Gordon, 92, 237, 337,
  345, 348
Craig, Helen, 99
Crawford, Don, 213
Cronyn, Hume, 321
Crucible, The, 62–65, 73, 261,
  313, 453–54, 462–63
Cry of the Peacock, 44
Cummings, E. E., 318

Daily Worker, The, 236, 267
Dallas, Tex., 123
Danton's Death, 290
Da Ponte, Lorenzo, 37, 173–74,
  392
Dark Is Light Enough, The, 219,
  226, 318
Darkness at Noon, 135
Darrieux, Danielle, 154
David, Thayer, 189
Davidson, John, 168
Days Without End, 18
Dean, James, 151
Death of a Salesman, 125, 209,
  261, 399
  Kazan and, 65, 75, 77, 225,
    454–55, 462
Death of Cuchulain, The, 97
Deaths and Entrances, 341
Deburau, Jean, 38, 39
Deep Blue Sea, The, 161, 162,
  201
De Filippo, Eduardo, 176, 210,
  337–38, 383
De Filippo, Titina, 337
Degen, Michael, 423

De Mille, Agnes, 84
Denham, Reginald, 204, 206–7
Dent, Alan, 335
De Paolis, Alessio, 393
Deputy, The, 416, 418
Desailly, Jean, 39, 372
De Sica, Vittorio, 273
Desire Under the Elms, 215,
    402–3
Desperate Hours, The, 214–16
De Vega, Lope, 370–71, 374
Diary of Anne Frank, The, 279,
    324–25
Dickens, Charles, 22–25, 198,
    277
  as acted by Emlyn WIlliams,
    89–90
Dickinson, Emily, 85–86
Dillman, Bradford, 264
Diversion of Angels, 341
Doctor Strangelove, 412
Doctor's Dilemma, The, 220, 320
Dog in the Manger, 370–71, 374
Doll's House, A, 120
Don Giovanni, 173, 175, 387
"Don Juan in Hell," 29
Doña Rosita, 429
Donahue, Vincent, 323
Double Inconstancy, 45
Douglas, Robert, 278
Downer, Alan, 404
Downes, Olin, 321
Dracula, 217
Drake, Alfred, 175–77
Drama Quartet, 55, 58, 69
Dramatic Event, The, xxxiii, 322,
    347, 454–55
  reviewed, 229
Draper, Ruth, 88
Dressler, Marie, 411
Dreyfus Affair, The, 124
Dryden, John, 55
Dukes, Ashley, 82, 83, 99
Dullin, Charles, 71
Dumas, Alexandre, 232
Dumont, Margaret, 411
Dunne, J. W., 360

Dunnock, Mildred, 129, 226, 230
Dürrenmatt, Friedrich, 415
Duse, Eleonora, 42, 53, 54
D'Usseau, Arnaud, 110–13
Dybbuk, The, 194–96

Eager, Edward, 176
East Lynne, 355
East of Eden, 275
Easy Street, 439
Eatherly, Claud, 419
Ebeling, George, 224, 253
Eckart, Jean, 191
Eckart, William, 191
Edmonds, Louis, 189
Edward II (Brecht), 21
Eglevsky, André, 36
Ehrenburg, Ilya, 310, 314
Eisenhower, Dwight, 63, 284,
    408
Eisler, Hanns, 447
Electra, 40, 42
Electra (Giraudoux), 145
Eliot, T. S., 10, 72, 95, 112, 195,
    346, 369
  The Cocktail Party, 10, 17, 117,
    169–72, 201
  The Confidential Clerk, 120,
    141–45, 170, 171
  The Family Reunion, 171,
    176, 349
  Murder in the Cathedral, 171
  Pirandello, and, 170
  Shaw and, 144
  Sweeney Agonistes, 342–43
Embezzled Heaven, 358
Emmet, Katherine, 52
Emperor's Clothes, The, 65
Enchanted, The (Intermezzo),
    100, 145, 371–72
End as a Man, 124–27, 457–58
Endgame, 379
Engels, Friedrich, 396
Enters, Warren, 190, 214
Epic theatre, 414
Epstein, Alvin, 302

Ermine, 44
Eternal Return, 103
Ethan Frome, 118
Evans, Edith, 321, 349, 466
Evans, Maurice, 93
Evergreen Review, The, 378–82
Excursion, 118
Expressionism, 26–27, 176, 267, 274, 414, 415
   in modern French plays, 367–71

False Secrets, The, 38–39
Family Reunion, The, 171, 176, 349
Fanny, 196
Farrar, Elizabeth, 254
Fast, Howard, 310*n,* 462–63, 464
Father, The, 218
Faulkner, William, 8, 296
Feder, Abe, 210
Federal Theatre, 123, 190, 250, 362
Fehling, Juergen, 414, 429
Felsenstein, Walter, 391, 392
Fergusson, Francis, 96
Fernandez, Ramon, 194
Ferrer, Mel, 147
Festival of American Dance, 85
Feydeau, Ernest, 405, 432
Field, Betty, 111, 113
Fields, Joseph, 276, 278
Fields, W. C., 299, 411, 412
Films, 121, 285, 335–38, 368, 411
   of Chaplin, 35–37, 84–85, 166, 377, 401, 410, 435–43
   of the Marx Brothers, 411
   from Shakespeare, 103–6, 235–37, 238, 335, 366–67
Filumena Marturano, 337–38
Finnegan's Wake, 94, 301
Fitch, Clyde, 233
Fitzgerald, F. Scott, 325
Fitzgerald, Geraldine, 320
Fitzgerald, Walter, 241–42, 459
Fleming, Gerry, 189

Fletcher, John, 79
Flies, The, 145
Flight into Egypt, 11, 67
Flowering Peach, The, 207–11, 303, 459
Fonda, Henry, 138
Fontanne, Lynn, 316–17, 374
Foote, Horton, 117–19
Forbes-Robertson, Johnston, 53, 54, 349
Ford, Paul, 163
Ford, Ruth, 288–89
Foreign languages in the theatre, 40–43
Forza del Destino, La, 388, 389–93
Fouqué, Friedrich, 146
Four Poster, The, 320–21
Fourberies de Scapin, Les, 83
Franciosa, Anthony, 326
Franco, Francisco, 382
Frau Flinz, 421
Freud, Sigmund, 48, 107, 298
   Civilization and Its Discontents, 123
Frisch, Max, 415
From the American Drama, 406
Fry, Christopher, 10, 101–2, 145–46, 221
   as adaptor of *Tiger at the Gates,* 239
   The Dark is Light Enough, 219, 226, 318
Funt, Julian, 159–61

Gabel, Martin, 318–19, 326
Galileo, 71, 443–49
Gallup, Donald, 394*n*
Galsworthy, John, 350
Gambler, The, 176
Gantillon, Simon, 98–99
Garbo, Greta, 133
García Lorca, Federico, *xxxviii–xxxix,* 37, 429–30
Garfein, Jack, 126
Garnett, Constance, 293

Garrick, David, 54, 91, 307
  The Clandestine Marriage,
    188–90
Gates, Larry, 60
Gay, John, 101–3
Gazzara, Ben, 126–27, 229, 230
Gazzo, Michael V., 326–27
Gelin, Daniel, 154
Gerard, Rolf, 60, 393
Gershwin, George, 79–80, 286
Gersten, Berta, 209
Get Away Old Man, 359
Ghelderode, Michel de, 380
Ghosts, 193
Gibbs, Wolcott, 159, 363–64
Gide, André, 149–51
Gielgud, John, 102, 105, 317, 333,
    349, 467
Gierow, Karl Ragnar, 394
Gillette, William, 57
Gioconda Smile, The, 10
Giraudoux, Jean, 7, 38, 83, 100,
    247, 283, 371
  Amphitryon 38, 145
  Ondine, 7, 145–48
  Siegfried, 46, 145
  Tiger at the Gates, 145, 238–
    42, 458–59
Girl of the Golden West, The,
    38
Girl on the Via Flaminia, 159,
    164
Girl with the Green Eyes, The,
    233
Gish, Lillian, 118
Glass Menagerie, The, 127, 210,
    413
Gluck, Christoph Willibald von,
    389
Glyndebourne Opera, 390
Goethe, Johann von, 99, 197n
Goetz, Augustus, 149–51
Goetz, Ruth, 149–51
Gogol, Nicolai, 301
Gold Rush, The, 84
Goldberg, Arthur, 388, 392
Golden Apple, The, 191

Goldoni, Carlo, 175
Goldstein, Jennie, 77
Good Woman of Setzuan, The,
    384
Goodrich, Frances, 324
Gordon, Ruth, 327, 465
Gorelik, Mordecai, 210
Graham, Martha, 84–87, 317,
    338–41, 378
Grant, Cary, 192
Granville-Barker, Harley, 91,
    307
Grass, Guenter, 415, 422
Grass Harp, The, 8–12
Gravet, Fernand, 155
Great Dictator, The, 401, 439
Great Sebastians, The, 313, 316–
    17
Greek National Theatre, 40–43,
    86
Greene, Graham, 200–3
Greenwood, Joan, 142
Grimm, Friedrich, 38
Grotjahn, Martin, 377
Group Theatre, 65, 81, 138, 321
Gruendgens, Gustav, 414
Guinness, Alec, 178
Guthrie, Tyrone, 269–72, 308,
    327, 348, 390, 465–66
Guys and Dolls, xxxv, 323–24,
    406–8
Gwenn, Edmund, 224

Hackett, Albert, 324
Hackett, Buddy, 216
Hacks, Peter, 415, 418–19
Hagen, Uta, 30–31, 159, 162,
    206
  in *The Cocktail Party*, 171
  in *A Month in the Country*,
    294
Haggard, Stephen, 32
Hambleton, T. Edward, 319
Hamlet, 335, 423–25, 428
Hammerstein, Oscar 2nd, 122,
    192, 197, 277, 327, 408

Hammerstein, Oscar 2nd (*continued*)
  Oklahoma!, 78, 178, 354, 405
Hampden, Walter, 65
Hamsun, Knut, 266
Harlequin Refined by Love, 38–39
Harris, Jed, 64–65, 66, 73, 227
Harris, Julie, 132–34, 254–57
Harrison, Rex, 61, 283
Hart, John, 54
Hart, Lorenz, 192, 408
Hart, Moss, 48, 286
Harvey, 277
Hatfield, Hurd, 77
Hatful of Rain, A, 326–27
Hauptmann, Gerhardt, 414
Hawkins, William, 3
Hayden, Terese, 98–100
Hayes, Alfred, 159
Hayes, Joseph, 214–15, 217
Hayes, Richard, 460
Hazel Flagg, 191
Hazlitt, William, 55, 345
Heckart, Eileen, 74, 205, 230
Heflin, Van, 260
Heggen, Thomas, 73, 163
Helena, 418
Hellman, Lillian, 49–52, 64, 66, 255, 257, 470
Helpmann, Robert, 34
Hemingway, Ernest, 17, 253
Henderson, Florence, 199–200
Henry IV (Pirandello), 380
Henry IV (Shakespeare), 21, 366–67
Henry V, 20, 335, 362, 366
Henry VI, 335
Hepburn, Audrey, 148, 213
Hepburn, Katharine, 31–34
Herter, Christian, 385
Hesterberg, Trude, 421
Heyme, Hansguenther, 425–28
Heyse, Hans Joachim, 429
Heyward, DuBose, 79–80, 286
Hiken, Gerald, 252
Hiller, Wendy, 284–85

Hingle, Pat, 227, 230
Hinkson, Mary, 341
Hirsch, John, 444, 446–49
Hiss, Alger, 50, 136, 314
Hitchcock, Alfred, 178, 192
Hitler, Adolf, 152, 414, 416
  effect of on German theatre, 413–14
Hochhuth, Rolf, 415–16
Hochwaelder, Fritz, 177
Hodes, Stuart, 86
Hofstra College, 92–93
Holloway, Stanley, 283–84
Holloway, Sterling, 9
Holm, Hanya, 285
Home Is the Hero, 183–86
Homer, 69
Homolka, Oscar, 219–21
Homosexuality in the theatre, 228–29, 261
Horan, Robert, 84
Houghton, Norris, 319
Houseman, John, 104, 136–38
Howard, Sidney, 138
Howe, George, 23
Huie, W. B., 419
Human Comedy, The, 359
Humphrey, Cavada, 237
Hunt, Hugh, 203
Hunt, Leigh, 54
Hunter, Kim, 52
Hurok, Sol, 246
Huxley, Aldous, 10
Hyman, Earle, 329–30

Ibsen, Henrik, 127, 193, 218, 221, 234, 251, 362
  The Master Builder, 218–21, 225
  O'Neill compared to, 17
Iceman Cometh, The, xxxiv, 17
Immoralist, The, 149–52
Importance of Being Earnest, The, 217, 298
In Any Language, 30–31

In Search of Theatre, 19, 466
In the Matter of J. Robert Oppenheimer, 416
In the Summer House, 127–31
Indiana University, 123
Inge, William, 71–74, 322, 323, 454
Inherit the Wind, 317
Inishfallen, Fare Thee Well, 26, 96
Innkeepers, The, 312
Institute for Advanced Studies in the Theatre Arts, 384
Intermezzo (The Enchanted), 100, 145, 371–72
Invitation au Château, L', 44, 179
Ionesco, Eugène, 377
Irving, Henry, 53, 237, 321
I've Got Sixpence, 48
Ives, Burl, 225–27, 229, 230

J'accuse!, 124
Jackson, Anne, 168, 275
Jacobowsky and the Colonel, 353*n*, 358
Jaffe, Sam, 132
James, Henry, 38, 144–45, 246, 248–49, 405
Jamison, Marshall, 325
Jamois, Marguerite, 98
Jessner, Leopold, 414
John Brown's Body, 68–71
Johnson, Samuel, 28, 55–56
Jonson, Ben, 33, 292, 368–69
Joseph II, Emperor, 387
Jourdan, Louis, 151
Journey's End, 26
Jouvet, Louis, 99, 145–47, 240, 368, 372
Joyce, James, 297, 301
Joyce, Peggy Hopkins, 438–41
Julius Caesar, *xxxv*, 103–6, 237
Jung, Carl, 341
Juno and the Paycock, 282

Kabuki theatre, 384
Kafka, Franz, 118, 176, 313
Kaiser, Georg, 261, 415
Kammerspiele (East Berlin), 418
Kasznar, Kurt, 302, 465
Kaye, Danny, 157
Kazan, Elia, 11, 64–65, 68, 81, 258, 462, 463
    Afer the Fall and, 399
    Camino Real and, 75–78
    Cat on a Hot Tin Roof, and, 224–31, 455
    compared with other directors, 65, 126, 130, 185–86, 272, 459
    Death of a Salesman and, 65, 73, 75, 226, 454–55
    Tea and Sympathy and, 109–10
Kazan, Molly, *see* Thacher, Molly Day
Kean, 232
Kean, Edmund, 54, 236
Keith, Ian, 93–94
Kelly, Nancy, 206
Kemble, John Phillip, 54
Kempton, Murray, 461
Kennedy, Arthur, 65
Kennedy, John F., assassination of, 419
Kerman, Joseph, 173
Kerr, Deborah, 109, 110
Kerr, Jean, 166
Kerr, John, 109, 186, 188
Kerr, Walter, 3, 97–98, 211, 289, 290, 464
    as director, 168
    on *Richard III*, 332
    on *Waiting for Godot*, 297–98, 300
    See also New York Herald Tribune, The
Kidd, Michael, 191
Killers, The, 17
Kilty, Jerome, 237–38
King, Martin Luther, 448
King and I, The, 192, 198

King Oedipus (Yeats), 366
King of Hearts, 166–68
King Lear, 82, 304–8, 332
Kingsley, Sidney, 216
Kipphardt, Heinar, 415, 416–17
Kirstein, Lincoln, 175
Kiss Me Kate, 406
Klugman, Jack, 137
Koestler, Arthur, 67
Komische Oper (East Berlin),
    390, 392, 420
Konn, Charles, 86
Konya, Sandor, 388
Kortner, Fritz, 414, 421
Krafft-Ebing, Richard von, 298
Kramer, Hilton, 322
Krauss, Werner, 414
Kronenberger, Louis, 134, 325
Krushchev, Nikita, 382
Krutch, Joseph Wood, 363
Kurnitz, Harry, 318
Kutschera, Frank, 423–24

Labiche, Eugène, 405
Ladies of the Corridor, 110, 117,
    132
Lady Vanishes, The, 192
Lahr, Bert, 284, 298, 300, 302–4,
    469
Lalique, Suzanne, 243
Lamb, Charles, 348, 353–54
Landau, Jack, 190
Landestheater Halle, 422
Lang, Pearl, 341
Lark, The, 254–57, 460–61
Larkin, Peter, 147
Late Mattia Pascal, The, 46
Later Ego, The, 346
Latouche, John, 191
Laughton, Charles, 32, 58
    The Caine Mutiny Court Mar-
        tial and, 138–41
    as Galileo, 444
    John Brown's Body and, 69–
        71
    as reader, 88

Laurence, Paula, 137–38
Lawrence, D. H., 75, 231
Lawson, John Howard, 435
Leachman, Cloris, 168
Lecoq, Jacques, 39
Lecouvreur, Adrienne, 38
Le Gallienne, Eva, 177
Legend of Lovers, 44, 176
Legouvé, Ernest, 232
Le Massena, William, 213
Lenin, Vladimir, 315
Leo X, Pope, 81
Léocadia, 44
Lerner, Alan Jay, 283–85
Lert, Ernst, 175
Lessing, Gotthold, 464
Letter to the World, 84–86
Lewis, C. S., 270
Lewis, "Monk," 92
Lewis, Robert, 9–10, 81, 328–29
Lichtenberg, G. C., 55
Life, 279, 362
Life with Father, 355
Lillie, Beatrice, 29–30
Limelight, 36–37
Lindfors, Viveca, 288–90
Little Glass Clock, The, 316
Little Hut, The, 178–79
Living Room, The, 200–3
Lloyd, Marie, 349
Loeb, Philip, 224
Loesser, Frank, 323
Loewe, Frederick, 283–85
Logan, Joshua, 73, 126, 163,
    185, 275–76
    Fanny, 196–200
London, George, 175, 393
Long Day's Journey into Night,
    395, 403–4
Long Player, The, 335
Look Back in Anger, 399
Lorre, Peter, 414
Losey, Joseph, 443
Love, Phyllis, 230, 322
Love for Three Oranges, 300
Love of Four Colonels, The, 58–
    61, 283, 313

Love Punished (*The Rehearsal*), 43–46
Loy, Myrna, 192
Lucas, Jonathan, 191
Lulli, Jean Baptiste, 243
Lumet, Sidney, 320
Lunatics and Lovers, 216
Lunt, Alfred, 147, 175, 316–17, 374
Luv, 405

Macaulay, Thomas, 83
Macbeth, 47, 92–94, 235
McCarthy, Desmond, 320
McCarthy, Joseph, 26, 192, 256, 261, 461, 470
MacCarthy, Kevin, 268
McClintic, Guthrie, 127, 130, 219, 226, 317
McCord, Bert, 455
McCormick, Myron, 323
McCullers, Carson, 128, 322
McDowell, Roddy, 320
McGehee, Helen, 340
MacGrath, Leueen, 60, 241
Machiavelli, Niccolò, 81–84
McKenna, Siobhan, 282, 466
MacKaye, Percy, 98–99
Macken, Walter, 183–84
Madam Will You Walk, 138
Madam's Late Mother, 376
Mademoiselle Colombe, 7, 44n, 132–34, 240, 458
Magarshack, David, 291
Magic and the Loss, The, 159–61
Magic Flute, The, 78, 173, 178, 354
Mahagonny, 419
Main Street, 113
Major Barbara, 61
Malden, Karl, 215
Maltese Falcon, The, 336
Man, Beast, and Virtue, 33
Man for All Seasons, A, 446
Man Who Came to Dinner, The, 166

Manchester Guardian, The, 348
Mandragola, 81–84
Mankiewicz, Joseph, 106
Mann, Daniel, 151–52
Mann, Dolores, 213
Mann, Thomas, 197n
Mansfield, Jayne, 325
Mao Tse-tung, 382
Marat/Sade, 417–18, 420, 425–28
Marceau, Marcel, 342, 383
Marivaux, Pierre, 38, 45–46
Marlowe, Christopher, 21, 269–71
Marre, Albert, 282
Marriage of Figaro, The, 173, 175
Marshall, E. G., 65, 176, 268, 302, 303, 453–54, 469
Marshall, Sarah, 278
Marshall, William, 237
Martin, Mary, 319
Martin, Ruth and Thomas, 175, 392
Martínez Sierra, Gregorio, 326
Martínez Sierra, María, 326
Marty, 272–73
Marx, Groucho, 213
Marx, Harpo, 344
Marx, Karl, 48, 63, 320, 396
Marx Brothers, 205, 411
Mason, James, 105
Mason, Reginald, 60
Massey, Raymond, 70
Master Builder, The, 218–21, 225
Matchmaker, The, 269–71, 327–28, 465–66
Matheson, Murray, 264, 464
Matthau, Walter, 113
Maugham, W. Somerset, 263
Maurer, Peggy, 223
Maurette, Marcelle, 313, 469
Mauriac, François, 202
Maya, 98–100
Mayakovsky, Vladimir, 425

Medea (Anouilh), 45
Medea (Jeffers), 226
Meeker, Ralph, 73
Meisner, Sanford, 81, 83, 321
Melchinger, Siegfried, 197n
Member of the Wedding, The,
9, 127, 129, 184, 197
Memory of Two Mondays, A,
261, 464
Mencken, H. L., 127
Menjou, Adolphe, 441
Menotti, Gian-Carlo, 321–22,
389
Merchant of Venice, The, 20
Mercury Theatre, 138
Messel, Oliver, 26, 132, 178–79,
350
Metropolitan Opera, 172, 174–
75, 193, 385–94
staging at, 389–91
Meyer, Jean, 243, 251
Middle of the Night, 272–76
Midsummer Night's Dream, A,
71, 198
Mielziner, Jo, 176, 186, 224
Mikado, The, 164
Mikulicz, Miss, 430
Miller, Arthur, 261, 266, 279,
312, 395, 399
After the Fall, 399
The Crucible, 62–65, 73, 261,
313, 453–54, 462–63
Death of a Salesman, 125, 209,
261, 454–55
A View from the Bridge, 258–
61, 462–64
Miller, Betty, 162
Miller, Gilbert, 203
Miller, Henry, *xxxix*
Millionairess, The, 31–34
Miner, Worthington, 185
Minotis, Alexis, 41
Misanthrope, Le, 134, 368, 374
Miss Julie, 288–90
Mister Johnson, 328
Mr. Pickwick, 22–25
Mister Roberts, 73, 163

Mitford, Nancy, 178
Mitropoulos, Dmitri, 42
Mizener, Arthur, 79
Modern Times, 36
Moissi, Alexander, 414
Molière, 83, 167, 292
Le Bourgeois Gentilhomme,
242–45
Monroe, Marilyn, 398
Monsieur Verdoux, 25, 35–37,
435
Montague, C. E., 55, 348
Montgomery, Robert, 215
Month in the Country, A, 291–
95, 333n, 432, 464, 467–68
Moon for the Misbegotten, A,
16–19
Moon Is Blue, The, 168
More Stately Mansions, 394–404
Morgan, Charles, 113n
Moross, Jerome, 191
Morrison, Paul, 142
Mother Courage, 242, 415
Mourning Becomes Electra, 164,
395, 400, 403
Moviegoer, 434
Mozart, Wolfgang Amadeus, 78,
172, 387, 389
Muni, Paul, 317
Murder in the Cathedral, 171
Murrow, Edward R., 421
Music, 429
Musset, Alfred de, 38
Mutiny on the Bounty, 141, 164
My Fair Lady, xxxv, 283–86
My Three Angels, 132

Nash, Ogden, 353n, 355–57
Nathan, George Jean, 3, 346,
363, 408
Nation, The, 245, 353, 358
National Theatre Conference,
366
Natwick, Mildred, 9, 136
Nausée, La, 176
Neal, Patricia, 52, 100

Neher, Caspar, 393
Nelson, Portia, 191
Nelson, Ruth, 9
Nesbitt, Cathleen, 117
Neumann, Natanya, 87
Neveux, George, 176, 370–71, 374
New Leader, The, 229, 265, 394, 423, 455
New Masses, 114
New Republic, The, xxxiii, xxxiv, 195, 295, 443, 456, 465
New Statesman, The, 186
New Tenant, The, 379–80
New York Daily Mirror, The, 297
New York Daily News, The, 169, 297
New York Herald Tribune, The, 97, 169, 298, 455
    See also Kerr, Walter
New York Post, The, 327, 461–62
New York Times, The, xl, 34, 75, 124, 255, 319, 443
    on *The Caine Mutiny Court Martial,* 139
    on *Camino Real,* 75
    on *The Cherry Orchard,* 253
    on *The Dybbuk,* 196
    on Eliot, 169
    on *The Teahouse of the August Moon,* 163
    on *Waiting for Godot,* 297
    See also Atkinson, Brooks
New Yorker, The, 114, 159, 279, 363
Newman, Paul, 215
Nietzsche, Friedrich, 85, 298
Night in Venice, A, 14–15
Night Journey, 85–86, 341
Night Rider, 70
Night with Guests, 417
Nights of Wrath, 369
Nilsson, Birgit, 388
No Time for Sergeants, 277
Noah, 207

Noelte, Rudolf, 429–34
Noguchi, Isamu, 339
Noh plays, 384
Nolan, Lloyd, 138

Obey, André, 145, 207
O'Brien, Edmund, 105
O'Casey, Sean, 25–28, 177, 346, 360
    Juno and the Paycock, 282
    Odets compared to, 210
    O'Neill compared to, 17
    on poetic drama, 96
    Purple Dust, 360
    Red Roses for Me, 265–68, 353n, 360–61
    The Star Turns Red, 26, 360
    Within the Gates, 26, 360
O'Connell, Arthur, 74
Odets, Clifford, 207–11, 261, 266, 273, 350, 361
Oedipus, 42, 366, 465
Oenslager, Donald, 116, 137
Off Broadway, *xxxiii–xxxv, xxxix–xl,* 186
    Broadway and, 97, 187
    demise of, 97–98
Offenbach, Jacques, 392, 418
Oh, Men! Oh, Women!, 166–68
Oklahoma!, 78, 178, 354, 355, 405
Old Vic, 362–67
Olivier, Laurence, 100–2, 333–35, 349, 365, 407
On the Waterfront, 258–60
On Your Toes, 192–93, 199
Once in a Lifetime, 49
Ondine, 7, 145–48
One Touch of Venus, 353n, 355–57
O'Neill, Eugene, *xl,* 404, 442
    Anna Christie, 17, 210, 357
    compared to other playwrights, 17, 399, 400
    The Iceman Cometh, xxxiv, 17
    language of, 17–18

O'Neill, Eugene (*continued*)
  Long Day's Journey into Night, 395, 403–4
  A Moon for the Misbegotten, 16–19
  More Stately Mansions, 394–404
  Mourning Becomes Electra, 164, 395, 400, 403
  A Touch of the Poet, 395
Opera News, 173
Ophuls, Max, 152
Oppenheimer, J. Robert, 417
Oresteia, 400
Orwell, George, 67, 266
Osborne, John, 416
O'Shaughnessy, John, 265, 267–68
Othello, 64, 407
  reviewed, 235–38
Otto, Teo, 393
Our Mutual Friend, 89
Our Town, 327
Oxford Book of Modern Verse, The, 361

Page, Geraldine, 119, 151–52, 219, 317
Pagnol, Marcel, 196–97, 199
Pajama Game, xxxv
Palitzsch, Peter, 428–29
Pallenberg, Max, 414
Palmer, Lilli, 61
Paradise Lost, 211n
Parisienne, 99
Parker, Dorothy, 110–13
Partisan Review, 353, 462
Pascal, Gabriel, 284
Patrick, John, 163, 165
Paxinou, Katina, 42, 43
Peace, 418
Peale, Norman Vincent, 408
Pearce, Alice, 10
Peck Seymour, 443
Peking Opera, 382–85
Penn, Leo, 161

Perelman, S. J., 353n, 355–57
Perichole, La, 392
Pernould, Régine, 461
Persecution and Assassination of Marat as Performed by the Inmates of the Asylum of Charenton under the Direction of the Marquis de Sade, The, 417–18, 420, 425–28
Persoff, Nehemiah, 132
Peter Pan, 319
Phèdre, 193, 292
Phoenix Theatre, 138, 218, 220, 319
  A Month in the Country at, 291, 293–95
  Strindberg at, 288–89
  "Photograph of the Colonel, The," 381
Pickford, Mary, 155–56
Pickwick Papers, The, 22–24, 89
Picnic, 72–74, 215, 230, 454
Pinza, Ezio, 199
Pipe Dream, 327
Pirandello, Luigi, 8, 61, 103, 130, 175, 218, 281, 283
  Anouilh and, 46, 212
  Eliot and, 170
  Henry IV, 380
  Man, Beast, and Virtue, 33
  O'Neill compared to, 17
  Six Characters in Search of an Author, 269–72, 302, 465
  Tonight We Improvise, 271
Piscator, Erwin, 271, 414, 421
Plainte contre l'Inconnu, 176
Playbill, Bentley article in, xxxiii, xxxv–xl
Player Queen, The, 94–97
Players Theatre, The, 187
Playfair, Nigel, 102
"Plays for Puritans," xxxvii
Playwright as Thinker, The, 353
Playwright at Work, 127
Playwrights Company, The, 24, 114, 206, 366

Plough and the Stars, The, 96
Plutarch, 104
Politics: theatre and, 241, 247, 260–61, 382, 385, 410–11, 416
    See also Communism
Pollock, Gordon W., 265
Ponder Heart, The, 276–78
Porgy and Bess, 78–80, 178, 285, 407
Potter, H. C., 116
Pound, Ezra, 140, 266
Power, Tyrone, 70
Prescott Proposals, The, 313
Preston, Edna, 200
Preston, Robert, 159
Prévert, Jacques, 39
Price, Gerald, 200
Priestley, J. B., 26, 346, 353n, 359–60
Prince, The, 83
Prince of Homburg, The, 290
Private Lives, 168, 405
Prokoviev, Sergei, 300
Proscenium Productions, 187, 213
Proust, Marcel, 292, 361
Provincetown Playhouse, 98
Public Garden, The, 344
Public Prosecutor, The, 177
Puccini, Giacomo, 389, 393
Purgatory, 94–97
Purple Dust, 360
Purviance, Edna, 440
Pygmalion, 283–86, 336

Quadrille, 317
Quayle, Anthony, 444–45, 448, 466
Queen's Gambit, The, 233
Queen's Quarterly, 465
Quintero, Jose, 131, 159–60, 162

Rabbit Race, The, 416
Rachel, 346

Rachel (Elisa Félix), 348
Racine, Jean, 193
Rae, Charlotte, 191
Raffaelli, Michel, 424, 428
Raimu, 244
Rainmaker, The, 317
Rains, Claude, 32, 142
Rajk, Làslò, 312
Rake's Progress, The, 78
Rascoe, Burton, 364
Rasumny, Mikhail, 132
Rattigan, Terence, 161
RCA Victor, 173
Reclining Figure, 318–19
Red Letter Nights, 211n
Red Roses for Me, 265–68, 353n, 360–61
Redgrave, Michael, 240, 293, 333n, 467–68
Redman, Joyce, 287
Reggiani, Serge, 154
Rehearsal, The (Love Punished), 43–46
Reigen (Round Dance; La Ronde), 152
Reinhardt, Max, 86, 152, 271, 362, 414
Réjane (Gabrielle Charlotte Réju), 348
Religion in theatre, 194–96, 201–3, 208
Renaud, Madeleine, 39, 372, 374, 376
Renoir, Pierre, 241
Repertory Theatre of Lincoln Center, 443, 447–49
Resurrection, 124
Retrial of Joan of Arc, The, 461
Richard II, 21, 348
Richard III, 91, 168, 184, 332–35
Richards, I. A., 41
Richards, Paul, 127
Richardson, Ralph, 334
Richter, Gerd, 428
Reiger, Roswitha, 430

Ring Round the Moon (*L'Invitation au Château*), 44, 179
Rip Van Winkle, 355
Ritchard, Cyril, 34, 319, 393
Ritt, Martin, 209, 261, 464
Robbins, Jerome, 191, 193, 319
Robertson, Tom, 232–33
Robinson, Earl, 320
Robinson, Edward G., 274, 275
Rodgers, Richard, 78, 122, 178, 191–92, 277, 327, 408
Rogoff, Gordon, 385
Romains, Jules, 368
Rome, Harold, 196
Romeo and Juliet, 335–36, 389, 401
Ronde, La, 152–55
Room Service, 278
Roosevelt, Eleanor, 321
Rose and Crown, 26
Rose Tattoo, The, 67, 129
Rosenberg, Ethel, 312, 462
Rosenberg, Julius, 312, 462
Rosenthal, Andrew, 262, 464–65
Ross, Anthony, 68
Ross, David, 223, 253–54
Ross, Elizabeth, 131
Rossellini, Roberto, 30
Rossini, Gioacchino, 175
Rosten, Norman, 328
Rothschild, Bethsabe de, 85, 338
Round Heads, 422
Roussin, André, 179
Rule, Janice, 209
Runyon, Damon, 323, 407
Ruzzante (Angelo Beolco), 83
Ryan, Robert, 136

Sabrina Fair, 114
Saint Joan, 33, 124, 202, 254–56, 460–61
Saint of Bleecker Street, The, 321
Saint-Denis, Michel, 366
Saks, Gene, 137, 219
Salacrou, Armand, 369
Salmi, Albert, 322

Salt, Waldo, 320
San Quentin News, The, 378
Sandhog, 320
Sarah Bernhardt, 308
Sarcey, Francisque, 249
Saroyan, William, 261, 321, 359–60
Sartre, Jean-Paul, 46, 145, 232, 299
Saturday Review, The, 328*n*
Scarecrow, The, 98–99
Schary, Dore, 295–96
Schiller Theater, 420, 425–26
Schisgal, Murray, 405
Schnabel, Stefan, 60
Schneider, Alan, 186
Schneider, Rolf, 419
Schnitzler, Arthur, 152–55
School for Scandal, The, 188
Schroeder, Ernst, 427
Schroeter, Renate, 424
Schwartz, Delmore, 275, 296, 367
Scourby, Alexander, 294
Scribe, Eugène, 232–34
Seagull, The, 218, 220
Second Mrs. Tanqueray, The, *xxxvi*
Seigner, Louis, 244
Seldes, Marian, 282
Sennett, Mack, 435
Seven Year Itch, The, 325
Seyler, Athene, 102
Shadow Line, The, 184, 397
Shakespeare, William, 28
    acting in plays of, 56, 93–94, 237–38
    Antony and Cleopatra, 198, 401
    on Broadway, *xxxv*, 362–67
    Coriolanus, 135–38, 189, 220
    directorial interpretation of, 19–21, 46–47
    films, 103–6, 235–38, 366–67
    Julius Caesar, 103–6, 237
    Macbeth, 47, 92–94, 235
    Off Broadway, *xxxiv–xxxv*
    Othello, 64, 235–38, 407
    politics in, 104, 135–36

Shakespeare, William (*cont.*)
  Richard II, 21, 348
  Richard III, 91, 168, 184, 332–35
  staging of, 91–93
Sharaff, Irene, 193
Shaw, George Bernard, 16, 28, 218, 350, 405
  acting in plays of, 32–33
  Caesar and Cleopatra, 61
  as critic, 54, 299, 303, 345
  The Doctor's Dilemma, 220, 320
  Eliot and, 144
  films and, 336
  Major Barbara, 61
  The Millionairess, 31–34
  other playwrights compared to, 116
  political views of, 25
  Pygmalion, 283–86, 336
  quoted, *xxxvii,* 47
  Saint Joan, 33, 124, 202, 254–56, 460–61
  on Shakespeare, 56, 135
  Widowers' Houses, 29
Shaw, Irwin, 363
Sheridan, Richard Brinsley, 83
Sherwood, Madeleine, 227, 230
Short, Sylvia, 189
Show, 414
Show Boat, 191
Showbill, Bentley letter to, *xxxiii–xxxiv*
Shubert, Lee, 354
Shulman, Max, 319
Shumlin, Herman, 176–77, 415
Sidestreet Story, 337
Siegfried (Giraudoux), 46, 145
Silk Stockings, 313
Silver Cord, The, 117
Silver Tassie, The, 26
Silvers, Phil, 284
Sing Me No Lullaby, 313, 319, 469–70
Six Characters in Search of an Author, 269–72, 302, 465
Skin of Our Teeth, The, 327

Skulnik, Menasha, 208–9, 303, 459
Slezak, Walter, 199, 200
Smith, Art, 219
Smith, Lois, 325
Smith, Milton, 232
Smith, Oliver, 131, 191, 285
Smith, Robert Paul, 319
Smithers, William, 127
Sneider, Vern, 163, 165
Snob, The, 167, 429, 431
Sokolow, Anna, 268, 455
Song of Bernadette, 358
South Pacific, 122
Southern, Terry, 399
Sparer, Paul, 237
Spellman, Francis Cardinal, 323
Spender, Stephen, 465
S.R.O.: The Most Successful Plays in the History of the American Stage, 353*n,* 354–55
Staatsoper (East Berlin), 391–92
Stanislavsky, Constantin, 57, 66, 125, 223, 291, 330, 339
  on *A Month in the Country,* 291
Stanley, Janice, 74
Stanley, Kim, 317*n,* 322
Stapleton, Maureen, 67, 119, 323, 453
Star Turns Red, The, 26, 360
Stein, Gertrude, 231
Steinbeck, John, 275, 327
Sternhagen, Frances, 213
Sternheim, Carl, 167, 414, 429, 431
Stevens, Leslie, 323
Stevens, Wallace, 342
Stevenson, Adlai, 113, 382
Stewart, David, 151
Stiller, Jerry, 137, 189
Stix, John, 237
Stokowski, Leopold, 390
Storch, Arthur, 127
Straight, Beatrice, 65
Strange Interlude, 395, 399

Strasberg, Lee, 81, 125, 226
Strasberg, Susan, 100, 325
Straus, Oscar, 155
Strauss, Johann, 14
Streetcar Named Desire, A, 48,
        72, 76, 77, 118, 225
    advertising of, 126
    language in, 210
    as social-historical drama, 402
Strindberg, August, *xxxiv*, 218, 362
    Miss Julie, 288–90
    O'Neill compared to, 17, 400
    The Stronger, 288–89
Stritch, Elaine, 193, 230, 322
*Strong Are Lonely, The (Das heilige
    Experiment)*, 177
Strongbox, The, 431
Stronger, The, 288–89
Strudwick, Shepherd, 320
Sullavan, Margaret, 117, 162
Sullivan, Joyce, 268
Summer and Smoke, 118, 184
Sunday Times, The, 346
Sunset and Evening Star, 265
Sweeney Agonistes, 342–43
Sweet Bird of Youth, 402
Sweet Thursday, 327
Swerling, Jo, 323
Swinarski, Konrad, 425–27
Symons, Arthur, 345, 348
Synge, J. M., 96

Tabori, George, 11, 65, 288–89
Tales of Hoffman, 392–93
Tamburlaine the Great, 269–71,
        308, 466
Taming of the Shrew, The, 48
Tandy, Jessica, 113, 321
Tartuffe, 167
Tate, Nahum, 82
Taylor, Bayard, 99
Taylor, Charles, 159
Taylor, Samuel, 114
Tchelitchev, Pavel, 147
Tea and Sympathy, *xxxvi*, 108–10,
        114, 126, 151, 163, 185

Tea and Sympathy (*continued*)
    parallels of to *Cat on a Hot
        Tin Roof*, 226, 228, 230
*Teahouse of the August Moon,
    The*, 163–65, 278, 328
Television, 121
    in Germany, 422
Tender Trap, The, 319
Tetzel, Joan, 220
Thacher, Molly Day, 229, 265,
        266, 455
Theater der Gegenwart, 197n
Theater der Zeit, 418, 425
Theater Heute, 417, 423
Theaterarbeit, 21
Theatre Arts, 147, 385
Theatre Digest, 69
Theatre for a Voyage, 339
Theatre Guild, 60, 113n, 176,
        249, 316, 366
Theatre Incorporated, 362, 365
Theatre of Commitment, The, *xxxiii*,
        124, 455
Theatre of Purity, *xxxvi–xl*
"Theory of the Stage, A," 345
*Thieves' Carnival (Thieves'
    Ball)*, 44, 211–14
Third Person, 262–64, 464
Thomas, Parnell, 26
Thomassin, 38
Thomson, Virgil, 10
Thorndike, Sybil, 349
Three Men on a Horse, 166
Three Sisters, The, 128, 218,
        286, 287, 290
    contrast with *The Cherry Or-
        chard*, 251–54
    reviewed, 221–24, 429, 431–34
Threepenny Opera, The, *xxxiv*,
        101–2, 153, 191, 421
Thurber, James, 191
*Tiger at the Gates (The Trojan
    War Will Not Take Place)*,
        145, 238–42, 458–59
Time, 362, 363
Time Limit, 313
Time of the Cuckoo, The, 66

Time of Your Life, The, 321
Times, The (London), 173
Times Literary Supplement, The, 301–2n, 304
Tiny Alice, 413
Tobacco Road, 108
Tocqueville, Alexis de, 120
Todd, Mike, 12–15
Toller, Ernst, 267
Tolstoy, Leo, 193
Tone, Franchot, 168, 286–87
Tonight We Improvise, 271
Torchbearers, The, 166
Toronto Star, The, 382
Touch of the Poet, A, 395
Traveler Without Luggage, 46
Travelling Lady, 317n
Trial, The, 176
Trial of Joan of Arc, The, 461
Trip to Bountiful, The, 117–19
Trovatore, Il, 389
Tucker, Richard, 388
Turandot, 389, 393
Turgenev, Ivan, 291–95
Turner, W. J., 155, 175
Twelfth Night, 174
Twenty-seven Wagons Full of Cotton, 322
Tyler, Parker, 461
Tynan, Kenneth, 59n, 419, 421

Ulbricht, Walter, 418
Ulysses, 301
Uncle Vanya, 286–87, 366
Underhill, John Garrett, 326
Undine, 146
Ustinov, Peter, 58–61, 349

Valency, Maurice, 147, 233–34
Valentino, Rudolph, 155–56
Valère, Simone, 372
Van Druten, John, 48, 127, 128
Van Fleet, Jo, 119
Varden, Evelyn, 207
Verdi, Giuseppe, 389, 392

Verdon, Gwen, 191
Vie de Molière, 194
View from the Bridge, A, 258–61, 462–64
Voice of America, 404
Volpone, 368–69, 372
Voltaire, 38
Von Furstenberg, Betsy, 282
Voskovec, George, 60, 287

Wager, Michael, 237
Wagner, Richard, 389
Waiting for Godot, 280, 296–304, 378, 381, 468–69
Walbrook, Anton, 154
Wallace, Henry, 25, 124
Wallach, Eli, 77, 100, 133
Walser, Martin, 415, 416, 422, 428
Walton, William, 335
War and Peace, 193
Warren, Robert Penn, 70
Warriner, Frederic, 189
Warshaw, Robert, 261
Washington Square, 405
Waters, Ethel, 177–78
Watteau, Antoine, 38
Watson, Douglas, 142
Watts, Richard, Jr., 3
Waverley, Richard, 419
Way of the World, The, 188–90, 213
Wayne, David, 163, 278
Weaver, Fritz, 189, 282
Webster, Margaret, 33, 127, 177, 390
Wedekind, Frank, 414, 430
Wegwerth, Manfred, 418
Weigel, Helene, 421, 425
Weill, Kurt, 101, 356
Weiss, Peter, 415, 417, 422, 426–27
Welles, Orson, xxxv, 19, 105, 235–38, 318
    as director, 305–8
    as Lear, 304–8

Wellesley College, 188
Welty, Eudora, 276 – 78
Werfel, Franz, 353, 358
West, Mae, 411
Wexley, John, 312
What Every Woman Knows, 320
White Devil, The, 282
Whiting, Jack, 191
*Who's Afraid of Virginia
    Woolf?,* 413
Wickwire, Nancy, 189, 252
Widowers' Houses, 29
Wild Duck, The, 154
Wilde, Oscar, *xxxix,* 59, 83, 129,
    149, 217, 290
Wilder, Thornton, 269–70, 327–
    28
Will Success Spoil Rock Hunter?,
    325–26
Williams, Emlyn, 88, 293, 333*n,*
    464, 467
Williams, Tennessee, 128, 299,
    322, 395
    Camino Real, 74–78, 119, 455
    Cat on a Hot Tin Roof, 224–
        31, 261, 264, 412, 413, 455
    The Glass Menagerie, 127,
        210, 413
    The Rose Tattoo, 67, 129
    A Streetcar Named Desire, 48,
        72, 76, 77, 118, 126, 210,
        225, 402, 454–55
    Summer and Smoke, 118, 184
    Sweet Bird of Youth, 402
Willingham, Calder, 124–26,
    456–58
Wilson, J. Dover, 21
Wilson, Sandy, 318

Winchell, Walter, 316, 364
Winckelmann, Johann, 86
Winters, Shelley, 326 – 27
Wischnewski, Siegfried, 424
Wisconsin, University of, 123
Within the Gates, 26, 360
Witness, 258
Witness for the Prosecution, 217
Wolfe, Thomas, 71
Wolfson, Victor, 117–18
Woman of Paris, A, 435–43
Wonderful Town, 78
*Words Upon the Window Pane,
    The,* 94, 95, 97
Worlock, Frederick, 320
Worsley, T. C., 21, 186–87
Wouk, Herman, 139–41

Yeats, William Butler, 27, 266,
    361, 366, 384
    staging of, 94–97
Yordan, Philip, 353*n,* 357–58
You Can't Take It With You,
    277, 357, 409–10
Young, Gig, 168
Young, Stanley, 22–25
Young, Stark, 82, 117, 195, 224,
    252, 333, 363, 364
Young and Beautiful, The, 325
Young Woodley, 108
*Youth, Maturity, Old Age, and
    Death,* 344

Zola, Emile, 124, 314
Zorina, Vera, 193
Zweig, Stefan, 368